Professional XML Schemas

Kurt Cagle
Jon Duckett
Oliver Griffin
Stephen Mohr
Francis Norton
Nikola Ozu
Ian Stokes-Rees
Jeni Tennison
Kevin Williams

Wrox Press Ltd. ®

Professional XML Schemas

Published by Wrox Press Ltd,
Arden House, 1102 Warwick Road, Acocks Green,
Birmingham, B27 6BH, UK
Printed in the United States
ISBN 1-861005-47-4

Trademark Acknowledgements

Credits

Authors
Jon Duckett
Oliver Griffin
Stephen Mohr
Francis Norton
Nikola Ozu
Ian Stokes-Rees
Jeni Tennison
Kevin Williams

Contributing Author
Kurt Cagle

Category Manager
Dave Galloway

Technical Architect
Victoria Hudgson

Technical Editors
Phillip Jackson
Chris Mills
Andrew Polshaw
James Robinson

Author Agent
Marsha Collins

Project Manager
Vicky Idiens

Indexing
Michael Brinkman

Technical Reviewers
Arnaud Blandin
Michael Corning
Paul Freeman
Sebastian Gignoux
Oli Gauti Gudmundsson
Susan Henshaw
Chris Houston
Mario Jeckle
Rick Jelliffe
Thomas B. Passin
Jeff Rafter
Eddie Robertson
David Schultz
Jeni Tennison

Production Manager
Simon Hardware

Production Coordinator
Mark Burdett

Production Assistant
Abbie Forletta

Cover
Dawn Chellingworth

Proof Readers
Miriam Robinson
Chris Smith
Fiver Locker
Keith Westmoreland

About the Authors

Kurt Cagle

Kurt Cagle is a writer and developer specializing in XML and Internet-related issues. He has written eight books and more than one hundred articles on topics ranging from Visual Basic programming to the impact of the Internet on society, and has consulted for such companies as Microsoft, Nordstrom, AT&T and others. He also helped launch Fawcette's XML Magazine and has been the DevX DHTML and XML Pro for nearly two years.

Jon Duckett

Jon has been working with XML since editing and co-authoring Wrox's first XML title in 1998. Having worked in Wrox's Birmingham UK offices for over 3 years, Jon recently moved to Sydney to get a different view from his window.

Jon would like to thank his family and friends for their support. He would also like to thank everyone at Wrox for making this possible.

Oliver Griffin

Oliver has worked in the UK publishing industry since graduating from St Anne's College, Oxford in 1989. He began programming at the dawn of the personal computer age, and in 1997 decided to combine his interest in technology and publishing by forming Griffin Brown Digital Publishing Ltd. with Alex Brown. Based in Cambridge, England, the company has become a world leader in the application of XML to document management, particularly within the academic and STM (Scientific, Technical and Medical) sectors.

Oliver is responsible for managing the company and leading the consulting team in a variety of work including DTD and schema development, transformation and workflow design. He also runs training courses in XML and XSLT.

When he's not working, Oliver enjoys flying, rowing, drawing and playing the piano.

I'd like to thank Victoria Hudgson for asking me to write this chapter, and the team at Wrox who helped me to do so. I'd also like to thank my mother Jacqueline, and my sisters Jessica and Miranda who have given me so much support.

Stephen Mohr

Stephen Mohr is a software systems architect with Omicron Consulting, Philadelphia, USA. He has more than ten years' experience working with a variety of platforms and component technologies. His research interests include distributed computing and artificial intelligence. Stephen holds BS and MS degrees in computer science from Rensselaer Polytechnic Institute.
For my wife, Denise, and my sons James and Matthew.

Francis Norton

Francis Norton works at iE (http://www.ie.com) as a senior consultant where he has a special interest in the application of XML technologies to the many challenges of cross-platform applications. His interests include running, cooking, travel and rather too much reading.

I'd like to thank Victoria and Vicky at Wrox, and my editors and technical reviewers – this is all new to me, so if it works, blame them – if not, blame me.

I'd also like to thank my colleagues and employers at iE for giving me the space and opportunities to pursue my technical interests, and in particular, the late and much-missed Tim Mulcahy for his experience, friendship and support.

Nikola Ozu

Nikola Ozu is a systems and information architect who lives in Wyoming at the end of a dirt road – out where the virtual community is closer than the nearest town, but still only flows at 24kBps and doesn't deliver pizza.

Recent work has included the use of XML for both production and publishing of text and bibliographic databases, an architectural vocabulary, and a new production and delivery system for hypermedia. He designed and developed an early hypertext database, a monthly CD-ROM product called *Health Reference Center* in 1990, followed by advanced versions of the similar *InfoTrac*. Given that large text databases were involved, some intimate involvement with SGML was unavoidable. Previous work has ranged from library systems on mainframes to telecom equipment, industrial robots, games, toys, and other embedded microsystems.

When not surfing the Net, he surfs crowds, the Tetons, and the Pacific; and climbs or sculpts wherever there is rock. He enjoys these even more when accompanied by his teenage son, who also likes mosh pits, skating in the Mission at midnight, and the freedom of the mountains and waves (liquid, crystalline, sonic, and photonic).

Many thanks to my editors at Wrox, the astute technical reviewers (especially Jeni Tennison), and my friends Vic & Joan Wagner and Deanna Bauder for their help with this project.

In memory of Douglas Adams, master of the modern five-volume trilogy. He has apparently taken his towel and gone after Ford Prefect's expense account. We have just lost a whole bunch of grins, giggles, and guffaws. So long, and thanks for all the fish, fun, and 42!

To Noah: *May we always think of the next $(2^3 - 1)$ generations instead of just our own 2^0.*

Ian Stokes-Rees

Ian is the Engineering Manager for DecisionSoft Ltd., an Oxford UK based XML company and creators of XML Script. Ian has been working with XSDL since the first working draft and has been involved in the modeling and production of schemas for various applications. He has also been heavily involved in the integration of XML into the business process of many DecisionSoft clients and as such has been working on X-Meta, an XML meta data repository, which facilitates information modeling and integration of business rules with data definitions. He is particularly excited by the several open souce XML and Java projects underway and (usually) enjoys fiddling with his home computer network. Ian can be reached at jstokes@ieee.org and is happy to hear from readers.

Ian enjoys the student buzz of Oxford, where his wife Emily is a graduate student in Anthropology. As many weekends as possible are spent walking in Wales, or otherwise being occupied with the Scout Association or his local church.

Jeni Tennison

Jeni Tennison is a freelance consultant in XML, XSLT and XML Schemas. She is a regular contributor on XSL-List and was an invited speaker on XSLT design patterns at XSLT UK '01 and is one of the people behind the EXSLT initiative. She lives with her partner, vast Lego collection and two cats in Nottingham, England.

Thanks to the authors of Professional XML Schemas, for teaching me so much about them.

Kevin Williams

Kevin's first experience with computers was at the age of 10 (in 1980) when he took a BASIC class at a local community college on their PDP-9, and by the time he was 12, he stayed up for four days straight hand-assembling 6502 code on his Atari 400. His professional career has been focussed on Windows development – first client-server, then onto Internet work. He's done a little bit of everything, from VB to Powerbuilder to Delphi to C/C++ to MASM to ISAPI, CGI, ASP, HTML, XML, and any other acronym you might care to name, but these days, he's focusing on XML work. Kevin is a Senior System Architect for Equient, an information management company located in Northern Virginia. He may be reached for comment at kevin@realworldxml.com.

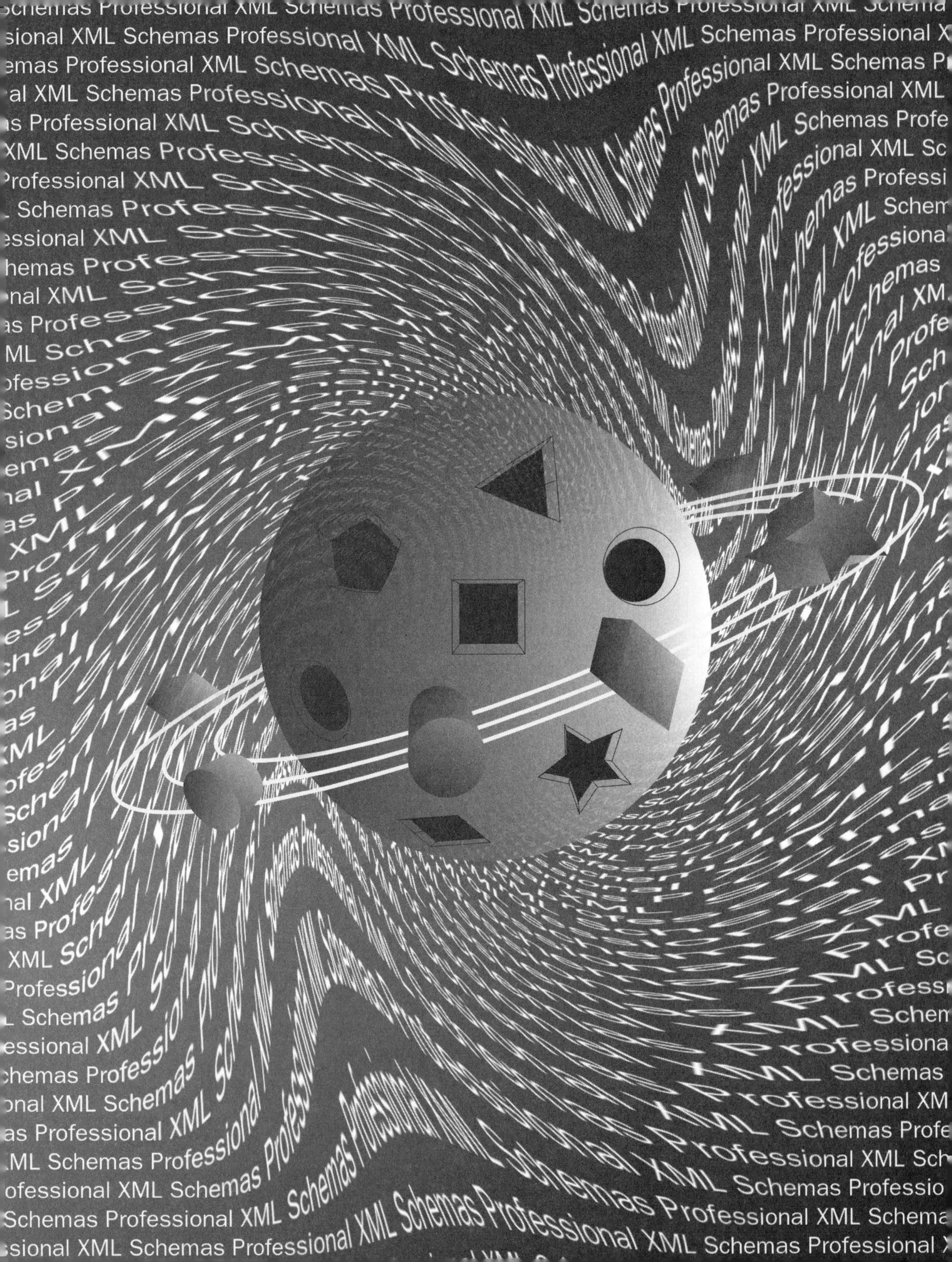
Professional XML Schemas

Table of Contents

Table of Contents

Table of Contents

Table of Contents

Table of Contents

Table of Contents

Table of Contents

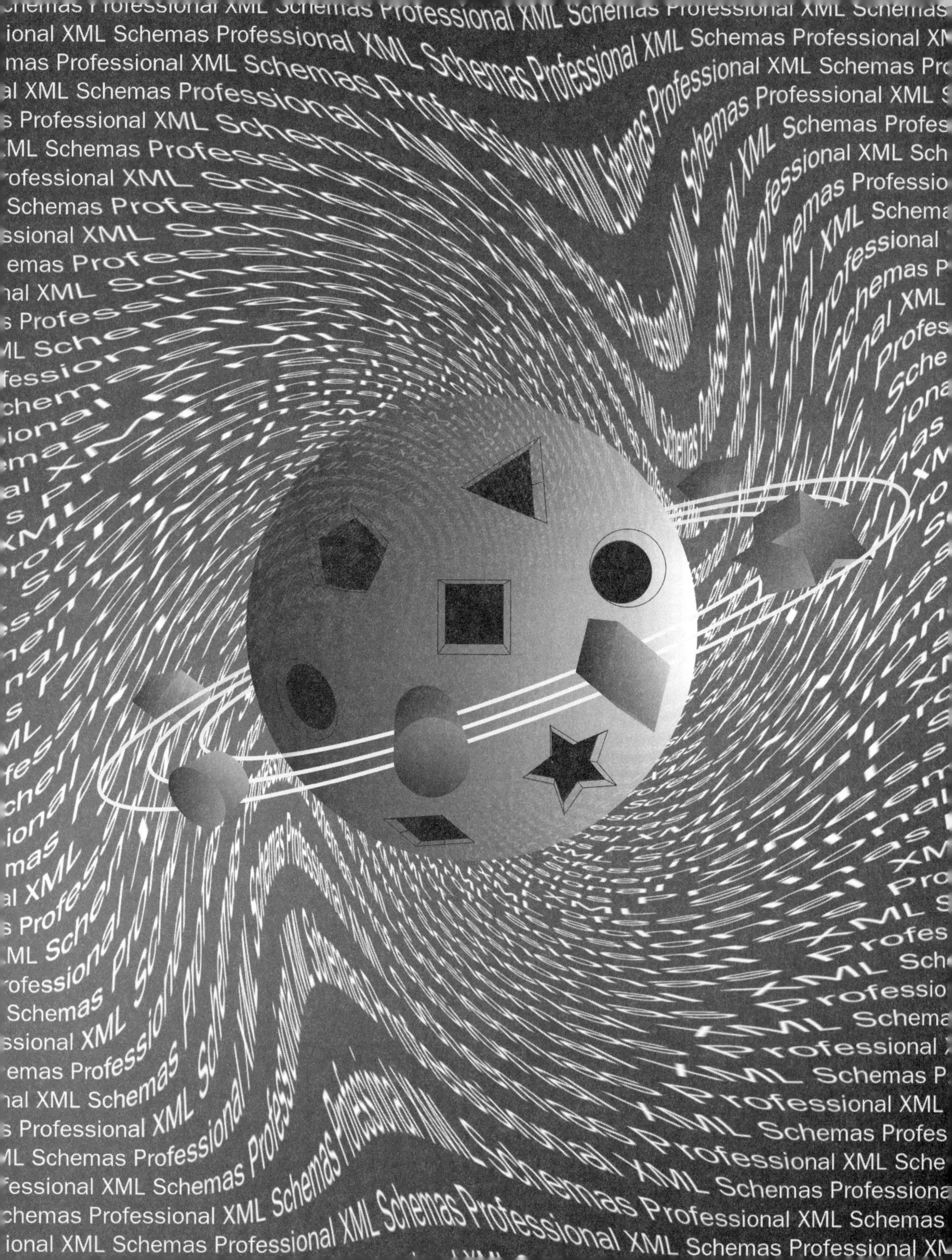
Professional XML Schemas

Introduction

Since its inception in 1998, the use of XML has mushroomed, with vocabularies created to represent seemingly every possible human endeavor. The problem with all these vocabularies is ensuring that we know which vocabulary is being used and enforcing adherence to it. DTDs, using SGML-based syntax, do provide some of this necessary validation. However, DTDs have some severe limitations; apart from not being an XML-based language, they also have no strong data typing and limited functionality with regards to specifying the sequence and occurrence of elements. The W3C introduced XML Schemas as a replacement for DTDs, with the aim of overcoming these shortcomings and providing a more powerful XML validation language. On May 2nd 2001, the W3C made XML Schema a full Recommendation, and within weeks several tools became available with support for this new language.

What Does This Book Cover?

This book exhaustively details the W3C XML Schema language – every element, attribute, and datatype is explained. More importantly, this book explains the various structures and how and where to use them. The fact that XML Schemas have support for XML Namespaces is one of their great advantages, and all the details of how to work with XML Schemas and Namespaces together are covered. Some of the parsers and tools that were available when this book went to press are also detailed.

The second half of this book is devoted to the use of XML Schemas in a practical context. We examine data modeling techniques, and how these techniques impact on our schema design. We look at designing and using schemas in three broad areas where XML plays an important role. Firstly, in the world of databases, we cover how to move from a database schema to an XML schema. Secondly, in the world of document management, we see how to design schemas for marking up documents in XML. And finally, we'll look at designing schemas for XML messages, and how to work with SOAP. Other chapters will look at the use of XML Schemas together with alternative schema technologies, such as Schematron. The last chapter in the book focuses on a more experimental area – *Schema-Based Programming*.

Who Is This Book For?

Any experienced XML developer who may have no knowledge of XML Schema at all can follow this book. Knowledge of other programming languages is not required, neither is knowledge of the language used for DTDs, although you will find this helpful. A good understanding of XSLT is necessary to follow the chapters on *Schema and XSLT* (10) and *Schema-Based Programming* (16). It is helpful but not necessary for Chapter 14. You will find an understanding of working with databases and database modeling helpful for Chapter 12.

You will find this book invaluable if you need to:

❑   Understand the XML Schema Recommendation and use schemas for validation

❑   Write your own vocabularies using XML Schema

❑   Work with regular datasets, where you're mapping database schema or object models to XML data

❑   Agree schemas for B2B transactions

❑   Write applications that read and write schemas

What You Need to Use This Book

The main requirement for working with the XML Schemas and XML instance documents presented in this book is a validating parser. Appendix D details some of these parsers and explains how to use them. We recommend using XSV (XML Schema Validator), which is freely available for download, or can even be used online. However, the choice of parser doesn't really matter as long as it supports the W3C XML Schema Recommendation. Some tools support more parts of the specification than others – you can check Appendix D for some details, but be aware that many were in beta at the time of writing, and you should consult the relevant documentation for up-to-date information. Some chapters also require the use of an XSLT-compliant parser, of which there are many available.

The code included in this book can be downloaded from http://www.wrox.com/. More details are given in the *Support, Errata, and P2P* section of this Introduction.

How Is This Book Structured?

The first nine chapters of the book focus on describing the fundamentals of the XML Schema language – what all the elements and attributes are, how to use the syntax, as well as core design issues. The remaining seven chapters talk about issues when using schemas and applying them in real-world situations. There is a chapter-by-chapter breakdown below:

1. **Getting Started with XML Schemas**
This chapter covers many of the fundamental aspects of XML Schemas. We cover the difference between simple and complex datatypes and show how to use element and attribute declarations for specifying what the allowed content of an instance document is. We also cover how to make annotations and how to specify a schema to use in an instance document. Finally, we look at validation with a specific validating parser – XSV.

2. **Datatype Basics**

The various datatypes that XML Schemas provide are included here. Some of the theory is explained first – the properties of the datatypes. We then explain what atomic, list, and union datatypes are and how to use them, before describing the built-in primitive and derived types.

3. **Creating Content Models**

Here we discuss the use of complex types and how we build content models using them. We also cover model groups and attribute groups, and how to define null values. We end this chapter introducing the XML Schema fundamentals that will be explained in later chapters.

4. **Deriving New Types**

In this chapter, we start by looking at the constraining facets of the built-in datatypes, and then move on to focus on one in particular – `pattern` – and how to use XML Schema regular expressions. These allow us to restrict datatypes by specifying, for instance, that only certain characters may appear in a specific order. We then cover the more standard methods of restricting and extending existing datatypes, using the various facets, such as `length`, `minLength`, and `maxLength`. Finally we cover how to derive complex types by both restriction and extension, and how this functionality mimics that provided by many object-oriented languages.

5. **Some Useful Datatypes**

In this chapter, we give examples of deriving our own datatypes and derive types that you might want to reuse in your applications. We cover various ISO standards and types such as names, addresses, and telephone numbers. We also cover how to derive useful types concerned with web technologies, such as those needed for e-mail addresses, domain names, and IP addresses.

6. **XML Schemas and Namespaces**

Starting with a quick overview of the Namespaces in the XML Recommendation, we move on to look at how this is used within XML Schemas. We explain what the three different namespaces of W3C XML Schema are and what they are used for and cover issues such as the scope of namespaces and namespace defaulting. The various attributes available to XML Schemas that affect namespacing are covered here too.

7. **Schema Design Fundamentals**

Rather than introducing any new syntax, this chapter consolidates what has been covered so far, and discusses how your schemas should be structured depending on your needs. We can make schemas as prescriptive or proscriptive as we like, but their use normally defines which method we should use. We discuss issues of consistency – how we should name our elements and group declarations together for easy discovery. We cover datatype and structure reuse and grouping to organize your schemas better.

8. **Creating Schemas from Multiple Documents**

Quite often it makes sense to use multiple schemas to validate your XML document. Some data structures will be used in different applications and it helps to put them all in one place and include them as necessary. There are a number of issues with using multiple schemas, and we examine these along with the various methods of working with multiple schemas.

9. Identity Constraints, Normalization, and Document Fragments

Identity constraints in XML Schemas are far more powerful than the simple ID/IDREF relationship provided with XML and DTDs. They allow the author to specify that only values within a certain range of nodes are unique, for instance, and these identity constraints may apply to any datatype, not just IDs. We can also key/value relationships, which enable us to normalize the information and save on repetition.

10. Schema and XSLT

The fact that XML Schemas are written in XML means that they can be manipulated in the same way as any other XML document. We can transform them using XSLT, which is an enormously powerful technique, and in this chapter, we focus on two examples that utilize this. First, we create a stylesheet for extracting documentation from a schema and presenting it as HTML. Second, we take information from both an XML instance document and the schema to which it conforms and use this to create an HTML form for editing the instance document.

11. XML System Modeling

In this chapter we look at the broad issues involved when modeling XML applications, and how this impacts on XML Schema design. Modeling XML data can often be somewhere between relational database design and object-oriented design. In this chapter, we cover many of the topics that are needed for successful modeling – those of relationships, inheritance, information modeling, business process analysis, and more.

12. Creating XML Schema for an Existing Database

The majority of data used in modern applications is held in relational database management systems, and usually we still prefer to store our data in such a way. However, XML models its data in a different way from that employed by most of these systems, and a common task is to move data between these two worlds. In this chapter we discuss how to take a database schema and move to an XML Schema that represents the same, or a subsection of that data.

13. W3C XML Schemas for Document Management

This chapter discusses how to design and create schemas for document-centric applications. 'Printed' documents often have different requirements from data-centric XML documents, and we look at some of these differences. Issues such as future-proofing and ease for the document authors are considered and they are discussed in the context of an practical example.

14. Schematron and Other Schema Technologies

Although extremely powerful, some validation issues have not been resolved with W3C XML Schema. Here we discuss Schematron and a few other alternative technologies and the extra validation powers they can bring to your schemas. We discuss some of the differences between Schematron and XML Schema, followed by how we can co-locate the two technologies so that they can be used together. Other technologies, such as Examplotron, are also investigated.

15. E-Commerce Case Study

When XML Schemas are used in B2B applications, they allow businesses to communicate effectively details of business transactions. By making these schemas public, different business partners can agree exactly on what data needs to be exchanged and how. In this chapter we show a specific example of this using SOAP. We very briefly describe the structure of a SOAP message and then build up the design of the XML Schema used. There is also a brief glance into the future of web services with UDDI and WSDL.

16. **Schema-Based Programming**

This final chapter details ongoing work with an experimental research project known as Schema-Based Programming. The idea behind this is to implement everything in an application – the application state and behavior – within XML and XSLT, using the Model-View-Controller design pattern. The chapter introduces the ideas and motivation behind this work, and illustrated it in practice with a sample application.

At the end of the book, we also have some appendices. They are detailed below:

A. **Schema Element and Attribute Reference**

In here we have a reference to all of the elements of the W3C XML Schema Structures Recommendation. We also include the schema instance attributes (for example, `xsi:schemaLocation` and `xsi:type`).

B. **Schema Datatypes Reference**

In here we list all of the built-in datatypes for XML Schemas and the facets that allow us to restrict these datatypes to create new ones.

C. **UML Reference**

This is a reference to the Unified Modeling Language – UML. UML is used in several chapters in this book when discussing application design. This reference should fill any gaps in your knowledge when reading these chapters.

D. **Tools and Parsers**

In this appendix we discuss the use of the different XML Schema-compliant validating parsers available, as well as investigating some of the authoring tools, which can ease the creation of schemas and instance documents.

E. **Bibliography and Further Reading**

In here are many of the references used throughout this book put in one place for easy reference later. Most of these are URLs.

Conventions

To help you get the most from the text and keep track of what's happening, we've used a number of conventions throughout the book.

For instance:

> **These boxes hold important, not-to-be forgotten information, which is directly relevant to the surrounding text.**

While this style is used for asides to the current discussion.

As for styles in the text:

❑   When we introduce them, we **highlight** important words

❑   We show filenames, and code within the text like so: `sample.xml`

- ❑ Text on user interfaces is shown as: File | Save

- ❑ URLs are shown in a similar font, thus: http://www.w3.org/

- ❑ Namespace URIs, however, are shown like this: http://www.w3.org/2001/XMLSchema .

- ❑ When referring to chapter sections or titles, we italicize it, thus: *Introduction*

We present code in two different ways. Code that is important is shown thus:

```
In our code examples, the code foreground style shows new, important, and
    pertinent code
```

Code that is an aside, or has been seen before is shown thus:

```
Code background shows code that's less important in the present context,
    or has been seen before.
```

In addition, when something is to be typed at a command line interface (for example, a DOS/Command prompt), then we use the following style to show what is typed, and what is output:

> **xsv regexp.xml**

Support, Errata, and P2P

The printing and selling of this book was just the start of our contact with you. If there are any problems whatsoever with the code or any explanation in this book, we welcome any input. A mail to support@wrox.com should elicit a response within two to three days (depending on how busy the support team are).

In addition to this, we also publish any errata online, so that if you have a problem, you can check on the Wrox web site first to see if we have updated the text at all. First, pay a visit to http://www.wrox.com/, then, click on the Books | By Title(Z-A), or Books | By ISBN link on the left hand side of the page. See the screenshot below:

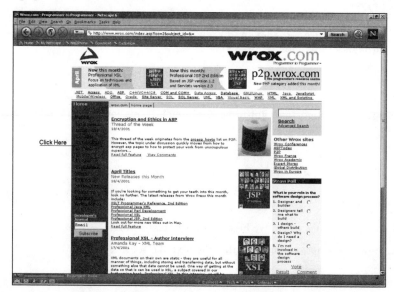

Navigate to this book (the ISBN is 1861005474, if you choose to navigate this way) and then click on it. As well as giving some information about the book, it also provides options to download the code, view errata, and ask for support. Just click on the relevant link. All errata that we discover will be added to the site and information on changes to the code that have to be made for newer versions of software may also be included here – as well as corrections to any printing or code errors.

All of the code for this book can be downloaded from our site. It is included in a zip file, and all of the code samples in this book can be found within, referenced by chapter number.

In addition, at http://p2p.wrox.com/, we have our free "Programmer to Programmer" discussion lists. There is already one called xml_schemas, and either someone at Wrox, or someone else in the developer community, should answer any questions that you post. Navigate to http://p2p.wrox.com/xml, and subscribe to a discussion list from there. All lists are moderated and so no spam or irrelevant e-mails should come from us.

Tell Us What You Think

We've worked hard to make this book as useful to you as possible, so we'd like to know what you think. We're always keen to know what it is you want and need to know.

We appreciate feedback on our efforts and take both criticism and praise on board in our future editorial efforts. If you've anything to say, let us know via:

feedback@wrox.com

Or via the feedback links on:

http://www.wrox.com/

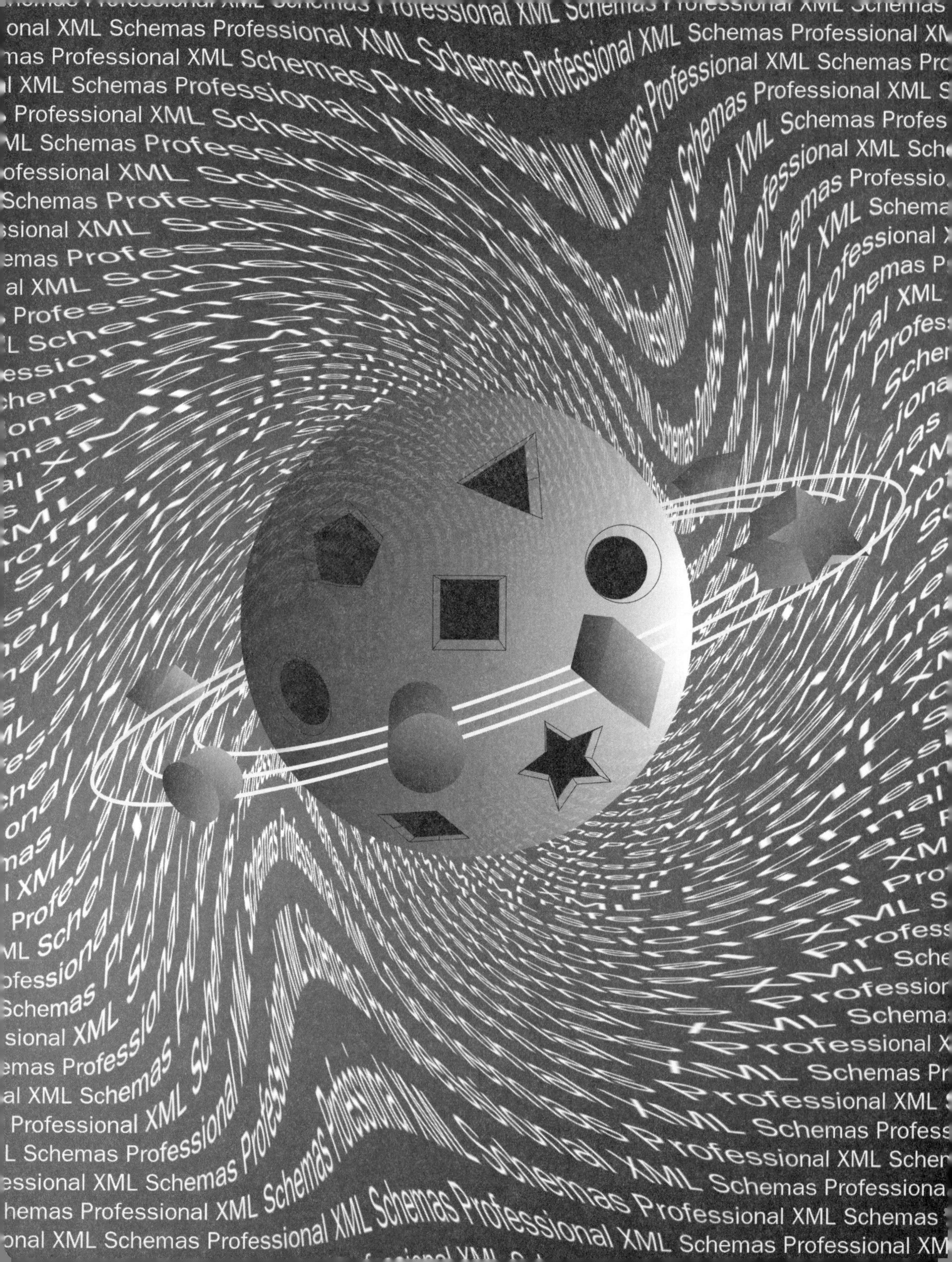
Professional XML Schemas

Getting Started with XML Schemas

This chapter introduces the W3C's XML Schema Recommendation and covers the mechanisms by which XML Schema allows us to define the elements and attributes we want to allow in our XML documents. We will also see how we can constrain element content and attribute values to have a particular datatype.

In particular this chapter will cover:

❑ The aims behind the W3C XML Schema specification

❑ How to create a simple XML Schema

❑ How to declare elements and attributes

❑ How to use some of the built-in simple datatypes: `string`, `integer` and `date`

❑ How to validate an XML document against a schema

This chapter will serve simply as a starting point for you. There are lots of other topics that you need to understand in order to take full advantage of XML Schemas, and as we go through the chapters of this book, you will be building up your experience and writing increasingly complex schemas.

> *To get you familiar with these concepts, the XML documents in this chapter do not use XML Namespaces, and the markup we are creating does not belong to a namespace. If you wish to write documents that make use of namespaces make sure that you read Chapter 6 before writing your schemas.*

Why do we Need Schemas?

XML is intended to be a self-describing data format, allowing authors to define a set of element and attribute names that describe the content of a document. As XML allows the author such flexibility, we need to be able to define what element and attribute names are allowed to appear in a conforming document in order to make that document useful. Furthermore, we need to be able to indicate what sort of content each of these elements and attributes are allowed to contain. Only then can people share the meaning of the markup used in an XML document, be it for human or application consumption.

Sometimes authors require flexibility in what markup they can use to describe a document's content, while at other times they may be forced to adopt a very specific structure. For example, if we were working on an application for a publishing company, we might define a set of elements such as Book, Chapter, Heading1, Heading2, Heading3, Paragraph, Table, CrossReference, and Diagram. Each Book element would be allowed to contain any number of Chapter elements, which in turn would contain Heading and Paragraph elements. The Paragraph elements may then contain text, tables, cross references and diagrams. In such a case, the people marking up the book's content need a flexible way of indicating what information is held within each element as no two books are going to have exactly the same content. By contrast, if we were writing an e-commerce system, it would be the job of an application, rather than a human, to create and process the XML documents. Each part of the process would require a different type document, one structure for catalogs, one for purchase orders, one for receipts, and so on. In such situations, rather than there being a requirement for flexibility, the application would expect a predictable, rigid structure; it would need certain pieces of information in order to fulfill any given task.

As XML becomes more widely used in applications, there is an increasing demand for support of primitive datatypes found in languages like SQL, Java, Visual Basic or C++ (the concepts of strings, dates, integers, and so on). XML Schema introduces a powerful type mechanism that not only allows us to specify primitive datatypes, but also types of structures, allowing us to integrate principles of object-oriented development such as inheritance into our schemas.

> **A schema defines the allowable contents of a class of XML documents. A class of documents refers to all possible permutations of structure in documents that will still conform to the rules of the schema.**

Background to XML Schemas

When XML was created, it was written as a simplified form of an existing markup language, called SGML, which was used for document markup. SGML, however, was so complex that it was not widely adopted, and browser manufacturers made it clear that they were not going to support it in their products. The simpler relative, XML, became a popular alternative, and was soon adopted by all kinds of programmers, not just those involved in document markup. When XML 1.0 became a W3C recommendation, it contained a mechanism for constraining the allowable content of a class of XML document, which you are probably familiar with, in the form of **Document Type Definitions** or **DTDs**. The syntax of DTDs, however, fell short of the requirements of those who were putting XML to new uses, in particular data transfer, and as a result the W3C wanted to create an alternative schema language, namely XML Schema.

The W3C XML Schema Working Group has had the incredibly tough task of creating a schema specification that would satisfy a wide range of users, from programmers to content architects, many of whom have been waiting for XML Schema with much anticipation because they see it as a much more powerful way to define document structures. Indeed, it has been a long time in coming, and there was a gap of over two years between the working group releasing a set of requirements they aimed to achieve with the new schema language, back in February 1999, and the recommendation's release in May 2001.

In the time the W3C have taken to release the XML Schema Recommendation, a number of alternative schema technologies have been released. While this one is likely to achieve wide support because of its endorsement by the W3C, the competing technologies offer alternative approaches to constraining allowable contents of an XML document. This book mainly focuses on the W3C XML Schema Recommendation, although we do look at some of the other schema efforts in Chapter 14.

The aims of the W3C XML Schema Working Group were to create a schema language that would be more expressive than DTDs and written in XML syntax. In addition it would also allow authors to place restrictions on the allowable element content and attribute values in terms of primitive datatypes found in languages such as SQL and Java.

In terms of defining structure of documents, the aims included:

- Providing mechanisms for constraining document structures and content

- Allowing tighter or looser constraints upon classes of documents than those offered by DTDs

- The ability to validate documents composed from markup belonging to multiple namespaces

- Mechanisms to enable inheritance for element, attribute, and datatype definitions, so that they can formally represent *kind-of* relations (for example, a car is a *kind-of* vehicle)

- Mechanism for embedded documentation

In terms of offering primitive data typing, the aims included:

- Support for primitive datatypes such as byte, date, and integer, as found in languages like SQL and Java

- Definition of a type system that would support import and export of data as XML to and from relational, object and OLAP database systems

- The ability to allow users to define their own datatypes that derive from existing datatypes by constraining certain of their properties, such as range and length

The full requirements can be seen at: http://www.w3.org/TR/NOTE-xml-schema-req

The result is a powerful and flexible language for expressing permissible content of a class of XML documents. The added capabilities, however, come at a cost: the resulting language is complicated, especially when we begin to experiment with its more advanced aspects.

The W3C XML Schema Recommendation

The W3C Recommendation for XML Schema comes in three parts:

❑ **XML Schema Part 0: Primer** The first part is a descriptive, example-based document, which introduces some of the key features of XML Schema by way of sample schemas. It is easy to read, and is a good start for getting to grips with XML Schemas and understanding what they are capable of. It can be read at http://www.w3.org/TR/xmlschema-0/.

❑ **XML Schema Part 1: Structures** The next part describes how to constrain the structure of XML documents – where the information items (elements, attributes, notations, and so on) can appear in the schema. Once we have declared an element or an attribute, we can then define allowable content or values for each. It also defines the rules governing schema-validation of documents. It can be read at http://www.w3.org/TR/xmlschema-1/.

❑ **XML Schema Part 2: Datatypes** The third part defines a set of built-in datatypes, which can be associated with element content and attribute values; further restricting allowable content of conforming documents and facilitating the management of dates, numbers, and other special forms of information by software processing of the XML documents. It also describes ways in which we can control derivation of new types from those that we have defined. It can be read at http://www.w3.org/TR/xmlschema-2/.

As we shall see throughout the course of this chapter and the rest of the book, there are a number of advantages to using XML Schemas over DTDs. In particular:

❑ As they are written in XML syntax (which DTDs were not), we do not have a new syntax to learn before we can start learning the rules of writing a schema. It also means that we can use any of the tools we would use to work with XML documents (from authoring tools, through SAX and DOM, to XSLT), to work with XML Schemas.

❑ The support for datatypes used in most common programming languages, and the ability to create our own datatypes, means that we can constrain the document content to the appropriate type required by applications, and / or replicate the properties of fields found in databases.

❑ It provides a powerful class and type system allowing an explicit way of extending and re-using markup constructs, such as content models, which is far more powerful than the use of parameter entities in DTDs, and a way of describing classes of elements to facilitate inheritance.

❑ The support for XML Namespaces allows us to validate documents that use markup from multiple namespaces and means that we can re-use constructs from schemas already defined in a different namespace.

❑ They are more powerful than DTDs at constraining mixed content models.

Getting Started with XML Schemas

The best way to start learning the syntax for XML Schemas is to jump in with an example. To start with, we will create a schema for the following simple document:

```
<?xml version = "1.0" ?>
<Customer>
    <FirstName>Raymond</FirstName>
    <MiddleInitial>G</MiddleInitial>
    <LastName>Bayliss</LastName>
</Customer>
```

A document conforming to a schema is known as an instance document, so let's have a look at an XML Schema for this instance document; we will go through it line by line in a moment (name the file Customer.xsd):

```
<?xml version = "1.0" ?>
<schema xmlns = "http://www.w3.org/2001/XMLSchema">
    <element name = "Customer">
        <complexType>
            <sequence>
                <element name = "FirstName" type = "string" />
                <element name = "MiddleInitial" type = "string" />
                <element name = "LastName" type = "string" />
            </sequence>
        </complexType>
    </element>
</schema>
```

> XML Schema files are saved with the .xsd extension.

As you can see, the Customer.xsd schema is itself an XML document, and the root element of any XML Schema document is an element called schema. In the opening schema tag we declare the namespace for the XML Schema Recommendation:

```
<schema xmlns = "http://www.w3.org/2001/XMLSchema">
```

The next line indicates how we declare our first element, the Customer element:

```
    <element name = "Customer">
...
    </element>
```

As XML is intended to be a self-describing data format, it is hardly surprising that we declare elements using an element called element, and we specify the intended name of the element as a value of an attribute called name. In our case, the root element is called Customer, so we give this as the value of the name attribute.

We will come back to the `complexType` element that appears on the next line in just a moment, but looking further down the schema we can see the declarations for the three other elements that appear in the document: one called `FirstName`, one called `MiddleInitial`, and one called `LastName`.

```
<sequence>
    <element name = "FirstName" type = "string" />
    <element name = "MiddleInitial" type = "string" />
    <element name = "LastName" type = "string" />
</sequence>
```

You may be able to guess from the way in which the elements are declared, nested inside an element called `sequence`, that they would have to appear in that same order in a conforming document. The `sequence` element is known as a **compositor**, and we are required to specify a compositor inside the `complexType` element – we will meet other types of compositor in Chapter 3.

In addition, the element declarations carry a `type` attribute, whose value is `string`. XML Schema introduces the ability to declare types such as `string`, `date` and `integer`, as we would find in languages such as SQL and Java; this is how we specify such types.

Let's now come back to the element we have not looked at yet, called `complexType`, which contains the declarations of the elements that appear as children of the `Customer` element in our sample XML document. XML Schema makes a distinction between simple types and complex types.

The Difference Between Simple and Complex Types

There are two kinds of type in XML Schema: simple types and complex types, both of which constrain the allowable content of an element or attribute:

- ❑ **Simple types** restrict the text that is allowed to appear as an attribute value, or text-only element content (text-only elements do not carry attributes or contain child elements)

- ❑ **Complex types** restrict the allowable content of elements, in terms of the attributes they can carry, and child elements they can contain

Let's have a closer look at what this means.

Simple Types

All attribute values and text-only element content simply consists of strings of characters. The ability for XML Schema to support datatypes means that we can place restrictions on the characters that can appear in attribute values and text-only element content.

An example of such a restriction is the representation of a Boolean value, in which case XML Schema only allows the character strings: `true`, `false`, `1`, or `0`. After all, an instance document should not be allowed to use values such as "maybe" or "4" in attributes or elements that are supposed to represent a Boolean value. Alternatively, if we wanted to represent a byte, we would only want characters that are an integer whose value is between −128 and 127, so that 1445 would not be allowed and neither would ff23.

An XML Schema aware processor is required to support a number of **built-in simple types** that are considered common in programming languages and databases, and a number of datatypes that the working group thought were important to XML document authors. This is why we were allowed to specify that the content of the `FirstName`, `MiddleInital`, and `LastName` elements were **strings** (which places very little restriction on the allowable text of the element content):

```
<element name = "FirstName" type = "string" />
<element name = "MiddleInitial" type = "string" />
<element name = "LastName" type = "string" />
```

In addition to the built-in simple types, XML Schema allows us to derive our own simple types that restrict the allowable content of the built-in simple types already defined in XML Schema.

We will look into all of the built-in simple types in the next chapter. The rest of this chapter will stick to using the built-in types of `string`, `date`, and `integer`.

Complex Types

Complex types define the attributes an element can carry, and the child elements that an element can contain. Whenever we want to allow an element to carry an attribute or contain a child element, we have to define a complex type.

The `Customer` element declared in the `Customer.xsd` example is allowed to contain three child elements (`FirstName`, `MiddleInitial`, and `LastName`), and therefore needs to be a complex type. We gave the `Customer` element a complex type using the `complexType` element nested inside the element that declared `Customer`. We then declared the number of child elements the element `Customer` is allowed to contain inside the `complexType` element and its compositor `sequence`, like so:

```
<complexType>
   <sequence>
      <element name = "FirstName" type = "string" />
      <element name = "MiddleInitial" type = "string" />
      <element name = "LastName" type = "string" />
   </sequence>
</complexType>
```

Note that we cannot just nest the other element declarations inside each other. The following would *not* be allowed:

```
<element name = "Customer">
   <element name = "FirstName" type = "string" />
   <element name = "MiddleInitial" type = "string" />
   <element name = "LastName" type = "string" />
</element>
```

This is not allowed because we need to define the complex type in order for the `Customer` element to contain child elements.

The complex type defined above is known as an **anonymous complex type**. This is because it is nested within the element declaration (`Customer`, in this case). If we wanted more than one element to contain the *same* child elements and carry the *same* attributes, then we would create a **named complex type**, which would apply the same restrictions to the content of our new element. We look at named complex types in Chapter 3.

Let's quickly add to the `Customer` element in our example XML document, by giving it an attribute called `customerID`, so that we can see how we declare attributes. We want the new document to look as follows:

```
<?xml version = "1.0" ?>
<Customer customerID = "24332">
    <FirstName>Raymond</FirstName>
    <MiddleInitial>G</MiddleInitial>
    <LastName>Bayliss</LastName>
</Customer>
```

To add the attribute we can just declare it within the `complexType` definition, after the closing sequence compositor tag and just before the closing `complexType` tag:

```
<?xml version = "1.0" ?>
<schema xmlns = "http://www.w3.org/2001/XMLSchema">
    <element name = "Customer">
        <complexType>
            <sequence>
                <element name = "FirstName" type = "string" />
                <element name = "MiddleInitial" type = "string" />
                <element name = "LastName" type = "string" />
            </sequence>
            <attribute name = "customerID" type = "integer" />
        </complexType>
    </element>
</schema>
```

We declare an attribute using an element called `attribute`. As with the element declaration, it carries an attribute called `name` whose value is the name of the attribute. Remember the value of an attribute is always a simple type; in this case we want our `customerID` attribute to be represented as an integer, so we can use the built-in type of `integer` to restrict the value of the attribute to an integer value.

> **Note the distinction that elements and attributes are declared, while simple and complex types are defined.**

Let's start to look at each of the schema constructs in greater depth.

Element Declarations

The declaration of an element involves associating a name with a type. Earlier, we saw how to declare an element using an element called `element`, and that it's name is given as the value of the `name` attribute that the element declaration carries. The type meanwhile would be a simple type if the element had text-only content, otherwise it would be a complex type. The type of the element can be given in one of two ways:

- ❑ A type definition can be anonymous, and nested inside the element declaration, as we saw with the child elements of `Customer` in the first example.

- ❑ A type can be referred to, by putting the name of the type as the value of a `type` attribute, as we have been doing with the value `string`.

In the following example we can see a mix of the two approaches. The `Address` element declaration contains an anonymous type, while the child elements are all given a simple type of `string`:

```
<element name = "Address">
   <complexType>
      <sequence>
         <element name = "Street" type = "string" />
         <element name = "Town" type = "string" />
         <element name = "City" type = "string" />
         <element name = "StateProvinceCounty" type = "string" />
         <element name = "Country" type = "string" />
         <element name = "ZipPostCode" type = "string" />
      </sequence>
   </complexType>
</element>
```

Here is an example of an `Address` element that conforms to this schema:

```
<Address>
   <Street>10 Elizabeth Place</Street>
   <Town>Paddington</Town>
   <City>Sydney</City>
   <StateProvinceCounty>NSW</StateProvinceCounty>
   <Country>Australia</Country>
   <ZipPostCode>2021</ZipPostCode>
</Address>
```

If we do not specify a type, then the element can contain any mix of elements, attributes and text. This is known as the **ur-type** type in XML Schema, although you do not actually refer to it by name, it is just the default if you do not specify a type.

Global versus Local Element Declarations

It is important to distinguish between the global and local element declarations:

❑ **Global element declarations** are children of the root `schema` element

❑ **Local element declarations** are nested further inside the schema structure and are not direct children of the root `schema` element

Once elements have been declared globally, any other complex type can use that element declaration, by creating a **reference** to it. This is especially helpful when an element and its content model are used in other element declarations and complex type definitions, as they enable us to re-use the content model (A content model simply refers to anything within an element declaration that affects the structure of the element in the instance document. This could be attributes or other elements within an element).

You should be aware that, if your instance documents make use of namespaces, there are greater differences between local and global element declarations. This is because when you use namespaces, globally declared elements must be explicitly qualified in the instance document, whereas local declarations should not always be qualified. We look into the issues that this introduces and the ways in which it might affect how you write XML Schemas in Chapter 6.

Imagine that we wanted to alter our `Customer.xsd` schema so that we could represent name and address details for customers as below. Note we have also added a containing element for the name details called `Name`:

```
<?xml version = "1.0" ?>
<Customer customerID = "242552">
    <Name>
        <FirstName>Raymond</FirstName>
        <MiddleInitial>G</MiddleInitial>
        <LastName>Bayliss</LastName>
    </Name>
    <Address>
        <Street1>10 Elizabeth Place</Street1>
        <Town>Paddington</Town>
        <City>Sydney</City>
        <StateProvinceCounty>NSW</StateProvinceCounty>
        <Country>Australia</Country>
        <ZipPostCode>2021</ZipPostCode>
    </Address>
</Customer>
```

We also want it to be able to use the same schema to validate details about employees. In this case the details would be contained in an `Employee` element, although the child elements of each are the same:

```
<?xml version = "1.0" ?>
<Employee employeeID = "133">
    <Name>
        <FirstName>Raymond</FirstName>
        <MiddleInitial>G</MiddleInitial>
        <LastName>Bayliss</LastName>
    </Name>
    <Address>
        <Street1>10 Elizabeth Place</Street1>
        <Town>Paddington</Town>
        <City>Sydney</City>
        <StateProvinceCounty>NSW</StateProvinceCounty>
        <Country>Australia</Country>
        <ZipPostCode>2021</ZipPostCode>
    </Address>
</Employee>
```

Seeing as both the `Customer` and `Employee` elements contain a `Name` element and an `Address` element, both of which have the same content models, we can define the `Name` and `Address` elements globally, and then use a reference to the global declarations inside the declarations for the `Customer` and `Employee` elements. When we want to create a reference to a globally declared element, we use the `ref` attribute on the element declaration, whose value is the name of the element that we are referencing.

In order to use references to elements we have declared, we will qualify all of the elements defined by XML Schema using a **namespace prefix** (We will look into the reasons behind this in Chapter 6). This is what the schema looks like now:

```
<?xml version = "1.0" ?>
<xs:schema xmlns:xs = "http://www.w3.org/2001/XMLSchema">

    <xs:element name = "Customer">
        <xs:complexType>
            <xs:sequence>
                <xs:element ref = "Name" />
                <xs:element ref = "Address" />
            </xs:sequence>
            <xs:attribute name = "customerID" type = "integer" />
        </xs:complexType>
    </xs:element>

    <xs:element name = "Employee">
        <xs:complexType>
            <xs:sequence>
                <xs:element ref = "Name" />
                <xs:element ref = "Address" />
            </xs:sequence>
            <xs:attribute name = "employeeID" type = "integer" />
        </xs:complexType>
    </xs:element>

    <xs:element name = "Name">
        <xs:complexType>
            <xs:sequence>
                <xs:element name = "FirstName" type = "string" />
                <xs:element name = "MiddleInitial" type = "string" />
                <xs:element name = "LastName" type = "string" />
            </xs:sequence>
        </xs:complexType>
    </xs:element>

    <xs:element name = "Address">
        <xs:complexType>
            <xs:sequence>
                <xs:element name = "Street1" type = "string" />
                <xs:element name = "Town" type = "string" />
                <xs:element name = "City" type = "string" />
                <xs:element name = "StateProvinceCounty" type = "string" />
                <xs:element name = "Country" type = "string" />
                <xs:element name = "ZipPostCode" type = "string" />
            </xs:sequence>
        </xs:complexType>
    </xs:element>

</xs:schema>
```

Firstly you will notice the use of the xs: prefix on all of the elements defined by XML Schema. This is declared in the root schema element:

```
<xs:schema xmlns:xs = "http://www.w3.org/2001/XMLSchema">
```

Next you can see that both the Customer element and the Employee element declarations contain a reference to the Name and Address elements:

```
<xs:element name = "Employee">
    <xs:complexType>
        <xs:sequence>
            <xs:element ref = "Name" />
            <xs:element ref = "Address" />
        </xs:sequence>
        <xs:attribute name = "employeeID" type = "integer" />
    </xs:complexType>
</xs:element>
```

This enables re-use of element declarations and saves repeating the element declarations inside each element. Any other element or complex type definition in the schema could use these globally defined elements. It is helpful whenever we have an element that may appear in more than one place in a document instance.

It is important to note, however, that any globally defined element can be used as the root element of a document. The only way of enforcing only one root element in a document is to only have one globally defined element, and to carefully nest all other element declarations inside complex type definitions. The benefits of this approach are that we can create a structure that can be used to validate fragments of documents without having to define separate schemas for each fragment, and that it allows us to define one schema for several classes of document. So, we would be able to validate the following document against this schema:

```
<?xml version = "1.0" ?>
<Address>
    <Street1>10 Elizabeth Place</Street1>
    <Town>Paddington</Town>
    <City>Sydney</City>
    <StateProvinceCounty>NSW</StateProvinceCounty>
    <Country>Australia</Country>
    <ZipPostCode>2021</ZipPostCode>
</Address>
```

This document is considered valid because the Address element has been declared globally. This may not be desirable, and we will see other approaches as we go through the book. We look into this topic more in Chapter 7.

Note that an element declaration that carries a ref attribute cannot also carry a name attribute, nor can it contain a complex type definition.

Element Occurrence Indicators

By default, when we declare an element in an XML Schema it is required to appear once and once only. However there are times when we might want to make the appearance of an element in a document optional. For example, we might want to make the MiddleInitial child element of our Customer element optional in case the customer does not have a middle name. Indeed there may be times when we want an element to be repeatable; for example, we might want to allow several MiddleInitial elements if the customer has several middle names.

To replicate the functionality offered by the cardinality operators in DTDs, namely ?, *, and +, which indicate how many times an element could appear in an instance document, XML Schema introduces two occurrence constraints which take the form of attributes on the element declaration: minOccurs and maxOccurs. Their value indicates how many times the element can appear, and are a lot simpler to use than the cardinality operators in DTDs because we just specify a minimum and maximum number of times that an element can appear. The maxOccurs attribute can also take a value of unbounded, which means that there is no maximum number of times the element can appear in the document instance.

The following table shows the mapping of DTD cardinality operators to the equivalent values of minOccurs and maxOccurs XML Schema attributes:

Cardinality Operator	minOccurs Value	maxOccurs Value	Number of Child Element(s)
[none]	1	1	One and only one
?	0	1	Zero or one
*	0	unbounded	Zero or more
+	1	unbounded	One or more

Let's look at some examples. To start, if we want an element to appear once and once only, then we do not have to add anything to the declaration, as the default values for both attributes if not included are 1. However, for clarity we could explicitly state that the MiddleInitial element must appear once and only once:

```
<element name = "MiddleInitial" type = "string" minOccurs = "1"
         maxOccurs = "1" />
```

If we wanted to make the element optional, so that the element could appear but is not required to do so, and that when it did appear it could only appear once we could use the following:

```
<element name = "MiddleInitial" type = "string" minOccurs = "0"
         maxOccurs = "1" />
```

If we wanted to require at least one MiddleInitial element, yet allow no more than 4 we could use the following:

```
<element name = "MiddleInitial" type = "string" minOccurs = "1"
         maxOccurs = "4" />
```

If we wanted to make sure that there were at least two MiddleInitial elements, but that there were no upper limits on the number of times the element could appear, we could use the following:

```
<element name = "MiddleInitial" type = "string" minOccurs = "2"
         maxOccurs = "unbounded" />
```

> **Note that you cannot declare minOccurs and maxOccurs on global elements, only on local element declarations.**

While we cannot use the minOccurs and maxOccurs attributes on a global element declaration, we can add them to a local element declaration that references a global declaration using the ref attribute:

```
<?xml version = "1.0" ?>
<schema>

   <element name = "Customer">
      <complexType>
         <sequence>
            <element ref = "FirstName" minOccurs = "0" maxOccurs = "1" />
            <element ref = "MiddleInitial"
                     minOccurs = "0" maxOccurs = "unbounded" />
            <element ref = "LastName" minOccurs = "1" maxOccurs = "1" />
         </sequence>
         <attribute name = "customerID" type = "integer" />
      </complexType>
   </element>

   <element name = "FirstName" type = "string" />
   <element name = "MiddleInitial" type = "string" />
   <element name = "LastName" type = "string" />

</schema>
```

Here the `FirstName` is optional, the `MiddleInitial` element is optional although it can appear as many times as the document author requires, and the `LastName` is required.

Value Constraints on Element Content – Default and Fixed Content

With DTDs we could supply a default attribute value for an attribute that was left empty in an instance document, but there was no equivalent mechanism for elements. With XML Schema, we can supply a default value for text-only element content.

If we specify a default value for an element, and that element is empty in the instance document, an XML Schema aware processor would treat the document as though it had the default value when it parses the document. In the following example we have a fragment of an XML instance document, which is used to profile a member's subscription to a web site:

```
<MailOut>
   <Subscribe></Subscribe>
</MailOut>
```

We want the default content of the `Subscribe` element to be `yes`, so we add a `default` attribute to the element declaration, whose value is the simple element content we want:

```
<element name = "Subscribe" type = "string" default = "yes" />
```

Once parsed, if the `Subscribe` element were empty in the instance document, the schema processor would treat the `Subscribe` element as if it had contained the string `yes`.

There is another attribute that we can add to an element declaration, called `fixed`. When `fixed` is used on an element declaration, the element's content must either be empty (in which case it behaves like `default`), or the element content must match the value of the `fixed` attribute. If the document contained a value other than that expressed by the `fixed` attribute it would not be valid.

For example, if we wanted a `SecurityCleared` element to either contain the `boolean` value of `true`, or if empty to be treated as if it contains `true`, we would use the fixed attributes like this:

```
<element name = "SecurityCleared" type = "boolean" fixed = "true" />
```

Therefore, the following would be valid:

```
<SecurityCleared>true</SecurityCleared>
```

As would either of these:

```
<SecurityCleared></SecurityCleared>
<SecurityCleared />
```

In either of the above cases, the processor would treat the element as if it had the content `true`. However, the three examples below would not be valid:

```
<SecurityCleared>false</SecurityCleared>
<SecurityCleared>no</SecurityCleared>
<SecurityCleared><UserID>001</UserID></SecurityCleared>
```

It should be noted that the value of the element is measured against the permitted values for the datatype. We will look at datatypes in more detail in the next chapter, but the examples here are not valid because the only allowed values for a `boolean` whose value is `true`, are the string `true` or the value 1. The following would be a valid example, because 1 is an allowed value for the datatype:

```
<SecurityCleared>1</SecurityCleared>
```

This would be helpful in preventing any documents being validated if they explicitly contained any content other than the string `true`.

Note that we could not add both a `default` and a `fixed` attribute to the same element declaration.

> Together the **default** and **fixed** attributes are known as value constraints, because they constrain the values allowed in element content.

Attribute Declarations

We declare attributes in a similar way to declaring elements. The key differences are:

❑ They cannot contain any child information items. Attribute values are always simple types.

❑ They are unordered; we cannot specify the order in which attributes should appear on a parent element.

This means that the value of the type attribute on an attribute declaration is always a simple type – a restriction upon the value of the attribute. If we do not specify a type, then by default it is the simple version of the ur-type definition, whose name is **anySimpleType**. This represents any legal character string in XML that matches the Char production in the XML 1.0 Recommendation, but we need to be aware that if we need to use characters such as angled brackets ([ ]) or an ampersand (&), these should be escaped using the escape characters or numeric character references defined in the XML 1.0 Recommendation.

Attributes are added to an element inside the complex type definition for that element; they are added after the content of the element is defined within the complex type:

```xml
<?xml version = "1.0" ?>
<schema>
   <element name = "Customer">
      <complexType>
         <sequence>
            <element name = "FirstName" type = "string" />
            <element name = "MiddleInitial" type = "string" />
            <element name = "LastName" type = "string" />
         </sequence>
         <attribute name = "customerID" type = "integer" />
      </complexType>
   </element>
</schema>
```

Here we can see that we have added the customerID attribute to the Customer element by including its declaration at the end of the complex type.

Global versus Local Attribute Declarations

As with element declarations, attribute declarations can either be local or global. If they are global declarations they are direct children of the schema element, meaning that any complex type definition can make use of the attribute.

> As with global and local element declarations, you should be aware that, if your instance documents make use of namespaces, there are greater differences between local and global attribute declarations. This is because globally declared attributes must be explicitly qualified in the instance document, whereas local declarations should not always be qualified. We look into the issues that this introduces and the ways in which it might affect how you write XML Schemas in Chapter 6.

Occurrence of Attributes

By default, when we declare an element to carry an attribute, its presence in an instance document is optional. While there is no provision for minOccurs and maxOccurs attributes on our attribute declarations, because an attribute can only appear once on any given element, we might want to specify that an attribute *must* appear on a given element.

If we want to indicate that an attribute's presence is required, or explicitly state that an attribute is optional, we can add an attribute called `use` to the attribute declaration, which can take one of the following values:

❑   `required` when indicating that an attribute must appear

❑   `optional` when it can either appear once or not at all (the default value)

❑   `prohibited` when we want to explicitly indicate that it must not appear

> **Note that we cannot add the `use` attribute to globally declared attributes.**

For example, if we just want to ensure that an attribute is present on the element, we can just add the `use` attribute to the attribute declaration with a value of `required`:

```
<attribute name="dateReceived" use="required" />
```

If the attribute is optional, we can use the value of `optional`, although this is not required as it is the default value:

```
<attribute name="child" use="optional" />
```

Value Constraints on Attributes

As we would expect from working with attributes in DTDs, we can supply default and fixed content for an attribute's value in the XML Schema. This works rather like the value constraints on the element declarations.

If an attribute is not included in an element in an instance document, we can use the schema to tell the processor: "When processing the document, treat the element as if it had this attribute with the value given in the schema". We give an attribute a default value by adding the `default` attribute to the attribute declaration, like this:

```
<attribute name = "currency" default = "US$" />
```

> **If you have a `default` value for an attribute, then the `use` value must be set to `optional`.**

Imagine that we wanted to be able to validate an XML document in the following format:

```
<CreditAccount currency = "US$">
    <AccountName>Ray Bayliss</AccountName>
    <AccountNumber>27012</AccountNumber>
    <Amount>200.00</Amount>
</CreditAccount>
```

In this example, we want to ensure that if the `CreditAccount` element does not have the `currency` attribute in the instance document, the processor acts as though the attribute is there, and that its value is `US$`. Here is an extract from a schema that will ensure this behavior:

```
<element name = "CreditAccount">
   <complexType>
      <sequence>
         <element name = "AccountName" type = "string" />
         <element name = "AccountNumber" type = "integer" />
         <element name = "Amount" type = "string" />
      </sequence>
      <attribute name = "currency" default = "US$" />
   </complexType>
</element>
```

If we want to indicate that the value of an attribute is the same as the value we prescribe in the schema, whether or not the attribute is present in the instance document, we can use the fixed attribute on the element declaration, like so:

```
<attribute name = "currency" fixed = "US$" />
```

If the attribute does not appear in the document, the value of fixed would act as the default attribute, and the processor would treat the document as though the attribute were there and had the value specified.

For example, if the CreditAccount element was declared to have the following attribute declaration:

```
<element name = "CreditAccount">
   <complexType>
      <sequence>
         <element name = "AccountName" type = "string" />
         <element name = "AccountNumber" type = "integer" />
         <element name = "Amount" type = "string" />
      </sequence>
      <attribute name = "currency" fixed = "US$" />
   </complexType>
</element>
```

Then the following document instance would not be valid because the currency attribute has a value of AUS$ not US$:

```
<CreditAccount currency = "AUS$">
   <AccountName>Ray Bayliss</AccountName>
   <AccountNumber>2701 2202</AccountNumber>
   <Amount>200.00</Amount>
</CreditAccount>
```

If the attribute were missing, the schema processor would treat the CreditAccount element as though it was carrying a currency attribute whose value is US$.

Note that you could not add both a default and a fixed attribute to the same attribute declaration.

> **Together the default and fixed attributes are known as value constraints, because they constrain the value of the attribute.**

Annotations

XML Schema offers two kinds of annotation to a schema, both of which appear as children of an element called annotation:

❏ documentation is rather like the ability to add comments. Using the documentation element, we can add information that will help us and others understand the intended purpose of our documents.

❏ appinfo offers a place in which we can provide additional information to a processing application.

As with all areas of programming, the use of comments is very important (even if they can be a nuisance to add at the time of writing). Of course they help the original author when they come back to use the schema later, but their use is also important for anyone else wanting to use the schema to help them understand the constructs – whether they are authoring documents according to the schema or writing an application to process documents according to the schema. As such, they will be especially helpful if the document author or programmer is not used to the schema syntax.

If we intend that others should use our schema, we should provide enough information in documentation elements to clarify any ambiguity regarding the intended purpose of an element or type. Additional information may also help users get to grips with a schema quicker.

Good use of documentation could make the difference in getting our schema adopted by a group of users over an alternative schema that is not as well documented.

DTD authors are allowed to use comments using the same syntax used for XML comments:

```
<!-- comment goes here -->
```

Indeed, we can include comments in this form in an XML Schema because it is an XML document itself, but this is not a good way of documenting the XML Schema for these reasons:

❏ By putting documentation in a documentation element, you can add structured documentation including markup such as XHTML, whereas XML comments cannot.

❏ You can easily make the schema self-documenting by adding a stylesheet to it.

❏ XML parsers can ignore comments. By providing an explicit documentation element, the information becomes available to any processing application. If the processing application is an authoring tool, it can pass on information from the documentation element to document authors allowing them to use the markup as it is intended

The annotation element can appear at the beginning of most schema constructs, although it will most commonly be used inside element, attribute, simpleType, complexType, group, and schema elements. Where we place the annotation and its child documentation will affect what the documentation applies to.

In our simple Customer example that we have been looking at through this chapter, we could provide copyright and author information at the root of the schema, and indicate to document authors that the MiddleInitial element is optional, although if the Customer has a middle name we should use it:

```
<?xml version = "1.0" ?>
<xs:schema xmlns:xs = "http://www.w3.org/2001/XMLSchema">
   <xs:annotation>
      <xs:documentation>
         Schema for customer name information.
         Used in Professional XML Schemas
         Copyright Wrox Press Ltd 2001, all rights reserved
         1102 Warwick Road, Acocks Green, Birmingham, B27 6BH. UK
      </xs:documentation>
   </xs:annotation>
   <xs:element name = "Customer">
   <xs:annotation>
      <xs:documentation>
         MiddleInitial is optional, but should be used if the customer has a
         middle name to help distinguish between customers with like names.
      </xs:documentation>
   </xs:annotation>
      <xs:complexType>
         <xs:group ref = "NameGroup" />
      </xs:complexType>
   </xs:element>
   <xs:group name = "NameGroup">
      <xs:sequence>
         <xs:element name = "FirstName" type = "xs:string" />
         <xs:element name = "MiddleInitial" type = "xs:string" />
         <xs:element name = "LastName" type = "xs:string" />
      </xs:sequence>
   </xs:group>
</xs:schema>
```

The appinfo child of the annotation element is designed to pass information to a processing
application, stylesheet, or other tool. This will be a particular advantage to schema users if XML
Schema compliant parsers implement a way of passing this information to an application, because those
who used XML 1.0 processing instructions to pass information to the processing application often had to
write custom parsers in order to do this. Therefore, a lot of developers who could have made use of
processing instructions ended up putting that information in application code, making the resulting
application less flexible. By allowing information to be put into the appinfo element, programmers can
either pass information to the application about how the section of a conforming document should be
processed, or they can add extra code inside the appinfo elements.

The appinfo element is subject to the same rules for appearing in an XML Schema as the
documentation element, as they are both contained in the annotation element. This means that it
can be used within most schema constructs. In the following example we have nested some script inside
the appinfo element, which is intended to indicate to an application what action to take, depending
upon which of a choice of two elements a document instance contains:

```
<xs:group name="CreditOrDebitGroup">
   <xs:annotation>
      <xs:appinfo>
         if (currentNode.firstChild != "Credit")
            docParser.load(debitURL);
         else
            document.write("Your account will be credited within 24
                        hours.");
```

```
        </xs:appinfo>
      </xs:annotation>
    <xs:choice>
       <xs:element name = "Credit" type = "CreditType" />
       <xs:element name = "Debit" type = "DebitType" />
    </xs:choice>
  </xs:group>
```

The script buried inside the `appinfo` element can be passed to an application that is using the schema to validate an instance of the document. In this case, the script in the `appinfo` element can be passed to a processing application to indicate how to handle each element in the choice group, depending upon which element the document contains.

We look at annotation in more detail in Chapter 10 on Schemas and XSLT. There is also an interesting example of using the `appinfo` element to contain Schematron rules in Chapter 14.

Validating an Instance Document

Having understood some of the basics for writing XML Schemas, we should look at how we validate document instances. You may have noticed that none of the sample XML documents in this chapter have indicated a link to the XML Schema they are supposed to correspond to. They have not included an equivalent of the Document Type Declaration (whether it refers to inline definitions or an external DTD). This is because there is no direct link of any kind between an instance document and its XML Schema.

A document author can indicate where a copy of the schema they used to write the document can be found using the `xsi:schemaLocation` attribute, whose value is a URL, but there is no requirement for the processor to use the indicated schema. For example we could use the following to indicate where the `Customer.xsd` file can be found:

```
<?xml version = "1.0" ?>
<Customer xmlns:xsi = "http://www.w3.org/2001/XMLSchema-instance"
          xsi:schemaLocation = "http://www.wrox.com/ProXMLSchemas/
          Customer.xsd">

   ...
</Customer>
```

Note that we have had to declare the XML Schema for Instance Documents namespace and its prefix `xsi:` in order to use the `schemaLocation` attribute (as the `schemaLocation` attribute is defined in that namespace).

> **Parsers can ignore or override the suggestion in the `schemaLocation` attribute; they may decide to use a different schema or use a cached copy of the suggested schema.**

Sometimes it is helpful to be able to validate a document against a different schema than that which it was authored against. Therefore we can leave it up to the program that hands the XML document to the parser to say which schema to use to validate it.

Note also that we have not so far been indicating the intended namespace to which our schema belongs. This means that the markup we have been creating does not belong to a namespace. In this case we need to use the `xsi:noNamespaceSchemaLocation` attribute on the root element, like this:

```
<?xml version = "1.0" ?>
<Customer xmlns:xsi = "http://www.w3.org/2001/XMLSchema-instance"
          xsi:noNamespaceSchemaLocation = "Customer.xsd">
...
</Customer>
```

This indicates to the parser where it can find a copy of the schema that doesn't belongs to a namespace.

How the XML Schema Recommendation Specifies Validity

The XML Schema Recommendation does not indicate *how* an XML Schema aware processor should validate a document, so before we look at validation it is worthwhile taking a moment to understand how the XML Schema Recommendation determines validity. The XML Schema Recommendation is written in terms of an abstract model (rather like the DOM Recommendation). This corresponds to information items as defined in the **XML Information Set**.

The purpose of the XML Information Set (or **infoset**) is to provide a consistent set of definitions that can be used in other specifications that refer to information held within a well-formed XML document.

Any well-formed XML document has an **information set** (as long as it also conforms to the XML Namespaces Recommendation). This in turn means that an XML Schema and all instance documents must be well-formed in order for them to be processed by a parser. After all, a document that is not well-formed does not have an information set.

The infoset presents an XML document's information set as a modified tree. We should be clear however, that the XML Schema Recommendation does not require that an XML Schema aware processor's interfaces make the infoset available as a tree structure – the document may just as equally be accessed by an event-based approach (such as that implemented in SAX processors) or a query-based interface. However, the term information set can be treated as analogous to the term **tree**.

An XML document's information set consists of a number of **information items**, each of which can be treated as analogous to a **node** on the tree. An information item is an abstract representation of some part of a document, and each information item has a set of associated properties. At minimum, a well-formed XML document will have a document information item. There are 14 information items in all; here are the ones that we are most concerned with:

❑ The **document information item** is the unique element in which all other markup is nested within a well-formed XML document. In the case of an XML Schema document, the document information item would correspond to the `schema` element.

❑ An **element information item** exists for every element that appears in an XML document.

❑ An **attribute information item** exists for each attribute, whether specified or defaulted, of each element in the document.

❑ A **character information item** exists for each data character in the document, whether literally or as a character reference, or within a CDATA section. Each character is a logically separate information item, although many processing applications chunk characters into larger groups.

❑ A **namespace information item** exists for each namespace that is in the scope for that element.

By talking in terms of an abstract tree representation, the schema specification can then ensure that each information item in an instance document respects the constraints imposed by the corresponding information item in the schema. This is known as **local schema-validity**.

There is a second level of schema validity, which represents the overall validation outcome for each item. This is where the local schema-validity of an information item corresponds with the results of the schema-validity assessments performed upon its descendents, if it has any. So, a parent element is checked against the schema-validity assessments of its child information items.

Therefore, the XML Schema Recommendation does not have to worry about how the validating processor is implemented. As long as the information items are locally schema-valid, and they correspond with child information items, an instance document will be valid. At each stage, augmentations (in the form of properties) may be added to the information items in the information set to record the outcome and help the processor achieve its task.

So, each of the components that make up any schema are used to determine whether an element or attribute in an instance document is valid. In addition, a processor may check augmentations (such as default values) placed upon those elements, attributes, and their descendents.

Validating with XSV

At the time of writing, XML Schema has only recently become a full W3C recommendation, and there are limited tools available for validating instance documents using the final recommendation. A proliferation of compliant tools is expected to follow, but many are in still in beta version. Check out Appendix D for full discussion of XML Schema tools and XML Schema-compliant parsers. For now, however, we are just going to focus on one, XSV.

XSV (XML Schema Validator) is an ongoing open source project, developed at the University of Edinburgh in the UK by Henry Thompson and Richard Tobin (Henry Thompson is also co-author of the XML Schema Recommendation, Part 1). Written in Python, it is available for download either as source, or as a Win32 executable. Alternatively, you can use it as an online utility. XSV is available from:

❏   http://www.ltg.ed.ac.uk/~ht/xsv-status.html (for download)

❏   http://www.w3.org/2001/03/webdata/xsv (to use online)

> *The easiest way to use XSV is via the online web form. You can validate schemas on their own by simply uploading the file from your own machine, but if you want to validate instance documents against your schema, then you need to be able to make them available online. If this is difficult for you – if you are behind a firewall for example – then you may prefer to download XSV and install it on your own machine.*

Since this is ongoing work, there are frequent updates to the tool, and full details concerning which parts of the XML Schema recommendation are implemented is available from the first URL above. At the time of writing, this tool appears to be the one most fully conformant with the W3C recommendation.

> *Warning: One of the main limitations of XSV at the time of writing is its lack of support for validating simple types. The only checks that XSV makes on simples types are on length and enumerations.*

The download comes in the form of a self-installing executable for Win32. If you're working on a Unix platform, however, you'll need to download and compile the source files. Alternatively, you could check out some of the tools discussed in Appendix D, such as Turbo XML from TIBCO Extensibility Solutions.

Validating a Schema

Let's start by validating a simple schema, name.xsd:

```
<?xml version = "1.0" encoding = "UTF-8"?>
<xs:schema xmlns:xs = "http://www.w3.org/2001/XMLSchema">
    <xs:element name = "Name">
        <xs:complexType>
            <xs:sequence>
                <xs:element name = "firstName" type = "xs:string" />
                <xs:element name = "middleInitial" type = "xs:string" />
                <xs:element name = "lastName" type = "xs:string" />
            </xs:sequence>
        </xs:complexType>
    </xs:element>
</xs:schema>
```

If you try validating this schema online, then you should see something like this:

Using the downloaded version of XSV, you can check that this is a valid schema by simply running it from the command line with a -i flag:

(Note that you'll need to have the folder in which XSV is installed included in your PATH variable). The output here isn't immediately obvious, so let's take a quick look at it (see the screenshot below). You can see that we are looking at a schema file here rather than an XML instance document since it says instanceAccessed='false', and that the target is [standalone schema assessment]. Note that no schema errors are listed.

If you are running IE5 or above, you get a more user-friendly version of this and you can redirect the XML output to another file, including a stylesheet for display, with the command:

> xsv -o xsv-out.xml -s xsv.msxsl -i name.xsd

If you have MSXML 3 installed, you should replace xsv.msxsl with the XSLT 1.0 compliant version of the stylesheet, xsv.xsl. You can then view the result in your browser:

Note that you can use xsv -? *for information on all the possible flags.*

So that covers the basic ways of using XSV. Now let's take a look at some of the error messages that occur if our schema *isn't* error free. Suppose, for example, we make a simple typographical mistake, such as spelling the name attribute wrongly, or forgetting to close one of the elements:

```
<?xml version = "1.0" encoding = "UTF-8"?>
<xs:schema xmlns:xs = "http://www.w3.org/2001/XMLSchema">
   <xs:element name = "Name">
      <xs:complexType>
         <xs:sequence>
            <xs:element nsme = "firstName" type = "xs:string" />
            <xs:element name = "middleInitial" type = "xs:string" />
            <xs:element name = "lastName" type = "xs:string" />
         </xs:sequence>
      <xs:complexType>
   </xs:element>
</xs:schema>
```

In this case, XSV warns us that we have an undeclared attribute nsme, on our element element, and that we have a complexType declaration out of place:

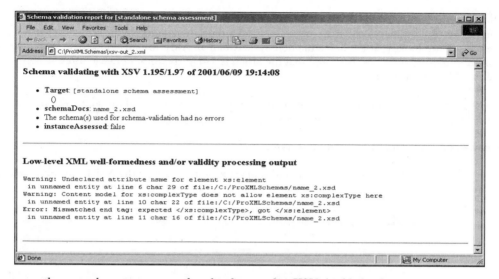

The reason the second error message takes this form is that XSV thinks that because we have forgotten to add a / in our closing tag, we are trying to nest a second complexType element inside the first, which is not allowed. Note that XSV also gives us the line number of each error. While the mistakes may be quite obvious in our simple schema, this information becomes very helpful when working with more complex examples.

Validating an Instance Document

Now let's try validating an instance document against our simple schema:

```
<?xml version = "1.0" encoding = "UTF-8"?>
<Name xmlns:xsi=" http://www.w3.org/2001/XMLSchema-instance"
      xsi:noNamespaceSchemaLocation="name.xsd">
   <firstName>John</firstName>
   <middleInitial>J</middleInitial>
   <lastName>Johnson</lastName>
</Name>
```

Here, we have used the xsi:noNamespaceSchemaLocation attribute to indicate the location of the schema document to which the XML instance document conforms. In this case, it is in the same directory. Note that if you're validating this with the online version of XSV, both the XML file and the schema file need to be accessible over the web. Here's what the results look like for this file, name.xml:

The things to look out for here are the statement that there are no schema-validity problems in the target, and that the "Validation was strict": this means that the instance document has correctly validated against the schema. If you see the validation described as "lax", then you'll know that your document has not been validated, though it may be well formed. Note also the line at the bottom of the output, "Attempt to import a schema document from http://apache.wrox.co.uk/name.xsd for no namespace succeeded". This means that XSV has successfully found and loaded the correct schema document.

Let's take a look at an instance document with some problems, so you can see how XSV reports errors in document validation. Here, we've simply slipped in an extra `title` element that is not declared in our schema:

```
<?xml version = "1.0" encoding = "UTF-8"?>
<Name xmlns:xsi="http://www.w3.org/2001/XMLSchema-instance"
      xsi:noNamespaceSchemaLocation="name.xsd">
   <title>Dr</title>
   <firstName>John</firstName>
   <middleInitial></middleInitial>
   <lastName>Johnson</lastName>
</Name>
```

Let's try this one with our local version of XSV. In this case, we don't use the `-i` flag, as we are validating an instance document, not a schema, so we use the command:

> xsv -o xsv-out.xml -s xsv.msxsl name_2.xml

And this is what the output looks like:

In the first part of the output, we see the line, "2 schema-validity problems were found in the target". If you look at the section below, where the problems are listed in detail, you can clearly see that there is a `title` element that is not allowed according to the schema, and XSV was expecting the `firstName` element to appear in its place. The first number after the file name (in this case 4) indicates the line number on which the error occurred. Again, this information can be very useful when debugging schemas.

The output prefixes all of the element names with {None} to indicate that these elements are not part of a namespace. We'll be seeing how to create schemas with a target namespace in Chapter 6.

In the final part of this chapter, we'll be tying together the ideas that we have met so far in a slightly more complex example.

Example Schema: Delivery Receipt

In this example, we'll see how to create a schema for a delivery receipt called `DeliveryReceipt.xsd`. The schema contains constructs for names, addresses, and delivery items.

The delivery receipt is held within a root element called `DeliveryReceipt`, which has two attributes, `deliveryID` and `dateReceived`. The customer's name and address are then held within an element called `Customer`. Finally, the delivered items will be held within an `Items` element.

Here is a sample document marked up according to the `DeliveryReceipt.xsd` schema called `DeliveryReceipt.xml`:

```xml
<?xml version = "1.0" ?>
<DeliveryReceipt deliveryID = "44215" dateReceived = "2001-04-16"
  xsi:noNamespaceSchemaLocation = "http://file_Location/DeliveryReceipt.xsd"
  xmlns:xsi = "http://www.w3.org/2001/XMLSchema-instance">
  <Customer>
    <Name>
      <FirstName>Ray</FirstName>
      <MiddleInitial>G</MiddleInitial>
      <LastName>Bayliss</LastName>
    </Name>
    <Address>
      <AddressLine1>10 Elizabeth Place</AddressLine1>
      <AddressLine2></AddressLine2>
      <Town>Paddington</Town>
      <City>Sydney</City>
      <StateProvinceCounty>NSW</StateProvinceCounty>
      <ZipPostCode>2021</ZipPostCode>
    </Address>
  </Customer>
  <Items>
    <DeliveryItem quantity = "2">
      <Description>Small Boxes</Description>
    </DeliveryItem>
  </Items>
</DeliveryReceipt>
```

Note how we indicate to a parser that it will be able to find a schema to validate the document using the `xsi:noNamespaceSchemaLocation` attribute in the root element. We use this because the constructs in the schema do not belong to a namespace. In order to use this attribute, we also need to declare the namespace for the XML Schema for instance documents:

```
<DeliveryReceipt deliveryID = "44215" dateReceived = "2001-04-16"
  xsi:noNamespaceSchemaLocation = "http://file_Location/DeliveryReceipt.xsd"
  xmlns:xsi = "http://www.w3.org/2001/XMLSchema-instance">
```

Now let's see the schema that we use for our Delivery Receipt documents. The schema is called
DeliveryReceipt.xsd:

```
<?xml version="1.0" encoding="UTF-8"?>
<xs:schema xmlns:xs = "http://www.w3.org/2001/XMLSchema">
   <xs:element name = "DeliveryReceipt">
      <xs:complexType>
         <xs:sequence>

            <xs:element name = "Customer">
               <xs:complexType>
                  <xs:sequence>
                     <xs:element ref = "Name" />
                     <xs:element ref = "Address" />
                  </xs:sequence>
               </xs:complexType>
            </xs:element>

            <xs:element name = "Items">
               <xs:complexType>
                  <xs:sequence>
                     <xs:element ref = "DeliveryItem"
                                 minOccurs = "1" maxOccurs = "unbounded"/>
                  </xs:sequence>
               </xs:complexType>
            </xs:element>

         </xs:sequence>
         <xs:attribute name = "deliveryID" type = "xs:integer" />
         <xs:attribute name = "dateReceived" type = "xs:date" />
      </xs:complexType>
   </xs:element>

   <xs:element name = "Name">
      <xs:complexType>
         <xs:sequence>
            <xs:element name = "FirstName" type = "xs:string" />
            <xs:element name = "MiddleInitial" type = "xs:string"
                              minOccurs = "0" maxOccurs = "1" />
            <xs:element name = "LastName" type = "xs:string" />
         </xs:sequence>
      </xs:complexType>
   </xs:element>

   <xs:element name = "Address">
      <xs:complexType>
         <xs:sequence>
            <xs:element name = "AddressLine1"  type = "xs:string" />
            <xs:element name = "AddressLine2" type = "xs:string"
                        minOccurs = "0" maxOccurs = "1" />
            <xs:element name = "Town" type = "xs:string" />
```

```
            <xs:element name = "City" type = "xs:string"
                        minOccurs = "0" maxOccurs = "1" />
            <xs:element name = "StateProvinceCounty" type = "xs:string" />
            <xs:element name = "ZipPostCode"  type = "xs:string" />
        </xs:sequence>
    </xs:complexType>
</xs:element>

<xs:element name = "DeliveryItem">
    <xs:complexType>
        <xs:sequence>
            <xs:element name = "Description"  type = "xs:string" />
        </xs:sequence>
        <xs:attribute name = "quantity" type = "xs:integer" />
    </xs:complexType>
</xs:element>

</xs:schema>
```

There are a few things we should note about this schema:

❑ We have defined the `Name`, `Address`, and `DeliveryItem` elements globally, which also means that this schema could be used to validate documents only containing these elements

❑ We build the `Customer` element's content model using references to the globally declared `Name` and `Address` elements

Let's take a closer look at the schema. We start off declaring the namespace for XML Schema, which we use to prefix all of the elements defined by the XML Schema Recommendation:

```
<xs:schema xmlns:xs = "http://www.w3.org/2001/XMLSchema">
```

We then define the root element `DeliveryReceipt`. Because it contains `Customer` and `Items` element elements (as opposed to being a text-only element), we have had to associate it with complex type using the `complexType` element. This also contains a `sequence` compositor, requiring that the `Customer` element appear before the `Items` element.

Between the closing `sequence` and `complexType` elements, we declare the two attributes that are carried by the `DeliveryReceipt` element: `deliveryID`, whose type is an `integer`, and `dateReceived`, whose type is a date type:

```
    <xs:element name = "DeliveryReceipt">
        <xs:complexType>
            <xs:sequence>

                <xs:element name = "Customer">
                    ...
                </xs:element>

                <xs:element name = "Items">
                    ...
                </xs:element>
```

```
            <xs:attribute name = "deliveryID" type = "xs:integer" />
            <xs:attribute name = "dateReceived" type = "xs:date" />
        </xs:complexType>
    </xs:element>
```

Inside the declaration of the DeliveryReceipt element we have a declaration of the Customer and Items elements. Both Customer and Items contain child elements, so we need to use a complexType element inside each of them, along with a compositor, which is the sequence element, to indicate the order in which they can appear. Customer and Items are made up of references to globally declared elements using the ref attribute:

```
    <xs:element name = "Customer">
        <xs:complexType>
            <xs:sequence>
                <xs:element ref = "Name" />
                <xs:element ref = "Address" />
            </xs:sequence>
        </xs:complexType>
    </xs:element>

    <xs:element name = "Items">
        <xs:complexType>
            <xs:sequence>
                <xs:element ref = "DeliveryItem"
                            minOccurs = "1" maxOccurs = "unbounded"/>
            </xs:sequence>
        </xs:complexType>
    </xs:element>
```

We have already seen how we defined the Name and Address elements earlier in the chapter. The third globally declared element is the DeliveryItem element, which can occur one or more times. Note that we had to declare the occurrence constraints on the reference to the element, however, because you cannot add them to global declarations.

The DeliveryItem element also holds a quantity element, which is declared between the closing sequence and complexType elements. The quantity attribute has a type of integer:

```
    <xs:element name = "DeliveryItem">
        <xs:complexType>
            <xs:sequence>
                <xs:element name = "Description"  type = "xs:string" />
            </xs:sequence>
            <xs:attribute name = "quantity" type = "xs:integer" />
        </xs:complexType>
    </xs:element>
```

We specify the simple built-in string datatype on the Description element to restrict the allowable content of text-only elements; if we not did associate them with a type they could hold any well-formed combination of elements, attributes and characters that we had defined in the schema.

Summary

In this chapter we have looked at the basics of the W3C XML Schema syntax, and how we can declare which elements and attributes are allowed to appear in our XML documents. We have seen that in order to declare an element or an attribute, we must associate its name with a type, and how XML Schema introduces two categories of types:

❑   Simple types: which restrict text-only element content and attribute values

❑   Complex types: which are required to indicate when an element contains child elements and carries attributes

We have briefly touched on some of the other features that make XML Schema such a powerful language:

❑   The built-in types such as string, date and integer, which will make integration of XML with applications and data sources a lot easier

❑   The annotation mechanism for commenting and passing information to processing applications

We also alluded to some of the more complicated features we will be seeing in coming chapters, such as the use of namespaces, named complex types and different compositors.

Having addressed the basics of the element and attribute declarations and the differences between simple and complex types in XML Schema, you can go on to look at the built-in types in more depth in the next chapter. In Chapter 3, we'll move on to see how we can build more complicated structures.

Datatype Basics

The basic benefit of XML – the ability to describe one's own vocabulary – is greatly enhanced by the use of XML Schema datatypes. These can ensure for example: that numeric data is really numeric, strings are a specific format, or otherwise validate the format and/or value of an element or attribute. Pre-defined XML Schema datatypes make provisions for various forms of commonly used values such as dates, times, and URI references, as well as providing the basis for more complex and user-defined data structures.

Strong data typing and the ability to create modern object-oriented (OO) structures are imperative for most of the newer uses of XML (such as SOAP or ebXML). These new applications can now use most of the datatypes used in traditional programming languages, plus the conceptual and maintenance benefits of OO inheritance of datatypes and structures.

The use of strong data typing has advantages beyond the description and validation of documents and web pages. Once web sites serve pages in XML, rather than HTML, web spiders will be able to extract much more meaningful information from these sites. For example:

❑   Numeric datatypes allow price comparison services that can calculate currency conversions, taxes, and/or multi-item costs.

❑   Users searching for date-sensitive items (like newspaper articles or a specific event) can use standardized dates, and search for specific dates or ranges of dates.

❑   Type-specific searching can also apply to other specific datatypes such as URIs and user-derived datatypes such as ISBNs, UPCs, and part numbers.

Existing free-text searches can't differentiate the *May* Company, *May* Day, the merry month of *May*, a place called *May*, or a person's name. Nor can these searches ignore the many appearances of the permissive verb "*may*" – which is rarely the target of a search, and often included in the "stop words" list (terms ignored when searching). The use of XML Schema datatypes will permit much more focused searching, reducing the huge lists of online search engine results. Type-specific searching is an awesome benefit of XML Schema's strong data typing.

First, we will look at the basic principles of schema datatypes, and then we will look at the two dozen or so built-in datatypes provided as part of XML Schema.

Datatypes in XML – An Overview

XML 1.0 and its DTDs provided a few simple datatypes, but none were numeric types, and validation mechanisms quite limited. There have been proposals to add some additional type checking to DTDs (such as DT4DTD), but these are beyond the scope of this book. Early schema proposals such as SOX and XML-Data provided various sets of pre-defined types, which informed the development of the W3C Schema Recommendation. The lack of strong data typing was one of the principle reasons for the development of XML Schema. Indeed, datatypes are so significant that they comprise half of the XML Schema specification, and they may be used independently from the rest of the XML Schema specification.

XML Schema datatypes are defined in XML Schema Part 2: Datatypes, which became a W3C Recommendation in May 2001. It is available at http://www.w3.org/TR/xmlschema-2.

These datatypes are based upon those in XML 1.0 DTDs, Java, SQL, the ISO 11404 standard on language-independent datatypes, existing Internet standards, and earlier schema proposals.

It would be useful to have a link to an online version of the ISO 11404 standard, but like most ISO documents, it is only available as expensive paper. You can find ordering information for this at http://www.iso.ch/cate/d19346.html.

In the last chapter, we saw how we could use the XML Schema built-in datatypes, such as `string` and `integer`, in our element declarations, for example:

```
<element name = "FirstName" type = "string" />
```

We also saw how we could create our own types rather than those from XML Schema, using the `complexType` element, like this:

```
<element name = "Customer">
    <complexType>
       <sequence>
          <element name = "FirstName" type = "string" />
          <element name = "MiddleInitial" type = "string" />
          <element name = "LastName" type = "string" />
       </sequence>
    </complexType>
</element>
```

Complex types and simple types are defined in Part 1 of the XML Schema specification (http://www.w3.org/TR/xmlschema-1). These concepts are about defining structures in your schemas. Here is a quick reminder of the difference between simple and complex types:

❑   **simple types** – a simple string that doesn't contain any child elements, but might be constrained to be numeric or otherwise specially-formatted (attribute values are always simple types)

❑   **complex types** – element values that contain other elements or have attributes, and can be constrained in a similar fashion to simple types

The second part of the specification independently defines the set of **built-in datatypes**. These are all simple types. In the next chapter we'll move on to see how we create our own complex content models using `complexType` and other schema constructs, but for this chapter, we'll be focusing on the set simple datatypes provided for us by XML Schema. Before we get stuck into the details of the different datatypes, let's spend a bit of time reviewing the basic ideas behind XML Schema datatypes in general.

Properties of XML Schema Datatypes

All datatypes are composed of three parts:

❑ A **value space** – the set of distinct and valid values, each corresponding to one or more string representations (for example, the number 42 is a single value)

❑ A **lexical space** – the set of lexical representations, that is, the string literals representing values (for example, any of the strings "42" or "forty-two" or "0.42E2" or even "0.42 10^2" could represent the value of 42)

❑ A set of **facets** – the properties of the value space, individual values, and/or lexical items

To illustrate the difference between lexical and value spaces, we'll look at a snippet of XML data where the first child element (`Name`) is declared to be a `string` datatype, the second (`Population`) uses the `decimal` datatype, and the third is a `date` datatype (`DateAdmission`).

```
<State>
    <Name>Wyoming</Name>
    <Population>469557</Population>
    <DateAdmission>1890-07-10</DateAdmission>
</State>
```

In the `Name` element, the value and lexical spaces are identical – the value of a string is the same as its lexical representation.

On the other hand, the `Population` element is represented in XML as a string, but its value is the mathematical concept of "four hundred and sixty nine thousand, five hundred and fifty seven". The string 469557 in the above example is just one possible lexical representation. We could also have used 469557.0 or 4695.57e2 to represent the same value.

The `DateAdmission` element is also represented as a string, like all elements in XML. This one conforms to an international (ISO) standard, and represents a value of July 10th, 1890. ISO dates are similar to the common data processing or Japanese format preference (*yyyy-mm-dd*). We will look at this and other built-in derived datatypes in the next chapter.

All comparisons, calculations, ordering, and the like are generally applied to the *value* of the datatype. There may be several alternative lexical representations for a given value.

Value Spaces

Each datatype has a range of possible values. These value spaces are implicit for many datatypes. For example, a floating-point number can range from negative to positive infinity. A string can contain any finite-length sequence of legal XML characters. An integer allows a value of zero, or any positive or negative whole number, but wouldn't allow fractional values.

Lexical Spaces

A lexical space is a set of string literals that *represent* the values of a datatype. These literals are always "text" characters, which may be any of the XML-legal subset of Unicode.

Remember that XML strings can use almost any Unicode 3.0 character in the range from #x0000 to #x10FFFF, excluding all ASCII control characters (#x0000 to #x001F) except the tab (#x09), newline / line-feed (#x0A), and carriage-return (#x0D) characters. Also excluded are character values in the range #xD800 to #xDFFF, and all of those values greater than #xFFFD.

By definition, strings only have one lexical representation, but numeric values may have several equivalent and equally valid lexical representations. For example, 100, 100.0, and 1.00e2 are obviously different lexical values, but they all have identical numeric values in the floating-point number value space. Date / time combinations may also have multiple representations of the same moment in different time zones, such as 2000-12-31T23:01-01:00 and 2001-01-01T00:01Z (both equivalent to the first minute of the recent turn of the millennium along the Prime Meridian).

To facilitate the *lexical* comparison of data, each datatype has a single **canonical representation**, as specified in the XML Schema Recommendation. This is the single lexical representation that should be used if such comparisons are needed. These canonical representations are critical to the creation and comparison of signed and verifiable documents in XML. They are similar in concept to Canonical XML.

Canonical XML *is a W3C Recommendation [2001-03-15] that is available at http://www.w3.org/TR/xml-c14n. This specification describes a way to generate a single common physical representation (the "canonical form") of some XML data that might have multiple physical representations, depending upon the use of entities and/or namespaces. If two instances of XML data have the same canonical form, they are considered to be equivalent.*

Secure and non-refutable business, legal, or financial transactions rely upon the ability to compare XML data instances and document any differences. Checksums and other methods may also be used to ensure that the data is not inadvertently or maliciously changed. It is a good idea to use the canonical representation of datatypes whenever possible (which will save some transformation time if Canonical XML is required).

Facets

A facet is one of the defining properties of a datatype. It distinguishes that datatype from others. Facets include properties such as the length of a string, the number of items in a list, or a range of minimum and maximum numeric values.

The abstract and intrinsic properties that define the characteristics of a value space are known as **fundamental facets**. These include: **equality**, **order**, **bounds**, **cardinality**, and the age-old **numeric / non-numeric** dichotomy.

Optional limits upon permissible values of a datatype's value space are called **constraining facets**. These include ranges of numeric values, string lengths, and can even use regular expressions to describe legal values. These facets can be used to **restrict** the permissible value space to create a new datatype, called a **derived datatype**. We'll see more about what this means in the next section, and in the next chapter, we'll see how to go about deriving our own new types.

Primitive versus Derived Datatypes

XML Schema provides two basic kinds of **built-in** datatype:

❑   **primitive datatypes** – those that are not defined in terms of other datatypes

❑   **derived datatypes** – types that are defined in terms of existing datatypes

It is worth noting that with the XML Schema built-in datatypes, the distinction between primitive and derived is really rather arbitrary.

Primitive datatypes cannot themselves be defined from any smaller components. They form the basis from which all other datatypes are derived, and they are defined only by the W3C in the XML Schema specification. A string of characters is probably the universal primitive type, and it is known as the string datatype in XML Schema. We've already used this in the last chapter. Floating-point numbers are based upon the well-known mathematical concept of real numbers, and correspond to the XML Schema primitive types named float and double. The entire set of built-in primitive datatypes will be described later in this chapter.

A **derived datatype** is one that is defined in terms of an existing datatype, known as its **base type**. New types may be derived from either a built-in primitive datatype or another derived datatype. Derived types inherit their value space from their base type, and may also constrain the derived value space to be an explicit subset of the base type's value space.

For example, integers are a subset of real numbers. Therefore, the XML Schema integer type is derived from the floating-point number type, which is its base type. We can in turn derive an even more restricted type of integer, negativeInteger:

```
<xs:simpleType name="negativeInteger" base="xs:integer">
   <xs:maxInclusive value="-1" />
</xs:simpleType>
```

The above is an example of an XML Schema structure known as a **Simple Type Definition** that uses the simpleType element to describe a derived integer datatype that is limited to negative values. The elements that describe the bounds of legal negative integer values are facets (properties) of this datatype. We will have an in-depth discussion of these and other facets in the next chapter, when we look at deriving types in more detail.

Datatypes can be derived in one of three ways:

❑   By **restriction**, where limits are placed on the base type's constraining facets. The negativeInteger datatype is an example of this – it is restricted to the set of negative integers. It is essentially a subset of the integer datatype.

❑   By **list**, where the derived datatype is a list of space separated values of the base datatype. For example, NMTOKENS, which is a list of NMTOKEN values.

❑   By **union**, where there are two or more base datatypes, and the value space derived datatype is formed from the union of the value spaces of the base types.

Complex types have a further method of derivation: by extension. We'll be looking at this in Chapter 4.

As with the primitive types, the W3C has defined a set of built-in derived datatypes that are so common that it was felt they should be an integral part of the XML Schema specification. These will also be described in detail later in this chapter.

Built-in Types versus User-Defined

As we have seen, XML Schema provides a set of predefined datatypes, known as **built-in types**. Only the W3C can add to these types by amending the XML Schema specification. These built-in types include both primitive and derived types, as described above. By definition, all primitive types are built-in types. The handful of built-in derived datatypes was believed to be so universal that they would end up being reinvented by most schema designers.

However, one of the great advantages of XML Schema is that you can derive your own datatypes, which are not a part of the specification, but are based on existing datatypes. These are called **user-defined datatypes**. These are always derived datatypes.

We could look at the relationship of datatypes and structures in XML Schema in terms of physical chemistry. Datatypes can be seen as the "sub-atomic particles" (primitive datatypes) and "atoms" or "elements" (derived datatypes) that are the basis of all the larger "compounds" (structures) in a schema.

Kinds of Datatype

Datatypes in XML Schema can be categorized as:

- ❑ **Atomic types** – these have *values* that are defined to be indivisible. All the built-in primitive types are atomic, but derived types can also be atomic.

- ❑ **List types** – these are whitespace-delimited lists of values of an atomic type. Lists are derived types; the type that makes up the list is its base type.

- ❑ **Union types** – these allow values and lexical representations to be any one of a set of alternatives. These are also derived types.

Now let's briefly look at each of these categories in turn.

Atomic Datatypes

An atomic type is one that has a *value* that cannot be divided, at least not within the context of XML Schema.

> **Atomic types are indivisible types, and may be either primitive or derived – an "atomic" type is *not* analogous to a "primitive" type.**

For example, numbers and strings are atomic types since their values cannot be described using any smaller pieces. The former is pretty obvious, but can't a string be defined in terms of a smaller component, namely characters? While this is true in the abstract sense, XML Schema has no concept of a character as a datatype – and therefore a string is atomic.

```
<atom>This string is as fine as we can slice textual data - there are no character
'atoms' in XML Schema.</atom>

<another_atom>1927-01-16</another_atom>
<!-- dates are XML Schema datatypes -->

<yet_another_atom>469557</yet_another_atom>
<!-- as are numbers -->
```

In the above example elements, the first (atom) is an atomic primitive type (a string). The second element
(another_atom) is an atomic derived type. Most date and time types *could* be derived from a single dateTime
primitive type, though in XML Schema they are all primitive types. The third example element
(yet_another_atom) is an atomic derived type (it is the integer datatype that is derived from the float
primitive type).

List Datatypes

A list type has a *value* that is comprised of a finite-length sequence of atomic values. This type can be considered a
special case of the more general aggregate or collection datatypes, such as those described in ISO 11404. Unlike
most programming languages, an XML Schema list type cannot have items that are other lists.

> **List types are always derived types, with values delimited by whitespace character(s).**

List types are just like the IDREFS or NMTOKENS attribute types defined in the XML 1.0 Recommendation.
Therefore, a list type must allow the presence of whitespace, but can't use any whitespace within the individual
values of list items. Another important consideration about a list type is its length – this descriptive value is always
the number of items in the list, and has no relation to the number of characters that represent the items.

The base type of a list type is known as its **itemType**. For example, we can define a simple user-derived list type for
generic sizes:

```
<simpleType name="sizenums">
   <list itemType="decimal" />
</simpleType>
```

This new datatype might then be used within a more specific ShoeSizes element in a document (assuming that
its type is declared as sizenums):

```
<ShoeSizes>8 8.5 9 9.5 10 10.5 11 12 13</ShoeSizes>
```

On the other hand, the use of whitespace as a delimiter can cause problems when we want to create lists of strings.
We can use this to provide a very simplistic datatype that treats each space-delimited sub-string as a "word":

```
<simpleType name="sizenames">
   <list itemType="string" />
</simpleType>
```

This datatype might then be used as an alternate to the numeric approach. Again, just assume that the `sizenames` type is used for `ShoeSizes`:

```
<ShoeSizes>Small Medium Large</ShoeSizes>
```

This works as we'd expect – the value of this element is a list of three items: `Small`, `Medium`, and `Large`. However, a problem could arise if we want to add a fourth size (`Extra Large`) to our list:

```
<ShoeSizes>Small Medium Large Extra Large</ShoeSizes>
```

Because of the space character between `Extra` and `Large`, this will be interpreted as a list of *five* items, rather than the four we'd intended to use. The solution in this case would be to use a hyphen to connect the two words to make a single list item:

```
<ShoeSizes>Small Medium Large Extra-Large</ShoeSizes>
```

This use of a connector character may not be acceptable in all cases, which means that lists of string items must always be based upon space delimited "words", and can never be "phrases". The assertion made in the text of the following example can never be true for the value of a list datatype – it will be interpreted as a list of *seven* items:

```
<BadList>this is all a single list item</BadList>
```

List types can be a very useful way to represent collections of numbers, or standard XML 1.0 attribute types like `IDREFS` or `NMTOKENS`. On the other hand, they are all but worthless for manipulation of textual data that involves anything more than words – sentences and larger groupings of text cannot be represented with an XML Schema list datatype.

Union Datatypes

A union type can have different value and lexical spaces comprised of those from any one of a set of alternative datatypes (which may be a mixture of atomic and/or list types). This is conceptually similar to the use of the `union` datatype in C/C++. Union types are very powerful, providing for multiple equivalent representations of the same data. For example, we can use a name ("Wyoming"), an abbreviation ("Wyo."), or an enumerated value ("WY").

> **Union types are always derived types, and must be comprised of at least two alternative datatypes.**

The base types of a union type are known as its **member types**. The order in which these memberTypes are specified is significant to validation of the datatype. That is, each member type is examined in sequence and the first match is used for validation.

As an example of a union datatype, we can extend the list datatype example in the previous section to allow two different valid forms of shoe sizes:

```
<simpleType name="sizename" >
   <restriction base="xs:string" >
      <enumeration value="XS" />
      <enumeration value="S" />
      <enumeration value="M" />
      <enumeration value="L" />
      <enumeration value="XL" />
      <enumeration value="XXL" />
      <enumeration value="XXXL" />
      <enumeration value="4XL" />
      <enumeration value="5XL" />
   </restriction>
</simpleType>

<simpleType name="sizenames">
   <list itemType="sizename" />
</simpleType>

<simpleType name="sizenums">
   <list itemType="decimal" />
</simpleType>

<simpleType name="union.ShoeSize">
   <union memberTypes="sizenames sizenums"/>
</simpleType>
```

We'll assume that the ShoeSizes element is defined as having the union.ShoeSize type. The "union." part of the name could be just "u.", or anything else (it's just part of the datatype *name*). The more verbose form simply emphasizes the nature of this union datatype, and is similar to a traditional programming practice in naming datatypes.

An excerpt of XML data that conforms to the above schema fragment is:

```
<ShoeSizes>8 8.5 9 9.5 10 10.5 11 12 13</ShoeSizes>
<ShoeSizes>S M L XL</ShoeSizes>
```

The first of these was from our list example in the previous section. It remains a valid form, with the addition of the letter sizes alternative in this example of a union datatype.

We touched upon another example of a union datatype a little earlier in this chapter. We can provide for three different common forms of naming states of the United States: a spelled-out name, commonly used abbreviations, and U.S. Postal Service (USPS) address codes. In the following example, we create three simple enumerated datatypes for these alternatives, plus the union datatype that brings them together:

```
<simpleType name="US_State_Names">
   <restriction base="xs:string">
      <enumeration value="Alabama" />
         . . .
      <enumeration value="Wyoming" />
   </restriction>
</simpleType>

<simpleType name="US_State_Abbreviations">
   <restriction base="xs:string">
```

```
            <enumeration value="Ala" />
            ...
            <enumeration value="Wyo" />
        </restriction>
    </simpleType>

    <simpleType name="USPS_State_Codes">
        <restriction base="xs:string">
            <enumeration value="AL" />
            ...
            <enumeration value="WY" />
        </restriction>
    </simpleType>

    <simpleType name="union.US_States">
        <union memberTypes="USPS_State_Codes US_State_Names
                US_State_Abbreviations" />
    </simpleType>
```

With this union datatype, we can represent a U.S. State using any of the three alternative forms:

```
<state>WY</state>
<state>Wyo</state>
<state>Wyoming</state>
```

Union types could also be used as a method of multi-lingual validation, wherein datatype and element names for an XML data structure can be expressed in different languages, but validated according to a single schema.

Simple datatypes may *not* have attributes, or include elements and other markup (such as comments or processing instructions). For example, neither of the following could be an instance of a simple datatype:

```
<not_simple>A string can <em>only</em> contain characters.</not_simple>
<not_simple_either attribute="value" />
```

Since the first example uses common HTML text with embedded formatting elements, it must be defined as a complex type, complete with a content model. The use of an attribute forces the `<not_simple_either>` element to use a complex type, also.

Namespaces for Built-in Datatypes

XML Schema datatypes are designed for use with both XML Schema Structures and the XML Schema definition language (XSDL). Since these datatypes are useful beyond schemas (such as within XML data instances, or in another XML-based specification), they are specified separately from structures. A by-product of this separation is the fact that the alternative schema languages for XML such as RELAX/TREX and Schematron can simply specify that XML Schema datatypes are used, and not re-invent the wheel of datatypes.

XML Schema uses the W3C Recommendation for **Namespaces in XML**, *which is available at* http://www.w3.org/TR/REC-xml-names/.

When using the entire XML Schema specification, the built-in datatypes share a general namespace:

```
http://www.w3.org/2001/XMLSchema
```

If we want to use only the datatypes from XML Schema, ignoring Structures and the rest, we can instead use the following namespace:

```
http://www.w3.org/2001/XMLSchema-datatypes
```

Usually, we would declare the namespaces for XML Schema in the `schema` element:

```
<xs:schema xmlns:xs="http://www.w3.org/2001/XMLSchema" >
  ...
</xs:schema>
```

These declarations could also have been made in an ancestor element.

Now that we've had an overview of datatypes in XML Schema, let's look at the primitive datatypes in greater detail.

Built-in Primitive Types

XML Schema has 19 built-in primitive datatypes. These may be grouped into four categories: **string types**, **encoded binary data types**, **numeric types**, and **date/time types**.

There are four string primitive datatypes:

- ❑ `string` – a finite-length sequence of UCS characters
- ❑ `anyURI` – a standard Internet URI
- ❑ `NOTATION` – declare links to external non-XML content
- ❑ `QName` – a legal `QName` string (name with qualifier), as defined in "`Namespaces in XML`"

Three primitive datatypes for encoded binary data:

- ❑ `boolean` – a two-state "`true`" or "`false`" flag
- ❑ `hexBinary` – binary data encoded as a series of pairs of hexadecimal digits
- ❑ `base64Binary` – base64 encoded binary data

Three numeric primitive datatypes:

- ❑ `decimal` – a decimal number of arbitrary precision (number of significant digits)
- ❑ `float` – a 32-bit single-precision IEEE 754-1985 floating-point number
- ❑ `double` – a 64-bit double-precision IEEE 754-1985 floating-point number

Lastly, there are nine date/time primitive datatypes:

❑   `duration` – a duration of time

❑   `dateTime` – a specific instance in time, using the Gregorian calendar

❑   `date` – a specific Gregorian calendar date

❑   `time` – an instance of time that recurs every day

❑   `gYearMonth` – a Gregorian calendar year and month

❑   `gYear` – a Gregorian calendar year

❑   `gMonthDay` – a Gregorian calendar month and day

❑   `gMonth` – a Gregorian calendar month

❑   `gDay` – a Gregorian calendar date (a single day within a month)

Let's take a look at some examples of these, and describe various aspects in more detail.

String Types

These four primitive datatypes include the generic "string of characters" datatype; plus three special types of name strings: the Internet URI reference, the XML 1.0 NOTATION attribute type, and the "qualified name" string from "*Namespaces in XML*".

string

This most universal of datatypes is simply a finite-length string of legal XML characters. For example:

```
<string>The    motto is: "plus ça change, plus c'est la même
    chose"</string>
<another_string> 1 2 3 4 </another_string>
```

Remember that almost any Unicode character can be used in an XML string.

anyURI

The `anyURI` type is any absolute or relative Uniform Resource Identifier (URI) reference, which *may* also have an optional fragment identifier. URIs are classified as using a specific *scheme*, or format, which is identified as the first part of the URI string, namely those characters up to the first "colon-slash-slash" (://) sequence. For example, the following link attribute values illustrate four different valid URI schemes:

```
<an_element link="http://www.w3.org" />
<an_element link="ftp://ftp.is.co.za/rfc/rfc2396.txt" />
<an_element link="mailto://sales@wrox.com" />
<an_element link="telnet://melvyl.ucop.edu" />
```

Each of these URI schemes has its own syntax rules, but, as the name suggests, these specific types of URIs and their validation are outside the scope of the `anyURI` datatype – any kind of URI is acceptable.

Data of this type is transformed according to the rules in *§5.4* of *XLink 1.0* (*Locator Attribute*), and is therefore not limited to a standard URI string, which uses only ASCII characters. The lexical representation of this datatype must be transformed to a string that is a legal URI-reference as defined in *§4* (*URI References*) of RFC 2396, and amended by RFC 2732 (*IPv6 Addresses in URLs*).

> *XLink 1.0* (*the XML Linking Language*) *is defined at* http://www.w3.org/TR/xlink/, *and is a Recommendation, dated 2001-06-27. The above RFCs for* **URIs** *are available online at* http://www.ietf.org/rfc/rfc2396.txt *and* http://www.ietf.org/rfc/rfc2732.txt. *These supercede the earlier RFC 1738* (**URL**) *and RFC 1808* (**Relative URLs**). *See also RFC 2141* (**URNs**) *at* http://www.ietf.org/rfc/rfc2141.txt.

An example of some `anyURI` data that must be transformed into the more limited set of legal URI characters might be the following:

```
<an_element link="http://www.Wide Open Spaces.org" />
```

Using a URI character escape (`%20`) to represent the space characters, the above link would be transformed into the more limited set of legal URI characters:

```
http://www.Wide%20Open%20Spaces.org
```

This transformation is a good way to connect the broad international character support of XML with an older ASCII-based Internet standard.

NOTATION

This datatype is equivalent to the `NOTATION` attribute type as defined in the XML 1.0 Recommendation. It is used to declare links to external non-XML content (for example, binary image data) and associate such content with the external application that handles it.

This primitive datatype *may not be used directly in a schema* – it must be used indirectly via a derived type. Its value must be a legal XML name, and it must match a notation declared elsewhere in the schema, using the `notation` element. For example, we might need to declare viewers for JPEG and PNG images:

```
<xs:notation name="jpeg" public="image/jpeg" system="JPEG_Viewer.exe" />
<xs:notation name="png" public="image/png" system="PNG_Viewer.exe" />

<xs:simpleType name="notation.Image" >
   <xs:restriction base="xs:NOTATION">
      <xs:enumeration value="jpeg"/>
      <xs:enumeration value="png"/>
   </xs:restriction>
</xs:simpleType>
```

XML data conforming to the above schema constraint could be one of two kinds of data (a JPEG or PNG image), which requires an associated processing application. The use of the `NOTATION` datatype constrains the syntax of the string data using an enumerated type. These values (`jpeg` and `png`) must correspond to the value of a `name` attribute in an associated `xs:notation` element elsewhere in the same schema. The validating parser using the schema will enforce these constraints.

For compatibility with XML 1.0, this datatype should only be used for attribute values.

QName

This datatype is used for XML qualified names, as defined in "*Namespaces in XML*". The lexical representation of a QName is the concatenation of two NCName strings (a namespace prefix and a local name), separated by the namespace delimiter (:) character.

An NCName is a legal XML name that excludes the otherwise legal colon character (:), and will be described in its own section, later in this chapter.

The following element name is an example of a qualified name:

```
<ns_prefix:the_local_part> ... </ns_prefix:the_local_part>
```

When this element name is used, it must be used in a context that is within the scope of a namespace declaration corresponding to the namespace prefix (ns_prefix). This prefix can then be resolved into a namespace name (which is of the anyURI datatype), via the namespace declaration. The *value* of each qualified name is a pair of names: the namespace name (a URI), and the local name (an NCName).

One of the most common uses of the QName datatype is within XML Schema declarations. Almost every element and attribute will be declared to be of a certain type – this type is often a qualified name of the XML Schema (or user-defined) datatype. For example, we used a QName for both the base type of our restriction element in the last section, and the value of its associated base attribute.

```
<xs:restriction base="xs:NOTATION">
```

Encoded Binary Types

The second group of primitive types is used to encode binary data. These three primitive datatypes are used for binary data, either a single bit (boolean) or an encoded stream of bytes (hexBinary or base64Binary).

boolean

This datatype is the equivalent of a single binary bit: its value may only be true or false. These values are represented by either the lower-case ASCII strings "true" and "false", or the single ASCII digits "1" and "0" (true and false, respectively).

```
<an_element flag1="true" flag2="1" />
<!-- two flags, equivalent values -->

<an_element flag3="false" flag4="0" />
<!-- two flags, equivalent values -->
```

The first example above illustrates the two lexical forms of the true value; the second shows the two forms of false.

Canonical form: Use the unambiguous, though more verbose, string form ("true" or "false") – the shorter single digit form is prohibited.

hexBinary

This datatype is used to represent binary data as a series of two-character hexadecimal strings, using the ASCII digits and the letters "A" through "F".

```
<an_element>312D322D33</an_element>
```

This example shows the hexBinary encoding of the ASCII string "1-2-3". This datatype can be used to represent arbitrary binary data as a set of finite-length sequences of binaryoctets (8-bit bytes).

Canonical form: Use only upper-case letters ("A" through "F") – lower-case letters are prohibited.

base64Binary

This datatype is used to represent binary data as a series of a limited set of ASCII characters: the 52 upper and lower case letters, 10 digits, the plus sign (+) and forward slash (/). Binary streams are grouped into 24-bit values, which are then split into 6-bit values that are represented by one of the above 64 ASCII characters. The equals sign (=) is used as a padding character to encode data that is not an even integer multiple of 24-bit values. This encoding scheme is defined in §6.8. *(Base64 Content-Transfer-Encoding)* of RFC 2045.

> **RFC 2045,**"**Multipurpose Internet Mail Extensions (MIME) Part One: Format of Internet Message Bodies**", *is available at http://www.ietf.org/rfc/rfc2045.txt*.

For example:

```
<an_element>MS0yLTM=</an_element>
```

This shows the base64Binary encoding of "1-2-3", including a "=" padding byte at the end to make it an even multiple of three byte input values.

Numeric Types

The third, and arguably most significant group of primitive types (because they can represent real dollars – in addition to physical reality!) includes some fundamental numeric types.

Although numbers may be seen conceptually as a hierarchy derived from a single mathematical concept, there are three primitive XML Schema datatypes for numeric data. All three types represent real numbers. The first is a generic signed decimal number, and the other two are range-limited subsets of real numbers in the form of single or double-precision IEEE floating-point numbers.

decimal

This datatype allows decimal numbers of arbitrary precision, using the ten ASCII digits (the character values #x30 through #x39), plus a period or full stop (.) as the decimal point. The ASCII plus (+) and minus (–) characters are used to represent positive or negative numbers. For example:

```
<an_element num1="-1.23" num2="3.1416" num3="+00042.00" num4="100.00" />
```

The above are all legal representations of decimal numbers – the sign may be omitted, in which case "+" will be assumed. Leading and trailing zeroes are optional.

> *A "minimally conforming" processor must support* at least 18 decimal digits. *It is up to the application to set a limit (if any) upon the number of digits that can be handled, so good documentation of such a limit is imperative, if* decimal *XML data is to be exchanged.*

This datatype is essential for financial and other applications that demand exact numeric values, without the rounding-off and approximation that is inherent in the two IEEE floating-point types. These types are better used when such precision is not necessary.

Canonical form: The decimal point is required, and a leading plus sign is *not* permitted. All leading and trailing zeroes must be omitted, except that at least one digit (which may be a zero) must appear on either side of the decimal point.

float

This datatype corresponds to standard IEEE single-precision 32-bit floating-point numbers.

> *The IEEE Standard for Binary Floating-Point Arithmetic (IEEE 754-1985) is available at* http://standards.ieee.org/reading/ieee/std_public/description/busarch/754-1985_desc.html.

IEEE floating-point numbers are comprised of a mantissa, and an optional exponent. If the exponent is used, it must be separated from the mantissa by the letter "E" (upper or lower-case). Positive and negative numbers can be indicated by a leading plus or minus sign. If the sign character is omitted, then the number is assumed to be positive. The mantissa must be an integer whose absolute value is less than 2^{24}. The exponent is an integer that must have a value between -149 and 104, inclusive. There are also five special values in a float's value space: positive and negative zero (represented as "0" and "-0"), positive and negative infinity ("INF" and "-INF"), and not a number ("NaN").

For example, the following are all legal float values:

```
<an_element num1="-1E4" num2="12.78e-1" num3="NaN" answer="42" />
```

Canonical form: For the mantissa, the decimal point is required, and a leading plus sign is *not* permitted. All leading and trailing zeroes must be omitted, except that at least one digit (which may be a zero) must appear on either side of the decimal point. The exponent must be indicated using an upper case "E", and leading zeros and/or plus sign are *not* permitted.

double

This datatype corresponds to standard IEEE double-precision 64-bit floating-point numbers.

The mantissa must be an integer whose absolute value is less than 2^{53}. The exponent is also an integer between -1075 and 970, inclusive. The same five special values as defined for the float type are also valid.

For example, the following are all legal `double` values (all of the previous `float` examples would be legal values for `double`, as well):

```
<an_element num1="-1E666" num2="3.1416" num3="12.78e-1040" num4="-INF" />
```

Canonical form: This has the same restrictions as the `float` type.

Date/Time Types

The last group of primitive types includes all of XML Schema's date and time datatypes.

These primitive datatypes are used for dates (using the Gregorian calendar) and times (using a 24-hour clock, with minutes, seconds, and an optional time zone). It is important to realize that although this calendar system is a *de facto* world standard, other calendar systems (such as Chinese, Muslim, Mayan, Hebrew, etc.) remain in widespread use. Because calendars may be based upon either the sun or the moon, it is not possible to easily convert dates from one system to another.

The lexical representations used for these types are based upon the ISO 8601 standard.

> As with most (if not all) ISO standards, **ISO 8601:Representations of dates and times** *is* not available on the WWW. As usual, a paper version can be ordered from the ISO at *http://www.iso.ch*.

Mixed calculations, like adding a month to a specific date, may depend upon the sequence of calculation, and esoterica such as leap seconds may also need to be considered. We will just do overview of the date/time datatypes in this section, and will return to the more complex aspects of dates and times in Chapter 5.

duration

This datatype is the duration of time, as specified in *§5.5.3.2* of ISO 8601. Its lexical representation is the ISO 8601 extended format: PnYnMnDTnHnMnS. The upper-case letters P, Y, M, D, T, H, M, and S in this format are called designators. The "P" stands for "period" (as in duration) and is required to be the first character of any `timeDuration` string. The recurring "n" represents a number, so nY is the number of years, nM the number of months, nD of days, T is the date/time separator, nH is hours, the second nM is minutes, and nS is seconds. Seconds may be any decimal number of arbitrary precisions. For example:

```
<an_element duration="P12Y10M2DT0H40M27.87S" />
<an_element duration="P12Y10M2DT40M27.87S" />
```

Both of the above examples represent a `timeDuration` of 12 years, 10 months, 2 days, 0 hours, 40 minutes, and 27.87 seconds – the latter illustrating one of the truncated forms (hours have been omitted).

An optional preceding minus sign (–) is also allowed, to indicate a negative duration; if the sign is omitted, a positive duration is assumed.

dateTime

This datatype is a specific instance in time, using the Gregorian (Common Era, or CE) calendar, as specified in *§5.4* of ISO 8601. Its primary lexical representation uses the ISO 8601 extended format, and several abbreviated versions. These acceptable formats for dateTime include:

❑ *yyyy-mm-dd*T*hh:mm:ss* – the shortest form, where time resolution is seconds and no time zone is specified (the meaning of the individual parts of the string should be obvious: *year-month-day*, the letter "T" to separate date and time, followed by a time in *hours:minutes:seconds*.

❑ *yyyy-mm-dd*T*hh:mm:ss.fff...f* – another form without time zone information, but adding a fractional value for seconds (*fff...f*). There may be as many digits to the right of the decimal point as desired to provide higher resolution values for the time.

❑ *yyyy-mm-dd*T*hh:mm:ss*Z – this is basic form, with the letter as a suffix to indicate that the date/time of the Coordinated Universal Time (UTC), also known in international aviation circles as "Zulu time". Of course, a fractional value for seconds could also be used with this form.

❑ *yyyy-mm-dd*T*hh:mm:ss±hh:mm* – this is the form that specifies that time zone as an offset to UTC, where negative numbers are used for time zones West of the Prime Meridian, and positive numbers represent offsets to the East. The optional seconds fraction can be used here, too.

For example, the following are all representations of the first moment of the new millennium (to the nearest thousandth of a second):

```
<a_moment>2001-01-01T00:00:00.001</a_moment>
<a_moment>2001-01-01T00:00:00.001Z</a_moment>
<a_moment>2000-12-31T17:00:00.001-07:00</a_moment>
```

Dates in XML are always represented using numbers, in the form "yyyy-mm-dd", where "yyyy" is the year, "mm" is the month, and "dd" is the day of the month. This minimizes any confusion based upon language or cultural differences.

The year is always represented using at least four digits, with leading zeros as needed. However, the year "0000" is *not* valid. Years after 9999 CE (Common Era, known to some as *anno Domini*, or AD) can be represented by adding digits on the left of the year, as needed:

```
<InTheYear2525 times10="25250-01-01" />
```

A minus sign may precede the year to indicate dates that are BCE (Before Common Era, also known as BC), for example:

```
<JuliusCaesar born="-0100-07-01" died="-0044-03-15" />
```

The month and day are always represented using two digit numbers, again with leading zeros as needed. A month may only use values from "01" to "12". The day of the month depends upon the given month, and ranges from a minimum of "01" to a maximum of between "28" and "31" (inclusive).

The literal "T" is simply the time indicator/separator character.

Times are represented in the form "hh:mm:ss.fff", where "hh" is the hour (24-hour clock), "mm" is the minutes, "ss" is the seconds, and "fff" is the fractional seconds (this optional field may be one or more digits of arbitrary precision). Hours, minutes, and seconds are always represented using two digit numbers, with leading zeros as needed. Hours will always be in the range "00" to "23", minutes range from "00" to "59", and seconds range from "00" to "60". The extra second is used when a leap second is announced. These restrictions do not apply to durations of time, which may use arbitrarily large values for any of these time components.

The "±hh:mm" at the end is an optional time zone adjustment factor. Alternatively, the letter "Z" may be used to indicate UTC, otherwise known (to Anglophones at least) as Greenwich Mean Time (GMT).

There is a great deal of esoterica associated with dates and times, ranging from leap seconds, to the limited scope and compatibility of various calendar systems. The definitive source for leap seconds and other ongoing adjustments to UTC is the International Earth Rotation Service (IERS) hosted by the U.S. Naval Observatory (USNO) at http://maia.usno.navy.mil/. Their master clock and time reference is at http://tycho.usno.navy.mil/time.html.

Two good academic sources of information about calendars and time are **Date Miscellany** *by Dr J R Stockton [2001-05-21] at http://www.merlyn.demon.co.uk/miscdate.htm, and* **A Summary of the International Standard Date and Time Notation** *by Markus Kuhn [2000-04-17] at http://www.cl.cam.ac.uk/~mgk25/iso-time.html.*

The ISO 8601 dates are based upon the Gregorian calendar (first established in 1582 CE), but this system has only been widely used for the last few hundred years. It was an adjustment of the Julian calendar, which had been used for about 1600 years (since 46 BCE). Of course, we're currently in the late 5700s according to the lunisolar Hebrew calendar, and it is 4699 in the Chinese lunar calendar. Neither of these calendar systems permit simple transformations into the Gregorian calendar, so, like the international convention of using UTC for time, it is probably best to represent all dates using the Gregorian calendar for maximum interoperability.

Canonical form: The time zone adjustment is *not* permitted. Times may either use the UTC indicator ("Z") or omit any time zone designation (an indeterminate local time is then assumed).

date

This datatype is a specific Gregorian calendar date. Its lexical representation uses the leftmost portion of the dateTime format, up to the "T" time indicator ("yyyy-mm-dd"). For example, the first day of the new millennium is:

```
<an_element moment="2001-01-01" />
```

A date string will always be at least 10 characters, since years must use at least four digits, and the month and day are always represented as two-digit numbers. Even though this datatype does not represent a specific time of day, it may use the optional time zone adjustment ("±hh:mm"). For example, the above date in the US Mountain Time zone would be:

```
<an_element moment="2001-01-01-07:00" />
```

Canonical form: None specified. However, to be consistent with other date/time datatypes, the time zone adjustment should not be used, and all times should only be expressed in UTC (ending with a "Z") or local time.

time

This datatype is an instance of time that recurs every day. Its lexical representation uses the rightmost portion of the `dateTime` format, without the "T" time indicator ("hh:mm:ss.fff±hh:mm"). For example, the following are all representations of the first second of a new day in Greenwich, England:

```
<an_element first_second="00:00:01" />
<an_element first_second="00:00:01Z" />
<an_element first_second="19:00:01-05:00" />
```

As an option, more precise times can be represented using an arbitrary number of fractional digits for seconds (the ".fff" in the pattern shown in the first paragraph), such as:

```
<a_very_precise_time>12:42:03.0275787</a_very_precise_time>
```

Canonical form: The time zone adjustment is *not* permitted. Times may either use the UTC indicator ("Z") or omit any time zone designation (an indeterminate local time is then assumed). Midnight is always represented as "00:00:00".

gYearMonth

This datatype allows values that are a specific Gregorian calendar year and month. Its lexical representation uses the leftmost portion of the `dateTime` format ("yyyy-mm"). For example, the year-month of the XML Schema Recommendation publication is:

```
<an_element year_month="2001-05" />
```

The various aspects of the year are the same as previously discussed for the `dateTime` and `date` types. The month must be a two-digit number from "01" to "12", inclusive. Even though this datatype does not represent a specific time of day, it may use the optional time zone adjustment ("±hh:mm").

Canonical form: None specified. However, to be consistent with other date/time datatypes, the time zone adjustment should not be used, and all times should only be expressed in UTC (ending with a "Z") or local time.

gYear

This datatype allows values that are a specific Gregorian calendar year. Its lexical representation is four or more numeric digits, with leading zeros as needed. Even though this datatype does not represent a specific time of day, it may use the optional time zone adjustment ("±hh:mm").

For example, the last year of the 20th century was:

```
<an_element year="2000" />
```

A minus sign may precede the year to indicate dates that are BCE (Before Common Era, also known as BC), for example:

```
<JulianCalendar established="-0046" />
<an_element year="-0357" />
<an_element year="-10000000" />
```

These examples show the years 46 BCE, 357 BCE and 10,000,000 BCE.

Canonical form: None specified. However, to be consistent with other date/time datatypes, the time zone adjustment should not be used, and all times should only be expressed in UTC (ending with a "Z") or local time.

gMonthDay

This datatype allows values that are a specific day within a month in the Gregorian calendar. Its lexical representation uses the middle portion of the dateTime format, with two leading hyphens to indicate the left truncation ("--mm-dd"). For example, the month-day values for US Independence Day (July 4th) and Christmas (December 25th) are:

```
<US_IndependenceDay month_day="--07-04" />
<Christmas month_day="--12-25" />
```

As usual, the month and day must be two-digit numbers within the appropriate range of values. Even though this datatype does not represent a specific time of day, it may use the optional time zone adjustment ("±hh:mm").

Canonical form: None specified. However, to be consistent with other date/time datatypes, the time zone adjustment should not be used, and all times should only be expressed in UTC (ending with a "Z") or local time.

gMonth

This datatype allows values that are a specific Gregorian calendar month. Its lexical representation is a two-digit number in the range of 1 to 12, with two leading and trailing hyphens to indicate the left and right truncations ("--mm--"). For example, the month of U.S. Thanksgiving Day (November) is represented as:

```
<an_element month="--11--" />
```

Canonical form: None specified. However, to be consistent with other date/time datatypes, the time zone adjustment should not be used, and all times should only be expressed in UTC (ending with a "Z") or local time.

gDay

This datatype allows values that are a single day within any Gregorian calendar month. Its lexical representation is a two-digit number in the range of 1 to 31, preceded by four hyphens to indicate the left truncation of dateTime format ("----dd"). For example, a bill due on the 15th of each month (the 15th) is represented like this:

```
<MonthlyDueDate value="----15" />
```

Canonical form: None specified. However, to be consistent with other date/time datatypes, the time zone adjustment should not be used, and all times should only be expressed in UTC (ending with a "Z") or local time.

Built-in Derived Types

Now that we've looked at the primitive XML Schema datatypes, let's move on to the derived types. The 25 built-in derived types can be split into two categories: those derived from the primitive `string` base type, and those derived from the `decimal` type.

Twelve built-in datatypes are derived from the `string` primitive type:

- ❑ `normalizedString` – a string where each whitespace character (tab, carriage return, or newline / line-feed) is replaced with a space character
- ❑ `token` – a string where all whitespace characters are converted to single spaces; plus leading and trailing spaces are removed, and multiple consecutive spaces are replaced with a single space character
- ❑ `language` – a natural language identifier string
- ❑ `Name` – any legal XML 1.0 name
- ❑ `NCName` – a legal XML 1.0 "non-colonized" name, as defined in "*Namespaces in XML*"
- ❑ `ID` – a unique value that identifies the associated element
- ❑ `IDREF` – a reference to another element via its `ID` attribute value
- ❑ `IDREFS` – a list comprised of `IDREF` values
- ❑ `NMTOKEN` – a string comprised of any legal XML name characters, but without the initial character restrictions of an XML name
- ❑ `NMTOKENS` – a list comprised of `NMTOKEN` values
- ❑ `ENTITY` – a string that is a legal `NCName`, and refers to the name of an unparsed entity that is declared in a DTD
- ❑ `ENTITIES` – a list comprised of `ENTITY` values

The seven datatypes above with all upper-case names (`ID`, `IDREF`, etc.) are equivalent to the like-named XML 1.0 attribute types. For compatibility with XML 1.0 DTDs, these datatypes should only be used for attribute values, and not for element content.

There are thirteen built-in datatypes derived from the `decimal` primitive type:

- ❑ `integer` – any integer number
- ❑ `negativeInteger` – any integer number with a value < 0
- ❑ `positiveInteger` – any integer number with a value > 0
- ❑ `nonNegativeInteger` – any integer number with a value ≥ 0
- ❑ `nonPositiveInteger` – any integer number with a value ≤ 0
- ❑ `byte` – an 8-bit signed integer number
- ❑ `short` – a 16-bit signed integer number
- ❑ `int` – a 32-bit signed integer number

- ❑ `long` – a 64-bit signed integer number
- ❑ `unsignedByte` – a non-negative 8-bit integer number
- ❑ `unsignedShort` – a non-negative 16-bit integer number
- ❑ `unsignedInt` – a non-negative 32-bit integer number
- ❑ `unsignedLong` – a non-negative 64-bit integer number

The hierarchy of those types derived from the `string` and `decimal` types are shown in the following two diagrams. First we have all the `string` types, most derived by restrictions placed upon another type, but with three types that are instead derived by list:

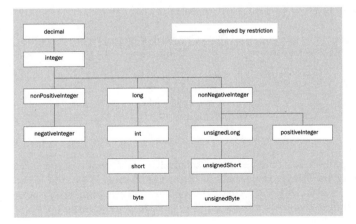

The `token` type is arguably the most significant of these types, since it is the basis for the rest of the built-in derived string types. On the other hand, several of these types (`NMTOKEN`, `ENTITY`, etc.) are primarily used for compatibility with existing data that uses the simple XML 1.0 DTD datatypes.

Secondly, we can see that the `integer` type (derived from the `decimal` type) is the basis for all other built-in derived numeric types:

Let's look at some examples and details of these datatypes.

string Types

These twelve built-in datatypes are all derived from the `string` primitive type, with various additional limitations upon the values of the strings. Several of these types are primarily for compatibility with XML 1.0 attribute types (as used in DTDs).

normalizedString

This datatype is derived from the `string` type. Data declared to be this type will have all whitespace characters converted to space characters before validation – more specifically, all tabs (#x09), carriage returns (#x0D), and line feeds (#x0A) are replaced with single space characters (#x20).

Thus these two instances of XML data would be considered to have equivalent values after parsing (but before validation):

```
<an_element>
      This is a normalized string                 (in English)
</an_element>

<an_element> This is a normalized string  (in English) </an_element>
```

The second example shows the result of the parser's transformation of the tabs and newlines in the first example, if this element were declared to be of the `normalizedString` datatype.

token

This datatype is derived from the `normalizedString` type. The value and lexical spaces of this datatype only allow strings that:

❑ do not contain any tab (#x09), carriage return (#x0D), or line feed (#x0A) characters

❑ have neither leading nor trailing space characters

❑ have no internal substrings of two or more space characters

For example, except for a different word ("token" instead of "normalized"), this would be the result if either of the two examples in the previous section were declared to be the `token` type:

```
<an_element>This is a token string (in English)</an_element>
```

This illustrates the difference between the processing implied for the `normalizedString` and `token` datatypes.

language

This datatype is derived from the `token` type, though it is further constrained to include no space characters. The pattern describing this datatype conforms to the Language ID string as specified in RFC 3066 – which has replaced RFC 1766, as allowed in XML 1.0 (Second Edition). Most languages can be represented with a simple two-letter code. The newer three-character language codes accommodate more languages, but are still not universally used.

RFC 3066: "**Tags for the Identification of Languages**" *[2001-01] is available at* http://www.ietf.org/rfc/rfc3066.txt. *The older* RFC 1766 *[1995-03] is available at* http://www.ietf.org/rfc/rfc1766.txt.

Some examples of the `language` datatype are:

```
<LanguageForATC>en</LanguageForATC>
<LanguageOfOrigin>en-GB</LanguageOfOrigin>
<an_element xml:lang="en-US" > ... </an_element>
```

The first of these shows an element that has its content constrained to be the `language` datatype. The second illustrates the proper format for a country-specific version of a language ("British English" in this case). The third exploits a little-known attribute defined in the XML 1.0 REC, which also uses values of this type to describe the human language ("American English" in this example), used in the content of the associated element and its children.

name, NCName

The `name` and `NCName` datatypes both describe legal XML name strings. The latter is a more restrictive version of `name` that simply prohibits the use of the colon (`:`) within the name (also known as a "non-colonized name"). The `NCName` datatype is necessary to describe the local part of a namespace-qualified name in XML Schema, but probably has limited utility for applications that aren't concerned directly with the syntax of XML names.

For example, both of the following examples are legal XML names that conform to the `name` datatype:

```
<somens:an_element_name> ... </somens:an_element_name>
<an_element_name> ... </an_element_name>
```

The first of these is also a valid `QName`, that is, a namespace-qualified name (see the **Primitive Datatypes** section earlier in this chapter). The latter example is a non-qualified (or "non-colonized") name that conforms to the `NCName` datatype, as well as the more general `name` datatype.

ID

This datatype is equivalent to the `ID` attribute type as defined in the XML 1.0 REC. It is used to provide a unique identifier for an element, and is derived from the `NCName` type (and thus must be a legal XML name, but without the use of any colon characters). For example:

```
<an_element its_id="AGENT_ID_007" />
```

Remember that XML names cannot begin with a digit, so no matter how tempting, the value of an `ID` datatype can't be used to directly represent a numeric key value.

The following validity constraints apply to data of this type:

❑ The value of the `ID` string must uniquely identify its associated element

❑ An element may only have one attribute of the `ID` type

❑ An `ID` value must be used once, and only once, in a document instance (they are, after all, intended to be used as unique identifiers)

A single `ID` attribute value may be the target of multiple `IDREF` attributes within the same document.

IDREF

This datatype is equivalent to the IDREF attribute type as defined in the XML 1.0 REC. It is used to refer to another element, which has an ID attribute with the same value as the IDREF attribute, and is also derived from the NCName type.

```
<another_element codename="AGENT_ID_007" />
```

The value of the IDREF string must match the value of an element or attribute of type ID, somewhere within the same document instance (such as the ID example above). If no match is found, then the data would be considered invalid (no matter whether it is validated using a DTD or an XML Schema).

IDREFS

This datatype is equivalent to the IDREFS attribute type as defined in the XML 1.0 REC. It is simply a whitespace-delimited list of IDREF values. For example, we can expand the previous IDREF example to allow multiple values:

```
<another_element codename="M Q AGENT_ID_006 AGENT_ID_007 AGENT_ID_009" />
```

Like all other list types, the value of an IDREFS type may not include any whitespace character, other than those used as the list item delimiters.

For more on the uses of ID, IDREF, and IDREFS in the context of XML Schemas, see Chapter 9, "Identity Constraints, Normalization and Document Fragments".

NMTOKEN

This datatype is equivalent to the NMTOKEN attribute type as defined in the XML 1.0 REC. A NMTOKEN is a legal XML name string that doesn't have the constraint placed upon the initial character. For example, either of these are valid NMTOKEN values:

```
<an_element name="AGENT_007" />
<an_element name="007" />
```

As its name suggests, it is derived from the token type, so all whitespace characters are converted to spaces, and spaces are trimmed from both ends and compressed within the string. This is slightly less constrained than the similar NCName datatype.

NMTOKENS

This datatype is simply a whitespace-delimited list of NMTOKEN values. It is equivalent to the XML 1.0 NMTOKENS attribute type. For example:

```
<an_element name="M Q 006 007 009" />
```

This is derived (by list) from the NMTOKEN type, and so all of that type's characteristics also apply here.

ENTITY

This datatype is derived from the NCName type, and is equivalent to the ENTITY attribute type as defined in the XML 1.0 REC. The ENTITY value must match an unparsed entity name that's declared in a notation element in the schema. This datatype should only be used for attribute values to maintain XML 1.0 compatibility.

ENTITIES

This datatype is derived (by list) from the ENTITY type, and so is simply a whitespace-delimited list of ENTITY values. It is equivalent to the ENTITIES attribute type as defined in the XML 1.0 REC.

decimal Types

These datatypes are all derived from the primitive decimal base type. All of these provide further constraints upon ranges of values and their representations.

integer

This datatype is derived from the decimal type, with the decimal point and fractional values disallowed. For example, the "ultimate answer" and its negative (in various forms) are:

```
<an_element value="42" />
<an_element value="+00000042" />
<an_element, value="-42" />
<an_element value="-042" />
```

The integer datatype may use a leading plus or minus sign, and can also have leading zeros.

Canonical form: Leading zeros and/or the plus sign (+) are *not* permitted.

nonPositiveInteger, nonNegativeInteger

These datatypes are derived from the integer type and have similar lexical and canonical forms, but are constrained to have values less than or equal to zero (*value* 0), or greater than or equal to zero (*value* 0), respectively.

```
<an_element value="-42" />
<!-- value is a nonPositiveInteger -->

<an_element value="+42" />
<!-- a nonNegativeInteger -->

<an_element value="0" />
<!-- both nonPositive and nonNegativeInteger -->
```

Canonical form: A leading minus sign is required for all nonPositiveInteger values, while the optional leading plus sign is prohibited for a nonNegativeInteger value. Leading zeros are *not* permitted for either type.

positiveInteger, negativeInteger

These datatypes represent integer values that are greater than zero ($value > 0$) or less than zero ($value < 0$), respectively. The `positiveInteger` type is derived from the `nonNegativeInteger` type, and `negativeInteger` is similarly derived from the `nonPositiveInteger` type.

```
<an_element value="0042" />
<!-- a positiveInteger -->

<an_element value="-42" />
<!-- a negativeInteger -->
```

Canonical form: The optional leading plus sign is prohibited for a `positiveInteger` value. Leading zeros are *not* permitted for either type.

long, int, short, byte

These datatypes are all signed integers. The `long` type is derived from the `integer` type, the `int` type is derived from the `long` type, and so on. They are all constrained to finite and inclusive ranges of values as shown in the following table:

Datatype	Minimum	Maximum
long	-9,223,372,036,854,775,808	+9,223,372,036,854,775,807
int	-2,147,483,648	+2,147,483,647
short	-32,768	+32,767
byte	-128	+127

The following examples may be valid for more than one type:

```
<an_element value="42" />
<!-- valid for any of these types -->

<an_element value="-42000" />
<!-- valid only for long/int -->

<an_element value="4200000000" />
<!-- can only be valid for a long -->
```

Canonical form: The optional leading plus sign and leading zeros are prohibited for any of these types.

unsignedLong, unsignedInt, unsignedShort, unsignedByte

These datatypes are all unsigned integers. The `unsignedLong` type is derived from the `nonNegativeInteger` type, the `unsignedInt` type is derived from the `unsignedLong` type, and so on. They are all constrained to inclusive ranges that have a minimum value of zero, and maximum values as shown in the following table:

Datatype	Maximum
unsignedLong	18,446,744,073,709,551,615
unsignedInt	4,294,967,295
unsignedShort	65,535
unsignedByte	255

These examples may also be valid for multiple types:

```
<an_element value="42" />
<!-- valid for any of these types -->

<an_element value="42000" />
<!-- valid for unsignedLong/unsignedInt/unsignedShort -->

<an_element value="4200000000" />
<!-- valid for unsignedLong or unsignedInt -->
```

Canonical form: The optional leading zeros are prohibited for any of these types.

We will revisit many of these built-in types in the next chapter, when we discuss more details of the constraints that define these types (such as minimum and maximum values, or regular expression patterns).

Summary

In this chapter, we have looked at the basic properties of XML Schema datatypes, examples of their use, and their history.

We looked at the three components of a datatype:

❑ value space
❑ lexical space
❑ facets

We also looked at the different kinds of datatypes:

❑ primitive datatypes (always built-in)
❑ derived datatypes (either built-in or user-derived)

A brief overview of complex datatypes followed a more detailed discussion of simple datatypes, and their three forms:

❑ atomic types
❑ list types
❑ union types

The latter half of the chapter was a quick reference to the built-in datatypes, both primitive and derived. These commonly used string, encoded binary data, numeric, and date/time datatypes are available for use in any schema, and related XML data. We will revisit a sampling of these types in the next chapter when we look at their facets (properties) in more detail.

The built-in types may suffice for many situations, but there will inevitably be the need for a slightly different type of string type, or a different range of numbers. Complex database structures may be translated to complex user-derived types. Simple, but constrained, types like ISBNs, UPCs, or SKUs can be described as simple user-derived types.

In the next chapter, we will discuss user-derived types, the facets that define these types, and inheritance of types, using abstract and final types.

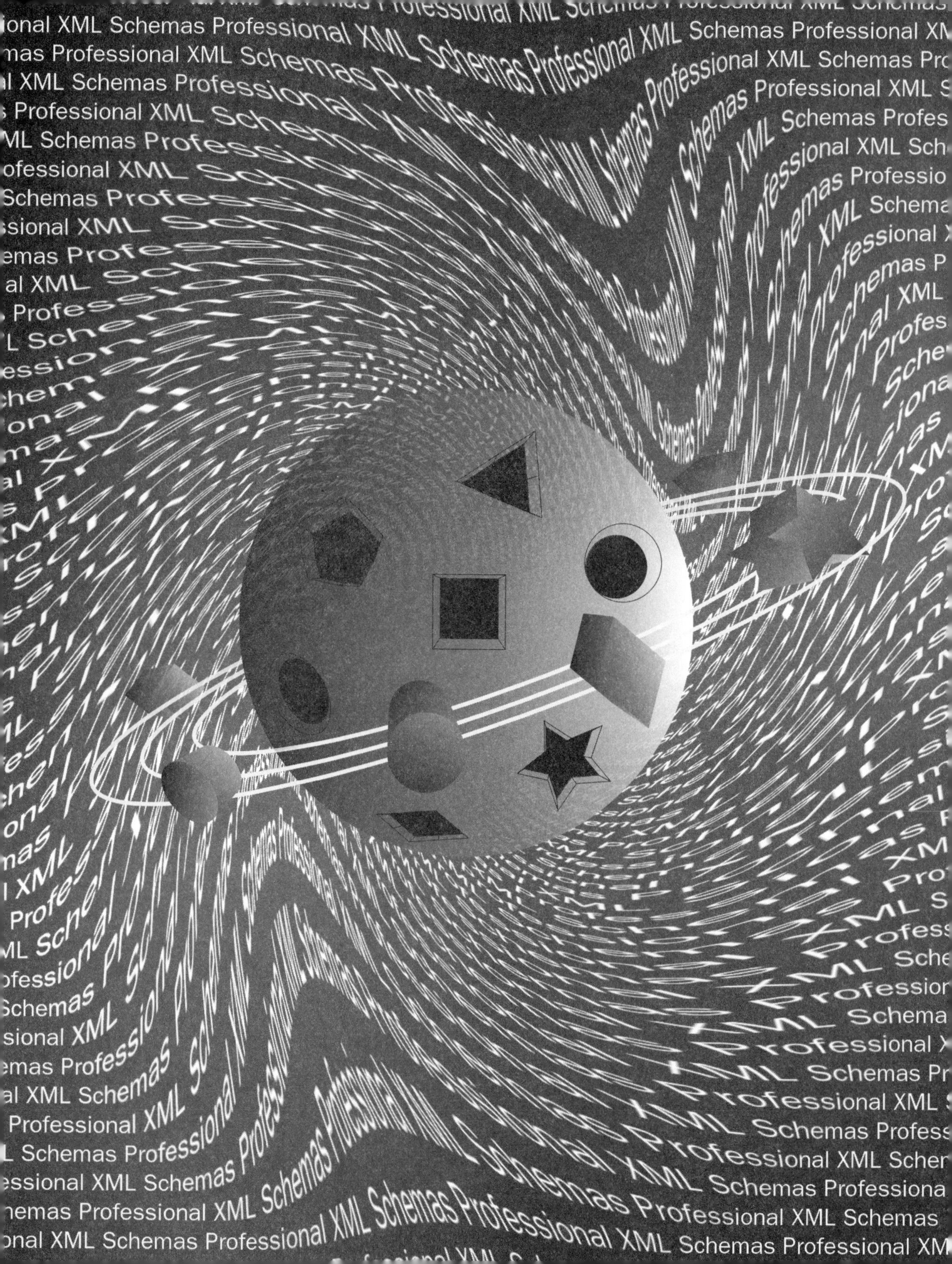
Professional XML Schemas

Creating Content Models

In Chapter 1, we saw that XML Schema makes a distinction between simple types and complex types. Simple types define the allowable content for text-only element content and attribute values. If we want an element to carry an attribute or contain child elements, however, we have to define a complex type, which makes up an element content model.

The content models we have been using so far have been quite basic. In Chapter 1, we started off by declaring elements and attributes, seeing how to control their occurrence and learning how we give them default values. In those examples the elements had to appear in the order in which they were declared. We then moved on in Chapter 2 to look at how we control the text-only content of elements and values of attributes using XML Schema's pre-defined datatypes.

In this chapter, we will start looking more closely at complex types, and how we can create more advanced content models for elements. In order to create more advanced content models we will learn about named complex types, and how to define model groups for use inside those complex types. On the way you will start to see there are some helpful mechanisms to facilitate re-use of constructs in XML Schema.

In particular, we'll be looking at:

- ❑ Anonymous and named complex type definitions
- ❑ Model groups
- ❑ Attribute groups
- ❑ Content specifications

By the end of this chapter, you will have seen how XML Schema allows us to define complex content models. We will finish the chapter with a look at some of the other features of XML Schema that you will meet in later chapters, and see how all of the different schema components that we have introduced so far fit together.

Complex Type Definitions

As you should now be aware, whenever you want to declare an element to carry an attribute or contain child elements, you have to define a complex type. The complex types we met back in Chapter 1 are known as **anonymous complex types**. They are associated with one particular element because their definitions are nested inside the element declaration using an element called `complexType` like so:

```
<?xml version = "1.0" ?>
<xs:schema xmlns:xs = "http://www.w3.org/2001/XMLSchema">
    <xs:element name = "Customer">
        <xs:complexType>
            <xs:sequence>
                <xs:element name = "FirstName" type = "xs:string" />
                <xs:element name = "MiddleInitial" type = "xs:string" />
                <xs:element name = "LastName" type = "xs:string" />
            </xs:sequence>
        </xs:complexType>
    </xs:element>
</xs:schema>
```

Here we can see that the element has a name, `Customer`, and is associated with the complex type that is defined within the element declaration. This means that the `Customer` element can contain only the three child elements declared within the `complexType` element. Furthermore, the child elements must appear in the order in which they are declared because they appear inside the `sequence` element.

This is fine if we are only going to want to use this particular content model with the `Customer` element. If we are likely to want to use the same content model in another element, however, we should give the complex type a name, creating a **named complex type**. We can then use its content model with other elements.

To see how we define a named complex type, let's look at an equivalent to the anonymous complex type we have just seen. We define the complex type globally, as a child of the `schema` element, and give it a `name` attribute, whose value is the name we are giving to the complex type. The rest of the complex type is defined just as it was in the other example. Now we can simply use the name of the complex type as the value of the `type` attribute in an element declaration, as we have done here with `Customer`:

```
<?xml version = "1.0" ?>
<xs:schema xmlns:xs = "http://www.w3.org/2001/XMLSchema">

    <xs:complexType name = "NameType">
        <xs:sequence>
            <xs:element name = "FirstName" type = "xs:string" />
            <xs:element name = "MiddleInitial" type = "xs:string" />
            <xs:element name = "LastName" type = "xs:string" />
        </xs:sequence>
    </xs:complexType>

    <xs:element name = "Customer" type = "NameType" />

</xs:schema>
```

Remember that an element declaration is an association between a name and a type. Here we have declared an element called Customer, whose type is NameType. In an instance document the Customer element can only contain the markup defined by the NameType complex type.

Note that it doesn't matter whether we define the complex type before or after the element declaration, as long as it is present in the schema document. Indeed, now we have defined the complex type globally and given it a name, we could have any number of elements associated with this type. For example, we could use the same complex type with an element called Employee like so:

```
<xs:element name = "Employee" type = "NameType" />
```

This is similar to the way in which global element declarations can be re-used in other element declarations and complex type definitions – a globally declared *and* named complex type can be associated with several element declarations.

Recall that an instance document can be validated against the schema as long as its root element is globally declared. This means that if we have more than one globally declared element in a schema, then we can validate different sorts of instance documents against the schema, with different root elements. Look at the following example, where we have a globally declared CustomerList element, with an anonymous complex type which indicates that the CustomerList element can contain one or more Customer elements. The Customer element is also globally defined, and is used as a reference in the anonymous complex type:

```
<?xml version = "1.0" ?>
<xs:schema xmlns:xs = "http://www.w3.org/2001/XMLSchema">

    <xs:element name = "CustomerList">
        <xs:complexType>
            <xs:sequence>
                <xs:element ref = "Customer"
                            minOccurs = "1" maxOccurs = "unbounded" />
            </xs:sequence>
        </xs:complexType>
    </xs:element>

    <xs:element name = "Customer" type = "NameType" />

    <xs:complexType name = "NameType">
        <xs:sequence>
            <xs:element name = "FirstName" type = "xs:string" />
            <xs:element name = "MiddleInitial" type = "xs:string" />
            <xs:element name = "LastName" type = "xs:string" />
        </xs:sequence>
    </xs:complexType>

</xs:schema>
```

You might expect that a valid instance of this document would contain a list of customers, with at least one or more Customer elements inside the CustomerList. However, because Customer has also been defined globally, a valid document instance could consist simply of a Customer element. To get around this problem, rather than defining the Customer element globally, we can use declare it instead where before we had a reference to it:

```
<xs:element name = "CustomerList">
    <xs:complexType>
        <xs:sequence>
            <xs:element name = "Customer" type = "NameType"
                        minOccurs = "1" maxOccurs = "unbounded" />
        </xs:sequence>
    </xs:complexType>
</xs:element>
```

As we shall see in the next chapter, we can derive new types from a named complex type by extending or restricting the named complex type. This is a powerful mechanism in representing object-oriented concepts such as inheritance and polymorphism. However, we should only really need to create named complex types if it is important to represent classes in our document structures, and if we need to make use of these concepts for element content. This is because named complex types introduce a lot of complexity that is not required when creating an element content model. An alternative is named **model groups**, which we'll see shortly.

Compositors

So far we have not looked too closely at the use of the sequence element. We have seen that when we have element declarations nested inside a sequence element, the corresponding elements in a conforming instance document are required to appear in the same order in which they are declared. For example, we have been declaring the FirstName, MiddleInitial, and LastName elements inside a sequence element:

```
<xs:sequence>
    <xs:element name = "FirstName" type = "xs:string" />
    <xs:element name = "MiddleInitial" type = "xs:string" />
    <xs:element name = "LastName" type = "xs:string" />
</xs:sequence>
```

In the instance document the elements must appear in that order, like so:

```
<FirstName>Raymond</FirstName>
<MiddleInitial>G</MiddleInitial>
<LastName>Bayliss</LastName>
```

The following would **not** be valid because the elements do not appear in the same order as which they were declared:

```
<LastName>Bayliss</LastName>
<FirstName>Raymond</FirstName>
<MiddleInitial>G</MiddleInitial>
```

The sequence element is known as a **compositor** because it has created a **group** of element declarations. It provides a rule for all elements declared within it – in the instance document, the elements must occur in the same order as which they are declared.

sequence is just one of three compositors that can be used to group together element declarations, the other two being all and choice. Each of these compositors conveys different rules governing how the elements declared within it can appear in an instance document.

Here are the rules for each of the compositors:

❑   sequence indicates that the elements declared inside it must appear in the order in which they are declared

❑   choice means that any one of the elements declared inside it can occur in the instance document, but only one of them

❑   all allows the elements to occur in any order, but they can only occur once or not at all

Suppose our example used a choice compositor, rather than sequence:

```
<xs:element name = "Customer">
   <xs:complexType>
      <xs:choice>
         <xs:element name = "FirstName" type = "xs:string" />
         <xs:element name = "LastName" type = "xs:string" />
      </xs:choice>
   </xs:complexType>
</xs:element>
```

This creates a group containing the FirstName and LastName elements, only one of which would be allowed to appear as a child of the Customer element in an instance document, but not both.

We could also have defined the complex type using the all compositor:

```
<xs:element name = "Customer">
   <xs:complexType>
      <xs:all>
         <xs:element name = "FirstName" type = "xs:string"
                     minOccurs = "0" maxOccurs = "1" />
         <xs:element name = "LastName" type = "xs:string"
                     minOccurs = "0" maxOccurs = "1" />
      </xs:all>
   </xs:complexType>
</xs:element>
```

Note that the occurrence indicators on the element declarations are set to minOccurs = "0" and maxOccurs = "1". The result of this is that an instance document can contain the FirstName and LastName elements in any order, and both are optional. Any of the following would be allowed in a Customer element in an instance document:

```
<Customer><FirstName></FirstName></Customer>
<Customer><LastName></LastName></Customer>
<Customer><FirstName></FirstName><LastName></LastName></Customer>
<Customer><LastName></LastName><FirstName></FirstName></Customer>
```

If we had not set the occurrence indicators on the element declarations to minOccurs = "0" and maxOccurs = "1", both elements are either required to appear. The default value for both of these attributes is 1. Note that you *cannot* set a value for minOccurs or maxOccurs of higher than 1 inside the all compositor.

Combining Compositors

If you want to combine more than one compositor along with child elements within a complex type definition, you can do so with the sequence and choice elements. For example, we might want to offer document authors a choice of child elements for an IceCream element. The first child could be either Strawberry or Chocolate, and the second child element could be either Cone or Tub:

```
<xs:element name = "IceCream">
   <xs:complexType>
      <xs:sequence>
         <xs:choice>
            <xs:element name = "Strawberry" type = "xs:string" />
            <xs:element name = "Chocolate" type = "xs:string" />
         </xs:choice>
         <xs:choice>
            <xs:element name = "Cone" type = "xs:string" />
            <xs:element name = "Tub" type = "xs:string" />
         </xs:choice>
      </xs:sequence>
   </xs:complexType>
</xs:element>
```

To achieve this, we have nested two choice compositors inside a sequence compositor. The only restriction for the ability to nest compositors is on the all group:

> A complex type can only contain one all compositor, and the all element must appear as the first child of the complexType element. We cannot combine the all compositor with either choice or sequence.

Repeating Compositors

When a complexType element contains a choice or sequence compositor as a child, the choice or sequence elements can carry minOccurs and maxOccurs attributes allowing the declarations inside to be repeated. You cannot, however, use these occurrence constraints with the all compositor (except to make an element optional with minOccurs=0). For example, if we wanted to allow a repeating set of names, where a document instance might look like this:

```
<Customers>
      <FirstName>Raymond</FirstName>
      <MiddleInitial>G</MiddleInitial>
      <LastName>Bayliss</LastName>
      <FirstName>Bob</FirstName>
      <LastName>Wilson</LastName>
      <FirstName>Alex</FirstName>
      <MiddleInitial>S</MiddleInitial>
      <LastName>Frazier</LastName>
      <FirstName>Martin</FirstName>
      <LastName>Watkins</LastName>
</Customers>
```

We could add `minOccurs` and `maxOccurs` attributes to the sequence compositor like so:

```
<xs:schema xmlns:xs = "http://www.w3.org/2001/XMLSchema">

<xs:element name = "Customers">
   <xs:complexType>
      <xs:sequence minOccurs = "1" maxOccurs = "unbounded">
         <xs:element name = "FirstName" type = "xs:string" />
         <xs:element name = "MiddleInitial" type = "xs:string"
                     minOccurs = "0" maxOccurs = "unbounded" />
         <xs:element name = "LastName" type = "xs:string" />
      </xs:sequence>
   </xs:complexType>
</xs:element>

</xs:schema>
```

This indicates that the child elements can appear repeatedly.

Named Model Groups

The compositors we have just looked at create what the XML Schema Recommendation refers to as **model group schema components**. This is a somewhat confusing use of terminology and you might like to stick with the term compositor, because it is also possible to create a **model group definition**, which contains one or more compositor inside it just like those we have seen in the previous section.

A model group definition appears inside a `group` element, which should be defined globally (a direct child of the `schema` element), rather than in a `complexType` element. The `group` element can be given a name, so that it can be referred to elsewhere in the schema. As a result, model groups are very helpful in creating re-usable content. The `sequence`, `choice`, or `all` compositors are then nested inside the `group` element. Here is how we could create a named model group for the name information we have been using throughout the chapter:

```
<?xml version = "1.0" ?>
<xs:schema xmlns:xs = "http://www.w3.org/2001/XMLSchema">

   <xs:element name = "Customer">
      <xs:complexType>
         <xs:group ref = "NameGroup" />
      </xs:complexType>
   </xs:element>

   <xs:group name = "NameGroup">
      <xs:sequence>
         <xs:element name = "FirstName" type = "xs:string" />
         <xs:element name = "MiddleInitial" type = "xs:string" />
         <xs:element name = "LastName" type = "xs:string" />
      </xs:sequence>
   </xs:group>

</xs:schema>
```

The named model group is defined globally, and its name is the value of the name attribute on the group element that contains it. We have used it in the content model for the Customer element, using the ref attribute of a group element, whose value is the name of the group.

Let's look at another example with a choice group:

```
<?xml version = "1.0" ?>
<xs:schema xmlns:xs = "http://www.w3.org/2001/XMLSchema">

    <xs:element name = "Customer">
        <xs:complexType>
            <xs:group ref = "FirstOrLastNameGroup" />
        </xs:complexType>
    </xs:element>

    <xs:group name = "FirstOrLastNameGroup">
        <xs:choice>
            <xs:element name = "FirstName" type = "xs:string" />
            <xs:element name = "LastName" type = "xs:string" />
        </xs:choice>
    </xs:group>

</xs:schema>
```

Here we have created a named model group that allows either a FirstName element or a LastName element (but not both) to appear in an instance document. Having defined the group, we can then use it inside any other complex type definition in this schema.

Named model groups are very helpful for creating re-usable building blocks within our schema. Having defined the named model group, we can reference it in any number of complex types. For example, if you are going to use a lot of names in your schema, by creating a named model group for these elements you do not need to define them each time you want to use them in a content model. This reproduces the functionality of parameter entities in DTDs, which were often used to define re-usable content models.

Below, we can see an example of using the named model group as a building block in a schema. Here, not only can the Customer element contain the child elements that are defined in the named model group, but it should also contain another element after it. Here we are using the named model group inside an anonymous complex type to build up the content model for the Customer element:

```
<xs:element name = "Customer">
    <xs:complexType>
        <xs:sequence>
            <xs:group ref = "FirstOrLastNameGroup" />
            <xs:element name = "FirstPurchase" type = "xs:string" />
        </xs:sequence>
    </xs:complexType>
</xs:element>
```

Here, the Customer element declaration contains an anonymous complex type definition, because we want the Customer element to contain child elements. Inside the complex type definition, we use the sequence compositor to indicate that the contents of the named model group definition should appear as the first children of the Customer element, and then the new FirstPurchase element should follow.

An example of a conforming document instance might be:

```
<Customer>
   <FirstName>Ray</FirstName>
   <FirstPurchase>Tin whistle</FirstPurchase>
</Customer>
```

Or:

```
<Customer>
   <LastName>Bayliss</LastName>
   <FirstPurchase>Spinning top</FirstPurchase>
</Customer>
```

Model groups and compositors are very helpful tools in creating element content models, and are an important way of indicating order or choice of elements. If we are likely to re-use the group, we should create a named model group, otherwise we should just use compositors inside our complex type definitions.

Repeating Model Groups

Just as the `sequence` and `choice` compositors could carry the `minOccurs` and `maxOccurs` attributes, so can the `group` element. This helps us build truly flexible and powerful content models. For example, to create the repeating name structure we saw in the section on *Repeating Compositors*, we could create a repeatable named model group, like so:

```
<?xml version = "1.0" ?>
<xs:schema xmlns:xs = "http://www.w3.org/2001/XMLSchema">

    <xs:element name = "Customers">
       <xs:complexType>
          <xs:group ref = "NameGroup" minOccurs = "1"
                    maxOccurs = "unbounded"/>
       </xs:complexType>
    </xs:element>

    <xs:group name = "NameGroup">
       <xs:sequence>
          <xs:element name = "FirstName" type = "xs:string" />
          <xs:element name = "MiddleInitial" type = "xs:string"
                    minOccurs = "0" maxOccurs = "1" />
          <xs:element name = "LastName" type = "xs:string" />
       </xs:sequence>
    </xs:group>

</xs:schema>
```

Note you cannot place the occurrence constraints on the global definitions of the named model group, but you can when you reference them in the complex types.

Attribute Groups

In the same way that we can create named model groups, we can also group together attribute declarations and give them a name. This can be helpful when a number of elements should carry the same set of attributes. For example, imagine we used an XML file as a persistent store of contact details (customers, employees, and suppliers) in the following form, and that several people could add to, or modify the store:

```
<Contacts>
   <Customers>
      <Customer customerID = "c143">Customer details go here.</Customer>
      <Customer customerID = "c144">Customer details go here.</Customer>
      <Customer customerID = "c144">Customer details go here.</Customer>
   </Customers>
   <Employees>
      <Employee employeeID = "e0012">Employee details go here.</Employee>
      <Employee employeeID = "e0013">Employee details go here.</Employee>
      <Employee employeeID = "e0014">Employee details go here.</Employee>
   </Employees>
   <Suppliers>
      <Supplier supplierID = "s0001">Supplier details go here.</Supplier>
      <Supplier supplierID = "s0002">Supplier details go here.</Supplier>
      <Supplier supplierID = "s0003">Supplier details go here.</Supplier>
   </Suppliers>
</Contacts>
```

Because several people can add and modify the entries, we might decide to keep a record of who had added the entries to the XML file, the date on which they were added, and when they were last modified. Rather than declare `dateCreated`, `lastModified`, and `author` attributes within the complex type definition for the `Customer`, `Employee`, and `Supplier` elements, we could create an attribute group and reference this group from within the complex type definitions. This would also have the advantage that, should we decide to store a new type of contact, say an advertiser, we could add the same set of attributes to the new type of contact.

Attribute groups must be defined globally, using the `attributeGroup` element, which carries a `name` attribute whose value is the name of the attribute group:

```
<xs:attributeGroup name = "createdAttrGroup">
   <xs:attribute name = "author" type = "xs:string" use = "required" />
   <xs:attribute name = "dateCreated" type = "xs:date" use = "required" />
   <xs:attribute name = "lastModified" type = "xs:date" use = "required" />
</xs:attributeGroup>
```

Having defined the attribute group called `createdAttrGroup`, we could then use it in several different complex type definitions, like so:

```
<xs:element name = "Customer">
   <xs:complexType>
      <xs:sequence>
         <xs:element name = "FirstName" type = "xs:string" />
         <xs:element name = "MiddleInitial" type = "xs:string" />
         <xs:element name = "LastName" type = "xs:string" />
```

```
            </xs:sequence>
            <xs:attribute name = "customerID" type="xs:string" use ="required" />
            <xs:attributeGroup ref = "createdAttrGroup" />
        </xs:complexType>
    </xs:element>

    <xs:element name = "Employee">
        <xs:complexType>
            <xs:sequence>
                <xs:element name = "FirstName" type = "xs:string" />
                <xs:element name = "MiddleInitial" type = "xs:string" />
                <xs:element name = "LastName" type = "xs:string" />
            </xs:sequence>
            <xs:attribute name = "employeeID" type="xs:string" use ="required" />
            <xs:attributeGroup ref = "createdAttrGroup" />
        </xs:complexType>
    </xs:element>
```

Note how the reference to the `attributeGroup` is after the closing element of the compositor, but before the closing `complexType` element. This is exactly where we place local attribute declarations within a complex type definition. The `attributeGroup` must have a `ref` attribute that has as its value the name of the attribute group that we want the element to carry.

An example `Customer` element might now look like this:

```
<Customer customerID = "c12442" author = "e0012"
          dateCreated = "2001-05-27" lastModified = "2001-05-27" >
    <FirstName>Raymond</FirstName>
    <MiddleInitial>G</MiddleInitial>
    <LastName>Bayliss</LastName>
</Customer>
```

All of the attributes must appear on the `Customer`, `Employee`, and `Supplier` elements, as their declarations all carry the use attribute with a value of `required`. If we wanted to add either a `default` or `fixed` value for them, we could have done this also. The simple types of the attributes constrain the allowable values of attributes; note that the values of the `dateCreated` and `lastModified` attributes will have to conform to the built-in `date` simple type, which we met in the last chapter.

Element Content Specifications

Recall that if we do not associate a type with the name of an element declaration, the default is the **ur-type** definition, which is known as `anyType`. For an element, it is rather like the equivalent of using the ANY keyword in a DTD, although (unlike the ANY keyword in a DTD) it can also contain elements that have not been defined in the schema. This is why we need to define the allowable content of elements with types (be they simple or complex), so that we can specify what can occur in a document instance.

Rarely will we want to allow an element to contain just any content; more often we will want to provide a **content specification**. We may want to specify an element's content specification as:

- ❑ **Element content** – which allows the element to have child elements, but no character data between opening and closing tags
- ❑ **Mixed content** – which allows child elements and character data between opening and closing tags
- ❑ **Empty** – which means that the element cannot contain child elements or anything between the opening and closing tags, although they can carry attributes
- ❑ **Text-only** – which allows character data between the opening and closing element tags, but the element cannot contain any elements

All of these are commonly used in XML. The only content specification we will not have dealt with by the end of this chapter (which you are likely to require) is that of a text-only element that carries an attribute, which because of the way they are declared will be dealt with in the next chapter.

We have already seen how we deal with text-only content, by associating the name of an element with a simple type (as we did with the FirstName, MiddleInitial, and LastName elements). If we want an element to carry attributes or have child elements, then we will need to define a complex type. Whether or not the complex type is named does not matter, although a named complex type can be re-used in different element declarations as we saw at the beginning of the chapter.

Let's see how we use different complex type definitions, model groups, and attribute groups to create different content models.

Element Content

When a content specification is said to have element content, it refers to an element being allowed to have child elements. The Customer element that we have been looking at throughout the chapter has had element content:

```
<Customer customerID = "c00014">
   <FirstName>Bob</FirstName>
   <MiddleInitial>J</MiddleInitial>
   <LastName>Winters</LastName>
</Customer>
```

We have defined the content model for the Customer element in several different ways throughout the chapter. Let's quickly review the approaches we have taken. We will raise some of the characteristics of each approach here, although there are many more issues that we need to be aware of when we start to use namespaces in our instance documents. We will come back to look at this more in Chapter 6.

The first approach used an anonymous complex type and the sequence compositor:

```
<xs:element name = "Customer">
   <xs:complexType>
      <xs:sequence>
         <xs:element name = "FirstName" type = "xs:string" />
         <xs:element name = "MiddleInitial" type = "xs:string" />
         <xs:element name = "LastName" type = "xs:string" />
      </xs:sequence>
```

```
            <xs:attribute name = "customerID" type = "xs:string" />
      </xs:complexType>
</xs:element>
```

This approach has the benefit that it keeps all of the element declarations together inside the `Customer` element declaration, making the schema easy to read. However, the content model can only be used with this `Customer` element.

The second approach used a named complex type:

```
<xs:element name = "Customer" type = "NameType" />
<xs:complexType name = "NameType">
   <xs:sequence>
      <xs:element name = "FirstName" type = "xs:string" />
      <xs:element name = "MiddleInitial" type = "xs:string" />
      <xs:element name = "LastName" type = "xs:string" />
   </xs:sequence>
   <xs:attribute name = "customerID" type = "xs:string" />
</xs:complexType>
```

With the named complex type, any element can re-use the content model that we have defined. Any element that is declared to have this type will automatically have the same child element declarations and attribute declarations. While it requires that we look across the schema to find the corresponding type, it can result in a smaller schema when the same content model is re-used in different elements.

The third solution was the named model group. This allowed us the benefits of re-using the group of elements with different elements. It also showed how model groups are helpful as building blocks within an XML Schema. Here we not only re-use the group in a `Customer` and `Employee` element, but we also add another optional `Title` element just to the customer records (not employees), indicating whether they are a `Mr`, `Mrs`, `Ms`, `Dr`, or `Sir`:

```
<xs:element name = "Customer">
   <xs:complexType>
      <xs:sequence>
         <xs:element name = "Title" type = "xs:string" />
         <xs:group ref = "NameGroup" />
      </xs:sequence>
   </xs:complexType>
</xs:element>

<xs:element name = "Employee">
   <xs:complexType>
         <xs:group ref = "NameGroup" />
   </xs:complexType>
</xs:element>

<xs:group name = "NameGroup">
   <xs:sequence>
      <xs:element name = "FirstName" type = "xs:string" />
      <xs:element name = "MiddleInitial" type = "xs:string" />
      <xs:element name = "LastName" type = "xs:string" />
   </xs:sequence>
</xs:group>
```

It is simple to add another element to the content model for the Customer element and is useful, as we are able to re-use the model group. So, not only are model groups important for expressing *order of* or *a choice of* elements, they also help us create an extensible, yet re-usable content model.

Mixed Content

Mixed content is a combination of child elements and character data, and is often used in viewable documents when document authors need to add extra meaning or emphasis to a piece of text. For example, look at the following snippet of XHTML taken from the W3C's HTML Home Page:

```
<div class="preface">
<p>This is <acronym title="World Wide Web Consortium">W3C</acronym>'s
home page for <acronym title="HyperText Markup Language">HTML</acronym>.
Here you will find pointers to our specifications for HTML, guidelines
on how to use HTML to the best effect, and pointers to related work
at W3C. When W3C decides to become involved in an area of Web technology or
policy, it initiates an activity in that area. HTML is one of
many Activities currently being pursued. You can learn more about
the HTML Activity from the <a href="Activity">HTML Activity
Statement</a>.</p>
</div>
```

The paragraph element p contains a mix of text, acronym elements and a (link) elements.

With DTDs we could specify which elements were allowed to appear within mixed content in a document instance, but we could not constrain the order in which they appeared or the number of times they occurred. With XML Schema, both the order and the number of times an element occurs in a mixed content model must agree with the specified content model.

Let's look at another example. Here we have a query acknowledgement document, which is not only intended for viewing by the customer, but can also be processed by an application. The acknowledgement is automatically generated in response to a customer enquiry, and uses the customer name, the department that will answer the query, and a query ID within the text:

```
<AutomaticQueryAck>
Thank you for your enquiry, <FirstName>James</FirstName>. Your question will be
answered as soon as possible by a member of our <Department>Finance</Department>
department. Your enquiry ID is <EnquiryRefNo>1346355</EnquiryRefNo>.
</AutomaticQueryAck>
```

So, how do we define mixed content so that we can have this greater control over order and occurrence of elements within a given parent element? Of course, we will have to define a complex type, because we want to have text *and* child elements. To indicate that the complex type contains a mix of the two, we add an attribute called mixed to the complexType element whose value is set to true:

```
<xs:element name = "AutomaticQueryAck">
    <xs:complexType mixed = "true">
        <xs:sequence>
            <xs:element name = "FirstName" type = "xs:string" />
            <xs:element name = "Department" type = "xs:string" />
            <xs:element name = "EnquiryRefNo" type = "xs:integer" />
        </xs:sequence>
    </xs:complexType>
</xs:element>
```

After declaring the `AutomaticQueryAck` element, we define an anonymous complex type with the `mixed` attribute whose value is set to `true` (the default value being `false`). Then we have the `sequence` compositor, because we want to make sure that the child elements will appear in a set order, inside of which we declare the elements. Now we would be able to validate the document instance as having the required child elements in that order.

Empty

Empty elements do not have any element content, but are allowed to carry attributes. They are ideal for placeholders. If we want to define a complex type whose content is empty, we define a type that allows only elements in its content, but then we do not actually declare any elements within the type, which makes it empty:

```
<xs:element name = "Placeholder">
   <xs:complexType />
</xs:element>
```

Here the `Placeholder` element cannot contain any text, and cannot carry any attributes. The only two ways of representing this element in an instance document are:

```
<Placeholder />
<Placeholder></Placeholder>
```

If we want to add attributes we can do so by simply adding them in the complex type definition like so:

```
<xs:element name = "Placeholder">
   <xs:complexType>
      <xs:attribute name = "placeRef" type = "xs:string" />
   </xs:complexType>
</xs:element>
```

Now the element can carry an attribute called `placeRef`, like so:

```
<Placeholder placeRef = "placeholder1" />
```

We will look at how to add an attribute to an element that has text-only content in the next chapter.

Any Content

We have seen that XML Schema allows schema authors to develop tight or loose structures. We can allow flexibility such as mixed content and repeating model groups, and we can tie down allowable content from empty elements to strict order of required child elements. There are times, however, when it is useful to allow an element to contain any of the elements that have been declared, or to carry any of the attributes declared in the schema, or indeed another schema. Times when such a decision is appropriate include:

❑   The start of a project when it is in development and we start getting ideas together, although these should be tightened up as soon as possible with further constraints as it can lead to errors creeping into the project.

❑   When we expect an element's content to change because we intend to release new versions of the schema, and we want to allow an area for updated elements.

❑ When we want to allow for a section of markup that has come from another schema, be it the one we've created, a related schema from our business domain or indeed when we want to include something like XHTML.

❑ When we want to allow part of the document to be unconstrained (possibly such as a memo or notes field).

If we wanted to allow an element to contain any well-formed XML regardless of whether there was a schema for it we could use the following:

```
<xs:element name = "ExtensionSpace">
   <xs:complexType mixed = "true">
      <xs:sequence>
         <xs:any minOccurs = "1" maxOccurs = "unbounded"
                 processContents = "skip" />
      </xs:sequence>
   </xs:complexType>
</xs:element>
```

Here we have used the occurrence constraints minOccurs and maxOccurs to indicate that we must have at least one undeclared element in the ExtensionSpace element, although there is no upper limit on the number of times new elements can appear within the ExtensionSpace element. We have also said that that the ExtensionSpace element can have mixed content by using a mixed attribute a value of true.

The processContents attribute tells the processor what to do with any content in the ExtensionSpace element in the instance document. It can take three values:

Value	Meaning
skip	(The default) indicates that the processor should not try to validate the content within this element
strict	Indicates that the processor should validate the contents of the element according to the namespace given
lax	Indicates that the processor should try to validate the contents of the element when it can

In this case, the processor should not try to validate the content of the ExtensionSpace element because the processContents attribute has a value of skip.

Let's look at an example of an instance document; the ExtensionSpace element can contain any well-formed XML, as long as it contains a minimum of one element:

```
<ExtensionSpace><Note>Here is an extension</Note> to some <Language>XML</Language>
that I made up myself. It can sit in the <XMLElement>ExtensionSpace</XMLElement>
without a problem, because it can have any element content.</ExtensionSpace>
```

Indeed, it could take something more structured:

```
<ExtensionSpace>
    <Age>23</Age>
    <LastPurchase>Alarm Clock</LastPurchase>
</ExtensionSpace>
```

As long as the XML is well formed it does not matter what we put in the ExtensionSpace element.

In our schema, we can also specify a namespace from which the markup must come:

```
<xs:element name = "XHTMLSection">
    <xs:complexType>
        <xs:sequence>
            <xs:any namespace = "http://www.w3.org/1999/xhtml"
                    minOccurs = "0" maxOccurs = "unbounded"
                    processContents = "lax" />
        </xs:sequence>
    </xs:complexType>
</xs:element>
```

Here the XHTMLSection element has been declared so that it can contain any well-formed XHTML. However, it does not need to contain anything, as we have set the minOccurs value to 0 this time. We have also indicated that the processor should validate any content of the XHTMLSection element according to the namespace we have given.

The namespace attribute can take any of the following values:

Value	Meaning
http://www.w3.org/1999/xhtml (or any other namespace)	The namespace(s) specified. We can even give a whitespace separated list of namespaces if we want to allow markup from a combination of them.
##any (the default)	Means the XML can come from any namespace. (Because this is the default, we left the namespace attribute off in the first example.)
##local	Refers to any XML that is not qualified by a namespace prefix.
##other	Refers to XML that is not from the same target namespace as this schema document.
##targetNamespace	Is a shorthand form for any XML from the namespace of this schema document.

We can also use a mix of ##targetNamespace with ##local or a given namespace. Going back to our XHTMLSection element, we could have something like the following:

```
<XHTMLSection>
    <p>This paragraph is written in
        <a href = "http://www.w3.org/MarkUp/">XHTML</a>.
```

```
        We can include any XHTML in here as long as it:
    </p>
    <ul>
        <li>conforms to the XHTML specification</li>
        <li>is well-formed XML</li>
    </ul>
</XHTMLSection>
```

Our processor may now attempt to validate this markup against the namespace given, but it is not required to because we set a value of lax for the processContents attribute. Note that if we had given processContents a value of strict we would have to find a copy of the schema to give to the processor and it would need to contain the relevant top-level elements that we had used in the section.

If we wanted to allow the XHTMLSection to contain any attribute from the XHTML namespace we could have added the anyAttribute element to the complex type definition like so:

```
<xs:element name = "XHTMLSection">
    <xs:complexType>
        <xs:sequence>
            <xs:any namespace = "http://www.w3.org/1999/xhtml"
                minOccurs = "0" maxOccurs = "unbounded"
                processContents = "strict" />
        </xs:sequence>
        <xs:anyAttribute namespace = "http://www.w3.org/1999/xhtml" />
    </xs:complexType>
</xs:element>
```

Now the XHTMLSection element would also be allowed to carry any XHTML attribute.

The any element and any attribute are known as **wildcards**, because they allow any content from the specified namespace (or any namespace if none is provided).

Nil Values

Generally speaking, we may think that an empty element has no significance. If we have an empty element whose content is supposed to be of a certain type, however, then a schema processor might object to the empty value because it does not conform to the datatype of the element. For example, suppose we had a Quantity element that had an integer datatype, and an instance document contained an empty Quantity element like so:

```
<Quantity></Quantity>
```

A processor might not validate the instance document because an empty string is not a valid integer. To get around this problem, XML Schema allows us to make an element **nillable**.

A nil value allows a processor to differentiate between a zero-length string, a zero value, and an undefined value. It can be seen as analogous to the use of 0 versus NULL in SQL. From the start, one of the main aims of XML Schema was to define a type system that would support import and export of data as XML to and from databases, this is an important addition to XML Schema in supporting types where a field does not contain a value.

If the element in question in the instance document carries the attribute xsi:nil with a value of true, then the processing application will not complain:

```
<Quantity xsi:nil = "true"></Quantity>
```

The xsi: prefix is from the XML Schema for Instance Documents namespace, which we'll see more of in Chapter 6 when we look at namespaces in more detail. We have to declare this namespace and use this prefix in our instance documents that contain nil values because the nil attribute is defined in the XML Schema for Instances namespace. We can add the required namespace declaration to any instance document that uses the nil mechanism, like so:

```
<?xml version = "1.0" ?>
<PurchaseOrder xmlns:xsi = "http://www.w3.org/2001/XMLSchema-instance">
    <ItemsOrdered>
        <Quantity xsi:nil = "true"></Quantity>
    </ItemsOrdered>
    ...
</PurchaseOrder>
```

The xsi:nil attribute can also be used to explicitly signal to a processing application that there is no value there. For example, if a document representing a purchase order used the Quantity element to indicate the number of products ordered, and there was not a value for it, we would have to go back and check the intended order – there is no point trying to process it.

Note that, while there can be no element content in such an element, it may still carry other attributes, which require the element to be present in the instance document.

To use the nil mechanism, we simply add a nillable attribute to the element declaration:

```
<xs:element name = "Quantity" type = "xs:integer" nillable = "true" />
```

Now we can use the xsi:nil attribute in an instance document, and the processor will not generate an error. If it comes across an empty Quantity element that uses the xsi:nil attribute with a value of true, it will not raise an error because it does not treat the empty element as a zero-length string (which would not a be valid integer). There is no equivalent mechanism for attribute values.

Example Schema: Contacts

Having seen the various ways in which we can build up schema constructs, let's build a slightly more complicated schema than those we have shown in the previous examples. It will also give us the opportunity to use some of the built-in datatypes we looked at in the previous chapter. The schema we are going to create ContactList.xsd contains contact information: names, addresses, phone and fax numbers, and email addresses.

The contact's details are all held in a root element called ContactList. Each individual contact's details are then held in an element called Contact. There will be two attributes on each Contact element: dateCreated, and dateModified. Inside the Contact element are containing elements for the four different types of information:

❑ Name will hold FirstName, MiddleInitial, and LastName elements

❑ HomeAddress will hold the contact's home address as element content

- ❑ WorkAddress will hold the contact's work address details using the same element content as the HomeAddress element
- ❑ EContact holds an email address, and various phone-based methods of communication

Here is a sample document called ContactList.xml marked up according to the ContactList.xsd schema:

```xml
<?xml version = "1.0" ?>
<ContactList
      xmlns:xsi ="http://www.w3.org/2001/XMLSchema-instance"
      xsi:noNamespaceSchemaLocation ="ContactList.xsd">
   <Contact dateCreated = "2001-03-15" dateModified = "2001-05-31">
      <Name>
         <FirstName>Ray</FirstName>
         <MiddleInitial>G</MiddleInitial>
         <LastName>Bayliss</LastName>
      </Name>
      <HomeAddress>
         <AddressLine1>10 Elizabeth Place</AddressLine1>
         <AddressLine2></AddressLine2>
         <Town>Paddington</Town>
         <City>Sydney</City>
         <StateProvinceCounty>NSW</StateProvinceCounty>
         <ZipPostCode>2021</ZipPostCode>
      </HomeAddress>
      <WorkAddress>
         <AddressLine1>The Example Corporation</AddressLine1>
         <AddressLine2>14 Townsend Close</AddressLine2>
         <Town>Alexandria</Town>
         <City>Sydney</City>
         <StateProvinceCounty>2050</StateProvinceCounty>
         <ZipPostCode></ZipPostCode>
      </WorkAddress>
      <EContact>
         <Email>rayb@example.org</Email>
         <HomeTel>0293283828</HomeTel>
         <WorkTel>0224482000</WorkTel>
         <CellPhone>0415512012</CellPhone>
      </EContact>
   </Contact>

   <!-- more contact details go here -->

</ContactList>
```

So, let's look at the schema; we will review it more closely in a moment, although you should note a few things:

- ❑ We have defined a named model for the address details, so that they can be re-used
- ❑ The schema only has one globally defined element, which means that we can determine what the root element of an instance document should be
- ❑ There are some elements declared in the schema that do not occur in the instance document we have just seen, such as Fax and Pager in the EContact element

Here is `ContactList.xsd`:

```xml
<?xml version = "1.0" ?>
<xs:schema xmlns:xs = "http://www.w3.org/2001/XMLSchema">

    <xs:element name = "ContactList">
        <xs:complexType>
            <xs:sequence>
                <xs:element name = "Contact" type = "ContactDetailsType"
                            minOccurs = "0" maxOccurs = "unbounded" />
            </xs:sequence>
        </xs:complexType>
    </xs:element>

    <xs:complexType name = "ContactDetailsType" >
            <xs:sequence>
                <xs:element name = "Name">
                    <xs:complexType>
                        <xs:sequence>
                            <xs:element name = "FirstName" type = "xs:string" />
                            <xs:element name = "MiddleInitial" type = "xs:string"
                                        minOccurs = "0" maxOccurs = "1" />
                        <xs:element name = "LastName" type = "xs:string" />
                        </xs:sequence>
                    </xs:complexType>
                </xs:element>

                <xs:element name = "HomeAddress" minOccurs = "0"
                            maxOccurs = "1">
                    <xs:complexType>
                        <xs:group ref = "AddressGroup" />
                    </xs:complexType>
                </xs:element>

                <xs:element name = "WorkAddress" minOccurs = "0"
                            maxOccurs = "1" >
                    <xs:complexType>
                        <xs:group ref = "AddressGroup" />
                    </xs:complexType>
                </xs:element>

                <xs:element name = "EContact">
                        <xs:complexType>
                            <xs:sequence>
                                <xs:element name = "Email" type = "xs:string"
                                            minOccurs = "0" maxOccurs = "1" />
                                <xs:element name = "HomeTel" type = "xs:integer"
                                            nillable = "true" minOccurs = "0"
                                            maxOccurs = "1" />
                                <xs:element name = "WorkTel" type = "xs:integer"
                                            nillable = "true" minOccurs = "0"
                                            maxOccurs = "1" />
                                <xs:element name = "CellPhone" type = "xs:integer"
                                            minOccurs = "0" maxOccurs = "1" />
                                <xs:element name = "Fax" type = "xs:integer"
                                            minOccurs = "0" maxOccurs = "1"/>
```

```
                                  <xs:element name = "Pager" type = "xs:integer"
                                              minOccurs = "0" maxOccurs = "1"/>
                          </xs:sequence>
                      </xs:complexType>
                  </xs:element>

          </xs:sequence>
          <xs:attribute name = "dateCreated" type = "xs:date"
                        use = "required" />
          <xs:attribute name = "dateModified" type = "xs:date" />
      </xs:complexType>

      <xs:group name="AddressGroup">
          <xs:sequence>
              <xs:element name = "AddressLine1"  type = "xs:string" />
              <xs:element name = "AddressLine2" type = "xs:string"
                          minOccurs = "0" maxOccurs = "1" />
              <xs:element name = "Town" type = "xs:string" />
              <xs:element name = "City" type = "xs:string"
                          minOccurs = "0" maxOccurs = "1" />
              <xs:element name="StateProvinceCounty" type = "xs:string" />
              <xs:element name="ZipPostCode"  type = "xs:string" />
          </xs:sequence>
      </xs:group>

  </xs:schema>
```

Let's take a look through the schema in detail and see what we have done. We start off declaring the namespace for XML Schema:

```
<xs:schema xmlns:xs = "http://www.w3.org/2001/XMLSchema">
```

We then define the root element `ContactList`. Because it contains `Contact` elements (as opposed to being a text-only element), we have had to associate it with complex type – in this case it is an anonymous complex type nested within the element declaration. So that we can declare the `Contact` element, we add a compositor to this complex type. We associate the `Contact` element with a named complex type called `ContactDetailsType`, which we see next. Because there can be many `Contacts` in the files, the `Contact` element has a `maxOccurs` value of `unbounded`.

```
<xs:element name = "ContactList">
    <xs:complexType>
        <xs:sequence>
            <xs:element name = "Contact" type = "ContactDetailsType"
                        minOccurs = "0" maxOccurs = "unbounded" />
        </xs:sequence>
    </xs:complexType>
</xs:element>
```

An alternative approach to defining the content model of the `Contact` element would have been to use a named model group instead of a named complex type.

Next we have the named complex type `ContactDetailsType`, in which we declare the four container elements `Name`, `HomeAddress`, `WorkAddress`, and `EContact`. These child elements of `Contact` must appear in the order stated, as denoted by the sequence group, although `HomeAddress` and `WorkAddress` are both optional and if present can only appear once (as denoted by the `minOccurs` = `"0"` and `maxOccurs` = `"1"` occurrence constraints). We come back to look at each declaration and their respective content models shortly.

The last thing to note here is that, at the bottom of the complex type just after closing the sequence compositor, we have the two attribute declarations, which allow the `Contact` element to carry the `dateCreated` and `dateModified` attributes. When we first add a contact it might not have a `dateModified` attribute, but we have required the use of the `dateCreated` attribute. Furthermore, the value of each of them must match the restrictions imposed by the built-in simple `date` type:

```xml
<xs:complexType name = "ContactDetailsType" >
    <xs:sequence>
        <xs:element name = "Name">
            . . .
        </xs:element>
        <xs:element name = "HomeAddress" minOccurs = "0"
                    maxOccurs = "1">
            . . .
        </xs:element>
        <xs:element name = "WorkAddress" minOccurs = "0"
                    maxOccurs = "1" >
            . . .
        </xs:element>
        <xs:element name = "EContact">
            . . .
        </xs:element>
    </xs:sequence>
    <xs:attribute name = "dateCreated" type = "xs:date"
                use = "required" />
    <xs:attribute name = "dateModified" type = "xs:date" />
</xs:complexType>
```

The first element declared inside the `ContactDetailsType` is the `Name` element. The contents of this element should be familiar; they are the same as for the `Customer` element we have looked at throughout the chapter. It is a good example of how we can nest complex type definitions and model groups within each other to create more complicated content models.

Remember that we specify the simple built-in string datatype to restrict the allowable content of text-only elements, because if we did not associate them with a type they could hold any well-formed combination of elements, attributes and characters that we had defined in the schema:

```xml
<xs:element name = "Name">
    <xs:complexType>
        <xs:sequence>
            <xs:element name = "FirstName" type = "xs:string" />
            <xs:element name = "MiddleInitial"  type = "xs:string"
                        minOccurs = "0" maxOccurs = "1" />
            <xs:element name = "LastName"  type = "xs:string" />
        </xs:sequence>
    </xs:complexType>
</xs:element>
```

Next we declare the `HomeAddress` and `WorkAddress` elements. Both share the same content model, so we will define a named model group called `AddressGroup` that they can both utilize. Both of these elements are optional:

```
<xs:element name = "HomeAddress" minOccurs = "0"
           maxOccurs = "1">
    <xs:complexType>
       <xs:group ref = "AddressGroup" />
    </xs:complexType>
</xs:element>
<xs:element name = "WorkAddress" minOccurs = "0"
            maxOccurs = "1" >
    <xs:complexType>
       <xs:group ref = "AddressGroup" />
    </xs:complexType>
</xs:element>
```

The last element in the `ContactDetailsType` is the `EContact` element. This holds another anonymous complex type because `EContact` holds several of its own child elements. Apart from the `Email` element, which has a string type, all of the others are of the XML Schema built-in integer type:

```
<xs:element name = "EContact">
     <xs:complexType>
        <xs:sequence>
           <xs:element name = "Email" type = "xs:string"
                       minOccurs = "0" maxOccurs = "1" />
           <xs:element name = "HomeTel" type = "xs:integer"
                       nillable = "true"
                       minOccurs = "0" maxOccurs = "1" />
           <xs:element name = "WorkTel" type = "xs:integer"
                       nillable = "true"
                       minOccurs = "0" maxOccurs = "1" />
           <xs:element name = "CellPhone" type = "xs:integer"
                       minOccurs = "0" maxOccurs = "1" />
           <xs:element name = "Fax" type = "xs:integer"
                       minOccurs = "0" maxOccurs = "1"/>
           <xs:element name = "Pager" type = "xs:integer"
                       minOccurs = "0" maxOccurs = "1"/>
        </xs:sequence>
     </xs:complexType>
</xs:element>
```

Because the telephone numbers are integer types, we cannot include these elements in the instance document if they do not contain a valid integer. If the elements are empty, the parser will throw an error, because an empty string is not a valid integer. If we wanted to allow these elements to appear in a document without any content, we would have to have used the nil mechanism we saw earlier.

Having closed the `ContactDetailsType` named complex type, we just have to define the `AddressGroup` used by both the `HomeAddress` and `WorkAddress` elements. It contains a `sequence` compositor, and the element declarations for the address fields. Some of these are optional, such as `AddressLine2` because not every address needs as many lines. If these optional elements did appear as empty elements in an instance document, however, it would not matter because they are of the `string` type:

```
<xs:group name="AddressGroup">
  <xs:sequence>
    <xs:element name = "AddressLine1"  type = "xs:string" />
    <xs:element name = "AddressLine2" type = "xs:string"
              minOccurs = "0" maxOccurs = "1"  />
    <xs:element name = "Town"  type = "xs:string" />
    <xs:element name = "City" type = "xs:string"
              minOccurs = "0" maxOccurs = "1"  />
    <xs:element name="StateProvinceCounty" type = "xs:string" />
    <xs:element name="ZipPostCode"  type = "xs:string" />
  </xs:sequence>
</xs:group>
```

You can test the `ContactList.xml` instance document against the schema using the XSV tool we discussed in Chapter 1. Remember, if you are running IE5 or above, you can redirect the XML output to view in your browser, with the command:

> **> xsv -o xsv-out.xml -s xsv.msxsl ContactList.xml**

(Remember, if you have MSXML 3 installed, you should replace `xsv.msxsl` *with the XSLT 1.0 compliant version of the stylesheet,* `xsv.xsl`*.)*

Schema Review

Having seen the majority of the features that XML Schema offers, we shall spend the last few pages of this chapter introducing some of the features we have yet to meet, and then reviewing what we have learned. After all, having seen many of the different types of markup that XML Schema allows us to use in the last three chapters, when writing schemas to constrain document instances, we will be in a better position to see how they fit together.

Features We Still Have to Meet

There are a number of schema constructs and mechanisms that we still have to meet, which we shall briefly mention over the next couple of pages. They will be covered in depth in the coming chapters, but it is good to be aware of the possibilities that XML Schema introduces so that you understand their power, and so that you know where to look for a particular feature. In particular we should look at:

❑   Identity constraints

❑   Namespace support

❑   The ability to derive new types from existing types

❑   Using constructs from other schemas

Identity Constraints

There are two kinds of identity constraint introduced by XML Schema, neither of which were available to authors of DTDs. The identity constraints are:

❑ Uniqueness constraint mechanism: which ensure that values in an instance document are unique

❑ `key` and `keyref` mechanisms: which define keys and references

Both of these features make use of a simplified subset of XPath syntax to define ranges of the document over which they apply, and both apply to the text-only contents of elements and values of attributes in addition to their datatype (not instead of). Identity Constraints are covered fully in Chapter 9.

Uniqueness Constraint Mechanism

The uniqueness constraint mechanism allows us to ensure that the values of a type of element or attribute are unique across a document instance. Furthermore, we are able to specify a range in which they are required to be unique, so we may only choose that they are unique from a certain point in the hierarchy down.

While XML 1.0 defined ID types for use with attributes, and their values had to be unique, the values had to be unique across a whole document and did not work with elements.

The uniqueness constraint mechanism is ideal for such things as ensuring unique product or inventory identifiers, ensuring unique usernames or passwords, or any other value that we do not want to be repeated in document instances.

key and keyref Mechanisms

The `key` and `keyref` mechanisms allow us to define a one-to-one or one-to-many relationship. Keys act as a unique identifier within a given part of the hierarchy of an XML document, and can be applied to any type of element or attribute. Their references must then point to a key that exists within the document.

While the XML ID and IDREF datatypes allow us to define relationships between information items, the `key` and `keyref` mechanisms introduced by XML Schema offer schema authors the ability to define much richer kinds of relationships.

The relationships expressed in keys and their references help us in the representation of data when it is imported from and exported to relational databases, while letting us maintain the structure imposed by the relational model – the key, acting as a primary key would in a database, and the `keyref` acting as a foreign key. As we shall see in Chapter 9, they also allow us to employ normalization techniques on our XML files.

Namespace Support

The schemas we have developed in this chapter create markup that does not belong to any particular namespace. There will be many kinds of XML documents that do not need to be validated according to a particular namespace, and that do not make use of namespaces. However, the lack of support for namespaces in DTDs was one of their weaknesses. The namespace support in XML Schema has some distinct purposes:

❑ To validate an instance document that makes use of namespaces against markup that explicitly belongs to that namespace

❑ To validate document instances that are created using markup from several namespaces

❑ To allow a schema author the ability to specify the intended namespace of markup that we are creating

❑ To allow a schema author to require that elements and attributes must or must not be qualified in instance documents

The use of namespaces, however, introduces a whole new level of complexity into schema authoring and both require and deserve a chapter of their own. In Chapter 6, we will quickly review the XML Namespaces Recommendation, and then look at how using namespaces in our documents affects the way in which we write our schemas.

Deriving Complex Types

Not only can we define complex types that can represent an element's content model, but we can also derive new types from those that we have already created or that others have defined. This allows us to create rich class structures in our element hierarchies, and represent features of object-oriented development such as inheritance and polymorphism. It also helps us derive new types from those that are made available through standards-based schemas if they are not ideally suited to our needs.

We have to be careful when restricting existing complex types, as there are a lot of details that we need to be aware of. Unless we particularly want the object-oriented mapping with our structures, creating named model groups is a simpler approach to defining content models. We look at the issues involved in deriving new types, and indeed restricting the ability to derive new types, from those we have created in the next chapter.

Using Constructs from Other Schemas

When you think about the name of XML, it is puzzling that the first description language, DTD, is not itself extensible. When writing a DTD, all markup declarations and definitions had to be included in the DTD or a parameter entity. With XML Schemas, there are a number of ways to extend the schema:

❑ Re-use parts of schemas in other schemas

❑ Define complex structures that can be re-used in different schemas

❑ Derive our own, new datatypes from existing ones

❑ Reference multiple schemas from a single document instance

These abilities are based upon two key features of XML Schema: their support for XML Namespaces and the new constructs; `import`, `include`, and `redefine`. These new features allow us to share standard vocabularies with greater ease. We can even tailor existing schemas to our individual needs if they are not exactly what we want, adding and removing elements, and attributes from content models.

The ability to re-use our own markup also means that we can take a modular approach to our schema development and re-use common constructs that appear in several schemas. Along with namespace support this also enables us to validate instance documents that were written according to more than one schema, and helps those who want to use industry standard or already developed schemas. We look at creating schemas from multiple documents in Chapter 8.

Having seen the remaining features that XML Schema offers schema authors, let's review how the pieces of the schema recommendation fit together.

The 13 Schema Constructs

Now that we are familiar with the abilities of XML Schema, and have been introduced to the majority of the features, we should take another quick look at how the schema specification splits up what it calls the **schema components**.

We looked at how XML Schema is described in terms of an abstract model based upon the information items defined in the infoset, when we looked at validating schemas in Chapter 1. There are 13 building blocks in XML Schema that comprise the abstract model, which are divided into three categories:

Primary Components:

- ❑ Simple Type Definitions
- ❑ Complex Type Definitions
- ❑ Attribute Declarations
- ❑ Element Declarations

Type definitions may either have names or be anonymous, while elements and attributes must have names.

Secondary Components:

- ❑ Attribute group definitions
- ❑ Identity-constraint definitions
- ❑ Model group definitions (named model groups)
- ❑ Notation declarations

All of the secondary components must be given a name.

Helper components:

- ❑ Annotations
- ❑ Model groups (created by compositors but not in a group element)
- ❑ Particles
- ❑ Wildcards
- ❑ Attribute uses

Helper components are used in other components. They belong in the context in which they are declared, and cannot be referenced by name for use in other element content models, text-only element content or attribute values.

Summary

In this chapter we have built upon what we have learnt in the previous chapter and looked at how to create more complex element content models. We have seen:

❑   How we can name complex types, so that they can be re-used with different elements

❑   How to use model groups as building blocks for either named or anonymous complex types

❑   How compositors can be used in both complex types and named model groups to indicate choice and order of elements

These are the basic constructs from which we can allow complicated content models to appear in instance documents. (We cover some general practices for defining content models in Chapter 7.) We then moved on to look at how we could use the nil mechanism in XML Schema along with the `xsi:nil` attribute in instance documents to distinguish between empty element content and zero-length strings. We ended the chapter looking at some of the features we still have to meet. In the next chapter we go on to look at how we can derive new types from existing ones.

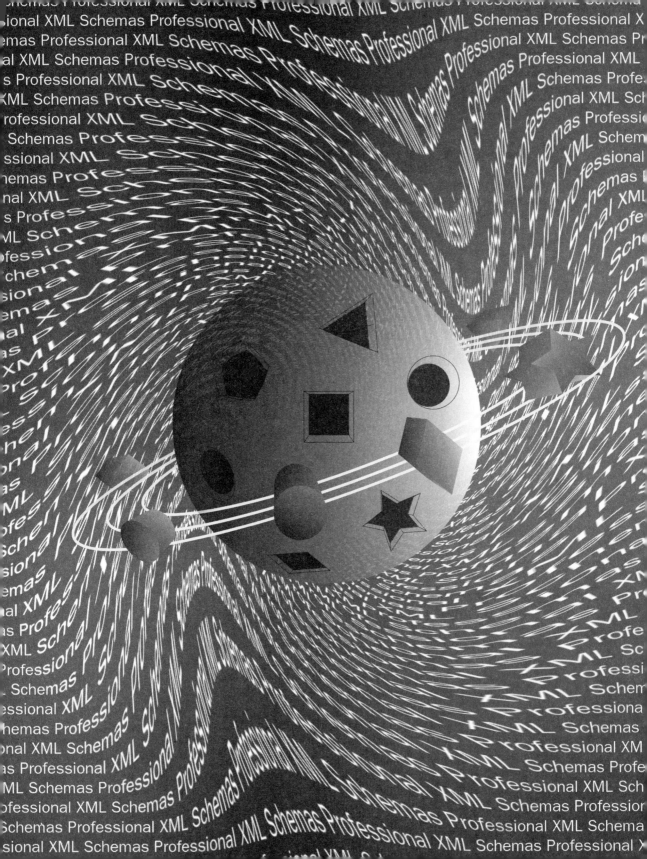

Deriving New Types

A derived type is one that is defined in terms of an existing type (its base type). A base type may be either a built-in primitive type, or another derived type. Simple types may be derived by restriction, list, or union, using the Simple Type Definition (the simpleType element). Complex types can be derived by restriction or extension, using the Complex Type Definition (complexType element). The built-in datatypes are a large step beyond those few provided in DTDs, but the ability to create user-defined types is an even greater leap.

In this chapter, we look at how we can derive our own simple and complex types, and how these types can be used to build other more complex datatypes. These hierarchies of types are much like those of object-oriented (OO) classes, and have the same advantage of leveraging existing definitions. The advantage of XML Schemas is that with this more detailed validation information, less application-specific code needs to be written.

Let's begin by looking at the facets (properties) of datatypes.

Facets of Datatypes

As we saw in Chapter 2, every XML Schema datatype has various defining properties, known as facets. They are always one of two types:

❑ **Fundamental facets** – the intrinsic abstract properties of a datatype.

❑ **Constraining facets** – optional limits upon the value and/or lexical space of a datatype.

We will examine the implications of these facets, and see how we can use these properties to define new types of our own. The following sections are supplemented by tables later in this chapter, which correlate these facets with all the built-in primitive and derived datatypes, as well as some of the example types we create in this, and the next, chapter.

Fundamental Facets

There are five fundamental facets, which are shared by *all* datatypes:

❑ **Equality** – different values can be compared and determined to be equal (A=B or B=A) or not (A≠B or A!=B).

❑ **Order** – numbers and some other datatypes may have ordered values, which allows the use of greater-than (A>B) and less-than (A<B) comparisons.

❑ **Bounds** – ordered datatypes may be constrained to be within a finite range of values (min ≤ A ≤ max), or have a single explicit upper or lower bound for an open-ended range of values that extend to positive or negative infinity (-∞ ≤ A ≤ max or min ≤ A ≤ ∞).

❑ **Cardinality** – the permissible number of values within the value space: none, one, two, forty-two, many (∞), and so on.

❑ **Numeric/non-numeric** – the age-old dichotomy between values that conform to the mathematical concept of numbers, and those that comprise all other forms of data.

The fundamental facets of a datatype, determine which comparisons and other operations can be performed upon data of that type. For example, it is not possible to compare the values of two items for a greater-than or less-than relationship if that datatype is not ordered. If the datatype cannot be bounded, the minInclusive facet is irrelevant.

Let's look at the details of these fundamental facets.

Equality

This facet applies to all datatypes, whether they are numeric or not.

The equality (and non-equality) of numbers is a fundamental mathematical concept. Whether the same value is represented as "0.4e1" or "4.0" or "4", the value remains the same (4=4=4). Conversely, this value (4) cannot be equal to another other value within the set of integers. Differences in precision may affect the real-world comparison of real numbers for equality, but such numbers still have that potential.

The concept of equality is much less obvious when describing string or date/time values. XML Schemas are case-sensitive, like XML 1.0 in general, therefore the string "YES" is *not* equal to "yes", "Yes", or "yEs". Therefore, string equality in this context implies an exact match of two strings – identical lengths of identical characters of matching case, except for those familiar with the case-sensitive UNIX operating system, However most of the Anglo-centric computing community has become conditioned to think of most string matching (particularly that involving names) as a generally case-insensitive operation. Alphabetized lists in printed publications, such as directories or dictionaries, also ignore the case of letters.

> *Even within the European languages, string matching is not always as simple as it seems. Accented characters (such as è, é, ê) or diacritic characters (such as ë) may or may not be sorted with their base characters (e). In some languages, all accented characters come after "z", when sorting lists of words – in others, these characters may be sorted within the alphabet, but not necessarily adjacent to their corresponding base character.*

> *Non-European languages often have no concept of upper- and lower-case letters. Indeed, even the basic concept of letters is nonsensical for languages represented by ideograms. These include East Asian languages such as Chinese, Japanese, and Korean (a group of languages and a common writing system that is called "CJK", for short).*

Another complication of string matching, is that many accented and ideographic characters can have multiple representations. For example, the letter "n" with a tilde accent can be represented in ASCII (or for an input device like a keyboard) as the two-letter sequence, "~n". An alternative representation, using the Latin-1 encoding, would be a single accented letter, "ñ". In XML Schemas, we can also use a character or entity reference to represent this "same" character. By definition, these characters are only equal if they are of the same form – "~n" is *not* equal to "ñ", even though these are different lexical representations of the same character and value.

All datatypes are presumed to have an equality facet, this never needs to be explicitly declared in a schema therefore – it is an intrinsic part of XML Schema.

Order

This facet also applies to both numeric and some non-numeric datatypes. Like equality, numeric order is intrinsic to the mathematical definition of numbers. For example, it is always true that 42>13, or 42<43, or (N-1)<N<(N+1), and so on. The set of integers {-∞...-2, -1, 0, 1, 2 ...∞} is a good example of a set of ordered values. All numeric datatypes in W3C XML Schema are completely ordered, that is they have the property of **total order**.

Strictly speaking, the XML Schemas string datatypes are all considered unordered (no particular character is considered to be greater or less than another character), nothing However prevents an application from imposing its own sense of order upon a datatype.

> *The order of characters, or strings of characters, usually depends on the* encoded *numeric value of the characters. These UCS code point values are depicted in Unicode as 4-digit hexadecimal numbers in the form "U+nnnn". For example, the code point for the digit "0" (ASCII zero, or U+0030) is less than that for an upper-case "A" (U+0041), "A" is less than "a" (U+0061), "e" (U+0065) is less than "è" (U+00E9 in the Latin-1 encoding), and so on.*

> *Don't assume however, that upper-case letters are always less than lower-case letters. While this is true for the ASCII and Latin-1 encodings, the Latin Extended -A and -B encodings mix the two cases together. Also remember that the concept of case doesn't even exist in many non-Latin alphabets.*

The built-in date/time datatypes have what is called **partial order** – there are certain ambiguous values that may or may not fit into an ordered set of values. For example, if we speak of midday or noon as "12:00" (local time), how can this be compared with "12:00Z" (noon UTC)? The latter probably isn't the same as local noon, and could be either less than or greater than the local time shown in the first example.

The ordered Schema Component

The order facet of a datatype is either inherent in XML Schemas (a "Schema Component" named ordered, as in the case of built-in primitive types) or in the case of a derived type, is inherited from its base type. There are three possible values for this component (that is, three kinds of order):

❑   false – this datatype is unordered.

❑   partial – this datatype is partially ordered, some comparisons may be possible, but there may be ambiguous values that cannot be compared.

❑   total – this datatype is totally ordered, and all values may be used in comparisons.

List datatypes are always unordered. Union datatypes may be ordered only if all member datatypes share the same type of ordering, and they all share a common ancestor type (no ordering is possible between different datatypes).

As we saw above, all numeric datatypes are totally ordered. All primitive string and binary encoding datatypes (`string`, `anyURI`, `hexBinary`, and so on) and the primitive `boolean` type are unordered. Partial ordering applies to all of the date/time datatypes, because of the optional time zone value, which can prevent precise comparison of date/time values.

Bounds

This facet only applies to ordered datatypes (numeric or date/time), but not string or binary encoding types. The value space of these datatypes may be constrained to have either lower or upper bounds, or both. These may be either inclusive or exclusive bounds.

The `float` and `double` primitive datatypes are bounded (because they represent finite 32- and 64-bit IEEE floating-point numbers), but the other primitive numeric type (`decimal`) is not bounded. The built-in derived datatypes are also divided into the infinite value spaces of `integer` and such like, plus the bounded types that are based upon finite computer hardware and language datatypes (`byte`, `short`, `int`, and so on).

The bounded Schema Component

The bounds facet of an ordered datatype is either inherent (the `bounded` Schema Component), or is inherited from its base type. This is a `boolean` value:

- ❑   `false` – the datatype is unbounded.
- ❑   `true` – the datatype is bounded (upper, lower, or both).

If we define an atomic datatype and specify `minInclusive` or `minExclusive` and either `maxInclusive` or `maxExclusive`, then our datatype is bounded (the attribute value is `true`). Otherwise, the datatype is unbounded.

List types are bounded if `length`, or both `minLength` and `maxLength`, are present.

Union datatypes may be bounded only if all member datatypes are both ordered and bounded (that is, they all have `bounded="true"`).

Cardinality

All value spaces have an associated concept of cardinality, in other words, the number of values within the value space. A value space may be finite or "countably infinite", or in theory, "uncountably infinite". There aren't any datatypes that are uncountably infinite in XML Schemas.

By definition, all bounded datatypes have a finite or countably infinite value space. One unbounded datatype (`boolean`) also has a finite value space. All other unbounded types are countably infinite. A string or decimal number type of this kind could theoretically be of infinite length or precision, but the software environment, available memory, or some other aspect of the implementation of XML Schema datatypes imposes the real limits.

> *A "minimally conforming" XML processor must support* at least 18 digits *for the decimal type, but there is no such minimum requirement for the length of a string type. It should be a very, very large number in almost all XML implementations However, aside from PDAs perhaps.*

The cardinality Schema Component

The cardinality facet of an ordered datatype is either inherent (this Schema Component), or is inherited from its base type. This is an enumerated value:

- ❑   finite – datatype has a finite value space.

- ❑   countably infinite – this datatype has an infinite value space.

This facet is probably most interesting to set theorists, but it does have some implications for the practical application of XML data. In fact, it is likely that most real world use of XML Schema datatypes will depend entirely upon user-derived types that have been artificially restricted to ensure interoperability (precision of decimal numeric calculations, maximum string lengths, and so on). In doing this, we no longer need to deal with anything, but datatypes that have finite cardinality, and this facet becomes irrelevant.

Numeric/Non-Numeric

A datatype and its associated value space are classified as numeric if the values can be considered numeric quantities in some number system. Remember that XML isn't limited to ASCII digits (those with hexadecimal values in the range from x30 to x39). Any of the several sets of Unicode number characters (that is, those in the "Nd" class) can be used to represent numeric values.

> The so-called Arabic numerals used in the ASCII character set, and familiar to most all of us, are not *actually used in modern Arabic. Unicode does have two different forms of the ten modern Arabic digits, as well as those of many other languages. Yet, any of these representations of the number "one" would still have a value that was "1" in a mathematical sense.*

Any datatype that doesn't have a numeric value space is, of course, considered non-numeric.

Constraining Facets

Constraining facets are those that limit the *value space* of a derived datatype, which in turn limits that datatype's lexical space. Strictly speaking, *primitive* types don't have constraining facets, but these may be added by creating a simple derived datatype that is **derived by restriction** from a primitive type.

There are several constraining facets that may be applied to any appropriate derived datatype:

- ❑   length, minLength, maxLength
- ❑   whiteSpace
- ❑   pattern
- ❑   enumeration
- ❑   minExclusive, maxExclusive, minInclusive, maxInclusive
- ❑   totalDigits, fractionDigits

Let's look at the definitions and details of these constraining facets.

length, minLength, maxLength

These three facets all deal with the number of units of length of a datatype, the value of which must always be a non-negative integer. The nature of the units will vary, depending on the base datatype.

For those derived from one of the string types (such as string or QName), these units are the number of Unicode code points ("characters"). It is important to remember that each Unicode character may be represented in a form that is 8, 16, or 32-bits long, or even variable-length sequences of 8-bit values.

Those types used for encoding binary data (hexBinary, base64Binary) use the number of octets (8-bit bytes) of the binary data as for these three length values.

As might be expected, list types simply use the number of items in the list.

A fixed number of units can be specified using the length facet. For example, if we wanted to constrain some string datatype, such as a US Social Security Number (SSN) to always be an 11-character string, we could define the datatype like so:

```
<xs:simpleType name="USA_SSN">
    <xs:restriction base="xs:string">
        <xs:length value="11" />
    </xs:restriction>
</xs:simpleType>
```

Any of the following values would therefore, be valid for an ssn element that uses the USA_SSN datatype:

```
<ssn>123-45-6789</ssn>
<ssn>abcdefghijk</ssn>
<ssn>$   2345.42</ssn>
```

Only the first of these is really in the correct form for an SSN – we will need to apply some other constraints to ensure that all strings of this type conform to a "nnn-nn-nnnn" pattern. We can do this sort of thing using regular expressions and the pattern constraining facet, which we'll come to later. Neither of the following would However, be considered valid:

```
<ssn>42</ssn>
<ssn>123-45-6789-000</ssn>
```

The former is too short for a valid USA_SSN string, and the latter string is too long.

The minLength and maxLength facets are the minimum and maximum number of units permitted for the datatype, respectively. For example, a vehicle license (registration) plate might have a "number" (usually a mix of letters and numbers) that can be anything from one to nine characters:

```
<xs:simpleType name="USA_LicensePlate">
    <xs:restriction base="xs:string">
        <xs:minLength value="1" />
        <xs:maxLength value="9" />
    </xs:restriction>
</xs:simpleType>
```

Any of the following values would therefore be valid for an element declared to use the USA_LicensePlate datatype:

```
<LicensePlate>123456789</LicensePlate>
<LicensePlate>1ABC123</LicensePlate>
<LicensePlate>ABC-1234</LicensePlate>
<LicensePlate>LICENSE42</LicensePlate>
```

As before, strings that are invalid by this description, would include a zero-length string, and those longer than the prescribed nine characters. Once again, we can apply further constraints to this kind of datatype using `pattern` and other constraining facets.

whiteSpace

This constraining facet dictates what, if any, whitespace transformation is performed upon the XML instances data, before validation constraints are tested. The normalization of whitespace in attribute values was defined in XML 1.0, but XML Schemas have extended this to element content as well. We want to be able to use simple types for both attributes and elements, and this extension allows consistent validation of both kinds of XML data.

There are three valid values for the `whiteSpace` facet:

❏ `preserve` – no changes will be made. This is required by XML 1.0 for element content.

❏ `replace` – all instances of tab (#x09), carriage return (#x0D), or line feed (#x0A) characters are replaced with space (#x20) characters. This corresponds to regular attribute value normalization.

❏ `collapse` – after transforming tabs, carriage returns and so on (just like `replace`), any spaces at the beginning or end of the string are removed, and any internal runs of multiple spaces are converted to a single space character. This is like the normalization of tokenized attribute values from lists, such as the `IDREFS` and `NMTOKENS` types.

For all datatypes that have been derived by list, the value of `whiteSpace` is fixed as `collapse`, and cannot be changed. This is also true for all atomic datatypes other than `string`.

The `string` datatype always has a `whiteSpace` value of `preserve`. Two other built-in datatypes derived from `string` (`token` and `normalizedString`), exploit the other two values of `whiteSpace`. Any other type that is derived by restriction from `string` may use any of the three values.

The definition of the built-in derived datatype called `token`, is a good example of the use of the `whiteSpace` facet:

```
<xs:simpleType name="token">
   <xs:restriction base="xs:normalizedString">
      <xs:whiteSpace value="collapse" />
   </xs:restriction>
</xs:simpleType>
```

In fact, the `whiteSpace` facet is the only significant difference between `token` and its `normalizedString` base type:

```
<xs:simpleType name="normalizedString">
   <xs:restriction base="xs:string">
      <xs:whiteSpace value="replace" />
   </xs:restriction>
</xs:simpleType>
```

As usual, datatypes that are derived by union do not use this facet directly, but rather they inherit the behavior of the individual member type of the union, that is used for validation of a particular instance of XML data.

These two elements have equivalent data, if declared as a `normalizedString` datatype:

```
<NormalString> S P A C E S are kept, but newlines and tabs aren't
</NormalString>
<NormalString> S P A C E S are kept,
   but newlines and tabs aren't </NormalString>
```

The `token` datatype goes a step further, causing multiple whitespace characters to be compressed into a single space character, and the removal of beginning and ending whitespace:

```
<Token>
    Beginning/ending a n d multiple internal spaces get squeezed, also
</Token>
<Token>
       Beginning/ending  a n d  multiple internal spaces get squeezed,
           also
</Token>
```

The above two instances of XML data have equivalent values (after whitespace compression), as do the following two elements:

```
<Token>2000-12-16</Token>
<Token>   2000-12-16
  </Token>
```

Several built-in datatypes (such as `ID`, `IDREF`, `IDREFS`, `NMTOKEN`, and so on) are similar to the `token` datatype in their use of the whitespace compression features of the `whiteSpace` facet.

pattern

This facet is an *indirect* constraint upon the datatype's value space, which requires the string literals used in the datatype's *lexical* space to match a specific pattern. The value of a pattern must be a regular expression (**regex**). The regex language used in XML Schemas are similar (but *not* identical) to the one defined for the Perl programming language. Although we include an example of XML Schemas regexes here, they will be described in detail later in this chapter.

If we wanted to constrain our earlier USA_SSN datatype further to be an 11-character hyphen-delimited numeric string, we could use the following pattern to replace our earlier string `length` constraint:

```
<xs:simpleType name="USA_SSN">
   <xs:restriction base="xs:string">
      <xs:pattern value="[0-9]{3}-[0-9]{2}-[0-9]{4}" />
   </xs:restriction>
</xs:simpleType>
```

The numbers above that are enclosed within square brackets ([0-9]) specify a range of values, and those in the curly braces (such as {3} or {4}) dictate the valid number of digits, with each group separated by a literal hyphen character (-). Based on the example above, an element using our USA_SSN datatype would look something like this:

```
<ssn>123-45-6789</ssn>
```

The above example is a simple regex, but regexes in XML Schemas can become quite complicated and powerful, though they are not quite as comprehensive as those in Perl. We'll continue to use some simple patterns in this chapter's examples, but the details will wait until later in this Chapter.

enumeration

This facet is very much like the DTD specification of the enumerated values of an attribute type. XML Schemas extend this useful datatype to element content as well. Enumeration limits a value space to a specific set of values – if a value isn't specified in the set in the schema, it isn't valid.

In Chapter 2, we had a simple datatype that included a superset of these four enumerated values:

```
<xs:simpleType name="Sizes">
  <xs:restriction base="xs:string">
    <xs:enumeration value="S" />
    <xs:enumeration value="M" />
    <xs:enumeration value="L" />
    <xs:enumeration value="XL" />
  </xs:restriction>
</xs:simpleType>
```

The order in which the enumerated values are declared is insignificant, so using this facet does *not* impose an additional or different order relation on the value space – any ordered property of the derived datatype remains the same as that of its base type.

minExclusive, minInclusive, maxExclusive, maxInclusive

These four facets can only apply to ordered or partially ordered datatypes, such as numbers and dates or time. In fact, only two of these facets may be used for a single datatype – a single minimum bound (using either minExclusive or minInclusive) and/or a choice of a maximum bound (maxExclusive or maxInclusive). Any simple numeric or date/time datatype that is derived by restriction is likely to use one or more of these facets. The bounds of value space may be defined in either of two ways:

❑ An **exclusive** bound means that the bounding value is *not* included in the value space. For all values V in the value space, minExclusive < V < maxExclusive.

❑ An **inclusive** bound is one that *is* included within the value space. For all values V in the value spece, minInclusive ≤ V ≤ maxInclusive.

Of course, these two types of bounds are not coupled – a lower bound might be *ex*clusive, while the upper bound is *in*clusive. We must choose between the two types of bounds for each end of the spectrum though – it is never possible for a bound to be both *in*clusive and *ex*clusive! Also, by definition, the upper (max) bound must always be greater than or equal to the lower (min) bound.

The boundaries of a datatype are declared using these elements within the restriction child of a simpleType element (as are most constraining facets). For example, the built-in derived datatype for negative integers is defined within XML Schemas as follows:

```
<xs:simpleType name="negativeInteger" id="negativeInteger">
  <xs:annotation>
    <xs:documentation
        source="http://www.w3.org/TR/xmlschema-2/#negativeInteger" />
```

```
      </xs:annotation>
      <xs:restriction base="xs:nonPositiveInteger">
          <xs:maxInclusive value="-1" id="negativeInteger.maxInclusive"/>
      </xs:restriction>
  </xs:simpleType>
```

This example shows a value space that is **bounded above** (has a finite maximum value), but is *not* **bounded below** (there is no minimum value – it is an open-ended range of values that extends to negative infinity). Any value in the range "-∞ ≤ value < 0" would be valid for this datatype.

These facets can even be used to constrain a datatype to be a single constant value:

```
<xs:simpleType name="TheAnswer">
    <xs:restriction base="xs:integer">
        <xs:minInclusive value="42" />
        <xs:maxInclusive value="42" />
    </xs:restriction>
</xs:simpleType>
```

This simple range checking is essential for many applications of XML. Alternatively, we could have used an enumerated datatype (as shown in the previous section) with a single value for the same purpose.

More complicated value checking, such as interrupted ranges, must be handled indirectly using datatypes derived by union, or by applying the pattern constraint to the lexical representation of the datatype.

totalDigits, fractionDigits

These two facets apply to all datatypes derived from the decimal type. They are somewhat similar to the printf() format string specification in the C/C++ programming languages. In XML Schemas, totalDigits is the *maximum* number of decimal digits allowed for the entire number (which must always be a positive integer), and fractionDigits is the maximum number of digits in the fractional portion of the number (always a *non-negative* integer that is less than or equal to the value of totalDigits). This is similar to the printf() precision field (like the 2 of the "%4.2f" format string).

> **These two facets are inextricably related – the value of fractionDigits must never be greater than that of totalDigits.**

For example, a scientific instrument measurement application might only accept non-negative values with precision up to three decimal places, and limited to a maximum of nine digits in total. This could be described as a simple XML Schema datatype that is derived by restriction:

```
<xs:simpleType name="Datapoint">
    <xs:restriction base="xs:decimal">
        <xs:totalDigits value="9" />
        <xs:fractionDigits value="3" />
    </xs:restriction>
</xs:simpleType>
```

This indirectly constrains the range of values – there could never be an absolute value that is greater than 999,999,999 since it would use more than the nine digits allowed a number that used all three digits to the right of the decimal point would However, be limited to a maximum 999,999.999 absolute value. So, we might also want to include some bounds facets to keep values limited to a specific minimum and maximum values, regardless of precision:

```
<xs:simpleType name="Datapoint">
   <xs:restriction base="xs:decimal">
      <xs:totalDigits value="9" />
      <xs:fractionDigits value="3" />
      <xs:minInclusive value="0" />
      <xs:maxInclusive value="999999.999" />
   </xs:restriction>
</xs:simpleType>
<xs:element name="datum" type = "Datapoint">
```

By this definition, any of the following would be valid amounts for the `Datapoint` datatype:

```
<datum>0</datum>
<datum>0.01</datum>
<datum>2345.42</datum>
<datum>9999.99</datum>
```

The following would *not* be valid:

```
<datum>-42</datum>
<datum>0.0001</datum>
<datum>1234567890</datum>
```

The first is a negative number (which we just prohibited), the second has too many digits to the right of the decimal point (violating the `fractionDigits` constraint), and the last one exceeds the allowable total number of digits (the `totalDigits` constraint).

Now, let's look again at the built-in datatypes from Chapter 2, and their constraining facets.

Constraining Facets of Built-in Datatypes

In this section, we have two tables illustrating which constraining facets can be used with each of the built-in datatypes.

The datatypes are grouped into the same four categories as used in Chapter 2: *string, encoded binary, numeric,* and *date/time*. We will also group some related facets together: `length`, `minLength`, and `maxLength` are always used together; as are `minExclusive`, `minExclusive`, `minInclusive`, `maxExclusive`, and `maxInclusive`; plus the `totalDigits`, and `fractionDigits` pair.

Primitive Datatypes

This table shows the constraining facets for the built-in primitive datatypes:

Datatypes	length	minLength	maxLength	whiteSpace	pattern	enumeration	minExclusive	maxExclusive	minInclusive	maxInclusive	totalDigits	fractionDigits
String Types												
string	X	X	X	preserve	X	X						
anyURI	X	X	X	collapse	X	X						
NOTATION	X	X	X	collapse	X	X						
QName	X	X	X	collapse	X	X						
Binary Encoding Types												
boolean				collapse	X							
hexBinary	X	X	X	collapse	X	X						
base64Binary	X	X	X	collapse	X	X						
Numeric Types												
decimal				collapse	X	X	X	X	X	X	X	X
float				collapse	X	X	X	X	X	X		
double				collapse	X	X	X	X	X	X		
Date/Time Types												
duration				collapse	X	X	X	X	X	X		
dateTime				collapse	X	X	X	X	X	X		
date				collapse	X	X	X	X	X	X		
time				collapse	X	X	X	X	X	X		
gYear				collapse	X	X	X	X	X	X		
gYearMonth				collapse	X	X	X	X	X	X		
gMonth				collapse	X	X	X	X	X	X		
gMonthDay				collapse	X	X	X	X	X	X		
gDay				collapse	X	X	X	X	X	X		

An X indicates that the facet can be used with this datatype, and any legal value is allowed. In the whiteSpace column, we have used either preserve or collapse to indicate the fixed value for the given facet-datatype combination.

Derived Datatypes

This table shows the constraining facets for the built-in derived datatypes, and any other types, which may be derived there from. Those cells marked with an X indicate that the facet can be used with this datatype, and any legal value is allowed. This means, for example, you can't set a maxExclusive value of greater than zero on a negativeInteger:

Datatypes	length	minLength	maxLength	whiteSpace	pattern	enumeration	minExclusive	maxExclusive	minInclusive	maxInclusive	totalDigits	fractionDigits
Types Derived from string												
normalizedString	X	X	X	replace	X	X						
token	X	X	X	collapse	X	X						
language	X	X	X	collapse	X	X						
Name	X	X	X	collapse	X	X						
NCName	X	X	X	collapse	X	X						
ID	X	X	X	collapse	X	X						
IDREF	X	X	X	collapse	X	X						
IDREFS	X	X	X	collapse		X						
NMTOKEN	X	X	X	collapse	X	X						
NMTOKENS	X	X	X	collapse		X						
ENTITY	X	X	X	collapse	X	X						
ENTITIES	X	X	X	collapse		X						
Types Derived from decimal												
integer				collapse	X	X	X	X	X	X	X	0
negativeInteger				collapse	X	X	X	X	X	X	X	0
positiveInteger				collapse	X	X	X	X	X	X	X	0
nonNegativeInteger				collapse	X	X	X	X	X	X	X	0
nonPositiveInteger				collapse	X	X	X	X	X	X	X	0

Table continued on following page

Datatypes	length	minLength	maxLength	whiteSpace	pattern	enumeration	minExclusive	maxExclusive	minInclusive	maxInclusive	totalDigits	fractionDigits
byte				collapse	X	X	X	X	X	X	X	0
short				collapse	X	X	X	X	X	X	X	0
int				collapse	X	X	X	X	X	X	X	0
long				collapse	X	X	X	X	X	X	X	0
unsignedByte				collapse	X	X	X	X	X	X	X	0
unsignedShort				collapse	X	X	X	X	X	X	X	0
unsignedInt				collapse	X	X	X	X	X	X	X	0
unsignedLong				collapse	X	X	X	X	X	X	X	0

Note that the `fractionDigits` facet is set equal to zero for all of the number types. This is because they are all integer types and cannot, therefore, have any values after the decimal point.

The `pattern` facet of the `language` datatype allows either a two-letter string (upper or lower-case permitted); or the string literals "I-", "i-", "X-", or "x-", followed by at least one (but maybe more) alphanumeric string that is one to eight letters long. For example, an obscure Northern California dialect and the language of babies could be identified using the following language tags:

```
en-US-boontling
x-gibberish
```

The `NCName` datatype allows an initial XML legal name character, except for the colon, followed by any legal XML name character, except for the colon.

We will look at the XML Schemas regular expression syntax used for the `pattern` facet in the next section.

Regular Expressions

As we saw earlier in this chapter, the `pattern` datatype facet has a value that is a specially formatted string called a **regular expression** (commonly abbreviated as "**regex**" or "regexp" or "RE"). This pattern can be used to validate instance data for any datatype, be it in the form of an attribute value or an element's content. This facet can be used to assert that only those values matching the regex are valid values for that datatype. Remember that this is an indirect constraint upon the value space of a datatype, since it is the lexical (string) representation against which the pattern is matched.

> **A regular expression is a formally defined string that uses special character sequences to describe a pattern that explicitly describes a set of string values (which are considered to match the pattern).**

XML Schema regexes are designed to work with Unicode characters, rather than simple ASCII characters, and are largely based upon those used in the Perl programming language. These were in turn derived from earlier UNIX regex syntax.

> *The definition of XML Schema regexes is in **Appendix F** of* XML Schema Part 2: Datatypes *at http://www.w3.org/TR/xmlschema-2/#regexs. Examples of these are in **Appendix D** of* XML Schema Part 0: Primer *at http://www.w3.org/TR/xmlschema-0/#regexAppendix.*
>
> *Unicode regexes are defined in a Unicode Technical Report (*UTR#18, Unicode Regular Expression Guidelines*), available online at http://www.unicode.org/unicode/reports/tr18/. The implications of character case mappings are discussed in another technical report (*UTR#21, Case Mappings*) at http://www.unicode.org/unicode/reports/tr21/, and the use of canonical character forms and character value normalization are discussed in* UTR#15, Unicode Normalization Forms *at http://www.unicode.org/unicode/reports/tr15/.*
>
> *Articles and links for Perl regular expressions are at http://www.perl.com/reference/query.cgi?regexp. Detailed documentation of Perl regex syntax is at: http://www.perl.com/CPAN-local/doc/manual/html/pod/perlre.html.*

There are other notable implementations of regular expressions, but all of these are slightly different (using different delimiters or other pattern syntax, and some having other major differences in form and features). Rather than spend time with a history of regular expressions, let's dive right into the structure and specifics of XML Schemas regular expressions.

XML Schema Regexes

It is important to understand that the XML Schemas regular expression was designed primarily in support of datatype validation – it is *not* a generalized Unicode regular expression (which is an extension of UNIX/Perl regular expressions intended to work with Unicode characters instead of simple ASCII strings).

Basic Grammar

Like XML 1.0 itself, XML Schemas regular expressions are based upon Unicode characters, and/or groups of characters. We will look at some of the specific implications of Unicode support later in this chapter.

There is a major difference in XML Schema regular expressions from Perl regular expressions. Perl is based upon traditional text-oriented structures such as word/line/paragraph. Regular expressions in XML Schemas are applied to the entire lexical representation of a datatype as a single string (which may contain newline and other whitespace characters).

> *From now on, until we reach the **Regex Syntax Comparison** section, when we use the term " regular expressions" or "regexes", we mean an XML Schemas regular expression string.*

A regular expression is an assertion about some data – if the assertion is true, the data is said to match the regex. A regular expression is comprised of zero or more of these alternative assertions, called **branches**. A regular expression with no branches is just an empty string, and such a pattern can only be matched by another empty string.

If any branch of a regular expression is true, the entire regular expression is considered to be true.

Each branch is a separate assertion about the data, the results of which are logically ORed to produce a result for the regular expression as a whole. As one might expect, and in keeping with XML 1.0 DTD syntax, these branches are separated by the usual "alternative" character – the vertical bar (|). For example, we might declare an anonymous simple string datatype for which *any one of three* literal string patterns (Small, Medium, or Large) are acceptable :

```
<xs:simpleType>
    <xs:restriction base="xs:string">
        <!-- string must match one of these three patterns (logical OR) -->
        <xs:pattern value="Small|Medium|Large" />
    </xs:restriction>
</xs:simpleType>
```

There is no provision within the regex syntax for logically ANDed results. XML Schemas permit multiple pattern facets to constrain a single datatype, However which is derived in multiple steps. This provides the equivalent of ANDed results, since the patterns for each step of the type derivation must be true for the data to be considered valid. An example using these ANDs to specify upper case ASCII characters only is shown below (in this case, however, the very last expression only would have sufficed):

```
<!-- string must match all three patterns (logical AND) -->
<xs:simpleType name="Uppercase_ASCII_Letters" >
    <xs:restriction>
        <xs:simpleType>
            <xs:restriction>
                <xs:simpleType>
                    <xs:restriction base="xs:string">
                        <xs:pattern value="[\p{L}]" />
                    </xs:restriction>
                </xs:simpleType>
                <xs:pattern value="[\p{Lu}]" />
            </xs:restriction>
        </xs:simpleType>
        <xs:pattern value="[A-Z]" />
    </xs:restriction>
</xs:simpleType>
```

The above, rather contrived, example shows how we might use ANDed patterns to narrow-down a datatype's value space (from all Unicode letters, to upper-case letters, to just upper-case ASCII letters). Of course, if not for the sake of illustration, we could have just done this directly with a single simple type constrained with the "[A-Z]" value for pattern.

String matching of all kinds, including that used in regular expressions, can be classified as greedy or non-greedy. Greedy string matching attempts to find the largest sub-string that matches the pattern. For example, the regular expression ".*abc.*" would match almost everything, due to the ".*" pattern (match zero or more lines). A non-greedy match would settle for the first good match (in this case "abc").

XML Schema regular expression use *non*-greedy string matching.

Each individual branch of a regular expression is comprised of zero or more concatenated **pieces**. These pieces consist of an **atom**, which may be followed by an optional **quantifier** string. The quantifier string is not unlike the cardinality operator in a DTD (such as ?, *, or +), but may specify a more precise range of occurrences. The SSN example in the earlier `pattern` facet section, illustrates the use of quantifiers (shown in **bold** below):

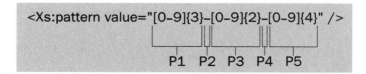

This regular expression constrains the string to be a 3-digit number, followed by a 2-digit number, and then a 4-digit number (and separated by hyphens). The regular expression is comprised of five pieces. Two of them (P2 and P4) are the simplest sorts of expression – simple atoms that dictate that the tested sub-string must match a single literal hyphen (–) character. The other three pieces (P1, P3, and P5) illustrate atoms with quantifiers. We will delve into the different forms of quantifier strings later in this chapter.

Atoms

A regex atom can be:

❑ A **normal character** (a normal Unicode character, that is).

❑ A **character class.**

❑ Another regular expression, enclosed in parentheses.

Atoms are the crux of regular expression string matching. The simple case is the one-for-one matching of normal character(s). For example, the following pattern could only be matched if the instance string were also the same seven characters "abc*def":

```
<xs:pattern value="abc*def" />
```

An XML Schemas regex atom may also specify a character class, which can be a character range (an explicit range of numeric values), a category of character (such as letter, number, symbol, and so on), or a named block of characters (like Greek, Thai, Currency Symbols, and so on). We will show how to specify these other types of regular expression atoms in a little while.

Meta Characters

Certain characters, called **meta characters**, have special meaning in a regular expression. Instead of matching just a single normal character, meta characters are used for regular expression operators, count or sub-expression delimiters, and as shorthand for special character sequences. The following table shows the XML Schemas regular expression meta characters (all of which will be explained in more detail later in this section):

Meta character	Use/Meaning
.	Match any character, except end-of-line (#x0D and/or #x0A) – same as [^\n\r]
\	Begin escape sequence
?	Zero or one occurrences
*	Zero or more occurrences
+	One or more occurrences
{ }	Enclose a numeric quantifier or character group
( )	Enclose a regular expression (may be the atom of another regex)
[ ]	Enclose a character class expression

Any character that is not one of the above meta characters is considered to be a normal character that simply matches another identical single character in the instance data. certain specific types of regular expressions use the following characters in a special way However, so these may be thought of as a hybrid of meta and normal characters. These three characters should be used with caution:

Hybrid	Use/Meaning
^	Begin a negative character group
–	1) Begin a character class subtraction
	2) Separate the minimum/maximum values that define a range of character values
,	Separate the minimum/maximum values for number of occurrences of an atom

As we'll see a little later in this chapter, these can be represented using a two-character literal form that begins with a backslash (\) character, like "\-" or "\}" (which escape the – and } characters, respectively).

Character Classes

A character class is a regex atom that defines a set of characters, any of which can be matched by a single character of the same value in the instance data. This may be expressed as either a **character class expression**, or a **character class escape sequence**.

Character Class Expressions

A character class expression is simply a **character group**, enclosed in square brackets. For example, if we wanted to allow any single upper case ASCII letter, we could use this pattern:

```
<xs:pattern value="[A-Z]" />
```

In this case, the character group includes all character values from upper case A (#x41) to Z (#x5A). This also shows one of the ways to express a **character range**, that is, as a set of minimum and maximum character values (based upon their UCS code point values).

Character Ranges

There are three kinds of character ranges:

- ❏ **s-e range** – specifies the starting and ending values of a contiguous range of character values (like the example in the previous section).

- ❏ **single normal character** – match a single character.

- ❏ **single character reference** – match a single character, as represented by an XML 1.0 character reference (such as using the character or entity reference strings © or © for the copyright symbol).

The example in the last section uses the "s-e range" form, a contiguous range of character values beginning with the *min* value and up to and including the *max* value. This kind of range is expressed as a string, which begins with the minimum acceptable value (*min*), followed by a single hyphen (-), and ending with the maximum acceptable value (*max*), and where *max* ≥ *min*:

```
<xs:pattern value="[min-max]" />
```

Any single normal character will match only that character. For example, only a single "A" character can match the following regular expression:

```
<xs:pattern value="A" />
```

There are three special regex characters (- [ ]) that cannot be used for the single normal character form of the character range. Ranges that need to include these values must use the single character escape, which will be described in just a few sections from here. For example, we can match either the opening or closing square bracket with the following:

```
<xs:pattern value="[\[\]]" />
```

Character references may also be used as an alternative to the direct keying of, say, a special symbol character. Therefore, the next two patterns are equivalent, and either would match the same character:

```
<xs:pattern value="©" />
<xs:pattern value="&#xA9;" />
```

Multiple ranges may be concatenated together to form the values of a single, but *not* contiguous, character range, such as the set of all upper-case Latin-1 letters:

```
<xs:pattern value="[A-ZÀ-ÖØ-Ý   ••   •   • • ]" />
```

Just as the top-level branches of a regular expression are combined with an explicit logical OR, a character group has an implicit OR between multiple character ranges and/or single characters. Therefore, the above pattern allows any one of the letters in the upper case ASCII range (A-Z), or the two ranges of accented letters (À-Ö and Ø-Ý), or any members of the list of eighteen single Latin-1 letters (••   •   • • If).

Character Groups

There are also three different kinds of character groups:

❑ **Positive character group** – match one of a set of characters that are defined by one or more character ranges and/or character class escapes.

❑ **Negative character group** – match any character *except* those specified in the character group, that is; use a logical NOT of a positive character group.

❑ **Character class subtraction** – match any character in a group, minus those specified in a secondary character class expression.

The preceding example was a positive character group comprised of all upper case ASCII letters. We could allow any ASCII letter by adding a second character range to the character group expression:

```
<xs:pattern value="[A-Za-z]" />
```

We can easily invert our positive character group to be a negative character group, simply by preceding the above character ranges with a caret (^) character:

```
<xs:pattern value="[^A-Za-z]" />
```

A character class subtraction allows the use of standard character ranges with a few specific characters being disallowed. For example, American telephones have three-letter strings labeling eight of the number keys (for example "ABC" on the "2" key, "DEF" on the "3" key). A quick multiplication shows room for only 24 of the 26 letters in the alphabet, and indeed, standard phones do not include the letters "Q" and "Z" on their keypads. We can express this more limited alphabet with the following character class subtraction:

```
<xs:pattern value="[A-Z-[QZ]]" />
```

This regular expression allows any upper-case ASCII letter, except "Q" or "Z" – no caret character is included.

Character Class Escapes

A character class escape is a short string that represents a pre-defined character class. Valid escape sequences may be:

❑ **Single character escape** – the value of the escape string is a single character code point.

❑ **Multi-character escape** – shorthand for a specific set of characters.

❑ **Category escape** – the one or two-character name of a Unicode "General Category"; one of seven kinds of categories, such as letters, numbers, symbols, and so on.

❑ **Block escape** – the Unicode name of a group (block) of characters, such as BasicLatin, Tibetan, MusicalSymbols, etc. (see Blocks-4.txt in the Unicode 3.0 database for the current list).

The first two kinds of character class escape are probably familiar, since they use common escape strings, such as "\n" to represent a newline (#x0A) character, or "\s" to represent any of the four XML whitespace characters (#x09, #x0A, #x0D, or #x20). The latter two depend upon values from the Unicode database.

The Unicode 3.0 database is available online at: http://www.unicode.org/Public/3.1-Update/ UnicodeCharacterDatabase-3.1.0.html (revision 3.1.0 as of 2001-02-28). General Categories and other properties for all Unicode characters can be found at http://www.unicode.org/Public/3.1-Update/PropList-3.1.0.txt. The Blocks-4.txt file can be downloaded from: http://www.unicode.org/Public/3.1-Update/.

Single Character Escapes

A single character escape can be used to represent a single character. These are useful for difficult-to-key characters such as end-of-line or control characters, and are also more compact than XML character references.

Also, all regex meta characters have corresponding escapes, so these characters can be used as simple literal values within the regular expression. The following table shows all seventeen of the pre-defined single character escape-sequences:

Escape Sequence	Represents
\n	A newline character (line-feed)
\r	A return character (carriage return)
\t	A tab character (horizontal tab)
\\	A single \ character (backslash)
|	A single | character (vertical bar)
\.	A single . character (period or full-stop)
\-	A single – character (hyphen or dash)
\^	A single ^ character (caret)
\?	A single ? character (question mark)
*	A single * character (asterisk)
\+	A single + character (plus sign)
\{	A single { character (open curly brace)
\}	A single } character (close curly brace)
\(	A single (character (open parenthesis)
\)	A single) character (close parenthesis)
\[	A single [character (open square bracket)
\]	A single] character (close square bracket)

Of course, any of these escapes can instead use a more verbose character reference.

Multi-Character Escapes

Multi-character escape sequences are used to represent a not-necessarily contiguous group of characters. These are shorthand expressions for some of the most commonly used regular expressions.

The following table shows six of the pre-defined multi-character escape-sequences and their regex equivalents:

Escape Sequence	Equivalent Regex	Description
.	[^\n\r]	Any character except a newline
\s	[#x20\t\n\r]	An XML 1.0 whitespace character
\i	[\p{L}_:]	Any legal Name1 (intial name) character
\c	[\p{L}_:\p{Nd}-.]	Any legal name (NameChar) character
\d	[\p{Nd}]	Any decimal digit (*not* limited to ASCII)
\w	[#x0000-#x10FFFF]-[\p{P}\p{Z}\p{C}]]	Any Unicode character, *except* a punctuation, separator, or other character

> **The first multi-character escape in the table (.) does *not* have the same meaning as the same character in a UNIX or Perl regular expression.**

We have omitted five multi-character escapes from this table in the interest of a good markup practice. Any of the last five escapes in the table above has a corresponding upper-case version that simply means to match the complement of the pattern shown in the table. For example, we could use \S to refer to any *non*-whitespace character (it is equivalent to [^\s]), or \D to refer to any *non*-digit (same as [^\d]), and so on.

The syntax described in the above paragraph is a very bad idea. This shorthand saves only a few characters – at the expense of clarity of code and future readability. The use of the explicit negation operator character (^) is strongly encouraged, since it offers documentation of the intent of the pattern and therefore greatly eases maintenance of the schema.

The use of different case letters for different purposes is a long-standing tradition in the C programming world, but ignores years of cognitive and usability research that shows that our memory of such case-sensitivity is less than perfect. Furthermore, such a distinction may be meaningless to many, if not most, of the world's population. This is not the first (nor is it likely to be the last) time that the W3C has ignored the XML design considerations of programming ease and human legibility in favor of an arguably unnecessary abbreviated representation (and also contradicting the "terseness ... is of minimal importance" design requirement).

Of course, any of these escapes could be replaced with the much more verbose un-escaped regular expression.

Category Escapes

There are seven varieties of the "General Category" property, as defined in Unicode 3.0:

- ❑ Letters
- ❑ Marks
- ❑ Numbers
- ❑ Punctuation
- ❑ Separators
- ❑ Symbols
- ❑ Other

Each of these is further subdivided into sub-categories, as shown in the following table of names:

Name	Category / Sub-category
	Letters
L	All letters
Lu	Upper-case letters
Ll	Lower-case letters
Lt	Title case letters
Lm	Modifier letters (mostly for Asian languages)
Lo	Other letters
	Marks
M	All mark characters
Mn	Non-spacing marks
Mc	Spacing/combining marks (mostly for Asian languages)
Me	Enclosing marks
	Numbers
N	All number characters
Nd	Decimal digits (the ten ASCII digits, *plus* some alternate forms)
Nl	"Letter" numbers (such as runes or Roman numerals)
No	Other numbers
	Punctuation
P	All punctuation characters

Table continued on following page

Name	Category / Sub-category
Pc	Connector punctuation (only used for the two forms of the Katakana middle dot)
Pd	Dash punctuation (almost any kind of hyphen-like character)
Ps	Opening punctuation
Pe	Closing punctuation
Pi	Initial quote punctuation
Pf	Final quote punctuation
Po	Other punctuation
Separators	
Z	All separator characters
Zs	Word (space) separators
Zl	Line separators
Zp	Paragraph separators
Symbols	
S	All symbol characters
Sm	Math symbols
Sc	Currency symbols
Sk	Modifier symbols (such as accent marks and other diacritic characters)
So	Other symbols
Other	
C	All Others
Cc	Control characters
Cf	Formatting characters
Co	Private Use characters
Cn	Unassigned characters

These abbreviated category names are used in the category escape form of the character class escape. For example, to match any kind of number character, we'd use this regex pattern:

```
<xs:pattern value="\p{N}" />
```

The first two characters of the character group (\p) indicate that this is a Unicode property-based expression, using either a category escape or a block escape (see the next section). The name of the category (N) must be one of the strings in the above table – no other values are permitted.

As with the multi-character escape strings, the complement of a group can be specified explicitly using [^\p{N}] to match all non-numbers, or implicitly with its "magical" upper-case form \P{N}.

Block Escapes

Another form of regex pattern value that depends upon the Unicode Database is the block escape. Unicode characters have been organized in named groups, called blocks, such as the alphabet for a distinct language or a set of mathematical symbols. For example:

```
<xs:pattern value="\p{IsBasicLatin}" />
<xs:pattern value="\p{IsGreek}" />
<xs:pattern value="\p{IsKatakana}" />
<xs:pattern value="\p{IsCurrencySymbols}" />
```

These are very useful when used with character class subtractions. For example, when representing some text from ancient Rome, we might want to prevent the use of the "U" character (which wasn't used until much later) and the ASCII control characters:

```
<xs:pattern value="[\p{IsBasicLatin}-[Uu\p{Cc}]]" />
```

This regex allows any regular (non-control) ASCII character, except "U" or "u". The first part of the character class subtraction establishes the character block that is allowed. The second part (after the minus sign) describes the character group to be subtracted from this block. In this example, we explicitly mention the forms of the letter "U", and use a category escape to subtract the ASCII control characters.

The following table shows a few of the more commonly used Unicode character blocks (all code point values are in hexadecimal and correspond to the typical "U+nnnn" Unicode representation):

Begin Value	End Value	Block Name
0000	007F	BasicLatin
0080	00FF	Latin-1Supplement
0100	017F	LatinExtended-A
0180	024F	LatinExtended-B
0370	03FF	Greek
0400	04FF	Cyrillic
0600	06FF	Arabic
0E00	0E7F	Thai
2000	206F	GeneralPunctuation
20A0	20CF	CurrencySymbols
2200	22FF	MathematicalOperators
30A0	30FF	Katakana
3100	312F	Bopomofo
4E00	9FFF	CJKUnifiedIdeographs

The block name in a block escape regex is always preceded by the literal string "Is" (such as "\p{IsArabic}").

Quantifiers

A quantifier defines the possible number of occurrences of a matching character for a given atom. There are two forms of quantifier: the three familiar DTD cardinality operators (?, *, +), or a numeric range of valid occurrence counts.

Quantifier	Meaning
?	Zero or one occurrences
*	Zero or more occurrences
+	One or more occurrences
{*min*,*max*}	At least *min* occurrences, at most *max* occurrences
{*equ*}	Exactly *equ* occurrences
{*min*, }	At least *min* occurrences
{0,*max*}	From zero to no more than *max* occurrences
{0,0}	Exactly zero occurrences (a special case of {*min*,*max*}, the empty string)

For example, to match a string of any length (including the empty string) that is comprised exclusively of lower-case ASCII letters, we could use the following pattern:

```
<xs:pattern value="[a-z]*" />
```

Below is an example of element content that matches the above pattern:

```
<example>qwertyuiop</example>
```

The pattern above would *not* match the following example, since it includes white space, digits, and upper-case letters:

```
<example>The 5th Element</example>
```

Another pattern allows one or more occurrences of the letter "Z", but nothing else:

```
<xs:pattern value="Z+" />
```

Any of the following would be acceptable instances of data conforming to the above pattern:

```
<example>Z</example>
<example>ZZZ</example>
<example>ZZZZZZZZZZZZZZZZZZZZZZZZZZ</example>
```

The numeric quantifier form is more powerful than the three DTD-like quantifiers. Any non-negative range of occurrence counts may be specified, using one of the formats from the above table. A single matching value may be specified, and minimum and/or maximum values may also be used.

We could limit the sleepy pattern of the previous example to allow only one to three Zs, using the following pattern:

```
<xs:pattern value="Z{1,3}" />
```

The first two of the prior instance data examples (the Z and ZZZ element content) would also conform to this more restrictive pattern, but the third example would not match. This is a very useful feature of XML Schemas regular expressions, particularly for describing structured numeric strings like US Social Security Numbers (SSNs):

```
<xs:pattern value="\d{3}-\d{2}-\d{4}" />
```

This regex matches all strings that are exactly eleven characters long, in the form of three numeric digits, followed by a hyphen (-), two more digits, another hyphen, and ending with four more numeric digits.

There is however, a problem with this example. XML Schemas regexes are based upon Unicode, the \d multi-character escape will not only match the ten ASCII digits, but a few sets of alternate forms of these ten digits (such as numbers in circles). We need to change this pattern to explicitly allow only the ten ASCII digits, using this character class expression:

```
<xs:pattern value="[0-9]{3}-[0-9]{2}-[0-9]{4}" />
```

A similar caution applies when dealing with letters. We can use a category escape to allow zero or more occurrences of any letter character:

```
<xs:pattern value="[\p{L}]*" />
```

If the intention is to limit matching characters to the set of ASCII letters, then it is necessary to explicitly specify them as a character class expression that includes two character groups (as we've seen before):

```
<xs:pattern value="[A-Za-z]*" />
```

At the risk of excessive repetition, consider as a reminder that the whole raison d'être of an XML Schemas regex is to match Unicode characters, *not* the traditional notion of simple ASCII text.

Regex Syntax Comparison

Although there have been numerous implementations of regexes over the past few decades, none have been exactly like any of the others. The UNIX grep utility program, for instance, was once considered the standard, but has since been surpassed in popularity by the Perl language. Indeed, many programmers today view regexes as almost synonymous with Perl, since Perl regexes are so powerful and so widely used for text manipulation and WWW server-side programming. The XML Schema Recommendation, explicitly cites Perl as its basis for regexes.

The other regex specification that has an impact upon regex processing for XML Schemas is that of Unicode. There are many aspects of Unicode that are different from traditional ASCII-based regexes, so we will also briefly look at the Unicode technical reports that address regexes, and related issues like case mapping and character value normalization.

Unicode

Unicode Technical Report #18 ("*UTR#18, Unicode Regular Expression Guidelines*") specifies three levels of support for regex engines:

❑   **Level 1: Basic Unicode Support** – support Unicode characters as 16-bit codes, simple matching of code point values.

❑   **Level 2: Extended Unicode Support** – handle combined characters, internationalized word-breaks, canonical character forms, and surrogate groups (still locale-independent).

❑   **Level 3: Locale-Sensitive Support** – handle characters differently based upon locale (such as treating "ch" as a single character, or "ss" as equivalent to "ß"). Also sorts characters depending upon local norms (for example, the same accented character may appear in different places relative to the unaccented form, depending upon the language being represented). Also provides different values for character categories (certain punctuation symbols may not be treated as such, certain characters in a block may not be used for a specific language, and so on)

While XML Schemas strive to support at least level 1 of Unicode's regex features, not everything has been implemented. For example, Unicode end-of-line characters include, not only the two supported in XML 1.0 (U+000A and U+000D), but also additional characters like PS (U+2029) and LS (U+2028). Also, in keeping with the spirit of XML 1.0 case-sensitivity, XML Schemas don't support any kind of case-less matching, much less the extended case-folding as specified in *UTR#18*.

Level 2 support is stated as being a desirable improvement in later versions of XML Schemas Unicode regexes use an extended BNF syntax that will be familiar to those who've used XML 1.0 DTDs, or read the XML 1.0 specification. Some differences between XML Schema regexes and those of Unicode Level 1 are shown in the following table:

Pattern	XML Schema	Unicode	Explanation
a b	Matches the string "a b"	Match "a" followed by "b"	BNF relies upon a space between individual terms of an expression – this is implicit in XML Schema regexes
ab	Match the string "ab"	Terminal character	

Pattern	XML Schema	Unicode	Explanation
\uFFFF	Illegal regex – the first two characters (\u) are an illegal meta character string	The Unicode form of a hex character reference	XML Schema regexes must use the hexadecimal character reference («)
[A-Z,a-z,0-9]	Illegal regex – the comma is considered a literal and is used twice	Match any ASCII letter or digit	Unicode supports insignificant commas to improve readability
[A-Za-z0-9]	Match any ASCII letter or digit	Match any ASCII letter or digit (commas *not* needed)	
{ALL}	Illegal regex – ALL is not a valid character category or block name	Match any Unicode character	
{ASSIGNED}	Illegal regex – ASSIGNED is not a valid character category or block name	Match any assigned Unicode character	^\p{Cn} is the XML Schema regex equivalent
{UNASSIGNED}	Illegal regex – UNASSIGNED is not a valid character category or block name	Match any unassigned Unicode character	\p{Cn} is the XML Schema regex equivalent
{Latin}	Illegal regex – Latin is not a valid block name	Match all BasicLatin and other Latin characters, Latin is the name of a collection of several block names	See *Annex A. Character Blocks* in *UTR#18*
	\p{Lu}	{Lu}	Match upper-case letters
	&#x201A	\u201A	Represent a character (code point) in hexadecimal

The last two rows of the table show examples of the XML Schemas and Unicode forms of comparable regexes – same meaning, different syntax.

Perl

The Perl regex module supports more complex regular expressions than those specified in XML Schemas. The following table shows the main differences between the regex syntax of XML Schema and Perl:

Pattern	XML Schema	Perl	Explanation
^	Negation operator	Match beginning of line	All XML Schema regexes match from the beginning of the string
$	No special meaning	Match end of line	All XML Schema regexes match to the end of string
\033 and \xAB	An illegal match string (the first two characters of each are illegal meta character strings, the latter two would be simple character match strings)	These are the Perl (and C) forms of octal and hex character references	XML Schema regexes must use the hexadecimal character reference («)
\i	Match initial XML name character		
\c	Match an XML name character	Match an ASCII control character (form is "\cx")	
\p{}			Match Unicode character class name
Zero-width assertions	Not available	Yes	
Look-ahead / -behind	Not available	Yes	
Back references	Not available	Yes	
Non-greedy + and *	Not available	Yes (option)	

Regular Expressions Summary

In this section, we've discussed the basic syntax of regular expressions for XML Schema, their Unicode implications, and compared them with the well-known Perl regular expressions. We've also seen some examples of their ability to provide much more stringent validation of datatypes. Although we kept things simple for the sake of illustration, very complicated regexes are not uncommon, and may allow very complex data structures to be validated for content, as well as syntax and structure. Regexes and the pattern facet, are some of the most significant additions to XML technology, and a strong argument for the use of XML Schema.

A key aspect of XML Schema datatypes is the mechanism whereby an XML data instance can select its own datatype association for validation, using the xsi:type attribute.

The xsi:type Attribute

Usually, the validation of an XML data instance refers to components in a schema that associate an element or attribute with its datatype (either a Simple or Complex Type Definition). An element within an instance of XML data However, may use the special xsi:type attribute to explicitly declare its associated datatype. Then, when the instance data is validated, the XML Schema processor will use the specified datatype for that element.

The xsi:type attribute value must always be a QName corresponding to either a built-in or user-derived datatype. The namespace prefix must also have been declared, and the element using the xsi:type attribute must be within the scope of that namespace.

In the next section of this chapter, we will look at deriving datatypes from other complex types. An example of this, might be a simple street address that is extended for additional addressing information required in a specific country. This excerpt of an invoice shows how the XML data instance indicates which datatype (GBR_Address or USA_Address) will be used to validate the two MailAddress elements:

```
<?xml version="1.0" ?>
< Invoice
    xmlns:xsi="http://www.w3.org/2001/XMLSchema-instance"
    <MailAddress xsi:type="GBR_Address">
     ...
    </eg:MailAddress>

    <BillAddress xsi:type="USA_Address">
     ...
    </BillAddress>
</Invoice>
```

We use two namespaces here. The namespace above with the xsi: prefix is needed for the xsi:type attribute from XML Schema. The second namespace (eg: prefix) is used to highlight those elements that we've defined for our various examples. You can ignore the other details of the above example for the moment – the important thing is the illustration of the use of the xsi:type attribute to select a datatype for validation of an element's content.

Datatype Inheritance

XML Schema has added several object-oriented (OO) features to its datatypes, including inheritance from other datatypes (or "derivation" in XML-ese). Simple derived types inherit the facets of their base type, and can have additional restrictions upon the derived type. A complex type can be derived by either restriction or extension, whereas a simple type can be derived by restriction, list, or union. Datatypes can also use **abstract type** definitions, and after a certain point may be declared to be hereafter unchangeable (that is, a **final type**).

Schemas may designate some elements to be substitutions for other elements, using **substitution groups**. Elements in the group can be substituted for a particular element, called the **head element**. All these substitute elements must be the same type as the head element, or use a type that is derived from it.

135

Or, sometimes a single-use type is needed within another type or element definition. This one-shot type doesn't really need a name, so XML Schemas make a provision for **anonymous types** – types without a name and just defined within a declaration using `simpleType` or `complexType` elements without a name attribute. We will also look at some special attributes that connect a type in an XML data instance with a dynamic content model or datatype definition in a schema.

In Chapter 2, a diagram showed the relationship of the built-in derived datatypes. As implied by that tree, XML Schema datatypes are organized in a hierarchy.

A key aspect of XML Schema types is the mechanism whereby an XML data instance can select its own type association for validation, using the `xsi:type` attribute.

Type Hierarchy

Like much of XML, XML Schema datatypes are organized as a simple hierarchical tree. The abstract type that serves as the root of the tree is known as the **ur-type,** and is represented as a datatype called `anyType`. This datatype does not constrain its content in any way, and can be used just like any other type when mixed element and text content is permissible. In fact, `anyType` is the default datatype for any element that doesn't explicitly reference another type.

The first branches of the type tree are split between the two main kinds of type:

❑   Simple type – attribute values or text-only element content; a secondary ur-type called `anySimpleType` serves as the root of the simple datatype sub-tree.

❑   Complex type – element, or element and text content. These are all user-derived datatypes, and in the abstract, are all considered to be derived by restriction from the root ur-type.

As discussed in Chapter 2, there are three ways we can derive new simple types:

❑   As a restriction upon another simple base type ("derived by restriction").

❑   As a list of multiple instances of a simple base type ("derived by list").

❑   As a union of multiple simple base types ("derived by union").

Complex types are also derived in three different ways:

❑   As an extension of a simple or complex base type ("derived by extension").

❑   As a restriction upon another complex base type.

❑   As a restriction upon the ur-type (the `anyType` pseudo-datatype).

Derivation by either restriction or extension is very much like object inheritance in an object-oriented (OO) language such as C++ or Java – aspects of one type or class are inherited by another, with additional restrictions or some additions being applied to the derived type or class.

Most user-derived types will probably be created in the abstract using a Simple or Complex Type Definition, before being named, and then used by reference in other type definitions. XML Schema types However need not be named to be useful.

Deriving Simple Types

As we saw in Chapter 2, simple types may be derived by restriction, list, or union:

❑ restriction – the new datatype is a subset of an existing type.

❑ list – derived from one other datatype, with zero or more individual values of that type, delimited by one or more white space character(s) between values.

❑ union – derived from at least two alternative datatypes, either/any of which may be used to validate an element or attribute that is declared to be of the union type.

The example datatypes from Chapter 2 are a good summary of all three types of simple object derivation – datatypes derived by restriction (size and sizenum), list (list.size and list.sizenum), and union (union.ShoeSize):

```
<simpleType name="size" >
   <restriction base="xs:string" >
      <enumeration value="S" />
      <enumeration value="M" />
      <enumeration value="L" />
      <enumeration value="XL" />
   </restriction>
</simpleType>
<simpleType name="list.size">
   <list itemType="size" />
</simpleType>

<simpleType name="sizenum">
   <restriction base="xs:decimal" >
      <minInclusive value="3.0" />
      <maxInclusive value="15.0" />
      <pattern value="[0-9]{1,2}(.[0-9])?" />
   </restriction>
</simpleType>
<simpleType name="list.sizenum">
   <list itemType="sizenum" />
</simpleType>

<simpleType name="union.ShoeSizes">
   <union memberTypes="list.size list.sizenum" />
</simpleType>
```

The use of the union datatype (union.ShoeSizes) allows either of the two following datatypes to be used for two different instances of a single element type:

```
<AvailableSizes>S M L</AvailableSizes>
<AvailableSizes>8 8.5 9 9.5 10 10.5 11 12 13</AvailableSizes>
```

The names of the list and union datatype examples use an explicit prefix to emphasize the different derivations – there is no requirement to use this naming style, and of course the type names are not limited to just plain ASCII text.

Deriving Complex Types

Unlike simple types, a complex type may derive by extension from an existing simple or complex type, or by restriction upon another complex type.

A new element needs to be investigated, namely the `complexContent` element. We will look at this, and the related `simpleContent` element, in the following sections. These two elements can only be used as part of a Complex Type Definition – they do not apply to simple types.

Restrictions Upon Element Content

As we've seen in our earlier discussions, there are essentially three types of content models:

- ❑ Text-only content – element can include character data, but no child elements.
- ❑ Element content – element can only include child elements.
- ❑ Mixed content – element can include a mixture of character data and/or child elements.

The simpleContent Element

The `simpleContent` element is used if the complex type may only have text content. The difference between this and a simple type is that it may carry one or more attributes. Like most XML Schema elements, an optional `id` attribute (of the `ID` datatype) is permitted. The only children that are permitted for this element are the `restriction` and `extension` elements. Here is a simple example, where we have a `Person` whose name is stored as a simple text content in the element, but also as an age as an attribute:

```
<xs:element name = "Person">
   <xs:complexType>
      <xs:simpleContent>
         <xs:extension base="xs:string">
            <xs:attribute name = "age" type = "xs:integer" />
         </xs:extension>
      </xs:simpleContent>
   </xs:complexType>
</xs:element>
```

Unlike most XML Schema elements, the `annotation` element cannot be used directly as a child of the `simpleContent` element.

The complexContent Element

The `complexContent` element is used to handle the other two types of content models: element and mixed content. The distinction between these two is made using the `mixed` attribute, which is a Boolean datatype. If the value of this attribute is true, then a mixed content model is allowed. Otherwise, this element is nearly identical to the `simpleContent` element – only the `restriction` and `extension` elements may be children of the `complexContent` element, and an optional `id` attribute is allowed. We'll see some examples illustrating the use of this element in the next section.

The restriction Element

Datatypes that are to be derived by restriction, whether a simple or complex type, must use the `restriction` element to contain the constraining facets that define this new datatype. This element has a required attribute, `base`, that is names the datatype that is being restricted. An optional `id` attribute is also allowed.

The extension Element

As we will see in the next section, datatypes that are derived by extension use the `extension` element to contain a revised content model and/or attribute list. This element also requires a `base` attribute to name the base type that is to be extended. An optional `id` attribute is also allowed.

Now that we've had a brief overview of the elements used to implement derived datatypes, let's look at the two different kinds of derivation for complex datatypes.

Deriving by Extension

Complex types may also be derived by extension from a simple type or another complex type. The only kind of extension supported by XML Schemas is the simple appending of additional schema components to an existing content model.

> **XML Schema datatypes that are derived by extension can only add attributes or append child elements to the existing content model.**

We have often used a simple definition of a mailing address in various examples earlier in this chapter and elsewhere in this book. Most of the time, we tend to use a simple US-centric address format. For the sake of this section, let us assume an even simpler address format, which just specifies the name, street, and city.

This basic address is described in the following simple little schema (which we might call "Address.xsd"):

```
<?xml version="1.0" ?>
<xs:schema xmlns:xs="http://www.w3.org/2001/XMLSchema" >

    <xs:complexType name="Address">
        <xs:sequence>
            <xs:element name="Name" type="xs:string" />
            <xs:element name="Street" type="xs:string"
                minOccurs="1" maxOccurs="3" />
            <xs:element name="City" type="xs:string" />
        </xs:sequence>
    </xs:complexType>

    <xs:element name="MailAddress" type="Address" />
    <xs:element name="BillAddress" type="Address" />

</xs:schema>
```

The following snippet of XML data illustrates a conformant `Address` element:

```
<?xml version="1.0" ?>
<MailAddress xmlns:xsi="http://www.w3.org/2001/XMLSchema-instance"
        xsi:noNamespaceSchemaLocation="Address.xsd">
    <Name>John Q. Public</Name>
    <Street>123 Fairview St.</Street>
    <City>Park Ridge</City>
</MailAddress>
```

We can now use this `Address` type to create three new derived complex types for specific additions to this address datatype: for Canada (CAN), Great Britain (GBR), and the United States (USA).

The effective content model of a complex type that is derived by extension is the combination of the base type's content model, *plus* the additions specified in the new datatype. These content models are merged in sequence, so an extended address is comprised of the common part (Name, Street, City), followed by the country-specific additions.

Canadian addresses require the name of a province, plus a postal code. For example, we could add the following at the end of the existing Address schema (just before the /schema end-tag):

```
<xs:simpleType name="CAN_PostalCode">
    <xs:restriction base="xs:string">
        <xs:pattern value =
            "[A-Z]{1}[0-9]{1}[A-Z]{1} [0-9]{1}[A-Z]{1}[0-9]{1}" />
        <!-- this allows codes in the form: "X9X 9X9" -->
    </xs:restriction>
</xs:simpleType>

<xs:complexType name="CAN_Address">
    <xs:complexContent>
        <xs:extension base="Address">
            <xs:sequence>
                <xs:element name="Province" type="xs:string" />
                <xs:element name="PostalCode" type="CAN_PostalCode"/>
            </xs:sequence>
        </xs:extension>
    </xs:complexContent>
</xs:complexType>
```

We have added a new simple type for the Canadian postal code, which is always in the alphanumeric form "X9X 9X9" (where "X" indicates an upper-case letter and "9" is a numeric digit). We've restricted the built-in string datatype using the pattern facet to achieve this.

The datatype that we are extending is a complex type therefore, with an element-only content model, we must indicate that the extended type also has complex content (using the complexContent element – more about this in a later section).

The following XML file (Address_1.xml) illustrates an Address element that conforms to the extended CAN_Address type:

```
<?xml version="1.0" ?>
<MailAddress xmlns:xsi="http://www.w3.org/2001/XMLSchema-instance"
        xsi:noNamespaceSchemaLocation="Address.xsd"
        xsi:type="CAN_Address">
    <Name>Trevelyn Smythe</Name>
    <Street>8185 Great White North Way</Street>
    <City>Thunder Bay</City>
    <Province>Ontario</Province>
    <PostalCode>M1A 3X9</PostalCode>
</MailAddress>
```

Our addresses in Great Britain will allow the optional name of a county (for example, Leicestershire or Northumberland) plus require a postcode (and again we simply append this to the ever-growing schema named Address.xsd):

```
    <xs:simpleType name="GBR_Postcode" >
     <!-- "AA99 9XX"/"AA9X 9XX"/"A99 9XX" -->
       <xs:restriction base="xs:string" >
       <!-- ^"AA" is postcode area (town) -->
          <xs:pattern value = "(([A-Z]{2}[0-9]{2})|([A-Z]{2}[0-9][A-Z])
                                |([A-Z][0-9]{2})) ([0-9][A-Z]{2})" />
             <!-- The above pattern value should be typed all on one line -->
       </xs:restriction>
    </xs:simpleType>

    <xs:complexType name="GBR_Address">
       <xs:complexContent>
          <xs:extension base="Address">
             <xs:sequence>
                <xs:element name="County" type="xs:string" minOccurs="0" />
                <xs:element name="Postcode" type="GBR_Postcode"/>
             </xs:sequence>
          </xs:extension>
       </xs:complexContent>
    </xs:complexType>
```

Note that British postcodes are of the alphanumeric form "XX99 9XX".

Everyone's favorite address in the UK is:

```
<?xml version="1.0" ?>
<MailAddress xmlns:xsi="http://www.w3.org/2001/XMLSchema-instance"
       xsi:noNamespaceSchemaLocation="Address.xsd"
       xsi:type="GBR_Address">
   <Name>Wrox Press Ltd.</Name>
   <Street>Arden House</Street>
   <Street>1102 Warwick Road</Street>
   <City>Birmingham</City>
   <Postcode>B27 6BH</Postcode>
</MailAddress>
```

Finally, we will add one more extended datatype for the US addresses:

```
    <xs:simpleType name="USPS_StateCode">
       <xs:restriction base="xs:string" >
          <xs:enumeration value="AL" />    <!-- Alabama -->
          <xs:enumeration value="AK" />    <!-- Alaska -->
<!-- skip the next 48 states (plus D.C. and some other territories) -->
          <xs:enumeration value="WY" />    <!-- Wyoming -->
       </xs:restriction>
    </xs:simpleType>

    <xs:simpleType name="USPS_ZIP">
       <xs:restriction base="xs:integer">
          <xs:minInclusive value="01000" />
          <xs:maxInclusive value="99999" />
       </xs:restriction>
    </xs:simpleType>

    <xs:complexType name="USA_Address">
```

```
          <xs:complexContent>
            <xs:extension base="Address">
               <xs:sequence>
                  <xs:element name="State" type="USPS_StateCode" />
                  <xs:element name="ZIP" type="USPS_ZIP"/>
               </xs:sequence>
            </xs:extension>
         </xs:complexContent>
      </xs:complexType>
```

The US Postal Service (USPS) has defined two-letter abbreviations for the 50 states, the District of Columbia, and various territories of the USA. We have omitted all, but three, from this example for the sake of brevity. The other USPS standard for mailing addresses in the US is a numeric postal code known as the zip code. Again, for simplicity, we will use the five-digit zip code, instead of the newer ZIP+4 scheme.

The following XML file conforms to the above schema for the US flavor of the Address element:

```
<?xml version="1.0" ?>
<MailAddress xmlns:xsi="http://www.w3.org/2001/XMLSchema-instance"
          xsi:noNamespaceSchemaLocation="Address.xsd"
          xsi:type="USA_Address">
   <Name>John Q. Public</Name>
   <Street>123 Fairview St.</Street>
   <City>Park Ridge</City>
   <State>IL</State>
   <ZIP>60068</ZIP>
</MailAddress>
```

Derived by Restriction

Complex datatypes may also be derived by restriction from a simple datatype or another complex type. We already dealt with simple datatypes derived by restriction earlier in this chapter; so let's turn our attention to complex types that are derived by restricting the content model of another complex datatype.

> **Restriction of complex types constrains the `element` and/or `attribute` declarations of an existing type.**

These new constraints cause the derived type to have values that are a subset of the base type's values. This implies that a processing application should be able to handle the derived type without any modification. The new schema is similarly compatible with the old, since all components of the base type definition must be repeated in the derived type definition.

For example, we could provide a less liberal form of our Address type, which only allowed one or two separate Street elements, instead of the three allowed earlier:

```
      <xs:complexType name="ShortAddress">
         <xs:complexContent>
            <xs:restriction base="Address" >
               <xs:sequence>
                  <xs:element name="Name" type="xs:string" />
                  <xs:element name="Street" type="xs:string"
```

```
                                        minOccurs="1" maxOccurs="2" />
                <xs:element name="City" type="xs:string" />
            </xs:sequence>
        </xs:restriction>
    </xs:complexContent>
</xs:complexType>
```

As you can see, the new derived datatype (ShortAddress) is declared using the very same sequence of child elements as its base type (Address). The changed maxOccurs facet of the Street element is the new, more restrictive, definition.

An additional, and arguably more powerful, datatype extension is possible using multiple schema files and the typical programming language inclusion mechanism. However, we won't go into this here, as Chapter 8 covers it in detail.

Substitution Groups

XML Schemas allow named groups of elements to be substituted for other elements, using a **substitution group**. This feature allows one global element to replace another, without requiring any changes to the markup or schema. This is a key advantage when working with an existing schema – the substitution group in the new schema simply replaces the global element of the same name in the old schema. Whereas a new complex datatype that is derived by extension can only add new elements to a content model, and one derived by restriction can only modify the existing model, a substitution group can be used to completely redefine an existing element's content model.

Substitution groups are somewhat similar to the OO concept of polymorphism – they can be used to provide different validation types for a given element or extensions to existing datatypes, just as different methods (of the same name, such as "+") in C++ can be used with different datatypes.

The target element of the substitution group is called the **head element**. It must be a global (which implies named, also) element. The datatype of an element in a substitution group must either be the same as the head element's type, or derived from the head element's type. The existence of a substitution group does *not* imply that the substitute elements must be used, nor does it preclude the continued use of the head type.

Instead of using the address datatypes derived by extension, as we did in the last section, we can use substitution groups to allow the use of a country-specific address anywhere that we are already able to use the Address element. For example, we can declare a substitution group for the Address head element, with three alternative elements:

```
<xs:element name="AddrCAN" type="CAN_Address"
    substitutionGroup="MailAddress"/>
<xs:element name="AddrGBR" type="GBR_Address"
    substitutionGroup="MailAddress"/>
<xs:element name="AddrUSA" type="USA_Address"
    substitutionGroup="MailAddress"/>
```

You can just add this to the end of the Address.xsd schema – in the code download this is Address_SG.xsd. The substitutionGroup attribute on these element declarations means that we can use one of these elements anywhere where we previously needed a MailAddress element.

Our previous US address examples could now use the concrete `AddrUSA` element (or one of the other substitutions), instead of the `MailAddress` head element, for example:

```
<?xml version="1.0" ?>
<AddrUSA xmlns:xsi="http://www.w3.org/2001/XMLSchema-instance"
         xsi:noNamespaceSchemaLocation="Address_SG.xsd">
   <Name>John Q. Public</Name>
   <Street>123 Fairview St.</Street>
   <City>Park Ridge</City>
   <State>IL</State>
   <ZIP>60068</ZIP>
</AddrUSA>
```

The substituted type is explicitly derived from its head type therefore, no `xsi:type` attribute is required in the instance data to select a datatype for validation.

Abstract Types

There is a mechanism in XML Schemas to force substitution for specific elements or datatypes, by preventing its appearance in any instance of XML data. This is accomplished by declaring the element or type to be `abstract` in its original definition. Elements that are declared abstract cannot appear in the instance document itself, but must be represented in the instance data by a member of the abstract element's derived type, or as a member of a substitution group. An abstract type requires that any elements of that type to instead use a derived type. As usual, the `xsi:type` attribute may also be used to explicitly associate the instance data with another derived type (that is not abstract).

Abstract types in XML Schemas are a little like abstract classes in Java or C++.

For example, we may want to prevent the `Address` type from being used in XML instance data, and force the use of one of the country-specific address elements, instead. We can do this for the datatype by changing the original definition of `Address` to include the `abstract` attribute:

```
<xs:complexType name="Address" abstract="true">
   <!-- the rest of the definition is exactly the same -->
</xs:complexType>
```

We must now explicitly declare a non-abstract datatype (derived from `Address`) for the `MailAddress` element:

```
<MailAddress xsi:type=" USA_Address">
   <!-- child elements omitted for clarity (they are unchanged) -->
</MailAddress>
```

If we had instead changed the element declaration for `MailAddress` to be abstract, and assuming the same substitution group as we used in the last section, we could then require the use of the concrete `AddrUSA` element (or one of the other substitutions), instead of the abstract `MailAddress`. The XML instance data conforming to this new revision would look just the same as the example in the previous section, but now the element substitution is required, instead of being optional.

Abstract types can be quite useful when we construct our own schema – for example, they can be used to force substitution of an element that is part of a substitution group. For example, we might want to be sure that a full address with country and zip code (or postcode) information is present, rather than the shorter version of this address from which the other types are derived.

There is no way to revise an existing schema to include the `abstract` attribute, However so this declaration is *not* very useful when working with an existing third party schema.

Controlling Datatype Derivation

At some point, we may want to prevent any further derivation or modification of a datatype. The XML Schemas mechanism to accomplish this purpose is a **final type** (using the `final` attribute and/or the `fixed` attribute).

Datatypes declared as `final` *in XML Schema are a lot like similarly declared classes in Java.*

The fixed Attribute

This attribute is used with simple type definitions to prevent any derived type from changing the value of a specific facet of the simple type.

Let's look at a variation on the definition of the USPS state code:

```
<xs:simpleType name="StateCode">
   <xs:restriction base="xs:string">
      <xs:length value="2" fixed="true" />
   </xs:restriction>
</xs:simpleType>
```

This allows any two-character state code (as before), but prevents any types derived from this specific datatype from using a longer or shorter string length. Other facets may still be changed – only `length` is affected by the above declaration.

The final Attribute

This attribute is used in a schema with complex type and element definitions to prevent any additional derivations from a given datatype. Once a datatype or element has been declared as `final`, any attempt to redefine it will result in a schema processing error.

There are three legal values for this attribute when used with a `complexType` element:

❑   `restriction` – prevents derivation by restriction.

❑   `extension` – prevents derivation by extension.

❑   `#all` – prevents any and all kinds of derivations.

For example, we could have declared the `Address` datatype to be final, like so:

```
<xs:complexType name="Address" final="#all">
   <!-- the rest of the definition is exactly the same -->
</xs:complexType>
```

If we had done this, we could not have derived the country-specific datatypes from this one. On the other hand, if we merely wanted to prevent any restricted versions of the Address datatype, but still allow extensions, we can just set the final attribute value to be restriction.

This attribute can also be used in a similar fashion with the element element; using the above three values plus a fourth legal value (substitution, which can be used to prevent a substitution group from changing the element's existing definition).

The finalDefault Attribute

This attribute can be included in the schema element, using any of the three values that have already been shown for the final attribute. If this attribute is present, its value will be used as the default value for any element and complexType elements in the schema, as if each had its own final attribute with that default value. This is a special case of an attribute default within XML Schemas – the value of the finalDefault is copied to any element that doesn't have an explicit final attribute.

The block Attribute

This attribute is used to control both the kinds of derived types and the use of substitution groups, much like the final attribute. The key difference is that the block attribute prevents the use of the xsi:type attribute in XML instance data from replacing an element's datatype association (while final prevents derivation of types or elements within a schema). For example, if we changed our ongoing Address example to use this attribute, we could block the use of the country-specific address datatype extensions (such as CAN_Address, GBR_Address, and so on):

```
<xs:complexType name="Address" block="extension">
    <!-- the rest of the definition is exactly the same -->
</xs:complexType>
```

This attribute uses the three values that have already been shown for the final attribute: restriction, extension, or #all (for both kinds of derivation). If we wanted to keep our special address type extensions, but still prevent any restricted versions of the Address datatype, we would use the restriction value. Similarly, the #all value prevents *any* use of xsi:type to replace a datatype.

The blockDefault Attribute

Like the finalDefault attribute, this can be included in the schema element, using any of the three values that have already been shown for the final attribute. As before, this attribute's value will affect all children of the schema, element, as if each had its own block attribute.

Summary

In this chapter, we've taken some of the basic derived datatype declarations from the previous chapters and looked at them in greater detail. We've seen that both simple and complex datatypes can be derived by restriction, while the latter can also be extended (derivation by extension) or replaced (using a substitution group).

We looked at the two kinds of datatype facets:

- ❑ The five fundamental facets (equality, order, bounds, cardinality, numeric/non-numeric).

- ❑ The twelve constraining facets (and their corresponding schema elements: `length`, `minLength`, `maxLength`, `whiteSpace`, `pattern`, `enumeration`, `minExclusive`, `maxExclusive`, `minInclusive`, `maxInclusive`, `totalDigits`, `fractionDigits`).

The `pattern` constraining facet is such a significant feature of XML Schema (and because it is different from the more familiar UNIX or Perl regexes) therefore, we devoted an entire section to the details of this facet – or more specifically to the XML Schema flavor of regular expressions.

We introduced the mechanism whereby an XML data instance can assert its own element-datatype associations using the `xsi:type` attribute.

Last, and certainly not least, the *Datatype Inheritance* section provided an overview of how datatypes can be developed in an object-oriented fashion. XML Schema uses similar concepts of derivation (inheritance), abstract and final types, and other ways to control derived datatypes. Different kinds of complex content can be described, using:

- ❑ `simpleContent` for text-only complex types (attributes are always allowed).

- ❑ `complexContent` for datatypes that allow element-only or mixed content (and attributes).

As we just saw in the previous section, there are several attributes (`fixed`, `final`, `finalDefault`, `block`, and `blockDefault`) that can be used with the `complexType` element to control further derivation of a datatype.

In the next chapter, we will create some useful user-derived types, such as more detailed and country-specific mailing addresses, some generic code types (such as ISO country, currency, or language codes), and Internet datatypes (like IP addresses and URIs).

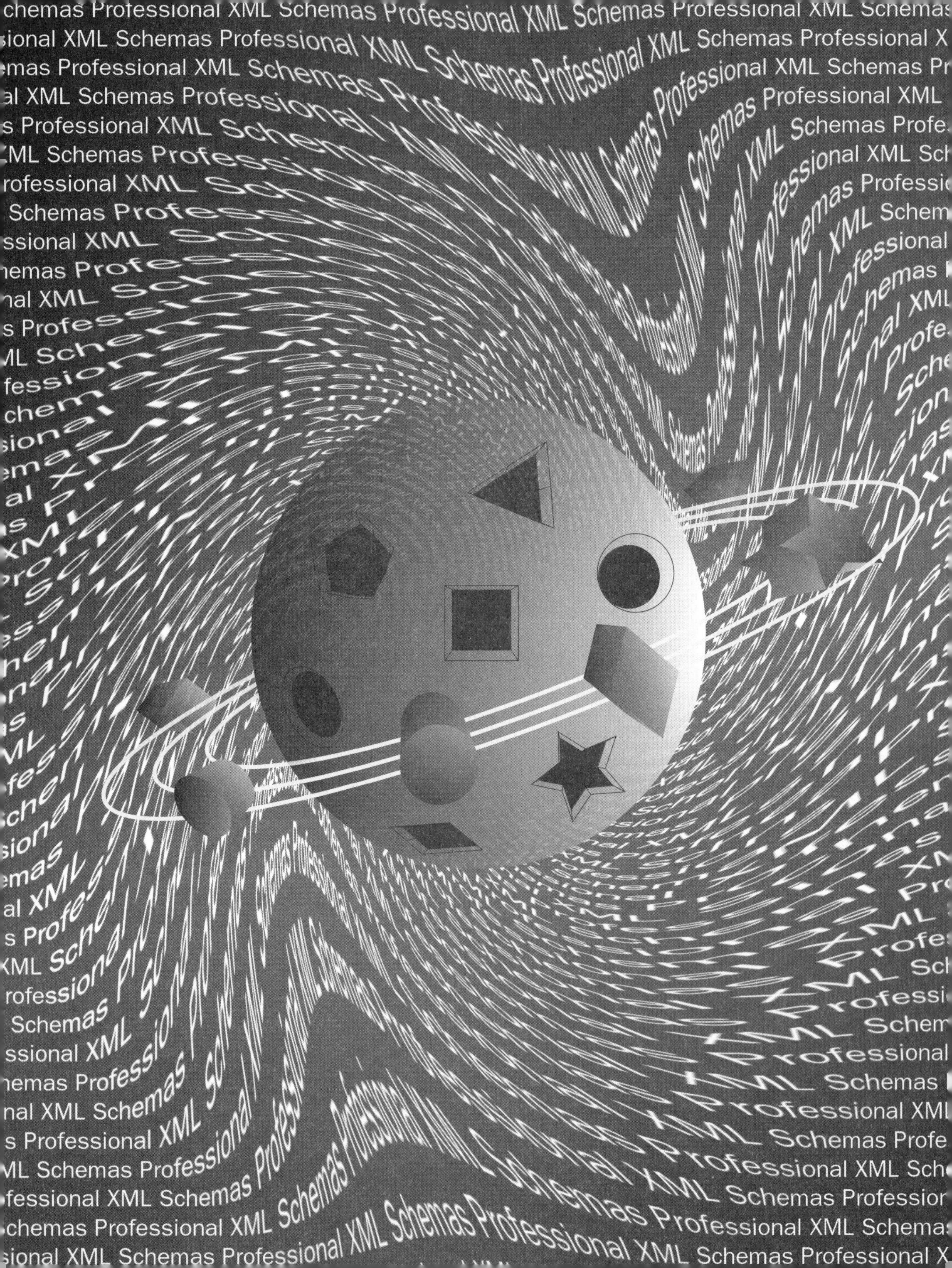
Professional XML Schemas

Some Useful Datatypes

We have already discussed the mechanisms of XML Schema datatypes in the last three chapters, and included numerous examples of both datatype definitions and their use in XML instance data. Now, let's apply some of this to more practical matters.

In this chapter, we will create some useful datatypes for use in e-commerce and other XML applications. These custom datatypes can be grouped into the following categories:

❑ Countries

❑ Internet Datatypes

❑ People

❑ Telephone Numbers

❑ Postal Addresses

❑ Geodetic Locations

The first category ("Countries") includes datatypes for three commonly used international (ISO) standards:

❑ ISO 3166 Country Codes

❑ ISO 4217 Currency Codes

❑ ISO 639 Language Codes

The "Internet Datatypes" category deals with a handful of *de facto* Internet Engineering Task Force standards, such as domain names and URIs. The other categories provide some common name and address datatypes, and include country-specific postal addresses for the United States, Canada, Mexico, and Great Britain. Last, but not least, we'll create some datatypes for "physical" (geodetic) locations using latitude and longitude.

Most of the examples in this chapter will use a subset of all possible values for a given datatype. For example, instead of listing all 50 US states, plus DC and various territories, we will just show a representative sample. The comprehensive lists can be found in example schema files available at http://www.wrox.com.

Sample Custom Datatypes

Before we get to the useful custom datatypes, we need to create a couple of more fundamental datatypes that will be used as the basis for several more complex types.

Some Simple Basic Types

Although XML Schema does provide a reasonable set of built-in datatypes, there are some very simple additions that we may use rather often when constructing other derived datatypes.

Curiously enough, XML Schema does *not* include the datatype that is probably the most universal type, that is, a single character. We can easily create this fundamental datatype by restricting a type derived from the built-in `string` type to have a one-character length:

```
<xs:simpleType name="Char">
   <xs:restriction base="xs:string">
      <xs:length value="1" />
   </xs:restriction>
</xs:simpleType>
```

Many commercial applications will want to use non-negative numbers (such as prices or weights) that are constrained to have only two digits to the right of the decimal point:

```
<xs:simpleType name="positiveDecimalN.2">
   <xs:restriction base="xs:decimal">
      <xs:minInclusive value="0" />
      <xs:fractionDigits value="2" />
   </xs:restriction>
</xs:simpleType>
```

Obviously, we could fill the entire book with such basic datatypes, but these two are included since they will be used later in the chapter. Let us now turn our attention to some more simple type definitions that will be used as the basis for some complex datatypes.

Countries

We are now going to create some datatypes that represent a few key facts about the various countries of the world. There is a multitude of data that *could* be described (such as population, Gross National Product, and so on), but we will focus upon three fairly universal items that are useful for e-commerce applications such as our Books Invoice system. The three datatypes we will attach to each country are:

- ❑ **Country code** – the 3-letter **ISO 3166** code for the country

- ❑ **Currency code** – the 3-letter **ISO 4217** code for the country's official (or most commonly used) currency

❑   **Language code** – one or more **ISO 639-2** language codes for the country's official language(s)

The syntax of these three codes is described in various places by both the ISO and the IETF. We will look at their syntax and informational resources, and construct some XML Schema datatypes that enforce their lexical formats and valid values.

This table shows a sample selection of some countries, their currencies, some languages (official and unofficial), and their related ISO codes:

ISO 3166 (xx)	ISO 3166 (xxx)	ISO 4217 *	Currency	Currency Symbol & Format	ISO 639-1	ISO 639-2	Country Name
vg	BVI	USD	US Dollar	$#,###.##	en-GB	eng	British Virgin Islands
ca	CAN	CAD	Canadian Dollar	$#,###.##	en	eng	Canada
cn	CHN	CNY	Yuan renminbi	Y#,###.##	zh	zho	China, People's Republic of
fr	FRA	EUR	Euro	•# ###,##	fr	fra	France
de	DEU	EUR	Euro	•#.###,##	de	deu	Germany
gb	GBR	GBP	Pound Sterling	£#,###.##	en-GB	eng	Great Britain
it	ITA	EUR	Euro	•#.###,##	it	ita	Italy
jp	JPN	JPY	Yen	¥#,###	ja	jpn	Japan
mx	MEX	MXP	Mexican Peso	$#,###.##	es	spa	Mexico
pr	PRI	USD	US Dollar	$#,###.##	es en	spa eng	Puerto Rico, Commonwealth of
za	ZAF	ZAR	Rand	R#,###.##	en af – zu	eng afr bnt zul	South Africa
us	USA	USD	US Dollar	$#,###.##	en-US es –	eng spa haw	United States of America
vi	VIR	USD	US Dollar	$#,###.##	en-US	eng	US Virgin Islands

Note: these codes are "real-world" labels, and are not entirely congruent with the ISO 4217 codes.

Let's look at these three ISO standards in more detail.

Country Codes (ISO 3166)

As you might expect, ISO 3166 Country Codes are used to label the countries of the world, using two- or three-letter codes from a controlled vocabulary. The two-character codes are maintained by the German national standards body, **die Deutsches Institut für Normung** (**DIN**). The three-character codes are maintained (and widely used) by the United Nations.

*The standard used here is **ISO 3166-1:1997 (E). Codes for the representation of names of countries and their subdivisions – Part 1: Country codes**. Online code lists are available at http://www.din.de/gremien/nas/nabd/iso3166ma/codlstp1/en_listp1.html (the two-character "Internet" codes) or http://www.un.org/Depts/unsd/methods/m49alpha.htm (the three-character codes). Another good resource for these codes is at http://www.oasis-open.org/cover/country3166.html. Alternatively, you can go to http://www.iso.ch/ to order a paper version of the official standard.*

As with ISO 639, there is an ongoing transition from two- to three-character codes. The former are still widely used for Internet domain addresses (such as bbc.co.uk and www.iso.ch – see the *Domain Names* section later in this chapter), and thus will continue to be used for some time.

The three-character codes are widely used in computer *and* real world applications. Broadcasts of the Olympics or the World Cup often identify national teams using these codes, and the oval national-origin plates that used to be common on motor vehicles in Europe are another example.

There are two alternatives to describing this data. The first and simplest approach just restricts the length of the code string and the characters that may be used therein:

```
<xs:simpleType name="iso3166_CountryCode">
   <xs:restriction base="xs:string">
      <xs:length value="3" />
      <xs:pattern value="[A-Za-z0-9]{3}" />
   </xs:restriction>
</xs:simpleType>
```

The use of both the length and pattern facets is something of a suspenders-and-belt approach for the sake of illustration – the length constraint is also implicit in the pattern. Obviously, the drawback to this method is the lack of an explicit list of valid values – any three-letter acronym would be accepted, without any regard to the current ISO code list. Thus, the second approach, while more rigid, and more long-winded, is probably the best:

```
<xs:simpleType name="iso3166_CountryCode">
   <xs:restriction base="xs:string">
      <xs:enumeration value="BVI" />    <!-- British Virgin Islands -->
      <xs:enumeration value="CAN" />    <!-- Canada -->
      <xs:enumeration value="CHN" />    <!-- China, People's Republic of -->
      <xs:enumeration value="FRA" />    <!-- France -->
      <xs:enumeration value="DEU" />    <!-- Germany -->
      <xs:enumeration value="GBR" />    <!-- Great Britain -->
      <xs:enumeration value="ITA" />    <!-- Italy -->
      <xs:enumeration value="JPN" />    <!-- Japan -->
      <xs:enumeration value="MEX" />    <!-- Mexico -->
      <xs:enumeration value="PRI" />    <!-- Puerto Rico, Commonwealth of -->
      <xs:enumeration value="USA" />    <!-- United States of America -->
      <xs:enumeration value="VIR" />    <!-- US Virgin Islands -->
      <xs:enumeration value="ZAF" />    <!-- South Africa -->
   </xs:restriction>
</xs:simpleType>
```

This list of country codes simply corresponds to the country table we saw earlier, but is by no means a comprehensive list of all possible country codes. There is an example schema file in the code download (ProSchemas.ISO3166_CountryCode.xsd), which provides the complete enumerated list of country codes (as of June 2001).

Now is a good time to go ahead and create another datatype for later use – a datatype that is nothing more than a simple list of ISO 3166 Country Codes:

```
<xs:simpleType name="iso3166_CountryCodes" >
   <xs:list itemType="iso3166_CountryCode" />
</xs:simpleType>
```

Except for specific Internet-related or legacy applications, the newer three-character language codes (or an extended form thereof) should be used whenever possible.

Currency Codes (ISO 4217)

ISO 4217 Currency Codes are usually derived from the two-letter form of an ISO 639 country code, with a third letter to represent the name of the currency. Although the ISO does maintain a list of currencies, their idea of an update cycle seems to be about once every five years, which isn't frequent enough to reflect the current state of the world. Since this datatype is concerned with money, it is important that such stale information is updated on a timely basis. Thus, various organizations try to maintain current lists of currency names, formats, and conversion rates outside of the ISO.

> *The ISO standard for the representation of currency codes and funds is **ISO 4217:1995 Codes**, with a printed version available at http://www.iso.ch/. Real-world lists of ISO 4217 codes and additions thereto are available at http://www.xe.com/iso4217.htm and http://www.thefinancials.com/vortex/CurrencyFormats.html. The former site also provides current conversion rates for several currencies, updated once every minute (including all of our examples; plus those of Australia, Switzerland, and Russia).*

The ISO has also defined numeric codes for these currencies, but in the spirit of XML we'll stick to the more mnemonic and memorable 3-letter codes.

We will continue to use the sample set of countries, as shown in the table in the preceding section. A datatype for currency codes is pretty straightforward – we'll just use an enumerated string datatype to represent the codes:

```xml
<xs:simpleType name="iso4217_Currency" >
    <xs:restriction base="xs:string" >
        <xs:enumeration value="CAD" />    <!-- Canadian dollar -->
        <xs:enumeration value="CNY" />    <!-- Chinese yuan renminbi -->
        <xs:enumeration value="EUR" />    <!-- Euro -->
        <xs:enumeration value="GBP" />    <!-- Pound Sterling -->
        <xs:enumeration value="JPY" />    <!-- Japanese yen -->
        <xs:enumeration value="MXP" />    <!-- Mexican peso -->
        <xs:enumeration value="USD" />    <!-- US dollar -->
        <xs:enumeration value="ZAR" />    <!-- South African rand -->
    </xs:restriction>
</xs:simpleType>
```

We can use these codes in various elements that involve money or other financial data. For example, we might want to have multiple `Price` elements for each product, one for each currency that our application can support. To simplify transformation and presentation of this data, we'll wrap the one or more `Price` elements in a `Prices` parent element:

```xml
<xs:complexType name="Amount" >
    <xs:simpleContent>
        <xs:extension base="positiveDecimalN.2" >
            <xs:attribute name="currency" type="iso4217_Currency" default="USD" />
        </xs:extension>
    </xs:simpleContent>
</xs:complexType>

<xs:element name="Prices">
```

```
    <xs:complexType>
       <xs:sequence>
          <xs:element name="Price" type="Amount" maxOccurs="unbounded" />
       </xs:sequence>
    </xs:complexType>
  </xs:element>
```

The `Amount` datatype is a complex type that *extends* a simple derived datatype (`positiveDecimalN.2`) with the addition of the `currency` attribute. This datatype can be used for prices (as it is in this example), item costs, taxes, or any other positive decimal number that is intended for interpretation as an amount of money. An example of an XML data instance that is valid according to this schema snippet is:

```
<Prices>
   <Price currency="CAD">89.95</Price>
   <Price currency="EUR">65.95</Price>
   <Price currency="GBP">47.99</Price>
   <Price currency="USD">59.99</Price>
</Prices>
```

The various examples so far have given us a consistent way to *identify* the currency associated with an invoice, or any other financial transaction, for that matter. Let's add another datatype which collects some of the information that is commonly associated with a given currency, such as symbols for presentation use, links to countries that use the currency, and so on:

```
<xs:element name="Currency" >
   <xs:complexType>
      <xs:attribute name="code"      type="iso4217_Currency"      use="required" />
      <xs:attribute name="symbol"    type="xs:string"             use="required" />
      <xs:attribute name="countries" type="iso3166_CountryCodes"  use="required" />
      <xs:attribute name="name"      type="xs:string"             use="required" />
   </xs:complexType>
</xs:element>

<xs:element name="Currencies" >
   <xs:complexType>
      <xs:sequence>
         <xs:element ref="Currency" maxOccurs="unbounded" />
      </xs:sequence>
   </xs:complexType>
</xs:element>
```

The declaration that the `Currency` element is a complex type without including a content model is shorthand for declaring an empty element. Since this element is not generically useful, and should only be used as a child of `Currencies`, we have used an anonymous complex type here.

The following XML data excerpt shows the use of these elements to describe the several currencies that we will continue to use for our illustrative examples:

```
<Currencies>
   <Currency code="CAD" symbol="$" name="Dollar" countries="CAN" />
   <Currency code="CNY" symbol="Y" name="Yuan"   countries="CHN" />
   <Currency code="EUR" symbol="•" name="Euro"   countries="DEU FRA ITA" />
```

```
            <Currency code="GBP" symbol="£" name="Pound"  countries="GBR" />
            <Currency code="JPY" symbol="¥" name="Yen"    countries="JPN" />
            <Currency code="MXP" symbol="$" name="Peso"   countries="MEX" />
            <Currency code="ZAR" symbol="R" name="Rand"   countries="ZAF" />
            <Currency code="USD" symbol="$" name="Dollar" countries="USA PRI BVI VIR" />
        </Currencies>
```

In the case of the Euro and the US Dollar, there are several countries that use each of these currencies. These whitespace-delimited lists of ISO 3166 Country Codes can be used to link from a currency to one or more countries. This might be used to verify that an invoice used the appropriate currency for an order, or that a refund is remitted in the correct currency. There is an inverse of this link in the Country datatype example we will create at the end of this section. These links are the beginning of an interlinked set of datatypes that can be used for a variety of purposes that are country-dependent.

Language Codes (ISO 639)

ISO 639 Language Codes use the Language Tag formats as specified in RFCs 3066 and 1766. Both of these RFCs describe the *syntax* of tags that are used to describe textual data as representing a specific human language (computer "languages" are explicitly excluded, sorry HAL). Lists of the actual tag strings are maintained by the ISO and also by the **Internet Assigned Numbers Authority** (**IANA**) – see http://www.iana.org for more details.

> **Language codes are needed for the xml:lang special attribute defined in XML 1.0, so an XML Schema built-in datatype (language) has been defined for this kind of data.**

A language tag is comprised of one or more parts. All tags include at least one alphabetic string of 1 to 8 ASCII characters ("A" to "Z", or "a" to "z"). There may optionally be one or more additional sub tags that are also 1 to 8 ASCII characters, and which may also include the ASCII numeric digits ("0" to "9"). If multiple sub tags are used, they must be separated by the ASCII hyphen ("-"). No whitespace or other characters are permitted in these tags, and these tags are *not* case-sensitive.

> *The standard is **ISO 639:1988 (E): Code for the representation of names of languages**. Code lists from the US Library of Congress are at http://lcweb.loc.gov/standards/iso639-2/termcodes.html. An overview of the standard is at http://lcweb.loc.gov/standards/iso639-2/langhome.html. Another source is at http://www.oasis-open.org/cover/iso639a.html. The "official" standard on paper can be ordered at http://www.iso.ch/.*

> *Tag syntax is defined in **RFC 3066: Tags for the Identification of Languages** [2001-01] at http://www.ietf.org/rfc/rfc3066.txt, and in the earlier **RFC 1766** of the same title [1995-03] at http://www.ietf.org/rfc/rfc1766.txt.*

The common practice is to use lowercase letters for simple two-character language codes. Local versions of these languages use an additional two-character ISO 3166 country code (in uppercase) to further qualify the exact language. For example, three peoples separated by a common language (British, Americans, and Australians) might indicate their version of English in the following fashion:

```
    <example xml:lang="en-GB" />
    <example xml:lang="en-US" />
    <example xml:lang="en-AU" />
```

We can even specify a dialect within a regional version of a language, like the following:

```
<example xml:lang="en-GB-cockney" />
<example xml:lang="en-US-boontling" />
```

Although XML 1.0 originally specified the older two-character language codes (ISO 639-1), there is a transition underway to the newer three-character codes (as defined in ISO 639-2). In fact, the Second Edition of the XML 1.0 Recommendation mentions the pending change, and implies that XML will specify the newer codes in the future. The earlier example would use these values in the new regime:

```
<example xml:lang="en-GBR" />
<example xml:lang="en-USA" />
<example xml:lang="en-AUS" />
```

Although `language` is a built-in datatype, we will soon enough want to make lists of these codes, so let's create a derived-by-list datatype for this purpose:

```
<xs:simpleType name="rfc3066_LanguageCodes">
    <xs:list itemType="xs:language" />
</xs:simpleType>
```

All new XML data should use the three-character ISO 639-2 language codes whenever possible, but we must continue to allow the use of the older two-letter codes, and the ever-present possibility that the alternative IANA language tags might also be used.

Example – Describe a Country

Just as we previously created a `Currency` element to describe various aspects of a specific currency, we'll also create a `Country` element to record information that is limited to a specific nation. As before, we will wrap the one or more `Country` elements in a `Countries` parent element:

```
<xs:element name="Country" >
    <xs:complexType>
        <xs:attribute name="code"      type="iso3166_CountryCode"    use="required" />
        <xs:attribute name="currency"  type="iso4217_Currency"       use="required" />
        <xs:attribute name="langs"     type="rfc3066_LanguageCodes"  use="required" />
        <xs:attribute name="multilang" type="xs:boolean"             default="false" />
        <xs:attribute name="name"      type="xs:string"              use="required" />
    </xs:complexType>
</xs:element>

<xs:element name="Countries" >
    <xs:complexType>
        <xs:sequence>
            <xs:element ref="Country" maxOccurs="unbounded" />
        </xs:sequence>
    </xs:complexType>
</xs:element>
```

As before, we've declared `Country` to be an empty element, using an anonymous complex type; and made a `Countries` container element to group information for one or more `Country` elements. Its attributes include the usual code, which is used as a unique ID to link to a specific country, the official currency, a list of languages (official, plus some others for illustrative purposes), and the name of the country. The other attribute (`multilang`) is a little cryptic, but it's intended to be used in conjunction with `langs` as a signal that the country is officially multi-lingual. If true, all listed languages should be used for packing labels and other commercial documents, else just the first language in the list should be used. Otherwise, this list of languages is primarily documentary information.

A valid XML data instance that conforms to this schema snippet (and uses all of the code datatypes we created in this section) is as follows:

```
<Countries>
   <Country code="BVI" currency="USD" langs="en-GB"
                                      name="British Virgin Islands" />
   <Country code="CAN" currency="CAD" langs="en-CA fr-CA" multilang="true"
                                      name="Canada" />
   <Country code="CHN" currency="CNY" langs="cn i-hakka"  name="China" />
   <Country code="FRA" currency="EUR" langs="fr"          name="France" />
   <Country code="DEU" currency="EUR" langs="de"          name="Germany" />
   <Country code="GBR" currency="GBP" langs="en-GB"       name="Great Britain" />
   <Country code="ITA" currency="EUR" langs="it"          name="Italy" />
   <Country code="JPN" currency="JPY" langs="jp"          name="Japan" />
   <Country code="MEX" currency="MXP" langs="es-MX"       name="Mexico" />
   <Country code="PRI" currency="USD" langs="es"          name="Puerto Rico" />
   <Country code="ZAF" currency="ZAR" langs="en-ZA afr xho zul bnt"
                                      name="South Africa" />
   <Country code="USA" currency="USD" langs="en-US es chr alg i-navajo apa"
                                      name="United States of America" />
   <Country code="VIR" currency="USD" langs="en-US" name="US Virgin Islands" />
</Countries>
```

Later in this chapter, we will construct some other datatypes, such as postal addresses, that are also country-specific. These will generally use an attribute of the `iso3166_CountryCode` type to refer to this "table". Such a reference could be used to provide a string containing the name of the country for a mailing label or similar address, to select the appropriate language for some output document, and/or to choose the appropriate currency for a transaction with a party in that country.

Now that we've created some simple standard code-based datatypes, let's move on to that other worldwide standard, the Internet.

Internet Datatypes

In addition to language codes, XML Schema has provided some other datatypes that represent standard Internet data structures and protocols, such as `anyURI` and `base64Binary`. We will create some new datatypes for some of the components of these, including numeric **IP addresses** and their symbolic **Domain Name Service** (**DNS**) counterparts. We'll also derive some types that restrict the subject data to a specific URI scheme, such as the familiar WWW hypertext (`http:`) or e-mail address (`mailto:`) schemes.

IP Addresses

There are now two types of IP addresses that are of interest: the current 32-bit address format (known as **IPv4**, the fourth version of IP addresses); and the new 128-bit **IPv6** addresses that are the future of Internet addressing.

> *IPv6 addresses are defined in **RFC 2373: IP Version 6 Addressing Architecture** [1998-07] at http://www.ietf.org/rfc/rfc2373.txt. Their use in URIs is described in **RFC 2732: Format for Literal IPv6 Addresses in URL's** [sic] [1999-12] at http://www.ietf.org/rfc/rfc2732.txt.*

IPv4 addresses are usually represented as a familiar "dotted-quad" string of decimal digits. These addresses can also be represented in other number bases, such as octal, but we will ignore these alternative forms in this chapter. For example, the following URL shows the use of a numeric IP v4 address:

```
<url>http://138.80.11.31:80/index.html</url>
```

Note that the number after the colon (80) is not part of the IP address, but is rather the port number portion of the URL.

The regular expression pattern that describes a generic numeric dotted-quad is fairly simple:

```
<xs:simpleType name="dottedQuad">
   <xs:restriction base="xs:string">
      <xs:pattern value="([0-9]*\.){3}[0-9]*" />
   </xs:restriction>
</xs:simpleType>
```

In reality, the individual numbers between the dots are limited to 3 digits, since each represents an 8-bit value (0 to 255). Four such values can be concatenated to provide a 32-bit address. Let's redo the pattern to make it a bit less permissive:

```
<xs:simpleType name="dotted3DigitQuad">
   <xs:restriction base="xs:string">
      <xs:pattern value="([0-9]{1,3}\.){3}[0-9]{1,3}" />
   </xs:restriction>
</xs:simpleType>
```

This new pattern allows each number to be from one to three ASCII digits. This still permits some illegal values (such as 321.999.1.42, where the first two numbers are out-of-range for IP addresses). We can make one more revision to the pattern to yield a regex that will constrain our dotted-quad to use 3-digit numbers in the range 0 to 255, thus producing a viable, if slightly verbose, ipv4_Address datatype:

```
<xs:simpleType name="ipv4_Address">
   <xs:restriction base="xs:string">
     <xs:pattern
         value="(([0-9]{1,2} | [1][0-9]{2} | [2][0-4][0-9] | [2][5][0-5])\.){3}
                 ([0-9]{1,2} | [1][0-9]{2} | [2][0-4][0-9] | [2][5][0-5])" />
   </xs:restriction>
</xs:simpleType>
```

Note: The `pattern` values shown in the above examples include some whitespace for clarity that is *not* permitted in a real XML Schema – be sure to remove all whitespace within these values before using this datatype (or just use the properly-formatted file from Wrox's web site, named `ProSchemas.IP_Address.xsd`).

Although various address pooling schemes have lessened the urgency, the IPv4 address space is almost completely exhausted and must be expanded. The solution, IPv6 addresses, is the future of the Internet. They can also have multiple representations, but there is one simple form that is most generically useful, upon which we will focus. Like an IPv4 dotted-quad, the 128 bits of an IPv6 are represented as a series of numbers separated by, in this case, colon (:) characters. Since we must encode rather large (128-bit) values, it is most convenient to break them into eight 4-digit hex numbers, each representing 16-bit values:

```
<url>http://[FEDC:BA98:7654:3210:FEDC:BA98:7654:3210]/index.html</url>
```

As with the port number string (:80) in the previous IPv4 example, the square bracket delimiters are part of the URI format, not the IPv6 address.

IPv6 addresses are easier to describe using a simple regex, than the shorter IPv4 addresses:

```
<xs:simpleType name="ipv6_Address">
   <xs:restriction base="xs:string">
      <xs:pattern value="([A-Fa-f0-9]{1,4}:){7}[A-Fa-f0-9]{1,4}" />
   </xs:restriction>
</xs:simpleType>
```

This pattern allows seven 1 to 4 digit hex numbers followed by a single colon (:), and ending with the eighth hex number.

We will use these datatypes later as part of the basis for some specific URI datatypes.

Domain Names

A simplistic validation test for domain names that are limited to the traditional six "top-level" domains is as follows:

```
<xs:simpleType name="ip_DomainName">
   <xs:restriction base="xs:string">
      <xs:pattern value="(((([A-Za-z0-9])|([A-Za-z0-9][A-Za-z0-9\-]*
                [A-Za-z0-9]))\.)+(com|edu|gov|mil|net|org)" />
   </xs:restriction>
</xs:simpleType>
```

Strictly speaking, the top-level part of a domain name can be any alphanumeric string, possibly including embedded hyphen character(s), and beginning with an upper- or lowercase ASCII letter.

```
<xs:simpleType name="ip_DomainName">
   <xs:restriction base="xs:string">
      <xs:pattern value="([A-Za-z0-9\-]+[A-Za-z0-9]\.)+
                    ([A-Za-z]([A-Za-z0-9\-]+[A-Za-z0-9])" />
   </xs:restriction>
</xs:simpleType>
```

159

Indeed, there have been recent additions to the six top-level domains that would not be permitted by the first of these patterns. Also, there have always been several alternate forms of domain names that don't fit the simple `foo.bar.com` pattern. For example, some domain names use a country specific form of the generic domain name (such as `www.mexicoweb.com.mx`), and others omit all of the common top-level names in favor of a geography-based domain name (such as `wyldweb.state.wy.us` or `www.bbc.co.uk`). We could extend the domain name pattern to include these kinds of domain names, but this exercise is left to the reader.

One of the most common and visible uses of domain names is within URLs, a concrete subset of URIs.

Uniform Resource Identifiers

One of the innovations of the WWW is its use of a simple text-based resource reference scheme – the **Uniform Resource Identifier** (**URI**), and extension of the earlier **Uniform Resource Locator** (**URL**). Several RFCs, written over a period of five years, have defined and refined the specifications for these special strings.

> *URIs are defined in RFC 2396: Uniform Resource Identifiers (URI): Generic Syntax [1998-08] at http://www.ietf.org/rfc/rfc2396.txt, which updates URLs as defined in RFCs 1738 and 1808, is amended by RFC 2732, and refers to RFC 2141.*
>
> *The concrete (URL) form is defined in two different RFCs: RFC 1738: Uniform Resource Locators (URL) [1994-12] at http://www.ietf.org/rfc/rfc1738.txt and RFC 1808: Relative Uniform Resource Locators [1995-06] at http://www.ietf.org/rfc/rfc1808.txt. The abstract form of a URI is a Uniform Resource Name, defined in RFC 2141: URN Syntax [1997-05], and available at http://www.ietf.org/rfc/rfc2141.txt.*

URNs have great potential in the world of XML applications, but we will focus upon the much more commonly used URLs.

All URIs must begin with a so-called "scheme", which determines the subsequent format of the URI. The basic format of a scheme name is:

```
<xs:simpleType name="uri_Scheme">
   <xs:restriction base="xs:string">
      <xs:pattern value="[A-Za-z]([A-Za-z0-9\+\-\.])*" />
   </xs:restriction>
</xs:simpleType>
```

Instead of allowing generic scheme names, we will only include a few of the more common ones in our examples:

```
<xs:simpleType name="uri_Scheme">
   <xs:restriction base="xs:string">
      <xs:enumeration value="ftp" />       <!-- File Transfer Protocol -->
      <xs:enumeration value="http" />      <!-- Hypertext Transfer Protocol -->
      <xs:enumeration value="mailto" />    <!-- E-mail address -->
      <xs:enumeration value="news" />      <!-- USENET newsgroup name -->
      <xs:enumeration value="telnet" />    <!-- TELNET protocol access -->
      <xs:enumeration value="urn" />       <!-- Uniform Resource Name (URN) -->
   </xs:restriction>
</xs:simpleType>
```

We can use an XML Schema union datatype to allow any of these three formats for data, typed as uri_Host. This way we can build structures based upon either an IP address or domain name, without worrying about which version we're using:

```
<xs:simpleType name="uri_Host">
   <xs:union memberTypes="ipv4_Address ipv6_Address ip_DomainName" />
</xs:simpleType>
```

The characters used in the path portion of a URL are limited:

```
<xs:simpleType name="uri_PathChars">
   <xs:restriction base="xs:string" >
      <xs:pattern value="((([A-Za-z0-9\-_\.!~\*&#x2D;\(\):@&#26;=\+$,/])
                        | ([%][A-Fa-f0-9]{2}))+ " />
   </xs:restriction>
</xs:simpleType>
```

A few more characters are used for the fragment and query parts of the URL:

```
<xs:simpleType name="uri_FragChars">
   <xs:restriction base="xs:string" >
      <xs:pattern value="([A-Za-z0-9\-_\.!~\*&#x2D;\(\):@&#26;=\+$,;/\?])+" />
   </xs:restriction>
</xs:simpleType>
```

Universal Resource Locators (URLs)

These four new datatypes are used in conjunction with a built-in datatype (nonNegativeInteger) to encode the six major parts of a URL (of which, only the scheme, host, and a simple path are required):

```
<xs:complexType name="url" >
   <xs:sequence>
      <xs:element name="Scheme" type="uri_Scheme" />
      <xs:element name="Host"   type="uri_Host" />
      <xs:element name="Port"   type="xs:nonNegativeInteger" minOccurs="0" />
      <xs:element name="Path"   type="uri_PathChars" />
      <xs:element name="Frag"   type="uri_FragChars" minOccurs="0" />
      <xs:element name="Query"  type="uri_FragChars" minOccurs="0" />
   </xs:sequence>
</xs:complexType>

<xs:element name="URL" type="url" />
```

Some examples of XML data that conform to this datatype include:

```
<URL>
   <Scheme>http</Scheme>
   <Host>www.w3.org</Host>
   <Port>80</Port>
   <Path>/TR/xmlschema-0</Path>
   <Frag>Intro</Frag>
</URL>
```

```
<URL>
   <Scheme>http</Scheme>
   <Host>www.google.com</Host>
   <Path>/search</Path>
   <Query>q=foo</Query>
</URL>
```

The first instance, properly formatted as a URL, would be: http://www.w3.org/TR/xmlschema-0/#Intro, while the second is http://www.google.com/search?q=foo.

e-mail Addresses (mailto:)

e-mail addresses are much older than the now more-familiar URLs. Since the advent of URIs, e-mail addresses are treated as instances of the `mailto` URI scheme.

> The `mailto` URI scheme is defined in **RFC 2368: The mailto URI scheme** *[1998-07] at http://www.ietf.org/rfc/rfc2368.txt, which updates RFCs 1738 and 1808.*

A very simple set of constraints is all that is needed to describe *singular* e-mail addresses:

```
<xs:simpleType name="mailto_Name" >
   <xs:restriction base="xs:string" >
      <xs:pattern value="([&#x21;-&#x7E; -[@,;:"\.\[\]\(\)\\&#x3C;&#x3E;]])*"/>
   </xs:restriction>
</xs:simpleType>

<xs:complexType name="uri_mailto" >
   <xs:sequence>
      <xs:element name="Name" type="mailto_Name" />
      <xs:element name="Host" type="uri_Host" />
   </xs:sequence>
</xs:complexType>

<xs:element name="Mailto" type="uri_mailto" />
```

The `pattern` value for the `mailto_Name` datatype uses a character class subtraction expression, which allows any "printable" ASCII character (that is, the range ! - ~), *minus* the characters listed in the latter portion ([@,;:"\.\[\]\(\)\\<>]). This disallows the following 13 characters: @ , ; : " . [ ] ( ) \ < > using meta-character escapes and character references, as needed.

Here is an example of an XML data instance that uses this datatype:

```
<Mailto>
   <Name>errata</Name>
   <Host>wrox.com</Host>
</Mailto>
```

Both the URI scheme and account-host separator character are constant string literals, so a formatted version of the above `Mailto` element would appear like so:

```
mailto://errata@wrox.com
```

Now let's look at some less technical, more human datatypes.

People

Company names are rarely divided into multiple elements, since the only common part is a legalistic suffix like "Inc.", "Ltd.", or "GmBH". However, people can often be classified on the basis of their names. Indeed, most directories of personal names are sorted by the so-called "last name" (or more properly, "family name").

Names

Human names can quickly become a very complicated subject. For instance, it is common to use only a single name in some cultures and countries (such as Brazil or Indonesia), while in the Anglophone parts of the world a person usually uses both given and family names, plus maybe one or two middle names. Other places (like the Iberian Peninsula and Latin America) may use rather long names that concatenate several generations of family and given names together, with a short (one or three name) form chosen from the entire list.

Another consideration is the presentation sequence of a name – in many Asian countries, names are typically shown in the "Family Given" order, while the opposite is common in Europe and the Americas.

> *The common use of "First Name" and "Last Name" as names for these elements reflects a Euro-centric bias that is possibly best avoided in international systems and trade, since it does not accurately reflect the several alternate forms of human names.*

Lastly, we will often want to include a personal title (such as "Dr.", "Mr.", "Frau", "Sra.", etc.) as part of a name, or the name may have a suffix such as "Jr." or "VIII" to denote some kind of generational label.

We will define a datatype that uses simple strings for these various parts of a person's name (see `ProSchemas.Person.xsd` in the download):

```xml
<xs:element name="PersonName" >
    <xs:complexType>
        <xs:choice>
            <xs:element name="SingleName"  type="xs:string" />
            <xs:sequence>
                <xs:element name="Prefix"     type="xs:string" minOccurs="0" />
                <xs:element name="GivenName"  type="xs:string" />
                <xs:element name="MiddleName" type="xs:string"
                            minOccurs="0" maxOccurs="unbounded" />
                <xs:element name="FamilyName" type="xs:string" />
                <xs:element name="Suffix"     type="xs:string" minOccurs="0" />
            </xs:sequence>
        </xs:choice>
    </xs:complexType>
</xs:element>
```

Some examples of XML data that conform to this datatype include:

```xml
<PersonName>
    <Prefix>Mr</Prefix>
    <GivenName>John</GivenName>
    <MiddleName>Q</MiddleName>
    <FamilyName>Public</FamilyName>
    <Suffix>Jr</Suffix>
</PersonName>
```

```
<PersonName>
    <GivenName>Jane</GivenName>
    <FamilyName>Doe</FamilyName>
</PersonName>
```

```
<PersonName>
    <SingleName>Madonna</SingleName>
</PersonName>
```

There is another bit of personal data that is even more personal than one's name.

Gender

Something as simple as the traditional male-female dichotomy does seem to lend itself to a special datatype – or does it? We could treat this kind of data as a simple Boolean variable named "female", with the false value implying "male" (no chauvinism intended!). However, what happens when we don't know an individual's gender? Treat all unknown cases as female? Probably not! We will at least want to add a value for "unknown", thus causing us to discard the simplistic Boolean approach.

We could use an Anglophone-centric approach, and label the genders "M" for male, and "F" for female. Of course, this makes little sense to those who don't think in English. The ISO has addressed this with yet another standard, using simple integer code numbers for the three choices we've already mentioned, plus a fourth option ("Not Specified", though we're unable to explain why the ISO felt it was important to distinguish this from "Not Known").

> *The ISO standard for human genders is **ISO 5218:1977 Information interchange --***
> ***Representation of human sexes**, available in printed form at http://www.iso.ch/. Numerous*
> *unofficial references provide documentation of the four values used, and there really isn't much else*
> *to this standard!*

The ISO 5218 specification takes great pains to assert that there is no gender bias implied by designating men as "1" and women as "2", though the author would argue that the reverse would have made more sense from a biological perspective. We can make a simple XML Schema datatype that can be used to validate these gender codes:

```
<xs:simpleType name="iso5218_GenderCode">
    <xs:restriction base="xs:nonNegativeInteger">
        <xs:enumeration value="0" />    <!-- Not Known -->
        <xs:enumeration value="1" />    <!-- Male -->
        <xs:enumeration value="2" />    <!-- Female -->
        <xs:enumeration value="9" />    <!-- Not Specified -->
    </xs:restriction>
</xs:simpleType>
```

Some people get a funny look when one mentions that the ISO has designated four different values for human gender, but in the real world there are at least *five* possible genders (plus the two unknown/unspecified values). Sadly, this often becomes a political and cultural minefield, but there is a consensus among medical doctors, psychologists, and sexologists that we should add at least three more gender codes to the ISO 5218 set.

```
<xs:simpleType name="realworld_GenderCode">
    <xs:restriction base="xs:nonNegativeInteger">
        <xs:enumeration value="0" />    <!-- Not Known -->
        <xs:enumeration value="1" />    <!-- Male -->
        <xs:enumeration value="2" />    <!-- Female -->
        <xs:enumeration value="3" />    <!-- Male-to-Female Transsexual -->
        <xs:enumeration value="4" />    <!-- Female-to-Male Transsexual -->
        <xs:enumeration value="5" />    <!-- True Neuter -->
        <xs:enumeration value="9" />    <!-- Not Specified -->
    </xs:restriction>
</xs:simpleType>
```

Let's not hold our breath that the ISO will acknowledge this reality any time soon; this second datatype is presented as a suggestion for those who deal with medical and other personal information databases that must make these distinctions.

Telephone Numbers

No matter what our gender, we are likely to want to speak with other people on the telephone. Names and telephone numbers are arguably the most ubiquitous database around – almost everyone keeps a personal phone directory.

We can describe telephone numbers, in the simplest terms, as non-negative integers that have seven or ten digits, which always begin with a digit in the range 2 through 9, but never 0 or 1 (which are reserved for operator, international dialing, and other access codes):

```
<xs:simpleType name="nanp_GenericPhoneNumber">
    <xs:restriction base="xs:positiveInteger">
        <xs:pattern value="[2-9](([0-9]{6})|([0-9]{9}))" />
    </xs:restriction>
</xs:simpleType>

<xs:element name="PhoneNumber" type="nanp_GenericPhoneNumber" />
```

A scrap of XML data that conforms to this description might look something like this:

```
<PhoneNumber>3135551212</PhoneNumber>
```

Since this simple datatype requires telephone numbers to be truly numeric, we can't use whitespace or any of the common separator characters such as a slash (/), a hyphen or dash (-), and/or a period or full-stop (.). We also cannot use alphanumeric phone "numbers", such as "1-800-CALL-ATT" or "1-800-FLOWERS". Furthermore, different numbering systems apply different constraints upon phone numbers, so let's look at some specific kinds of these.

Telephone numbers in the United States, Canada, Bermuda, and some Caribbean countries use the **North American Numbering Plan** (**NANP**). In the NANP, each phone number is comprised of three parts: the three-digit Area Code (also known as the "NPA" number), the three-digit Exchange number (in Telco-speak, the "NXX"), and the four-digit local number (that used to be the only number one needed to dial – ah, progress!). Each of these is subject to some further constraints.

For more about North American telephone numbers and Area Codes, see the NANP Administration website at http://www.nanpa.com/.

Let's create a more precise pattern for North American telephone numbers, using the modern "999", "999/999-9999", or "999.999.9999" formats, as well as the technically improper (but commonly used) "(999) 999-9999" format:

```
<xs:simpleType name="nanp_PhoneNumber">
   <xs:restriction base="xs:string">
      <xs:pattern value="([2-9]11) | ([2-9][0-9]{2}/[0-9]{3}-[0-9]{4})
                       | ([2-9][0-9]{2}\. [0-9]{3}\. [0-9]{4})
                       | (\([2-9][0-9]{2}\) [0-9]{3}-[0-9]{4})" />
   </xs:restriction>
</xs:simpleType>
```

Given this definition (and assuming an `element` declaration that uses the new datatype), the phone number from our previous XML data example would need to be changed to one of these forms:

```
<PhoneNumber>313/555-1212</PhoneNumber>
<PhoneNumber>313.555.1212</PhoneNumber>
```

This inclusion of presentation information (the slash and dash) does run counter to the basic XML philosophy that data structure and presentation should be separate. Let's back up and take a different approach to this. The following datatypes will use a combination of simple and complex types, and XML elements to segregate the three components of a NANP telephone number, plus an "extension" (which can be almost any string of ASCII numeric digits dialed after a connection is made):

```
<xs:simpleType name="nanp_NXX" >
   <xs:restriction base="xs:positiveInteger" >
      <xs:pattern value="[2-9][0-9]{2}" />    <!-- Phone# cannot begin with 0/1 -->
   </xs:restriction>
</xs:simpleType>

<xs:simpleType name="nanp_N11" >   <!-- see explanation in text below -->
   <xs:restriction base="xs:positiveInteger" >
      <xs:pattern value="[2-9]11" />   <!-- N11 phone# cannot begin with 0/1 -->
   </xs:restriction>
</xs:simpleType>

<xs:simpleType name="nanp_XXXX" >
   <xs:restriction base="xs:nonNegativeInteger" >
      <xs:pattern value="[0-9]{4}" />
   </xs:restriction>
</xs:simpleType>

<xs:simpleType name="nanp_Ext" >
   <xs:restriction base="xs:nonNegativeInteger" >
      <xs:pattern value="[0-9]*" />
   </xs:restriction>
</xs:simpleType>

<xs:complexType name="nanp_PhoneNumber_verbose" >
   <xs:choice>
      <xs:sequence>
```

```
            <xs:element name="AreaCode" type="nanp_NXX" />
            <xs:element name="Exchange" type="nanp_NXX" />
            <xs:element name="LocalNum" type="nanp_XXXX" />
            <xs:element name="Extension" type="nanp_Ext" minOccurs="0" />
        </xs:sequence>
        <xs:element name="N11Code" type="nanp_N11" />
    </xs:choice>
</xs:complexType>
```

Note: the old rule that "the second digit of an Area Code cannot be a 0 or 1" is no longer valid, and so this element now shares the same datatype as the local exchange (nanp_NXX).

This revised datatype requires a more verbose representation of telephone numbers (we'll just assume that we've declared a PhoneNumber element that now uses the nanp_PhoneNumber_verbose datatype):

```
<PhoneNumber>
    <AreaCode>313</AreaCode>
    <Exchange>555</Exchange>
    <LocalNum>1212</LocalNum>
</PhoneNumber>
```

Alternatively, a 3-digit Service Code (also known as an **N11 Code**), such as "411" or "911" may be used in place of a full US phone number:

```
<PhoneNumber>
    <N11Code>611</N11Code>
</PhoneNumber>
```

This additional structure might be considered overkill, but it does accurately represent the phone number from both a network and a geographic perspective. Automated dialers can optimize call routing based upon area code and exchange numbers. These also provide rudimentary geographic information, including the locations of fixed central offices and approximate distances between them (and thus between different areas and local exchanges). Presentation of the telephone number can now use whichever format is required by local custom or stylistic concerns.

We have also moved from the days of multiple people sharing a single party-line phone to each person having more than one phone, and a possible multitude of phone numbers. We'll also create a simple datatype that attempts to define the various descriptive labels that we might want to attach to a phone number:

```
<xs:simpleType name="phoneType" >
    <xs:restriction base="xs:string">
        <xs:enumeration value="HOME" />
        <xs:enumeration value="WORK" />
        <xs:enumeration value="CELL" />
        <xs:enumeration value="FAX" />
        <xs:enumeration value="PAGER" />
        <xs:enumeration value="BBS" />
    </xs:restriction>
</xs:simpleType>
```

Assuming that we add a type attribute to the PhoneNumber element, an instance of our complex datatype version would look like this:

```
<PhoneNumber type="WORK">
    <AreaCode>313</AreaCode>
    <Exchange>555</Exchange>
    <LocalNum>1212</LocalNum>
</PhoneNumber>
```

Of course, if we wanted to use this same attribute in the earlier version of `PhoneNumber`, it would require that we change the definition of that datatype from simple to complex, since elements declared to be simple datatypes couldn't use attributes.

Now let's look at another of the typical data structures associated with persons and companies.

Postal Addresses

A postal address is typically represented in three or four (or maybe more) lines, each of which may have some additional subdivisions. These include:

❑   Name of the addressee (*not* included in our address datatypes, since it's shared with other datatypes)

❑   Street address (usually includes a number and street name, and maybe some other information)

❑   City (town, village, or other locality)

❑   State (the US has 50, plus a single District, several Territories and some other USPS postal destinations – Mexico has 31 States and a single District, while Canada is divided into 10 Provinces and 3 Territories)

❑   ZIP Code (specific to the US – Great Britain uses "postcodes", and other countries often use generically-named "postal codes")

❑   Country

The simplest form of a US postal address is a collection of five child elements that are simple strings:

```
<xs:complexType name="postalAddress">
    <xs:sequence>
        <xs:element name="Street"   type="xs:string" maxOccurs="4" />
        <xs:element name="City"     type="xs:string" />
        <xs:element name="State"    type="xs:string" />
        <xs:element name="ZIP"      type="xs:string" />
        <xs:element name="Country"  type="xs:string" />
    </xs:sequence>
</xs:complexType>

<xs:element name="Address" type="postalAddress" />
```

We have allowed a maximum of four separate elements for the street address, since it isn't restricted to a single line, and often requires additional lines for an apartment number, building name, Post Office Box number, etc.

A couple of examples of this simple address format (assuming an `Address` element was defined using the `postalAddress` datatype as above) include:

```
<Address>
   <Street>710 Tenth Street</Street>
   <Street>Suite 100</Street>
   <City>Golden</City>
   <State>CO</State>
   <ZIP>80401</ZIP>
   <Country>USA</Country>
</Address>

<Address>
   <Street>POB 57</Street>
   <City>Moose</City>
   <State>WY</State>
   <ZIP>83012</ZIP>
   <Country>USA</Country>
</Address>
```

While this simple address format is quite adequate for many uses, it is sometimes useful to have some of the above information broken-down into smaller units for mass mailings, to more precisely describe specific locations, or to be able to correlate an address to some geographic datum like a voting district or other bounded area.

We will look at some more detailed representations of street addresses, some standard coding systems that can be used with postal addresses, and some implications for international addresses.

Street Addresses

As we just saw, the simplest way to tag street addresses uses a single `Street` element for each line of an address (excluding the codified data like state or postal code). Sometimes, however, we will need a more detailed division of the various relatively standard parts of a street address, perhaps for a messaging application:

```
<xs:complexType name="msgtype_PostalAddress" >
   <xs:sequence>
      <xs:element name="Street">
         <xs:complexType>
            <xs:attribute name="bldg"  type="xs:string" />
            <xs:attribute name="room"  type="xs:string" />
            <xs:attribute name="num"   type="xs:string" />
            <xs:attribute name="dir"   type="xs:string" />
            <xs:attribute name="name"  type="xs:string" use="required" />
            <xs:attribute name="type"  type="xs:string" />
            <xs:attribute name="quad"  type="xs:string" />
            <xs:attribute name="suite" type="xs:string" />
            <xs:attribute name="apt"   type="xs:string" />
         </xs:complexType>
      </xs:element>
      <xs:element name="PostOffice">
         <xs:complexType>
            <xs:attribute name="city"   type="xs:string" use="required" />
            <xs:attribute name="region" type="xs:string" />
            <xs:attribute name="code"   type="xs:string" use="required" />
            <xs:attribute name="country" type="iso3166_CountryCode"
                                          use="required" />
```

```
            </xs:complexType>
        </xs:element>
      </xs:sequence>
  </xs:complexType>

  <xs:element name="PostalAddress" type="msgtype_PostalAddress" />
```

A US address that uses this datatype structure would look like this:

```
<PostalAddress>
    <Street num="710" name="10th" type="ST" suite="100" />
    <PostOffice city="Golden" region="CO" code="80401" country=USA" />
</PostalAddress>
```

We'll revisit this datatype near the end of the chapter, when we show some examples of internationalized addresses.

Regions

Most countries are sub-divided into regions of some kind or another. These might be called "states" or "provinces" or "districts", but they all represent a political unit that can be used in a postal address (among other things). Often, the national postal authority will devise a set of standard abbreviations for these regions. In addition to simplifying mail routing, these are usually much more compact than their textual equivalents. The use of a limited and controlled vocabulary of these codes also improves the reliability of other address data, since misspelled or otherwise invalid values are rejected by the XML parser (in conjunction with our schema).

> *The Universal Postal Union (UPU) is an institution of the United Nations, based in Switzerland. It sets standards for international postal services, including postage rates and addressing formats. The latter are described for the 189 member nations at:*
> *http://www.upu.org/ap/layout.startup?p_language=AN&p_theme=addrsyst&p_content_ url=/ap/postcode.choice?p_language=AN.*
>
> *Alternatively, just go to the home page at http://www.upu.org, and click on "Postal Addresses".*

Canada is divided into 10 Provinces and 3 Territories. The following is an excerpt from the schema that represents these (ProSchemas.CAN_ProvinceCode.xsd):

```
<xs:simpleType name="can_ProvinceCode" >
   <xs:restriction base="xs:string" >
        ...<!-- More lines go here -->
      <xs:enumeration value="MB" />    <!-- Manitoba -->
      <xs:enumeration value="NB" />    <!-- New Brunswick -->
      <xs:enumeration value="NF" />    <!-- Newfoundland -->
      <xs:enumeration value="NT" />    <!-- Northwest Territories -->
      <xs:enumeration value="NS" />    <!-- Nova Scotia -->
      <xs:enumeration value="NU" />    <!-- Nunavut -->
      <xs:enumeration value="ON" />    <!-- Ontario -->
      <xs:enumeration value="PE" />    <!-- Prince Edward Island -->
      <xs:enumeration value="QC" />    <!-- Québec -->
      <xs:enumeration value="SK" />    <!-- Saskatchewan -->
          ...<!-- More lines go here -->
   </xs:restriction>
</xs:simpleType>
```

Great Britain has dozens of postcode areas, which could also be part of a hideous regular expression to validate the first two characters of the postcode (see the next section). The following is an excerpt from the complete schema list representation (see: `ProSchemas.GBR_PostcodeArea.xsd`, available with the download for this book):

```
<xs:simpleType name="gbr_PostcodeArea">
   <xs:restriction base="xs:string">
        ...<!-- More lines go here -->
     <xs:enumeration value="KT" />     <!-- Kingston Upon Thames -->
     <xs:enumeration value="KW" />     <!-- Kirkwall -->
     <xs:enumeration value="KY" />     <!-- Kirkcaldy -->
     <xs:enumeration value="L" />      <!-- Liverpool -->
     <xs:enumeration value="LA" />     <!-- Lancaster -->
     <xs:enumeration value="LD" />     <!-- Llandrindod Wells -->
     <xs:enumeration value="LE" />     <!-- Leicester -->
     <xs:enumeration value="LL" />     <!-- Llandudno -->
     <xs:enumeration value="LN" />     <!-- Lincoln -->
     <xs:enumeration value="LS" />     <!-- Leeds -->
        ...<!-- More lines go here -->
   </xs:restriction>
</xs:simpleType>
```

Mexico has 31 States and a single District. The following is an excerpt from the schema file that represents these (`ProSchemas.MEX_StateCode.xsd`):

```
<xs:simpleType name="mex_StateCode">
   <xs:restriction base="xs:string">
        ...<!-- More lines go here -->
     <xs:enumeration value="JAL" />      <!-- Jalisco -->
     <xs:enumeration value="MEX" />      <!-- México -->
     <xs:enumeration value="MICH" />     <!-- Michoacán de Ocampo -->
     <xs:enumeration value="MOR" />      <!-- Morelos -->
     <xs:enumeration value="NAY" />      <!-- Nayarit -->
     <xs:enumeration value="NL" />       <!-- Nuevo Léon -->
     <xs:enumeration value="OAX" />      <!-- Oaxaca -->
     <xs:enumeration value="PUE" />      <!-- Puebla -->
     <xs:enumeration value="QRO" />      <!-- Querétaro Arteaga -->
     <xs:enumeration value="QROO" />     <!-- Quintana Roo -->
        ...<!-- More lines go here -->
   </xs:restriction>
</xs:simpleType>
```

The US has 50 States, plus a single District, several Territories and some other extra-territorial (but still served by the USPS) postal destinations. The following is an excerpt from the representative schema (`ProSchemas.USA_StateCode.xsd`):

```
<xs:simpleType name="usa_StateCode" >
   <xs:restriction base="xs:string" >
        ...<!-- More lines go here -->
     <xs:enumeration value="MH" />     <!-- Marshall Islands -->
     <xs:enumeration value="MD" />     <!-- Maryland -->
     <xs:enumeration value="MA" />     <!-- Massachusetts -->
     <xs:enumeration value="MI" />     <!-- Michigan -->
     <xs:enumeration value="MN" />     <!-- Minnesota -->
```

```
          <xs:enumeration value="MS" />    <!-- Mississippi -->
          <xs:enumeration value="MO" />    <!-- Missouri -->
          <xs:enumeration value="MT" />    <!-- Montana -->
          <xs:enumeration value="NE" />    <!-- Nebraska -->
          <xs:enumeration value="NV" />    <!-- Nevada -->
                 ...<!-- More lines go here -->
      </xs:restriction>
  </xs:simpleType>
```

Postal Codes

Many countries use numeric or alphanumeric postal codes to improve mail-sorting efficiency. These have the side effect of being much more compact in many cases than their textual equivalent. In some cases, a portion of a postal code may have a unique relation with another part of the address, so the more verbose part can be omitted and automatically generated from the postal code.

Canadian postal codes are two fixed-length (3-character) codes separated by a single space:

```
<xs:simpleType name="can_PostalCode" >    <!-- "xnx nxn" -->
   <xs:restriction base="xs:string" >
       <xs:length value="7" />    <!-- 6 alphanumeric chars + 1 space -->
       <xs:pattern value="[A-Z][0-9][A-Z] [0-9][A-Z][0-9]" />
   </xs:restriction>
</xs:simpleType>
```

British postal codes are also comprised of two codes separated by a single space – the first code may be between two to four characters, whilst the latter's length is fixed at three characters:

```
<xs:simpleType name="gbr_Postcode" >
<!-- "AA99 9XX"/"A9 9XX"/"A99 9XX"/"AA9 9XX" -->
   <xs:restriction base="xs:string" >    <!-- "AA" is postcode area (town) -->
       <xs:pattern value="(([A-Z]{2}[0-9]{2})|([A-Z][0-9])|
                  ([A-Z][0-9]{2})|([A-Z]{2}[0-9])) ([0-9][A-Z]{2})" />
   </xs:restriction>
</xs:simpleType>
```

Mexican postal codes are simple five-digit numbers, with the first two digits representing a region, followed by three digits for zone and locality:

```
<xs:simpleType name="mex_PostalCode" >    <!-- "nnnnn" -->
   <xs:restriction base="xs:positiveInteger" >
       <xs:length value="5" />
   </xs:restriction>
</xs:simpleType>
```

Five-digit ZIP (Zone Improvement Plan) codes were created in the early 1960s by the USPS in order to improve mail sorting and delivery systems. In 1983, these codes were extended to form ZIP+4 Codes, which added four additional digits to help more precisely (in many cases, uniquely) locate a delivery address. Thus, a current definition of a ZIP code allows both regular and ZIP+4 codes:

```
<xs:simpleType name="usa_ZIP">    <!-- "nnnnn" or "nnnnn-nnnn" -->
   <xs:restriction base="xs:positiveInteger">
       <xs:pattern value="[0-9]{5}(-[0-9]{4})?" />
   </xs:restriction>
</xs:simpleType>
```

All of our examples will use the shorter ZIP code, but a properly formatted ZIP+4 code would also be accepted as valid.

The postalAddress Datatype – Revised

Now that we've added these more specific datatypes, we need to change to definition of the `postalAddress` datatype to include these new types. At the same time, we'll use our earlier `iso3166_CountryCode` datatype for the country and move it to an attribute.

First, we'll need to add some more datatypes that collect country-specific codes into union datatypes. Remember that union datatypes are those whose value spaces and lexical spaces are the union of the value spaces and lexical spaces of two or more other datatypes.

```xml
<xs:simpleType name="union.PostalRegion">
    <xs:union memberTypes="can_ProvinceCode gbr_PostcodeArea mex_StateCode
usa_StateCode"/>
</xs:simpleType>

<xs:simpleType name="union.PostalCode">
    <xs:union memberTypes="can_PostalCode gbr_Postcode mex_PostalCode usa_ZIP" />
</xs:simpleType>
```

Now we can validate addresses for any of the three NAFTA (North American Free Trade Agreement) countries, plus Great Britain, all using the same basic element structure:

```xml
<xs:complexType name="postalAddress">
    <xs:sequence>
        <xs:element name="Street"     type="xs:string" maxOccurs="4" />
        <xs:element name="City"       type="xs:string" />
        <xs:element name="Region"     type="union.PostalRegion" />
        <xs:element name="PostalCode" type="union.PostalCode" />
    </xs:sequence>
    <xs:attribute name="country" type="iso3166_CountryCode" use="required" />
</xs:complexType>

<xs:element name="Address" type="postalAddress" />
```

Two examples of addresses that both conform to this structure are:

```xml
<Address country="GBR">
    <Street>Arden House</Street>
    <Street>1102 Warwick Road</Street>
    <Street>Acocks Green</Street>
    <City>Birmingham</City>
    <Region>B</Region>
    <PostalCode>B27 6BH</PostalCode>
</Address>

<Address country="USA">
    <Street>29 S La Salle St</Street>
    <Street>Suite 520</Street>
    <City>Chicago</City>
    <Region>IL</Region>
    <PostalCode>60603</PostalCode>
</Address>
```

Another approach would be to use a complex type for the common data (`Street` and `City`), and then create several country-specific datatypes by extension of the common type:

```
<xs:complexType name="base_PostalAddress">
    <xs:sequence>
        <xs:element name="Street"      type="xs:string" maxOccurs="4" />
        <xs:element name="City"        type="xs:string" />
    </xs:sequence>
    <xs:attribute name="country" type="iso3166_CountryCode" use="required" />
</xs:complexType>

<xs:element name="PostalAddress" type="base_PostalAddress" />
```

Addresses in the USA would extend the `base_PostalAddress` type to add `State` and `ZIP` elements:

```
<xs:complexType name="usa_PostalAddress">
    <xs:complexContent>
        <xs:extension base="base_PostalAddress">
            <xs:sequence>
                <xs:element name="State" type="usa_StateCode" />
                <xs:element name="Zip"   type="usa_ZIP" />
            </xs:sequence>
        </xs:extension>
    </xs:complexContent>
</xs:complexType>
```

Mexican addresses are almost identical to US addresses, with only a minor difference in nomenclature ("postal code" instead of "ZIP code"), and different datatypes for the code values:

```
<xs:complexType name="mex_PostalAddress">
    <xs:complexContent>
        <xs:extension base="base_PostalAddress">
            <xs:sequence>
                <xs:element name="State"      type="mex_StateCode" />
                <xs:element name="PostalCode" type="mex_PostalCode" />
            </xs:sequence>
        </xs:extension>
    </xs:complexContent>
</xs:complexType>
```

Canadian addresses are very similar, but we should tag a Province using `Province`, rather than `State`; the postal code is also different:

```
<xs:complexType name="can_PostalAddress" >
    <xs:complexContent>
        <xs:extension base="base_PostalAddress">
            <xs:sequence>
                <xs:element name="Province"   type="can_ProvinceCode" />
                <xs:element name="PostalCode" type="can_PostalCode" />
            </xs:sequence>
        </xs:extension>
    </xs:complexContent>
</xs:complexType>
```

British addresses use similar elements, with different code datatypes, but there is no need for a `State` or a `Province` element:

```xml
<xs:complexType name="gbr_PostalAddress" >
   <xs:complexContent>
      <xs:extension base="base_PostalAddress">
         <xs:sequence>
            <xs:element name="Postcode" type="gbr_Postcode" />
         </xs:sequence>
      </xs:extension>
   </xs:complexContent>
</xs:complexType>
```

A completely different approach to tagging address data uses attributes in a message-oriented format. To save complexity (and a little bandwidth), many XML messaging systems prefer to use very few elements, with many attributes each. For example, we can reformat our address data like so:

```xml
<xs:element name="PostTo" >
   <xs:complexType>
      <xs:sequence>
         <xs:attribute name="co"  type="iso3166_CountryCode" use="required" />
         <xs:attribute name="pc"  type="union.PostalCode"    use="required" />
         <xs:attribute name="st1" type="xs:string" />
         <xs:attribute name="st2" type="xs:string" />
         <xs:attribute name="st3" type="xs:string" />
         <xs:attribute name="st4" type="xs:string" />
         <xs:attribute name="num" type="xs:string" />
         <xs:attribute name="box" type="xs:string" />
      </xs:sequence>
   </xs:complexType>
</xs:element>
```

This schema excerpt (and the others in this section) are available in the example file named ProSchemas.PostalAddress.xsd.

In the next section, we will see several instances of XML data that conform to these datatypes.

Example – NAFTA and British Addresses

The examples in this section take advantage of almost all the datatypes that we've created as examples throughout this chapter. Let's assume that an international company based in England sells its products (say, books) to customers in the three NAFTA countries: Canada, Mexico, and the USA. This implies the need to create shipping labels that conform to country-specific address formats. We will also use various special codes as defined by that country's national postal authority.

The definitive source for sample international address formats, postal code patterns and sub-codes, and official postal abbreviations for cities, states, provinces, etc. is the Universal Postal Union (UPU) at http://www.upu.org.

The official USPS (United States Postal Service) state and territorial abbreviations are listed at http://www.usps.gov/ncsc/lookups/usps_abbreviations.html.

All of the examples in the following sections show two XML data excerpts that conform to one of the different datatypes collected in the *xxx*_PostalAddress and PostTo datatypes. The first can be seen as an example of some "document-oriented" XML for print output & database. The second is an example of a more "message-oriented" (more attribute-based) version of the same data, such as what might be used with a mail-sorting robot or as part of a mail tracking system. These are followed by mailing label illustrations that could be easily generated from either data form using a simple XSL stylesheet.

Simple Child Element Form – Canadian (CAN), British (GBR), and Mexican (MEX) Addresses

The following XML excerpts conform to three of the simple versions of the PostalAddress datatype, using single or multiple Street elements that are common to all kinds of addresses.

In addition to these elements, Canadian addresses also include the name of a city or town, a Province (or Territory) code, and an alphanumeric postal code:

```
<PostalAddress country="CAN" xsi:type="can_PostalAddress">
   <Street>Box 8040</Street>
   <Street>Indian Flats Road</Street>
   <City>Canmore</City>
   <Province>AB</Province>
   <PostalCode>T1W 2T8</PostalCode>
</PostalAddress>

<PostTo co="CAN" pc="T1W 2T8" st1="Indian Flats Road" box="8040" />
```

> **The Alpine Club of Canada**
> Box 8040
> Indian Flats Road
> Canmore, Alberta T1W 2T8
> CANADA

The British version of the simple PostalAddress element omits the State or Province element used in the other address examples in this chapter. A simple table of postcodes and their full names can be part of a stylesheet, or perhaps supplied as default attribute values (which requires another revision to the schema). Since the first one or (usually) two letters of British postcodes correspond to a specific town or city, it would be possible to revise the schema to allow the omission of the City element, thus saving considerable storage with no loss of data. For this example though, we'll just leave the city name, as previously defined:

```
<PostalAddress country="GBR" xsi:type="gbr_PostalAddress">
   <Street>The Old Granary</Street>
   <Street>West Mill St</Street>
   <City>Perth</City>
   <Postcode>PH1 5QP</Postcode>
</PostalAddress>

<PostTo co="GBR" pc="PH1 5QP" st1="The Old Granary" st2="West Mill St" />
```

> **The Mountaineering Council of Scotland**
> The Old Granary
> West Mill St
> Perth, PH1 5QP
> GREAT BRITAIN

Mexican addresses include a city (or town), a State (or District) code, and a numeric postal code:

```
<PostalAddress country="MEX" xsi:type="mex_PostalAddress">
    <Street>Calle 3 No. 235 x 32A y 34 Col. Pensiones</Street>
    <City>Mérida</City>
    <State>AB</State>
    <State>YUC</State>
    <PostalCode>97219</PostalCode>
</PostalAddress>

<PostTo co="MEX" pc="97219" num="235" st1="Calle 3" st2="x 32A y 34 Col.
Pensiones" />
```

> **Ecoturismo Yucatan**
> Calle 3 No. 235 x 32A y 34 Col. Pensiones
> 97219 Mérida, Yucatán
> MEXICO

Now that we've seen a few examples of addresses that use versions of the *xxx*_PostalAddress datatypes, let's look at a slightly different approach to the same data.

US Address – Detailed Street Data Attribute Form

The following XML excerpts conform to the more complex, attribute-based versions of the *xxx*_PostalAddress datatype, and are followed by the usual mailing label examples.

US addresses are quite similar to Canadian addresses, with a city, state, and ZIP code all required. Unlike British postcodes, regular ZIP code boundaries can cross state lines, or be applied to multiple cities. Thus, it is necessary to store all three in this example of a more data-oriented, coded form:

```
<PostalAddress country="USA">
    <Street num="710" name="10th" type="ST" suite="100" />
    <PostOffice city="Golden" region="CO" code="80401" />
</PostalAddress>
```

> **The American Alpine Club**
> 710 – 10th Street, Suite 100
> Golden, CO 80401
> USA

The British address example from the previous section would not really benefit much from the more detailed division of street data here, but the separation of the area portion of the postcode allows us to omit the city ("Perth"):

```
<PostalAddress country="GBR">
    <Street name="The Old Granary" />
    <Street name="West Mill St" />
    <PostOffice region="PH" code="15QP" />
</PostalAddress>
```

Internet and postal addresses are important commercial datatypes, but the needs of science and navigation require a different system of physical "addresses".

Geodetic Locations

Physical locations on the Earth's surface are commonly described using a system of numbers called **latitude** and **longitude** (known as "**LatLong**"), plus **altitude** above a specific geodetic reference datum (such as sea level). LatLong values are polar (spherical) coordinates, representing the Earth at sea level as an imaginary perfect sphere.

> *The ISO standard for geodetic locations is* **ISO 6709:1983 Standard representation of latitude, longitude and altitude for geographic point locations**, *available in printed form at http://www.iso.ch/. As usual, the standard is not available online, but a useful summary is available at http://www.ftp.uni-erlangen.de/pub/doc/ISO/english/ISO-6709-summary.*

Latitudes can range from 0°0'0.00" (the Equator, represented in the third form below as "000000.00") to 90°0'0.00" (the North or South Pole, at "±900000.00"), and longitude ranges from 0°0'0.00" (the Prime Meridian) to 180°0'0.00" (the main part of the International Date Line in the Pacific Ocean, represented as "±1800000.00").

An optional altitude in meters may be appended to the LatLong position. Signed decimal numbers of arbitrary precision may be used for this value. Use positive (+) altitudes for points above and on the geodetic reference datum, and negative (–) altitudes for points below the reference point.

Latitude and longitude can be represented in one of three ISO 6709 formats:

Latitude	Longitude	Description
±DD.DD	±DDD.DD	Degrees and decimal degrees
±DDMM.MMM	±DDDMM.MMM	Degrees, minutes and decimal minutes
±DDMMSS.SS	±DDDMMSS.SS	Degrees, minutes, seconds and decimal seconds

The plus or minus (±) prefix is used to indicate position relative to the Equator for latitude, and relative to the Prime Meridian (Greenwich) for longitude. Use positive (+) latitudes for positions North of (or on) the Equator, and negative (–) latitudes for positions to the South. Positive (+) longitudes are for positions East of (or on) the Prime Meridian (Greenwich), and negative (–) longitudes for positions to the West (up to the 180th meridian).

Leading zeros must be used for degrees, minutes, or seconds of latitude and longitude (the decimal values may use one to two/three digits, depending upon the format).

The following is an XML Schema datatype that can be used to represent these different formats, and the three components of a geodetic position:

```
<xs:simpleType name="iso6709_LatLongAlt">
    <xs:annotation>
        <xs:appinfo>
units [Lat] = (±DD.dd | ±DDMM.mmm | ±DDMMSS.ss)
units [Long] = (±DDD.dd | ±DDDMM.mmm | ±DDDMMSS.ss)
units [Alt] = (±m~m.m~m)
        </xs:appinfo>
    </xs:annotation>
    <xs:restriction base="xs:string">
        <xs:pattern value="( [+-][0-9]{2}(\.[0-9]{2})?
                     | [+-][0-9]{2}[0-5][0-9](\.[0-9]{3})?
```

```
                                       |  [+-][0-9]{2}[0-5][0-9][0-5][0-9](\.[0-9]{2})?
                                     )
                                     ( [+-][0-9]{3}(\.[0-9]{2})?
                                       |  [+-][0-9]{3}[0-5][0-9](\.[0-9]{3})?
                                       |  [+-][0-9]{3}[0-5][0-9][0-5][0-9](\.[0-9]{2})?
                                     )
                                     ( [+-][0-9]+(\.[0-9]+)? )?" />
       </xs:restriction>
    </xs:simpleType>

    <xs:simpleType name="iso6709_Lat">
       <xs:restriction base="xs:string">
          <xs:pattern value="( [+-][0-9]{2}(\.[0-9]{2})?
                             |  [+-][0-9]{2}[0-5][0-9](\.[0-9]{3})?
                             |  [+-][0-9]{2}[0-5][0-9][0-5][0-9](\.[0-9]{2})? )" />
       </xs:restriction>
    </xs:simpleType>

    <xs:simpleType name="iso6709_Long">
       <xs:restriction base="xs:string">
          <xs:pattern value="( [+-][0-9]{3}(\.[0-9]{2})?
                             |  [+-][0-9]{3}[0-5][0-9](\.[0-9]{3})?
                             |  [+-][0-9]{3}[0-5][0-9][0-5][0-9](\.[0-9]{2})? )" />
       </xs:restriction>
    </xs:simpleType>

    <xs:simpleType name="iso6709_Alt">
       <xs:restriction base="xs:string">
          <xs:pattern value="([+-][0-9]+(\.[0-9]+)?)?" />
       </xs:restriction>
    </xs:simpleType>
```

Note: Remember, as with earlier examples, the whitespace in the above pattern is *not* permitted in a real XML Schema instance, but is included for clarity – remove all whitespace between the quotes that enclose the regexs (or use the example file ProSchemas.ISO6709_LatLongAlt.xsd).

We can define two different kinds of location elements – one using the combined and more compact ISO 6709 "LatLongAlt" format, and the second using explicit XML elements for each of the three:

```
<xs:element name="LatLong" type="iso6709_LatLongAlt" />

<xs:element name="Location">
   <xs:complexType>
      <xs:sequence>
         <xs:element name="Latitude" type="iso6709_Lat" />
         <xs:element name="Longitude" type="iso6709_Long" />
         <xs:element name="Altitude" type="iso6709_Alt" />
      </xs:sequence>
   </xs:complexType>
</xs:element>
```

Some example XML data instances that conform to these datatypes include (all of these show the same geodetic location of 40°15'N 116°30'E at 600' above sea level, which is Beijing, China):

```
<LatLong>+40.250+116.500</LatLong>
<LatLong>+40.250+116.500+182.88</LatLong>
```

and:

```
<Location>
    <Latitude>+401500</Latitude>
    <Longitude>+1163000</Longitude>
    <Altitude>+182.88</Altitude>
</Location>
```

In both these examples, we've converted the altitude of 600' to its SI equivalent (182.88 meters). The former style is probably the most generally useful approach to LatLong locations. It conforms to an ISO standard format, is compact, and it's relatively easy to reformat the data for presentation. The latter format might be more appropriate for use in a GIS (Geographical Information System), as an interchange format for GPS (Global Positioning System) data, or anytime calculations must be made using individual parts of this data.

Summary

In this chapter, we created a variety of generic datatypes that may be useful when constructing XML applications. Some were based upon international standards from the ISO, IETF, and UPU. Others were more country-specific, but all of them illustrated the various forms of XML Schema datatype derivation:

❑   restriction

❑   list

❑   union

❑   extension

The extensive use of the `pattern` constraining facet offers additional examples of regular expressions, which are one of the most powerful features of XML Schema validation. Although most of the datatype examples were simple types, there were also several complex types, such as the various forms of postal addresses.

Many of these derived datatypes are also available in XML Schema files at http://www.wrox.com. Here is a summary of where they can be found:

Datatype	Filename
base_PostalAddress	ProSchemas.PostalAddress.xsd
can_PostalAddress	ProSchemas.PostalAddress.xsd
can_ProvinceCode	ProSchemas.CAN_ProvinceCode.xsd
gbr_PostalAddress	ProSchemas.PostalAddress.xsd
gbr_PostcodeArea	ProSchemas.GBR_PostcodeArea.xsd
ip_DomainName	ProSchemas.IP_Address.xsd
ipv4_Address	ProSchemas.IP_Address.xsd
ipv6_Address	ProSchemas.IP_Address.xsd
iso3166_CountryCode	ProSchemas.ISO3166_CountryCode.xsd

Datatype	Filename
iso5218_GenderCode	ProSchemas.Person.xsd
iso6709_Alt	ProSchemas.ISO6709_LatLongAlt.xsd
iso6709_LatLongAlt	ProSchemas.ISO6709_LatLongAlt.xsd
iso6709_Lat	ProSchemas.ISO6709_LatLongAlt.xsd
iso6709_Long	ProSchemas.ISO6709_LatLongAlt.xsd
mex_PostalAddress	ProSchemas.PostalAddress.xsd
mex_StateCode	ProSchemas.MEX_StateCode.xsd
realworld_GenderCode	ProSchemas.Person.xsd
usa_PostalAddress	ProSchemas.PostalAddress.xsd
usa_StateCode	ProSchemas.USA_StateCode.xsd

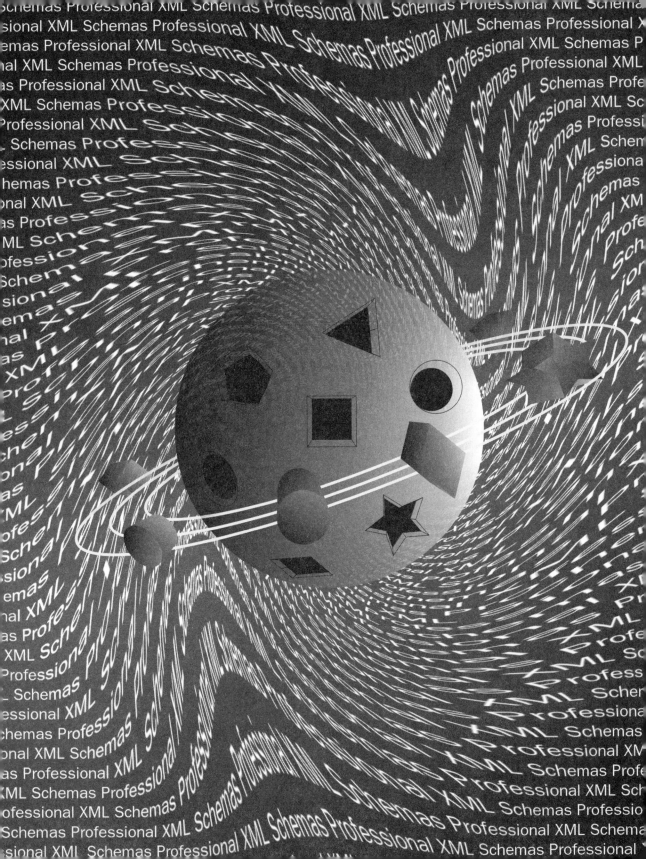

XML Schemas and Namespaces

So far in this book we have not really delved into the powerful namespace support offered in XML Schema. If you wanted to support namespaces with DTDs, it involved complicated workarounds that made the DTD very hard to read and hard for users to understand. The flexible support for XML Namespaces in XML Schemas is one of the powerful reasons why you should consider using XML Schemas over DTDs. In this chapter, we are going to look at the different areas in which XML Schema makes use of namespaces.

> **If you are using namespaces, you need to be aware of the way that if you declare elements and attributes globally as opposed to locally, it has an effect upon the way the element or attribute must appear in the instance document.**

Up to now, we have been writing schemas that do not belong to a namespace, so it is time to look at why we would want to specify a namespace, and how we can make our markup part of a defined namespace should we choose to do so. W3C XML Schema makes use of namespaces in three areas, and we shall look at each of these:

First, we need to use XML Namespaces in the schemas that we write to distinguish between the elements, attributes, and types that we are creating and the markup that is defined by the XML Recommendation. As we shall see shortly, this is the reason why we have been prefixing all of the XML Schema elements and type values in the book so far.

Second, the W3C XML Schema Recommendation defines three namespaces of its own, which we need to be familiar with. We have already met each of these, although we will take a closer look at why there are three namespaces and how we make full use of them:

- ❑ The main namespace we use is http://www.w3.org/2001/XMLSchema, the one that has been appearing in the root element of most of our XML Schemas.

- ❑ In Chapter 2 we also met the http://www.w3.org/2001/XMLSchema-datatypes namespace, which contains a copy of the built-in types that XML Schema defines (and which are also present in the main http://www.w3.org/2001/XMLSchema namespace). The point of this namespace is that you can use it in other alternative schema applications (such as Schematron, or Relax NG, which we will cover in Chapter 14), in which you want to use the datatypes defined in the W3C XML Schema Recommendation.

- ❑ The third namespace is the XML Schema for instances namespace (http://www.w3.org/2001/XMLSchema-instance), which is used with the xsi:type, xsi:nil, xsi:schemaLocation, and xsi:noNamespaceSchemaLocation attributes in instance documents.

Third, XML Schema makes use of XML Namespaces so that we can validate an instance document against mark up of a given namespace, or indeed a document that is marked up using elements and attributes from multiple namespaces. While this is a very powerful feature, it is also the most complicated area of namespace use in XML Schema. When we start making use of namespaces in our schemas, or have to write schemas for documents that explicitly use namespaces, there are some interesting choices that we have to make. The use of namespaces in a schema can potentially require a document author to know a lot more about the schema than we would like, or is often practical. So, we have to be careful with how we use namespaces.

By the end of this chapter, we will have seen:

- ❑ An overview of XML Namespaces

- ❑ How we distinguish between our markup and that of the XML Schema Recommendation in schemas that we write

- ❑ The namespaces that are defined by the XML Schema Recommendation

- ❑ How to create markup that belongs to a specific namespace

- ❑ How the use of namespaces in schemas affects our instance documents

- ❑ When to indicate that elements and attributes should be qualified in instance documents

- ❑ Pitfalls in using locally declared elements

- ❑ Pitfalls of using globally declared attributes

- ❑ How to write schemas that use constructs from different namespaces

- ❑ Guides of practice on how to use namespace in schemas

- ❑ When you might want to qualify elements and attributes as belonging to a namespace in instance documents

XML namespaces are slightly different from the namespaces conventionally used in computing, so before we look in depth at how XML Schema uses them, we will start with a refresher on what XML namespaces are and how they are used.

XML Namespace Refresher

This section is intended as a quick guide or refresher to the use of XML Namespaces. If you are familiar with their purpose and syntax, you can skip to *The Three Namespaces of XML Schema* section. The Namespaces in XML Recommendation was released in January 1999, and is considered as the other base XML specification for the use of XML along with the W3C XML 1.0 Recommendation. The Recommendation can be found at http://www.w3.org/TR/REC-xml-names. XML 1.0 Second Edition also explicitly addresses the use of namespaces within instance documents.

Why We Need XML Namespaces

With everyone being able to create their own XML elements and attributes for use in their problem domain, we need a way of identifying where markup has come from, so that:

❑   It can be recognized as belonging to a certain markup vocabulary

❑   If two elements or attributes from different vocabularies have been given the same name, they can be distinguished

In order to achieve this, elements and attributes used in XML documents need a way of universally being identified. We need to be able to make the elements and attributes that we use unique so that if someone else uses the same name for an element or attribute, it will be clear that it should be used as defined in our namespace. After all, there are going to be many different uses of element names such as `Name`, `Product`, `LineItem`, `Address`, `Account`, and so on. XML Namespaces offer us a way of uniquely identifying each name from a markup vocabulary.

How We Declare and Use Namespaces in XML Documents

A namespace is uniquely identified using a **Uniform Resource Identifier** (**URI**), and when elements and attributes are used in a document, they are associated with that namespace using a prefix. The intended use of the markup can therefore be distinguished from another element or attribute with the same name that is associated with a different URI.

In this book we have already made use of a few namespaces. Since Chapter 1 we have identified the namespace for XML Schema in the root `schema` element of the schemas we have been creating, and prefixed all elements that come from that schema with the prefix `xs:`, like so:

```
<?xml version = "1.0" ?>
<xs:schema xmlns:xs = "http://www.w3.org/2001/XMLSchema">
   <xs:element name = "Customer">
      <xs:complexType>
         <xs:sequence>
            <xs:element name = "FirstName" type = "xs:string" />
            <xs:element name = "MiddleInitial" type = "xs:string" />
            <xs:element name = "LastName" type = "xs:string" />
         </xs:sequence>
      </xs:complexType>
   </xs:element>
</xs:schema>
```

Here you can see that each of the elements declared in the W3C XML Schema Recommendation (schema, element, complexType, and sequence) have been prefixed with xs:. In addition, the built-in string type has been prefixed in the same way.

The xs characters are known as the **namespace prefix**, and the colon is used to separate the namespace prefix from the element or attribute name. The part after the colon is known as the **local part**.

We made the association between the prefix and the URI that identifies the namespace in the root schema element using:

```
xmlns:xs = "http://www.w3.org/2001/XMLSchema"
```

Here the xmlns attribute uses a colon to separate it from the prefix, and has the value of the URI for the namespace.

> **Note that a URI does not have to specify the location of a schema; it is only a unique identifier – although you can use a URL as a URI**

Declaring a Namespace

In order to associate a namespace with a prefix, we have to declare it. In order to declare a namespace we use **reserved attributes**. Remember from the XML Recommendation that we are not allowed to create an element or attribute name that begins with the characters xml in any combination of upper- or lowercase. These characters were reserved for use in developing XML related specifications, and this is a good example of why they were reserved.

XML Namespaces use attributes whose name begins with xml to declare a namespace in an XML document. When declaring a namespace the attribute must either be xmlns or use xmlns: as a prefix. The value of the attribute is a URI reference, which is the namespace name that uniquely identifies the namespace.

When we first used namespaces in this book, it was on the root schema element of the Customer.xsd file in the format:

```
<schema xmlns = "http://www.w3.org/2001/XMLSchema">
  ...
</schema>
```

In this example, the reserved attribute xmlns was given the value of the URI for the W3C XML Schema Recommendation. This had the effect of indicating to a processor that the entire markup from this document (unless otherwise explicitly qualified) belonged to the XML Schema Namespace.

After the first example in Chapter 1, we started prefixing all of the elements and type values from the XML Schema Namespace with xs: (the characters xs being the namespace prefix, and the colon separating the prefix from the local name).

The XML Schema Namespace was declared in the root element of the schema using a reserved attribute that was prefixed with xmlns:, the letters after the colon being the characters that would be used as the namespace prefix in the rest of the document (in this case xs). The value of the attribute was again the URI reference for the XML Schema Recommendation:

```
xmlns:xs = "http://www.w3.org/2001/XMLSchema"
```

This works because a namespace-aware processor should know that any attribute starting with `xmlns:` will be used to associate a namespace prefix with a URI reference for that namespace. If we had instead wanted to prefix the entire markup from the XML Schema Namespace with `xsd:`, we could have used:

```
xmlns:xsd = "http://www.w3.org/ 2001/XMLSchema"
```

The author of the XML document instance chooses the prefix associated with the namespace, but it cannot include the characters `xml` in any combination of case, nor can it contain a colon.

The Scope of a Namespace

When we declare a namespace in an instance document, it applies to the element in which it is specified, and all content within that element. In the following example, the namespace is declared in the root element, and therefore applies to the whole document:

```
<?xml version = "1.0" ?>
<xs:schema xmlns:xs = "http://www.w3.org/2001/XMLSchema">
    <xs:element name = "Customer">
        <xs:complexType>
            <xs:sequence>
                <xs:element name = "FirstName" type = "xs:string" />
                <xs:element name = "MiddleInitial" type = "xs:string" />
                <xs:element name = "LastName" type = "xs:string" />
            </xs:sequence>
        </xs:complexType>
    </xs:element>
</xs:schema>
```

Here all of the elements are prefixed indicating they each belong to the XML Schema Namespace.

It is also possible to use multiple namespaces in a document. For example, here we are mixing markup from our own `inventory` namespace with that defined in the XHTML Namespace:

```
<?xml version = "1.0" ?>
<inv:product xmlns:inv = "http://www.example.org/inventory"
             xmlns:xhtml = "http://www.w3.org/1999/xhtml">
    <inv:table>
        <inv:model>Kitchen Table</inv:model>
        <inv:wood>Pine</inv:wood>
        <inv:sizes>
          <xhtml:table>
           <xhtml:tr>
              <xhtml:th>Width</xhtml:th>
              <xhtml:th>Length</xhtml:th>
              <xhtml:th>Height</xhtml:th>
           </xhtml:tr>
           <xhtml:tr>
              <xhtml:td>35</xhtml:td>
              <xhtml:td>28</xhtml:td>
              <xhtml:td>26</xhtml:td>
           </xhtml:tr>
```

```
        <xhtml:tr>
            <xhtml:td>48</xhtml:td>
            <xhtml:td>32</xhtml:td>
            <xhtml:td>26</xhtml:td>
        </xhtml:tr>
        </xhtml:table>
        </inv:sizes>
    </inv:table>
</inv:product>
```

The URI that identifies the namespace for our inventory is `http://www.example.org/inventory` while the XHTML Namespace identified by the W3C is `http://www.w3.org/1999/xhtml`. Markup that comes from our inventory namespace has been associated with the `inv:` prefix, while markup from the XHTML Namespace has been associated with the `xhtml:` prefix. Both namespace declarations were put in the root element, like so:

```
<inv:product xmlns:inv = "http://www.example.org/inventory"
             xmlns:xhtml = "http://www.w3.org/1999/xhtml">
```

We could have declared the XHTML Namespace in the XHTML `table` element rather than the root, and all of the XHTML markup would have been in scope:

```
<inv:sizes>
    <xhtml:table xmlns:xhtml = "http://www.w3.org/1999/xhtml">
        <xhtml:tr>
            ... <!-- rest of table information goes here -->
        </xhtml:tr>
    </xhtml:table>
</inv:sizes>
```

However, we could not have declared our inventory namespace in the same element, because we were already using it before that point in the document.

Note that, if we did declare the XHTML Namespace in the `table` element that contained the XHTML table of sizes, and then wanted to use another XHTML table for prices like this:

```
<?xml version = "1.0" ?>

<inv:product xmlns:inv = "http://www.example.org/inventory">
    <inv:table>

        <inv:model>Kitchen Table</inv:model>
        <inv:wood>Pine</inv:wood>

        <inv:sizes>
            <xhtml:table xmlns:xhtml = "http://www.w3.org/1999/xhtml">
                <xhtml:tr>
                    ... <!-- rest of table about sizes goes here -->
                </xhtml:tr>
            </xhtml:table>
        </inv:sizes>

        <inv:price>
```

```
        <xhtml:table>
            <xhtml:tr>
                <xhtml:th>Currency</xhtml:th>
                <xhtml:th>Amount</xhtml:th>
                ... <!-- rest of table prices goes here -->
            </xhtml:tr>
        </xhtml:table>
    </inv:price>
```

```
    </inv:table>
</inv:product>
```

There would be a problem because the second XHTML `table` is not nested within the original namespace declaration and is therefore out of scope of the namespace declaration. We would either have to declare the namespace in the second `xhtml:table` element again, or move the namespace declaration so that it was in either the `inv:table` or `inv:product` element, and therefore within scope of both `xhtml:table` elements.

Unless we explicitly state otherwise, the attributes that an element carries are considered to be in no namespace (or the null namespace), although most applications treat them as though they are in the same namespace as the element that carries them. However, we can explicitly qualify one or more attributes on any element to indicate where they are from. Imagine we wanted to stick an XHTML `href` attribute on the `model` element – we could do so by qualifying it with the `xhtml:` prefix, but note we have to move the namespace declaration back in scope of the item that uses it:

```
<?xml version = "1.0" ?>
```

```
<inv:product xmlns:inv = "http://www.example.org/inventory"
             xmlns:xhtml = "http://www.w3.org/1999/xhtml">
    <inv:table>
```

```
        <inv:model xhtml:href = "http://www.example.org/kitchentable.html">
            Kitchen Table
        </inv:model>
        ...
    </inv:table>
</inv:product>
```

Scope also has an effect upon namespace defaulting.

Namespace Defaulting

The first example we used in this book showed a default namespace, indicating that the entire markup in the document belonged to the XML Schema Namespace, and therefore dispensing with the need to prefix all the elements in the document:

```
<schema xmlns = "http://www.w3.org/2001/XMLSchema">
    <element name = "Customer">
        <complexType>
            <sequence>
                <element name = "FirstName" type = "string" />
                <element name = "MiddleInitial" type = "string" />
                <element name = "LastName" type = "string" />
            </sequence>
        </complexType>
    </element>
</schema>
```

Here, the use of the reserved attribute xmlns (without the addition of the colon and a namespace prefix) allows us to create these default namespaces.

Let's look at another example using our table element from the inventory namespace, which contains markup from the XHTML Namespace. We need to identify the table element as being from the XHTML Namespace so that we can:

❑ Distinguish the table element that carries information about the wooden table in our inventory from the table element in XHTML that is used to define a table with columns and rows

❑ Associate the table with columns and rows with the XHTML Namespace so that an application will understand how to display that information

We will make our inventory namespace the default namespace:

```
<?xml version = "1.0" ?>
<product xmlns = "http://www.example.org/inventory">
   <table>

      <model>Kitchen Table</model>
      <wood>Pine</wood>

      <sizes>
         <xhtml:table xmlns:xhtml = "http://www.w3.org/1999/xhtml">
            <xhtml:tr>
               <xhtml:td>
                  <price currency = "AUS$">600.00</price>
               </xhtml:td>
            </xhtml:tr>
         </xhtml:table>
      </sizes>

   </table>
</product>
```

Here the default namespace for the whole document is the inventory namespace, and any element that is not prefixed with the xhtml: prefix is considered part of the inventory namespace. We have declared the XHTML Namespace in the XHTML table element, because this is the only place that XHTML markup exists in this document, although we could have declared it in the root element.

This means that even the price element that is nested in the xhtml:td element is part of the inventory namespace. It should be noted that this final use of namespaces could be frowned upon; some people would prefer it if we qualify everything when mixing namespaces like this.

If the Price element had not been present, however, we could have saved ourselves from even prefixing these elements by using two default namespaces. In the next example, we create a new default namespace in the table element, because all of the XML nested inside it belongs to that namespace:

```
<?xml version = "1.0" ?>
<product xmlns = "http://www.example.org/inventory">
   <table>

      <model>Kitchen Table</model>
      <wood>Pine</wood>

      <sizes>
         <table xmlns = "http://www.w3.org/1999/xhtml">
```

```
            <tr>
                <td>Details about the table... </td>
            </tr>
        </table>
    </sizes>

   </table>
</product>
```

The second default namespace applies for the XHTML `table` element and all of its children (those lines that are highlighted). However, as soon as we have closed the `table` element, the default becomes our inventory namespace again.

> **When an element is within scope of the default namespace, it is qualified by that namespace.**
>
> **Attributes, unless specifically prefixed, do not belong to a namespace – they are assumed to be part of the same namespace as the element that carries them.**

No Namespace

In the markup in the above examples, which mixed tables from our inventory with tables from the XHTML Namespace, we either explicitly prefixed each element, or the markup was within scope of a namespace declaration that used the `xmlns` attribute without a prefix or colon.

If we want to distinguish one set of markup from the other, there is no reason why we have to qualify both sets of markup. For example, if we had an application that was expecting markup from our inventory namespace, and it only needed to explicitly know if a document contained any markup from another namespace, then we could use the following:

```
<?xml version = "1.0" ?>
<product>
    <table>

        <model>Kitchen Table</model>
        <wood>Pine</wood>

        <sizes>
            <table xmlns = "http://www.w3.org/1999/xhtml">
                <tr>
                    ... <!-- rest of table about sizes goes here -->
                </tr>
            </table>
        </sizes>

    </table>
</product>
```

Setting the `xmlns` attribute to an empty string has the same effect as leaving it off completely:

```
<product xmlns = "">
```

Here our inventory markup does not belong to a namespace, our application is written already for the markup used in such documents. It only needs to know what markup to ignore because it is from a different namespace.

Uniqueness of Attributes

The XML Recommendation prohibits a well-formed XML document from containing two attributes with the same name. The following would not be allowed:

```
<Dimensions>
   <Vertical height="24inches" height="61cms" />
</Dimensions>
```

With XML Namespaces, things are different because we are qualifying the attributes with namespaces. Let's look at three cases and see what this allows us to do. First, we have a default namespace for the `Vertical` element, but the two `height` attributes that it carries are qualified as belonging to two different namespaces – the local parts of the attribute (the attribute names) have been bound to different namespace declarations. This allows us to work round the problem we previously encountered:

```
<Dimensions  xmlns="http://www.example.org/measurements"
             xmlns:inch="http://www.example.org/inches"
             xmlns:cm="http://www.example.org/cms" >
   <Vertical inch:height="24inches" cm:height="61cms" />
</Dimensions>
```

In the second case, the following would not be allowed because both namespace prefixes are bound to the same namespace name `http://www.example.org/measurements`:

```
<Dimensions  xmlns:inch="http://www.example.org/measurements"
             xmlns:cm="http://www.example.org/measurements">
   <Vertical inch:height="24inches" cm:height="60cms" />
</Dimensions>
```

although we are allowed to have the third case, where the default namespace name is the same as the qualified namespace name:

```
<Dimensions xmlns="http://www.example.org/measurements"
            xmlns:cm="http://www.example.org/measurements" >
   <Vertical height="24inches" cm:height="60cms" />
</Dimensions>
```

This is allowed, and often desirable, because the default namespace does not apply to attribute names.

The Three Namespaces of XML Schema

You might have noticed through the book so far that the XML Schema Recommendation defines markup that belongs to three different namespaces:

❑   http://www.w3.org/2001/XMLSchema

❑   http://www.w3.org/2001/XMLSchema-datatypes

❑   http://www.w3.org/2001/XMLSchema-instance

Let's quickly review the differences between each of the namespaces.

The XML Schema Namespace

The first namespace, `http://www.w3.org/2001/XMLSchema`, identifies the markup that is defined in the XML Schema Recommendation. It is the namespace that declared the elements such as `schema`, `element`, `attribute`, `complexType`, `group`, `sequence`, `choice`, and `all`, and attributes such as `name`, `ref`, `type`, `minOccurs`, `maxOccurs`, and `use`. It also contains the definitions of the built-in datatypes that we met in Chapter 2.

We met this namespace in Chapter 1 when we started prefixing elements and type values from the XML Schema Namespace. The reason why we started this was because an XML Schema is itself an XML document and we need to distinguish between the vocabulary defined by the W3C for use when writing XML Schemas, and the vocabulary we are creating in the schema. So, for example, when we use the `ref` attribute to indicate that we are referring to an element or type we have created, we need to make it clear that we are referring to an element or type we have created, not one that is part of the XML Schema Namespace. If we did not do this, a processor would expect that the element or type we were referring to would be part of the XML Schema Namespace and would not be able to find the appropriate definition, therefore the schema itself would not be valid.

By prefixing the elements and types from the XML Schema Namespace it is clear that they belong to the XML Schema Namespace, while those that we do not prefix belong in no namespace or the null namespace.

```
<?xml version = "1.0" ?>
<xs:schema xmlns:xs = "http://www.w3.org/2001/XMLSchema">

    <xs:element name = "Customer" type = "CustomerType" />

    <xs:complexType name = "CustomerType">
        <xs:sequence>
            <xs:element name = "FirstName" type = "xs:string" />
            <xs:element name = "MiddleInitial" type = "xs:string" />
            <xs:element name = "LastName" type = "xs:string" />
        </xs:sequence>
    </xs:complexType>

</xs:schema>
```

So, the markup that we have been creating does not belong to a particular namespace, which is why we were using the `xsi:noNamespaceSchemaLocation` attribute in our instance documents when indicating to a processor where it could find a schema that could be used to validate the document.

As we shall see later in the chapter, there are other ways around this if we are defining markup that will belong to a namespace, but so far in the book the schemas we have developed, like this one, do not belong to any namespace.

The XML Schema Datatypes Namespace

We met the second namespace in Chapter 2; it defines the XML Schema built-in types. It was not necessary to define this second namespace for the datatypes that we used in our schema, however. So, you might ask why you should not be separately distinguishing the datatypes namespace using something more along the lines of:

```
<xs:schema xmlns = "http://www.w3.org/2001/XMLSchema"
           xmlns:xsdatatypes = "http://www.w3.org/2001/XMLSchema-datatypes">

  <xs:element name = "myElement" type = "xsdatatypes:string" />

</xs:schema>
```

This is not necessary, because the main XML Schema Namespace also defines the built-in datatypes within the context of XML Schema. If we wanted to use the same datatypes outside the context of the XML Schema, however, we would use the second, more specific namespace. This allows other alternative schema languages and applications (such as Schematron or Relax NG) to use the datatypes defined by the XML Schema working group.

The XML Schema Instance Namespace

The third namespace http://www.w3.org/2001/XMLSchema-instance is defined for attributes that need to appear in instance documents, as opposed to in the schema. The prefix xsi: is usually associated with this namespace.

There are four attributes that we commonly use in instance documents associated with this namespace:

❑　When we want to indicate to a parser where it might find a copy of the schema(s) used to author the document, and the vocabulary defined in the schema belongs to a namespace, we could use the xsi:schemaLocation attribute in an instance document.

❑　When we want to indicate to a parser where it might find a copy of the schema(s) used to author the document, and the vocabulary defined in the schema does not belong to a namespace, we could use the xsi:noNamespaceSchemaLocation attribute in an instance document.

❑　When we want to indicate that we are using a complex type derived from the one associated with the element name in the schema, we use the xsi:type attribute in instance documents to indicate which derived types we are using in the instance document.

❑　When we want to indicate that an element has a nil value to distinguish between a zero-length string and no given entry for a field, we add the xsi:nil attribute to the element in the document instance. Remember that we need to do this when we are using a datatype such as an integer, because the parser would treat an empty element as an empty string, which would not be a valid integer value.

For example, here is an instance document that identifies where a schema can be found, and uses a nil value in an element to allow the processor to differentiate between a zero-length string and the integer datatype without a value:

```
<?xml version = "1.0"?>
<Customer xmlns:xsi = "http://www.w3.org/2001/XMLSchema-instance"
   xsi:schemaLocation = "http://www.example.org/schemas/customer.xsd">

   <FirstName>George</FirstName>
   <LastName>Watkins</LastName>
   <Age xsi:nil = "true"></Age>

</Customer>
```

Here we have declared the XML Schema instances namespace in the root `Customer` element, and used the `schemaLocation` attribute in the same root element to indicate to a parser where it might find a schema that could be used to validate this document instance. We have also used the `nil` attribute on the empty `Age` element. We first met the nil mechanism in Chapter 3.

Having seen the namespaces that are defined by XML Schema, we should move onto the third and most interesting topic of this chapter: declaring markup that belongs to a namespace and validating instance documents across multiple namespaces.

Defining Namespace for Markup

As we have already seen, namespaces can be used in XML documents to distinguish markup that belongs to different namespaces. When writing a schema we can indicate whether an element or attribute should be qualified in an instance document, be this explicitly using a prefix or implicitly by default. This is one of the key advantages of XML Schemas over DTDs, and it is this mechanism by which we can validate documents that contain markup belonging to more than one namespace.

When you write a schema, the elements, attributes, and types you use either belong to a namespace, or have no namespace. In the schemas we have been creating in this book so far, the declarations and definitions have not belonged to a namespace. When it comes to checking that an instance document conforms to a schema, however, a schema processor needs to check the use of elements and attributes against the declarations that it finds in one or more schemas. This means that, if an instance document contains markup declared in more than one schema, we will need to be able to distinguish which schema the processor should use when checking elements and attributes in the instance document. Also, if a document indicates that the elements and attributes it contains belong to a specific namespace, then the processor will try to check the document markup against the declarations and definitions that belong to that namespace. This means that if the schema does not inform the processor that the markup it defines belongs to the same namespace as that indicated in the instance document, the processor might not be able to validate the document. As we shall see, this is why it is important to require that a document instance specifies the namespaces that its elements and attributes belong to.

There are, however, a lot of complexities introduced when we start using namespaces. The choices you make can have a number of implications upon how you decide to structure your schemas and the appearance of elements and attributes in instance documents. In particular, as we shall see, where you declare an element in a schema will affect its representation in an instance document. For the rest of this chapter we will be focusing on indicating which namespace our markup belongs to in a schema, how we require that elements and attributes be qualified, and we will look at the effects this has upon instance documents.

Creating Vocabularies that Do Not Belong to a Namespace

In all of the examples we have been using in the book so far, neither the instance documents, nor the schemas indicate that the markup we have been creating belongs to a particular namespace. Let's look at how we indicate that elements, attributes, and types we declare and define do **not** belong to a namespace.

In the schemas, we have just avoided any mention of a namespace that our markup may belong to. For example, the simple example (`Customer.xsd`) we met in Chapter 1 looked like this:

```
<?xml version = "1.0" ?>
<xs:schema xmlns:xs = "http://www.w3.org/2001/XMLSchema">

    <xs:element name = "Customer" >
       <xs:complexType>
          <xs:sequence>
             <xs:element name = "FirstName" type = "xs:string" />
             <xs:element name = "MiddleInitial" type = "xs:string" />
             <xs:element name = "LastName" type = "xs:string" />
          </xs:sequence>
       </xs:complexType>
    </xs:element>

</xs:schema>
```

A conforming instance document would look something like this:

```
<?xml version = "1.0" ?>
<Customer xmlns:xsi = "http://www.w3.org/2001/XMLSchema-instance"
          xsi:noNamespaceSchemaLocation = "Customer.xsd">

   <FirstName>Ray</FirstName>
   <MiddleInitial>G</MiddleInitial>
   <LastName>Bayliss</LastName>
</Customer>
```

If an instance document that does not have a namespace wants to indicate to a processing application where it might find a copy of the schema, it should use the xsi:noNamespaceSchemaLocation attribute (as opposed to the xsi:schemaLocation attribute).

Creating Vocabularies that Belong to a Namespace

In order to indicate that elements, attributes, and types declared in a schema belong to a namespace, we have to add an attribute called targetNamespace to the root schema element, whose value is a target namespace, which represents the namespace that we want our markup to belong to.

As soon as we declare a target namespace, something interesting happens. Let's go back to the simple example (Customer.xsd) that we first met in Chapter 1, where we declared a Customer element and its content model. For the sake of this example, we are going to declare the LastName element globally as well, and then use it by reference in the content model for the Customer element. This schema is called CustomerA.xsd:

```
<?xml version = "1.0" ?>
<xs:schema xmlns:xs = "http://www.w3.org/2001/XMLSchema"
           targetNamespace = "http://www..example.org/Customers"
           xmlns = "http://www.example.org/Customers">

    <xs:element name = "Customer" >
       <xs:complexType>
          <xs:sequence>
             <xs:element name = "FirstName" type = "xs:string" />
             <xs:element name = "MiddleInitial" type = "xs:string" />
             <xs:element ref = "LastName" />
          </xs:sequence>
```

```
        </xs:complexType>
    </xs:element>

    <xs:element name = "LastName" type = "xs:string" />

</xs:schema>
```

Note how we have added the `targetNamespace` attribute to the `schema` element, and given it a value of `http://www.example.org/Customers`. We have also added a third attribute, `xmlns`, to indicate that the default namespace for this document is the `http://www.example.org/Customers` namespace. By making this the default namespace, we do not have to qualify elements, attributes, and types that we have declared and defined in this document when we want to use them again (for example, we do not have to qualify the reference to the globally declared `LastName` element because it is part of the default namespace for this document).

Here is a conforming document (`CustomerA.xml`). As you can see the order of elements is the same, but the namespace is being used in rather an interesting fashion:

```
<?xml version = "1.0" ?>
<cust:Customer xmlns:cust = "http://www.example.org/Customers"
               xmlns:xsi = "http://www.w3.org/2001/XMLSchema-instance"
               xsi:schemaLocation = "Customers.xsd">
    <FirstName>Ray</FirstName>
    <MiddleInitial>G</MiddleInitial>
    <cust:LastName>Bayliss</cust:LastName>
</cust:Customer>
```

Both the `Customer` element and the `LastName` element have been qualified as belonging to the http://www.example.org/Customers namespace.

Very importantly, this means that the following would NOT be a valid instance document according to this schema:

```
<?xml version = "1.0" ?>
<Customer xmlns = "http://www.example.org/Customers">
    <FirstName>Ray</FirstName>
    <MiddleInitial>G</MiddleInitial>
    <LastName>Bayliss</LastName>
</Customer>
```

Why is this the case? You may remember that back in Chapter 1, in both the *Global versus Local Element Declarations* and the *Global versus Local Attribute Declarations* sections, we warned that globally declared elements and attributes must be qualified, whereas locally declared elements and attributes need not always be qualified. You can ignore this requirement if your declarations and definitions do not belong to a namespace, because there is no namespace to qualify the globally declared elements and attributes with. However, as soon as you declare a target namespace for your schema, your instance documents will have to obey this requirement.

By introducing the `targetNamespace` attribute in `CustomerA.xsd`, we are required to qualify all elements and attributes that are declared globally in the schema, but we **must not** qualify locally declared elements and attributes.

Let's take a closer look at why this is happening.

Looking Behind Namespace Qualification

In order to understand why this interesting problem with namespace qualification occurs, we need to look at how the `targetNamespace` of the schema is being populated.

Let's look at another example of this schema, and see what happens this time. We are simply going to add two attributes and a named complex type to the schema and call it `CustomerB.xsd`:

```xml
<?xml version = "1.0" ?>
<xs:schema xmlns:xs = "http://www.w3.org/2001/XMLSchema"
           targetNamespace = "http://www.example.org/Customers"
           xmlns = "http://www.example.org/Customers">

    <xs:element name = "Customer" type = "CustomerType" />

    <xs:complexType name = "CustomerType">
        <xs:sequence>
            <xs:element name = "FirstName" type = "xs:string" />
            <xs:element name = "MiddleInitial" type = "xs:string" />
            <xs:element ref = "LastName" />
        </xs:sequence>
        <xs:attribute name = "clubCardMember" type = "xs:boolean" />
        <xs:attribute ref = "customerID" />
    </xs:complexType>

    <xs:element name = "LastName" type = "xs:string" />
    <xs:attribute name = "customerID" type = "xs:integer" />

</xs:schema>
```

The changes have been highlighted. So, let's take a look at the affect this has on the conforming instance document (`CustomerB.xml`):

```xml
<?xml version = "1.0" ?>
<cust:Customer xmlns:cust = "http://www.example.org/Customers"
               clubCardMember = "true"
               cust:customerID = "24427">
    <FirstName>Ray</FirstName>
    <MiddleInitial>G</MiddleInitial>
    <cust:LastName>Bayliss</cust:LastName>
</cust:Customer>
```

This example is even more interesting because, of the two new attributes, the only attribute that carries a prefix is the one that was declared globally, `customerID`, and therefore it has to be qualified. As with the last example, we still have to qualify the `Customer` and `LastName` elements because they are globally declared.

We could write this schema in another way, by qualifying the types that we have defined and the references to elements or attributes that we have declared (rather than the markup from the XML Schema Namespace). The conforming instance document would be the same; it just changes the default namespace of the schema from the `targetNamespace` to that of the XML Schema Recommendation (`CustomerC.xsd`).

```
<?xml version = "1.0" ?>
<schema xmlns = "http://www.w3.org/2001/XMLSchema"
        targetNamespace = "http://www.example.org/Customers"
        xmlns:cust = "http://www.example.org/Customers">

   <element name = "Customer" type = "cust:CustomerType" />

   <complexType name = "CustomerType">
      <sequence>
         <element name = "FirstName" type = "string" />
         <element name = "MiddleInitial" type = "string" />
         <element ref = "cust:LastName" />
      </sequence>
      <attribute name = "clubCardMember" type = "boolean" />
      <attribute ref = "cust:customerID" />
   </complexType>

   <element name = "LastName" type = "string" />
   <attribute name = "customerID" type = "integer" />

</schema>
```

By default, each globally declared element, attribute, and type is added to the target namespace, while the locally declared elements and attributes belong in no namespace and are interpreted according to their containing element. So, the `Customer` element, the `CustomerType` complex type, the `LastName` element, and the `customerID` attribute are all added to the target namespace. In order to associate the element and attributes in the instance document with the information items in a schema, they need to be qualified. Target namespaces in the schema therefore control the validation of corresponding namespaces in the instance. (Note that when we come to look at `elementFormDefault` and the `form` attribute, we need to give them a value of `qualified`, because this adds the child elements to the target namespace.)

Furthermore, globally declared elements are the only ones that can be used as a starting point for validation, which is why if you only have one globally declared element the schema will know which is the intended root element because there is only one element as a starting point.

Understanding Infoset Contributions to Namespace Qualification

If you remember back to the end of Chapter 1, we briefly looked at how XML Schema's validation mechanism is described in terms of an abstract information model defined in the infoset. Each well-formed XML document has an infoset, and validation is described in terms of comparing the information items in the instance document to the information items that represent the schema constructs. As soon as we introduce namespaces to instance documents, we add to the infoset in terms of:

❑   Namespace information items that correspond to the namespaces of the documents

❑   Namespace properties to each of the information items qualified by a namespace in the instance document

❑   Namespace properties to each of the information items representing schema constructs that are globally declared

In the information set that represents an instance document, each element and attribute information item carries three properties that are key to namespace resolution:

- ❑ local name: whose value is the local part of the element/attribute name, not including any namespace prefix or following colon

- ❑ prefix: whose value is the namespace prefix part of the element/attribute name. If the name is unprefixed, this property has no value

- ❑ namespace name: whose value is the namespace URI of the element/attribute. If the element does not belong to a namespace, this property has no value

Note that namespace-aware applications should use the namespace name rather than the prefix to identify elements.

> *XML Schema also allows processors to add a lot of new properties to the information items of an infoset representing an XML Schema, but you really do not need to know about these when authoring schemas.*

If the value of the local name and the namespace name properties in the infoset representing the instance document do not match up with the values represented in the infoset for the schema, then the document will not be validated.

Value of local name property of information item representing the source document	Value of the namespace name property of information item representing the source document	The declaration's local name	The target namespace of the schema component	Validates
Book	http://www.example.org/book	Book	http://www.example.org/book	Yes
Book		Book	http://www.example.org/book	No
Book	http://www.example.org/book	Book		No

Both parts of the namespace have to match up in order for a document to be valid.

Requiring that a document author needs to know which elements and attributes were declared globally and act upon that when writing an instance document is a tall order, certainly making the authoring of documents more difficult. There are, however, ways in which we can control how the instance document must appear.

Requiring All Elements and Attributes Be Qualified

There are two very helpful attributes we can add to the root schema element to indicate whether we want our elements and attributes to be qualified or not. These act as a global switch for the whole document, and indicate that all of the elements and attributes declared in the document (unless we specifically declare otherwise) should be qualified.

These two attributes are elementFormDefault and attributeFormDefault, and the default value for both is unqualified, which is why only globally declared elements and attributes need to be qualified in instance documents. Let's see what happens then, when we give these attributes a value of qualified.

Here is the same schema with elementFormDefault and attributeFormDefault set to qualified (CustomerD.xsd):

```
<?xml version = "1.0" ?>
<schema xmlns = "http://www.w3.org/2001/XMLSchema"
        targetNamespace = "http://www.example.org/Customers"
        xmlns:cust = "http://www.example.org/Customers"
        elementFormDefault = "qualified"
        attributeFormDefault = "qualified">

    <element name = "Customer" type = "cust:CustomerType" />

    <complexType name = "CustomerType">
       <sequence>
          <element name = "FirstName" type = "string" />
          <element name = "MiddleInitial" type = "string" />
          <element ref = "cust:LastName" />
       </sequence>
       <attribute name = "clubCardMember" type = "boolean" />
       <attribute ref = "cust:customerID" />
    </complexType>

    <element name = "LastName" type = "string" />
    <attribute name = "customerID" type = "integer" />

</schema>
```

Now let's look at how we could represent the instance document. We could qualify each element and attribute individually like so (CustomerD.xml):

```
<?xml version = "1.0" ?>
<cust:Customer xmlns:cust = "http://www.example.org/Customers"
               cust:clubCardMember = "true"
               cust:customerID = "24427">
   <cust:FirstName>Ray</cust:FirstName>
   <cust:MiddleInitial>G</cust:MiddleInitial>
   <cust:LastName>Bayliss</cust:LastName>
</cust:Customer>
```

But the following would NOT be valid:

```
<?xml version = "1.0" ?>
<Customer xmlns = "http://www.example.org/Customers"
          clubCardMember = "true"
          customerID = "24427">
   <FirstName>Ray</FirstName>
   <MiddleInitial>G</MiddleInitial>
   <LastName>Bayliss</LastName>
</Customer>
```

The problem with this is that we still need to explicitly qualify references to attributes on the root element like so because, as we have seen before, unqualified attributes are in the null namespace, rather than the default namespace:

```
<?xml version = "1.0" ?>
<Customer xmlns = "http://www.example.org/Customers"
          xmlns:cust = "http://www.example.org/Customers"
          cust:clubCardMember = "True"
          cust:customerID = "24427">
   <FirstName>Ray</FirstName>
   <MiddleInitial>G</MiddleInitial>
   <LastName>Bayliss</LastName>
</Customer>
```

So, what happens if we give `elementFormDefault` a value of `qualified` and either give `attributeFormDefault` a value of `unqualified`, or leave it off?

```
<?xml version = "1.0" ?>
<schema xmlns = "http://www.w3.org/2001/XMLSchema"
        targetNamespace = "http://www.example.org/Customers"
        xmlns:cust = "http://www.example.org/Customers"
        elementFormDefault = "qualified"
        attributeFormDefault = "unqualified">

   <element name = "Customer" type = "cust:CustomerType" />

   <complexType name = "CustomerType">
      <sequence>
         <element name = "FirstName" type = "string" />
         <element name = "MiddleInitial" type = "string" />
         <element ref = "cust:LastName" />
      </sequence>
      <attribute name = "clubCardMember" type = "boolean" />
      <attribute ref = "cust:customerID" />
   </complexType>

   <element name = "LastName" type = "string" />
   <attribute name = "customerID" type = "integer" />

</schema>
```

If we enter the above, the following instance document will still not work:

```
<?xml version = "1.0" ?>
<Customer xmlns = "http://www.example.org/Customers"
          customerID = "2442"
          clubCardMember = "true">
   <FirstName>Ray</FirstName>
   <MiddleInitial>G</MiddleInitial>
   <LastName>Bayliss</LastName>
</Customer>
```

Why? Because the schema is still expecting that we qualify the globally declared attribute name; it wants to see the following (CustomerE.xml):

```
<?xml version = "1.0" ?>
<Customer xmlns = "http://www.example.org/Customers"
          xmlns:cust = "http://www.example.org/Customers"
          clubCardMember = "true"
          cust:customerID = "2442">
   <FirstName>Ray</FirstName>
   <MiddleInitial>G</MiddleInitial>
   <LastName>Bayliss</LastName>
</Customer>
```

Notice how the clubCardMember attribute is not qualified, but the customerID attribute is, because the customerID attribute is globally declared.

We can work around the requirement to add qualifications to globally declared attributes by adding the attributes that we want to declare to an attribute group like so (CustomerF.xsd):

```
<?xml version = "1.0" ?>
<schema xmlns = "http://www.w3.org/2001/XMLSchema"
        targetNamespace = "http://www.example.org/Customers"
        xmlns:cust = "http://www.example.org/Customers"
        elementFormDefault = "qualified"
        attributeFormDefault = "unqualified">

   <element name = "Customer" type = "cust:CustomerType" />

   <complexType name = "CustomerType">
      <sequence>
         <element name = "FirstName" type = "string" />
         <element name = "MiddleInitial" type = "string" />
         <element ref = "cust:LastName" />
      </sequence>
      <attributeGroup ref = "cust:rootAttributes" />
   </complexType>

   <element name = "LastName" type = "string" />

   <attributeGroup name = "rootAttributes">
      <attribute name = "clubCardMember" type = "boolean" />
      <attribute name = "customerID" type = "integer" />
   </attributeGroup>

</schema>
```

Now the following instance document will be valid:

```xml
<?xml version = "1.0" ?>
<Customer xmlns = "http://www.example.org/Customers"
          customerID = "2442"
          clubCardMember = "true">
   <FirstName>Ray</FirstName>
   <MiddleInitial>G</MiddleInitial>
   <LastName>Bayliss</LastName>
</Customer>
```

> **Unless you want to explicitly have to qualify attributes, do not declare them globally.
> As document authors might not expect you to require that they qualify attributes, you
> are better off creating an attribute group and using that.**

Typical use for qualified attributes is when using them in a document that is not based on that
namespace. For example, the attributes from the XML Schema for Instances namespace (such as
`xsi:type` and `xsi:nil`) are all qualified attributes because they're designed to be used in a document
that doesn't use the `XMLSchema-instance` namespace throughout. In such cases you need to either
make the attributes global in the schema or say they're qualified either through
`attributeFormDefault` or the `form` attribute on the attribute definitions.

Just to re-iterate one last point that we met earlier but which might need re-enforcing. If we remove the
attributes, and just go back to the elements using a complex type definition, and remove the
`elementFormDefault` attribute from the root element (`CustomerG.xsd`):

```xml
<?xml version = "1.0"?>
<schema xmlns = "http://www.w3.org/2001/XMLSchema"
        targetNamespace = "http://www.example.org/Customers"
        xmlns:cust = "http://www.example.org/Customers">

   <element name = "Customer" type = "cust:CustomerType" />

   <complexType name = "CustomerType">
      <sequence>
         <element name = "FirstName" type = "string" />
         <element name = "MiddleInitial" type = "string" />
         <element name = "LastName" type = "string" />
      </sequence>
   </complexType>

</schema>
```

Here we are using local element declarations for the children of the `Customer` element. This means
that the following will not work in an instance document, because we are only expected to qualify
globally declared elements and attributes:

```xml
<?xml version = "1.0" ?>
<Customer xmlns = "http://www.example.org/Customers">
   <FirstName>Ray</FirstName>
   <MiddleInitial>G</MiddleInitial>
   <LastName>Bayliss</LastName>
</Customer>
```

The proper way of showing this in a document is (`CustomerG.xml`):

```
<?xml version = "1.0" ?>
<cust:Customer xmlns:cust = "http://www.example.org/Customers">
   <FirstName>Ray</FirstName>
   <MiddleInitial>G</MiddleInitial>
   <LastName>Bayliss</LastName>
</cust:Customer>
```

As we mentioned in the earlier section on *namespace defaulting*, some people frown on this particular usage of namespaces. There are three reasons for this. First, it means that the people using the schema need to know which elements are declared globally so that they know which they need to put in a namespace. Second, it means that two elements with the same name and both in no namespace could actually be from different vocabularies, and require different treatment; therefore people reading or writing processing applications to work with the XML need to look to the parent element to work out which vocabulary they're from.

The problem remains whether we use a named complex type or a named model group. The other way around this problem is to globally declare elements and then group them together using references (`CustomerH.xsd`):

```
<?xml version = "1.0" ?>
<schema xmlns = "http://www.w3.org/2001/XMLSchema"
        targetNamespace = "http://www.example.org/Customers"
        xmlns:cust = "http://www.example.org/Customers">

   <element name = "Customer">
      <complexType>
         <sequence>
            <element ref = "cust:FirstName" />
            <element ref = "cust:MiddleInitial" />
            <element ref = "cust:LastName" />
         </sequence>
      </complexType>
   </element>

   <element name = "FirstName" type = "string" />
   <element name = "MiddleInitial" type = "string" />
   <element name = "LastName" type = "string" />

</schema>
```

Note how we also have to qualify all of the elements, but this time we are allowed to use the default namespace mechanism.

```
<?xml version = "1.0" ?>
<Customer xmlns = "http://www.example.org/Customers">
   <FirstName>Ray</FirstName>
   <MiddleInitial>G</MiddleInitial>
   <LastName>Bayliss</LastName>
</Customer>
```

One drawback to declaring all elements globally is that we cannot create two elements with the same local name (but not in the same scope) and allow each to have a different content model.

> **Be careful using local declarations if `elementFormDefault` has a value of `unqualified`. Local declared elements should not be qualified.**

Summary of Rules to Remember when Using Namespaces

The rules and examples that we have just seen can take a while to get used to, and certainly complicate the use of namespaces in XML documents. Here is a summary of points to be remembered when working with namespaces:

❑   *When `elementFormDefault` has a value of `unqualified`*:

Be careful because locally declared elements must not be qualified.

❑   *When `elementFormDefault` has a value of `qualified`*:

We can use namespace defaulting on elements.

❑   *When `attributeFormDefault` has a value of `qualified`*:

We have to explicitly qualify all attributes, because they do not inherit the default namespace.

❑   *When `attributeFormDefault` has a value of `unqualified`*:

We have to explicitly qualify all globally declared attributes. If we do not want to qualify attributes, define attribute groups and create references to them.

❑   *When namespaces are required, XML Schema authors often use the following settings*:

`elementFormDefault` is given a value of `qualified` to allow namespace defaulting.

`attributeFormDefault` is given a value of `unqualified` or left as this is the default.

> **Attribute groups are used in favor of globally declared attributes.**

Note that people who come from a more OO programming-oriented background might choose to vary from these general guidelines if they view sub-elements as being like attributes.

Here is the final suggestion of the easiest way of declaring this schema (`CustomerI.xsd`):

```
<?xml version = "1.0" ?>
<schema xmlns = "http://www.w3.org/2001/XMLSchema"
        targetNamespace = "http://www.example.org/Customers"
        xmlns:cust = "http://www.example.org/Customers"
        elementFormDefault = "qualified"
        attributeFormDefault = "unqualified">

    <element name = "Customer">
        <complexType>
            <sequence>
                <group ref = "cust:CustomerGroup" />
```

```
            </sequence>
            <attributeGroup ref = "cust:rootAttributes" />
        </complexType>
    </element>

    <group name = "CustomerGroup">
        <sequence>
            <element name = "FirstName" type = "string" />
            <element name = "MiddleInitial" type = "string" />
            <element name = "LastName" type = "string" />
        </sequence>
    </group>

    <attributeGroup name = "rootAttributes">
        <attribute name = "customerID" use = "required" type="integer" />
        <attribute name = "clubCardMember" use = "required" type="boolean" />
    </attributeGroup>

</schema>
```

Here is the conforming instance document (`CustomerI.xml`):

```
<?xml version = "1.0" ?>
<Customer xmlns = "http://www.example.org/Customers"
          customerID = "2442"
          clubCardMember = "true" >
    <FirstName>Ray</FirstName>
    <MiddleInitial>G</MiddleInitial>
    <LastName>Bayliss</LastName>
</Customer>
```

Local Control of Namespace Qualification

If we want finer grained control over whether an element or attribute should be qualified in instance documents, we can control it at an element or attribute declaration level using the `form` attribute.

The `form` attribute takes the values of `qualified` and `unqualified`, just like `elementFormDefault` and `attributeFormDefault`. Its use in the schema overrides that of `elementFormDefault` and `attributeFormDefault`.

XML Schema itself does not require that attributes are qualified, however, there are times when qualification of attributes is required in instance documents, for example when the attribute is not from the same namespace as the rest of the document – rather like the use of `xsi:schemaLocation` in instance documents. By prefixing the attribute it specifically indicates that the `schemaLocation` attribute belongs to the XML Schema for instances namespace, rather than the namespace of the document in question.

If we just wanted the `customerID` element to be qualified in the example we have been looking at throughout this chapter, we would simply add the `form` attribute to the declaration of the attribute we want to be qualified:

```
       <attributeGroup name = "rootAttributes">
          <attribute name = "customerID" use = "required" type="integer"
                     form = "qualified" />
          <attribute name = "clubCardMember" use = "required" type="boolean" />
       </attributeGroup>
```

In the instance document we would now have to declare the namespace, even though we have made use of namespace defaulting:

```
<?xml version = "1.0" ?>
<Customer xmlns = "http://www.example.org/Customers"
     xmlns:cust = "http://www.example.org/Customers"
     cust:customerID = "2442"
     clubCardMember = "true" >
  <FirstName>Ray</FirstName>
  <MiddleInitial>G</MiddleInitial>
  <LastName>Bayliss</LastName>
</Customer>
```

Let's now turn our attention to how we can use markup in instance documents that comes from different namespaces.

Models and Issues for Local versus Global Declarations

You might think that you should declare elements globally if you are likely to want to re-use them in another part of the document. As we have seen, however, there are issues regarding namespaces that require us to think twice about this, as it can complicate the requirements for qualification in instance documents (which complicate the work of a document author).

We have seen that global versus local declarations have an effect on whether elements and attributes should be qualified in instance documents, and how we can control the requirement of qualification in instance documents. Therefore, we should take a look at the different ways in which we can declare content models for elements.

There has been quite a lot of discussion regarding the question of when to declare elements locally and when to declare them globally in the XML community. Various members of the XML-Dev list, in particular Roger Costello (who maintains an excellent schema resource at http://www.xfront.com/BestPractices.html), have contributed to the design of three models that describe issues regarding when to declare elements locally or globally. The three models are known as:

❑   Russian Doll Design

❑   Salami Slice Design

❑   Venetian Blind Model

In this section, we'll take a look at examples of the Russian Doll and Salami Slice designs first as they take almost opposite approaches from each other, and will follow those with a look at the characteristics of each of them. Then we will come back to look at the Venetian Blind Model, which is a compromise between the two.

We will continue with the customer example that we first used in Chapter 1, and have been looking at in this chapter, to illustrate these models. Throughout the examples, we will start by looking at XML Schemas that have the following settings on the root schema element:

```
elementFormDefault = "qualified"
attributeFormDefault = "unqualified"
```

The examples that follow this setting have filenames that end with _eq_au.xsd and _eq_au.xml. This is intended to be a quick reference to show that all *e*lements are required to be *q*ualified (hence eq) and *a*ttributes are *u*nqualified (hence au).

We will also look at what an instance document would look like with the following settings on the root schema element:

```
elementFormDefault = "unqualified"
attributeFormDefault = "unqualified"
```

The examples that follow this setting have filenames that end with _eu_au.xsd and _eu_au.xml. This is intended to be a quick reference to show that all *e*lements are required to be *u*nqualified (hence eu) and *a*ttributes are *u*nqualified (hence au).

Russian Doll Design

With the **Russian Doll Design**, the schema mirrors the structure of the instance document. For example, if we had the following document (RussianDoll_eq_au.xml):

```
<?xml version = "1.0" ?>
<Customer xmlns = "http://www.example.org/Customers"
          customerID = "2442"
          clubCardMember = "true" >
   <FirstName>Ray</FirstName>
   <MiddleInitial>G</MiddleInitial>
   <LastName>Bayliss</LastName>
</Customer>
```

In the schema, each element is declared inside its parent element in the same way that it would appear in the instance document (RussianDoll_eq_au.xsd):

```
<?xml version = "1.0" ?>
<schema xmlns = "http://www.w3.org/2001/XMLSchema"
        targetNamespace = "http://www.example.org/Customers"
        xmlns:cust = "http://www.example.org/Customers"
        elementFormDefault = "qualified"
        attributeFormDefault = "unqualified">

   <element name = "Customer">
      <complexType>
         <sequence>
         <element name = "FirstName" type = "string" />
         <element name = "MiddleInitial" type = "string"
                   minOccurs = "0" maxOccurs = "1" />
```

```
                <element name = "LastName" type = "string" />
            </sequence>
            <attribute name = "customerID" use = "required" type = "integer" />
            <attribute name = "clubCardMember" type = "boolean" />
        </complexType>
    </element>

</schema>
```

In the same way that the document has all of its components bundled together, so the schema bundles the declarations together. The child element declarations sit inside the containing element declaration like Russian Dolls inside a parent container. Because all elements are declared within the parent container, there are no `ref` attributes used, but it does mean that you might have to declare an element of the same name several times.

If the schema had a value of `unqualified` for `elementFormDefault` it would look like so (`RussianDoll_eu_au.xml`):

```
<?xml version = "1.0" ?>
<cust:Customer xmlns:cust = "http://www.example.org/Customers"
               customerID = "2442"
               clubCardMember = "true" >
    <FirstName>Ray</FirstName>
    <MiddleInitial>G</MiddleInitial>
    <LastName>Bayliss</LastName>
</cust:Customer>
```

Here, we use a prefix to qualify the `Customer` element, which is the only one that requires qualifying, while the other elements and attributes must not be qualified.

Salami Slice Design

As we indicated, the **Salami Slice Design** takes the opposite approach to the Russian Doll Design (this is also sometimes referred to as the **Flat Catalog Design**). With this approach, each element and attribute is declared globally. Content models are then pieced together to create the required structure by adding references to the element and attribute declarations inside the declaration of the parent.

This time, references to all of the elements that `Customer` can contain and the attributes that it can carry are added to the anonymous complex type definition in the `Customer` element's declaration. If we were dealing with the same document, the Salami Slice Design schema would look as follows (`SalamiSlice_eq_au.xsd`):

```
<?xml version = "1.0" ?>
<schema xmlns = "http://www.w3.org/2001/XMLSchema"
        targetNamespace = "http://www.example.org/Customers"
        xmlns:cust = "http://www.example.org/Customers"
        elementFormDefault = "qualified"
        attributeFormDefault = "unqualified">

    <element name = "FirstName" type = "string" />
    <element name = "MiddleInitial" type = "string" />
    <element name = "LastName" type = "string" />
```

```
      <attribute name = "customerID" type = "integer" />
      <attribute name = "clubCardMember" type = "boolean" />

      <element name = "Customer">
        <complexType>
          <sequence>
            <element ref = "cust:FirstName" />
            <element ref = "cust:MiddleInitial" minOccurs = "0"
              maxOccurs = "1" />
            <element ref = "cust:LastName" />
          </sequence>
          <attribute ref = "cust:customerID" use = "required" />
          <attribute ref = "cust:clubCardMember" />
        </complexType>
      </element>

  </schema>
```

Note how both occurrence constraints cannot be placed on the global declarations, and have to be placed on the references to the globally declared elements and attributes.

The declarations here are quite a lot longer than for the Russian Doll Design, but they are no longer bundled together as in the last example, so any of the elements can be re-used in other structures, just as they have been within Customer. Here, we are taking the individual slices needed to make up a content model. Sample XML code (SalamiSlice_eq_au.xml) is shown below:

```
<?xml version = "1.0" ?>
<cust:Customer xmlns:cust = "http://www.example.org/Customers"
               cust:customerID = "2442"
               cust:clubCardMember = "true" >
  <cust:FirstName>Ray</cust:FirstName>
  <cust:MiddleInitial>G</cust:MiddleInitial>
  <cust:LastName>Bayliss</cust:LastName>
</cust:Customer>
```

Note that if elementFormDefault had a value of unqualified the instance document would look like this – exactly the same as the last one (SalamiSlice_eu_au.xml):

```
<?xml version = "1.0" ?>
<cust:Customer xmlns:cust = "http://www.example.org/Customers"
               cust:customerID = "2442"
               cust:clubCardMember = "true" >
  <cust:FirstName>Ray</cust:FirstName>
  <cust:MiddleInitial>G</cust:MiddleInitial>
  <cust:LastName>Bayliss</cust:LastName>
</cust:Customer>
```

Having introduced the two designs, let's have a look at the characteristics of each.

Characteristics of Russian Doll Design

The Russian Doll Design provides a clean compact way of declaring schema components. It can be easier to read than the Salami Slice Design because related declarations are bundled together rather than being spread out, although if we have complicated content models we can end up with a very long element declaration. We will see how to split this up when we come to the third model.

The way that the Customer element's child elements and attributes are declared inside the Customer element's declaration means that there are some interesting side effects:

1. The child elements and attributes are **opaque** to other schema components and indeed other schemas. Because they are not globally declared, no other schema component within the same schema can make use of them by reference, nor can any other schema make use of them. So, the child elements or attributes of Customer cannot be referenced elsewhere in this or other schemas.

2. They have **localized scope**, which means that we could use a second FirstName element and let it have a different content model in the same document as long as it was used outside the scope of the Customer element.

3. The effects of a change to an element or attribute declared inside the content model would not affect any other element content models. The child declarations are therefore considered as being **decoupled** – they do not interact with each other, and the impacts of a change are not felt outside the context of the element in which they are declared. For example, if you change the FirstName or LastName elements, then the changes will not affect anything in the schema outside of the Customer element.

4. The way in which this kind of schema is constructed is very different from the way in which DTDs declare elements and attributes, which means that it can be difficult either to use a language such as XSLT to transform DTDs into schemas, or for humans to follow the patterns in each design. Furthermore, you cannot use the same design guidelines for both technologies.

Bearing in mind that all global elements need to be namespace qualified; if the schema declares elementFormDefault to be unqualified (which is the default), then only the Customer element should be qualified. In this case, the instance document would look like this (RussianDoll_eu_au.xml):

```
<?xml version = "1.0" ?>
<cust:Customer xmlns:cust = "http://www.example.org/Customers"
               customerID = "2442"
               clubCardMember = "true" >
   <FirstName>Ray</FirstName>
   <MiddleInitial>G</MiddleInitial>
   <LastName>Bayliss</LastName>
</cust:Customer>
```

The requirement to only qualify the Customer element in the instance, and not the child elements, can make matters more difficult for a number of reasons:

❑ First, document authors would need to know which elements and attributes to qualify.

❑ Second, if we are using XSLT we have to process ancestor elements in order to determine which vocabulary they belong to.

❑ Third, if we are using a SAX processor we need to record the context of the element or attribute in order to check which vocabulary it belongs to.

This approach also means that we cannot use namespace defaulting if we do not set `elementFormDefault` to `qualified`.

Characteristics of Salami Slice Design

The Salami Slice Design can end up being quite verbose in comparison to the compact Russian Doll Design **unless** you re-use a lot of elements by reference. While this means that all of the element declarations are clearly visible at the global level and can be re-used, in a large schema you end up with a lot of global declarations. The effects of this design are quite different from those of the Russian Doll Design:

1. The child elements and attributes are **transparent** and can be used by more elements than just the `Customer` element; other complex types can use the same elements and attributes by reference just like the `Customer` element does. Furthermore, because they have been declared globally, so other schemas can also use them.

2. Because each element and attribute is declared globally they all have **global scope**, which means that we could not have another element with the same name and a different content model, and we cannot have an attribute with a different simple type.

3. These declarations are considered **coupled** because if a change is made to any of the global elements it will affect any of the content models that make use of it.

4. This kind of approach is more like that used with DTDs, where each element or attribute has to be declared before it can be used in a content model. This approach has also been compared to that of cloning an object, having defined the element or attribute it can be used by reference. In which case two elements are clearly instances of the same class.

5. The `elementFormDefault` and `attributeFormDefault` settings have no effect on the Salami Slice Design because all elements and attributes are global, and these settings affect only local declarations.

Note that this also means that we can use namespace defaulting on elements even when `elementFormDefault` has a value of unqualified (which we could not when `elementFormDefault` was set to unqualified in the Russian Doll Design), although we still have to qualify the attributes:

```
<?xml version = "1.0" ?>
<Customer xmlns = "http://www.example.org/Customers"
          xmlns:cust = "http://www.example.org/Customers"
          cust:customerID = "2442"
          cust:clubCardMember = "true" >
   <FirstName>Ray</FirstName>
   <MiddleInitial>G</MiddleInitial>
   <LastName>Bayliss</LastName>
</cust:Customer>
```

From a processing point of view, whether validating an instance document or the schema itself, the Salami Slice Design introduces more work for the processing application that has to deal with the overhead of all of the references.

In summary, the Russian Doll and Salami Slice Designs differ in four important ways:

❑ The Russian Doll Design facilitates hiding (localizing) of namespace complexities, while the Salami Slice Design does not.

❑ The Salami Slice Design facilitates individual component re-use, while the Russian Doll Design does not.

❑ Changes made to the component elements of the Russian Doll Design will not have any effect outside their containing element, while changes to components of the Salami Slice Design will affect any other element declaration that uses them.

❑ The Russian Doll Design allows only one document element to be used, whereas the Salami Slice Design allows any globally defined element to be used as the document element of a conforming document.

The third approach that we mentioned, the Venetian Blind Model, creates a middle ground where namespace complexity is hidden, while still allowing a degree of component re-use.

Venetian Blind Model

The **Venetian Blind Model** encourages the use of `complexTypes` rather than just the declaration of elements. In this approach, we will be able to re-use the elements that make up the `Customer` element. For example, if we wanted to create elements called `Employee` and `Supplier`, both would be able to use the same child elements, because, while they are not individually declared globally, they can be re-used together as a group. The idea behind types and the Venetian Blind Model is analogous to the notion of defining a class and using the class to create an object.

Here we define the `complexType` called `NameType` to use in the `Customer` element (`VenetianBlindNCT_eq_au.xsd`):

```
<?xml version = "1.0" ?>
<xs:schema xmlns:xs = "http://www.w3.org/2001/XMLSchema"
           targetNamespace = "http://www.example.org/Customers"
           xmlns = "http://www.example.org/Customers"
           elementFormDefault = "qualified"
           attributeFormDefault = "unqualified">

  <xs:element name = "Customer" type = "NameType" />

  <xs:complexType name = "NameType">
    <xs:sequence>
      <xs:element name = "FirstName" type = "xs:string" />
      <xs:element name = "MiddleInitial" type = "xs:string"
                  minOccurs = "0" maxOccurs = "1" />
      <xs:element name = "LastName" type = "xs:string" />
    </xs:sequence>
    <xs:attribute name = "customerID" type = " xs:integer"
```

```
                    use = "required" />
        <xs:attribute name = "clubCardMember" type = "xs:boolean" />
    </xs:complexType>


</xs:schema>
```

Having abstractly defined the `NameType`, we can use it to define the allowable content of any element. The file is below (`VenetianBlindNCT_eq_au.xml`):

```
<?xml version = "1.0" ?>
<Customer xmlns = "http://www.example.org/Customers"
          xmlns:cust = "http://www.example.org/Customers"
          customerID = "2442"
          clubCardMember = "true" >
    <FirstName>Ray</FirstName>
    <MiddleInitial>G</MiddleInitial>
    <LastName>Bayliss</LastName>
</Customer>
```

By setting `elementFormDefault` to have a value of `qualified`, while keeping the default of `unqualified` for `attributeFormDefault`, we have neatly hidden the attributes in local declarations and they need not be qualified.

It will also minimize the namespace complexities of having to declare child elements' namespaces in an instance document when `elementFormDefault` is set to `unqualified` because the child declarations are not global – although the author still needs to qualify the root element. See below (`VenetianBlindNCT_eu_au.xml`):

```
<?xml version = "1.0" ?>
<cust:Customer xmlns:cust = "http://www.example.org/Customers"
               customerID = "2442"
               clubCardMember = "true" >
    <FirstName>Ray</FirstName>
    <MiddleInitial>G</MiddleInitial>
    <LastName>Bayliss</LastName>
</cust:Customer>
```

This is quite a contrast to the Salami Slice Design, which, by its very nature, requires all elements to expose their namespaces.

Imagine you chose to use the Salami Slice Design, and the document authors were getting frustrated with having to add prefixes to every element, you would have to completely re-design the schema to remove the requirement. If you had chosen the Venetian Blind Design, however, then you could have removed the requirement to qualify local elements simply by changing the value of `elementFormDefault`. It allows you to use `elementFormDefault` as a switch over the whole document.

As indicated, we could still use this abstract definition of a type in other elements; we can create as many elements of this class as we want:

```
<xs:element name = "Employee" type = "NameType" />
<xs:element name = "Supplier" type = "NameType" />
```

Another advantage of this approach is that, if we wanted to add a containing element into the structure:

```
<cust:Customer xmlns:cust = "http://www.example.org/Customers"
               customerID = "2442"
               clubCardMember = "true" >
    <Name>
        <FirstName>Ray</FirstName>
        <MiddleInitial>G</MiddleInitial>
        <LastName>Bayliss</LastName>
    </Name>
</cust:Customer>
```

We could change the content model of just the `Customer` element (and no other elements that use the same type) to include a `Name` element, and then set the `Name` element to be of the type `NameType`:

```
<xs:element name = "Customer">
    <xs:complexType>
        <xs:sequence>
            <xs:element name = "Name" type = "NameType" />
        </xs:sequence>
    </xs:complexType>
</xs:element>
```

This design maximizes the re-use of the child elements. We group the individual components, as we did with the Russian Doll Design, but then create a type definition for the groups, rather than re-use element declarations so that the set of elements can be re-used together.

Going Deeper into the Venetian Blind Model

The following schema is intended to validate instance documents that capture the name and address details of either `Customers` or `Employees`, both of which are people, and `Suppliers`, which are companies. We are using the Venetian Blind Model of declaring named complex types for content models. In doing so, we want to make the content models of the name and address details available to other parts of the schema (and indeed other schemas), which means they have to be declared globally. This allows us to share the `PersonType` between employees and customers, *and* allows us to re-use the `NameType` and `AddressTypes` in a new `CompanyType`. In effect, both instances of people should be created from the same class, while the suppliers need to be treated as companies, and are therefore created from a different class, which makes use of the common classes of `NameType` and `AddressType` within that class.

This does come at a price though; if we change the way we declare a name in one place, it will affect all instances of name. So, we must always be aware of the scope that changes to any globally declared component will have.

Here is the schema (`CustomerAndSupplier_eq_au.xsd`):

```
<xs:schema xmlns:xs = "http://www.w3.org/2001/XMLSchema"
        xmlns = "http://www.example.org/complexTypeExample"
        targetNamespace = "http://www.example.org/complexTypeExample"
        elementFormDefault = "qualified"
        attributeFormDefault = "unqualified">
```

```
        <xs:element name = "Customer" type = "PersonType" />
        <xs:element name = "Employee" type = "PersonType" />
        <xs:element name = "Supplier" type = "CompanyType" />

<!-- Note we do not use the prefix when declaring types
     only when referring to them -->

    <xs:complexType name = "PersonType">
        <xs:sequence>
            <xs:element name = "Name" type = "NameType" />
            <xs:element name = "Address" type = "AddressType" />
        </xs:sequence>
        <xs:attribute name = "customerID" type = "xs:integer"
                      use = "required" />
        <xs:attribute name = "clubCardMember" type = "xs:boolean" />
    </xs:complexType>

    <xs:complexType name = "CompanyType">
        <xs:sequence>
            <xs:element name = "CompanyName" type = "xs:string" />
            <xs:element name = "Contact" type = "NameType" />
            <xs:element name = "Address" type = "AddressType" />
        </xs:sequence>
        <xs:attribute name = "companyID" type = "xs:integer" />
    </xs:complexType>

    <xs:complexType name = "NameType">
        <xs:sequence>
            <xs:element name = "FirstName" type = "xs:string" />
            <xs:element name = "MiddleInitial" type = "xs:string" />
            <xs:element name = "LastName" type = "xs:string" />
        </xs:sequence>
    </xs:complexType>

    <xs:complexType name = "AddressType">
        <xs:sequence>
            <xs:element name = "AddressLine1" type = "xs:string" />
            <xs:element name = "AddressLine2" type = "xs:string"
                        minOccurs = "0" maxOccurs = "1" />
            <xs:element name = "Town" type = "xs:string" />
            <xs:element name = "City" type = "xs:string" />
            <xs:element name ="StateCountyRegion" type = "xs:string" />
            <xs:element name ="PostalZipCode" type = "xs:string" />
        </xs:sequence>
    </xs:complexType>

</xs:schema>
```

There are seven schema components that become available to other parts of this schema or other schemas:

❑   The Customer element and its content model

❑   The Employee element and its content model

❑   The Supplier element and its content model

❑ The `PersonType` named complex type, and its content model of name and address details

❑ The `CompanyType` named complex type, and its content model of contact and address details, and company name and company ID

❑ The `NameType` named complex type and its child elements

❑ The `AddressType` named complex type and its child elements

Here is one conforming document instance for the new `Supplier` element (`CustomerAndSupplierA_eq_au.xml`):

```xml
<?xml version = "1.0" ?>
<Supplier xmlns = "http://www.example.org/complexTypeExample"
     companyID = "2442">

   <CompanyName>Widget Wonders</CompanyName>

   <Contact>
       <FirstName>Dominic</FirstName>
       <MiddleInitial>R</MiddleInitial>
       <LastName>White</LastName>
   </Contact>

   <Address>
       <AddressLine1>20 The Crescent</AddressLine1>
       <Town>Acocks Green</Town>
       <City>Birmingham</City>
       <StateCountyRegion>West Midlands</StateCountyRegion>
       <PostalZipCode>B27 6PH</PostalZipCode>
   </Address>

</Supplier>
```

As we can see, this is a flexible design in allowing re-use of schema components. We can make use of the same complex types in different content models. Also the requirement to qualify any element other than the root element can be turned on and off with the `elementFormDefault` attribute; if we give it a value of qualified we can make use of default namespaces in the instance document.

Here is a second conforming document instance. Note, however, that we still have the `customerID` and `clubCardMember` attributes attached, and this time we are dealing with an `Employee` element (`CustomerAndSupplierB_eq_au.xml`):

```xml
<?xml version = "1.0" ?>
<Employee xmlns = "http://www.example.org/complexTypeExample"
         customerID = "2442"
         clubCardMember = "true" >

   <Name>
       <FirstName>Dominic</FirstName>
       <MiddleInitial>R</MiddleInitial>
       <LastName>White</LastName>
   </Name>

   <Address>
```

```
        <AddressLine1>20 The Crescent</AddressLine1>
        <Town>Acocks Green</Town>
        <City>Birmingham</City>
        <StateCountyRegion>West Midlands</StateCountyRegion>
        <PostalZipCode>B27 6PH</PostalZipCode>
      </Address>

    </Employee>
```

Here we can see that we have to be very careful about how we split up types and the scope of the content model that they are representing. In particular, we have two unnecessary attributes on the `Employee` element, namely `customerID` and `clubCardMember`, and we do not have an `employeeID` attribute. Let's look a little closer.

Issues with Complex Types and the Venetian Blind Model

Complex types and the Venetian Blind Model give us a lot of flexibility in writing schemas. However, the use of complex types in this model raises some issues regarding when to use named complex types to define parts of element content models. You need to exercise caution when working on the scope of complex types, and take into consideration how you might want to extend the model in the future.

We will take a quick look at two final examples that illustrate how you need to be careful in selecting what becomes part of a type, and how named model groups can play an important role within the Venetian Blind Model.

We Can Only Associate Each Element Name with One Type

In the last example that we saw, we needed to add different attributes to the `Customer` and `Employee` elements. The problem was that when we added the `Employee` element to the schema, we went to use the same complex type as the one that we had used in the `Customer` element:

```xml
<xs:element name = "Customer" type = "PersonType" />
<xs:element name = "Employee" type = "PersonType" />

<xs:complexType name = "PersonType">
  <xs:sequence>
    <xs:element name = "Name" type = "ct:NameType" />
    <xs:element name = "Address" type = "ct:AddressType" />
  </xs:sequence>
  <xs:attribute name = "customerID" type = "xs:integer"
                use = "required" />
  <xs:attribute name = "clubCardMember" type = "xs:boolean" />
</xs:complexType>
```

When defining the `PersonType`, attribute declarations were added that were specific to a `Customer` and it was called a general `PersonType` – it was specific to customers, not all people.

> **XML Schema does not allow you to use named complex types as well as anonymous complex types in the same element; you can only associate each element name with one complex type.**

This means that we must be careful when defining named complex types and make sure that they associate everything you need to associate with an element, while at the same time making it general enough for re-use.

We could not, for example, split off the declarations of the elements from the attributes and create a named complex type for the element content and then add an anonymous complex type as well to hold the attributes for the different element type. The following would not be allowed:

```
<xs:element name = "Employee" type = "PersonType">
   <xs:complexType>
      <xs:attribute name = "customerID" type = "xs:integer" />
      <xs:attribute name = "clubCardMember" type = "xs:boolean" />
   </xs:complexType>
</xs:element>
```

Rather, we have to separate out the complex type definitions in another way. For example, we could create a `PersonType`, and then extend it to create a separate `CustomerType` and `EmployeeType`:

```
<xs:element name="Customer" type="CustomerType" />
<xs:element name="Employee" type="EmployeeType" />

<xs:complexType name="PersonType">
   <xs:sequence>
      <xs:element name="Name" type="NameType" />
      <xs:element name="Address" type="AddressType" />
   </xs:sequence>
</xs:complexType>

<xs:complexType name="CustomerType">
   <xs:complexContent>
      <xs:extension base="PersonType">
         <xs:attribute name="customerID" type="xs:integer"
                       use="required" />
         <xs:attribute name="clubCardMember" type="xs:boolean" />
      </xs:extension>
   </xs:complexContent>
</xs:complexType>

<xs:complexType name="EmployeeType">
   <xs:complexContent>
      <xs:extension base="PersonType">
         <xs:attribute name="employeeID" type="xs:integer"
                       use="required" />
      </xs:extension>
   </xs:complexContent>
</xs:complexType>
```

This works fine for adding attributes, and is probably the best solution for this particular problem. But it will not work in all circumstances, because we are not allowed to extend a type with elements that are required to come before those that already exist – we can only add to the end of an element content model.

Alternatively, we could create a `Customer` element and an `Employee` element that use a separate `NameType` and `AddressType`, like so:

```
   <xs:element name = "Customer">
      <xs:complexType>
         <xs:sequence>
            <xs:element name = "Name" type = "NameType" />
            <xs:element name = "Address" type = "AddressType" />
         </xs:sequence>
         <xs:attribute name = "customerID" type = "xs:integer"
                       use = "required" />
         <xs:attribute name = "clubCardMember" type = "xs:boolean" />
      </xs:complexType>
   </xs:element>

   <xs:element name = "Employee">
      <xs:complexType>
         <xs:sequence>
            <xs:element name = "Name" type = "NameType" />
            <xs:element name = "Address" type = "AddressType" />
         </xs:sequence>
         <xs:attribute name = "employeeID" type = "xs:integer"
                       use = "required" />
      </xs:complexType>
   </xs:element>
```

The point to be aware of here is the scope of your complex types and what they are intended to model. If you are trying to represent a person in the complex type, stick to elements that represent the person only, and add other items outside of the complex type.

We should also look at what happens when we add to the content model defined in the NameType.

Complex Types and Model Groups as Building Blocks

The next issue we encounter occurs when we decide we want to add to the NameType with a new element. As the example stands, we would have to derive a new type. There are two methods of deriving types, which we met in Chapter 4: restriction and extension. However, both have interesting limitations.

If we want to add elements to a complex type by extension, we can only do so at the end of the content model. The reason for this seems to be so that it makes implementation of parsers and processors that are XML Schema aware easier. If we wanted to add a Title element to the beginning of the NameType, however, we cannot do so by extension, we would have to define a completely new type. Also note that if we want to restrict a complex type, we still need to repeat all of the declarations in the new complex type.

Essentially this is only a problem when we are going to want to extend complex types with elements that might be required to appear before those that already exist in the content model. However, it is also something to consider when creating re-usable blocks of schema. Therefore, it is worth noting that there can be advantages to using named model groups to create building blocks from which we write schemas rather than named complex types.

Named model groups make very effective building blocks in schemas, because they can allow more flexibility, especially in the way we can extend our content models. Let's take a closer look at the problem and how model groups solve it. If we use a named complex type it needs to be associated with an element:

```
   <xs:element name = "Name" type = "NameType" />
```

In this case, if we want to extend a type by adding new elements the extension mechanism only allows us to do so at the end of the type. Whereas if we use named model groups, we can nest the named model group inside another anonymous complex type or model group to extend the model wherever we want to add an element – even at the beginning of a group:

```
<element name = "Name">
   <complexType>
      <sequence>
      <!-- you can add a title of Mr, Mrs, Ms, Dr here -->
         <group ref = "NameGroup" />
      <!-- can add letters after someone's name here -->
      </sequence>
   </complexType>
</element>
```

When we use a model group we do not *have* to add to the end of it as we do with extension of complex types – we can create new structures that use the model group at the beginning or the end of that new structure.

We cannot do this with the complex type because each named complex type needs to be associated with an element. We would have to introduce another element to hold each type, which would then contain the child elements of that type and change the structure, like so:

```
<element name = "Name">
   <complexType>
      <sequence>
      <element name = "Title" type = "string" />
      <element name = "RestOfName" type = "ct:NameType" />
      </sequence>
   </complexType>
</element>
```

This latter example would only permit the following instance document:

```
<Name>
   <Title>Mr</Title>
   <RestOfName>
      <FirstName>Ray</FirstName>
      <MiddleInitial>G</MiddleInitial>
      <LastName>Bayliss</LastName>
   </RestOfName>
</Name>
```

If we took this a step further, and had two named model groups, we could add an element in between them to create a new content model, whereas with named complex types we would have to add two containing elements.

> **Complex types are much more geared towards data-oriented applications. Named model groups are particularly helpful for creating building blocks, which can then be used in complex types.**

Let's look at an example of this. We are going to add a `Title` element to the beginning of the `Name` element in the `Customer` elements only (not `Employee`). To add further to the example, we are also going to strip down the `Employee` element to the first line of the address and the zip or postal code. Here, bearing in mind that you have to repeat all of the declarations again when restricting a complex type, we are not creating any more work for ourselves by defining a new un-named model group inside the `Employee` element (`CustomerJ_eq_au.xsd`):

```
<xs:schema xmlns:xs = "http://www.w3.org/2001/XMLSchema"
        xmlns = "http://www.example.org/complexTypeExample"
        targetNamespace = "http://www.example.org/complexTypeExample"
        elementFormDefault = "qualified"
        attributeFormDefault = "unqualified">

   <xs:element name = "Customer">
      <xs:complexType>
         <xs:sequence>

            <xs:element name = "Name">
               <xs:complexType>
                  <xs:sequence>
                     <xs:element name = "Title" type = "xs:string" />
                     <xs:group ref = "NameGroup" />
                  </xs:sequence>
               </xs:complexType>
            </xs:element>

            <xs:element name = "Address">
               <xs:complexType>
                  <xs:group ref = "AddressGroup" />
               </xs:complexType>
            </xs:element>

         </xs:sequence>
         <xs:attribute name = "customerID" type = "xs:integer" />
         <xs:attribute name = "clubCardMember" type = "xs:boolean" />
      </complexType>
   </element>

   <xs:element name = "Employee">
      <xs:complexType>
         <xs:sequence>

            <xs:element name = "Name">
               <xs:complexType>
                  <xs:group ref = "NameGroup" />
               </xs:complexType>
            </xs:element>

            <xs:element name = "Address">
               <xs:complexType>
                  <xs:sequence>
                     <xs:element name = "AddressLine1" type = "xs:string" />
                     <xs:element name = "Town" type = "xs:string" />
                     <xs:element name = "City" type = "xs:string" />
                     <xs:element name ="StateCountyRegion"
                                 type = "xs:string" />
```

```
                    <xs:element name ="PostalZipCode" type = "xs:string" />
            </xs:sequence>
        </xs:complexType>
    </xs:element>


    </xs:sequence>
    <xs:attribute name = "employeeID" type = "xs:integer" />
    </xs:complexType>
</xs:element>

<xs:group name = "NameGroup">
    <xs:sequence>
        <xs:element name = "FirstName" type = "xs:string" />
        <xs:element name = "MiddleInitial" type = "xs:string" />
        <xs:element name = "LastName" type = "xs:string" />
    </xs:sequence>
</xs:group>

<xs:group name = "AddressGroup">
    <xs:sequence>
        <xs:element name = "AddressLine1" type = "xs:string" />
        <xs:element name = "AddressLine2" type = "xs:string"
                    minOccurs = "0" maxOccurs = "1"/>
        <xs:element name = "Town" type = "xs:string" />
        <xs:element name = "City" type = "xs:string" />
        <xs:element name ="StateCountyRegion" type = "xs:string" />
        <xs:element name ="PostalZipCode" type = "xs:string" />
    </xs:sequence>
</xs:group>

</xs:schema>
```

The resulting schema is quite a lot longer, but allows a lot more flexibility. The re-usable components are: Customer, Employee, NameGroup, and AddressGroup, and both Customer and Employee have different content models.

Because of this, unless we explicitly need the extra error checking that deriving a type provides, there should only be one layer in the complex type hierarchy. It is worth bearing in mind that we can achieve anything that the features of named complex types offer by simply using named model groups. The two things we need to consider here are as follows:

❑   While we have to add a complex type for the use of a named model group, we can add to the beginning of a named model group, but we cannot add to the beginning of a named complex type.

❑   When we want to perform a restriction on a named complex type, we have to repeat all of it anyway.

Let's summarize the advantages then of using named model groups in a Venetian blind design – they:

❑   Allow us to re-use content models within and across schemas

❑   Allow us to add elements to the beginning of the content model

❑   Hide namespace complexities because the child element declarations are not made globally

❑   Allow control over whether elements require namespaces using `elementFormDefault`

❑   Allow us to apply `minOccurs` and `maxOccurs` attributes to the element declarations, because the element declarations are not global

The only disadvantages with this approach are that we cannot re-use the element declarations that are inside the `group` by reference, and that it does not mirror the approach used by DTDs.

Summary

In this chapter we have built on what we have learnt about XML Schemas to allow us to validate an instance document that contains a namespace against a schema, and to allow us to write markup that belongs to part of a namespace.

We have seen that namespaces add a lot of complexity to both our schema authoring and to instance documents. The default requirement of XML Schema is that all globally declared elements and attributes in a schema are qualified in an instance document, while locally declared ones are not. This must be considered when writing schemas because it can have a serious effect on the ease of writing instance documents. In particular we are restricted in our ability to take advantage of default namespaces if some components of our schema are declared globally and others locally.

We can help control the effects of where we declare elements and attributes upon an instance document (and gain the ability to use namespace defaults) by setting `elementFormDefault` to `qualified`, while leaving `attributeFormDefault` unqualified and not declaring attributes globally – if necessary using an attribute group instead.

We have also seen three models for defining content models and deciding when to declare elements locally and globally, namely the Russian Doll Design (which largely follows the structure of the XML document), the Salami Slice Design (where we define every element and attribute globally as we would in a DTD and then use references to the global declarations in content models), and the Venetian Blind Design (which creates re-usable schema components, and can help reduce namespace complexities).

Finally, we looked at the idea of when to use named model groups rather than named complex types in the Venetian Blind Design, especially for creating small re-usable chunks of schemas. While complex types are helpful in creating classes of element content, we have to make sure that they contain everything that we require as they do not extend well – you are best off only allowing one layer of defined complex types in your type hierarchy.

Having investigated the issues regarding using a namespace in XML Schemas, we will go on to look at some common schema and document design issues, which will affect the way in which you write schemas. In previous chapters we have made it clear that schemas also allow us to validate instance documents that contain markup from several namespaces – this is something we cover later in the book. If you need to use multiple namespaces within your schema, or want to create schemas from multiple documents, these topics are covered in Chapter 8. However, next we'll take a look at the design issues that require consideration when creating schema vocabularies for just one namespace.

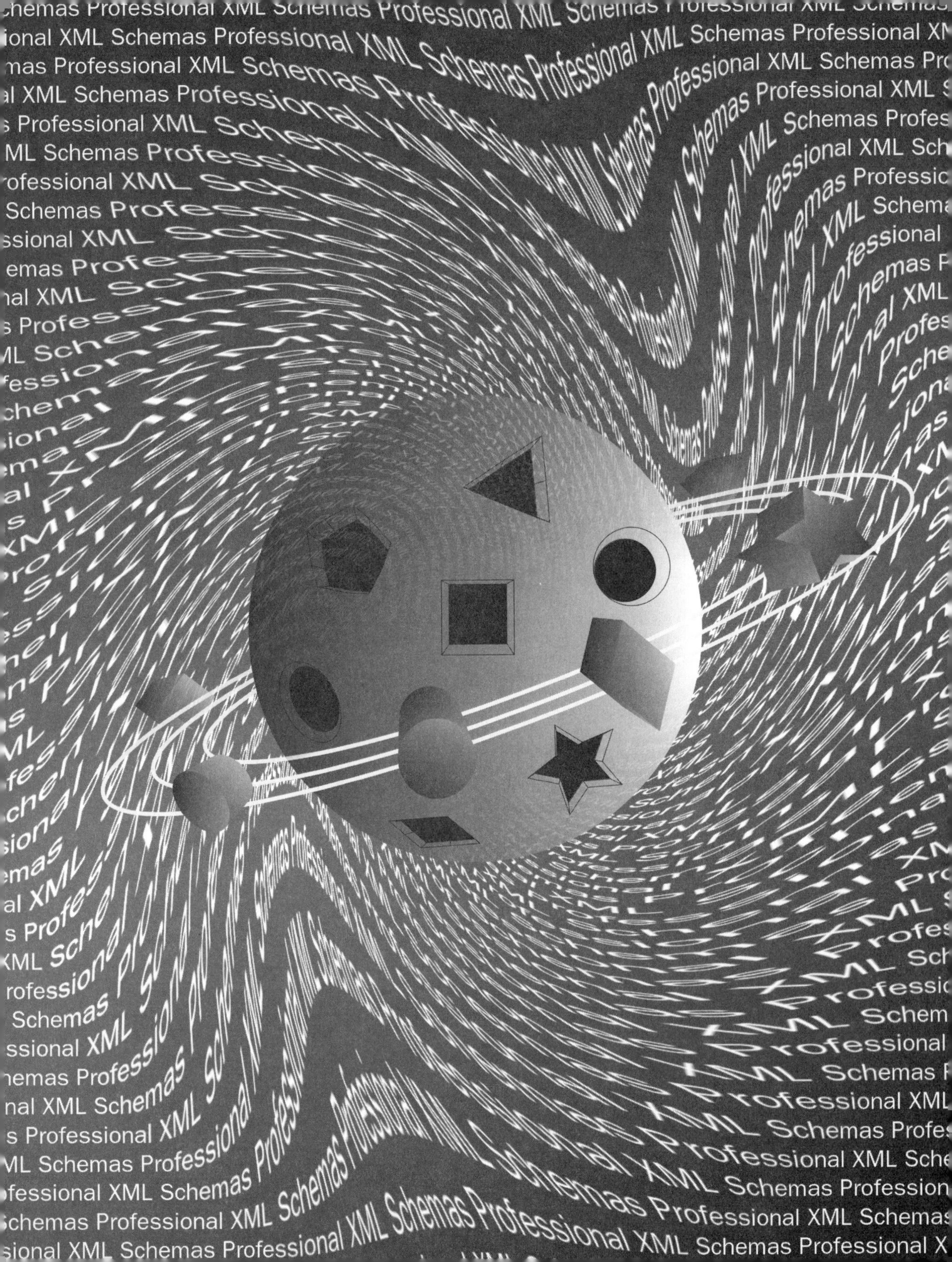
Professional XML Schemas

Schema Design Fundamentals

In this chapter we will be looking at two key issues: the design and structure of an XML document, and how we design a schema for that document structure. In particular we will be looking at design of content models, and how our design decisions have an impact upon how easy our schemas are to learn, use and process.

The topics of, firstly, designing a document structure, and secondly how the allowable structure is restricted in a schema, are quite separate; however, they often seem to get entangled and can affect each other. To help distinguish between the two topics, each section of this chapter will first look at document structures, and then at how we can represent these structures in an XML Schema. Throughout the chapter we will assess the impact upon of our decisions upon ease of learning, use and processing.

It is worth noting that the first aim of any schema is to capture all the data we need for our application, but this is a topic that we address in Chapter 11 so we won't cover it here. Furthermore, if we are dealing with a predefined document, we will not have the choice over how we represent the document structure, although we will have control over how to implement the design in the schema. Therefore, when looking at each of the structural issues in this chapter, we will see a clear separation between their design and how we deal with them in a schema.

The six sections of this chapter deal with the following issues:

❑   Naming conventions

❑   Consistent, predictable and re-usable structures

❑   Creating groups and hierarchical structures

❑   Allowing choice and controlling options

Before we look at each of these areas, however, we should look at an issue that lies beneath all schemas: how much flexibility an author is allowed over the content of a document structure.

Prescriptive versus Descriptive Models

Prescriptive or descriptive, restrictive or permissive, predictable or unpredictable – however we look at it, some schemas define a class of document that allows the author more control over how the defined markup can appear in an instance document, while others tightly restrict allowable content.

Without doubt, the subject and purpose of the data we are marking up should have the largest influence upon how we structure or represent it in XML. While one of XML's greatest strengths is its ability to mark up unstructured or semi-structured data, it is also commonly used in representations of highly structured data. So, the flexibility our schema offers should reflect the predictability of the data that document authors are marking up.

For example, if we are working on a project to mark up books or research papers, we are going to need to allow authors a certain amount of **flexibility** in the structure of a document. After all, we could never say that all books will have twelve Chapters, no more, no less. Nor could we say that a table can only appear after the first paragraph of a given chapter. We want the schema to give document authors **descriptive** powers. Schemas that have to deal with **unpredictable** structures are sometimes known as **permissive** schemas.

If we are working on a project that represents account transaction information, however, there is going to be a minimum amount of information that we require in order to process a transaction, so the structure is **predictable**. Indeed, any additional information would be surplus to requirements, so the schema can be quite **prescriptive** in how it allows authors to mark up data. Furthermore, we may require a consistent structure where information always appears in a fixed order so that a processing application can deal with it more efficiently. As such, the schemas are quite **restrictive** or **inflexible** about how a document can be written.

Before we really get started, we should note that there are an increasing number of tools being used to create and process XML documents. It is becoming less common for humans to deal with XML in its raw format, where they actually see the markup. We therefore have to place particular attention to how document structures, and restrictions placed upon allowable structures represented in schemas, can be processed by applications.

Processing XML Documents

In order to process a document, an application needs to be able to cope with all the possible structures the document will contain. It should also raise an error if the document does not match one of the allowed structures.

Because XML Schemas offer more powerful validation features than DTDs, such as supporting datatypes and allowing more flexible structures, more of the validation work that has traditionally been performed by application code can become the responsibility of the parser. The more business requirements we place in the schema, and the tighter its restrictions, the less validation code we have to write.

While W3C XML Schema does help bridge the divide between documents and data, especially with its ability to restrict order and occurrence of elements in mixed content, the requirements for order and sequence of elements will frequently depend upon whether we are dealing with documents or data. For many the bridge between these two types of document is being built to give structure to unstructured and semi-structured documents (allowing them to be processed), rather than the other way around.

> **Where we do have flexibility in the structure, then reducing the number of possible document structures allows us to optimize our code for the defined structure.**

With documents we tend to have a flat structure; the traditional application of markup languages was for display. Many of the constraints on such documents are to do with logical structure (you can only have line items in bulleted or numbered lists) and the house style. With this kind of structure, there is little chance of an application being able to construct a document. The advantage of humans adding this data to the document, however, is that applications can process it and use it.

In contrast, data-oriented schemas often represent internal data structures such as those imposed by a relational database, or properties of objects. In which case, we can often enforce strong constraints. These tight constraints make it possible for an application to create documents according to our required markup.

Naming Conventions

It should be obvious to you, as a user of XML, that element and attribute names should be as self-describing as possible, but there are a number of other concerns that we should be aware of when dealing with document structures and implementing them in schemas. Naming conventions apply equally to document design as they do to schema design; it is just that they are implemented in the schema.

The names we give our elements and attributes should always be **intuitive** to those who are going to have to use the markup. Points to consider in making a vocabulary intuitive include:

- ❑ As far as possible reflect the experience of those who have to use it.
- ❑ If we use abbreviations, only use standard abbreviations (such as Dr for Doctor), and even then only use them if they will make sense to those who have to use the document.
- ❑ Be aware of regional differences; for example, use of the name "Pants" can mean something quite different in the UK than it does in America.
- ❑ Use defined standards where possible, either standards created by a specific industry (such as ISBN numbers for books), or defined by a standards body such as ISO.

Some people like to use abbreviated names (such as cr for credit). The first reason given for this is to save on bandwidth and storage space, but the price of both is constantly falling so this need not be a concern unless we are dealing with very high volumes (gigabytes) of data. The second reason given is that it can be less intrusive on the content of a document, making it easier to read. However, this only really applies to reading text, and does not apply to finding data, if indeed users are working on the document with the markup visible. If you are still considering use of abbreviations, then you should also consider anyone else who is likely to have to use the markup, if you are hoping your schema will be adopted in your or by other trading partners, then it is clear that abbreviations will only encourage take up if they are standard abbreviations that are intuitive to users.

In order to make your names more intuitive you may decide to put extra information into the name. For example, if you are creating an element for an address, while you could just use the term Address, in cases where document contain more than one kind of address you could be more specific and use names such as BillingAddress and ShippingAddress. (This can be preferable to adding an attribute such as use to the element – see the later section *A Note About Attributes for Distinguishing Types of Element*.)

We should also try to add **consistency** to our names. This takes two forms: consistency within a type of name, and consistency across types of markup.

Consistency within a type of name refers to representing like items with similar names. For example, if we are going to create our own ID attribute for Customer, Employee, and Supplier elements, use similar names such as customerID, employeeID, and supplierID. If we are working with marking up documents, use something like Heading1 for primary headings, and then the authors will be able to expect that Heading2 and Heading3 element will apply to subheadings.

> It easier for users to learn your vocabulary if you use intuitive names, avoid abbreviations, if possible, and offer consistency within a type of name.

When it comes to consistency across types of markup, you will benefit from using a slightly different naming convention for elements and attributes. For example, this author's personal preference is to start elements with an upper-case letter and attribute with a lower-case letter; this way it is easy to distinguish between element names and attribute names at a glance.

Furthermore, because the names of our elements and attributes should be descriptive, they often contain more than one word, and can sometimes be quite long. To make names more readable, it helps if we use one of the following conventions:

- ❑ Use **camel case** where the first letter of each new word is capitalized for example:
- ❑ <PurchaseOrder orderNumber = "13832">
- ❑ Use **separating characters** such as a dash, underscore or dot notation between each new word, for example:
- ❑ Separate_words
- ❑ Hyphenate-words
- ❑ Dot.Notation

Whichever notation we choose, we should stick with it across a schema or set of schemas.

> Your vocabulary will be easier to use if you distinguish between names of elements and attributes, and start each new word in a name with an upper-case letter.

Another point to consider when devising names is whether we should **overload** names – that is, whether we should use of the same name for objects that appear in more than one type. For example, should we use a Name element to refer to individuals' names as well as company names? At a bare minimum, our naming should try to encourage one-to-one relationships between names of child information items and their parents.

Some people advocate the use of structured names that use dot notation to represent class-like data. For example, if there are names that crop up more than once, such as a `Title` for both a `Book` and a `Chapter`, that we could use a structure such as:

```
<Book>
    <Book.Title></Book.Title>
    <Book.Author></Book.Author>
        <Book.Chapter>
        <Book.Chapter.Title><Book.Chapter.Title>
        ...
        </Book.Chapter>
</Book>
```

While this kind of approach is appropriate in flat structures, and can help a user see the intent of an element, this is not necessary in XML as we can make use of XML's hierarchical structure to determine the context of an element. Furthermore, XML Schemas introduces the ability to define local elements and hence explicitly distinguish between two elements that share a name yet have different purposes. A preferable structure might be the following:

```
<Book>

    <TitleInformation>
        <Title>Miniature Bobbin Lace</Title>
        <Author>Roz Snowden</Author>
        <Publisher>Wrox Press</Publisher>
    </TitleInformation>

    <Chapter chapterNumber = "4">
        <Title indexMark = "i144">Creating Soft Furnishings</Title>
        ...
    </Chapter>

</Book>
```

One point we should consider, however, is that it *can* aid retrieval of information if we avoid relying on an application retaining the context of a name in order to distinguish it from another. For example, if we were using SAX to read the document with overloaded names, our application would have to remember the context of the item in order to determine the meaning. Alternatively, if we were using the DOM with methods such as `getElementsByTagName()`, we would have to navigate to an appropriate node before we could use it.

> **Always try to achieve a one-to-one mapping in names of parent and child items. It is easier for applications to retrieve data if you do not overload names.**

When it comes to working with an XML Schema, all of the above advantages of naming conventions help us to learn, use and process the schema. There are some additional points we can consider as well.

It can often help if we distinguish type, element, and group names. The preference of this author is to suffix a type name with the word `Type` and a group with the word `Group`. If it is a simple type, you could start the name with a lower case letter, and if it is a complex type, start it with an upper case letter. Furthermore, it is important that our name accurately names that type. For example, do not call a complex type a `PersonType` if it is specifically a `CustomerType`.

Remember that W3C XML Schema allows us to define different content models for elements of the same name in different parts of a document. Suffixing the name of your types with the word **Type** helps distinguish them from element or attribute names.

Whichever naming convention you choose to follow, you should stick to it rigidly throughout all of your documents.

Example of Two Elements with the Same Name and Different Content Models

In this example, we can see how XML Schemas allow us to define two different content models for elements of the same name. Here we have some book information that contains two elements called `Title`; one carries an attribute, which is required, the other does not (ex1sameName.xml):

```xml
<?xml version = "1.0" ?>
<Book xmlns = "http://www.example.org/books">

   <TitleInformation>
      <Title>Miniature Bobbin Lace</Title>
      <Author>Roz Snowden</Author>
      <Publisher>Wrox Press</Publisher>
   </TitleInformation>

   <Chapter chapterNumber = "4">
      <Title indexMark = "i144">Creating Soft Furnishings</Title>
      ...
   </Chapter>

</Book>
```

While the two `Title` elements have the same name, they are used in different contexts. Note how the `Title` element contained in the `Chapter` element (whose model is defined in the `ChapterType` complex type), carries an extra attribute, which as you will see from the schema below is required, while the `Title` element in the `TitleInformation` element does not. The lines that show the two different `Title` elements have been highlighted (ex1sameName.xsd):

```xml
<?xml version = "1.0" ?>
<xs:schema xmlns:xs = "http://www.w3.org/2001/XMLSchema"
           targetNamespace = "http://www.example.org/books"
           xmlns:book = "http://www.example.org/books"
           elementFormDefault = "qualified">

   <xs:element name = "Book">
      <xs:complexType>
         <xs:sequence>
            <xs:element name = "TitleInformation"
                  type = "book:TitleInformationType" />
            <xs:element name = "Chapter" type = "book:ChapterType"
                  minOccurs = "1" maxOccurs = "unbounded" />
```

```
          </xs:sequence>
        </xs:complexType>
    </xs:element>

    <xs:complexType name = "TitleInformationType">
        <xs:sequence>
            <xs:element name = "Title" type = "xs:string" />
            <xs:element name = "Author" type = "xs:string" />
            <xs:element name = "Publisher" type = "xs:string" />
        </xs:sequence>
    </xs:complexType>

    <xs:complexType name = "ChapterType">
        <xs:sequence>
            <xs:element name = "Title">
                <xs:complexType>
                    <xs:simpleContent>
                        <xs:extension base = "xs:string">
                            <xs:attribute name = "indexMark" type = "xs:ID"
                                use = "required" />
                        </xs:extension>
                    </xs:simpleContent>
                </xs:complexType>
            </xs:element>
        </xs:sequence>
        <xs:attribute name = "chapterNumber" type = "xs:integer" />
    </xs:complexType>

</xs:schema>
```

This shows how XML Schema allows us to re-use names, and give them different content models. Indeed both could have different child elements as well.

Consistency, Order, and Occurrence

If two structures are similar, they should have a **consistent structure**. This is sometimes known as **parallel design**.

The constituent structure can take two forms:

❑   Requiring the same items of information

❑   Requiring that the items of information appear in the same fixed order

It is common sense to require that two like structures should appear in a similar way. If we were to represent information, such as an address, in two different ways within the same document, it would only serve to confuse users, and create more possible structures that an application has to deal with. In this section, we will start by looking at how to create consistency in structures, use ordering for elements, and how and when to require the presence of markup in an instance document. We'll see how each of these issues affects the way users learn and use a vocabulary, and will then look at the implications for affects processing applications. Having addressed the issues that reflect document instances, we will then look at some helpful mixes of these constraints in XML Schemas.

Consistency, Order, and Occurrence in Document Structures

Let's look at each of these issues in turn and what they mean to someone who has to produce and use the document structures we define in our schemas. The balance between learning and using a schema can often be contradictory; what may be harder to learn becomes easier to use (once we have learned a restriction, we may be less likely to create an invalid document instance).

The advantages of a consistent structure are that it will make it easier to learn, because having learned one structure, others will follow the same pattern. This allows users to generalize, or predict the content model every time they come across it. For example, if every time someone has to work with a postal address structure we provide it in a consistent manner, users will soon become accustomed to the format we require for each address.

An effect of using a consistent structure is that it reduces the number of items of information we have to learn. For example, you could think of an address as being eight **chunks** of information, one parent item and seven child elements:

```
<BillingAddress>
    <AddressLine1></AddressLine1>
    <AddressLine2></AddressLine2>
    <Town></Town>
    <City></City>
    <StateCountyRegion></StateCountyRegion>
    <ZipPostCode></ZipPostCode>
    <Country></Country>
</BillingAddress>
```

Using a separate structure for billing, shipping, and suppliers, would make 24 chunks of information if the address structures were not the same. By re-using the address structure, we reduce the number of chunks we have to learn to ten (three parent elements and seven children).

The structure should also follow a users experience to make it **intuitive**. Do not be tempted to add information where a user would not expect it just so that we can re-use the constructs.

Parallel design should also highlight the differences between like items, so it is clear to users where the markup is going to differentiate. For example, if we were working on an application for a vehicle rental firm, there are going to be several kinds of vehicle that a customer can hire. However, there are also going to be common features to each kind of vehicle.

By keeping the information that is common to all vehicles in the structure for each of them (and in the same place within that structure), it will be easier to learn several different types of vehicle. All vehicles may have certain characteristics such as: make, model, engine capacity, fuel used, brake horsepower, number of passengers it can carry, and year registered.

Then there may be different information that is specific to each kind of vehicle; for example, we could be dealing with cars, minibuses, coaches, vans and trucks. Each of these types of vehicle in turn has special characteristics. For cars, we may wish to offer a category such as a saloon, sports, estate car, or sports utility vehicle. For minibuses, coaches, and trucks, you may wish to indicate the type of license needed to drive the vehicle. For vans and trucks, we may wish to indicate the maximum weight load and the volume they can carry.

By separating out the common class-like information, it makes it easy to learn the different types of vehicle quicker. Then by explicitly keeping non-general information separate, , we can make it easier to deal with the differences in vehicles.

> **The parallel design makes structures easier to learn and use because same structures are preserved across class-like structures, and differences are clearly marked.**

Another part of creating like structures is to enforce an order. Order is an interesting restraint for authors of instance document, as it can take longer to learn when you first come to use the schema. Remembering items in order, however, is a common memory improvement trick as users can chunk together items. For example, if you think about traffic lights, you tend to remember them as being red, yellow and green. The order can in fact help you learn something and use it. If you had an unordered list of things you *had* to include, it would be a lot harder to remember them all.

First, think about the user's expectations of how information is ordered. Will they expect it to be in a given order? For example:

❑   There may be ordering that reflects our business process

❑   People may be used to dealing with a specific order of information on forms

Often information might require or imply an order, such as a book's content having a table of contents and an introduction, before the main chapters, which in turn are followed by an index. Indeed, sometimes there are patterns we become accustomed to in everyday life:

❑   Addresses following the convention: House Number, Street, Town, City, State, Zip Code

❑   Meals following the pattern: starter, main course, dessert on a menu

❑   Things associated with a calendar (such as seasons, months, or days of the week)

❑   Things associated with time (breakfast, lunch, dinner or AM before PM)

❑   Rankings (charts, and competition results)

Other times, if there is no expected order, we will just need to ask ourselves whether specifying an order will make the items easier to remember.

On the flip side of this argument, sometimes we need flexibility and order might only serve to hinder document authors. For example, in a paragraph of a normal text, we cannot specify the order of references, cross-references and index marks. Under each heading we cannot specify an order of paragraphs, tables, images or diagrams, bulleted lists.

Here are some questions we can ask ourselves when considering whether to enforce ordering:

❑   Does the data allow an order to be specified?

❑   Does the data naturally follow an order?

❑   Will specifying an order help fit in with users' expectations?

❑   Will specifying an order help prevent items being missed during use?

The final thing to consider in this section is when items of information are required. This might be determined in advance, because you should already know what information you need to model in your document structure. When items that are required and are optional are mixed together, then it can be difficult for document authors to learn and remember which instances require a value and which don't. However, this is often a requirement of information you are trying to represent– for example, some people do not have middle names, some addresses are shorter than others. Where possible, it is a good idea to always require a value for of an element or attribute, if we tend to require a value in most instances. Our application should be able to ignore the items that it does not need. Clauses in required information, such as "...you always need to give an ID value to an employee, unless they are temporary employees from an agency working for less that 1 week" only serve to confuse document creation. If we cannot provide data in such cases, then it can be helpful to provide a **null** option, so that it is clear that the information is not available.

Effects of Consistency, Order, and Occurrence Upon Processing Requirements

What are the issues regarding processing of the data? By creating similar structures, we can re-use the code that will process like structures. For each element that uses the same content model (in particular the same complex type) we can process it with the same code. In this way, the re-use ties in very well with both component-based and service-based architectures. If we are not using such a programming model, we can still re-use the same code each time we come across it, and create common methods or functions for processing that data.

Regarding order, as with any restriction, the tighter we are able to constrain the structures of the documents, the more we can optimize our code for that structure. Specifying order is particularly good for reducing possible document structures. For example, if element A can contain child elements of X, Y and Z, then we will end up with the following options when we specify an order:

```
A ((X, Y?, Z?) | (X, Z?) | (Y, Z?) | Z)
```

Whereas if we do not specify an order, then we would end up with:

```
A ((X, ((Y, Z?)? | (Z, Y?)))
  | (Y, ((X, Z?)? | (Z, X?)))
  | (Z, ((X, Y?)? | (Y, X?))))
```

Order can be particularly useful when, for example, using schemas to dynamically generate forms for user input, or using them to describe an API we could indicate the order of parameters that have to be passed to a method.

Finally by requiring element content or attribute values, we are able to guarantee that an application will get the information it requires to do its job. We can place extra trust in the parser that all of the information the application needs to work with will be in an instance document. The addition of the nil mechanism is particularly helpful for dealing with information that is required, but for which there is no value.

Consistency, Order, and Occurrence in Schemas

In this section we will provide a quick refresher of the techniques we can use to implement consistency, and order and occurrence constraints, and move on to look at how we can combine some of these constraints.

In the last chapter, we saw how we can create named model groups when we want to re-use components of content models within a schema, and how we can model class-like information in named complex types. The allows us to create consistent instance documents.

We can control the order of elements using the sequence compositor, or allow items to appear in any order using all.

We can make elements optional or indeed require them to appear a fixed number of times in an instance documents using the minOccurs and maxOccurs occurrence constraints. If you have any doubts about how powerful this concept is, imagine restricting a GreenBottle element to appear inside a Wall between 1 and 10 times in a DTD:

```
<!ELEMENT GreenBottle (#PCDATA)>
<!ELEMENT Wall
   (GreenBottle, GreenBottle?, GreenBottle?, GreenBottle?, GreenBottle
    GreenBottle?, GreenBottle?, GreenBottle?, GreenBottle?, GreenBottle?,
    GreenBottle?, GreenBottle?,?)
```

We have also seen how we can require presence of attributes by adding the use attribute to their declarations.

So, let's see how we combine some of these constraints.

Re-Use

The way in which we can re-use XML Schema constructs is very powerful. In DTDs we were largely limited to re-using element already defined content models and parameter entities. With XML Schemas however, we can use a number of mechanisms. There are two types of re-use available to us:

❑ **Internal re-use** where we re-use schema components that we have already defined in the schema we are working with.

❑ **Cross-schema re-use** where we make use of schema components that have been globally defined in other schemas. We come back to re-using schema components from other schemas in the next chapter.

When internally re-using constructs, we can make use of the XML Schema's ability to:

❑ Reference elements and attributes that we have already declared (including their content model if we have already defined one)

❑ Define named complex types to represent element content models representing structures for classes of elements

❑ Define named model groups to help define content models by grouping together related elements

❑ Create new complex types by extending and restricting named complex types that we have already defined

❑ Employ attribute groups where several attributes apply to the same elements

❑ Use substitution groups to re-use the definition of the context in which an element can be placed

The three most common methods of re-use in most schemas, however, will be referencing elements and attributes, named model groups and complex types. We looked at when we should use a named model group, and when a complex type is more appropriate in the last chapter, because they have a great impact upon how we have to declare namespaces in instance documents.

The important points you should remember are:

- ❏ When defining class-like information, use a complex type
- ❏ If defining a re-usable structure, use a named model group

Let's quickly review how we could re-use these constructs for the following structure. Note how Customer and Employee have common Name, Address and EContact elements, but carry different attributes and have different elements after the three common elements:

```
<Customer customerID = "3223">
   <Name>...</Name>
   <Address>...</Address>
   <EContact>...</EContact>
   <AccountDetails>...</AccountDetails>
</Customer>
```

```
<Employee employeeID = "12700">
   <Name>...</Name>
   <Address>...</Address>
   <EContact>...</EContact>
   <JobRole>...</JobRole>
   <Department>...</Department>
</Employee>
```

At the simplest level, we could create elements for Name, Address and EContact globally and then reference them within the same document, as in the salami slice design we met in the last chapter:

```
<xs:element name = "Name" type = "NameType" type = "xs:string" />
<xs:element name = "Address" type = "AddressType" type = "xs:string" />
<xs:element name = "EContact type = "EContactType" type = "xs:string" />

<xs:element name = "Customer">
   <xs:complexType>
      <xs:sequence>
         <xs:element ref = "Name" />
         <xs:element ref = "Address" />
         <xs:element ref = "Econtact" />
         <xs:element name = "AccountDetails" type = "xs:string" />
      </xs:sequence>
   </xs:complexType>
   <xs:attribute name = "customerID" type = "xs:string" />
</xs:element>

<xs:element name = "Employee">
   <xs:complexType>
      <xs:sequence>
         <xs:element ref = "Name" />
         <xs:element ref = "Address" />
```

```
            <xs:element ref = "Econtact" />
            <xs:element name = "JobRole" type = "xs:string" />
            <xs:element name = "Department" type = "xs:string" />
        </xs:sequence>
    </xs:complexType>
    <xs:attribute name = "employeeID" type = "xs:string" />
</xs:element>
```

Here we are re-using the elements that we have declared by passing reference to them. To keep the example simple, we presume that each of these elements would just hold a string, although in reality each would likely have its own content model.

However, we could employ more efficient re-use if we were to use a named model group, however, so that all three elements were re-used together, so that we can refer to the group in each element. Here we define a `PersonGroup` containing the three elements that are common to each representation of a person:

```
<xs:group name = "PersonGroup">
   <xs:sequence>
      <xs:element name = "Name" type = "xs:string" />
      <xs:element name = "Address" type = "xs:string" />
      <xs:element name = "Econtact" type = "xs:string" />
   </xs:sequence>
<xs:group>

<xs:element name = "Customer">
   <xs:complexType>
      <xs:group ref = "PersonGroup" />
      <xs:element name = "AccountDetails" type = "xs:string" />
   </xs:complexType>
   <xs:attribute name = "customerID" type = "xs:string" />
</xs:element>

<xs:element name = "Employee">
   <xs:complexType>
      <xs:group ref = "PersonGroup" />
      <xs:element name = "JobRole" type = "xs:string" />
      <xs:element name = "Department" type = "xs:string" />
   </xs:complexType>
   <xs:attribute name = "employeeID" type = "xs:string" />
</xs:element>
```

In this case, both elements reference the same group, while the XML in an instance document would remain the same.

The final option would be to use a complex type to represent the three repeated elements. Here we have to extend the complex type that we have defined, creating new types for `Customer` and `Employee`:

```
<xs:complexType name = "PersonType">
   <xs:sequence>
      <xs:element name = "Name" type = "xs:string" />
      <xs:element name = "Address" type = "xs:string" />
```

```
            <xs:element name = "Econtact" type = "xs:string" />
        </xs:sequence>
    </xs:complexType>

<xs:element name = "Customer">
    <xs:complexType>
    <xs:complexContent>
        <xs:extension base = "PersonType">
            <xs:sequence>
                <xs:element name = "AccountDetails" type = "xs:string" />
            </xs:sequence>
            <xs:attribute name = "customerID" type = "xs:string" />
        </xs:extension>
    </xs:complexContent>
    </xs:complexType>
</xs:element>

<xs:element name = "Employee">
    <xs:complexType>
    <xs:complexContent>
        <xs:extension base = "PersonType">
            <xs:sequence>
                <xs:element name = "JobRole" type = "xs:string" />
                <xs:element name = "Department" type = "xs:string" />
            </xs:sequence>
        </xs:extension>
    <xs:attribute name = "employeeID" />
    </xs:complexContent>
    </xs:complexType>
</xs:element>
```

This will work fine, as long as we extend our class-like structures at the end of the base class they inherit from.

If we are working in a component-based or service-based architecture, then we are best only using a complex type to represent the whole of the information required by an object or service, and use named model groups for the common subcomponents. This is because each element can only be associated with one complex type. If we do not have a particular need for the representation of class-like information, then we will find that just using named model groups will gain the same functionality without the limitations of extending a complex type.

Re-use in Text-only Element Content Models

When we are talking about element values rather than content models, we have a choice of whether to declare an element that contains the restrictions within the element declaration, or whether to create a named simple type that restricts the element content.

The key question to ask when making this decision is whether you or another construct will be able to make use of the restriction. If you are likely to want to re-use the restriction, you are better off creating a simple type, whereas if the restriction only applies to the one element, defining it inline keeps the restriction with its intended element and therefore improves clarity of the structure.

For example, imagine we have an XML document where we want to place a restriction on the dates that can be used for the year when an account is due to be reviewed (ex2SimpleTypes.xml):

```
<Transaction currency = "AUS$">
   <Withdrawal>300.00</Withdrawal>
   <AccountHolderName>Martin Shaw</AccountHolderName>
   <AccountHoldingBranch>Martin Shaw</AccountHoldingBranch>
   <AccountNumber>3899 2913 2362 8411</AccountNumber>
   <AccountReviewYear>2003</AccountReviewYear>
</Transaction>
```

There is only one element to which the restriction applies, so by keeping it in the element declaration, we keep the schema simple and tidy. Here is how we could restrict the year that the review on the account is due to somewhere between the years 2001 and 2009 (ex2SimpleTypes.xsd):

```
<xs:element name = "AccountReviewYear">
   <xs:simpleType>
      <xs:restriction base = "xs:gYear">
         <xs:pattern value="200[1-9]"/>
      </xs:restriction>
   </xs:simpleType>
</xs:element>
```

However, if we are likely to want to place the same restriction on different element content, we should declare a named simple type. For example, if we wanted to limit the number of characters allowed as simple element content, rather like creating a fixed length field, then we are better off creating a simpleType to represent this and re-use it on different element declarations. So, if we wanted to limit the number of characters allowed to 256, say, we could specify a type called fixedLengthFieldType to the appropriate elements, like so:

```
<xs:simpleType name = "fixedLengthFieldType">
   <xs:restriction base = "string">
      <xs:minLength value = "0" />
      <xs:maxLength value = "256" />
   </xs:restriction>
</xs:simpleType>

<xs:element name = " AccountHolderName" type = "FixedLengthFieldType" />
<xs:element name = "AccountHoldingBranch" type = "FixedLengthFieldType" />
```

Here we are re-using the simpleType in two different elements that are used.

Declaring Order and Occurrence

Having seen the basics of how to declare a fixed order using sequence in the first chapter, let's start to look at some more complicated examples of content models, where we mix the sequence element with occurrence of attributes and elements.

Fixed Order All Elements Required

In this example, the Count elements are required to have the children One, Two, and Three, in that order.

❑   The sequence compositor specifies the order.

❑   None of these elements are optional because the default values of the occurrence constraints minOccurs and maxOccurs are 1.

```
<!-- ex3FixedOrder.xsd -->
<xs:element name = "Count">
   <xs:complexType>
      <xs:sequence>
         <xs:element name = "One" type = "xs:string" />
         <xs:element name = "Two" type = "xs:string" />
         <xs:element name = "Three" type = "xs:string" />
      </xs:sequence>
   </xs:complexType>
</xs:element>
```

So the following example (ex3FixedOrder.xml) would be a conforming structure:

```
<!-- ex3FixedOrder.xml -->
<Count>
   <One></One>
   <Two></Two>
   <Three></Three>
</Count>
```

But this would not:

```
<Count>
   <Two></Two>
   <One></One>
</Count>
```

Fixed Order Optional Elements

In order to make elements optional, we just add the minOccurs attribute with a value of 0:

```
<!-- Ch06 ex4OptionalElements.xsd -->
<element name = "Add">
   <complexType>
      <sequence>
         <element name = "Namespace" minOccurs = "0" maxOccurs = "1" />
         <element name = "FilePath" />
      </sequence>
   </complexType>
</element>
```

So, both of the following would be valid instances:

```
<Add>
   <Namespace>http://www.example.org/books</Namespace>
   <FilePath>http://www.example.org/books/books.xsd</FilePath>
</Add>
```

```
<Add>
   <FilePath>http://www.example.org/books/books.xsd</FilePath>
</Add>
```

> Remember that the **minOccurs** and **maxOccurs** attributes cannot occur on global element declarations.

Requiring Repeating Sequences of Elements

We can specify that a group of elements should be repeated a fixed number of times, or provide a range of times, by adding occurrence constraints to the compositor. For example, here we are requiring that the One, Two and Three elements be repeated three times, without a containing element:

```
<!-- ex5RepeatingSequences.xsd -->
<xs:element name = "RepeatingSequences" >
   <xs:complexType>
      <xs:sequence minOccurs = "3" maxOccurs = "3">
            <xs:element name = "One" type = "xs:string" />
            <xs:element name = "Two" type = "xs:string" />
            <xs:element name = "Three" type = "xs:string" />
      </xs:sequence>
   </xs:complexType>
</xs:element>
```

So, the following is the only allowable conforming instance document:

```
<!-- ex5RepeatingSequences.xml -->
<RepeatingSequences>
   <One>First came...</One>
   <Two>Second came...</Two>
   <Three>Third came...</Three>
   <One>First came...</One>
   <Two>Second came...</Two>
   <Three>Third came...</Three>
   <One>First came...</One>
   <Two>Second came...</Two>
   <Three>Third came...</Three>
</RepeatingSequences>
```

This type of structure would be ideal for representing comma-delimited formats as XML.

Require Both Elements or None

In order to require that either a group of child elements appear, or none of them can appear, again we can add occurrence constraints on the compositor. Here the elements that are declared inside the sequence element can either appear both together once, or not at all:

```
<!-- ex6BothOrNone.xsd -->
<?xml version = "1.0" ?>
<xs:schema xmlns:xs = "http://www.w3.org/2001/XMLSchema">

<xs:element name="Book">
    <xs:complexType>
        <xs:sequence minOccurs = "0" maxOccurs = "1">
            <xs:element name="Title" type="xs:string" />
            <xs:element name="Author" type="xs:string"  />
        </xs:sequence>
    </xs:complexType>
</xs:element>

</xs:schema>
```

So the following two examples would be allowed:

```
<Book>
</Book>
```

```
<Book>
    <Title>Professional XML Schema</Title>
    <Author>Nik Ozu et al.</Author>
</Book>
```

But the third is invalid because it only contains one of the child elements:

```
<Book>
    <Title>Professional XML Schema</Title>
</Book>
```

Requiring Elements in a Mixed Model

In the following example, imagine we are cataloguing scientific evidence. For easy reference to research work, we want to note a research paper's hypothesis, and the conclusion. We can allow a Hypothesis element to mark up the purpose of the research, and then use Conclusion element to determine whether the hypothesis was proven or disproved. Only one Hypothesis element may appear in the document, and only one Conclusion, and they should be in that order.

Here is an example of a research paper `ex7OrderedMixedContent.xml`. Note how the `Conclusion` element also carries an attribute called `accepted`, which has a `boolean` data type:

```
<ResearchPaper paperID = "43374">
In this paper, we will be testing the hypothesis that <Hypothesis>XML Schema
allows us to order elements in mixed content</Hypothesis>. With this example, we
have <Conclusion accepted = "true">proved that this is possible</Conclusion>.
</ResearchPaper>
```

Let's have a look at the schema for this example. We need to declare that the complex type associated with the `ResearchPaper` element can contain mixed content, which we do by giving the `mixed` attribute a value of `true`. We also need to add the `accepted` attribute to the `Conclusion` element, which contains text as well as carrying an attribute. We can do this by creating a new complex type as an extension of the `string` simple built-in type, adding to it an attribute of type `boolean`:

```
<xs:schema xmlns:xs = "http://www.w3.org/2001/XMLSchema">

    <xs:element name = "ResearchPaper">
        <xs:complexType  mixed = "true">
            <xs:sequence>
                <xs:element name = "Hypothesis" type = "xs:string" />
                <xs:element name = "Conclusion" type = "ConclusionType" />
            </xs:sequence>
            <xs:attribute name = "paperID" type = "xs:integer" />
        </xs:complexType>
    </xs:element>

    <xs:complexType name = "ConclusionType">
        <xs:simpleContent>
          <xs:extension base="xs:string">
              <xs:attribute name = "accepted" type = "xs:boolean" />
          </xs:extension>
        </xs:simpleContent>
    </xs:complexType>

</xs:schema>
```

This means we are not only able to validate the order of the elements in the mixed content model, but also the data type of the `accepted` attribute on the `Conclusion` element, while only allowing the `Conclusion` element to contain a string between the opening and closing tags.

Grouping and Hierarchy

Grouping related items involves making use of the way in which XML allows us to create hierarchical document structures nested to arbitrary depths. While we are limited to a rather flat structure when storing data in a relational database, or transferring data using positional file formats such as fixed width and comma delimited files, XML allows us to group related information items adding more depth and scope to the information we are making up.

There are two key uses of grouping that restrict structure:

❑ Grouping of related items of information

❑ Grouping lists of same information items

While, this may seem like a basic feature of using XML, but it has some interesting side effects that are worth noting.

Grouping Related Items of Information in Documents

On its own, a flat sequence of elements in an instance document would tell us nothing about the structure of the data. Nested structures allow us to indicate that an element appearing inside another element is part of, or owned by, the parent. For example, in the PersonType we saw earlier, we created a nested structure whereby a person had properties of a name, address, and e-contact details:

```
<xs:complexType name = "PersonType">
    <xs:sequence>
        <xs:element name = "Name" type = "xs:string" />
        <xs:element name = "Address" type = "xs:string" />
        <xs:element name = "Econtact" type = "xs:string" />
    </xs:sequence>
</xs:complexType>
```

These child elements declared in this type definition belonged to every representation of a person. Furthermore, if we had expanded our example, the Name element would have been composed of the first, and last names, which collectively describe that person's full name. Likewise the Address element would have contained items that described their precise address, and the Econtact details would have been made up of all the ways of getting in touch with the person electronically.

Not only does nesting elements indicate that the child elements are owned by all or part of the parent element, it also helps separate out information that would otherwise be at the same level. Compare the two following structures. In the first we have a flat structure where all of the Customer element's child elements are all siblings – they're at the same level of the hierarchy:

```
<Customer>
    <FirstName>Claire</FirstName>
    <LastName>Watson</LastName>
    <Street>40 Tower Street</Street>
    <Town>East Barnet Village</Town>
    <City>East Barnet</City>
    <State>Hertfordshire</State>
    <ZipCode>EN4 8UT</ZipCode>
    <Email>cwatson@myExample.org</Email>
    <HomeTelNo>02082082080</HomeTelNo>
    <WorkTelNo>02082222222</WorkTelNo>
</Customer>
```

In this representation, there is no way of distinguishing between the ZipCode and HomeTelNo, for example, because they are nested at the same level.

In the second example the structure is refined using the extra nested elements to separate out and group related information, like so:

```
<Customer>
   <Name>
      <FirstName>Claire</FirstName>
      <LastName>Watson</LastName>
   </Name>
      <Street>40 Tower Street</Street>
      <Town>East Barnet Village</Town>
      <City>East Barnet</City>
      <State>Hertfordshire</State>
      <ZipCode>EN4 8UT</ZipCode>
   </Address>
   <Econtact>
      <Email>cwatson@myExample.org</Email>
      <HomeTelNo>02082082080</HomeTelNo>
      <WorkTelNo>02082222222</WorkTelNo>
   </Econtact>
</Customer>
```

As you can see, this approach is more intuitive. Not only does the structure make it easier for users to work with marked up data, but also means that when marking up the document, authors have fixed places for each of the items to go. The marking up of data becomes less **ambiguous**. For example, details relating to the customer's address are grouped together in the one Address element, rather than having to look through all of the Customer element's child elements, or siblings of the Name element.

There is also another very important feature of creating this kind of hierarchy. If a user does not need to use one of the sections, they will not have to learn any of the sub-components. For example, if we do not need to use addresses, we will save having to learn five child elements, although we will know that the schema is capable of holding address details. The deeper the structure, the less of the markup we need to learn.

Grouping Same Information Items in Documents

Containing elements can also be very helpful whenever an element can be repeated. By grouping a list of the same elements together, the author can only place the multiple elements within a container.

For example, a typical purchase order will consist of details about both the customer and the products that they want to purchase. The product information in a purchase order can be represented with something like an Item or LineItem element. Because any purchase order may well contain several line items (or products) that the customer wants to order, we should group these together in a containing element that keeps them together:

```
<PurchaseOrder orderNumber = "po1410001" orderDate = "2001-05-14" />
   <Customer customerID = "c127772">
      ...
   </Customer>
   <LineItems>
      <LineItem lineNumber = "1" quantity = "3">
         <Product sku = "1450">
            <Name>Widgets</Name>
            <Price currency = "AUS$">1.45</Price>
```

```
            </Product>
        </LineItem>
        <LineItem lineNumber = "2" quantity = "5">
            <Product sku = "1450">
                <Name>Gromets</Name>
                <Price currency = "AUS$">2.45</Price>
            </Product>
        </LineItem>
    </LineItems>
</PurchaseOrder>
```

Here the users of the document will be able to go straight to the LineItems element to find out the information about products that the customer wants, and the details of the product itself can be found in the Product element. Indeed, we would do something similar in a bulleted or numbered list for a document.

> **We should add a containing element when the items of information relate to each other and belong to the same class of information, and when there are several occurrences of the same element representing a list.**

Because we have created these sub-sections of the document, it also means that they can be worked on individually.

Advantages of Grouping for Processing

When it comes to grouping of elements, processing applications will benefit from the use of the added structure for a number of reasons.

If only a subset of information from the document is required, and that subsection is held within a containing element, the application will be able to just look for that one containing element and take its child elements. It will then have a well-formed fragment of XML that it can deal with. All necessary information will be found within that element and there is no need to process the rest of the document.

For example, if we had an application that was working with the purchase order we have just seen, and its role was solely related to updating the inventory, then it would just be able to take the LineItems element and its children. All of the items that were ordered would be within that element, and there would be no need for it to process the rest of the document.

The containing element can also indicate context information to an application – that is, where the current node is within the hierarchy. The ability to detect context is especially important when elements have the same name, but have to be treated differently depending upon their context.

For example, a schema representing the API of a piece of software may describe methods of several objects. Furthermore, these objects may share common method names, such as Add(), each of which can take different parameters. If our XML represented a method using an element of the same name, we could have several elements called Add, each of which would have a different content model depending upon the parameters the method on that object took. By looking at the containing element, we would be able to tell what object the method relates to. This is illustrated below:

```
<XMLDomObject>
    <Add>
        <FilePath>http://www.example.org/schemas/books.xml</Namespace>
        <ValidateOnParse>False</ValidateOnParse>
    </Add>
    <!-- Other methods here -->
</XMLDOMObject>

<XMLSchemaObject>
    <Add>
        <Namespace>http://www.example.org/schemas/books</Namespace>
        <FilePath>http://www.example.org/schemas/books.xsd</FilePath>
    </Add>
    <!-- Other methods here -->
</XMLSchemaObject>
```

If we are working on an object-oriented application, all the information required to populate an object could be found within one element. If we are working with a database representation, the containing element could represent a table. If we are working on a document-based application, the containing element could represent a section of the document, such as a chapter.

Grouping also helps when working with document fragments. For example, if we do not want to retrieve the whole of a large file, we can select a node point represented by a containing element, and just request it and its children.

Creating Hierarchical Structures in Schemas

We have already seen the ways of creating a hierarchical structure in a schema. We have to define a complex type to be associated with any element that does not only have simple content. This can be an anonymous complex type definition nested inside the element declaration, or it can be a named complex type. We then use model groups or other elements with complex types to build up the structure. We looked into when you might want to use named complex types, and when you might want to use named model groups for building up content models at the end of the last chapter, so we won't be going into this again here.

Choice and Options

The examples we have been looking at so far have illustrated how we can create consistency in documents and employ the re-use mechanisms offered by XML Schema to achieve and enforce consistency, and create hierarchies. In this section, we will look at ways in which we can manage the flexibility that document authors often need to represent information in the form of choices of structure.

There are a number of different types of choice an author may require and ways in which we can manage the choice so that it is still easy to learn and use, and sometimes even predictable. Essentially, we are looking here at acceptable ways of **restricting the choice** of content a document author can make. While offering choice to authors, by carefully restricting the options they can use, we can prevent the schema from becoming over complicated.

By the end of the chapter, we will have seen how to allow flexibility in documents, while retaining enough predictability to make the schema easy to process. In some of these cases, the restrictions will even allow an application to author our documents.

A Choice of Fixed Values

If we have a fixed set of values that an element or attribute can contain, then we should restrict the appropriate attributes or elements to only be allowed those values. This will help in learning a schema, because the author does not have to guess what values are allowed, and will continue to be of help as more documents are authored.

As you can imagine, if a processing application only has to deal with a fixed set of values, then it will make it a lot easier to program for the possible outcomes. Furthermore, by putting this requirement in the schema, we will ensure that a validated document instance contains one of the values an application can handle, saving having to write validation code into the application.

Indeed, if the authors are using some kind of authoring tool or user interface, the permitted values could be displayed to the user so that they know what values a field an take. We often see these sort of fixed values on web site and application forms as drop-down lists when users are asked to enter which country they live in, or age range.

Handling Choices for Simple Content Using Enumeration

Attribute values always have simple types, and by nature they cannot hold complex content. Text-only elements also have simple types. So, when there is a fixed set of values that an attribute or text-only element can take, we should create an **enumerated simple type**. The ability to enumerate allowable values for text-only elements is not something that DTDs allow, and is a handy addition to XML Schema.

If we only have two choices of a simple type, then we should consider making the type a `boolean`. This will not always be a logical choice, for example, if we were dealing with just two sizes, we might be better off sticking with an enumeration of large and small, especially if that is what users will expect to see. When we are dealing with information that can be answered "yes" or "no" to, and this would be an intuitive question to ask, we should use `booleans` and many applications will be ready to work with this datatype.

When we are dealing with a simple type that only applies to one element or attribute, it can be nested within the declaration for the element or attribute. If it is likely to be used by several elements or attributes, we should create a named simple type so that we can benefit from re-use.

Enumerating A Simple Type

In this example, we enumerate allowable values for color and size of clothing garments. By creating two named simple types, we can apply the same choice of color and size to any garment we require. Indeed, we can apply them individually to different garments if both do not apply. In this case, we will illustrate how they are used, by allowing the choices to be applied to a t-shirt.

```xml
<!-- ex8EnumeratedSimpleType.xsd -->
<xs:element name = "Tshirt">
    <xs:complexType>
        <xs:sequence>
            <xs:element name = "Color" type = "clothesColorType" />
            <xs:element name = "Size" type = "clothesSizeType" />
        </xs:sequence>
    </xs:complexType>
</xs:element>
```

```
<xs:simpleType name="clothesSizeType">
    <xs:restriction base="xs:string">
        <xs:enumeration value="S" />
        <xs:enumeration value="M" />
        <xs:enumeration value="L" />
        <xs:enumeration value="XL" />
    </xs:restriction>
</xs:simpleType>

<xs:simpleType name="clothesColorType">
    <xs:restriction base="xs:string">
        <xs:enumeration value="Black" />
        <xs:enumeration value="White" />
        <xs:enumeration value="Green" />
        <xs:enumeration value="Blue" />
    </xs:restriction>
</xs:simpleType>
```

The content of any element or value of any attribute that uses these simple types will have to use one of these strings as a value. For example, we could have the following:

```
<Tshirt>
    <Color>Blue</Color>
    <Size>XL</Size>
</Tshirt>
```

However, this would not be allowed:

```
<Tshirt>
    <Color>LightBlue</Color>
    <Size>10</Size>
</Tshirt>
```

Here, the `Color` and `Size` elements contain values that have not been enumerated in the `simpleType`. This can be helpful in any case where there are limited values.

Choice of Structures

When you are dealing with highly structured data, you will not have to give your author many choices in the markup they can use. This will particularly be the case when dealing with representations of data held in relational databases, or when we are working with applications where each document tightly follows the internal structure of the application and we have a different document for each part of the process.

When the data we are marking up is less predictable, however, you need to allow an author a lot of choice or flexibility so that they can apply structure to a document. Yet, even when authors require a high degree of flexibility, there are usually restrictions we can put in place. For example, in HTML a `tr` tag should only have a child of a `td` tag, there should not be anything between the two, otherwise we would have something in the table row, yet outside of a table cell, or column. If we were writing your own document-based application, we could also restrict what can appear within the table. Likewise we can restrict what appears in a list item, so that it can only contain emphasis or cross references, not section headings, paragraphs or diagrams. Apart from these structural restrictions, choices in flat structures are often constrained in order to preserve a house style, or impose restrictions on where an author can talk about different things – such as a requirement for a scientific paper to start with an abstract.

If we have to allow different structures, limiting the choice will help users:

❑ If users only have to learn one structure in order to work with the type of document they are writing, it limits the amount of markup they have to learn and use. For example, if they do not have tables in their documents, they will not have to learn about any of the restrictions on how to use tables.

❑ If users have to deal with several different situations, then restricting the allowed options helps them make a choice, especially in a new or unfamiliar section, because they will have a narrow set of options on how to interpret the document.

As far as applications go, the less choices we offer, the fewer options an application will have to be able to deal with. The program will be able to deal with choices using conditional sections easier. It will be able to make authoring decisions based upon what it already knows.

If we have to allow a lot of flexibility, or a flat structure, it may not be possible for applications to author documents. By enforcing some degree of restrictions, however, we allow an application to work with unstructured or semi-structured data.

Handling Choices of Content Models

We always have to use a complex type to indicate a structural choice. When we start looking at limiting the choices of complex content, there are two main approaches that we can use:

❑ A choice group

❑ A substitution group

Both have different advantages in different situations.

A choice group allows us to enumerate the possible elements or content models that an element can contain. A choice group is ideal for representing either/or choices, and choices between several sibling nodes in a tree structure – the point in the tree where we decide which fork to go down. For example, if we are working on a purchase order, each line item may contain details of either a product or a service. It is likely that these will have different content models, because you buy a product once and it is yours, whereas a service could be bought in units of hours or days. Furthermore, we may need to indicate when we required a service, and whether it is at regular intervals.

It obviously helps a schema user if the choices are clearly kept together in some logical structure. For example, if there are not many nodes beneath the point at which our choice occurs, then the Russian Doll design (which we met in the last chapter) has the advantages of keeping the items in the choice together. As the content models grow, however, the benefits of nesting the content model inside the choices diminish because we can end up with a structure that is complicated and hard to follow. If we have a lot of choices, or the choices contain complicated content models, we are better off *only* indicating either the root of the choice or references to the choices within the choice element. Furthermore, if there are common structures between the options available to the author, or we are working within an object-oriented representation, then we will likely want to take advantage of the re-use mechanisms we have already seen, which means that we have to declare some of the named model groups and named complex types globally (and will not be able to nest all the declarations).

The substitution group, meanwhile, allows an element within a content model to be substituted for other elements either of the same type or derived from the same type. In a substitution group one element acts as the **head**; this is the element that can be replaced with other elements in the substitution group. The reference to the head not only validates the head, but also the elements that correspond to a member of the substitution group. Having defined an element to be part of a substitution group, wherever it appears in a content model, we can use the members of a substitution group to replace the head. We should note that there are some limitations with using the substitution group:

❑ All the elements that take part in the substitution group must be of the same type or derived from the same type as the head element. Substitution groups should only be used for elements with relatively similar content models.

❑ All members of a substitution group must be declared globally, so we will have to expose their namespaces in the instance document.

❑ The choices are no longer grouped together. To avoid confusion, we should keep the members of a substitution group that can replace the head together, and add a documentation element in the schema by the head.

❑ Elements that appear in a substitution group cannot appear anywhere else other than in place of the head element.

❑ As the schema evolves, the elements that may occur in the variable section will grow. The way that it grows may not always reflect the base type. If they do not reflect the base type, this could create an overly complex schema and confuse users.

❑ If there are a lot of differently named elements, we will need a lot of case code to determine how to deal with each one in the processing application.

Substitution groups do, however, have the distinct advantage of being more extensible, as you can add elements that can be used in the variable content section.

Recall that an abstract element cannot be instantiated in instance documents. So, in declaring the head element as being abstract, it acts as a placeholder because we are forced to use one of the members of the substitution group in the document rather than the head.

Substitution groups are especially helpful when the content model of the choices are largely the same, and there may just be one element in the hierarchy that differs from the others. Rather than repeating the content model for each child element, and having branches in our hierarchy that create very similar sequences of child nodes, we can allow different elements to be substituted in the place where the variation may occur.

Substitution groups are also helpful when it is unlikely that the author will have to make the choice; when there are uncommon circumstances that only occasionally require a different or content model take over from the norm. For example, in a sales system, we might use a substitution group to allow for the appearance of a Discount element, so that discounts could be applied in sales, to shop-soiled/ex-display goods, or for staff who are entitled to get discount.

Choice Groups Versus Substitution Groups

As you can tell from the examples, choice groups and substitution groups both have their benefits, but each is more suited to a different set of circumstances.

Choice groups are generally more helpful when:

- ❑ We are going to have to make the choices every time you use the schema
- ❑ There is a fixed set of choices
- ❑ Users need to be able to quickly see the options, or when we do not want the processing overhead of having to check a whole document for elements that can be substituted in place of this one
- ❑ Our choices clearly diverge and cannot be represented by an element of the same type
- ❑ The participating elements need to appear elsewhere in the document
- ❑ We need to hide namespace complexities without qualifying all elements (because elements in a substitution group have to be declared globally).

Substitution groups can be more helpful when:

- ❑ The choices are exceptions to the rule and only need to be used in rare circumstances.
- ❑ The element content model either has the same type can be derived from the same type.
- ❑ When there is likely to be a growing set of choices.
- ❑ When the choices apply to an element that occurs several times in the schema.
- ❑ When we want to offer a different choice in the middle of a content model. This can be better than creating a fork in the hierarchy, where the branches are the same except for the element that can be substituted, and therefore having to repeat the content models beneath that element.

Because substitution groups do not keep the alternative content models in the same place as the abstract element, it is especially important to document them, and to try to keep the location of elements that can take part in each substitution group together.

Choices Between Elements and Their Content Models

In the following examples, we will look at different ways of handling choices of elements; some with different content models, others with like structures.

Few Choices and Small Content Models

If we only need to offer limited choice and each choice has a small content model, we keep as many of the declarations inside the choice group as we can, like the Russian Doll design. This keeps all the options together.

For example, imagine that we only wanted to allow a Product element to contain either CD or Book details, like so:

```
<Product>
    <Book ISBN = "1-861001-34-7">
        <Title>Professional XML Schemas</Title>
        <Authors>
            <Author>Nik Ozu</Author>
            <Author>Jon Duckett</Author>
        </Authors>
        <Price>24.99</Price>
    </Book>
</Product>
```

Or:

```
<Product>
   <CD>
      <Title>Lovers Rock</Title>
      <Artists>
         <Artist>Sade</Artist>
      </Atists>
      <Price>24.99</Price>
   </CD>
</Product>
```

We can implement this in our schema by using a choice group to indicate that the product element must either contain a Book or CD element. The only items that a Product element can contain are now either a Book or CD. Note how the content models here follow the Russian Doll design that we met in the last chapter. Here, we have defined these within the choice compositor to keep the declarations together, especially seeing as there are only two choices:

```
<!-- ex9FewChoices.xsd -->
<xs:element name = "Product">
   <xs:complexType>

      <xs:choice>
         <xs:element name = "Book">
            <xs:complexType>
               <xs:sequence>
                  <xs:element name = "Title" type = "xs:string" />
                  <xs:element name = "Authors">
                     <xs:complexType>
                        <xs:sequence>
                           <xs:element name = "Author" type = "xs:string"
                              minOccurs = "1" maxOccurs = "unbounded" />
                        </xs:sequence>
                     </xs:complexType>
                  </xs:element>
                  <xs:element name = "Price" type = "xs:decimal" />
               </xs:sequence>
               <xs:attribute name = "ISBN" type = "xs:string" />
            </xs:complexType>
         </xs:element>

         <xs:element name = "CD">
            <xs:complexType>
               <xs:sequence>
                  <xs:element name = "Title" type = "xs:string" />
                  <xs:element name = "Artists">
                     <xs:complexType>
                        <xs:sequence>
                           <xs:element name = "Artist" type = "xs:string"
                              minOccurs = "1" maxOccurs = "unbounded" />
                        </xs:sequence>
                     </xs:complexType>
                  </xs:element>
                  <xs:element name = "Price" type = "xs:decimal" />
               </xs:sequence>
```

```
                <xs:attribute name = "ASIN" type = "xs:string" />
            </xs:complexType>
        </xs:element>
      </xs:choice>
   </xs:complexType>
</xs:element>
```

Notice how both the `Book` and the `CD` details follow similar structures, which mean that the content model for each is both easier to learn and follows the same structure for processing applications.

The Russian Doll design works well when there are limited choices and the declarations do not nest very deep. If we had a lot of choices, however, we could declare each content model separately either in an element, a named model group, or a named complex type, and use them from within the `choice`.

Several Choices Or Larger Content Models

If we have to deal with a lot of choices, or if the content models are quite complicated, then we will not be able to see the options clearly in a Russian Doll design. In which case, we could use the Venetian Blind approach or Salami Slice design. These also allow us to re-use sections of the content models between elements.

For example, if our `Product` element could contain CDs, DVDs, videos, computer games, and gift vouchers, then it would not be possible to see all the options clearly with the Russian Doll design. In the following example, we pass references to the elements, so we can easily see the available options, and can then follow the schema to the point where we declare each of them:

```
<!-- ex10ManyChoices.xsd -->
<xs:element name = "Product">
   <xs:complexType>
      <xs:choice>
         <xs:element ref = "Book" />
         <xs:element ref = "CD" />
         <xs:element ref = "DVD" />
         <xs:element ref = "Video" />
         <xs:element ref = "ComputerGame" />
         <xs:element ref = "GiftVoucher" />
      </xs:choice>
   </xs:complexType>
</xs:element>

<xs:element name = "Book">...</xs:element>
<xs:element name = "CD">...</xs:element>
<xs:element name = "DVD">...</xs:element>
<xs:element name = "Video">...</xs:element>
<xs:element name = "ComputerGame">...</xs:element>
<xs:element name = "GiftVoucher">...</xs:element>
```

When using the `choice` group, we can combine a choice with a number of elements that can potentially contain different element content models or types, they do not even have to be related – they can be **independent**, or **loosely-coupled**.

Using Substitution Groups to Handle Choice Between Elements

In the following example, we want the document author to be able to use a `Tshirt`, `Sweater`, or `JoggingPants` element, wherever the `Garment` element is allowed in a schema. Note that each of them is of the same type, the `GarmentDetailsType`, which gives details about the item, and enumerates allowable sizes. This saves us from having to repeat the details for each content model in the element declaration.

```
<!-- ex11SubsGroup.xsd -->
<xs:annotation>
    <xs:documentation>
        Note that the Garment element must be substituted for an element
        in the Garment substitution group.
    </xs:documentation>
</xs:annotation>

<xs:element name = "Garment" type = "GarmentDetailsType" abstract="true" />

<xs:element name = "TShirt" type = "GarmentDetailsType"
    substitutionGroup = "Garment" />
<xs:element name = "Sweater" type = "GarmentDetailsType"
    substitutionGroup = "Garment" />
<xs:element name = "JoggingPants" type = "GarmentDetailsType"
    substitutionGroup = "Garment" />

<xs:complexType name = "GarmentDetailsType">
    <xs:sequence>
        <xs:element name = "Quantity" type = "xs:string" />
        <xs:element name = "DesignNumber" type = "xs:integer" />
        <xs:element name = "Size" type = "clothesSizeType" />
    </xs:sequence>
</xs:complexType>

<xs:simpleType name="clothesSizeType">
    <xs:restriction base="xs:string">
        <xs:enumeration value="S" />
        <xs:enumeration value="M" />
        <xs:enumeration value="L" />
        <xs:enumeration value="XL" />
    </xs:restriction>
</xs:simpleType>
```

Note that, having declared the `Garment` element as being `abstract` and part of a substitution group, wherever it appears in the schema, we have to substitute one of the other elements. This is because an `abstract` element must be substituted by another element that is within the same substitution group, as long as it is of the same type or derived from the same type. For example, the following could appear in place of a `Garment` element in the instance document:

```
<TShirt>
    <Quantity>100</Quantity>
    <DesignNumber>114</DesignNumber>
    <Size>S</Size>
</TShirt>
```

Note that we do not explicitly define a substitution group as a separate component – indeed, we do not need to specify anything in the head element. Rather, we use the substitutionGroup *attribute placed upon members of the group that can be substituted for the head element.*

Flexible Combinations of Order and Occurrence

Having looked earlier in the chapter at how we can specify order and occurrence of elements, we should look at ways in which we can allow the document author flexibility of these options: how we can give them choice over when and whether an element appears in the instance document.

Fixed Order Flexible Occurrence

Suppose we have a Meal element that can contain one or more of the elements Starter, MainCourse and Dessert, but only one of each, and they must occur in that order. In a DTD we would have to express this as follows:

```
((Starter, MainCourse?, Dessert?) | (Starter, Dessert?)
| (MainCourse, Dessert?) | Dessert)
```

XML Schema does make this kind of flexible occurrence much simpler; if we put them in a sequence group, it becomes a lot easier to follow:

```
<complexType>
   <sequence>
      <element name = "Starter" type = "integer"
         minOccurs = "0" maxOccurs = "1" />
      <element name = "MainCourse" type = "integer"
         minOccurs = "0" maxOccurs = "1" />
      <element name = "Dessert" type = "integer"
         minOccurs = "0" maxOccurs = "1" />
   </sequence>
</complexType>
```

It can be see that the example given only allows three options, if we went on with four courses, a DTD would look like this:

```
((Starter, MainCourse?, Dessert?, Beverage?) | (MainCourse, Dessert?, Beverage?) |
(Dessert, Beverage?) | Beverage)
```

The greater the number of options you select the more complex the DTD has to become, Whereas in XML Schema we only have to add an extra element declaration:

```
<complexType>
   <sequence>
      <element name = "Starter" type = "integer"
         minOccurs = "0" maxOccurs = "1" />
      <element name = "MainCourse" type = "integer"
         minOccurs = "0" maxOccurs = "1" />
      <element name = "Dessert" type = "integer"
         minOccurs = "0" maxOccurs = "1" />
      <element name = "Beverage" type = "integer" />
   </sequence>
</complexType>
```

Here any combination of Starter, MainCourse, Dessert, and Beverage are allowed, as long as, when present, they appear in the order declared.

Flexible Order and Occurrence

Things get really complicated when elements can appear in any order. If we want to allow Starter, MainCourse, and Dessert to appear in any order, we would have to express it in a DTD as follows:

```
((Starter, ((MainCourse, Dessert?)? | (Dessert, MainCourse?))) | (MainCourse,
((Starter, Dessert?)? | (Dessert, Starter?))) | (Dessert, ((Starter,
MainCourse?)? | (MainCourse, Starter?)))))
```

This shows the power of the all group, which allows us to do things that are either not possible with DTDs, or are very complex. If we do not want to specify the order in which they appear, we can do so as follows:

```
<complexType>
   <all>
      <element name = "Starter" type = "integer"
         minOccurs = "0" maxOccurs = "1" />
      <element name = "MainCourse" type = "integer"
         minOccurs = "0" maxOccurs = "1" />
      <element name = "Desert" type = "integer"
         minOccurs = "0" maxOccurs = "1" />
   </all>
</complexType>
```

Now that is a lot simpler. The all group allows any of the elements to appear in the model, in any order, and they can appear once or not at all.

This is what would it look like if we did not have the all group:

```
<complexType>
   <choice>
      <group ref = "r:SMD" />
      <group ref = "r:SDM" />
      <group ref = "r:MSD" />
      <group ref = "r:MDS" />
      <group ref = "r:DSM" />
      <group ref = "r:DMS" />
   </choice>
</complexType>

<complexType>
   <group name = "SMDGroup">
      <sequence>
         <element name = "Starter" type = "integer"
            minOccurs = "0" maxOccurs = "1" />
         <element name = "MainCourse" type = "integer"
            minOccurs = "0" maxOccurs = "1" />
         <element name = "Desert" type = "integer"
            minOccurs = "0" maxOccurs = "1" />
      </sequence>
   </group>
```

```
    </complexType>
<complexType>
    <group name = "MSDGroup">
        <sequence>
            <element name = "MainCourse" type = "integer"
                minOccurs = "0" maxOccurs = "1" />
            <element name = "Starter" type = "integer"
                minOccurs = "0" maxOccurs = "1" />
            <element name = "Desert" type = "integer"
                minOccurs = "0" maxOccurs = "1" />
        </sequence>
    </group>
</complexType
<complexType>
    <group name = "MDSGroup">
        <sequence>
            <element name = "MainCourse" type = "integer"
                minOccurs = "0" maxOccurs = "1" />
            <element name = "Desert" type = "integer"
                minOccurs = "0" maxOccurs = "1" />
            <element name = "Starter" type = "integer"
                minOccurs = "0" maxOccurs = "1" />
        </sequence>
    </group>
</complexType
<complexType>
    <group name = "DMSGroup">
        <sequence>
            <element name = "Desert" type = "integer"
                minOccurs = "0" maxOccurs = "1" />
            <element name = "MainCourse" type = "integer"
                minOccurs = "0" maxOccurs = "1" />
            <element name = "Starter" type = "integer"
                minOccurs = "0" maxOccurs = "1" />
        </sequence>
    </group>
</complexType
<complexType>
    <group name = "DSMGroup">
        <sequence>
            <element name = "Desert" type = "integer"
                minOccurs = "0" maxOccurs = "1" />
            <element name = "MainCourse" type = "integer"
                minOccurs = "0" maxOccurs = "1" />
            <element name = "Starter" type = "integer"
                minOccurs = "0" maxOccurs = "1" />
        </sequence>
    </group>
</complexType
```

And that is only with three choices! As you can see, this not only requires a lot of effort to learn, but also to process and use. It is a lot easier if we can say "Any of these elements can appear once or not at all in any order", as we can with the `all` group.

You can imagine how complex things could get if we wanted to allow any combination of the following:

```
<complexType>
  <all>
    <element name = "Starter" type = "integer"
       minOccurs = "0" maxOccurs = "1" />
    <element name = "MainCourse" type = "integer"
       minOccurs = "0" maxOccurs = "1" />
    <element name = "Potatoes" type = "integer"
       minOccurs = "0" maxOccurs = "1" />
    <element name = "Vegetable" type = "integer"
       minOccurs = "0" maxOccurs = "1" />
    <element name = "Desert" type = "integer"
       minOccurs = "0" maxOccurs = "1" />
    <element name = "Beverage" type = "integer"
       minOccurs = "0" maxOccurs = "1" />
  </all>
</complexType>
```

> The `all` group with `minOccurs = "0"` allows us to have any combination of the items in the group, once or not at all, in any order.

There are some important restrictions with the all group, however, which we must remember to observe:

❑ An `all` group must appear as the sole child at the top of a content model

❑ An `all` group does not allow us to declare an element such as `Starter` outside the group as a means of enabling it to appear more than once

❑ We can only declare elements as children of `all`

Getting Around Restrictions of the all Compositor

There are ways to get around many of the restrictions imposed by the `all` group. If we introduced a difference between choices from a set menu and an à la carte menu, we might want the `Starter`, `MainCourse`, and `Dessert` elements to appear more than once. For good measure, we should also allow customers to order a `Beverage`.

The following example would be illegal for two reasons:

❑ The `all` is not the sole child of at the top of the content model

❑ `Starter` occurs outside the `all` group

```
<complexType name = "SetMealType">
  <sequence>
    <element name = "Starter" type = "integer" />
    <element name = "MainCourse" type = "integer" />
    <element name = "Desert" type = "integer" />
  </sequence>
</complexType>
```

```
<complexType name = "AlaCarteType">
   <sequence>
      <all>
         <element name = "Starter" type = "integer"
            minOccurs = "0" maxOccurs = "1" />
         <element name = "MainCourse" type = "integer"
            minOccurs = "0" maxOccurs = "1" />
         <element name = "Desert" type = "integer"
            minOccurs = "0" maxOccurs = "1" />
      </all>
   </sequence>
   <sequence>
      <all>
         <element name = "AlchoholicBeverage" type = "integer"
            minOccurs = "0" maxOccurs = "1" />
         <element name = "SoftBeverage" type = "integer"
            minOccurs = "0" maxOccurs = "1" />
         <element name = "Water" type = "integer"
            minOccurs = "0" maxOccurs = "1" />
      </all>
   </sequence>
</complexType>
```

If we wanted to allow such a combination, we could use the following schema:

```
<!-- ex12FlexibleOrder.xsd
     Declare a MealType named complex type and DrinksType complex type: -->

<complexType name = "DrinksType">
   <all>
      <element name = "AlchoholicBeverage" type = "integer"
         minOccurs = "0" maxOccurs = "1" />
      <element name = "SoftBeverage" type = "integer"
         minOccurs = "0" maxOccurs = "1" />
      <element name = "Water" type = "integer"
         minOccurs = "0" maxOccurs = "1" />
   </all>
</complexType>

<complexType name = "MealType">
   <all>
      <element name = "Starter" type = "integer"
         minOccurs = "0" maxOccurs = "1" />
      <element name = "MainCourse" type = "integer"
         minOccurs = "0" maxOccurs = "1" />
      <element name = "Desert" type = "integer"
         minOccurs = "0" maxOccurs = "1" />
   </all>
</complexType>

<!-- Use the MealType in two elements that allow you to either select from
     the set meal menu or the A la Carte Menu: -->

<complexType name = "r:MenuSelectionType">
   <choice>
```

```
            <element name = "AlaCarte" type = "r:MealType" />
            <element name = "SetMeal" type = "r:MealType" />
        </choice>
</complexType>

<!-- Combine the choice of the Meal with Beverage. While we have not made
        them optional elements, both are allowed to be empty because all does
        not force any of the child elements to appear in the instance document:
-->

<complexType name = "OrderType">
    <sequence>
        <element name = "MealSeletction" type = "r:MenuSelectionType" />
        <element name = "Beverage" type = "r:DrinksType" />
    </sequence>
</complexType>

<element name = "Order" type = "r:OrderType" />
```

This would be incredibly complicated to model in a DTD, at least without specifying order for the child elements of the meal and beverage types.

> **Remember that an attribute must be optional in order to use the default or fixed attributes.**

A Note About Attributes for Distinguishing Types of Element

Some schemas try to make use of **attributes** to indicate choices in document structure. They add a lot of flexibility in how a processing application should treat the element. For example they will use a construct such as:

```
<Order client = "trade">...</Order>
<Order client = "public">...</Order>
<Order client = "staff">...</Order>
```

The problem with role attributes is that they are difficult to program for. The program has to check both the element and the value of the role attribute in order to determine how to process the element. When processing a document with the DOM, we could not just use getElementsByTagName() to retrieve the elements we wanted, we would have to check the attributes as well to filter for those that were relevant.

This kind of structure can be avoided in XML Schema because:

❑   If the two roles are different enough the elements should probably have different names

❑   We can associate the same named model groups or complex types with different element names so that the structures can be re-used

However, as we will discover later in the book, it can be easier to update a schema that uses role attributes. If you use role attributes, you should always enumerate the values so that users cannot make up their own and the processing application will know the different options.

While one of the reasons for using role attributes was that they allow us to create new structures from the same components, so that they can be treated differently, we can now do the same thing by either adding in a child element or attaching the same complex types to different elements.

Do not confuse the use of role attributes with those that provide default values for child elements, which are otherwise overridden.

Summary

This chapter was largely divided into two sections, the first looking at different ways in which we can create consistency in our document structures, the second looking at effective ways of dealing with choice.

While we want our schemas to be easy to learn, use and process, these goals can provide a conflict of interest. While schemas constrain the allowable content of a class of XML document instances, we could constrain our documents so tightly that they are no longer able to mark up the appropriate range of information they are designed to deal with. The more we constrain the schema, the less flexible it becomes. For processing requirements, however, and to make the schema easier to use we have to add a degree of constraint.

When looking at consistency, we addressed both naming conventions and structural consistency. Structural consistency encourages us to use similar structures for like information – to aid learning, use and processing. We saw how this could be implemented using a number of re-use techniques provided by XML Schema. In particular we looked at creating model groups, complex types, and how the position in which we declare the elements and attributes in the schema, affects their re-use.

In the second section, we addressed a number of ways in which we could provide document authors flexibility in markup, while still limiting their choices to a manageable level, both for processing and learning. These involved:

- ❑ Grouping related elements together and grouping same elements
- ❑ Restricting use of optional elements and attributes
- ❑ Offering fixed choices of simple content through enumeration in a user-derived `simpleType`
- ❑ Specifying fixed choices of elements within a `choice` group
- ❑ Using substitution groups to define alternative element content

The choices that face schema authors when trying to constrain documents using XML Schemas are many and varied. Through this chapter we have seen some key techniques that will help schema authors constrain document content without removing required flexibility.

In the next chapter we will go on to look at how we can create schemas from multiple namespaces and documents, which will introduce new concepts to the re-use and consistency we have met so far.

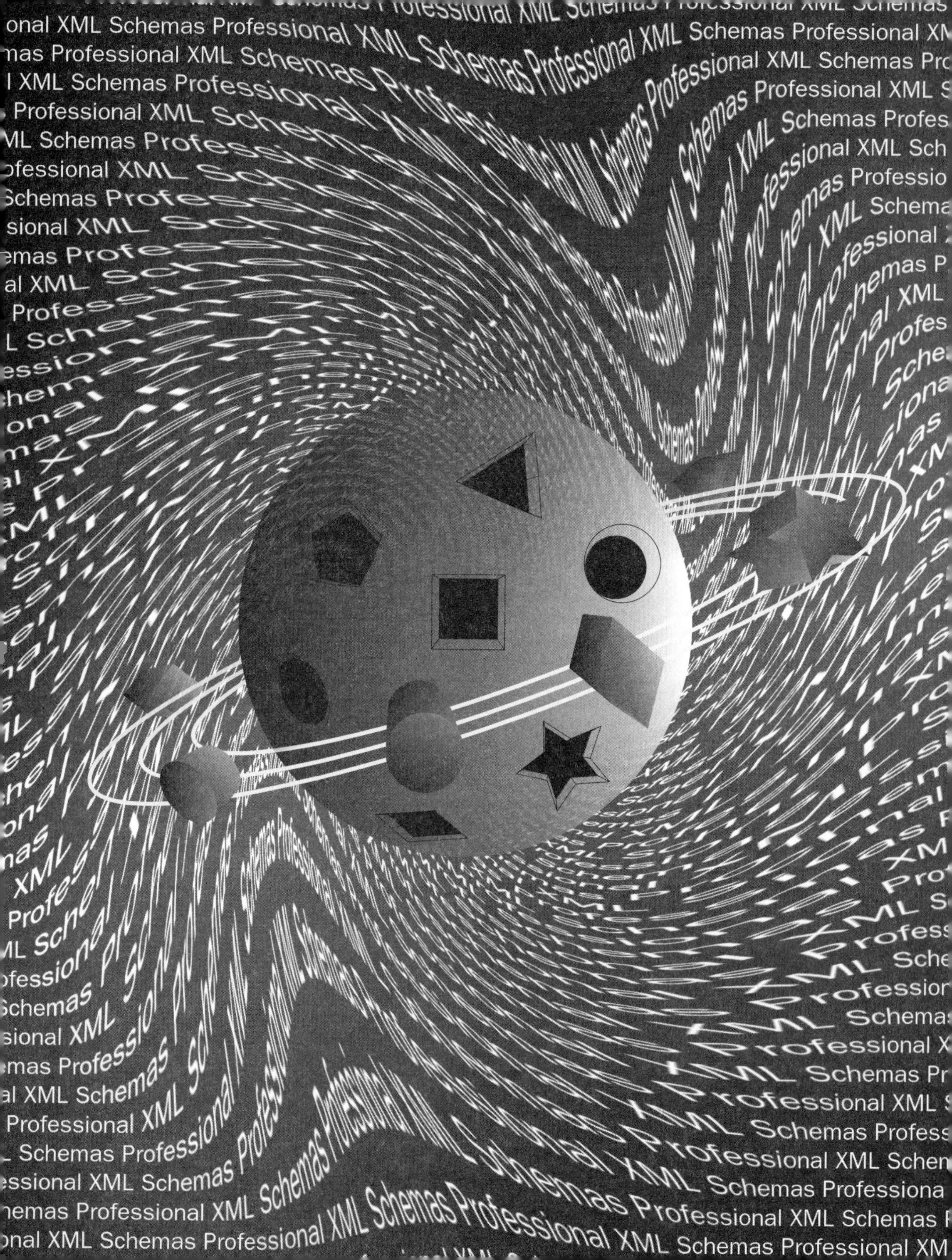
Professional XML Schemas

Creating Schemas From Multiple Documents

In this chapter we will be looking at different ways in which we can employ schema constructs in multiple schema documents, and across different namespaces. W3C XML Schema provides several mechanisms by which we can pull in definitions and declarations from other schemas and re-use them within another schema, whether these are schemas that we have written (allowing us to re-use our own markup), or those written by others that may at first seem outside of our control.

The ability to create schemas from multiple documents has two key advantages:

❑ Firstly we are able to modularize the development of our own schemas, which means we can re-use common schema components, create our own type libraries, and potentially keep the size of our schemas down.

❑ We can borrow constructs from other author's schemas and schemas developed by standards bodies, and likewise others can borrow constructs from our schemas (which is important if we are hoping that our schema will become adopted by others).

While looking at creating a schema from multiple other schemas, we are also forced to look at issues regarding namespaces; after all, if we are to reuse markup from different schemas, then sometimes we will inherently be dealing with different namespaces. This has important implications on how we use markup from other namespaces, and how we split up the namespaces we create.

If we want to re-use a schema, but need to change some of the constructs to tailor the schema to our exact needs, the W3C XML Schema specification also provides a number of facilities for changing the definitions and declarations before we re-use them. We will be looking at the different ways in which we can change the form of instance documents as we pull definitions and declarations into schemas that we are creating. Whether this is a minor tweak to permissible structures within an entire schema we would like to make use of, or alterations to a specific type that is relevant to our business domain, there are ways in which we can change permissible content – even if a schema is from a different namespace.

In all, we will look at:

- ❑ How we can re-use information across schemas

- ❑ How many namespaces we should use

- ❑ When we should hide or expose namespaces

- ❑ What the default namespace of our schema should be

- ❑ How to alter schema constructs we want to re-use

- ❑ How to define constructs that allow for extensibility of our design

- ❑ How to protect our own markup, both in terms of ownership and permission to derive types from our definitions

- ❑ Modularizing schema development

The first thing we need to do, then, is to see what we can borrow from other schemas and how we can use those constructs in the schemas that we are authoring.

Why Create Modular Schemas

By carefully designing and constructing our schemas, we not only gain from re-use within the schema, as we saw in the last chapter, we can also gain re-use of constructs across schemas. This enables us to write tight, compact schemas, which focus on an area of our business, with minimum effort.

When a schema is modularized, it is split into a collection of abstract modules that each provides a class or specific type of functionality. These modules act like a set of building block schemas. Other schemas that satisfy business needs can then borrow from these modular schemas, facilitating re-use of constructs across an organization and, as a by-product, encouraging interoperability if different departments and applications use similar structures.

Once we have these building blocks in place, it means that we can:

- ❑ Rapidly develop new schemas from the core building blocks

- ❑ Have standard structures for entities that are reflected across an application or organization

- ❑ Update classes of information from one schema and have the changes to the data structure represented across all of your schemas

- ❑ Allow different departments to use the same markup and include it within their own namespace

- ❑ Enhance interoperability between information in different parts of an application or organization

For example, we may use the same structure for addresses throughout a system; in which case we can create an address type that can be used in each schema that allows a document to contain a representation of an address. Similarly, customer and employee records may follow some common structure to represent information such as names, addresses or contact details; again, we can define a schema for this class of information and re-use it within other schemas.

To see an example of the advantages of modularization, by way of motivation for creating our own modular schemas, let's take a look at how and why the W3C have decided to modularize the XHTML Recommendation.

Modularization of XHTML

XHTML was modularized because there was a need to support an increasing number of Internet-aware appliances alternative to the standard desktop computer. The splitting up of the schema for XHTML allows platform developers to select which modules are applicable to their platform, and then fully support those modules. This in turn allows authors and architects of documents to select the subsets of markup that are appropriate to their device platform. For example, a text-only or embedded device would have no need to support image maps, so they could avoid implementing that module.

Each module defines a set of element types, attribute list declarations, and content models, and any of these can be empty. There are four core modules that each conforming processor is required to support, and then a number of optional ones. Each optional module is termed a **point of conformance** and if the application wants to offer any of the facilities in that module, they must support it fully. The author can then be sure that the subsection will be implemented on the platform they are writing for, and only use those subsections that are relevant to that platform. The underlying principle is that devices should not be required to support the full range and every permutation of XHTML elements that are required for each type of device. Therefore, they can just support the subset that they require.

The four core modules that any conforming processor is required to work with are the:

- ❑ Structure Module
- ❑ Text Module
- ❑ Hypertext Module
- ❑ List Module

Here are some of the modules that are optional in XHTML. Assuming that you are familiar with HTML, you should be able to see how these modules correspond to functionality offered by HTML, which is not required by all kinds of application:

- ❑ Forms module
- ❑ Table module
- ❑ Image module
- ❑ Client-side image map module
- ❑ Server-side image map module
- ❑ Object module
- ❑ Frames module
- ❑ Scripting module
- ❑ Meta-information module

As you can probably guess, the forms module includes markup for working with and creating forms, the table module for adding tables to pages, and so on.

This is a good example of how we can split up our schemas so that the applications that are required to work with XHTML only need to support the facilities that are relevant to them. The implementation of this will be described further when we explain how many namespaces should be used.

How We Can Re-Use Information Across Schemas

Any named, globally declared schema component can be re-used in other schemas: element and attribute declarations, named complex types, named simple types, named model groups, and attribute groups. The ways in which W3C XML Schema allows schema authors to borrow markup declarations and definitions from other schemas are governed by the target namespace of the schema that we are borrowing from. There are different methods for using schema components from the same target namespace as the document being created, than when working with constructs that reside in a different target namespace. This distinction is a requirement of processors that may need to validate instance documents that have come from multiple namespaces. We have more flexibility and control if the schema whose constructs we wish to use is in the same namespace as the schema we are writing, or has no namespace, but there are methods, which we will see later, of restricting re-use and derivation whoever is borrowing the constructs.

> A schema with no target namespace has no **targetNamespace** attribute on the schema element, or if it is present it has no value.

In order to look at examples of creating schemas from multiple namespace, we will be working with a pair of schemas throughout the chapter, and illustrating their uses in different namespaces. The re-usable schemas we will be looking at are:

❑   TypeLib.xsd which is a type library of the simple types, complex types, and elements that are commonly used in the schemas we create

❑   Products.xsd which contains declarations and definitions used in schemas that represent products and services

We will be using these common schemas to create other schemas, such as a customer list and a catalog.

Below is TypeLib.xsd, while not solely a library of simple and complex types (there is an element declaration in there too), it forms common components we will be using throughout other schemas. Note that, at the moment, it has no namespace, although we will be changing the namespace declarations as we look at different scenarios.

```
<xs:schema xmlns:xs = "http://www.w3.org/2001/XMLSchema"
           elementFormDefault = "qualified">

<xs:simpleType name = "fixedLengthField24Type">
   <xs:restriction base = "xs:string">
      <xs:minLength value = "0" />
      <xs:maxLength value = "24" />
   </xs:restriction>
</xs:simpleType>
```

```xml
<xs:simpleType name = "fixedLengthField256Type">
   <xs:restriction base = "xs:string">
      <xs:minLength value = "0" />
      <xs:maxLength value = "256" />
   </xs:restriction>
</xs:simpleType>

<xs:element name = "Customer">
   <xs:complexType>
      <xs:sequence>
         <xs:element name = "Name" type = "NameType" />
         <xs:element name = "Address" type = "AddressType" />
         <xs:element name = "EContact" type = "EContactType"
            minOccurs = "0" maxOccurs = "1" />
         <xs:element name = "AccountNumber" type = "xs:integer" />
      </xs:sequence>
      <xs:attribute name = "customerID" type = "xs:string" />
   </xs:complexType>
</xs:element>

<xs:complexType name = "NameType">
   <xs:sequence>
      <xs:element name = "FirstName" type = "fixedLengthField24Type" />
      <xs:element name = "MiddleInitial" type = "fixedLengthField24Type"
         minOccurs = "0" maxOccurs = "1" />
      <xs:element name = "LastName" type = "fixedLengthField24Type" />
   </xs:sequence>
</xs:complexType>

<xs:complexType name = "AddressType">
   <xs:sequence>
      <xs:element name = "Street" type = "fixedLengthField24Type" />
      <xs:element name = "Town" type = "fixedLengthField24Type" />
      <xs:element name = "City" type = "fixedLengthField24Type"
         minOccurs = "0" maxOccurs = "1" />
      <xs:element name = "StateRegionCounty"
         type = "fixedLengthField24Type" />
      <xs:element name = "ZipPostalCode" type = "fixedLengthField24Type" />
      <xs:element name = "Country" type = "fixedLengthField24Type" />
   </xs:sequence>
</xs:complexType>

<xs:complexType name = "EContactType">
   <xs:sequence>
      <xs:element name = "Email" type = "xs:string"
         minOccurs = "0" maxOccurs = "1" />
      <xs:element name = "HomeTel" type="xs:integer"
         minOccurs = "0" maxOccurs = "1" />
      <xs:element name = "WorkTel" type="xs:integer"
         minOccurs = "0" maxOccurs = "1" />
      <xs:element name = "CellPhone" type="xs:integer"
         minOccurs = "0" maxOccurs = "1" />
      <xs:element name = "Fax" type="xs:integer"
         minOccurs = "0" maxOccurs = "1"/>
      <xs:element name = "Pager" type="xs:integer"
         minOccurs = "0" maxOccurs = "1"/>
```

```
      </xs:sequence>
   </xs:complexType>

   </xs:schema>
```

As can be seen, it contains two simple types:

- ❑ `fixedLengthField24Type` – a `string` with a maximum length of 24 characters
- ❑ `fixedLengthField256Type` – a `string` with a maximum length of 256 characters

An element declaration:

- ❑ `Customer` – this contains the name, address, e-contact, and account number details of a customer

Three complex types, which are used in the `Customer` element, but are also available for other purposes:

- ❑ `NameType` – which contains a content model for describing peoples' names
- ❑ `AddressType` – which contains a content model for describing all kinds of addresses
- ❑ `EContactType` – which contains a content model for forms of electronic communication including phone, fax, and email

Let's look at the second schema we will be using, `Products.xsd`, which contains the components to describe the products, and services that our fictional company offers, and the price of these. Note that the `Products.xsd` schema uses the fixed length field types that we defined in `TypeLib.xsd` (we shall see how this affects our design shortly):

```
<xs:schema xmlns:xs = "http://www.w3.org/2001/XMLSchema"
           elementFormDefault = "qualified">

<xs:complexType name = "ProductType">
   <xs:sequence>
      <xs:element name = "ProductName" type = "fixedLengthField24Type" />
      <xs:element name = "Description" type = "fixedLengthField256Type" />
      <xs:element ref = "Price" />
   </xs:sequence>
   <xs:attribute name = "sku" type = "xs:ID" />
</xs:complexType>

<xs:complexType name = "ServiceType">
   <xs:sequence>
      <xs:element name = "ServiceName" type = "fixedLengthField24Type" />
      <xs:element name = "Description" type = "fixedLengthField256Type" />
      <xs:element ref = "Price" />
   </xs:sequence>
   <xs:attribute name = "sid" type = "xs:ID" />
</xs:complexType>

<xs:element name = "Price">
   <xs:complexType>
```

```
            <xs:attribute name = "currency" type="xs:string" />
            <xs:attribute name = "units" type="priceUnitsType" />
        </xs:complexType>
    </xs:element>

    <xs:simpleType name = "priceUnitsType">
        <xs:restriction base = "xs:string">
            <xs:enumeration value = "perUnit" />
            <xs:enumeration value = "perHour" />
            <xs:enumeration value = "perDay" />
            <xs:enumeration value = "onceOnlyCharge" />
        </xs:restriction>
    </xs:simpleType>

</xs:schema>
```

As you can see, `Products.xsd` contains two complex types:

❑ `ProductType` – that defines a content model for elements that describe products we sell

❑ `ServiceType` – that defines a content model for elements that describe services we offer

An element declaration:

❑ `Price` – that is used to indicate prices of products and services. This carries two attributes, one for the currency, the other for the units in which we are charging whose value is an enumerated simple type.

A simple type declaration:

❑ `PricePerUnits` – that is an enumerated type indicating the units in which we can be charged

So, let's see how we benefit from using these example schemas.

Schemas from the Same Namespace or No Namespace

If the schema that we want to borrow constructs from is within the same namespace as the schema we are creating, there are two mechanisms we can use:

❑ The **include** mechanism, which brings in all the declarations and definitions from the other schema into the one we are writing.

❑ The **redefine** mechanism, which not only brings in the declarations and definitions from the other schema, but also lets us alter them if we so desire/need.

We shall look at `include` first as it is the simpler of the two.

Using the include Mechanism

The include mechanism uses an element called `include` to bring all of the declarations of the external schema into the schema we are creating. For schema authors, the effect is that of copying and pasting the content of the external schema where the included element was, because the local name of the elements in the included schema are being qualified by a declaration for the same namespace as that of the schema that includes the constructs.

Later in the chapter we will see that, if there is no `targetNamespace` *for the schema we are borrowing from, when we use the* `include` *mechanism,* **namespace coercion** *takes place, which means that the constructs become part of the namespace we are writing.*

> **If the schema we include borrows from other schemas, we only have to reference the topmost schema for it to pull in other schemas it references.**

To see how we use the `include` mechanism in practice we will create a schema for a simple catalog. The catalog will borrow components that describe the details of the products and services that we offer from the `Product.xsd` schema. Remember that this schema also makes use of the fixed field length types from `TypeLib.xsd`:

When we introduced the schemas, they were no namespace schemas, so we will change the declaration of the root `schema` element in `Product.xsd` to the following. We need to make its target namespace the same as the target namespace of the schema we are about to write, which will be `http://www.example.com/ECommerce`. Note also for this example, `elementFormDefault` has been given a value of `qualified`, so that we can use a namespace defaulting to qualify elements in the instance document.

```
<xs:schema xmlns:xs = "http://www.w3.org/2001/XMLSchema"
           targetNamespace = "http://www.example.com/ECommerce"
           xmlns = "http://www.example.com/ECommerce"
           elementFormDefault = "qualified">
```

We have to do exactly the same for the `TypeLib.xsd` schema too. You can find the files for this example inside the `Ch07_ex1_Include` folder, in with the downloadable code for this book available from http://www.wrox.com/.

Before we look at the `Catalog.xsd` schema, and how it includes these other two schemas, let's take a look at the format for the catalog information. Here is an example of an instance document:

```
<?xml version = "1.0" ?>
<Catalog  xmlns = "http://www.example.com/ECommerce"
          publishDate = "2001-04-18">
   <Products>
       <Product sku = "p2140">
          <ProductName>Widgets</ProductName>
          <Description>Y'know those funny little widgetty things that
          all programmers seem to want to buy in examples.</Description>
          <Price currency = "AUS$" units = "perUnit">1.45</Price>
      </Product>
      <!-- More product details go here -->
   </Products>
   <Services>
     <Service sid = "s12">
        <ServiceName>Delivery</ServiceName>
        <Description>How you get our wonderful products...</Description>
```

```
          <Price currency = "AUS$" units = "onceOnly">12.00</Price>
       </Service>
       <!-- More service details go here -->
    </Services>
</Catalog>
```

Onto the `Catalog.xsd` schema... We already have complex types to define the content model for product and service elements in the `Product.xsd` file, along with a declaration for the `Price` element that they both use.

The job of the `Catalog.xsd` schema is to include the other two schemas, declare the containing elements for the whole `Catalog`, `Products`, and `Services` holders, and individual `Product` and `Service` elements, and to apply appropriate occurrence constraints.

Note that, the target namespace of the schemas we are including is the same as the one for this schema, that `elementFormDefault` has been given a value of `qualified` so that we can use namespace defaulting in the instance document, and that the `include` elements which bring in the other schemas' declarations and definitions are the children of the `schema` element.

```
<xs:schema xmlns:xs = "http://www.w3.org/2001/XMLSchema"
           targetNamespace = "http://www.example.com/ECommerce"
           xmlns = "http://www.example.com/ECommerce"
           elementFormDefault = "qualified">

<xs:include  schemaLocation = "http://location_of_schema/Products.xsd" />
<xs:include  schemaLocation = "http://location_of_schema/TypeLib.xsd" />

<xs:element name = "Catalog">
   <xs:complexType>
      <xs:sequence>
         <xs:element name = "Products">
            <xs:complexType>
               <xs:sequence>
                  <xs:element name = "Product" type = "ProductType"
                        minOccurs = "0" maxOccurs = "unbounded" />
               </xs:sequence>
            </xs:complexType>
         </xs:element>
         <xs:element name = "Services">
            <xs:complexType>
               <xs:sequence>
                  <xs:element name = "Service" type = "ServiceType"
                        minOccurs = "0" maxOccurs = "unbounded" />
               </xs:sequence>
            </xs:complexType>
         </xs:element>
      </xs:sequence>
      <xs:attribute name = "publishDate" type = "xs:date" />
   </xs:complexType>
</xs:element>

</xs:schema>
```

This schema is also known as the **main** schema. At the beginning of the main schema, we include the two schemas that we want to re-use the constructs from:

```
<xs:include  schemaLocation = "http://location_of_schema/Products.xsd" />
<xs:include  schemaLocation = "http://location_of_schema/TypeLib.xsd" />
```

The include element must be a top-level element, a direct child of the schema element. The include element can carry an attribute called schemaLocation, which provides a hint to a processing application of where it might find a copy of the schema. The W3C XML Schema Recommendation does not specify how a processor should interpret the include element. It may choose to pull in the included schemas as it loads the main schema, or it may choose to do so when they are used, if at all.

Having declared the schemas that can be imported, we define the Catalog element, which is the root element of the catalog XML files. Inside this declaration, we have an anonymous complex type, which holds the Products and Services element declarations – these are containers for all of the products and services that we offer.

Note how the Product element declaration is associated with the ProductType. The ProductType is the complex type that was defined in the Products.xsd schema.

```
<xs:element name = "Product" type = "ProductType"
            minOccurs = "0" maxOccurs = "unbounded" />
```

Likewise the Service element is associated with the ServiceType complex type, which we defined in the Products.xsd schema as well.

```
<xs:element name = "Service" type = "ServiceType"
            minOccurs = "0" maxOccurs = "unbounded" />
```

Having included the two other schemas we can use any of the named, globally declared or defined constructs from these schemas.

If we trace back and look at the definitions of these complex types, we can see why we had to import the TypeLib.xsd schema as well. Both of the complex types we used in the Catalog schema use the maxFieldLength24Type and maxFieldLength256Type simple types that we defined in the TypeLib.xsd schema, which was why we needed to include that schema as well.

This would have worked exactly the same had the Products.xsd schema included the TypeLib.xsd schema itself, rather than relying on us to do it. This is because, if we include a schema that includes another schema, both get included in the parent document.

Using the redefine Mechanism

If the schema we want to re-use constructs from belongs to the same namespace as the one we are creating there is another technique we can use to bring in the constructs from another schema. The redefine element allows us to modify:

❑ Simple and complex types, in which case the modifications must be extensions or restrictions of the same base type.

❑ Named model groups and attribute groups, which would have to be supersets or subsets of the original groups.

❑ Annotations, this is an important one to remember, especially if we are changing the meaning of a type or group.

To use the redefine mechanism, we use a new `redefine` element for each type, group, or annotation that we want to modify. However, the redefine mechanism performs an implicit `include` as well, so there is no need to either explicitly include the schema, or redefine every declaration we want to use.

> **When we redefine a schema component, all instances of that type or group within the schema you are writing and from the schema that is imported – even if only referenced – take on the redefined type or group.**

Suppose that we wanted to contract out some of the services that we offer. In our catalog, we want to add a `ContractedTo` element, to indicate who was the contractor responsible for providing that service, so that services looked like this:

```
<Service sid = "s12">
  <ServiceName>Delivery</ServiceName>
  <Description>How you get our wonderful products...</Description>
  <Price currency = "AUS$" units = "perHour">12.00</Price>
  <ContractedTo>UPS</ContractedTo>
</Service>
```

Rather than using an `include` element, we could use a `redefine` element, and derive a new `ServiceType`, which would be used by the schema when the `Products.xsd` schema was implicitly included. We derive new types, when redefining them, in exactly the same way that we did in Chapter 3 when we looked at defining our own types.

Having derived a new complex type for the `ServiceType` using the extension mechanism, when we refer to it later in the schema, we will be able to use the new `ContractedTo` element we have defined. If the type was used anywhere else in the schema, the elements it is associated to would also be redefined. The files for this example can be found in the `Ch07_ex2_redefine` folder.

```
<xs:schema xmlns:xs = "http://www.w3.org/2001/XMLSchema"
           targetNamespace = "http://www.example.com/ECommerce"
           xmlns = "http://www.example.com/ECommerce"
           elementFormDefault = "qualified">

  <xs:include schemaLocation = "http://location_of_schema/TypeLib.xsd" />
  <xs:redefine schemaLocation = "http://location_of_schema/Products.xsd">
    <xs:complexType name = "ServiceType">
      <xs:complexContent>
        <xs:extension base = "ServiceType">
          <xs:sequence>
            <xs:element name = "ContractedTo" type = "xs:string"/>
          </xs:sequence>
        </xs:extension>
      </xs:complexContent>
    </xs:complexType>
  </xs:redefine>
```

```
<xs:element name = "Catalog">
    <xs:complexType>
        <xs:sequence>
            <xs:element name = "Products">
                <xs:complexType>
                    <xs:sequence>
                        <xs:element name = "Product" type = "ProductType"
                            minOccurs = "0" maxOccurs = "unbounded" />
                    </xs:sequence>
                </xs:complexType>
            </xs:element>
            <xs:element name = "Services">
                <xs:complexType>
                    <xs:sequence>
                        <xs:element name = "Service" type = "ServiceType"
                            minOccurs = "0" maxOccurs = "unbounded" />
                    </xs:sequence>
                </xs:complexType>
            </xs:element>
        </xs:sequence>
        <xs:attribute name = "publishDate" type = "xs:date" />
    </xs:complexType>
</xs:element>

</xs:schema>
```

This is an especially powerful way of adding to schemas that we have already defined, and updating our own schemas. We must be careful, however, that when we redefine a group or type that we do not break other definitions that make use of them.

Unqualified Elements

Earlier in the chapter, we made note of the fact that we were setting elementFormDefault to have a value of qualified. This is important because we have to qualify any element that is defined globally in an instance document, but we should not qualify locally declared elements (unless elementFormDefault has a value of qualified). So, we have been making things easier for ourselves so far.

Let's take a look at these examples without elementFormDefault taking a value of qualified. The files for this example are in the folder Ch07_example3_unqualified_include. All of the schemas in that folder therefore have specified elementFormDefault to be unqualified (which is the default, so it could have been left off the schema element altogether). The schema element of each of these examples has the following structure:

```
<xs:schema xmlns:xs = "http://www.w3.org/2001/XMLSchema"
        targetNamespace = "http://www.example.com/ECommerce"
        xmlns = "http://www.example.com/ECommerce"
        elementFormDefault = "unqualified">
```

This means that the two globally declared elements: Catalog from the Catalog.xsd schema and Product from Product.xsd must be explicitly qualified, while the others should not. Like so:

```
<?xml version = "1.0" ?>
<ecom:Catalog  xmlns:ecom = "http://www.example.com/ECommerce"
    publishDate = "2001-04-18">
  <Products>
    <Product sku = "p2140">
      <ProductName>Widgets</ProductName>
      <Description>Y'know widgetty things</Description>
      <ecom:Price currency = "AUS$" units = "perUnit">1.45</ecom:Price>
    </Product>
  </Products>
  <Services>
    <Service sid = "s12">
      <ServiceName>Delivery</ServiceName>
      <Description>How you get our wonderful products...</Description>
      <ecom:Price currency = "AUS$" units = "perHour">12.00</ecom:Price>
    </Service>
  </Services>
</ecom:Catalog>
```

As you can imagine, this would soon start to become quite complicated to track if we had to manually author the instance documents, and would require careful checking if we were writing an application to cope with such namespace complexities. Not only do we have to check which elements and attributes have been declared globally in the schema we are referencing, but also any schemas that they use. Therefore, by setting elementFormDefault to have a value of qualified, we are able to not only use namespace defaulting, but also save an author having to check through each of the schemas.

Why Use include and redefine

The include and redefine mechanisms are especially powerful when creating our own modular schemas. Because we are limited to using them within the same namespace as the target namespace of our schema, they are more helpful for internal work.

> *While there is nothing, in theory, to stop us from adding to a namespace defined by someone else, we would not be able to guarantee interoperability of our files, because our partners would not share our extra definitions and declarations.*

The include and redefine mechanisms help us to:

- ❑ Re-use schema constructs across several schemas

- ❑ Keep the size of schema document down

- ❑ Create schemas to represent each class of entity that we may meet in the real world

- ❑ Only use sections of the schema that are relevant to the class of document or target application we are dealing with

Inclusion is a powerful mechanism when working with schemas that we have already written, but is less likely to be of use when we want to borrow markup that someone else has created, as an external schema is not likely to inhabit the same namespace. We can still, however, incorporate markup defined in another namespace using the import mechanism.

Schemas from a Different Target Namespace

If the schema from which we want to borrow is outside of our control or in a different namespace, then we can use the **import** mechanism, which uses an element called import to bring definitions and declarations of the external schema into the new schema that we are working with. When we import schema constructs from several namespaces, it means that we can create instance documents that can be validated across multiple namespaces. Therefore, we will be forced to use namespace prefixes in the schema and take a closer look at the effect on our instance documents.

The import element may carry two attributes:

❑ Firstly, it is required to carry an attribute called namespace, which indicates the namespace to which the schema belongs.

❑ Secondly, we can provide an optional schemaLocation attribute to indicate to the processor where it might find a copy of the schema (just as we did with the include element). It is a good idea to provide one if we can, even if it is a copy of the schema on your server (in case the original is not available – although we must make sure we keep this up-to-date).

Once we have imported a schema, all of the globally declared schema components can be used within the schema we are creating. For example, we can use a named complex type from the schema we have imported to derive new types (provided the author has not forbidden it, an ability we look at in the *Protecting Our Markup – Re-Use* section).

To use the components from the other schemas, we have to declare the namespace from which they have come, along with a prefix to qualify the local names of those schema components in the root schema element, just as we would for any other namespace declaration. Then, when we want to use globally defined components from the other schema in the one we are writing, we just use the prefix that qualifies them with the namespace from which they have come.

Note that we have to use a new import element for each schema that we want to import constructs from, and declare a new namespace and namespace prefix for each namespace we are borrowing from.

Using the import Mechanism

To demonstrate working with markup that someone else has defined, we will use the same examples we have looked at so far, but we will place the declarations and definitions of TypeLib.xsd and Products.xsd in the http://www.wrox.com/ECommerce namespace, while keeping the catalog schema in the http://www.example.com/ECommerce namespace. To do this, we start by changing the schema element in TypeLib.xsd and Products.xsd to the following (note that the default and target namespaces are the same):

```
<xs:schema xmlns:xs = "http://www.w3.org/2001/XMLSchema"
           targetNamespace = "http://www.wrox.com/ECommerce"
           xmlns = "http://www.wrox.com/ECommerce"
           elementFormDefault = "qualified">
```

Both are the same, because the Products.xsd schema borrows from the TypeLib.xsd schema and would likely be in the same namespace.

So, now we move onto the new `Catalog.xsd` schema. Note how we have to define the new namespace along with a prefix, and import the schemas so that we can qualify which namespace the complex types that we are borrowing from belong to:

```xml
<xs:schema xmlns:xs = "http://www.w3.org/2001/XMLSchema"
           targetNamespace = "http://www.example.com/ECommerce"
           xmlns = "http://www.example.com/ECommerce"
           elementFormDefault = "qualified"
           xmlns:wrox = "http://www.wrox.com/ECommerce">

    <xs:import  schemaLocation = "http://file_Location/Products.xsd"
       namespace = "http://www.wrox.com/ECommerce" />
    <xs:import  schemaLocation = "http://file_Location/TypeLib.xsd"
       namespace = "http://www.wrox.com/ECommerce" />

    <xs:element name = "Catalog">
        <xs:complexType>
            <xs:sequence>
                <xs:element name = "Products">
                    <xs:complexType>
                        <xs:sequence>
                            <xs:element name = "Product" type = "wrox:ProductType"
                                minOccurs = "0" maxOccurs = "unbounded" />
                        </xs:sequence>
                    </xs:complexType>
                </xs:element>
                <xs:element name = "Services">
                    <xs:complexType>
                        <xs:sequence>
                            <xs:element name = "Service" type = "wrox:ServiceType"
                                minOccurs = "0" maxOccurs = "unbounded" />
                        </xs:sequence>
                    </xs:complexType>
                </xs:element>
            </xs:sequence>
            <xs:attribute name = "publishDate" type = "xs:date" />
        </xs:complexType>
    </xs:element>

</xs:schema>
```

If we look at this a little more closely, we can see that we have defined three separate namespaces in the root schema element:

- `http://www.w3.org/2001/XMLSchema`, which is the XML Schema namespace

- `http://www.example.com/ECommerce`, which is the target and default namespace for this schema

- `http://www.wrox.com/ECommerce`, which is the namespace that we are borrowing `ProductType` and `ServiceType` from

We have also given `elementFormDefault` a value of `qualified` so that we can hide
namespace complexities:

```
<xs:schema xmlns:xs = "http://www.w3.org/2001/XMLSchema"
           targetNamespace = "http://www.example.com/ECommerce"
           xmlns = "http://www.example.com/ECommerce"
           xmlns:wrox = "http://www.wrox.com/ECommerce"
           elementFormDefault = "qualified">
```

Next up, as a direct child of the `schema` element, we use the import element to bring in the two
schemas that we are borrowing constructs from. We have given the `import` element both the optional
`schemaLocation` attribute (to indicate to the application where it can find the schema if it needs to do
so), and the `namespace` attribute, which is required and is the namespace that we are borrowing the
markup from.

```
<xs:import  schemaLocation = "http://file_Location/Products.xsd"
    namespace = "http://www.wrox.com/ECommerce" />
<xs:import  schemaLocation = "http://file_Location/TypeLib.xsd"
    namespace = "http://www.wrox.com/ECommerce" />
```

Remember we had to include both schemas because the `Product.xsd` *schema uses simple types
from the* `TypeLib.xsd` *schema. This raises some interesting issues regarding schema dependencies,
which we will come back to later in the chapter.*

You can then see that we have had to prefix the types that we are borrowing from the schemas which
we have imported with the prefix that was associated with the namespace in the root `schema` element:

```
<xs:element name = "Catalog">
    <xs:complexType>
        <xs:sequence>
            <xs:element name = "Products">
                <xs:complexType>
                    <xs:sequence>
                        <xs:element name = "Product" type = "wrox:ProductType"
                            minOccurs = "0" maxOccurs = "unbounded" />
                    </xs:sequence>
                </xs:complexType>
            </xs:element>
            <xs:element name = "Services">
                <xs:complexType>
                    <xs:sequence>
                        <xs:element name = "Service" type = "wrox:ServiceType"
                            minOccurs = "0" maxOccurs = "unbounded" />
                    </xs:sequence>
                </xs:complexType>
            </xs:element>
        </xs:sequence>
        <xs:attribute name = "publishDate" type = "xs:date" />
    </xs:complexType>
</xs:element>

</xs:schema>
```

Finally, here is an example of an instance document that uses the imported types. Note how we have to qualify the elements that have come from the imported namespace, because we set elementFormDefault to have a value of qualified.

```xml
<?xml version = "1.0" ?>
<Catalog  xmlns = "http://www.example.com/ECommerce"
    xmlns:wrox = "http://www.wrox.com/ECommerce"
    publishDate = "2001-04-18">
    <Products>
        <Product sku = "p2140">
            <wrox:ProductName>Widgets</wrox:ProductName>
            <wrox:Description>Y'know widgetty things</wrox:Description>
            <wrox:Price currency = "AUS$" units = "perUnit">1.45</wrox:Price>
        </Product>
    </Products>
    <Services>
        <Service sid = "s12">
            <wrox:ServiceName>Delivery</wrox:ServiceName>
            <wrox:Description>
                How you get our wonderful products...
            </wrox:Description>
            <wrox:Price currency = "AUS$" units = "perHour">12.00</wrox:Price>
        </Service>
    </Services>
</Catalog>
```

To finish off our look at import, we should have a look at what happens when we do not give elementFormDefault a value of qualified.

Unqualified Elements

When we imported the two helper schemas into our main schemas, each of the schemas had an elementFormDefault attribute on its root schema element. This helped hide namespace complexities. If we had removed the elementFormDefault attribute or specified its default value of unqualified, we would have had the following declarations in the root elements of the helper schemas:

```xml
<xs:schema xmlns:xs = "http://www.w3.org/2001/XMLSchema"
           targetNamespace = "http://www.wrox.com/ECommerce"
           xmlns = "http://www.wrox.com/ECommerce"
           elementFormDefault = "unqualified">
```

Then in our Catalog.xsd schema we would have had the following:

```xml
<xs:schema xmlns:xs = "http://www.w3.org/2001/XMLSchema"
           targetNamespace = "http://www.example.com/ECommerce"
           xmlns = "http://www.example.com/ECommerce"
           xmlns:wrox = "http://www.wrox.com/ECommerce"
           elementFormDefault = "unqualified">
```

As with using the include mechanism, without specifying that elementFormDefaults have a value of unqualified, we have to specifically qualify the globally declared elements. Our resulting Catalog.xml file would therefore look like this:

```
<?xml version = "1.0" ?>
<ecom:Catalog  xmlns:ecom = "http://www.example.com/ECommerce"
    xmlns:wrox = "http://www.wrox.com/ECommerce"
    publishDate = "2001-04-18">
    <Products>
        <Product sku = "p2140">
            <ProductName>Widgets</ProductName>
            <Description>Y'know widgetty things</Description>
            <wrox:Price currency = "AUS$" units = "perUnit">1.45</wrox:Price>
        </Product>
    </Products>
    <Services>
        <Service sid = "s12">
            <ServiceName>Delivery</ServiceName>
            <Description>How you get our wonderful products...</Description>
            <wrox:Price currency = "AUS$" units = "perHour">12.00</wrox:Price>
        </Service>
    </Services>
</ecom:Catalog>
```

Again, as you can see we have to qualify the root `Catalog` element as belonging to the
`http://www.example.com/ECommerce` namespace, and we also have to qualify the `Price` elements,
although this time we have to associate them with the `http://www.wrox.com/ECommerce`
namespace, because we have imported them from that namespace (as opposed to including them from
the same namespace).

Having seen how we can make use of schema components declared in both the same, and different
namespaces, we should ask ourselves how many namespaces we should be using in our own
schema development.

How Many Namespaces Should We Use

As you start to develop multiple schemas, you may ask yourself whether you should be creating them in
one or more namespaces. For example, if we are writing schemas for several different departments we
might be tempted to place the schema constructs in different namespaces.

The question of when to split up namespaces is an interesting one. Remember that we indicate the
namespace that each schema's constructs are intended to reside in using the `targetNamespace`
attribute on the `schema` element. As we have seen, the ways in which we can re-use constructs depends
upon whether the constructs are within the same or a different schema and namespace.

There are three different design approaches that can be used to answer the question of how many
namespaces you should use:

❑   **Heterogeneous namespace design**: where each schema has its own separate namespace

❑   **Homogeneous namespace design**: where we create a single namespace for the schemas of any
    given project, sometimes known as an **umbrella namespace**

❑   **Chameleon namespace design**: where we create several schemas that have no namespace, and
    use them like building blocks for creating larger schemas – known as **main** schemas – which
    do have a namespace. This allows us to re-use the smaller schemas, known as **supporting**
    schemas, in different namespaces; because when they are included in the main schemas, they
    become part of the main schema's namespace

We have already seen examples that make use of the `Product.xsd` and `TypeLib.xsd` schemas to create the `Catalog.xsd` schema from the same namespace and different namespaces, so we will quickly go through those two scenarios before focusing on the third, which is new and poses some interesting issues.

Heterogeneous Namespace Design

In the heterogeneous design we would create separate namespaces for each of the schemas we were creating, so we will create three namespaces:

- ❏   http://www.example.com/Product
- ❏   http://www.example.com/TypeLib
- ❏   http://www.example.com/Catalog

First, here is the root `schema` element for the `TypeLib.xsd` schema in the `http://www.example.com/TypeLib` namespace:

```
<xs:schema xmlns:xs = "http://www.w3.org/2001/XMLSchema"
           targetNamespace = "http://www.example.com/TypeLib"
           xmlns = "http://www.example.com/TypeLib"
           elementFormDefault = "qualified">
```

In the earlier examples, the `TypeLib.xsd` schema was in the same namespace as the `Product.xsd` schema, in this example all of our schemas are in different namespaces, so we need to alter the `Product.xsd` schema to import the `TypeLib.xsd` schema, which contains the definitions of `fixedFieldLength24Type` and `fixedFieldLength256Type`, which are used in `Product.xsd` which is in the `http://www.example.com/Product` namespace:

```
<xs:schema xmlns:xs = "http://www.w3.org/2001/XMLSchema"
           targetNamespace = "http://www.example.com/Products"
           xmlns = "http://www.example.com/Products"
           xmlns:tl = "http://www.example.com/TypeLib"
           elementFormDefault = "qualified">

<xs:import namespace =  "http://www.example.com/TypeLib"
     schemaLocation =  "http://file_location/TypelLib.xsd" />

<xs:complexType name = "ProductType">
   <xs:sequence>
      <xs:element name = "ProductName"
         type = "tl:fixedLengthField24Type" />
      <xs:element name = "Description"
         type = "tl:fixedLengthField256Type" />
      <xs:element ref = "Price" />
   </xs:sequence>
   <xs:attribute name = "sku" type = "xs:ID" />
</xs:complexType>

<xs:complexType name = "ServiceType">
   <xs:sequence>
      <xs:element name = "ServiceName"
         type = "tl:fixedLengthField24Type" />
```

```
            <xs:element name = "Description"
                type = "tl:fixedLengthField256Type" />
            <xs:element ref = "Price" />
        </xs:sequence>
        <xs:attribute name = "sid" type = "xs:ID" />
    </xs:complexType>

    <xs:element name = "Price">
        <xs:complexType>
            <xs:simpleContent>
                <xs:extension base="xs:decimal">
                    <xs:attribute name = "currency" type="xs:string" />
                    <xs:attribute name = "units" type="priceUnitsType" />
                </xs:extension>
            </xs:simpleContent>
        </xs:complexType>
    </xs:element>

    <xs:simpleType name = "priceUnitsType">
        <xs:restriction base = "xs:string">
            <xs:enumeration value = "perUnit" />
            <xs:enumeration value = "perHour" />
            <xs:enumeration value = "perDay" />
            <xs:enumeration value = "onceOnlyCharge" />
        </xs:restriction>
    </xs:simpleType>

</xs:schema>
```

The third and final schema is the `Catalog.xsd` schema. This now only needs to import the one `Products.xsd` schema. We do not need to import the `TypeLib.xsd` schema, because the `Products.xsd` schema has imported it.

```
<xs:schema xmlns:xs = "http://www.w3.org/2001/XMLSchema"
            targetNamespace = "http://www.example.com/Catalog"
            xmlns = "http://www.example.com/Catalog"
            xmlns:prod = "http://www.wrox.com/Products"
            elementFormDefault = "qualified">

    <xs:import  schemaLocation = "http://file_location/Products.xsd"
        namespace = "http://www.wrox.com/Products" />

    <xs:element name = "Catalog">
        <xs:complexType>
            <xs:sequence>
                <xs:element name = "Products">
                    <xs:complexType>
                        <xs:sequence>
                            <xs:element name = "Product" type = "prod:ProductType"
                                minOccurs = "0" maxOccurs = "unbounded" />
                        </xs:sequence>
                    </xs:complexType>
                </xs:element>
                <xs:element name = "Services">
                    <xs:complexType>
```

```
            <xs:sequence>
                <xs:element name = "Service" type = "prod:ServiceType"
                    minOccurs = "0" maxOccurs = "unbounded" />
            </xs:sequence>
        </xs:complexType>
    </xs:element>
    </xs:sequence>
    <xs:attribute name = "publishDate" type = "xs:date" />
    </xs:complexType>
</xs:element>

</xs:schema>
```

And here is a sample document, remember that this one has `elementFormDefault` set with a value of `qualified` on all schemas:

```
<?xml version = "1.0" ?>
<Catalog  xmlns = "http://www.example.com/Catalog"
    xmlns:prod = "http://www.example.com/Products"
    publishDate = "2001-04-18">
    <Products>
        <Product sku = "p2140">
            <prod:ProductName>Widgets</prod:ProductName>
            <prod:Description>
                Y'know those widgetty things that do really exciting stuff.
            </prod:Description>
            <prod:Price currency = "AUS$" units = "perUnit">1.45</prod:Price>
        </Product>
    </Products>
    <Services>
        <Service sid = "s12">
            <prod:ServiceName>Delivery</prod:ServiceName>
            <prod:Description>
                How you get our wonderful products...
            </prod:Description>
            <prod:Price currency = "AUS$" units = "perHour">12.00</prod:Price>
        </Service>
    </Services>
</Catalog>
```

There is also another folder in the examples, where `elementFormDefault` has a value of `unqualified` in all of its schemas, called `Ch07_ex6_heterogeneous_unqualified`, for which the instance document follows. The main difference being that we only have to qualify the globally declared elements in the first schema we are calling, and then explicitly qualify all elements from other schemas because their markup is in a different namespace (it does not matter whether they were locally or globally declared).

```
<?xml version = "1.0" ?>
<cat:Catalog  xmlns:cat = "http://www.example.com/Catalog"
    xmlns:prod = "http://www.example.com/Products"
    publishDate = "2001-04-18">
    <Products>
        <Product sku = "p2140">
            <prod:ProductName>Widgets</prod:ProductName>
```

```
                <prod:Description>Y'know widgetty things</prod:Description>
                <prod:Price currency = "AUS$" units = "perUnit">1.45</prod:Price>
        </Product>
    </Products>
    <Services>
        <Service sid = "s12">
                <prod:ServiceName>Delivery</prod:ServiceName>
                <prod:Description>
                    How you get our wonderful products...
                </prod:Description>
                <prod:Price currency = "AUS$" units = "perHour">12.00</prod:Price>
        </Service>
    </Services>
</cat:Catalog>
```

So, to summarize the effects of the heterogeneous namespace design upon instance documents:

❑   Elements from each namespace must be explicitly qualified, when we set
    elementFormDefault to qualified

❑   Globally declared elements and attributes from the main schema must be explicitly qualified,
    and all elements and attributes from other namespaces must be explicitly qualified, when we
    set elementFormDefault to unqualified

❑   For each namespace that was used in the schema and for which there is corresponding
    markup in the instance document, we must declare the namespace and associate it with a
    namespace prefix

This is powerful when we want to import markup from someone else's schema, although there are
complications for the author of the instance document if they have to indicate which namespace each
element came from.

Homogeneous Namespace Design

We have already seen an example of the Homogeneous Namespace Design in the first example, when
we were using include, the examples for this are in the Ch07_example1_include folder. We can use
either include or redefine to bring in elements from the same namespace, which as we have seen
allows us more flexibility in re-using markup.

Because the schemas all declare markup in the same namespace, we do not need to add a namespace
attribute to the include element.

Again with each schema, we set elementFormDefault to have a value of qualified so that we can
see the effects it is having on the instance documents.

Here is the root element and the two include elements to remind you:

```
<xs:schema xmlns:xs = "http://www.w3.org/2001/XMLSchema"
           targetNamespace = "http://www.example.com/ECommerce"
           xmlns = "http://www.example.com/ECommerce"
           elementFormDefault = "qualified">

    <xs:include  schemaLocation = "http://file_location/Products.xsd" />
    <xs:include  schemaLocation = "http://file_location/TypeLib.xsd" />
```

And this is what the instance document looked like, with just one default namespace to cover all of the elements in the document:

```
<?xml version = "1.0" ?>
<Catalog  xmlns = "http://www.example.com/ECommerce"
    publishDate = "2001-04-18">
    <Products>
        <Product sku = "p2140">
            <ProductName>Widgets</ProductName>
            <Description>Y'know widgetty things</Description>
            <Price currency = "AUS$" units = "perUnit">1.45</Price>
        </Product>
    </Products>
    <Services>
        <Service sid = "s12">
            <ServiceName>Delivery</ServiceName>
            <Description>How you get our wonderful products...</Description>
            <Price currency = "AUS$" units = "perHour">12.00</Price>
        </Service>
    </Services>
</Catalog>
```

When elementFormDefault had been left off the root schema element or given a value of unqualified (as shown in the examples in the folder Ch07_example3_unqualified_include) things got more complicated because we had to qualify each globally declared element or attribute, and only those that were globally declared no matter what schema they were in. For example, in this case we had to qualify the Price elements and the Catalog element only.

```
<?xml version = "1.0" ?>
<ecom:Catalog  xmlns:ecom = "http://www.example.com/ECommerce"
    publishDate = "2001-04-18">
    <Products>
        <Product sku = "p2140">
            <ProductName>Widgets</ProductName>
            <Description>Y'know widgetty things</Description>
            <ecom:Price currency = "AUS$" units = "perUnit">1.45</ecom:Price>
        </Product>
    </Products>
    <Services>
        <Service sid = "s12">
            <ServiceName>Delivery</ServiceName>
            <Description>How you get our wonderful products...</Description>
            <ecom:Price currency = "AUS$" units = "perHour">12.00</ecom:Price>
        </Service>
    </Services>
</ecom:Catalog>
```

In this situation, we do not need to separately qualify the namespaces of the elements imported using the type definitions from the other supporting schemas because all of the schemas are from the same namespace. This certainly makes the instance document easier to use and understand.

Chameleon Design

The third design is the Chameleon Design. This is a particularly interesting design because we only define a namespace for the main schema, while the supporting schemas are written as no namespace schemas. When re-using components from schemas that do not have a namespace, we can use the `include` or `redefine` mechanism. The effect of the chameleon design is that, when we include the no-namespace schemas in the main schema, the declarations and definitions from the supporting schemas become **namespace coerced** into the main schema, so it is just as if they have been defined in the namespace of the main schema.

So in this example, the `Catalog.xsd` schema has a `targetNamespace` of `http://www.example.com/Ecommerce`, while `Product.xsd` and `TypeLib.xsd` do not have a target namespace.

Here is the start of the `Catalog.xsd` schema:

```
<xs:schema xmlns:xs = "http://www.w3.org/2001/XMLSchema"
           targetNamespace = "http://www.example.com/ECommerce"
           xmlns = "http://www.example.com/ECommerce"
           elementFormDefault = "qualified">

    <xs:include schemaLocation = "http://file_location/Products.xsd" />
    <xs:include schemaLocation = "http://file_location/TypeLib.xsd" />
```

While here is the start of the `Product.xsd` and `TypeLib.xsd` schemas:

```
<xs:schema xmlns:xs = "http://www.w3.org/2001/XMLSchema"
           elementFormDefault = "qualified">
```

The effect of this is that we can just put a default namespace in the root element of the schema and it can be used to qualify all of the elements and attributes in the document:

```
<?xml version = "1.0" ?>
<Catalog  xmlns = "http://www.example.com/ECommerce"
    publishDate = "2001-04-18">
    <Products>
        <Product sku = "p2140">
            <ProductName>Widgets</ProductName>
            <Description>Y'know widgetty things</Description>
            <Price currency = "AUS$" units = "perUnit">1.45</Price>
        </Product>
    </Products>
    <Services>
        <Service sid = "s12">
            <ServiceName>Delivery</ServiceName>
            <Description>How you get our wonderful products...</Description>
            <Price currency = "AUS$" units = "perHour">12.00</Price>
        </Service>
    </Services>
</Catalog>
```

If the root `schema` element on these schemas did not carry the `elementFormDefault` attribute with a value of `qualified`, we would have to explicitly qualify just the globally declared elements. So, again we would have to declare the `Catalog` and `Price` elements. This is slightly easier than when they are from different namespaces, but does require that the document author know which elements are globally declared in the supporting schemas as well as the main schema.

```
<?xml version = "1.0" ?>
<ecom:Catalog  xmlns:ecom = "http://www.example.com/ECommerce"
    publishDate = "2001-04-18">
    <Products>
        <Product sku = "p2140">
            <ProductName>Widgets</ProductName>
            <Description>Y'know widgetty things</Description>
            <ecom:Price currency = "AUS$" units = "perUnit">1.45</ecom:Price>
        </Product>
    </Products>
    <Services>
        <Service sid = "s12">
            <ServiceName>Delivery</ServiceName>
            <Description>How you get our wonderful products...</Description>
            <ecom:Price currency = "AUS$" units = "perHour">12.00</ecom:Price>
        </Service>
    </Services>
</ecom:Catalog>
```

As you can imagine, this technique is very helpful when creating parts of schemas that have to be used in schemas from different namespaces.

When using chameleon design, we should avoid using globally declared attributes in the chameleon schema. This is because we will have to qualify the attribute in the instance document. This can pose particular problems if we end up with unqualified elements and qualified attributes. Not only does it make it difficult for authors to follow which attributes have to be qualified (when they are only used to using qualified attributes in special circumstances), but in particular it will cause problems for namespace-aware applications that do not have access to the schema, and therefore cannot interpret which element belongs to which namespace.

Which Approach is Best?

As you can see, the different approaches to how many namespaces you use impact upon the readability of the document, and the amount that authors have to learn in order to use them.

With all schemas, if `elementFormDefault` is not given a value of `qualified`, then document authors have the complexity of having to check which elements and attributes are defined globally, and which are defined locally, so that they know which ones require qualifying. This means that if we borrow constructs from other schemas, the document authors will need to check the design of those schemas to see whether they require qualifying.

When we are using the homogeneous design we can either include components from other schemas (whose target namespace is the same) to use them as declared in the other schema, or we can redefine them if we need to alter any of the components before using them. Having made these components available to our schema, then the setting of `elementFormDefault` is the most complicated problem we face. Once the components have been included into the new schema, then we will be able to use them as if they had been declared in that schema. It adds slight complication for the author of the documents in that they have to check the supporting schemas, so it is a good idea to make sure they are easily available for authors. Alternatively, we can save users of your schema the trouble of checking supporting schemas by documenting use of what references to other schemas contain and what needs to be qualified.

Clearly, if we want to borrow markup constructs that someone else has defined in a different namespace, we will have to put up with the complexities of using different namespaces. When we are using a schema that has been developed by a standards body, we should import schema components following the heterogeneous design. For example, if we are going to incorporate some XHTML markup into our schema so that we can render it in a browser, we should maintain the namespace that the XHTML markup comes from rather than trying to make it part of our namespace. There are two good reasons for doing this:

❑ Firstly, if we want to make use of a processing application that can already work with these components, it will need to know that it can deal with those elements (for example, an XHTML-aware browser would understand `xhtml:table` not `PO:table`).

❑ Secondly, it will align with versioning of the standard, whereas if we were going to include some of the markup in your schema, we would have to make sure that our version reflected those of the standard.

If we are thinking of creating several namespaces for the schemas we are working on, perhaps using one namespace for each department within our organization, then benefits of re-use from schemas in other namespaces will have to be measured against the complexity of authoring documents that are aware of and comply to these namespaces. The requirement for the document authors to qualify the namespaces for the components they want to use does somewhat complicate matters. Of course, there are going to be occasions when this is useful, for example, if we are retrieving data from different departments, and want to qualify where the records of the information are coming from, then the namespace qualification will indicate the owners of the document. We look at the benefits of hiding and exposing namespaces in the next section.

Of course, if we want to be able to create schemas that belong to several namespaces, such as one for each different department being dealt with, then we can make use of chameleon components in our design to help get around the complexities of namespace issues. By defining the components that we want to be available to the different departments in the chameleon schema, different schemas in different namespaces can use the same constructs, but it means that the constructs are coerced into the namespace of the main schema that borrows from them.

The creation of a library of chameleon schemas can effectively speed up the development and deployment of new schemas, as authors can borrow common constructs that would otherwise have to be re-created.

The chameleon design using namespace schemas is particularly good for internal schemas. However, we should carefully consider the implications before adopting it for schemas that will be used industry-wide, or with trading partners. There are two points to consider here:

❑ As soon as we make schema components available to be coerced into other namespaces that we define, they will also be available for other schema authors to do the same. So a competitor could take our schema and create one tailored from the basic constructs we have defined to their needs.

❑ If we want other people to adopt the structure we use, but require that their markup be qualified by a different namespace (perhaps to indicate ownership of the data in the XML), then chameleon schemas may help them use our structure in their namespace.

Because chameleon components are from no namespace, we can also use `redefine` to include the constructs and alter any of the components we need to. When using `redefine` with no-namespace schemas, the components are still coerced into the same namespace as the main schema.

Whichever approach we use, it will make things easier for authors of instance documents if our schemas do not borrow from schemas that contain global declarations, or all of the declarations are global. As soon as we start mixing the two, things will get more complicated. This means that it will be easiest to borrow named model groups and complex types whose components are declared locally.

If our schemas do borrow components from other schemas, we should be careful to document where copies of the schemas can be found. Furthermore, if we borrow from schemas that in turn borrow from other schemas, we should make it clear in the top-level schema so that users are forewarned about the nested use and potential complexities.

When We Should Hide or Expose Namespaces

Depending on the purpose of our instance documents, there are benefits to either hiding or exposing your namespaces in instance documents. By default, in an instance document we have to qualify names of every schema component that has been defined globally within an XML Schema, but we should not qualify those that are defined locally.

In Chapter 5, we looked at three different models for creating schemas:

❑   Russian Doll – in which elements are declared as they appear in the schema

❑   Salami Slice – which most closely resembled the model used in DTDs where all elements are declared before they could be used in a content model

❑   Venetian Blind – which allows us to reuse named schema components, where some elements are locally declared

Our choice of which approach to use had significant effect upon how we used namespaces in instance documents. Both Russian Doll and Venetian Blind techniques require knowledge about which schema components have been declared globally, and therefore which have to be qualified by a namespace in instance documents. In the Russian Doll design, all components have to be qualified by a namespace, since they were all defined globally (although this often meant qualifying attributes as well as elements). This means we could use default namespaces in the instance documents (whereas we cannot with the other two approaches).

While Russian Doll design may be particularly helpful for those working with XSLT and W3C XML Schema, or those wanting to construct their schemas using a similar structure to that of DTDs, there are significant re-use advantages with the different ways in which we could use the Venetian Blind model. In order to get around the complexities of the Russian Doll and Venetian Blind techniques (knowing which components had been globally declared), we could use the elementFormDefault attribute on the root schema element as a global switch for whether names should be qualified in instance documents (and therefore allowed the use of default namespaces).

So, let's look at some of the reasons as to why we might want to qualify our namespaces in instance documents.

There are some clear advantages in hiding namespaces in our instance documents, such as:

❑   When people are going to be reading marked up instance documents with the markup visible. By exposing namespaces it adds complexity to our documents and makes them more difficult to read. This is especially useful if those users are not familiar with XML.

❑   When we might need to be able to make changes to the schema without impacting upon the instance documents; because even if the source of the schemas changes in the future, the namespaces are hidden from the instance document.

❑   The document does not need to know where the components have come from, therefore making it easier to write processing applications.

❑   When we do not want users to know which schema our markup has come from.

There are also good reasons and situations when we might want to expose namespaces, such as when:

❑   There is ambiguous content, and there may be two elements of the same name (consumer's name versus the producer's name).

❑   An application is not namespace aware, or does not have access to the original schemas, in which case namespace defaulting need not affect the names of elements (and as long as we do not use globally declared attributes will not affect the names of attributes either).

❑   An application has to be able to deal with many different sorts of document, using namespaces to help indicate the type of document.

❑   Ownership of the information is important, we can use the namespace of the document or certain elements to indicating the owner of information contained within the element. This can be for a number of reasons such as:

   ❑   copyright purposes or when we syndicate content

   ❑   when working with data from multiple sources, to indicate which source data has come from

More often than not, we tend to require use of namespaces for all elements (through the use of `elementFormDefault` in the schema). We find that this is because it makes it easier to author instance documents because all elements need to be qualified and you can make use of default namespaces. Furthermore, it is easy to strip the namespaces from the instance documents if this is required, whereas it is much harder to get the appropriate information to put them in once they have been written.

This leads us to an interesting question regarding the schema, which remember is an XML document itself.

Should Our Default Namespace be the targetNamespace or XML Schema Namespace

Throughout the book we have seen plenty of examples where we have declared default namespaces in our schema documents. We can declare a default namespace in any element within an XML document and it will apply to all of its children (unless explicitly qualified otherwise), although mainly we have been doing this in the root `schema` element. This started off from the requirement to be able to create named schema components without a processor interpreting our named components as part of the XML Schema namespace, and therefore not being able to find them.

There are different options of which namespace to use as the default namespace for the schema:

❑   Use the `targetNamespace` as the default namespace for the schema document

❑   Use the W3C XML Schema namespace as the default namespace for the schema document (unless you are designing a schema with no `targetNamespace`)

❑   Use no default namespace declaration at all, which means we would have to qualify everything

Up to now, we have not paid too much attention to which default namespace, if any, we should use. So, let's look at this problem using a simple example schema.

We'll start by making the XML Schema namespace the default namespace. We come to the included schema (which just contains the AddressType complex type) shortly.

```
<?xml version = "1.0" ?>
<schema xmlns = "http://www.w3.org/2001/XMLSchema"
        targetNamespace = "http://www.example.com/Customer"
        xmlns:cust = "http://www.example.com/Customer"
        elementFormDefault = "qualified">

    <include schemaLocation = "Address.xsd" />

    <element name = "Customer">
        <complexType>
            <sequence>
                <element name = "Name" type = "cust:NameType" />
                <element name = "Address" type = "cust:AddressType" />
            </sequence>
        </complexType>
    </element>

    <complexType name = "NameType">
        <sequence>
            <element name = "FirstName" type = "string" />
            <element name = "MiddleInitial" type = "string"
                minOccurs = "1" maxOccurs = "unbounded" />
            <element name = "LastName" type = "string" />
        </sequence>
    </complexType>

</schema>
```

The default namespace is the namespace for XML Schema. This certainly makes our schemas more readable from the point of view of seeing the XML Schema markup.

Because we are using a type we have defined in this schema, the NameType, we have to declare a namespace that is the same namespace as the target namespace and associate it with a prefix, in this case we have associated the prefix cust: with the namespace http://www.example.com/Customer. This is because we cannot refer to the type without qualifying that it is not in the same namespace as the XML Schema namespace. Because the namespace that we have declared is the same as that of the target namespace, the processor will know when it comes across a type prefixed with cust:, it is one defined in the current schema document.

Using this approach we have to remember to qualify types and references to constructs that we have defined ourselves, in this schema with the cust: prefix, as they are not from the XML Schema namespace.

We have also included the AddressType from the Address.xsd schema. We have prefixed this with cust: too, because Address.xsd is a chameleon schema and will become coerced into the namespace of the including schema:

```
<include schemaLocation = "Address.xsd" />
```

Because `Address.xsd` is a no-namespace schema, we have to do the opposite from the previous example, and qualify elements and simple types from the XML Schema namespace, this has been the most common approach used in the book so far. The result looks like this:

```
<?xml version = "1.0" ?>
<xs:schema xmlns:xs = "http://www.w3.org/2001/XMLSchema"
           elementFormDefault = "qualified">

   <xs:complexType name = "AddressType">
      <xs:sequence>
         <xs:element name = "Street" type = "xs:string" />
         <xs:element name = "Town" type = "xs:string" />
         <xs:element name = "City" type = "xs:string"
            minOccurs = "0" maxOccurs = "1" />
         <xs:element name = "StateRegionCounty" type = "xs:string" />
         <xs:element name = "ZipPostalCode" type = "xs:string" />
         <xs:element name = "Country" type = "xs:string" />
      </xs:sequence>
   </xs:complexType>

</xs:schema>
```

Because of the absence of a `targetNamespace` attribute, the components defined in this schema (in this case a named complex type) do not belong to a namespace.

You might say that this is somewhat harder to read than the previous example, but you soon get used to seeing the prefix on the schema components.

At the point at which the `Address.xsd` schema is included, the `AddressType` is coerced into the target namespace of the including schema. In this case `AddressType` automatically becomes part of the `http://www.example.com/Customer` namespace – hence we prefix the `AddressType` with `cust:` in the `Customer.xsd` schema:

```
<element name = "Address" type = "cust:AddressType" />
```

It is important to note that we must remember to qualify the namespace of included chameleon types and elements if our including schema is qualifying its own components.

The mixing of when schemas use one namespace as the default and when they use another can become confusing, and it is better to adopt one standard and stick with it. If you are going to use chameleon schemas, then you will be using the approach where you qualify markup from the XML Schema namespace.

Of course, if we wanted to, we could qualify the entire markup, regardless of which namespace we use. If we had done this is the previous example, we would have ended up with something that looked like this:

```
<?xml version = "1.0" ?>
<xs:schema xmlns:xs = "http://www.w3.org/2001/XMLSchema"
           targetNamespace = "http://www.example.com/Customer"
           xmlns:cust = "http://www.example.com/Customer"
           elementFormDefault = "qualified">
```

```
      <xs:include schemaLocation = "Address.xsd" />

      <xs:element name = "Customer">
        <xs:complexType>
          <xs:sequence>
            <xs:element name = "Name" type = "cust:NameType" />
            <xs:element name = "Address" type = "cust:AddressType" />
          </xs:sequence>
        </xs:complexType>
      </xs:element>

      <xs:complexType name = "NameType">
        <xs:sequence>
          <xs:element name = "FirstName" type = "xs:string" />
          <xs:element name = "MiddleInitial" type = "xs:string"
             minOccurs = "1" maxOccurs = "unbounded" />
          <xs:element name = "LastName" type = "xs:string" />
        </xs:sequence>
      </xs:complexType>

  </xs:schema>
```

This can be a good idea when working with multiple schemas, as we know that every element and type has to be qualified, leaving less room for error.

The real danger is the effect of unqualified elements and qualified attributes, in particular for other namespace-aware applications that don't have access to a schema to enable them to interpret which element is in which namespace.

Name Collisions

When we are creating schemas from multiple documents, if we do not preserve their original namespaces we run a risk of name collisions, where two schemas may use the same element or attribute names.

The risks of name collisions are especially high when working with chameleon component schemas. One suggestion that has come from the XML community for solving situations where we are going to have to deal with namespace collisions is the notion of creating **proxy schemas**. This technique involves including the no-namespace schema in a namespaced proxy schema and then importing the proxy schema into the schema where the collision is likely to occur. This will be less of a problem when we are dealing with schemas that we have created as we can avoid namespace collisions in the first place by careful naming of elements. When we are dealing with schemas created by others, however, such as when two departments have used the same name to mean different things, this can be a helpful technique.

Let's look at an example that shows conflicts of the element Component. In the first example, it is referring to object-oriented software development and a component of software. In the second, it refers to an electronic component:

```
<Component>
   <ComponentName>SimpleShoppingCart</ComponentName>
   <ComponentType>C++ COM+ component</ComponentType>
   <ComponentMethods>
```

```
        <ComponentMethod>AddItem</ComponentMethod>
        <ComponentMethod>RemoveItem</ComponentMethod>
        <ComponentMethod>CheckOut</ComponentMethod>
    </ComponentMethods>
    <ComponentAuthor>Bob Winters</ComponentAuthor>
</Component>
```

```
<Component>
    <Type>5kHz Resistor</Type>
    <Description></Description>
    <Make>Maplin</Make>
</Component>
```

Here is the proxy for the software component, `SoftwareComponent.xsd`. It is called `SoftwareComponentProxy.xsd`:

```
<xs:schema xmlns:xsd = "http://www.w3.org/2001/XMLSchema"
           targetNamespace = "http://www.example.com/software_proxy">
    <xs:include schemaLocation = "SoftwareComponent.xsd" />
</xs:schema>
```

Here is the proxy for the electronics component, `ElectronicsComponent.xsd`. It is called `ElectronicsComponentProxy.xsd`:

```
<xs:schema xmlns:xsd = "http://www.w3.org/2001/XmlSchema"
           targetNamespace = "http://www.example.com/electronics_proxy">
    <xs:include schemaLocation = "ElectronicsComponent.xsd" />
</xs:schema>
```

Now we can make use of both of these components, and require that they are namespace qualified to distinguish the two by importing them into the schema and by setting `elementFormDefault` to qualified:

```
<xs:schema xmlns:xsd = "http://www.w3.org/2001/XMLSchema"
    targetNamespace = "http://www.example.com/new_schema_using_proxies"
    xmlns:sp = "http://www.example.com/software_proxy"
    xmlns:ep = "http://www.example.com/electronics_proxy"
    elementFormDefault = "qualified">

    <xs:import namespace = "http://www.example.com/software_proxy"
        schemaLocation = "SoftwareComponentProxy.xsd" />
    <xs:import namespace = "http://www.example.com/electronics_proxy"
        schemaLocation = "ElectronicsComponentProxy.xsd" />

...<!--  rest of schema goes here ... -->

</xs:schema>
```

A resulting document instance would then qualify the use of each of these as follows where the namespace is provided as a default for that element:

```
<Component xmlns = "http://www.example.com/software_proxy">
    <ComponentName>SimpleShoppingCart</ComponentName>
    <ComponentType>C++ COM+ component</ComponentType>
    <ComponentMethods>
        <ComponentMethod>AddItem</ComponentMethod>
        <ComponentMethod>RemoveItem</ComponentMethod>
        <ComponentMethod>CheckOut</ComponentMethod>
    </ComponentMethods>
    <ComponentAuthor>Bob Winters</ComponentAuthor>
</Component>
```

Or as follows, using namespace prefixing:

```
<ep:Component xmlns:ep = "http://www.example.com/electronics_proxy">
    <ep:Type>5kHz Resistor</ep:Type>
    <ep:Description></ep:Description>
    <ep:Make>Maplin</ep:Make>
</ep:Component>
```

This approach is better than relying on context to determine use, because we cannot always rely on the context of an element to describe the meaning of an element and how it is processed. It also means that we can still `redefine` definitions and declarations, if we want to, before putting them in the proxy schema.

There are distinct advantages to allowing applications to create or at least choose whether to use these proxy schemas when we are going to be dealing with documents from different namespaces. If a potential collision is detected, it could decide to make use of a proxy schema by matching element declarations.

An alternative approach to resolving name collisions would be to add an ID attribute, with a value that is a Globally Unique Identifier (GUID), to the declaration that is ambiguous or could be misconstrued so that the application could know the intended meaning. Indeed, we could even combine the two approaches so that an application knew where to find the original chameleon component regardless of whether it is part of a proxy schema.

Altering Schema Constructs

We have seen how we can make use of schema constructs defined and declared in other schemas, and indeed some of the problems that relate to the namespaces to which they belong. So, what happens if we want to make use of a construct from another schema, but it is not quite how we want it?

Perhaps there is a schema that nearly suits a task that you are about to face, but it has a few elements that you do not require. Or perhaps there is not quite enough detail for your purpose? How can you go about bending, or altering, the constructs that someone else has come up with to suit your purpose?

Methods of Altering Markup that We Import and Include

There are three different ways in which we can alter markup once we have imported it:

- ❑ **Deriving** a new content model: The new content model is derived from a base type; it is a member type of the base type's class. Derivation allows us to either extend or restrict content.

- ❑ **Redefining** the content model: Which allows us to extend or restrict a type as we pull it in from another schema within the same target namespace, and uses that definition wherever it is used (even within the schema it was originally in).

- ❑ **Substitution Groups**: Where we make a new element part of a substitution group so that we can replace the given element with another element that is derived from the same type.

Note that we can also define new content models using globally defined elements, attributes, named model groups and attribute groups, but this is not strictly changing those constructs. Rather it is using them like building blocks to define our own new schema components.

> **When we want to change the name of elements or attributes (rather than add or remove them to or from a content model), we have to reconstruct them ourselves because there is nothing that we can do to remove and replace a name in one step.**

Deriving New Types and Element Content Models

You can derive a new type or content model using `extension` and `restriction` elements that we have met in previous chapters. Let's briefly re-cap what these allow us to do:

Extension

Using extension you can create a new type, derived from an existing type (known as the base type), by adding elements or attributes to the content model of the existing type.

In this example, we have a schema called `TypeLib.xsd` containing two complex types, one called `NameType`, the other `AddressType`. We will include the complex types from this schema, in a new schema called `Customer.xsd`. `Customer.xsd` will then use the `AddressType` as it is, but will extend the `NameType` to create a `LongNameType` with an extra element and attribute. The files for this example are in the folder `Ch07_example11_extension`.

Here is `TypeLib.xsd`:

```xml
<?xml version = "1.0" ?>
<xs:schema xmlns:xs = "http://www.w3.org/2001/XMLSchema"
           elementFormDefault = "qualified">

   <xs:complexType name = "NameType">
      <xs:sequence>
         <xs:element name = "FirstName" type = "xs:string" />
         <xs:element name = "MiddleInitial" type = "xs:string"
            minOccurs = "0" maxOccurs = "1" />
         <xs:element name = "LastName" type = "xs:string" />
```

```
            </xs:sequence>
        </xs:complexType>

    <xs:complexType name = "AddressType">
        <xs:sequence>
            <xs:element name = "Street" type = "xs:string" />
            <xs:element name = "Town" type = "xs:string" />
            <xs:element name = "City" type = "xs:string"
                minOccurs = "0" maxOccurs = "1" />
            <xs:element name = "StateRegionCounty" type = "xs:string" />
            <xs:element name = "ZipPostalCode" type = "xs:string" />
            <xs:element name = "Country" type = "xs:string" />
        </xs:sequence>
    </xs:complexType>

</xs:schema>
```

We will be including the two types from this schema into our `Customer.xsd` schema. `Customer.xsd` uses the two complex types in the children of the `Customer` element. However, we want to add a `Suffix` element to the end of the elements used in the `NameType`, and add an attribute for a nickname to the root element of the type. So, we extend the type that we have imported and create a new type called `LongNameType`, which is derived from the imported `NameType`:

```
<?xml version = "1.0" ?>
<xs:schema xmlns:xs = "http://www.w3.org/2001/XMLSchema"
            targetNamespace = "http://www.example.com/Customer"
            xmlns = "http://www.example.com/Customer"
            elementFormDefault = "qualified">

    <xs:include schemaLocation = "http://file_location/TypeLib.xsd" />

    <xs:element name = "Customer">
        <xs:complexType>
            <xs:sequence>
                <xs:element name = "Name" type = "LongNameType" />
                <xs:element name = "Address" type = "AddressType" />
            </xs:sequence>
        </xs:complexType>
    </xs:element>

    <xs:complexType name = "LongNameType">
        <xs:complexContent>
            <xs:extension base = "NameType">
                <xs:sequence>
                    <xs:element name = "Suffix" type = "xs:string" />
                </xs:sequence>
                <xs:attribute name = "nickName" type = "xs:string" />
            </xs:extension>
        </xs:complexContent>
    </xs:complexType>

</xs:schema>
```

Here, you can see that we have extended the included NameType and created the LongNameType, which is used associated with the Name element. The AddressType element is also used in the Address element remains as it appeared in TypeLib.xsd.

Here is a document instance that uses the new LongNameType and the original AddressType in the Name and Address elements:

```
<Customer xmlns = "http://www.example.com/Customer">
    <Name nickName = "Bobby">
        <FirstName>Robert</FirstName>
        <MiddleInitial>Winters</MiddleInitial>
        <LastName>Winters</LastName>
        <Suffix>III</Suffix>
    </Name>
    <Address>
        <Street>40 Leighton Road</Street>
        <Town>Paddington</Town>
        <City>Sydney</City>
        <StateRegionCounty>New South Wales</StateRegionCounty>
        <ZipPostalCode>2021</ZipPostalCode>
        <Country>Australia</Country>
    </Address>
</Customer>
```

Here are some points to remember about extending types:

❑   We can only add elements to the end of the type. So, we could not have added a Title element before the FirstName element.

❑   We can only extend a type when the base type definition does not have a final attribute with a value of extension or all.

❑   We cannot add a second attribute whose type is or is derived from ID to the same element or type, if one already exists.

Restriction

When we restrict a type, we create a new type by further restricting the allowable components inherited from the base type. You can use restriction you create a new type that removes elements or attributes from the base a complex type, or to further restrict the facets of a simple type.

In this example we will use the same TypeLib.xsd schema that we met in the last example of extension. It contains a definition of the AddressType and the NameType. However, in the schema that includes the TypeLib.xsd types, we will create a new type derived from NameType that restricts the content model to only containing the FirstName and LastName elements, we will not include the option of containing a MiddleInitial element. The files for this example are in the Ch07_example12_restriction folder.

Here is the Customer.xsd schema that restricts the NameType from TypeLib.xsd:

```
<?xml version = "1.0" ?>
<xs:schema xmlns:xs = "http://www.w3.org/2001/XMLSchema"
            targetNamespace = "http://www.example.com/Customer"
            xmlns = "http://www.example.com/Customer"
```

```
                    elementFormDefault = "qualified">

    <xs:include schemaLocation = "http://file_location/TypeLib.xsd" />

    <xs:element name = "Customer">
       <xs:complexType>
          <xs:sequence>
             <xs:element name = "Name" type = "ShortNameType" />
             <xs:element name = "Address" type = "AddressType" />
          </xs:sequence>
       </xs:complexType>
    </xs:element>

    <xs:complexType name = "ShortNameType">
       <xs:complexContent>
          <xs:restriction base = "NameType">
             <xs:sequence>
                <xs:element name = "FirstName" type = "xs:string" />
                <xs:element name = "MiddleInitial" type = "xs:string"
                   minOccurs = "0" maxOccurs = "1" />
                <xs:element name = "LastName" type = "xs:string" />
             </xs:sequence>
          </xs:restriction>
       </xs:complexContent>
    </xs:complexType>

</xs:schema>
```

When we restrict a complex type, we create a content model that is a subset of the base type's content model. It is a member type of the base type.

Inside the `restriction` element, we simply have to repeat all of the components of the base type that are allowed to be included in the restricted type.

redefine

Redefine only works with schemas that have no namespace or are from the same target namespace as the document we are using. It replicates and adds to the functionality offered by `include`. Using `redefine` we can redefine any of the components that we include, either by extension or restriction *before* they become part of the schema, and the new definitions will apply wherever the original component occurred as well as wherever it is used in the new schema.

In this example, we are going to change `TypeLib.xsd` so that it contains a definition of a `CustomerType`. We are doing this because we will redefine the `NameType` to illustrate how the `redefine` also changes the use of the `NameType` where it is used within this schema. The files for this example are in the folder `Ch07_example13_redefine`.

Here is the new `TypeLib.xsd` file, with the definition of the `CustomerType`:

```
<?xml version = "1.0" ?>
<xs:schema xmlns:xs = "http://www.w3.org/2001/XMLSchema"
          elementFormDefault = "qualified">
```

```
<xs:complexType name = "CustomerType">
   <xs:sequence>
      <xs:element name = "Name" type = "NameType" />
      <xs:element name = "Address" type = "AddressType" />
   </xs:sequence>
</xs:complexType>

<xs:complexType name = "NameType">
   <xs:sequence>
      <xs:element name = "FirstName" type = "xs:string" />
      <xs:element name = "MiddleInitial" type = "xs:string"
         minOccurs = "0" maxOccurs = "1" />
      <xs:element name = "LastName" type = "xs:string" />
   </xs:sequence>
</xs:complexType>

<xs:complexType name = "AddressType">
   <xs:sequence>
      <xs:element name = "Street" type = "xs:string" />
      <xs:element name = "Town" type = "xs:string" />
      <xs:element name = "City" type = "xs:string"
         minOccurs = "0" maxOccurs = "1" />
      <xs:element name = "StateRegionCounty" type = "xs:string" />
      <xs:element name = "ZipPostalCode" type = "xs:string" />
      <xs:element name = "Country" type = "xs:string" />
   </xs:sequence>
</xs:complexType>

</xs:schema>
```

Next let's look at the Customer.xsd schema, which uses the definitions from TypeLib.xsd, but also changes the use of the NameType wherever it occurs in either schema. We have done this by restricting the allowable contents of the NameType within the redefine element. The restriction is the same as the one that we created in the last example, but this time it will have an effect on the schema that is implicitly included when we use redefine.

We use the CustomerType in the Customer elements that are part of the new CustomerList element. You can see that the rest of the schema is included when we perform the redefine because we are still using other types than the NameType.

```
<?xml version = "1.0" ?>
<xs:schema xmlns:xs = "http://www.w3.org/2001/XMLSchema"
           targetNamespace = "http://www.example.com/Customer"
           xmlns = "http://www.example.com/Customer"
           elementFormDefault = "qualified">

   <xs:redefine schemaLocation = "http://file_location/TypeLib.xsd">
   <xs:complexType name = "NameType">
      <xs:complexContent>
         <xs:restriction base = "NameType">
            <xs:sequence>
               <xs:element name = "FirstName" type = "xs:string" />
               <xs:element name = "LastName" type = "xs:string" />
            </xs:sequence>
```

```
            </xs:restriction>
          </xs:complexContent>
      </xs:complexType>
  </xs:redefine>

    <xs:element name = "CustomerList">
       <xs:complexType>
          <xs:sequence>
             <xs:element name = "Customer" type = "CustomerType"
                minOccurs = "0" maxOccurs = "unbounded" />
          </xs:sequence>
       </xs:complexType>
    </xs:element>

</xs:schema>
```

In the conforming document instance we cannot use the `MiddleInitial` element that was defined in the `NameType`, because we have redefined it. Here is a sample XML document that conforms to this schema:

```
<CustomerList  xmlns = "http://www.example.com/Customer">
    <Customer>
       <Name>
          <FirstName>Robert</FirstName>
          <LastName>Winters</LastName>
       </Name>
       <Address>
          <Street>40 Leighton Road</Street>
          <Town>Paddington</Town>
          <City>Sydney</City>
          <StateRegionCounty>New South Wales</StateRegionCounty>
          <ZipPostalCode>2021</ZipPostalCode>
          <Country>Australia</Country>
       </Address>
    </Customer>
</CustomerList>
```

Whereas the following would not, because we have the middle initial element inside the `Name` element, which was no longer allowed when we redefined the schema whose types we were including.

```
<CustomerList>
    <Customer>
       <Name>
          <FirstName>Mark</FirstName>
          <MiddleInitial>J</MiddleInitial>
          <LastName>Walters</LastName>
       </Name>
       <Address>
          <Street>10 Elizabeth Road</Street>
          <Town>Newtown</Town>
          <City>Sydney</City>
          <StateRegionCounty>New South Wales</StateRegionCounty>
          <ZipPostalCode>4021</ZipPostalCode>
          <Country>Australia</Country>
       </Address>
    </Customer>
</CustomerList>
```

The way that `redefine` allows us to extend or restrict types before we include their components in our schema, and have those changes reflected in the included schema, is a powerful tool. The usual rules over extending and restricting these types apply, but have the added advantage that they are changed in the source as well.

Substitution Groups

If you remember from Chapter 4, using a substitution group allows a globally declared element to be replaced by another element or selection of elements without altering the markup for the element we want to replace. This is especially helpful when working with other people's schemas, because we can take an element that they have declared and allow our own extensions to replace their element or type. We simply declare another global element (or set of elements) to be part of the substitution group using a `substitutionGroup` attribute whose value is the name of the globally declared element that it can replace. The two caveats to using a substitution group are that:

❑ The elements must be declared globally (which can be restrictive)

❑ They must be either of the same type or derived from the same type

In this example, we have another new `TypeLib.xsd` schema; this time it contains a `PersonType` (rather than a `CustomerType` as in the last example), which builds a content model that uses the `NameType` and `AddressType` also used in that schema.

We also declare an element called `Customer` whose type is `PersonType`. When this schema is included into another schema, we will allow a number of other elements to be substituted for the Customer element, both of which have the same type. The files for this example are in the folder `example14_substitutionGroup`.

Here is the new `TypeLib.xsd` file:

```xml
<?xml version = "1.0" ?>
<xs:schema xmlns:xs = "http://www.w3.org/2001/XMLSchema"
           elementFormDefault = "qualified">

    <xs:element name = "Customer" type = "PersonType" />

    <xs:complexType name = "PersonType">
       <xs:sequence>
          <xs:element name = "Name" type = "NameType" />
          <xs:element name = "Address" type = "AddressType" />
       </xs:sequence>
    </xs:complexType>

    <xs:complexType name = "NameType">
       <xs:sequence>
          <xs:element name = "FirstName" type = "xs:string" />
          <xs:element name = "MiddleInitial" type = "xs:string"
             minOccurs = "0" maxOccurs = "1" />
          <xs:element name = "LastName" type = "xs:string" />
       </xs:sequence>
    </xs:complexType>

    <xs:complexType name = "AddressType">
       <xs:sequence>
```

```
                <xs:element name = "Street" type = "xs:string" />
                <xs:element name = "Town" type = "xs:string" />
                <xs:element name = "City" type = "xs:string"
                   minOccurs = "0" maxOccurs = "1" />
                <xs:element name = "StateRegionCounty" type = "xs:string" />
                <xs:element name = "ZipPostalCode" type = "xs:string" />
                <xs:element name = "Country" type = "xs:string" />
            </xs:sequence>
        </xs:complexType>

    </xs:schema>
```

Next we come to the new schema called `Contacts.xsd`, which uses the `PersonType` and `Customer` element from the `TypeLib.xsd` schema. In this schema, we create a substitution group whereby we can use the `Employee` or `Supplier` element wherever `Customer` appears, because they declared to be part of the same substitution group where `Customer` is the head element, and are of the same type as `Customer`.

Here is the `Contacts.xsd` schema where we have used the `Customer` element inside a new `Contact` element, which forms part of a contact list.

```
<?xml version = "1.0" ?>
<xs:schema xmlns:xs = "http://www.w3.org/2001/XMLSchema"
           targetNamespace = "http://www.example.com/Customer"
           xmlns = "http://www.example.com/Customer"
           elementFormDefault = "qualified">

    <xs:include schemaLocation = "http://file_location/TypeLib.xsd" />

    <xs:element name = "ContactsList">
        <xs:complexType>
            <xs:sequence>
                <xs:element name = "Contact" minOccurs = "0"
                    maxOccurs = "unbounded">
                    <xs:complexType>
                        <xs:sequence>
                            <xs:element ref = "Customer" minOccurs = "0"
                                maxOccurs = "1" />
                        </xs:sequence>
                    </xs:complexType>
                </xs:element>
            </xs:sequence>
        </xs:complexType>
    </xs:element>

    <xs:element name = "Employee" substitutionGroup = "Customer"
        type = "PersonType" />
    <xs:element name = "Supplier" substitutionGroup = "Customer"
        type = "PersonType" />

</xs:schema>
```

The `Employee` and `Supplier` types do not have to have identical types to the `Customer` element's type, although if they differ they do have to be derived from that type. However, if our types stray too far from the original, we will somewhat lose the predictability of our document structures, and make them harder to learn. After all, when a type deviates from its base type enough, we may as well create a completely new type.

Here is an example XML document that uses both the `Customer` element, and a member of its substitution group:

```
<ContactsList xmlns = "http://www.example.com/Customer">
    <Contact>
        <Employee>
            <Name>
                <FirstName>Robert</FirstName>
                <LastName>Winters</LastName>
            </Name>
            <Address>
                <Street>40 Leighton Road</Street>
                <Town>Paddington</Town>
                <City>Sydney</City>
                <StateRegionCounty>New South Wales</StateRegionCounty>
                <ZipPostalCode>2021</ZipPostalCode>
                <Country>Australia</Country>
            </Address>
        </Employee>
    </Contact>
    <Contact>
        <Customer>
            <Name>
                <FirstName>Robert</FirstName>
                <LastName>Winters</LastName>
            </Name>
            <Address>
                <Street>40 Leighton Road</Street>
                <Town>Paddington</Town>
                <City>Sydney</City>
                <StateRegionCounty>New South Wales</StateRegionCounty>
                <ZipPostalCode>2021</ZipPostalCode>
                <Country>Australia</Country>
            </Address>
        </Customer>
    </Contact>
</ContactsList>
```

Forcing Substitution with Abstract Elements and Types

As we saw in Chapter 4, it is possible to force substitution of an element or type by declaring the element or type to be `abstract`. When the element is declared abstract, it cannot appear in the instance document itself, but a member of the element's substitution group is forced to appear in the instance document where the abstract element was. When a type is declared as being abstract, all instances of the element must use `xsi:type` to indicate a derived type that is not abstract.

This is not as useful when working with imported schemas because we cannot add the `abstract` attribute onto someone else's declaration. However, it is useful in our own schemas to enforce substitution for one of the elements we have declared as part of a substitution group. Here either the `Replacement1` or `Replacement2` elements must substitute the `Original` element.

```
<xs:element name = "Original" abstract = "true"/>
<xs:element name = "Replacement1" substitutionGroup = "Original" />
<xs:element name = "Replacement2" substitutionGroup = "Original" />
```

Or for a type, things get more complicated.

```
<xs:schema xmlns:xs = "http://www.w3.org/2001/XMLSchema"
           targetNamespace = "http://www.example.com/albums">

   <xs:element name = "Album" type = "AlbumType" />
   <xs:complexType name = "AlbumType" abstract = "true" />

   <xs:complexType name = "CD">
      <xs:complexContent>
         <xs:extension base = "AlbumType" />
      </xs:complexContent>
   </xs:complexType>

   <xs:complexType name = "Vinyl">
      <xs:complexContent>
         <xs:extension base = "Album" />
      </xs:complexContent>
   </xs:complexType>

</xs:schema>
```

Here you can see that we have an empty `complexType` definition with just a `name` attribute and that we have made it `abstract` to force a type to be substituted.

There is nothing to prevent the `Album` element appearing in the instance document, but because we require that its type is a derived type, we need to use an `xsi:type` attribute in the document element with the value being the derived type we are using:

```
<Album xmlns = "http://www.example.com/albums"
       xmlns:xsi = "http://www.w3.org/2001/XMLSchema-instance"
       xsi:type = "CD" />
```

Allowing for Extension of Our Model

There are times when we or other users might want to be able to extend content models that we have defined in our schema. It is important to consider this when designing our schemas. We could allow users to `redefine` the element but this only works if the schema is in the same target namespace, or if our schema had no namespace. So, how can we extend an existing content model or allow for it:

❑   Substitution groups – which we have just seen, but we shall revisit for purposes of extending a content model

❑   Any – adding a wildcard that allows for extension in a given place within the content model

Let's start by revisiting the substitution group solution.

Substitution Groups

We have just looked at how we can use substitution groups to alter content, but what do they mean in terms of creating an extensible model?

If an element has been defined globally in a schema and has a named type, we can then import or include that schema into our own. Having done so, we can extend or restrict the type that element has, to create a new content model. Finally we can indicate that other elements can be used to substitute for the globally declared element, and they can use this newly derived content model, hence allowing us to change the content model for the DTD that is outside our control.

We can see an example of this by extending the example we just saw with substitution groups. In that example we were using elements of the same type. Here we are also defining a new content model for the Supplier element as well. You can find the files for this example in the example16_extension_with_substitutionGroup folder.

This Contacts.xsd schema not only allows us to use an Employee or Supplier element instead of the Customer element, it also allows us to add an extra element onto the content model for the Supplier element, because we have derived a new type called PersonAndCompanyType from the PersonType.

```
<?xml version = "1.0" ?>
<xs:schema xmlns:xs = "http://www.w3.org/2001/XMLSchema"
          targetNamespace = "http://www.example.com/Customer"
          xmlns = "http://www.example.com/Customer"
          elementFormDefault = "qualified">

   <xs:include schemaLocation = "http://file_location/TypeLib.xsd" />

   <xs:element name = "ContactsList">
      <xs:complexType>
         <xs:sequence>
            <xs:element name = "Contact" minOccurs = "0"
               maxOccurs = "unbounded">
               <xs:complexType>
                  <xs:sequence>
                     <xs:element ref = "Customer" minOccurs = "0"
                        maxOccurs = "1" />
                  </xs:sequence>
               </xs:complexType>
            </xs:element>
         </xs:sequence>
      </xs:complexType>
   </xs:element>

   <xs:element name = "Employee" substitutionGroup = "Customer"
      type = "PersonType" />
   <xs:element name = "Supplier" substitutionGroup = "Customer"
      type = "PersonAndCompanyType" />

   <xs:complexType name = "PersonAndCompanyType">
      <xs:complexContent>
         <xs:extension base = "PersonType">
            <xs:sequence>
               <xs:element name = "CompanyName"/>
            </xs:sequence>
         </xs:extension>
      </xs:complexContent>
   </xs:complexType>

</xs:schema>
```

Here is a sample XML document that uses the `Supplier` element that has the new `PersonAndCompany` type:

```
<ContactsList>
    <Contact>
        <Supplier>
            <Name>
                <FirstName>Robert</FirstName>
                <LastName>Winters</LastName>
            </Name>
            <Address>
                <Street>40 Leighton Road</Street>
                <Town>Paddington</Town>
                <City>Sydney</City>
                <StateRegionCounty>New South Wales</StateRegionCounty>
                <ZipPostalCode>2021</ZipPostalCode>
                <Country>Australia</Country>
            </Address>
            <CompanyName>The Example Organization</CompanyName>
        </Supplier>
    </Contact>
</ContactsList>
```

This demonstrates how we can modify a schema without changing the original schema and enables us to make changes to schemas that are outside of our control.

There are a couple of disadvantages to this approach that we should note:

❑ We can only append elements onto the end of the existing content model – it is not possible to add elements before the content model.

❑ It is unpredictable; someone else could extend our content models without us knowing by using the type substitution mechanism. So, if we write an application that is designed to process such documents, it must be able to deal with situations where it can have more than the given markup. We will see methods of controlling extension of markup shortly.

The alternative is to provide a given place for extension with the `any` element.

Using Unknown Content

There are reasons why we might want to allow a wildcard into our schema. For example, if we know that our model is likely to be extended, then there are advantages to making it possible for users to add elements or attributes in a defined place. By limiting where we allow users to do this, or at least providing them with a defined place in which to do it, it also helps us in our application construction because the application can be told to avoid information in this section if it does not understand it.

When we allow an `any` or `anyAttribute` wildcard in our schema, we can control the namespace from which the elements and/or attributes come from, and how the processor should treat these elements.

For example, if we only wanted them to be able to extend our schema with elements and attributes we had defined, we could only allow them to use markup defined in the schema containing the wildcard. If we wanted to allow them to use any XHTML markup, we could include a namespace for XHTML.

The `namespace` attribute can take the following values to control the namespace from which our markup can come:

❑   `##targetNamespace` to indicate that it should only accept markup from the target namespace for this schema

❑   `##other` to indicate that it should accept markup from any namespace other than the target that the schema uses

❑   A whitespace-separated list of URIs if we want to specify more than one namespace

❑   `##any` to indicate that it can take markup from any namespace

❑   `##local` to indicate that it can use any non-qualified elements

To control how the processor treats these elements and attributes you can use the `processContents` attribute; it can take the following values:

❑   `strict` – which tells the processing application that it should validate the elements within an element of this type

❑   `lax` – which tells the processor to validate them when possible

❑   `skip` – which tells the processor not to try to validate the contents of the `any` element

If we want to validate the content of elements from another namespace then they would either have to have been declared in the schema itself, or be included or imported from another schema.

For instance, if we want to extend the definition of our `Description` element to contain any XHTML tag, we could declare a type that we could associate with the `Description` element:

```
<xs:element name = "Description" type = "XHTMLType" />

<xs:complexType name="XHTMLType" mixed="true">
  <xs:sequence>
     <xs:any namespace="http://www.w3.org/1999/xhtml"
       minOccurs="0" maxOccurs="unbounded"
     processContents="skip"/>
  </xs:sequence>
</xs:complexType>
```

Now wherever we declare an element to have the XHTMLType type, it accepts any elements from the `http://www.w3.org/1999/xhtml` namespace. Furthermore, because the type has been marked as mixed content and the any element can occur an unbounded number of times, it can contain mixed content and as many of the elements from this namespace as the user wants.

We should think of any as being a way of adding flexibility to our rigid structures, and through careful use of it, we could control where extra markup can appear. This will help the evolution of our schema and as people find things they need to add into it, we can then plan revisions for those who submit the requests. This is known as an open content schema, because it allows instance documents to include information beyond what is already declared in them. There is an example of one of these in Chapter 12.

The best way of controlling where the unknown content may appear is in an element declaration; in a sequence group, this means that:

❑ We know the name of the element that will contain the unknown content

❑ We will know the exact position of the element containing the unknown content

❑ It will not be available to be part of a substitution group because it is defined locally

If we define a type so that we can use it with several elements, then we should add the `block` attribute with a value of `#all` so that users cannot derive new types from this type.

The `anyAttribute` gives the same functionality for attribute definitions as `any` does for elements.

Protecting Our Markup – Controlling Re-Use

When we have gone to the effort of creating a schema, there are a number of reasons why we might want to protect the markup that we have defined:

❑ To give credit to the author who originally developed the schema

❑ To prevent changes and additions that may break an application

❑ To indicate ownership of information in a given element or attribute

There are a number of ways in which we can protect markup:

❑ Enforcing use of namespaces

❑ Declaring Types to be `final` Types

❑ Block derivation and substitution groups

Let's look at the different types of control these approaches offer.

Enforcing Namespace Qualification

Enforcing namespace qualification requires document users to qualify the elements and attributes as belonging to part of our namespace when used in instance documents. This is helpful for indicating when documents use definitions and declarations as defined in our namespace, in which case they will be qualified by our namespace; or when they have been altered, in which case the altered components will be part of a different namespace or no-namespace.

We have already seen several examples of how we can enforce namespace qualification in instance documents in either of two places:

❑ At a global level for an entire schema inside the `schema` element using `elementFormDefault` and `attributeFormDefault`

❑ At the individual element and attribute level using the `form` attribute on the declarations

The global control acts as a default for the whole document, so if we need finer grained control, the individual local controls will take precedence.

Preventing Derivation of Types

We have seen that XML Schemas offer a lot of flexibility in deriving new types from existing ones. But there are times when we will want to prevent other schema authors from being able to derive new types or content models from our definitions and declarations.

Final Types

If we want to control the derivation of a datatype, we can do this through the use of a `final` attribute on either a `complexType` or `element` declaration. This attribute can take one of three values:

❑   `restriction` – which prevents restriction of the type

❑   `extension` – which prohibits extension of the type

❑   `#all` – which prevents extension or restriction of the type

For example, say we wanted to define more than one type of vehicle; we could define a base type with the minimum number of elements and attributes required to describe a vehicle, and then derive specific types of vehicle from the base class. In this case, if we are allowing people to define new types of vehicle, we want to be able to restrict the minimum information that we require to define a vehicle. Therefore, we would prevent restriction of the type and guarantee that we had our minimum number of information items.

Alternatively, we may have defined a general item of information and want to make other classes more specific; in this case we would use `extension` to prevent our class from being extended any further.

If we want to prevent both extension and restriction, then we can use `all`.

There is also `finalDefault`, which can be used on the `schema` element as the default control for when types can be derived. It takes the same values as the `final` attribute.

Fixed Attribute for SimpleTypes

If we want finer grained control over the individual facets of a simple type, then we can use the `fixed` attribute. When `fixed` has a value of `true`, it prevents a facet from being modified – although the other facets of the type can be added or modified.

For example, here we have created a simple type called `fixedLengthFieldType`, to have a maximum length of 256 characters. We have fixed this facet so that it cannot be extended.

```
<xs:simpleType name = "fixedLengthFieldType">
   <xs:restriction base = "xs:string">
      <xs:maxLength value = "256" fixed = "true" />
   </xs:restriction>
</xs:simpleType>
```

While we are able to add other facets or modify them, this one remains fixed at a maximum of 256 characters. So, you can imagine that there could be a scenario where we wanted to make sure that there were at least 5 characters in a field, but we would want to maintain that there was a restriction of a maximum of 256 characters. In this case we can add a minimum length facet to a new type derived from this one:

```
<xs:simpleType name = "minCharsFixedLengthFieldType">
   <xs:restriction base = "fixedLengthFieldType">
      <xs:minLength = value "5" />
   </xs:restriction>
</xs:simpleType>
```

When deriving this new type, we cannot change the `maxLength` facet.

Block for Control in Instance Documents

We have seen in previous chapters how, in an instance document, an element may have a content model defined by any type derived from the type associated with the element name in the schema (the type substitution mechanism). While the `final` attribute controls what users can do in the schema (such as create a new type derived from one you have defined), the `block` attribute controls what derivations and substitution groups may be used in instance documents via type substitution.

If our processing application is expecting a fixed content model, and is not able to cope with this potential sort of fluctuation; (when we are at risk of someone else creating derived types that may be substituted in the instance document), then we can add the `block` attribute. The `block` attribute can take the same values as `final` to prevent this kind of substitution occurring in conforming instance documents:

❑ `restriction` prevents derivations-by-restriction appearing in an instance document

❑ `extension` would prevent derivations-by-extension appearing in an instance document

❑ `#all` would prevent derivations-by-restriction or extension appearing in an instance document

Again, there is a `blockDefault` attribute that can be used on the `schema` element as a default for every type definition and element declaration in the schema.

Modularizing Schemas

As you will have gathered from the abilities to re-use schema components, particularly those from different schemas, there are strong possibilities for the modularized development of schemas. Indeed, as illustrated by the chameleon design, there are strong advantages to creating separate schemas that we can re-use, although you have to be very careful about the namespace from which the schema components come and whether they have been defined locally or globally.

In this final section, we will look at some final issues regarding the development of modularized schemas.

When a schema is modularized, it is split into a collection of abstract modules that each provides a class or specific type of functionality. Other schemas that satisfy business needs can then borrow from these modular schemas, facilitating re-use of constructs across your organization and as a by-product, encouraging interoperability if different departments and applications use similar structures.

Creating Our Own Modularized Schemas

We have already seen how we can make use of components within other schemas to facilitate re-use of declarations and definitions from those schemas. Using this principle, we can modularize our own schema development to facilitate re-use of components between schemas.

Once we have these building blocks in place, it means that we can:

❑ Rapidly develop new schemas from the core building blocks

❑ Have standard structures for entities that are reflected across an application or organization

❑ Update classes of information from one schema and have the changes to the data structure represented across all of our schemas

❑ Allow different departments to use the same markup and include it within their own namespace

❑ Enhances interoperability between information in different parts of an application or organization

For example, we may use the same structure for addresses throughout a system, in which case we can create an address type. Similarly, customer and employee records may follow some common structure to represent information such as names, addresses or contact details; again, we can define a schema for this class of information and re-use it within other schemas.

If we are developing a document-based application, we can develop chameleon components for standard constructs that appear in different types of document, as we saw with the example of XHTML at the beginning of the chapter. For another example, we could define modules for paragraphs, lists, tables, indexes, bibliographies, etc. Then we could use these chameleon components in more specific schemas such as schemas for articles, books, academic papers, presentations, etc.

If we are using a component-based or object-oriented approach, then we will be trying to tie our document structures to the application's representation of the data. In which case, we will be able to define classes of information to represent objects used within the company, such as products, customers, accounts, etc.

If we are developing schemas that represent different namespaces, we will get particular benefit from creating no-namespace or chameleon schemas, because they will adopt the target namespace of the schema that uses them. If we look to only create schemas that have a target namespace when they represent an action that is occurring to these objects or entities, we will maximize re-use. For example, we will not have need for a customer on its own, we may need to add a new customer, or a customer may be placing an order, or we may even be storing customer details (in which case they become part of a table or store), but they are not required on their own. So, the lack of a namespace for the customer itself is not a problem; this is an ideal candidate for being a chameleon component or building block.

Granularity

One of the key questions that we need to ask ourselves is how granular we should make our schema components. While we could put each schema component in a separate component schema, this can have negative side effects. Remember that some processors are designed to pull in all of the schemas that they are going to need to use before starting processing. If the processor has large numbers of schemas to collect, it will need to locate and import the schemas before it can validate the document instance. Some other implementations may choose to keep the schemas in memory, in which case the operations may be quicker.

To help counter these problems, we can store related schema components in the same chameleon schemas to minimize the number of schemas that we are going to need to bring into the *main* schema. For example, if we are going to need Name and Address constructs in the same documents, we will be able to put them together in the same schema.

Dependencies

When we start working across multiple schemas, including or importing constructs from other schemas into the new ones we write, it makes it very easy to update a component that is used by several schemas and have the changes reflected across all of them that use that component. However, it does mean that we create dependencies on these schema components. If we update one of these components in a supporting schema, the effects of any changes we make to it will not be localized to the one schema; it will affect all of the schemas that use the component in it.

So that we do not break applications that make use of schemas that share common components, we should make a list of dependencies. This should be kept with the supporting schema, so that, if someone goes to change it, they will know what other schemas will be affected by the change. This record could either be in a simple text file, XML file, or spreadsheet that is kept with the schema, or it could be made in an annotation element.

Noting dependencies works for internal re-use, but if we are expecting others to share our modularized approach, we cannot always work like this as those who use our structures may not be able to change their applications to work with new extensions as and when we want to. In which case we need to resort to some versioning mechanism. One way of preserving the integrity of schemas that we have already defined is to make a new schema that includes the component that we have already defined, and to extend or restrict its definition.

Documenting Dependencies in a Modular Set of Schemas

The dependencies that are created when a schema is built from other schemas should always be documented. This is especially important if we expect others to adopt the schema(s) that we have written. Users are less likely to adopt a modular schema approach designed by someone else if they have to trawl through several levels of included schemas to make sure that they have all of the necessary documents.

Hence, it is important to document the modules that are available if others are to adopt our design. Where there are dependencies, we should always record them in a documentation element at the start of the schema.

By doing this, we are, to a certain extent, exposing our internal logic to those who need to adopt our schema. We may therefore decide that modularization is practical for internal schemas, but not for the subset that we will be sharing with partners. In which case, we can still use the source code from the schema constructs that are in the chameleon components as a kind of library of markup.

Something else to be aware of when creating no-namespace chameleon components, is that while it makes it easier for us to create new schemas, it also makes it easier for those who are adopting our schema to coerce our components into their own schemas, making development of their own schemas easier. To prevent this, we could make the design a homogeneous namespace design, whereby all of the components had the same target namespace; although this would restrict us to a single namespace for our application or organization.

Summary

In this chapter we have looked further into the type and class system that W3C XML Schema offers, in particular how it can be used to create schemas from multiple document instances. We have seen how these abilities are far more flexible than those offered by DTDs using parameter entities.

The ability to create schemas that can validate document instances across multiple namespaces is a powerful addition to any XML developer's toolkit. However, there are cautions that need to be exercised when writing a schema, to prevent misuse of the markup that we are defining. With the ability to create types and element content models derived from those that we have already created, the same ability is offered to others.

In particular we have seen how we can:

❑ Include other schemas from the same namespace into our own schema, as if copying and pasting the declarations into our own document

❑ Import schemas from other namespaces, so that we can make use of their constructs, and create classes of documents from schema components that come from a range of namespaces

❑ Alter type definitions and element content models that we have borrowed from other schemas using extension, restriction, the redefine mechanism, and substitution groups

❑ Allow our content models to be extended through substitution groups and wildcards

❑ Prevent derivation of types by use of the `final` attribute

❑ Prevent type substitution in instance documents using `block`

❑ Enforce namespace qualification through the use of `elementFormDefault`, `attributeFormDefault`, and the `form` attribute

We have also seen the different ways in which our design can affect namespaces, and how we can:

❑ Use chameleon components that are coerced into the namespace of the schema that uses them

❑ Create schemas that require instance documents to maintain namespace qualification

❑ Make use of chameleon components to create a modular design for our schema development

W3C XML Schema gives us a lot more flexibility in how we design our schemas, but in doing so it adds a certain amount of complexity to the schema design process. It is important to think about the design and construction of our schemas, so that we really can control how conforming instance documents appear, and how others can use our definitions and declarations.

Identity Constraints, Normalization, and Document Fragments

In this chapter we will start by looking at the new identity constraints offered by W3C XML Schema and how they affect the way in which we author documents. These include both a uniqueness constraint, which indicates that a value should be unique within a document, and a mechanism for representing keys and their references, which is very helpful when working with database representations. The key mechanism also helps us to introduce some relational database techniques to our XML-based work.

On the way, we will look at how data integrity is preserved in databases using normalization techniques, and how these techniques can be translated onto XML Schemas and their instance documents, when we try to represent similar data structures in XML.

We will also look at how we deal with fragments of documents, rather than the whole document. When working with large files, we will often want to be able to work with a subsection of the document rather than the whole instance. We will look at issues related to how we split up our documents so that they can be worked on in parts.

In particular, we will be looking at:

❑ Uniqueness Constraints

❑ Using key and keyref mechanisms to represent relationships

❑ How database normalization techniques relate to schema authors, in particular the abilities introduced by XML Schemas to create references between entities

❑ Issues raised when we want to deal with document fragments

By the end of the chapter, we will have seen not only the advantages that identity constraints can bring to schema authors, but also the risks that using them can introduce.

Identity Constraints

There are two types of identity constraint offered by XML Schema:

❑ Uniqueness constraints, whereby we can require that an element's content or attribute's value is unique within a range of a document instance

❑ The key and keyref mechanism for describing relationships using keys and references, which are similar to the notion of primary keys and foreign keys in relational databases

While IDs have to be unique within an XML document, and they can be used in conjunction with IDREFs to represent relationships, the identity constraints in XML Schema allow a lot more power and flexibility over the constraints they impose upon a document, so we shall look in this section at both the syntax and some of the ways in which we can take advantage of them.

Throughout our investigation of identity constraints we will be using a document structure, which is detailed below. It is a staff list that contains information about employees and of the departments that they work in. If we were to include details of the department within each employee record, we would end up with significant repetition of department details. Instead we have one record for each employee, and one for each department, and define a relationship between each employee record and the department they work in so that we only have to provide each department's details once. The root StaffList element contains an Employees element, which contains the list of employees, and a Departments element, which contains the details of each department. Each department is given a unique ID, which is then referred to from employee records using an attribute called refDepartmentID held within an element called Department.

Here is an example of the structure that we will be using (stafflist.xml):

```
<?xml version = "1.0" ?>
<StaffList xmlns = "http://www.example.org/hr/stafflist">

   <Employees>

      <!-- list of employees -->

      <Employee employeeID = "14">
         <Name>
            <FirstName>Amy</FirstName>
            <LastName>Robertson</LastName>
         </Name>
         <Department refDepartmentID = "12"/>
         <JobTitle>Telesales Manager</JobTitle>
      </Employee>

      <Employee employeeID = "54">
         <Name>
            <FirstName>Roger</FirstName>
            <LastName>Stone</LastName>
         </Name>
```

```
            <Department refDepartmentID = "12"/>
            <JobTitle>Telesales Representative</JobTitle>
        </Employee>

    </Employees>

    <Departments>

        <!-- list of departments -->

        <Department departmentID = "12">
            <DepartmentTitle>Telesales</DepartmentTitle>
            <DepartmentManager refEmployeeID = "14" />
        </Department>

    </Departments>

</StaffList>
```

Here is the schema to define this class of document (stafflist1.xsd):

```
<?xml version = "1.0" ?>
<xs:schema xmlns:xs = "http://www.w3.org/2001/XMLschema"
           targetNamespace = "http://www.example.org/hr/stafflist"
           xmlns = "http://www.example.org/hr/stafflist"
           elementFormDefault = "qualified">

    <!-- Define the containing Employees and Departments elements as an
         anonymous complex type within the declaration of the StaffList
         element -->

    <xs:element name = "StaffList">
        <xs:complexType>
            <xs:sequence>

                <xs:element name = "Employees" minOccurs = "1" maxOccurs = "1" >
                    <xs:complexType>
                        <xs:sequence>
                            <xs:element ref = "Employee" minOccurs = "1"
                                maxOccurs = "unbounded" />
                        </xs:sequence>
                    </xs:complexType>
                </xs:element>

                <xs:element name = "Departments" minOccurs = "1"
                    maxOccurs = "1" >
                    <xs:complexType>
                        <xs:sequence>
                            <xs:element ref = "Department"
                                minOccurs = "1" maxOccurs = "unbounded" />
                        </xs:sequence>
                    </xs:complexType>
                </xs:element>

            </xs:sequence>
```

```
            </xs:complexType>
        </xs:element>


    <!-- Define the content model for each Employee element inside an
         anonymous complex type definition -->

    <xs:element name = "Employee">
        <xs:complexType>
            <xs:sequence>

                <!-- We may well want to re-use the content model for Name in
                     other elements, so we define a NameType type -->

                <xs:element name = "Name" type = "NameType" />

                <xs:element name = "Department">
                    <xs:complexType>
                        <xs:attribute name="refDepartmentID" type="xs:integer" />
                    </xs:complexType>
                </xs:element>

                <xs:element name = "JobTitle" type = "xs:string" />

            </xs:sequence>
            <xs:attribute name = "employeeID" type = "xs:integer" />
        </xs:complexType>
    </xs:element>

    <!-- Define the content model for department inside an anonymous
         complex type definition as we did with Customer -->
    <xs:element name = "Department">
        <xs:complexType>
            <xs:sequence>
                <xs:element name = "DepartmentTitle" type = "xs:string" />
                <xs:element name = "DepartmentManager">
                    <xs:complexType>
                        <xs:attribute name="refEmployeeID" type = "xs:integer" />
                    </xs:complexType>
                </xs:element>
            </xs:sequence>
            <xs:attribute name = "departmentID" />
        </xs:complexType>
    </xs:element>


    <!-- Define the NameType type -->
    <xs:complexType name = "NameType">
        <xs:sequence>
            <xs:element name = "FirstName" type = "xs:string" />
            <xs:element name = "LastName" type = "xs:string" />
        </xs:sequence>
    </xs:complexType>

</xs:schema>
```

Four things will be demonstrated with this example:

- Ensuring that the value of the `employeeID` attribute is unique for each employee
- Ensuring that the value of the `departmentID` attribute is unique for each department
- Expressing a relationship between the department that the employee works in, and a record containing details of the department; the allowed value the department an employee works in will be constrained to be that of an existing department
- Expressing a relationship between a department manager and an instance of an employee. Each employee will have to be managed by a manager who is already defined in the document.

Both the uniqueness and key mechanisms offered by W3C XML Schema make use of XPath, so we need to be familiar with the basic syntax of creating an XPath statement. So, before we look at how we enforce unique values and define relationships, we will look at the subset of XPath that is used by XML Schema.

Locating Nodes with XPath

Both types of identity constraints (the `unique`, and `key` and `keyref` mechanisms) introduced in XML Schema require that an author is able to specify an element or attribute whose content or value is a simple type. This is because, whether we are looking to express a key or that a value should be unique, we can only work with simple values – not complex content and element content models.

Furthermore, we need to be able to identify the elements or attributes in terms of nodes – in a generalized manner with regards to the structure a document can take, rather than with respect to a document instance. By this, we mean that we need to be able to identify all elements or attributes that can occur within a certain point in the hierarchy created in the document instance. After all, we cannot rely on each document instance matching another. We need a way of expressing something like:

> *"Find me the `employeeID` attribute of the `Employee` element, that is in turn a child of the `Employees` element in the `StaffList` element."*

Look at the hierarchy of the document structure is shown oveleaf. Here we have a `StaffList` element as the root element of the document. The `StaffList` element can contain two child elements: `Employees`, which is a container element for all of the employee records, and `Departments`, which is a container for the details of each department. Each `Employee` and `Department` then have child elements of their own, attributes being shown in brackets.

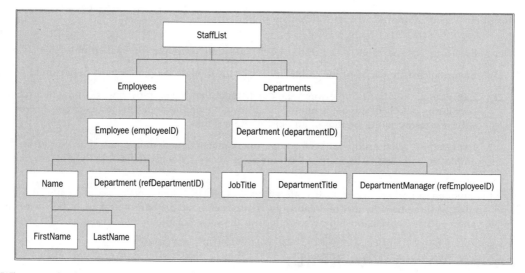

When we think in this abstract manner as illustrated in the diagram shown above, which we can think of as being similar to the approach taken by the DOM, we can indicate the three types of information needed to apply identity constraints.

For example, each Employee element is supposed to define a unique employee. In order to ensure that they are treated as being unique, they will each have a unique employeeID attribute on the Employee. This would mean that there couldn't be two Employee elements with the same value for the employeeID attribute, although there could be another employeeID attribute outside the Employees element with the same value. So, how do we define such an identity constraint?

In order to specify any identity constraint, we need to give three pieces of information:

❑ A context within which the constraint applies. In this case it is within the Employees element (because each Employee element in the Employees element must be unique.

❑ The elements (and these have to be elements) that are being uniquely identified by unique or key or that are referring elsewhere with keyref. For our example the Employee elements are unique.

❑ The value(s) that are used to uniquely identify the elements, whether they are elements or attributes. In our case, the employeeID attribute on the Employee element is what uniquely identifies that Employee element.

In order to define our ranges, and the locations of the information items within those ranges, we use XPath. W3C XML Schema only permits a subset of XPath to be used, to simplify the requirements of a conforming processor to identify a node set or specific node.

XPath was created to provide syntax and semantics that indicate or address a part of an XML document. The need for such syntax arose because there was a common requirement in both the XSLT and XPointer specifications that required a node set or individual node to be identified within the structure of a document. Rather than working on the syntax employed by a specific XML vocabulary,

XPath uses an abstract representation of the document similar to that of the DOM.

An XPath is rather like a file path or URL path, which navigates the hierarchy of the document. Here we are just providing a brief introduction to the subset of XPath used by XML Schemas so that we can get used to using it with the identity constraints of XML Schema.

We provide two XPath expressions when defining any identity constraint:

- ❑ The **selector**, which defines the elements that have unique values
- ❑ The **field**, which provides a path from the selected node to the individual element or attribute's node that we are constraining

There are two types of location path in XPath:

- ❑ A **relative location path** consists of a sequence of one or more location steps leave separated by a forward slash character (/). The steps are composed from left to right like a file path, rather like a file path going through a directory structure.
- ❑ An **absolute location path** consists of a forward slash character, which can be followed by a relative location path. A forward slash on its own selects the root node of the document containing the context node. If there is a relative path after it, then the location path selects the set of nodes that would be selected by the relative location path relative to the root node.

W3C XML Schema always uses relative XPaths, as we shall see, because where we declare the identity constraint within the schema document reflects the node within which our constraint applies. Each location step is separated from the next by a forward slash character. This is similar to the way a file path works; to indicate a folder called `Chaper8` within the `ProSchemas` folder, which is in the `Wrox` folder under `myDocuments`, we could use a path such as `C:\myDocuments\Wrox\ProSchemas\Chapter8`. To indicate the `LastName` element in our document structure, on the other hand, we might use something like this (s, is the namespace prefix for this XML document):

```
Employees/s:Employee/Name/LastName
```

Recall that the context of the XPath is important and that we should use relative XPaths. This is why we do not have the root element of `StaffList` in this example; we are assuming that `StaffList` is the context node.

If we want to locate an attribute, we use an @ symbol to prefix the attribute. So, if we wanted to identify the `refDepartmentID` attribute that is a child of the `Department` element, which is in turn a child of the `Employee` element, then we would do so like this:

```
Employees/s:Employee/Department/@refDepartmentID
```

Again we are assuming that the `StaffList` element is the context node.

> **We must namespace prefix all globally declared elements and attributes in our XPath statements.**

We have to be particularly careful with our use of XPaths when writing our XPaths using identity constraints, because of the way in which only globally declared elements become part of the target namespace of the schema. Those elements and attributes that are declared locally within a complex type or model group do not belong to the target namespace, rather they are in a null namespace – hence we have to set `elementFormDefault`, or the `form` attribute, to have a value of `qualified` if we want to be able to use default namespaces and reduce namespace complexities in instance documents.

The point we have to be aware of here is that XPath requires we always specify the namespace prefix for any elements that are in anything other than a null namespace. So in our examples, we have to declare all namespace prefixes for globally declared elements and attributes.

Let's go back to the example of wanting to ensure that each `Employee` element is unique within the `Elements` node. Remember that where we define the constraint defines the range in which the constraint applies. In this case we will define it within the definition of the `Employees` element. We then apply the selector as a relative XPath from the `Employees` element to the `Employee` element, which in this case is only one step:

```
s:Employee
```

This is the selector that refers to all the `Employee` elements that are children of `Employees`. Because it is globally declared we have to prefix it with the namespace associated with the target namespace of the schema. Here `Employee` now becomes the **context node**.

Now to identify the `employeeID` attribute we provide a second path to it from here:

```
@employeeID
```

Having already navigated to the `Employee` node set in the selector (the element we want the constraint to apply to), we specified the `employeeID` attribute of the `Employee` element as the field (the value that identifies the element in the selector).

Let's quickly look at a slightly more complicated example, where we ensure that want to use the `departmentID` attribute on the `Department` element indicates the department to which the employee belongs. We start by deciding the scope of the restriction. Again we want to specify this in the `Employees` element. We then specify the element to which we are applying the constraint, which is the `Employee` element:

```
s:Employee
```

And from the `Employee` element being the context node, we have to specify the field, which is the `departmentID` attribute on the `Department` element:

```
Department/@employeeID
```

Note that we could not have used `Employees/s:Employee/Department` in the first step, as we would have been using the `refDepartmentID` attribute to identify the `Department` element, not the `Employee` element.

It is important to note that identity constraints exist alongside the datatype declaration, and their lexical space is compared to see if they are equal or unequal, which means they are checked by value rather than by a string comparison. For example if we had two values that are both integers, such as 6 and 6.0, then they would be considered equal, but if their data types were strings then they would be different. This is an advantage W3C XML Schema identity constraints have over XML IDs, because the XML ID is the datatype. (See Chapter 2 for a description of value comparisons in simple types).

> **You will make lighter work for the processor if you narrow the scope in which an identity constraint applies, as it will have less of the document to check if it is processing the constraint.**

Having seen how we define a range within which our identity constraints apply, and a way of locating the relevant item from that range, we should now look at the individual identity constraints themselves.

Unique Values

There are many situations where we might need to ensure that a value within a document is unique. Many applications require unique identifiers to work with the data that they are processing. For example, we may require unique product codes to individually identify a type of product, user names/numbers to identify each user, or purchase order numbers to identify a purchase order. When we are working with document-based applications, there are similar requirements for unique values in chapter numbers, footnotes, and cross-references. It is also extremely helpful when working with representations of databases, and we want to ensure that a record has a key, because we can enforce the uniqueness of the key.

By enforcing unique values in the schema, we can ensure that a document instance does not contain two elements with the same content or two attributes with the same value. The limitation of this is that it only works across the document instance that is being validated by the schema, if we do not have each element or attribute whose value we want to ensure is unique within the document that is being processed, we will not be guaranteed of its uniqueness across an application. Therefore, the key to thinking about the uniqueness constraint is that it is for ensuring unique values *within* a document instance. While it will not work across a group of documents, it is still a powerful tool for any schema author, in particular it is a lot more powerful than using the XML ID type to ensure uniqueness.

A requirement of an XML ID type is that its value is unique within the document instance. However, there are a number of disadvantages with XML ID types; they:

- ❑ They only work as attribute values.
- ❑ They have to be unique across the whole document – we can only have one set of unique values within the document.
- ❑ They cannot start with a number or contain spaces.

W3C XML Schema identity constraints offer a lot more flexibility because:

- ❑ They can specify that an element's content or attribute's value be unique.
- ❑ The unique value can be any datatype and can start with a number.

❑ The value does not have to be unique across the whole document – we can specify a range within which the values should be unique.

❑ We can create composite IDs that are made up of a set of values, for example an ID for a unique address can contain a combination of house number, street, and town fields (which is especially helpful as there will be several identical house numbers, and there is usually more than one property on a street, so we can use a combination of the values for each of these).

W3C XML Schema uses an element called `unique` to ensure that an element's content or attribute's value is unique. The idea behind expressing a uniqueness constraint is that we can specify a range within which a value has to be unique. For example, take the sample structure we met at the beginning of the chapter:

```
<StaffList xmlns = "http://www.example.org/hr/stafflist>

    <Employees>

        <!-- list of employees goes here -->
        <Employee employeeID = "14">
           <Name>
               <FirstName>Amy</FirstName>
               <LastName>Robertson</LastName>
           </Name>
           <Department refDepartmentID = "12"/>
           <JobTitle>Telesales Manager</JobTitle>
        </Employee>
    ... more employee records ...
    </Employees>

    <Departments>
    <!-- ...department info goes here ... -->
        <Department departmentID = "12">
           <DepartmentTitle>Telesales</DepartmentTitle>
           <DepartmentManager refEmployeeID = "14" />
        </Department>
    </Departments>
</StaffList>
```

In this example, we might want to ensure that the value of the `employeeID` attribute on each `Element` attribute is unique. We also want to ensure that the value of the `departmentID` on each `Department` element is unique, but only to the list of departments. We do not want to eliminate the possibility that both an employee and a department could have the same identifiers – although it might make sense to use a prefix to ensure that they do not (such as e for employee, d for department, p for product IDs, s for suppliers, and so on).

To allow us to capture the items that we require to be unique in the schema, W3C XML Schema requires that we perform a there-step process in defining the uniqueness constraint:

❑ Locate the position for the constraint. It should be inside the definition of the element within which we want our constraint to apply. Our constraint is supposed to be within the `Employees` element, and we should be allowed to have the same value for an `employeeID` on a `Manager` element in the `Department` element.

❑ Define the selector, the element to which our constraint applies. In this case, the `Employee` element.

❑ Define the field that uniquely identifies an element. It is the `employeeID` attribute that we are using to uniquely identify each employee.

The selector and field make use of the XPath syntax to indicate which nodes we want to be unique, which we have already met:

```
<xs:unique name = "employeeIdentificationNumber">
   <xs:selector xpath = "Employees/s:Employee" />
   <xs:field xpath = "@employeeID" />
</xs:unique>
```

This is placed inside the definition of the `Employees` element, to indicate that each `Employee` element inside the `Employees` element is unique, as identified by their `employeeID` attribute. (This means that, if there were another `Employee` element outside the `Employees` element with an attribute called `employee ID` attribute, it could have the same value.)

It is also possible to specify that a *combination* of more than one value be unique. We can specify that combinations of simple element content or attribute values be unique, by simply adding more field elements to the uniqueness constraint. However, we can only do this within the same constraint if the nodes for which we want to ensure uniqueness lie within the same scope specified in the selector.

Let's look at an example to make this clearer. Say we wanted to make sure that the value of an address was unique. If we added the `Address` element to an employee record like so:

```
<Employee employeeID = "14">
   <Name>
      <FirstName>Amy</FirstName>
      <LastName>Robertson</LastName>
   </Name>
   <Address>
      <HouseNumber>10a</HouseNumber
      <Street>Walker Terrace</Street>
      <City>Grosse Pointe</City>
      <State>Michigan</State>
      <ZipCode>48236</ZipCode>
   </Address>
   <Department refDepartmentID = "12"/>
   <JobTitle>Telesales Manager</JobTitle>
</Employee>
```

we could have several common house numbers in different streets and there could be several streets with the same name in an area. We can ensure that an address is unique by combining the values of the `HouseNumber`, `Street`, and `ZipCode` elements using several `field` elements in the constraint:

```
<xs:unique name = "uniqueAddress">
   <xs:selector xpath = "s:Employee " />
   <xs:field xpath = "Address/HouseNumber" />
   <xs:field xpath = "Address/Street" />
   <xs:field xpath = "Address/ZipCode" />
</xs:unique>
```

This ensures that a combination of the content of the `HouseNumber`, `Street`, and `ZipCode` elements cannot be the same.

331

Identity constraint definitions must be unique within a schema, which is why they are given a name attribute. This has to be unique within the whole document regardless of namespaces. Therefore, we should carefully consider names when working with schemas from multiple namespaces, as we cannot allow two constraints with the same name to exist within a document.

We should also be careful when using uniqueness constraints in substitution groups and where wildcards are used. Processors may handle these situations differently, as they are difficult to express. To ensure that they are interpreted correctly, we should keep the range of the selector at the narrowest applicable level. Furthermore, this is another good reason for only allowing wildcard content in specific areas of your markup – preferably in a containing component so that it will not conflict with a specific path in an identity constraint.

Keys and Key References

One of the most significant aims of the XML Schema working group was to allow schema authors to create constraints on documents that represent relational database structure better. In such terms, we needed a more powerful way of representing relationships than that offered by the ID and IDREF datatypes from XML 1.0.

One problem was that the ID had to be unique to the whole document. This could be a particular problem if we were using a structure where tables of a database were represented as containing elements with child elements representing the rows of data within that table, and each row of data had an attribute that was an XML ID to indicate the primary key of the row. This problem here is that two rows (albeit in different tables) could not have the same ID, as seen below:

```
<Database>
   <Table1>
      <Row id = "1" firstField = "value1" secondField = "value2" />
      <Row id = "2" firstField = "value1" secondField = "value2" />
      <Row id = "3" firstField = "value1" secondField = "value2" />
   </Table1>
   <Table2>
      <Row id = "1" firstField = "value1" secondField = "value2" />
      <Row id = "2" firstField = "value1" secondField = "value2" />
      <Row id = "3" firstField = "value1" secondField = "value2" />
   </Table2>
</Database>
```

If the id attribute were an XML ID, then this example would not work because the two tables, both of which used an auto-incremented primary key in the database, now have conflicting values for the ID, not to mention that they are numbers and XML IDs cannot start with a number.

With XML Schemas, on the other hand, we have already seen how we can specify the scope of a uniqueness constraint, so we can specify the scope within which a key applies, and we can use numbers. The advantages XML Schemas have over the XML IDs and IDREFs are as follows:

❑   ID/IDREF relationships require a lot of processing resources to traverse the references, whereas key and keyref mechanisms in W3C XML Schema make use of the XPath syntax. This allows a processor to find the scope within which it will find the constraint, narrowing down the area it has to check.

❑　Using XML IDs, the ID is the datatype, so there is no way of expressing the datatype of the field you are recording. In W3C XML Schema, the identity constraint is determined alongside the datatype, so the value can still keep its datatype.

❑　Only attributes can be IDs, whereas in W3C XML Schema, both simple element content and attribute values can be keys.

If you remember the sample document we met at the beginning of the chapter, we wanted only to have to add the details of each department to the file once. There is a relationship, however, between each employee, and the department to which each belongs. We will indicate this relationship through two pieces of information. Firstly, the department will be uniquely identified by the departmentID on the Department element that contains the details of each department. We can then associate the employee with the relevant department details by referencing the department they work in using the refDepartmentID attribute carried by the Department element that is a child of Employee.

The syntax for defining a key is very similar to that for a uniqueness constraint:

```
<xs:key name = "KeyDepartmentByID">
   <xs:selector xpath = "Departments/s:Department" />
   <xs:field xpath = "@departmentID" />
</xs:key>
```

The key is the value of the departmentID attribute carried by the Department element used to describe a department's details. The selector and field elements work just the same as they did for the uniqueness constraint.

The name attribute on the key element is required to identify the key we are referring to within a reference. Therefore, the name of the key has to be unique to the document regardless of namespaces.

The key reference will then form the relationship back to a given key from the element in which it is used. The reference created from the refDepartmentID attribute would look like this:

```
<xs:keyref name="RefEmployeeToDepartment" refer="KeyEmployeeToDepartment">
   <xs:selector xpath = "Employees/s:Employee" />
   <xs:field xpath = "Department/@refDepartmentID" />
</xs:keyref>
```

Here the keyref element contains an attribute called refer whose value is the name of the corresponding key. This is an identity constraint because the reference must point back to a key that exists in the document instance. The selector and field work just the same as they did both for the uniqueness constraint and the key definition. Remember that the name has to be unique to the schema.

It is possible to specify an ordered list of fields to cater for multi-field/multi-part keys simply by adding more field attributes, just as we did with the combination uniqueness constraint.

An element or attribute whose value is used as a field in a key must be non-nillable.

One convention is to add Key to the beginning of a name for a key, and Ref to the beginning of a name of a keyref. Also our keys should describe the item they uniquely identify, as they may be referred to from different references, while the keyref should describe what it is pointing from and to. For example, our key is called KeyDepartmentByID, while the key ref is called RefEmployeeToDepartment.

Let's quickly review the schema that contains all of the relationships and the uniqueness constraints that we have just looked at to see where these have been placed within the schema. First, we should note the declaration of the target namespace associated with the target namespace of this schema. This is so that we can use the namespace prefix in the XPaths. After this, the highlighted sections illustrate where the identity constraints should go. Remember that where we position the identity constraint will affect the scope of the identity constraint – we must position the constraint within the element declaration whose children we want the scope to apply to.

```xml
<?xml version = "1.0" ?>
<!-- Example2.xsd -->
<xs:schema xmlns:xs = "http://www.w3.org/2001/XMLSchema"
           targetNamespace = "http://www.example.org/hr/stafflist"
           xmlns = "http://www.example.org/hr/stafflist"
           xmlns:s = "http://www.example.org/hr/stafflist"
           elementFormDefault = "qualified">

    <xs:element name = "StaffList">
        <xs:complexType>
            <xs:sequence>

                <xs:element name = "Employees" minOccurs = "1"
                    maxOccurs = "1" >
                    <xs:complexType>
                        <xs:sequence>
                            <xs:element ref = "Employee" minOccurs = "1"
                                maxOccurs = "unbounded" />
                        </xs:sequence>
                    </xs:complexType>

                    <xs:unique name = "employeeIdentificationNumber">
                        <xs:selector xpath = "s:Employee" />
                        <xs:field xpath = "@employeeID" />
                    </xs:unique>

                </xs:element>

                <xs:element name = "Departments" minOccurs = "1"
                    maxOccurs = "1">
                    <xs:complexType>
                        <xs:sequence>
                            <xs:element ref = "Department" minOccurs = "1"
                                maxOccurs = "unbounded" />
                        </xs:sequence>
                    </xs:complexType>
                </xs:element>

            </xs:sequence>
        </xs:complexType>
        <xs:keyref name = "RefEmployeeToDepartment"
```

```
                    refer = "KeyDepartmentByID">
            <xs:selector xpath = "Employees/s:Employee" />
            <xs:field xpath = "Department/@refDepartmentID" />
        </xs:keyref>

        <xs:key name = "KeyDepartmentByID">
            <xs:selector xpath = "Departments/s:Department" />
            <xs:field xpath = "@departmentID" />
        </xs:key>
    </xs:element>

    <xs:element name = "Employee">
        <xs:complexType>
            <xs:sequence>

                <xs:element name = "Name" type = "NameType" />
                <xs:element name = "Department">
                    <xs:complexType>
                        <xs:attribute name = "refDepartmentID"
                                type = "xs:integer" />
                    </xs:complexType>
                </xs:element>

                <xs:element name = "JobTitle" type = "xs:string" />

            </xs:sequence>
            <xs:attribute name = "employeeID" type = "xs:integer" />
        </xs:complexType>
    </xs:element>

    <xs:element name = "Department">
        <xs:complexType>
            <xs:sequence>
                <xs:element name = "DepartmentTitle" type = "xs:string" />
                <xs:element name = "DepartmentManager">
                    <xs:complexType>
                        <xs:attribute name="refEmployeeID" type="xs:integer" />
                    </xs:complexType>
                </xs:element>
            </xs:sequence>
            <xs:attribute name = "departmentID" />
        </xs:complexType>
    </xs:element>

    <xs:complexType name = "NameType">
        <xs:sequence>
            <xs:element name = "FirstName" type = "xs:string" />
            <xs:element name = "LastName" type = "xs:string" />
        </xs:sequence>
    </xs:complexType>

</xs:schema>
```

As you might imagine, the ability to represent keys and references has an important impact on the way we deal with XML documents that represent databases. In addition, it impacts on how we can apply principles of normalization to our XML documents; but before we look at that, here is another example to illustrate references to make sure that we are clear.

Maintaining Stable, Secure, and Accurate Data

The identity constraint mechanisms introduced by W3C XML Schema, in particular key and keyref, have important implications on design of XML documents because they allow us to create more powerful relationships between nodes of a document than are allowed with XML ID and IDREF datatypes.

One of the main goals of the XML Schema working group was to allow schema authors to create constraints on documents that represent relational database structures. With relational databases being by far the most common format for persistent data storage, this is hardly surprising. It means that we need to look at the facilities that an RDBMS system offers, the design practices that database designers use, and how these concepts apply to schema authors. In particular, we should look at the normal forms that offer a way of creating structures, as well as some of the rules that are implicitly built into an RDBMS that help preserve the stability, security, and accuracy of data.

> While we read through this section, we should keep in mind that the ability to follow the normalization rules in a relational database does not mean that our data structure should necessarily follow the structure of the database – after all, the structure of the XML document should be governed a lot more by the intended use of the document, and the ability to create hierarchical structures does not correspond to the two-dimensional way in which database designers must design their structures.

In this section, we will look at mechanisms employed by an RDBMS to help ensure that data remains stable, secure, and accurate. In particular, we will be looking at:

❑ Techniques implemented in RDBMSs, in particular types of data integrity

❑ Database design methods called normal forms

Dr. E. F. Codd, who was a researcher at IBM's San Jose Research Center, is largely credited for having devised the relational database model back in 1969. He was working in the field of applying algebra to solve problems related to storing large amounts of data. The results of his work are commonly known and codified as **normalization**. Many of the principles he discovered have been internalized into all major RDBMS products, meaning that relational database developers do not need to work through all of them, because many have already been put in place. Indeed, some developers are unaware that the requirement to specify a datatype for each field in a relational database, and the need to declare primary and foreign keys, come from the result of normalization.

> The process of normalization is removing fundamental logical inconsistencies from the design, using tables, keys, columns, and relationships, the aim being to simplify the structure of data so that performance is improved.

Many of the integrity rules that are built into RDBMSs, such as only having two dimensions that are linked with relationships and joins, the ability to allow a null field (one that contains no data – but is explicitly null), and the ability to determine strong datatypes, are not inherent in XML; so the rules of normalization do not port directly to our work with XML. However, with the new features added to W3C XML Schema, not only can documents be adapted where necessary to represent relational structures, XML developers can also take advantage of some of the practices to ensure that their data remains stable, secure, and accurate.

Clarifying Database Terms

In order to describe the normalization of data, we should quickly clarify some fundamental terms for those who are not familiar with relational databases:

- ❑ **Entity**: An entity in database terms (as opposed to XML terms) relates to a name for something that can be seen as a distinguishable object in the real world, and whose information is stored within a single table. The columns in the table represent attributes that describe the entity – information that is *about* the object. For example, a product will have a stock keeping unit number (SKU), a name, a description, and a price. A customer will have a name, address, and a customer ID number.

- ❑ **Primary key**: The primary key uniquely identifies an instance of an entity, or a row of data in a given table. So, the SKU or the customer ID, fields would be the primary keys for the `Product` and `Customer` tables respectively, and would uniquely identify each product or customer within the table. It is possible that a primary key corresponds to a combination of several attributes of an entity – known as a **concatenated primary key**. For example, a time alone could not identify a recurring event, and a date could not identify the event if a number of events occurred on the same day; however, a combination of date and time could.

- ❑ **Foreign key**: A foreign key maps to a primary key in a different table. So, a purchase order table may contain a foreign key column such as `OrdCustID`, which contains the primary key that identifies the customer that made a purchase. The corresponding primary key column (say, `CustID`) would be found in a `Customers` table. The foreign key represents the many of a one-to-many relationship.

We also need to look at some key issues that concern database designers:

- ❑ Data redundancy
- ❑ Functional Dependencies
- ❑ Properties of fields
- ❑ Atomicity

Data Redundancy

Data redundancy occurs when there is repetition of a piece of data. One of the goals of normalization is to reduce repetition of data. This is an important goal because:

- ❑ If there are two instances of a piece of data, then there is an increased chance that not all of the items will be updated correctly
- ❑ Duplicating data consumes more space than necessary

This can be a valuable aim in our work with XML as well. By making sure that each record only applies once, we reduce the risk of our data containing inconsistencies. We saw an example of this earlier in the chapter when looking at keys and their references to save us repeating department information for each employee.

Functional Dependencies

Functional dependencies are based on the storage and retrieval of data and are important for determining keys in databases.

> **A functional dependency occurs when, given the value of A, we can obtain the value of B. Node B is therefore considered to be functionally dependent upon Node A.**

In the following table we can see that the ProductName is functionally dependent upon the SKU number, and that they both would reside in the Product table of an Inventory database. The functional dependency is that the content of the SKU field determines the Product:

Inventory	->	Product	->	SKU	->	ProductName
Inventory	->	Product	->	244	->	Widget
Inventory	->	Product	->	246	->	Grommet

This is rather like considering the purpose of a document structure in XML and designing the structure so that it can be accessed in the way that is needed.

Properties of Fields

If we take a field of information in a relational database (that is, any given column item of a given table in a named database), then we are able to constrain what information that field can take. These are considered the **properties** of a field.

You can apply several properties to fields in a database. These constrain the allowable content that can go into such a field. In doing so, they prevent inappropriate use of data. The attributes reflect things such as the datatype, maximum lengths of the field, whether it is a primary key, and whether the value is nillable. For example, an employeeID field might contain attributes such as these (screenshot taken from MS SQL Server):

Typically if we were to express these kinds of properties in XML, we could use markup by expanding the structure. The simple content would be element content and the properties could be added to the element in question. For example:

```
<CustomerID datatype = "integer" maximumLength = "10"
    primaryKey = "true" nillable = "true" >2442</CustomerID>
```

While we could write an application to handle these attributes, there is no guarantee that a trading partner could make use of the added information that we have included. Furthermore, if we designed it to be used with a specific database, while it would work with the database for which it was designed, if another database did not offer the same functionality, the concept might fail. An example of this was introduced in Microsoft ADO 2.6 where it was possible to persist data to a stream that would include a schema in XDR (a Microsoft schema language).

As a result, when validation logic was required for an application to share information with a partner while working with DTDs, validation of this kind of information was performed by a custom-written parser or put into the application logic. Through the ability to add this information to a schema, we can put much of the validation work onto a conforming XML parser.

With XML Schema we can now add these properties using the schema. We can specify things like datatypes and maximum length of fields within datatypes, they can be declared nillable, and we can define keys using identity constraints, etc. Furthermore, by putting these information items in the XML Schema we can ensure interoperability with other products that support the W3C XML Schema Recommendation.

Atomicity

Atomicity refers to the granularity with which we store pieces of information. Atomic information items cannot be split up, and in both relational database fields and simple content of elements and attributes, the values contained are supposed to be atomic. While application logic could be written to further split up the information in the fields, as far as the data store is concerned, they are individual items of data.

For example, how many pieces of information are represented by the following value 2001-05-18T16:12:47? If it is a database field or simple XML content, then the answer is one: it represents a specific time on a given date. But it can also be seen as several pieces of information grouped together. If we want to work with any of these items of information separately, they should go in separate fields.

The more pieces of information we store in one value, the less flexible our data is in terms of our ability to process and share it. As far as our XML work goes, this means we should avoid losing data by ensuring each leaf node contains the atomic values that are, or will in the future, be required by an application.

Data Integrity

It is very important to ensure that the data in your application is accurate and consistent. Relational database theory commonly breaks down data integrity into four areas:

- ❑ **Entity integrity**
- ❑ **Domain integrity**
- ❑ **Referential integrity**
- ❑ **User-defined integrity**

Each of these can quite easily be applied to XML Schema, so we should look at how we can achieve this.

Entity Integrity

> **We achieve entity integrity when there are no duplicated rows or node sets of data.**

Each entity should be able to be identified uniquely. If we update a column or node set, we should be able to predict that it is the only one with that set of data (as long as uniqueness constraints have been applied). If entities are not constrained, any operations on this data will introduce inconsistencies in our data for two reasons:

❑   If we make any changes to an entity, these changes will not be made in all instances of the information.

❑   It would be impossible to distinguish between two different items if we wanted to perform an operation based on data in one of them.

Entity integrity is often enforced through the use of a **primary key** in a database – the rest of the data for any given row or node set may be identical, but the identifier ensures that it is different.

The use of a key identity constraint will enforce this uniqueness, as it also performs the same function as the unique identity constraint and will act as a primary key.

In order to be able to differentiate between items in XML we can add a **unique identifier** to uniquely identify an entity in a node set. For example, we may have two customers called John Doe who live at the same address – because one is John Doe Junior, the other John Doe Senior – but we do not have a column that will distinguish them as Junior and Senior:

```
<Customers>
    <Customer>
        <Name>
            <FirstName>John</FirstName>
            <LastName>Doe</LastName>
        </Name>
        <Address>
            <AddressLine1>40 Leighton Road</AddressLine1>
            <Town>Townsville</Town>
            <State>NSW</State>
            <ZipCode>408112</ZipCode>
        </Address>
    </Customer>
    <Customer>
        <Name>
            <FirstName>John</FirstName>
            <LastName>Doe</LastName>
        </Name>
        <Address>
            <AddressLine1>40 Leighton Road</AddressLine1>
            <Town>Townsville</Town>
```

```
            <State>NSW</State>
            <ZipCode>408112</ZipCode>
        </Address>
    </Customer>
</Customers>
```

If we tried to find a customer by name, or by address, we would get two matching records. This could mean that we end up billing the wrong account for goods that have not been ordered, change the wrong customer's address, or any number of events that could compromise the integrity of our data.

Through the use of a unique identifier, we can clearly distinguish between two customers that otherwise appear the same.

```
<!-- johndoe.xml -->
<Customers>
    <Customer customerID = "124441">
        <Name>
            <FirstName>John</FirstName>
            <LastName>Doe</LastName>
        </Name>
        <Address>
            <AddressLine1>40 Leighton Road</AddressLine1>
            <Town>Townsville</Town>
            <State>NSW</State>
            <ZipCode>408112</ZipCode>
        </Address>
    </Customer>
    <Customer customerID = "14662">
        <Name>
            <FirstName>John</FirstName>
            <LastName>Doe</LastName>
        </Name>
        <Address>
            <AddressLine1>40 Leighton Road</AddressLine1>
            <Town>Townsville</Town>
            <State>NSW</State>
            <ZipCode>408112</ZipCode>
        </Address>
    </Customer>
</Customers>
```

By adding the customerID attribute onto the customer element, we have ensured entity integrity.

Domain Integrity

> We can achieve domain integrity by ensuring values in any given column or node fall within acceptable ranges.

When we enter data into a field, not only must the data be correct, but it must also contain information that is appropriate for that field. W3C XML Schema allows us to do this through the addition of the ability able to specify simple types for element content or attribute values. It may require that we simply specify an existing built-in datatype (such as `string`, `number`, or `date`), or it might require us to define our own datatype.

Through careful use of simple types we can express constraints if they are required above those provided by the built-in types. Here are some common situations where it will help if we enforce our own datatypes to further constrain built-in types:

Type of information	Example	Datatype solution
Fixed formats	Social Security numbers, Zip Codes, Telephone Numbers	Use regular expressions to define the allowable character formats
Values from fixed lists	States, Job Roles, Departments	Use an enumerated simple type to define allowable values
True or false	Is active, Is Online, Has full clean driving license	Use the Boolean built-in simple type
Allowable ranges	Withdrawal amounts, Credit Limits, Minimum purchases	Use allowable ranges, `minInclusive`, `maxInclusive`, `minExclusive`, `maxExclusive` (and sometimes `totalDigits`, `fractionDigits`, and `length`)

For more information on creating your own datatypes see Chapters 4-5.

Referential Integrity

You achieve referential integrity when all foreign keys point to valid rows or node sets in the referenced table.

A foreign key is one that references or points to a row in another table. If you perform a lookup on an item of information where there is no corresponding foreign key, you will not be able to find the required data.

This is already enforced automatically in XML Schema through the requirement that a corresponding `key` be present in the file where any `keyref` is used. This does require, however, that the `key` be in the same document instance as the `keyref` that is pointing to it.

Beware that many database engines allow you to specify how to handle changes to one side of a relationship in terms of cascading updates and deletes. Cascading updates indicate that if the primary key changes all related rows on the many side, the foreign keys, will be updated, while cascading deletes suggest that if a row containing a primary key is deleted, that all other rows that point to it should also be deleted. There is no way of enforcing this in W3C XML Schema; you have to ensure that you write it into your application logic.

User-Defined Integrity

> **User-defined integrity ensures that data complies with applicable business rules.**

This is a catchall for the rules that did not neatly fit into the other categories. As we have seen, it is possible to use W3C XML Schema to enforce some of our business rules as well as define our own strong datatypes. These may be things like specifying a credit limit for accounts, or requiring a minimum number of purchases to be made.

Normal Forms

There are a number of rules collectively known as **normal forms**, which are the basis of many aspects of normalized database design. In this section we will look at the first three normal forms of normalization.

While going through this section we should bear in mind that relational databases only allow data to exist in two dimensions and require that relationships be defined to link related items of information. While this has an important effect on the integrity of data, it does neglect the fact that XML is designed so that it can create arbitrarily nested items of data. Therefore, the rules of normal forms and integrity do not and should not always hold true for XML documents.

Before we start, let's look at some of the problems we want to resolve. Let's take some data and represent it in a relational database table:

	EmployeeID	FirstName	LastName	JobTitle	Manager	DepartmentTitle	DepartmentManager
	1	Bob	Smith	Sales Person	Tom Shaw	Sales	Tom Shaw
	2	Karen	Stevens	Sales Person	Tom Shaw	Sales	Tom Shaw
	3	Bill	Williams	Database Admin	Tom Shaw	Sales	Tom Shaw
	4	Mark	Simmons	Database Admin	Mike Foster	Systems	Mike Foster
*	(AutoNumber)						

Alternatively, if it were represented in XML it might look as follows:

```xml
<?xml version="1.0"?>
<Employees>
  <Employee>
    <EmployeeID>1</EmployeeID>
    <Name>
        <FirstName>Bob</FirstName>
        <LastName>Smith</LastName>
    </Name>
    <JobTitle>Sales Person</JobTitle>
    <Manager>Tom Shaw</Manager>
    <DepartmentTitle>Sales</DepartmentTitle>
    <DepartmentManager>Tom Shaw</DepartmentManager>
  </Employee>
  <Employee>
    <!-- next employee in the list... -->
  </Employee>
</Employees>
```

This structure poses some problems though – let's look at the kind of problems that we are facing:

❑ It contains **repeating groups** (such as `DepartmentTitle`) – department information is repeated for each employee.

❑ We risk **inconsistency** – if a department manager changes name we would have to go back and check every record for each employee – if one of these is omitted, or done incorrectly, we introduce errors. Also, a bigger problem would arise if someone else with the same name as an existing employee joined the company – how would we distinguish between these two?

❑ If we lost a department, we would have to change the record of every employee that was in that department.

❑ If we wanted to add a department for which there were no employees yet, how would we go about this?

Crudely speaking, normalization is the process of taking the wider table and separating it out into a set of separate related tables with fewer columns. It will get over the problems we have just seen, but we also need to think about what it means in terms of XML.

First Normal Form

The first normal form states that we should:

> **Remove repeating forms/groups of data and put them in a separate table.**

We must not have multi-valued attributes, composite attributes, and their combinations. Attributes must be atomic values (simple and indivisible) and any attribute must be a single value from the domain of that group.

We do not actually face this problem in the example we have just seen, although we would have if we had recorded employees by department, like so:

	DepartmentID	DepartmentName	DepartmentManager	Employee1Name	Employee1JobTitle	Employee2Name	Employee2JobTitle
	1	Sales	Tom Shaw	Bob Smith	SalesPerson	Karen Stevens	SalesPerson
✱	(AutoNumber)						

An equivalent in XML might look like this:

```
<Departments>
   <Department id = "1">
      <DepartmentName>Sales</DepartmentName>
      <DepartmentManager>Tom Shaw</DepartmentManager>
      <Employee1>
         <EmployeeName>Bob Smith</EmployeeName>
         <EmployeeTitle>Salesperson</EmployeeTitle>
      </Employee1>
      <Employee2>
         <EmployeeName>Karen Stevens</EmployeeName>
         <EmployeeTitle>Salesperson</EmployeeTitle>
      </Employee2>
   </Department>
</Departments>
```

Here, `EmployeeTitle` is the multi-valued repeating attribute. This is not such a problem in XML documents, but as far as database tables go, we should separate out tables for employees:

	Department ID	DepartmentName	DepartmentManager	DepartmentManagerRef
▶	1	Sales	Tom Shaw	3
✳	(AutoNumber)			

	DepartmentID	EmployeeID	EmployeeName	EmployeeJobTitle
	1	1	Bob Smith	Sales Person
	1	2	Karen Stevens	Sales Person
⬦	1	3	Tom Shaw	Sales Manager
✳	0	(AutoNumber)		

Note how the new table gives each record a primary key so that the item can be identified, and so that we can maintain **entity integrity**.

XML can cope with this because we can add a containing employees element, but the important thing that we should look at in terms of XML is how we are going to be looking at the data – what are the **functional dependencies**. If we want to look at employees regardless of their department, then we should store the employee records separately, and reference the department entries as we did in the first example; whereas if we want to look at who works within each department, then the structure we just saw is better. Although we could still adjust it as follows to add a containing `Employees` element, and add a unique identifier to each `Employee` element using the `employeeID` attribute:

```
<Departments>
    <Department id = "1">
        <DepartmentName>Sales</DepartmentName>
        <DepartmentManager>Tom Shaw</DepartmentManager>
        <Employees>
            <Employee employeeID = "1">
                <EmployeeName>Bob Smith</EmployeeName>
                <EmployeeTitle>Sales person</EmployeeTitle>
            </Employee>
            <Employee employeeID = "2">
                <EmployeeName>Karen Stevens</EmployeeName>
                <EmployeeTitle>Sales person</EmployeeTitle>
            </Employee>
        </Employees>
    </Department>
</Departments>
```

Whatever we do, we still need to make sure that we have a unique identifier for each instance of an entity so that we can maintain entity integrity.

Second Normal Form

The second normal form states that:

> **No non-key attributes should depend on a portion of the primary key.**

This constraint only really applies when two or more columns or items of information define the primary key.

The idea is that if the primary key is formed from two separate items of information and that only one of the items of information that makes up the primary key is required to identify an attribute or information item that is part of the entity, then it should be put in a separate table.

As far as this translates to XML, then entities that are identified by a key composed of two different simple types should only be in the same containing element if the composite key value is required to identify the instance of the entity, otherwise they should be separated into separate containing elements.

Third Normal Form

The third normal form states that:

> **No attributes depend on other non-key attributes.**

All columns in the table must contain data about the entity that is uniquely identified by the primary key. This is the requirement that would suggest that we split employee information from department information. You should move any values that do not help define the item that is being uniquely identified by the primary key into another table.

The idea that the columns must contain data about only one thing is an extension of second normal form used to ensure that items that should be in their own table are in a separate table. .

Not all of the child information items of the Employee element represent information about the employee; therefore those that do not should be removed to another containing element. Using this approach, we should split information into two containing elements like so:

```
<StaffList>

    <!-- employees element contains details of each individual employee -->
    <Employees>

        <Employee id = "1">
            <Name>
                <FirstName>Bob</FirstName>
                <LastName>Smith</LastName>
            </Name>
            <JobTitle>Salesperson</JobTitle>
            <Department departmentID = "1" />
        </Employee>

    </Employees>

    <!--Departments element contains details of each individual department-->
    <Departments>

        <Department departmentID = "1">
```

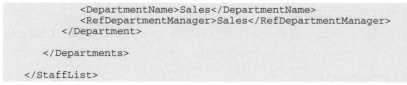

```
            <DepartmentName>Sales</DepartmentName>
            <RefDepartmentManager>Sales</RefDepartmentManager>
        </Department>

    </Departments>

</StaffList>
```

This structure should be familiar to you as the one we used at the start of the chapter.

Domain-Key Normal Form

The domain-key normal form is, theoretically, supposed to represent the ultimate normal form taking into account all possible dependencies and domain constraints. A relation is said to be DKNF if simply enforcing the domain constraints and key constraints on the relation can enforce all constraints and dependencies that should hold on the relation.

Obviously the normal forms do not immediately correspond to XML. But we can apply the thoughts behind them to structure, particularly containing elements, even though they do not transfer directly.

Applying Normalization to XML

As we have seen, the principles behind normalization can apply, or at least teach us valuable lessons, when working with XML documents. While we are not forced to keep to a strict two-dimensional representation of information, because we can make use of the hierarchical nature of XML, we can make use of references to achieve integrity of data and reduce data redundancy.

So, if we were to apply some kind of rules to the authoring of XML documents to achieve the same goals as normalization, what would these rules be? The following **grades** are just one suggested way of increasing the integrity of XML Documents. The higher the grade, the greater the integrity of the data. These grades only indicate levels and do not tie in directly with normal forms in database theory; they incorporate ideas from normal forms of relational databases, as well as those that are inbuilt database mechanisms.

We have split the two types of information up into two classes, and look at them in the context of three different grades of normalization below:

❑ **Document class requirements**: refer to the nature of the schema to be used on the XML document – how strict the constraints it will impose on the XML will be.

❑ **Structural normalization requirements**: refer to concepts that should be checked in terms of normal forms in database theory. Suggestions of ways to structure the data to maximize data integrity.

First Grade XML Normalization

Document class requirements: the document should be well-formed. At the most basic, an XML document is required to be well-formed. So, first grade normalization should, as a bare minimum, require that the document be well formed.

Structural Normalization Suggestions:

❑ If we have repeating element structures (structures consisting of more than one element), we place them in a containing element.

❑ The data in each simple type should be as atomic as required by the application.

Second Grade XML Normalization

Document class requirements: the document should be equally easy to validate using XML Schemas or DTDs.

Structural Normalization Suggestions:

- ❑ Each individual entity should have a unique identifier to ensure entity integrity.

- ❑ Relationships between related entities should be expressed using XML ID and IDREFs if we are working with a DTD, and key and keyrefs if we are working with an XML Schema.

- ❑ Each reference must point to a valid unique identifier.

- ❑ Each sibling element that shares the same parent element should be a constituent part of the containing element. (The exception to this would be wrapper elements – which would be treated as a holder for constituent parts.)

Third Grade XML Normalization

Document class requirements: document instances should ideally be validated by an XML Schema, which makes use of additional facilities over DTDs.

Structural Normalization Suggestions:

- ❑ Each child element or attribute should be directly related to the entity that is uniquely identified by the key of the parent element.

- ❑ Making a change to one unique node set should not affect the integrity of another node set.

- ❑ Each simple type should be given a datatype that describes its content.

XML Domain/key Norm (XML DKNF)

Document class requirements: document instances should be able to be validated by an XML Schema that does not contain any wildcards or substitution groups. All types should prevent derivation. Namespaces should be qualified.

Structural Normalization Suggestions:

- ❑ A unique key should be used to identify each node set.

- ❑ Domain integrity must be preserved.

- ❑ Business rules that can be enforced by a schema must be added.

Of course, as we pointed out at the beginning of this section, XML's ability to nest elements to arbitrary levels allows a lot of flexibility that relational databases do not. However, for those who are not from a database background, some of the ideas that have come from it are interesting and worth considering when designing XML structures.

Working with Document Fragments

In the final section of this chapter we will look at some of the issues regarding working with document fragments. Especially when working with large files, we will often want to work with a document fragment rather than a whole document instance. For example, if we are working with a document-based application that represents information such as books, we might want to be able to work on chapters individually. Alternatively, if we are dealing with data that is being persisted to a large file we might just want to work with a subsection of that document, such as an individual product from a catalogue or inventory. However, there are some considerations that schema authors should be aware of when writing schemas for documents, some of which are particularly important when using the identity constraints that are introduced by XML Schema.

As document size increases, the advantages of being able to work with fragments of these documents becomes clearer – let's look at the advantages of being able to work with such fragments:

Advantage of working with fragments	Example for document-based application	Example for data-oriented application
More than one person can work with the document at a given time, each working on subsections	Different chapters of a book can be worked on by authors, editors, and reviewers simultaneously	Different users of an application can alter different records from the same store at the same time
We can reuse and re-purpose the different sections	We could include a sample chapter of a book on a web site	We could use the details from an inventory to make a list of items that are on special offer
We can store the subsections separately in a system that allows user-management, locks, and security management, such as an XML Server	Chapters can go through an editorial process of revisions	Customer records can maintain information about previous addresses as well as new ones, which is often important for records that span long periods

The key requirements of working with document fragments are that the user should be able to get to the separate pieces of information that they require so that they can deal with them in isolation, and once they have finished with the fragment, they should be able to put them together again to create a larger document.

Working with Fragments

One of the advantages of the XML class and type reuse mechanisms is that they make it easier for a document fragment to conform to a given schema. By very nature, if the subsection of the document that represents a fragment is contained in an element that has a global declaration, then we can validate the fragment using the same schema that we use for the complete document.

The best way to break a document into fragments is though careful use of containing elements that correspond to an entity that needs to be dealt with discretely. For example, if we are dealing with a book, we are likely to want to work with subsections that are chapters. If we are dealing with an e-commerce system, then we are likely to want to deal with individual customers and products. Whatever the split is, our hierarchy should reflect the way in which we are going to use subsections of the document, and the element at the top of each hierarchy that we want to be able to work with separately should be globally declared if we want the same schema to be able to validate that fragment.

> **Each of the globally declared elements can act as a root element for a conforming document instance.**

In order to work with a fragment of this kind of document, we just need to attach a link to the schema, and we are ready to go.

While we can validate any well-formed fragment of an XML document from a globally declared element within a schema, there are still problems with working with well-formed fragments. The first of these relates to the use of XML `ID` and `IDREF` datatypes.

Problems with References and Uniqueness

When working with fragments of documents it is very important that the document does not contain references (whether these are XML `IDREF` or `IDREFS` types, or XML Schema `keyrefs`) that point back to `ID`s or `keys` that are outside of the document fragment.

This is because of the requirement in XML that an `IDREF` datatype points back to a valid `ID`, and because the XML Schema identity constraints require that an XML Schema `keyref` identity constraint has a value for its `refer` attribute that is the same as the vale of a `name` attribute on a corresponding key.

Here you can see that there are instantly going to be problems if:

❑ We have created cross-references in a document-based application that cross the subsections or fragments of a document that you are working with. For example, a table of contents would make references to all of the subject headings in a book. If we are just working on the table of contents without the chapters being in the same documents, then the references to the headings will not work. Furthermore if a document author tries to add a new reference, whose name is already used in another part of the document (say each chapter author tries to use `summary` as a key value, then it will not be unique to the document when reconstructed), there will be an error. On the other hand if an author wants to make a reference to a key that is not in the fragment, they are more likely to make an error – perhaps misspelling it, or even worse trying to use a completely inaccurate one.

❑ We have made heavy use of `key` and `keyref` relationships while trying to normalize our data in a persistent data store. Say we have used normalization principles to relate a purchase order to a customer; if we only collect the purchase order details and not the relevant customer details, the purchase order will try to correspond to a customer and will fail.

There are similar problems when working with a uniqueness constraint, in that if we are editing or authoring a fragment of a document, our fragment will only ensure uniqueness within the fragment; when it is returned to the parent document a collision of values may occur.

Let's look at the problems with the `ID` and `IDREF` datatypes first. We could try to get around the validation problems by editing the schema (either manually, by searching and replacing, or creating an XSL transform) to change all entries of `IDREF` to `NMTOKEN`s. But then we would have to change the appropriate ones back before re-inserting the fragment into the main document.

Alternatively we could create placeholders in the fragment that we are working with. The application would have to remove all elements that have a simple type of ID or IDREF, and elements with attributes whose value was of the type ID or IDREF, before they could be included in the document. If we did take this approach we would have had to add new schema declarations to handle the placeholders for ID and IDREF datatypes:

```
<xs:element name = "IDReferenceHolder">
   <xs:complexType>
      <xs:attribute name = "ID" type = "xs:ID" />
   </xs:complexType>
</xs:element>

<xs:element name = "IDREFReferenceHolder">
   <xs:complexType>
      <xs:attribute name = "IDREF" type = "xs:IDREF" />
   </xs:complexType>
</xs:element>
```

This could be quite a processor intensive job and a complicated add-on to the application. We would also have to resolve all XPaths to the instances of identity constraints and include placeholders for the elements and attributes involved in identity constraints.

In any case, neither of these solutions is a satisfactory solution when working with W3C XML Schema identity constraints.

> **You should avoid are using IDs and IDREFs datatypes in your schemas if you are going to be working with fragments.**

A better solution is to carefully position our schemas' identity constraints outside the range of the fragments we are using, therefore avoiding such problems because the identity constraints will not be processed. As long as the constraints are not in the fragment they will not affect it. This will mean that the constraints are not there for document authors to verify their integrity.

This will solve many types of situation. Although there are two problems that will certainly still apply if we are working with large document-based applications:

❑ An author will not be able to check that references work.

❑ There is no way of ensuring uniqueness throughout a full document instance – only the given fragment. If the author adds a new ID or value used in a key, they won't know if the value or name already exists elsewhere in the larger document.

You have to remember, however, that the advantage of working with fragments is that we do not have to deal with the whole document, and that this is a natural cost of saving bandwidth and freeing up the rest of the document resources. Especially when we are allowing work on fragments in order to facilitate work on different sections of the document at the same time, then there is nothing we can do to prevent another section being altered at the same time, so this is an acceptable process for ensuring that the keys and their references still remain intact and the document fragment can be validated.

What we can do is split validation into a two-step process. First we can validate the fragment of the document against the allowed structure for that section of the document in the schema, while the identity constraints are out of range of the fragment. Once this stage has been performed, we can then validate the document as a whole at the location of the rest of the file, with the fragment inserted. If the fragment is not valid according to the constraints, we do not allow it to be persisted until it does validate, and can offer the author indications of where their fragment is broken.

With regards to ensuring uniqueness, we can adopt naming conventions for the items that are supposed to be unique. These may include:

❑ Leaving the insertion of unique reference numbers (such as primary keys) to the point when the fragment is inserted into the main body of the document, and requiring that the application assign an available number.

❑ Adopting an ordered way of assigning unique identifiers that is unlikely to cause clashes. These may involve use of strategies such as incorporating the fragment author's initials, dates and/or times, or topic-related identifiers.

Problems with Multiple Schemas

Note that the idea of working with multiple schemas to validate subsections would not permit us to validate references that are not included in the fragment. Indeed it can introduce problems of its own if we have a schema for each fragment we are likely to use, and the whole document is validated by a schema that imports or includes these other schemas.

Firstly, the software that is processing the document needs to be aware of any imported schema components that the document uses. If schema components have come from external schemas, then it will need to be able to deal with those as well.

If we are using the same schema to validate all fragments, then this is not a concern, as the necessary declarations will be in the schema. If we are using multiple schemas, however, then we have to add the relevant include, redefine, or import elements to each schema that we are using in order to validate the fragment. To make life easier, we should place all of our include, redefine, and import elements as the first children of the root schema element, so that they can clearly be identified, and we should document them with an annotation element. Because there is potential for schemas to chain the import of other schemas (where we only include or import the topmost schema we will be using, and the other schemas in turn include or import other schemas), we should be careful to document the dependencies of all the schemas and not expect when a schema is used that the type library, for example, will already have been included.

If we were to use chameleon schemas, we would have to carefully look at a problem that could arise because our fragments would be in no namespace, while the main document would have a namespace. This would mean that our instance documents for fragments could not contain namespace qualifiers, whereas these could actually be required in the main document. Furthermore, the chameleon components would not be an option if they contained information that was supposed to be from multiple namespaces.

Context

The next problem we face is one of context. What is the intended context of a fragment, where does it appear in the larger structure? This needs to be known for two key reasons:

❑ So that the application or user knows/understands where the information comes from in the context of the larger document structure

❑ So that, once the fragment has been finished with, it can then be re-inserted into the larger document

By simply treating fragments as documents in their own right we have no context. This will not bother the parser, but if the user of the data wants to know the context (such as how deeply it is nested or what order it is within a set of fragments), then we cannot offer such information. Regarding putting the fragment back, it will require a unique identifier that will inform the user where the fragment came from. A simple solution for this would be an ordered unique identifier on the root element of the fragment, such as `customerID` on a `Customer` element containing customer details, or a `chapterNumber` attribute on a `Chapter` element that contains a chapter of a book.

One solution involves constructing a dummy document for the rest of the structure of the document that the fragment sits in. The dummy structure will contain an empty element for each element in the document. Elements will only have content where the element's simple content takes part in an identity constraint, whereas attributes will only be included if they are required, when their value takes part in an identity constraint, or when their type is an `ID` or `IDREF`.

This not only solves the problems of cross-references, but also that of context. It can, however, incur a large processing overhead when extracting the fragment from the document. While the extraction of fragments is more difficult, re-integration of fragments to the larger document will be far easier. We will have to assess the value of this approach in a couple of ways:

❑ Can we afford the extra bandwidth that the dummy document incurs? Will this negate some of the advantages of working with the document fragment?

❑ Can we cope with the processor resources required to create the dummy document if the load is heavy?

The other thing you can do to make sure that fragments can be re-integrated back into the whole document is to ensure that there is an identifier that indicates where the processing application should re-insert the fragment. This could be a sequential number, an alphabetical identifier, or a programmatic decision.

Summary

In this chapter we have looked at three key areas that affect our authoring of schemas. The first was the introduction of identity constraints. We saw how we could use these identity constraints to enforce uniqueness of a node or node set's value across a document instance. We also saw how we could use `key` and `keyref` mechanisms to show relationships between nodes in a document. These have two important effects on the other two topics we looked at in this chapter.

The second section of this chapter looked at issues that are raised by work with relational databases. We looked at the normal forms that impose structure on a database, which can now be replicated through the use of W3C XML Schema and its key and key reference system. We also looked at a number of other mechanisms that are often enforced by an RDBMS and that we don't see; these – along with the normal forms – protect the stability, security, and accuracy of data. Issues included different forms of data integrity, atomicity, and attributes on fields, which we implemented in terms of W3C XML Schema. Having looked at the individual issues in normalization, we developed some rough grades that we can follow to maintain integrity of our data.

Finally we looked at issues regarding fragments of documents. There are two key problems we face when dealing with fragments of documents. The first is that key and key reference mechanisms (both the new W3C XML Schema identity constraints), and the XML ID and IDREF datatypes require that the value of a reference be in a document instance. In particular, this problem raises serious questions about the use of relationships in XML documents that have to be treated as fragments. However, the key and keyref mechanisms offer a far more flexible solution than IDs and IDREFs, where we can place the reference out of range of the fragment that we are dealing with. The second is that we need a way of representing context of a document. This can be difficult unless there is an order to the document that the user of the document is aware of. This is, nevertheless a problem with any kind of fragment in XML, and one that we should just be aware of when dealing with sections of a document.

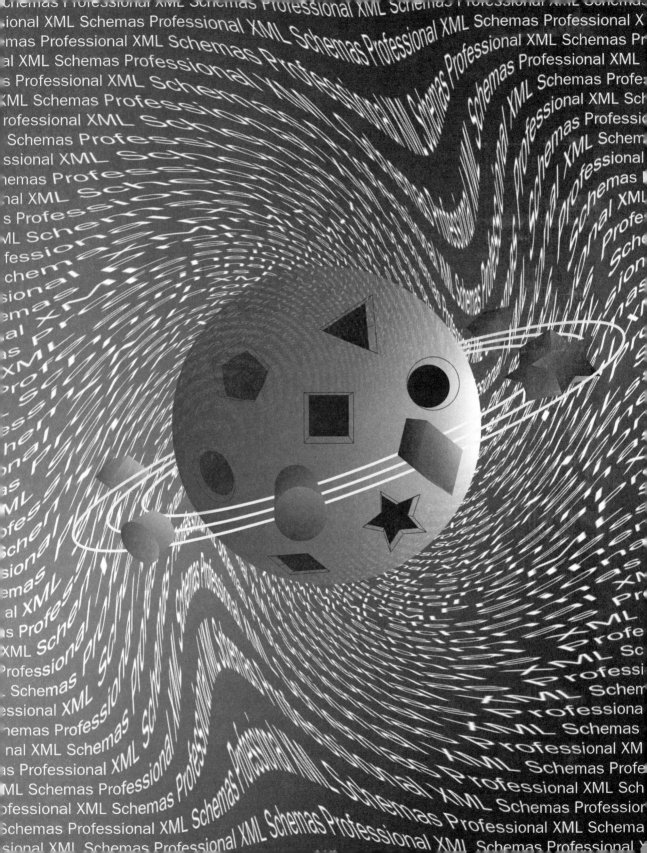

10

Schema and XSLT

It may seem odd to have a chapter on XSLT in a book on XML Schema. After all, one of them deals with transforming XML documents for output, while the other handles defining the structure of an XML document. They are not as incompatible as you might actually think, however, they are not as incompatible as you might actually think – because XML Schemas are themselves XML, XSLTs can be applied to them, allowing you to do all sorts of things with them:

- ❑   Create documentation about a schema.
- ❑   Extract application information from the schema.
- ❑   Create instances of a given schema, such as build a constructor.
- ❑   Present instances using information from a schema.
- ❑   Generate a basic schema from an XML document.

Additionally, schemas can provide lots of useful information to a stylesheet. With a schema and the concept of datatypes in place, you can use the meta-information that a schema provides to build components and determine actions based upon datatype, rather than just upon a specific element name. This is a powerful notion within XML, because it makes it possible to build an object-oriented flavor for the XML language. You could also use a schema to build a basic stylesheet that you can tweak later on.

Unfortunately, there isn't space in this chapter to go into all of these, so we will concentrate on the ways that you might use XSLT on a schema and on an instance of a schema Firstly, looking at creating schema documentation from a schema, and then at creating a form based on a schema with supplementary information from an instance document.

Creating Documentation

One of the primary purposes of a schema is to document a vocabulary. XML documents are only any good if the people that author them, read them and write, the programs that process them have a shared understanding about the elements and attributes that the XML uses.

Schema validation gets us part way there. It tells us that the documents that we write, adhere to the **syntax** of the vocabulary – that we have the right elements and attributes in the right place, that they have the right kind of value, that we've used the right case in the names and so on. It doesn't tell us about the **semantics** of the vocabulary, however what the elements and attributes mean, how they should be interpreted. For that, you need additional documentation; XML Schema supply this using the `xs:documentation` element.

The following extract from the `possibleHouseForSale.xsd` schema gives a good example of documentation in use:

```
<xs:complexType name="PossibleHouseForSale">
   <xs:annotation>
      <xs:documentation>
         This describes a house that is currently being explored to
         potentially put it on the market.
      </xs:documentation>
   </xs:annotation>
   <xs:sequence>
      <xs:element name="title" type="house:Title"/>
      <xs:element name="address" type="house:Address"/>
      <xs:element name="bedrooms" type="xs:nonNegativeInteger">
         <xs:annotation>
            <xs:documentation>
               This gives the number of bedrooms designated for the
               house (though of course not all bedrooms are necessarily
               used as such).
            </xs:documentation>
         </xs:annotation>
      </xs:element>
      <xs:element name="baths" type="house:BathCount"/>
      <xs:element name="houseStyle" type="xs:string">
         <xs:annotation>
            <xs:documentation>
               This is the architectural style of the house.
            </xs:documentation>
         </xs:annotation>
      </xs:element>
      <xs:element name="floors" type="xs:nonNegativeInteger">
         <xs:annotation>
            <xs:documentation>
               This is the number of formal floors that the house
               has (split-level houses are typically described as
               having two floors).
            </xs:documentation>
         </xs:annotation>
      </xs:element>
      <xs:element name="garageCars" type="xs:nonNegativeInteger">
         <xs:annotation>
```

```
            <xs:documentation>
                This describes the number of spaces that the garage has
                set aside for cars. If garageCars is zero, then there is
                no garage.
            </xs:documentation>
        </xs:annotation>
    </xs:element>
    <xs:element name="dateBuilt" type="xs:gYear">
        <xs:annotation>
            <xs:documentation>
                This is the year in which the house was built, as a four
                digit year (for instance, 1995).
            </xs:documentation>
        </xs:annotation>
    </xs:element>
    <xs:element name="condition" type="house:Condition"/>
</xs:sequence>
</xs:complexType>
```

The schema designer has given each element, attribute and, type, a human-readable description that describes what the meaning of each values is, not just what its format and arrangement is.

This is all very well and good, but we wouldn't want to force everyone to wade through the schema to find out all this information – we want the documentation to be readable and navigable. For example, we might want it to be an HTML page, or a nicely formatted PDF document. This is where XSLT comes in. XSLT's purpose in life is to transform XML into other formats; XML Schema is an XML format, so we can use XSLT to create documentation for the schema.

In the rest of this section, we'll look at how to create a stylesheet that turns a schema into an HTML page like the one shown below:

The stylesheet that creates this output from the input schema is discussed in detail in the next few sections. The stylesheet is quite long therefore we'll take it a section at a time, and examine how it works. Along the way, we'll see a few techniques that come in handy when working with schemas with XSLT.

Note that you can find the complete stylesheets from this chapter, along with all the code that accompanies this book, from http://www.wrox.com.

Schema Information

The first level in our documentation stylesheet is the overall look of the page and information about the schema at a global level. The following template sets up a couple of variables to hold the namespace and title for the XML Schema, and then creates an HTML page. It creates a small table to hold the important information about the schema – its target namespace and its version, if it has one – and then goes on to process the rest of the schema:

```
<xsl:template match="xs:schema">
   <xsl:variable name="ns">
      <xsl:value-of select="@targetNamespace" />
      <xsl:if test="not(@targetNamespace)">no namespace</xsl:if>
   </xsl:variable>
   <xsl:variable name="title">
      <xsl:text>XML Schema: </xsl:text>
      <xsl:value-of select="$ns" />
   </xsl:variable>
   <html>
      <head>
         <title><xsl:value-of select="$title" /></title>
         <link href="XMLSchema.css" type="text/css" rel="stylesheet" />
      </head>
      <body>
         <h1><xsl:copy-of select="$title" /></h1>
         <table>
            <tr>
               <th>target namespace</th>
               <td><xsl:value-of select="$ns" /></td>
            </tr>
            <xsl:if test="@version">
               <tr>
                  <th>version</th>
                  <td><xsl:value-of select="@version" /></td>
               </tr>
            </xsl:if>
         </table>
         <xsl:apply-templates />
      </body>
   </html>
</xsl:template>
```

The most important part of our documentation is, naturally, the human-readable annotations in the schema. If we come across these at the top level of the schema, we want to indicate a break in the documentation of the page, with a horizontal rule, and then include the documentation in a paragraph on its own:

```
<xsl:template match="xs:schema/xs:annotation">
  <hr />
  <xsl:apply-templates select="xs:documentation" />
</xsl:template>

<xsl:template match="xs:documentation">
  <p>
    <xsl:apply-templates />
  </p>
</xsl:template>
```

The rest of the page then goes through each of the top-level components in the schema and summarizes them.

Summarizing Components

The documentation for our schema, involves summarizing each of the components within it. We want to have a summary of each of the following types of components:

- element declarations (local and global)
- attribute declarations (local and global)
- simple type definitions
- complex type definitions
- model group definitions
- attribute group definitions
- notation declarations

The types of information that we need to give depend on the component. In general, it follows the pattern of having the name of the component followed by a table that gives any documentation for that component, its target namespace, and then component-specific information such as whether or not it's final.

If we take a look at the template to create documentation for a simple type, we can look more closely at the kind of information that might be given and how it's retrieved:

```
<xsl:template match="xs:element[@name]">
  <xsl:variable name="schema" select="ancestor::xs:schema" />
  <div class="element">
    <h2>
      <span class="label">(element)</span>
      <xsl:value-of select="@name" />
    </h2>
    <table>
      <xsl:apply-templates select="xs:annotation" />
      <tr>
        <th>target namespace</th>
        <td><xsl:apply-templates select="." mode="targetNamespace" /></td>
      </tr>
      <xsl:apply-templates select="@substitutionGroup" />
      <xsl:if test="@final or $schema/@finalDefault">
```

```
      <tr>
        <th>substitution group exclusions</th>
        <td>
          <xsl:apply-templates
           select="@final |
                    $schema/@finalDefault[not(current()/@final)]" />
        </td>
      </tr>
    </xsl:if>
    <xsl:if test="@block or $schema/@blockDefault">
      <tr>
        <th>disallowed substitutions</th>
        <td>
          <xsl:apply-templates
            select="@block |
                    $schema/@blockDefault[not(current()/@block)]" />
        </td>
      </tr>
    </xsl:if>
    <tr>
      <th>abstract</th>
      <td>
        <xsl:choose>
          <xsl:when test="@abstract = 'true' or
                          @abstract = 1">true</xsl:when>
          <xsl:otherwise>false</xsl:otherwise>
        </xsl:choose>
      </td>
    </tr>
    <tr>
      <th>nillable</th>
      <td>
        <xsl:choose>
          <xsl:when test="@nillable = 'true' or
                          @nillable = 1">true</xsl:when>
          <xsl:otherwise>false</xsl:otherwise>
        </xsl:choose>
      </td>
    </tr>
    <xsl:apply-templates select="@fixed | @default" />
    <xsl:apply-templates select="@type" />
  </table>
  <xsl:apply-templates select="xs:complexType" />
 </div>
</xsl:template>
```

Retrieving the Target Namespace

Getting the target namespace for a component is something that we need to do quite a lot, so it's worth adding utility templates to do it for us. For most components, it's simple: you get the value of the targetNamespace attribute on the xs:schema element of the schema, which we may as well store as a global variable as it means we only have to retrieve it once:

```
<xsl:variable name="targetNamespace"
              select="/xs:schema/xs:targetNamespace" />
```

```
<xsl:template match="*" mode="targetNamespace">
   <xsl:choose>
      <xsl:when test="$targetNamespace">
         <xsl:value-of select="$targetNamespace" />
      </xsl:when>
      <xsl:otherwise>no namespace</xsl:otherwise>
   </xsl:choose>
</xsl:template>
```

It's a little more complicated forelement and attribute declarations. If the element or attribute is at the top level of the schema, then it is in the target namespace of the schema. If, however, it occurs within a group or a complex type, then its target namespace depends on the value of its `form` attribute, if it has one, or the `elementFormDefault` or `attributeFormDefault` attribute on its ancestor `xs:schema` element if it doesn't. If this attribute is `qualified`, then the element or attribute takes the target namespace of the schema; if `unqualified` then it is in no namespace. The templates to get the target namespace for `xs:element` and `xs:attribute` are, therefore, as follows:

```
<xsl:template match="xs:element" mode="targetNamespace">
  <xsl:choose>
    <xsl:when
        test="$targetNamespace and
               (parent::xs:schema or @form = 'qualified' or
                ancestor::xs:schema/@elementFormDefault = 'qualified')">
      <xsl:value-of select="$targetNamespace" />
    </xsl:when>
    <xsl:otherwise>no namespace</xsl:otherwise>
  </xsl:choose>
</xsl:template>

<xsl:template match="xs:attribute" mode="targetNamespace">
  <xsl:choose>
    <xsl:when
        test="$targetNamespace and
               (parent::xs:schema or @form = 'qualified' or
                ancestor::xs:schema/@attributeFormDefault = 'qualified')">
      <xsl:value-of select="$targetNamespace" />
    </xsl:when>
    <xsl:otherwise>no namespace</xsl:otherwise>
  </xsl:choose>
</xsl:template>
```

Summarizing List Attributes

The template for `xs:element` above, gives information about the types of derivations that are allowed when substituting the element or adding `xsi:type` attributes in the instance. It does this by applying templates to the `final` attribute on the `xs:element`, if there is one, or the `finalDefault` attribute on the element declaration's ancestor schema, if there isn't one on the `xs:element`. The template in both these cases is the same.

To get a list of the relevant values, you need to have a way of iterating over these values. The easiest types of values to iterate over in XSLT are node values, so you need to have a node set consisting of the possible values for the `final` attribute on the element. The simplest way to do that in XSLT, is to define some inline XML that you access as a variable using the `document()` function.

In the following template, we iterate over the three relevant values with an `xsl:for-each` – if the `final` attribute is equal to the special value `##all`, then all three values are listed. Otherwise, the template only lists those values that appear in the value of the `final` attribute. The attribute value is normalized and spaces added to it, to ensure that other values that might appear in the attribute don't affect the result:

```
<xs:finalValues>
  <xs:value>extension</xs:value>
  <xs:value>restriction</xs:value>
</xs:finalValues>

<xsl:variable name="finalValues"
              select="document('')/*/xs:finalValues/xs:value" />

<xsl:template match="@final | @finalDefault">
  <xsl:variable name="final" select="concat(' ', normalize-space(), ' ')" />
  <xsl:call-template name="list">
    <xsl:with-param name="items"
         select="$finalValues[$final = ' ##all ' or
                         contains($final, concat(' ', ., ' '))]" />
  </xsl:call-template>
</xsl:template>

<xsl:template name="list">
  <xsl:param name="items" />
  <xsl:for-each select="$items">
    <xsl:value-of select="." />
    <xsl:if test="position() != last()">, </xsl:if>
  </xsl:for-each>
</xsl:template>
```

We use a similar approach to document the value of the `block` element on `xs:element`, the `final` and `block` attributes on `xs:complexType`, and the `final` attribute on `xs:simpleType`. The only things that change, are the items that appear in the list.

The other information that appears for element and attribute declarations, simple types and complex types involve standard XSLT mappings from elements and attributes to HTML for display. You can look at the full stylesheet for more details. We'll turn now to a couple of areas that are particularly tricky when creating documentation for, or indeed doing anything else with information from a schema.

Navigating Schemas

The first step in creating any stylesheet that pulls information out of a schema, whether it's documentation or application-specific information, is to set up the basics that will allow us to navigate within the schema.

There are two aspects to navigating schemas:

- ❑ navigating between components
- ❑ navigating between various schema documents

Navigating Between Components

XML Schema involve a lot of referencing of component to component. Element and attribute declarations refer to type definitions. Type definitions refer to other type definitions. Complex type definitions refer to attribute groups and so on.

In the HTML documentation, we're creating, a reference to a component involves creating a local link to an anchor at the point in the page where we talk about the component. When we create the section of the page dedicated to a particular component, we need to create an anchor with a unique ID within the page. The easiest unique ID to get our hands on is one that XSLT creates for you using the generate-id() function. It's handy to put the XSLT for creating an ID in a dedicated template, which we can refer to from elsewhere, because it means that if we need to change how IDs are created later on, we can do just by changing the template. The template's pretty simple given that we're just using the generated ID:

```
<xsl:template match="*" mode="id">
   <xsl:value-of select="generate-id()" />
</xsl:template>
```

When we generate the documentation for an element, for example, we can create an anchor that uses this ID:

```
<xsl:template match="xs:element[@name]">
   ...
   <xsl:variable name="id">
      <xsl:apply-templates select="." mode="id" />
   </xsl:variable>
   <div class="element">
      <h2 id="{$id}">
         <span class="label">(element)</span>
         <xsl:value-of select="@name" />
      </h2>
      ...
   </div>
</xsl:template>
```

When we come across a reference to an element, we need to use this same unique ID to link to the anchor. In order to find that ID, we need to find the xs:element node that the reference points to. You can use XPaths to find these nodes, but it's a lot easier and more efficient to use a key that can take you from the reference to the component that's being referenced.

Key Definitions

Keys are defined in XSLT using xsl:key. The name attribute gives the symbol space for the key, the match attribute gives the type of element that it indexes, and the use attribute gives the way of working out the value by which the element's indexed.

This set up performs the same kind of function as the xs:key element that we met in the last chapter. The name attribute on xsl:key is like the name attribute on xs:key. The match attribute performs the same kind of function as xs:selector and the use attribute does the same kind of thing as xs:field.

XML Schema use a number of symbol spaces for schema components:

- ❑ type definitions
- ❑ attribute declarations
- ❑ element declarations
- ❑ attribute group definitions
- ❑ model group definitions
- ❑ notation declarations

We need to create a key for each of these symbol spaces that matches the elements that declare or define the relevant component and uses the name of the component to index them. These elements can only occur at the top level of a schema, right underneath the xs:schema element – we don't want to match local declarations or definitions.

The key definitions are as follows:

```
<xsl:key name="typeDefinitions"
         match="/xs:schema/xs:simpleType" use="@name" />
<xsl:key name="typeDefinitions"
         match="/xs:schema/xs:complexType" use="@name" />

<xsl:key name="attributeDeclarations"
         match="/xs:schema/xs:attribute" use="@name" />

<xsl:key name="elementDeclarations"
         match="/xs:schema/xs:element" use="@name" />

<xsl:key name="attributeGroupDefinitions"
         match="/xs:schema/xs:attributeGroup" use="@name" />

<xsl:key name="modelGroupDefinitions"
         match="/xs:schema/xs:group" use="@name" />

<xsl:key name="notationDeclarations"
         match="/xs:schema/xs:notation" use="@name" />
```

With these key definitions in place, we can now use the key() function to access a schema component by its name. For example, to get hold of the PossibleHouseForSale complex type definition from above, we can use the following expression, and then examine it and transform it to our heart's content:

```
key('typeDefinitions', 'PossibleHouseForSale')
```

Unfortunately, things aren't quite this simple in XML Schema. As we discussed in Chapter 6, the components that you define or declare in a schema are identified by the target namespace of that schema as well as by their name. For example, the complex type definition that we gave above resides in a schema with a target namespace of http://www.wrox.com/proschema/possibleHouseForSale. When we reference the complex type, we use the prefix associated with that namespace. In the schema extract below, see how the type attribute of the element declaration uses the house prefix declared in the xs:schema element's start tag to point to the complex type definition:

```
<xs:schema xmlns:xs="http://www.w3.org/2001/XMLSchema"
    xmlns:house="http://www.wrox.com/proschema/possibleHouseForSale"
    targetNamespace="http://www.wrox.com/proschema/possibleHouseForSale"
    elementFormDefault="qualified"
    attributeFormDefault="unqualified">

<xs:element name="possibleHouseForSale" type="house:PossibleHouseForSale"/>

<xs:complexType name="PossibleHouseForSale">
  ...
</xs:complexType>

</xs:schema>
```

Fortunately, it's fairly easy to work out the target namespace of a schema by looking at the `xs:schema` element's `targetNamespace` attribute. We can use this to put together key values that include the namespace of the component as well as its local name. For example, the key value that we use for the `PossibleHouseForSale` complex type might be:

```
{http://www.wrox.com/proschema/possibleHouseForSale}PossibleHouseForSale
```

The revised key definitions are therefore:

```
<xsl:key name="typeDefinitions"
        match="/xs:schema/xs:simpleType"
        use="concat('{', ../@targetNamespace, '}', @name)" />
<xsl:key name="typeDefinitions"
        match="/xs:schema/xs:complexType"
        use="concat('{', ../@targetNamespace, '}', @name)" />

<xsl:key name="attributeDeclarations"
        match="/xs:schema/xs:attribute"
        use="concat('{', ../@targetNamespace, '}', @name)" />

<xsl:key name="elementDeclarations"
        match="/xs:schema/xs:element"
        use="concat('{', ../@targetNamespace, '}', @name)" />

<xsl:key name="attributeGroupDefinitions"
        match="/xs:schema/xs:attributeGroup"
        use="concat('{', ../@targetNamespace, '}', @name)" />

<xsl:key name="modelGroupDefinitions"
        match="/xs:schema/xs:group"
        use="concat('{', ../@targetNamespace, '}', @name)" />

<xsl:key name="notationDeclarations"
        match="/xs:schema/xs:notation"
        use="concat('{', ../@targetNamespace, '}', @name)" />
```

Resolving References

Whenever we come across a reference to a top-level component, we need to be able to resolve the reference and work out what component it is. For this we need a utility template. The utility template matches any kind of element in `resolve` mode, takes a `$qname` parameter, and gives back the resolved name in the same format that we used in the key definitions.

Working out what value to use to retrieve the key involves looking at the prefix used in the qualified name and discovering what namespace that prefix is associated with. We can do that by looking at the namespace nodes on the element we're looking at and finding the one whose name is the same as the prefix used in the reference (the string before the ':' in the qualified name). The expression for that is:

```
namespace::*[name() = substring-before($qname, ':')]
```

The rest of the qualified name gives the local name for the component. The utility template looks as follows:

```
<xsl:template match="*" mode="resolve">
   <xsl:param name="qname" />
   <xsl:text>{</xsl:text>
   <xsl:value-of
       select="namespace::*[name() = substring-before($qname, ':')]" />
   <xsl:text>}</xsl:text>
   <xsl:choose>
      <xsl:when test="contains($qname, ':')">
         <xsl:value-of select="substring-after($qname, ':')" />
      </xsl:when>
      <xsl:otherwise><xsl:value-of select="$qname" /></xsl:otherwise>
   </xsl:choose>
</xsl:template>
```

Linking in documentation

In the documentation that we're creating, we want to create HTML links to the part of the page that describes the component that's being referenced. For example, when we come across a type reference from an element, we want to link to the description of that type. To achieve this, we use the `resolve` template above to work out the key value to use with the key, identify the component using the `key()` function, and then apply templates to that component in `id` mode to work out the ID to use in the link. With element references, creating a link looks like:

```
<xsl:template match="xs:element[@ref]">
   <xsl:variable name="name">
      <xsl:apply-templates select="." mode="resolve">
         <xsl:with-param name="qname" select="@ref" />
      </xsl:apply-templates>
   </xsl:variable>
   <xsl:variable name="declaration"
                 select="key('elementDeclarations', $name)" />
   <xsl:variable name="id">
      <xsl:apply-templates select="$declaration" mode="id" />
   </xsl:variable>
   <a href="#{$id}">
      <xsl:value-of select="substring-after($name, '}')" />
   </a>
</xsl:template>
```

Making these links is something that we'll need to do often, so again it's worth making a utility template that will do it for us. This template uses `link` mode, takes a `$qname` parameter to give the string that's being resolved and a `$type` parameter to give the name of the key to use (which defaults to `'typeDefinitions'` since those are the most frequent kinds of references to resolve):

```
<xsl:template match="*" mode="link">
   <xsl:param name="qname" />
   <xsl:param name="type" select="'typeDefinitions'" />
   <xsl:variable name="name">
      <xsl:apply-templates select="." mode="resolve">
         <xsl:with-param name="qname" select="$qname" />
      </xsl:apply-templates>
   </xsl:variable>
   <xsl:variable name="id">
      <xsl:apply-templates select="key($type, $name)" mode="id" />
   </xsl:variable>
   <xsl:choose>
      <xsl:when test="string($id)">
         <a href="#{$id}">
            <xsl:value-of select="$qname" />
         </a>
      </xsl:when>
      <xsl:otherwise><xsl:value-of select="$qname" /></xsl:otherwise>
   </xsl:choose>
</xsl:template>
```

Stylesheets that do other things solely with schemas, such as extract application information, create template documents, or convert XML Schemas into different schema standards, also need to resolve references between schema components, but do other things with the results of this resolution. For example, a stylesheet that created a canonical schema might make a copy of the referenced component.

Navigating Between schemas

In real life, schemas are often made up of several modules. A schema can incorporate other schemas in three ways:

- ❑ by including it
- ❑ by redefining it
- ❑ by importing it

Importing allows a schema to use and reference components in other target namespaces, whereas including and redefining adds components in the target namespace of the existing schema. Adding documentation about each of these components involves applying templates to their content, which we can retrieve using the document() function.

The following template adds some information about included components by accessing the schema located via the schemaLocation attribute on xs:include. Any schemas that are included, redefined or imported into the included schema are themselves described after the included schema.

```
<xsl:template match="xs:include">
   <xsl:variable name="schema"
                 select="document(@schemaLocation, .)/xs:schema" />
   <xsl:variable name="ns">
      <xsl:value-of select="$targetNamespace" />
      <xsl:if test="not($targetNamespace)">no namespace</xsl:if>
   </xsl:variable>
   <h1>Included Schema</h1>
```

```
        <table>
          <tr>
             <th>schema location</th>
             <td><xsl:value-of select="@schemaLocation" /></td>
          </tr>
          <tr>
             <th>target namespace</th>
             <td><xsl:value-of select="$ns" /></td>
          </tr>
          <xsl:if test="$schema/@version">
             <tr>
                <th>version</th>
                <td><xsl:value-of select="$schema/@version" /></td>
             </tr>
          </xsl:if>
        </table>
        <xsl:apply-templates select="$schema/*[not(self::xs:include or
                                                   self::xs:import or
                                                   self::xs:redefine)]" />
        <xsl:apply-templates select="$schema/xs:include | $schema/xs:redefine" />
        <xsl:apply-templates select="$schema/xs:import" />
   </xsl:template>
```

For redefined schemas, the components within the xs:redefine have to be detailed as well as those within the referenced schema itself:

```
<xsl:template match="xs:redefine">
    <xsl:variable name="schema"
                  select="document(@schemaLocation, .)/xs:schema" />
    <xsl:variable name="ns">
       <xsl:value-of select="$targetNamespace" />
       <xsl:if test="not($targetNamespace)">no namespace</xsl:if>
    </xsl:variable>
    <h1>Redefined Schema</h1>
    <table>
       <tr>
          <th>schema location</th>
          <td><xsl:value-of select="@schemaLocation" /></td>
       </tr>
       <tr>
          <th>target namespace</th>
          <td><xsl:value-of select="$ns" /></td>
       </tr>
       <xsl:if test="$schema/@version">
          <tr>
             <th>version</th>
             <td><xsl:value-of select="$schema/@version" /></td>
          </tr>
       </xsl:if>
    </table>
    <xsl:apply-templates select="*" />
    <xsl:apply-templates select="$schema/*[not(self::xs:include or
                                               self::xs:import or
                                               self::xs:redefine)]" />
    <xsl:apply-templates select="$schema/xs:include | $schema/xs:redefine" />
    <xsl:apply-templates select="$schema/xs:import" />
</xsl:template>
```

Imported schemas might give only the namespace of the imported schema, not its location. The namespace for the schema is indicated via the namespace attribute on the xs:import. Otherwise, they can be treated in the same way as included schemas:

```
<xsl:template match="xs:import">
    <xsl:variable name="schema"
                select="document(@schemaLocation, .)/xs:schema" />
    <xsl:variable name="ns">
       <xsl:value-of select="@namespace" />
       <xsl:if test="not(@namespace)">no namespace</xsl:if>
    </xsl:variable>
    <h1>Imported Schema</h1>
    <table>
       <xsl:if test="@schemaLocation">
          <tr>
             <th>schema location</th>
             <td><xsl:value-of select="@schemaLocation" /></td>
          </tr>
       </xsl:if>
       <tr>
          <th>target namespace</th>
          <td><xsl:value-of select="$ns" /></td>
       </tr>
       <xsl:if test="$schema/@version">
          <tr>
             <th>version</th>
             <td><xsl:value-of select="$schema/@version" /></td>
          </tr>
       </xsl:if>
    </table>
    <xsl:apply-templates select="$schema/*[not(self::xs:include or
                                        self::xs:import or
                                        self::xs:redefine)]" />
    <xsl:apply-templates select="$schema/xs:include | $schema/xs:redefine" />
    <xsl:apply-templates select="$schema/xs:import" />
</xsl:template>
```

So getting the information from other schemas that you include, import or redefine is fairly easy. The real challenge is to find the appropriate element for a component, whether it's in the main schema, one of the included ones, or even if redefined. In the last section, we set up a number of keys for retrieving the components from a schema and created a template in link mode to resolve a reference and create a link to the relevant component:

```
<xsl:template match="*" mode="link">
    <xsl:param name="qname" />
    <xsl:param name="type" select="'typeDefinitions'" />
    <xsl:variable name="name">
       <xsl:apply-templates select="." mode="resolve">
          <xsl:with-param name="qname" select="$qname" />
       </xsl:apply-templates>
    </xsl:variable>
    <xsl:variable name="id">
       <xsl:apply-templates select="key($type, $name)" mode="id" />
    </xsl:variable>
    <xsl:choose>
```

```
        <xsl:when test="string($id)">
          <a href="#{$id}">
            <xsl:value-of select="$qname" />
          </a>
        </xsl:when>
        <xsl:otherwise><xsl:value-of select="$qname" /></xsl:otherwise>
      </xsl:choose>
  </xsl:template>
```

Currently, this template only works with one schema. The keys only retrieve components defined at the top level of the main schema. Instead, we need to have this template create links to redefined components, or to included and imported components as necessary. These searches always start from the main schema and identify the generated ID of a component based on its namespace, local name and type. We apply templates to the main schema element in getID mode to retrieve the ID:

```
<xsl:variable name="schema" select="/xs:schema" />

<xsl:template match="*" mode="link">
  <xsl:param name="qname" />
  <xsl:param name="type" select="'typeDefinitions'" />
  <xsl:variable name="name">
    <xsl:apply-templates select="." mode="resolve">
      <xsl:with-param name="qname" select="$qname" />
    </xsl:apply-templates>
  </xsl:variable>
  <xsl:variable name="id">
    <xsl:apply-templates select="$schema" mode="getID">
      <xsl:with-param name="ns"
                      select="substring-before(substring($name, 2), '}')" />
      <xsl:with-param name="localName"
                      select="substring-after($name, '}')" />
      <xsl:with-param name="type" select="$type" />
    </xsl:apply-templates>
  </xsl:variable>
  <xsl:choose>
    <xsl:when test="string($id)">
      <a href="#{$id}"><xsl:value-of select="$qname" /></a>
    </xsl:when>
    <xsl:otherwise><xsl:value-of select="$qname" /></xsl:otherwise>
  </xsl:choose>
</xsl:template>
```

Getting the ID involves searching the schema itself, and any other schemas that are associated with it. Searching a single schema just involves using the keys that we've set up on that schema. Some of these keys need to be modified though, to take into account redefined components. This involves adding more xsl:key elements for redefined types, groups and attribute groups:

```
<xsl:key name="typeDefinitions"
         match="/xs:schema/xs:redefine/xs:simpleType"
         use="concat('{', ../../@targetNamespace, '}', @name)" />
<xsl:key name="typeDefinitions"
         match="/xs:schema/xs:redefine/xs:complexType"
         use="concat('{', ../../@targetNamespace, '}', @name)" />

<xsl:key name="attributeGroupDefinitions"
```

```
        match="/xs:schema/xs:redefine/xs:attributeGroup"
        use="concat('{', ../../@targetNamespace, '}', @name)" />

<xsl:key name="modelGroupDefinitions"
        match="/xs:schema/xs:redefine/xs:group"
        use="concat('{', ../../@targetNamespace, '}', @name)" />
```

With those keys in place, we can access any component that is defined or redefined in the schema through a key. If that doesn't turn up anything, we need to search in the included, redefined and imported schemas themselves, by applying templates to the first of those elements, again in getID mode:

```
<xsl:template match="xs:schema" mode="getID">
  <xsl:param name="ns" />
  <xsl:param name="localName" />
  <xsl:param name="type" select="'typeDefinitions'" />
  <xsl:param name="targetNS" select="@targetNamespace" />
  <xsl:variable name="id">
    <xsl:if test="$targetNS = $ns">
      <xsl:value-of
        select="generate-id(
                  key($type,
                      concat('{', @targetNamespace, '}', $localName)))" />
    </xsl:if>
  </xsl:variable>
  <xsl:choose>
    <xsl:when test="string($id)"><xsl:value-of select="$id" /></xsl:when>
    <xsl:otherwise>
      <xsl:apply-templates mode="getID"
          select="(xs:include | xs:redefine | xs:import)[1]">
        <xsl:with-param name="ns" select="$ns" />
        <xsl:with-param name="localName" select="$localName" />
        <xsl:with-param name="type" select="$type" />
        <xsl:with-param name="targetNS" select="$targetNS" />
      </xsl:apply-templates>
    </xsl:otherwise>
  </xsl:choose>
</xsl:template>
```

The template for xs:import in getID mode involves applying templates to the xs:schema element for the imported schema, if there is one, again in getID mode. If this finds an ID for the reference, then we can return that. Otherwise, we need to move on to the next imported, included or redefined schema in the original schema:

```
<xsl:template match="xs:import" mode="getID">
  <xsl:param name="ns" />
  <xsl:param name="localName" />
  <xsl:param name="type" select="'typeDefinitions'" />
  <xsl:param name="targetNS" select="@namespace" />
  <xsl:variable name="id">
    <xsl:apply-templates select="document(@schemaLocation, .)/xs:schema"
                         mode="getID">
      <xsl:with-param name="ns" select="$ns" />
```

```
            <xsl:with-param name="localName" select="$localName" />
            <xsl:with-param name="type" select="$type" />
            <xsl:with-param name="targetNS" select="@namespace" />
        </xsl:apply-templates>
    </xsl:variable>
    <xsl:choose>
        <xsl:when test="string($id)"><xsl:value-of select="$id" /></xsl:when>
        <xsl:otherwise>
            <xsl:apply-templates mode="getID"
                select="following-sibling::*[self::xs:include or self::xs:redefine
                                            or self::import][1]">
                <xsl:with-param name="ns" select="$ns" />
                <xsl:with-param name="localName" select="$localName" />
                <xsl:with-param name="type" select="$type" />
                <xsl:with-param name="targetNS" select="$targetNS" />
            </xsl:apply-templates>
        </xsl:otherwise>
    </xsl:choose>
</xsl:template>
```

The template for xs:include and xs:redefine is almost the same as that for xs:import, with one difference: the $targetNS parameter remains as it was in the original schema, rather than changing as it does with xs:import. This is because the schemas referenced by xs:include and xs:redefine always use the same target namespace as the schema they're included in.

```
<xsl:template match="xs:include | xs:redefine" mode="getID">
    <xsl:param name="ns" />
    <xsl:param name="localName" />
    <xsl:param name="type" select="'typeDefinitions'" />
    <xsl:param name="targetNS" select="$targetNamespace" />
    <xsl:variable name="id">
        <xsl:apply-templates select="document(@schemaLocation, .)/xs:schema"
                             mode="getID">
            <xsl:with-param name="ns" select="$ns" />
            <xsl:with-param name="localName" select="$localName" />
            <xsl:with-param name="type" select="$type" />
            <xsl:with-param name="targetNS" select="$targetNS" />
        </xsl:apply-templates>
    </xsl:variable>
    <xsl:choose>
        <xsl:when test="string($id)"><xsl:value-of select="$id" /></xsl:when>
        <xsl:otherwise>
            <xsl:apply-templates mode="getID"
                select="following-sibling::*[self::xs:include or self::xs:redefine
                                            or self::import][1]">
                <xsl:with-param name="ns" select="$ns" />
                <xsl:with-param name="localName" select="$localName" />
                <xsl:with-param name="type" select="$type" />
                <xsl:with-param name="targetNS" select="$targetNS" />
            </xsl:apply-templates>
        </xsl:otherwise>
    </xsl:choose>
</xsl:template>
```

These templates for navigating between schemas are useful in other XSLT stylesheets that deal with schemas as well. Rather than getting the ID of a component, you might apply templates to it to get part of the result tree, but the basic pattern remains the same.

Creating a Form

The second example presented in this chapter involves creating a form from a schema and using information from an instance document to populate it. In the last example, we concentrated on processing a schema to get some information about it. Here, we'll look at taking an instance document and using information from the schema to get extra information about the instance.

The HTML page that we're working towards is shown in the screenshot below. Each element and attribute has a corresponding field, with the relevant value plucked from the instance document. Submitting the form updates the XML instance document. The schema provides extra information, for example limiting the values that a particular element can take, giving user-friendly names for the labels, and including placeholders for optional information. The HTML page is shown below:

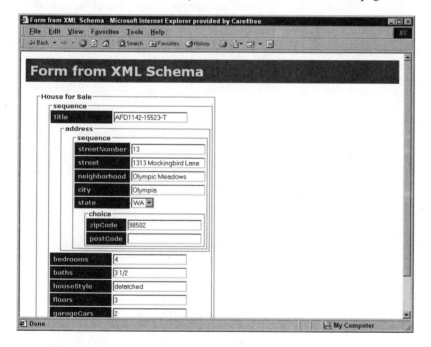

Accessing Schemas from Instances

In this stylesheet, the source document is an instance document that complies with a schema, but we're also going to have to access information from the schema document. Whenever you have more than one document involved in a stylesheet, it's worthwhile keeping the root node of each within a variable, so that's our first task. Getting the root node of the instance document is easy, since that's our source:

```
<xsl:variable name="instance" select="/" />
```

Getting the schema document is a little trickier. There are two ways to use this stylesheet:

- ❑ passing the filename of the schema document explicitly as a parameter
- ❑ leaving it up to the stylesheet to retrieve it for you

Whichever method is used the stylesheet retrieves the root node of the schema document using the `document()` function:

```
<xsl:param name="schemaDoc">
   <xsl:call-template name="schemaLocation">
      <xsl:with-param name="ns" select="namespace-uri($instance/*)" />
   </xsl:call-template>
</xsl:param>
<xsl:variable name="schema" select="document($schemaDoc, $instance)" />
```

The `$schemaDoc` parameter's default value is computed by calling a `schemaLocation` named template. This template takes a namespace URI as a parameter and searches through the schema locations (as given by `xsi:schemaLocation` or `xsi:noNamespaceSchemaLocation`) to find the location of the relevant schema for the namespace:

```
<xsl:variable name="noNamespaceSchemaLocation"
   select="normalize-space($instance/*/@xsi:noNamespaceSchemaLocation)" />
<xsl:variable name="schemaLocation"
   select="normalize-space($instance/*/@xsi:schemaLocation)" />

<xsl:template name="schemaLocation">
   <xsl:param name="ns" />
   <xsl:choose>
      <xsl:when test="$ns">
         <xsl:value-of
            select="substring-before(
                        substring-after(concat(' ', $schemaLocation, ' '),
                                        concat(' ', $ns, ' ')), ' ')" />
      </xsl:when>
      <xsl:otherwise>
         <xsl:value-of select="$noNamespaceSchemaLocation" />
      </xsl:otherwise>
   </xsl:choose>
</xsl:template>
```

The `xsi:schemaLocation` attribute gives a pair (or pairs) of values separated by spaces: the namespace of the schema and the location for the schema for that namespace. As shown in the above code, extracting the relevant location means taking the substring that occurs after the namespace within the schema location string, and then taking the substring before the first space in that string to get the schema location.

Generating Forms

As usual with a stylesheet, the first stage is to create a top-level template that generates the outline of the page. In this stylesheet, this top-level template matches the root node, creates the shape of the page, including the form. The action for the form is set through a parameter. Its content is held in a table (just to make it prettier):

```
<xsl:param name="action" select="'submitForm.asp'" />

<xsl:template match="/">
   <html>
      <head>
         <title>Form from XML Schema</title>
          <link href="XMLSchema.css" type="text/css" rel="stylesheet" />
      </head>
      <body>
         <h1>Form from XML Schema</h1>
         <form action="{$action}">
            <table>
               ...
            </table>
         </form>
      </body>
   </html>
</xsl:template>
```

Generating the content of the form involves setting in motion the general process that will be continued throughout the stylesheet. In the stylesheet we looked at in the first example, the order in which schema components were processed was based on where they were within the schema. The stylesheet worked through the schema component by component, producing a summary for each and pointing to the descriptions of components that were referenced further down the page.

Here, the process is different for two reasons. Firstly, the page that we're generating has a nested structure that follows the structure of an instance document rather than the structure of a schema. This means that we have to follow the references between components to navigate through the schema. Secondly, the page includes information from the instance document. As well as moving through the schema, looking at the components within it, we have to keep track of where we are within the instance document to work out what information should be given in the fields that we generate. However, the process is driven by the schema rather than the instance: the schema has to determine what content is going to appear because it might contain optional or alternative elements and attributes that the instance lacks.

Kicking off the process involves applying templates to the element declaration in the schema that corresponds to the document element in the instance and passing the instance document element as a parameter into that template. We can identify the relevant element declaration using the same key declarations as we used in the last section. To simplify matters, we'll assume that all the declarations are in a single schema rather than having to take account of included and imported schemas.

```
<xsl:template match="/">
   <html>
     <head>
       <title>Form from XML Schema</title>
       <link href="XMLSchema.css" type="text/css" rel="stylesheet" />
     </head>
     <body>
       <h1>Form from XML Schema</h1>
       <form action="{$action}">
         <table>
           <xsl:variable name="docElement" select="*" />
           <xsl:variable name="docElementQName"
               select="concat('{', namespace-uri(*), '}', local-name(*))" />
```

```
         <!-- change context so that the key searches in the schema
              rather than the instance document -->
         <xsl:for-each select="$schema">
           <xsl:apply-templates
               select="key('elementDeclarations', $docElementQName)">
             <xsl:with-param name="node" select="$docElement" />
           </xsl:apply-templates>
         </xsl:for-each>
       </table>
     </form>
   </body>
 </html>
</xsl:template>
```

The form that we're generating needs to contain, for each simple element and attribute, a label and a field that contains the value from the instance. We can work out whether an element has a simple value by looking at its type, which is either the `xs:complexType` or `xs:simpleType` in its content, or the type that it refers to through its `type` attribute.

```
<xsl:template match="xs:element">
   <xsl:param name="node" select="/.." />
   <xsl:param name="id" select="@name" />
   <xsl:variable name="typeName">
      <xsl:apply-templates select="." mode="resolve">
         <xsl:with-param name="qname" select="@type" />
      </xsl:apply-templates>
   </xsl:variable>
   <xsl:variable name="type" select="xs:complexType | xs:simpleType |
                                     key('typeDefinitions', $typeName)" />
   <tr>
      <xsl:choose>
         <xsl:when test="$type[self::xs:complexType]">...</xsl:when>
         <xsl:otherwise>...</xsl:otherwise>
      </xsl:choose>
   </tr>
</xsl:template>
```

If the element has a complex type, then it we can create a `fieldset` to hold the information from the various elements and attributes that it contains, and apply templates to the complex type to generate the content for the `fieldset`. The `legend` for the `fieldset` is the result of applying templates to the `xs:element` in `label` mode; we also use this template to generate the labels when the element is a simple type. We'll look in more detail at generating those labels in the next section.

```
<xsl:template match="xs:element">
  <xsl:param name="node" select="/.." />
  <xsl:param name="id" select="@name" />
  <xsl:variable name="typeName">...</xsl:variable>
  <xsl:variable name="type" select="xs:complexType | xs:simpleType |
                                    key('typeDefinitions', $typeName)" />
  <tr>
    <xsl:choose>
      <xsl:when test="$type[self::xs:complexType]">
        <td colspan="2">
```

```
          <fieldset>
            <legend><xsl:apply-templates select="." mode="label" /></legend>
            <xsl:apply-templates select="$type">
              <xsl:with-param name="node" select="$node" />
              <xsl:with-param name="id" select="$id" />
            </xsl:apply-templates>
          </fieldset>
        </td>
      </xsl:when>
      <xsl:otherwise>...</xsl:otherwise>
    </xsl:choose>
  </tr>
</xsl:template>
```

If the element is a simple type, then we want to generate a label/field pair in the table row. The content of the `label` comes from applying templates to the element in `label` mode, just as the `legend` for the `fieldset` did. If the type is in the XML Schema namespace, then it's a built in type, and the field is provided by the `createInput` named template. The same applies if the `xs:simpleType` element corresponding to the type given for the element can't be found. Otherwise, the stylesheet applies templates to the relevant simple type to create the field.

```
<xsl:template match="xs:element">
  <xsl:param name="node" select="/.." />
  <xsl:param name="id" select="@name" />
  <xsl:variable name="typeName">...</xsl:variable>
  <xsl:variable name="type" select="xs:complexType | xs:simpleType |
                                     key('typeDefinitions', $typeName)" />
  <tr>
    <xsl:choose>
      <xsl:when test="$type[self::xs:complexType]">...</xsl:when>
      <xsl:otherwise>
        <th>
          <label for="{$id}">
            <xsl:apply-templates select="." mode="label" />
          </label>
        </th>
        <xsl:choose>
          <xsl:when
              test="starts-with($typeName,
                                '{http://www.w3.org/2001/XMLSchema}')">
            <td>
              <xsl:call-template name="createInput">
                <xsl:with-param name="type"
                                select="substring-after($typeName, '}')" />
                <xsl:with-param name="value" select="$node" />
                <xsl:with-param name="id" select="$id" />
              </xsl:call-template>
            </td>
          </xsl:when>
          <xsl:otherwise>
            <td>
              <xsl:apply-templates select="$type">
                <xsl:with-param name="node" select="$node" />
                <xsl:with-param name="id" select="$id" />
```

```
              </xsl:apply-templates>
              <xsl:if test="not($type)">
                <xsl:call-template name="createInput">
                  <xsl:with-param name="type" select="'string'" />
                  <xsl:with-param name="value" select="$node" />
                  <xsl:with-param name="id" select="$id" />
                </xsl:call-template>
              </xsl:if>
            </td>
          </xsl:otherwise>
        </xsl:choose>
      </xsl:otherwise>
    </xsl:choose>
  </tr>
</xsl:template>
```

A similar template applies to generating label/value pairs for attributes. The node supplying the value for the relevant element or attribute is passed as a parameter, and this is fed into creating the value for the field again using a parameter.

Creating Labels

The labels that are used for the various parts of the form are generating by applying templates in `label` mode. Labels are used as the legends of fieldsets, as labels for fields in the form, as the displayed text in option lists, and so on.

The text that we use for these labels doesn't necessarily match the name of the component that we're looking at. For example, rather than having the element name `possibleHouseForSale` appear as the legend of a field set, we want to use the more approachable label "House for Sale". We need to access these more user-friendly labels somehow, and the best way to do that is to place them within the application information section of the annotation on the component. For the `possibleHouseForSale` element, for example, we might have:

```
<xs:element name="possibleHouseForSale" type="PossibleHouseForSale">
   <xs:annotation>
      <xs:appinfo>
         <form:label>House for Sale</form:label>
      </xs:appinfo>
   </xs:annotation>
</xs:element>
```

In terms of templates in `label` mode, then, the ideal label is one that comes from the application information in the schema. Other sources of possible label text are the `name` attribute on the component, if it has one, the `value` attribute if we're looking at an enumerated value or, as a last resort, the local name of the component (which comes into play if it's a model group). These possible sources can be accessed through a series of templates. Note that the one accessing the label in the `xs:appinfo` element is given an explicitly high priority, so that it overrides all the other possibilities if it matches:

```
<xsl:template match="*[xs:annotation/xs:appinfo/form:label]"
              mode="label" priority="1">
   <xsl:value-of select="xs:annotation/xs:appinfo/form:label" />
</xsl:template>
```

```
<xsl:template match="*[@name]" mode="label">
   <xsl:value-of select="@name" />
</xsl:template>

<xsl:template match="xs:enumeration" mode="label">
   <xsl:value-of select="@value" />
</xsl:template>

<xsl:template match="*" mode="label">
   <xsl:value-of select="local-name()" />
</xsl:template>
```

Creating Form Fields

The type of field that's generated for a component depends on the type of that component: a boolean value should give a checkbox, a set of enumerated values a drop-down list, and so on. If the HTML that we were creating used applets, we could even have different input types for dates and times.

Fields for built-in types are generated through a `createInput` named template. This takes three parameters: the datatype, the value for the field if there is one, and an `id` for naming the field. As it stands, it's very simple. If the type is `boolean` then it generates a checkbox, checking the checkbox if the value is one of the legal values for boolean `true` (`true` or 1). Otherwise, it just creates a text field with the relevant value:

```
<xsl:template name="createInput">
   <xsl:param name="type" select="'string'" />
   <xsl:param name="value" />
   <xsl:param name="id" />
   <xsl:choose>
      <xsl:when test="$type = 'boolean'">
         <input name="{$id}" type="checkbox">
            <xsl:if test="$value = 'true' or $value = '1'">
               <xsl:attribute name="checked">checked</xsl:attribute>
            </xsl:if>
         </input>
      </xsl:when>
      <xsl:otherwise>
         <input name="{$id}" value="{$value}" />
      </xsl:otherwise>
   </xsl:choose>
</xsl:template>
```

Creating the field for user-derived simple types is a little more complicated. Simple types can be derived in three ways: by restriction, by list and by union. Each of these methods of derivation allows different types of values to be selected within the field. For the purposes of this example, we'll concentrate on derivation by restriction as that is the most common and the simplest one to deal with. The field is generated by applying templates to the `xs:restriction` element via the `xs:simpleType` element:

```
<xsl:template match="xs:simpleType">
   <xsl:param name="node" />
   <xsl:param name="id" />
   <xsl:apply-templates select="xs:restriction | xs:list | xs:union">
```

```
            <xsl:with-param name="node" select="$node" />
            <xsl:with-param name="id" select="$id" />
        </xsl:apply-templates>
    </xsl:template>

    <xsl:template match="xs:simpleType/xs:restriction">
        <xsl:param name="node" />
        <xsl:param name="id" />
        <xsl:choose>
            <xsl:when test="xs:enumeration">
                <select name="{$id}">
                    <xsl:for-each select="xs:enumeration">
                        <option value="{@value}">
                            <xsl:if test="normalize-space($node) = @value">
                                <xsl:attribute name="selected">selected</xsl:attribute>
                            </xsl:if>
                            <xsl:apply-templates select="." mode="label" />
                        </option>
                    </xsl:for-each>
                </select>
            </xsl:when>
            <xsl:otherwise>
                <input value="{$node}" name="{$id}">
                    <xsl:if test="xs:length or xs:maxLength">
                        <xsl:attribute name="maxlength">
                            <xsl:value-of select="(xs:length | xs:maxLength)/@value" />
                        </xsl:attribute>
                    </xsl:if>
                </input>
            </xsl:otherwise>
        </xsl:choose>
    </xsl:template>
```

The above template for xs:restriction recognizes cases where there is a set of enumerated values for the element or attribute and in that case creates a drop-down list of values. The stylesheet generates the text for each option using the templates in label mode that we looked at in the last section. If the node in the instance document (which is still being passed into templates through the $node parameter) takes a particular value, then that value is selected by adding a selected attribute to the option.

If the restriction specifies a length or maxLength facet, then we can add a maxlength attribute to the input element that we create to make sure that the user doesn't enter a value that's longer than the allowed value for the element or attribute.

Other kinds of facets that might be specified in a restriction test the value that's given rather than change how it's specified. While these could be tested server-side, when the form is submitted, ideally we want to test the values client-side to prevent the user from submitting invalid values. We can do this by generating JavaScript using XSLT. For example, the schema might limit the values allowed with a range:

```
<xs:simpleType name="BathCount">
    <xs:restriction base="xs:integer">
        <xs:minInclusive value="1" />
        <xs:maxInclusive value="5" />
    </xs:restriction>
</xs:simpleType>
```

Translating this to some JavaScript, we want a function that tests whether a value is between 1 and 5 (inclusive), and raises an error if it isn't:

```
function test(value) {
    if (value < 1 || value > 5) {
        alert('invalid value');
    }
}
```

We can generate this function dynamically based on the schema, and indeed generate the name of the function that does the testing within the stylesheet:

```
<xsl:template match="xs:simpleType/xs:restriction">
  <xsl:param name="node" />
  <xsl:param name="id" />
  <xsl:choose>
    <xsl:when test="xs:enumeration">...</xsl:when>
    <xsl:otherwise>
      <input value="{$node}" name="{$id}">
        <xsl:if test="xs:length or xs:maxLength">...</xsl:if>
        <xsl:variable name="facets"
                      select="xs:*[not(self::xs:maxLength)]" />
        <xsl:if test="$facets">
          <xsl:variable name="function"
                        select="concat('test', generate-id())" />
          <xsl:attribute name="onblur">
            <xsl:value-of select="$function" />
            <xsl:text>(this.value);</xsl:text>
          </xsl:attribute>
          <script>
            function <xsl:value-of select="$function" />(value) {
                if (<xsl:text />
                <xsl:for-each select="$facets">
                  <xsl:apply-templates select="." />
                  <xsl:if test="position() != last()"> || </xsl:if>
                </xsl:for-each>
                <xsl:text />) {
                    alert('invalid value');
                }
            }
          </script>
        </xsl:if>
      </input>
    </xsl:otherwise>
  </xsl:choose>
</xsl:template>
```

The contents of the test are generated by applying templates to the relevant facets (those aside from the maxLength facet, which has already been catered for with the maxlength attribute on the input). Each facet generates a piece of JavaScript testing the value passed into the function against its value attribute. Most of these are straightforward, but testing the value against a regular expression involves a separate function that we won't examine here.

```
<xsl:template match="xs:minInclusive">
   <xsl:text />value &lt; <xsl:value-of select="@value" />
</xsl:template>

<xsl:template match="xs:maxInclusive">
   <xsl:text />value > <xsl:value-of select="@value" />
</xsl:template>

<xsl:template match="xs:minExclusive">
   <xsl:text />value &lt;= <xsl:value-of select="@value" />
</xsl:template>

<xsl:template match="xs:maxExclusive">
   <xsl:text />value >= <xsl:value-of select="@value" />
</xsl:template>

<xsl:template match="xs:length">
   <xsl:text />value.length &lt; <xsl:value-of select="@value" />
</xsl:template>

<xsl:template match="xs:pattern">
   <xsl:text>!matches(value, '</xsl:text>
   <xsl:value-of select="@value" />')<xsl:text />
</xsl:template>
```

Navigating Model Groups

The final aspect of using XSLT with schemas that we will touch on in this chapter is how to navigate between model groups, keeping track of the correspondence between the particles in the model groups in the schema and the elements in the instance document.

We can do this in XSLT with a two-stage process to guarantee that a particle in a model group is only processed with the nodes that it matches. The first stage involves testing how many nodes a particular particle matches; the second stage then passes the relevant nodes to that particle and lets it handle how those are processed. For a complex type, the stylesheet applies templates first to the complex type's attributes and then to the complex type's model group in `particle` mode:

```
<xsl:template match="xs:complexType">
   <xsl:param name="node" select="/.." />
   <xsl:param name="id" />
   <table>
      <xsl:apply-templates
            select="xs:attribute | xs:attributeGroup | xs:anyAttribute">
         <xsl:with-param name="node" select="$node" />
         <xsl:with-param name="id" select="$id" />
      </xsl:apply-templates>
      <xsl:apply-templates mode="particle"
            select="xs:choice | xs:sequence | xs:group | xs:all">
         <xsl:with-param name="nodes" select="$node/*" />
         <xsl:with-param name="id" select="$id" />
      </xsl:apply-templates>
   </table>
</xsl:template>
```

For sequences and choices, we want to create a fieldset that brackets off the model group from repetitions of that model group or from its previous and following particles:

```
<xsl:template match="xs:sequence | xs:choice" mode="particle">
  <xsl:param name="nodes" select="/.." />
  <xsl:param name="id" />
  <xsl:param name="count" select="1" />
  <tr>
    <td colspan="2">
      <fieldset>
        <legend>
          <xsl:apply-templates select="." mode="label" />
          <xsl:if test="$count > 1">
            <xs:text /> (<xsl:value-of select="$count" />)<xsl:text />
          </xsl:if>
        </legend>
        <table>
          <xsl:apply-templates select="." mode="particleRecurse">
            <xsl:with-param name="nodes" select="$nodes" />
            <xsl:with-param name="id" select="$id" />
            <xsl:with-param name="count" select="$count" />
          </xsl:apply-templates>
        </table>
      </fieldset>
    </td>
  </tr>
</xsl:template>
```

Working through the model group involves recursive templates for each of the types of model group. Each recursion tests to see how many elements the first particle in the model group matches by applying templates to it in test mode. The test mode template returns -1 if it doesn't match any elements, but should – for a sequence this indicates that the instance document is invalid. Otherwise, templates are applied to the particle in particle mode, with the elements that it matches passed as a parameter. The next step in the recursion depends on whether there are still particles in the model group left to process: if there are, then the $particles parameter to the template is set to the particles after the first. Otherwise, if there are still elements left to be dealt with by the model group, then the model group itself has templates applied to it again, incrementing the $count parameter by one.

```
<xsl:template match="xs:sequence" mode="particleRecurse">
  <xsl:param name="nodes" select="/.." />
  <xsl:param name="count" select="1" />
  <xsl:param name="id" />
  <xsl:param name="particles" select="xs:*[not(self::xs:annotation)]" />
  <xsl:variable name="matches">
    <xsl:apply-templates select="$particles[1]" mode="test">
      <xsl:with-param name="nodes" select="$nodes" />
    </xsl:apply-templates>
  </xsl:variable>
  <xsl:choose>
    <xsl:when test="$matches = -1">
      <xsl:message terminate="yes">invalid document</xsl:message>
    </xsl:when>
    <xsl:otherwise>
      <xsl:apply-templates select="$particles[1]" mode="particle">
```

```
            <xsl:with-param name="nodes"
                            select="$nodes[position() &lt;= $matches]" />
        <xsl:with-param name="id"
                            select="concat($id, '.sequence', $count)" />
    </xsl:apply-templates>
    <xsl:variable name="rest" select="$nodes[position() > $matches]" />
    <xsl:choose>
      <xsl:when test="$particles[2]">
        <xsl:apply-templates select="." mode="particleRecurse">
          <xsl:with-param name="nodes" select="$rest" />
          <xsl:with-param name="particles"
                          select="$particles[position() > 1]" />
          <xsl:with-param name="id" select="$id" />
        </xsl:apply-templates>
      </xsl:when>
      <xsl:when test="$rest">
        <xsl:apply-templates select="." mode="particle">
          <xsl:with-param name="nodes" select="$rest" />
          <xsl:with-param name="count" select="$count + 1" />
          <xsl:with-param name="id" select="$id" />
        </xsl:apply-templates>
      </xsl:when>
    </xsl:choose>
  </xsl:otherwise>
  </xsl:choose>
</xsl:template>
```

The template for choice works in a similar fashion. This time, though, the first particle that matches indicates that we can skip through the rest of the particles, and not matching just means that it's time for the next step in the recursion:

```
<xsl:template match="xs:choice" mode="particleRecurse">
  <xsl:param name="nodes" select="/.." />
  <xsl:param name="count" select="1" />
  <xsl:param name="id" />
  <xsl:param name="particles" select="xs:*[not(self::xs:annotation)]" />
  <xsl:variable name="matches">
    <xsl:apply-templates select="$particles[1]" mode="test">
      <xsl:with-param name="nodes" select="$nodes" />
    </xsl:apply-templates>
  </xsl:variable>
  <xsl:choose>
    <xsl:when test="not($matches) or $matches = -1">
      <xsl:apply-templates select="$particles[1]" mode="particle">
        <xsl:with-param name="id" select="concat($id, '.choice', $count)" />
      </xsl:apply-templates>
      <xsl:choose>
        <xsl:when test="$particles[2]">
          <xsl:apply-templates select="." mode="particleRecurse">
            <xsl:with-param name="nodes" select="$nodes" />
            <xsl:with-param name="particles"
                            select="$particles[position() > 1]" />
          <xsl:with-param name="id" select="$id" />
        </xsl:apply-templates>
        </xsl:when>
```

```
            <xsl:otherwise>
              <xsl:message terminate="yes">invalid document</xsl:message>
            </xsl:otherwise>
          </xsl:choose>
        </xsl:when>
        <xsl:when test="number($matches)">
          <xsl:apply-templates select="$particles[1]" mode="particle">
            <xsl:with-param name="nodes"
                            select="$nodes[position() &lt;= $matches]" />
            <xsl:with-param name="id" select="concat($id, '.choice', $count)" />
          </xsl:apply-templates>
          <xsl:for-each select="$particles[position() > 1]">
            <xsl:apply-templates select="." mode="particle">
              <xsl:with-param name="id"
                              select="concat($id, '.choice', $count)" />
            </xsl:apply-templates>
          </xsl:for-each>
          <xsl:variable name="rest" select="$nodes[position() > $matches]" />
          <xsl:if test="$rest">
            <xsl:apply-templates select="." mode="particle">
              <xsl:with-param name="nodes" select="$rest" />
              <xsl:with-param name="count" select="$count + 1" />
              <xsl:with-param name="id" select="$id" />
            </xsl:apply-templates>
          </xsl:if>
        </xsl:when>
      </xsl:choose>
    </xsl:template>
```

The template matching xs:element in particle mode either applies templates to the xs:element in normal mode repeatedly, once for each element passed into the template, or applies templates just once without any nodes being passed in (if the element isn't present in the instance document):

```
<xsl:template match="xs:element" mode="particle">
  <xsl:param name="nodes" select="/.." />
  <xsl:param name="id" />
  <xsl:variable name="ele" select="." />
  <xsl:choose>
    <xsl:when test="$nodes">
      <xsl:for-each select="$nodes">
        <xsl:apply-templates select="$ele">
          <xsl:with-param name="node" select="." />
          <xsl:with-param name="id">
            <xsl:value-of select="$id" />.<xsl:text />
            <xsl:value-of select="$ele/@name" />
            <xsl:if test="$nodes[2]">
              <xsl:value-of select="position()" />
            </xsl:if>
          </xsl:with-param>
        </xsl:apply-templates>
      </xsl:for-each>
    </xsl:when>
    <xsl:otherwise>
      <xsl:apply-templates select="$ele">
        <xsl:with-param name="id" select="concat($id, '.', $ele/@name)" />
      </xsl:apply-templates>
    </xsl:otherwise>
  </xsl:choose>
</xsl:template>
```

An integral part of the strategy for working through model groups is being able to work out how many elements in a list match a particular particle. This is calculated by applying templates to that particle in `test` mode. For sequences, we sum the number of elements matched by each of its particles in turn. Calculating this sum has to be done recursively by working through the particles one by one in a similar way to how they're worked through during the main part of the process. The `minOccurs` and `maxOccurs` attributes on the `xs:sequence` form the boundary conditions for the maximum and minimum number of times that the sequence can match elements in the set that it's passed.

```
<xsl:template match="xs:sequence" mode="test">
  <xsl:param name="nodes" select="/.." />
  <xsl:param name="count" select="1" />
  <xsl:param name="particles" select="xs:*[not(self::xs:annotation)]" />
  <xsl:param name="sum" select="0" />
  <xsl:variable name="minOccurs">
    <xsl:value-of select="@minOccurs" />
    <xsl:if test="not(@minOccurs)">1</xsl:if>
  </xsl:variable>
  <xsl:variable name="maxOccurs">
    <xsl:value-of select="@maxOccurs" />
    <xsl:if test="not(@maxOccurs)">1</xsl:if>
  </xsl:variable>
  <xsl:choose>
    <xsl:when test="$count > $maxOccurs">
      <xsl:value-of select="$sum" />
    </xsl:when>
    <xsl:otherwise>
      <xsl:variable name="matches">
        <xsl:apply-templates select="$particles[1]" mode="test">
          <xsl:with-param name="nodes" select="$nodes" />
        </xsl:apply-templates>
      </xsl:variable>
      <xsl:choose>
        <xsl:when test="$matches = -1">
          <xsl:choose>
            <xsl:when test="$count &lt;= $minOccurs">-1</xsl:when>
            <xsl:otherwise><xsl:value-of select="$sum" /></xsl:otherwise>
          </xsl:choose>
        </xsl:when>
        <xsl:when test="$particles[2]">
          <xsl:apply-templates select="." mode="test">
            <xsl:with-param name="nodes"
                            select="$nodes[position() > $matches]" />
            <xsl:with-param name="count" select="$count" />
            <xsl:with-param name="particles"
                            select="$particles[position() > 1]" />
            <xsl:with-param name="sum" select="$sum + $matches" />
          </xsl:apply-templates>
        </xsl:when>
        <xsl:otherwise>
          <xsl:apply-templates select="." mode="test">
            <xsl:with-param name="nodes"
                            select="$nodes[position() > $matches]" />
            <xsl:with-param name="count" select="$count + 1" />
            <xsl:with-param name="sum" select="$sum + $matches" />
          </xsl:apply-templates>
        </xsl:otherwise>
      </xsl:choose>
    </xsl:otherwise>
  </xsl:choose>
</xsl:template>
```

The test mode template for choices works in a similar way, but each repetition of the choice only involves adding the number of elements matched by the first particle in the choice that matches to the sum of elements that the choice matches.

```
<xsl:template match="xs:choice" mode="test">
  <xsl:param name="nodes" select="/.." />
  <xsl:param name="count" select="1" />
  <xsl:param name="particles" select="xs:*[not(self::xs:annotation)]" />
  <xsl:param name="sum" select="0" />
  <xsl:variable name="minOccurs">
    <xsl:value-of select="@minOccurs" />
    <xsl:if test="not(@minOccurs)">1</xsl:if>
  </xsl:variable>
  <xsl:variable name="maxOccurs">
    <xsl:value-of select="@maxOccurs" />
    <xsl:if test="not(@maxOccurs)">1</xsl:if>
  </xsl:variable>
  <xsl:choose>
    <xsl:when test="$count > $maxOccurs">
      <xsl:value-of select="$sum" />
    </xsl:when>
    <xsl:otherwise>
      <xsl:variable name="matches">
        <xsl:apply-templates select="$particles[1]" mode="test">
          <xsl:with-param name="nodes" select="$nodes" />
        </xsl:apply-templates>
      </xsl:variable>
      <xsl:choose>
        <xsl:when test="$matches = 0 or $matches = -1">
          <xsl:choose>
            <xsl:when test="$particles[2]">
              <xsl:apply-templates select="." mode="test">
                <xsl:with-param name="nodes" select="$nodes" />
                <xsl:with-param name="count" select="$count" />
                <xsl:with-param name="particles"
                                select="$particles[position() > 1]" />
                <xsl:with-param name="sum" select="$sum" />
              </xsl:apply-templates>
            </xsl:when>
            <xsl:when test="$count &lt;= $minOccurs">-1</xsl:when>
            <xsl:otherwise><xsl:value-of select="$sum" /></xsl:otherwise>
          </xsl:choose>
        </xsl:when>
        <xsl:otherwise>
          <xsl:apply-templates select="." mode="test">
            <xsl:with-param name="nodes"
                            select="$nodes[position() > $matches]" />
            <xsl:with-param name="count" select="$count + 1" />
            <xsl:with-param name="sum" select="$sum + $matches" />
          </xsl:apply-templates>
        </xsl:otherwise>
      </xsl:choose>
    </xsl:otherwise>
  </xsl:choose>
</xsl:template>
```

Finally, the test mode template for xs:element returns the number of elements from the list that it's passed that match the element. It does this by comparing the expanded name of the first element in the list with the expanded name indicated by the element declaration or reference. Again, we use the resolve and targetNamespace templates that we created near the start of this chapter to identify the expanded name of the element:

```
<xsl:template match="xs:element" mode="test">
  <xsl:param name="nodes" select="/.." />
  <xsl:param name="count" select="1" />
  <xsl:param name="sum" select="0" />
  <xsl:variable name="minOccurs">
    <xsl:value-of select="@minOccurs" />
    <xsl:if test="not(@minOccurs)">1</xsl:if>
  </xsl:variable>
  <xsl:variable name="maxOccurs">
    <xsl:value-of select="@maxOccurs" />
    <xsl:if test="not(@maxOccurs)">1</xsl:if>
  </xsl:variable>
  <xsl:choose>
    <xsl:when test="$count &gt; $maxOccurs">
      <xsl:value-of select="$sum" />
    </xsl:when>
    <xsl:otherwise>
      <xsl:variable name="nodeName"
                    select="concat('{', namespace-uri($nodes[1]), '}',
                                   local-name($nodes[1]))" />
      <xsl:variable name="eleName">
        <xsl:choose>
          <xsl:when test="@ref">
            <xsl:apply-templates select="." mode="resolve">
              <xsl:with-param name="qname" select="@ref" />
            </xsl:apply-templates>
          </xsl:when>
          <xsl:otherwise>
            <xsl:text>{</xsl:text>
            <xsl:apply-templates select="." mode="targetNamespace" />
            <xsl:text />}<xsl:value-of select="@name" />
          </xsl:otherwise>
        </xsl:choose>
      </xsl:variable>
      <xsl:variable name="match" select="$nodeName = $eleName" />
      <xsl:choose>
        <xsl:when test="$match">
          <xsl:apply-templates select="." mode="test">
            <xsl:with-param name="nodes" select="$nodes[position() > 1]" />
            <xsl:with-param name="count" select="$count + 1" />
            <xsl:with-param name="sum" select="$sum + 1" />
          </xsl:apply-templates>
        </xsl:when>
        <xsl:when test="$count &lt; $minOccurs">-1</xsl:when>
        <xsl:otherwise>
          <xsl:value-of select="$sum" />
        </xsl:otherwise>
      </xsl:choose>
    </xsl:otherwise>
  </xsl:choose>
</xsl:template>
```

The templates for xs:all model groups and named model groups (xs:group) follow similar patterns to these: a test mode template to see how many nodes it matches, a particle mode template to do the real processing, and a particleRecurse mode template to recurse over the particles in the model group.

Summary

In this chapter, we've gone into depth about how to use XSLT with XML Schemas in two representative ways:

❑   working through schemas on their own

❑   working through schemas in conjunction with an instance document

These two ways of processing schemas with XSLT form the basis of many useful transformations. We've looked at pulling out schema documentation and creating forms, but the same basic approaches apply to creating template instance documents, extracting information about schema adjuncts like Schematron and so on. Hopefully this chapter has given you a taste of how to go about processing schemas using XSLT and highlighted some of the pitfalls involved and how to get around them, especially:

❑   identifying schema components through references

❑   working with multiple schemas

❑   navigating through model groups while keeping track of instance elements

This chapter has also highlighted how useful annotations can be. The documentation part of an annotation can be used to provide human-readable information about a schema, or to provide help text about information within an instance. The application information that annotations offer can be used within XSLT or during any other processing to guide the process or again to provide user-friendly labels, including language-specific ones.

The range of ways in which you can use XSLT with XML Schema is testament to one of the biggest advantages that this schema language holds over DTDs: it's written in XML. It's due to this that XSLT, XML editors and other XML-based tools can be used with XML Schema just as they can with any other XML vocabulary.

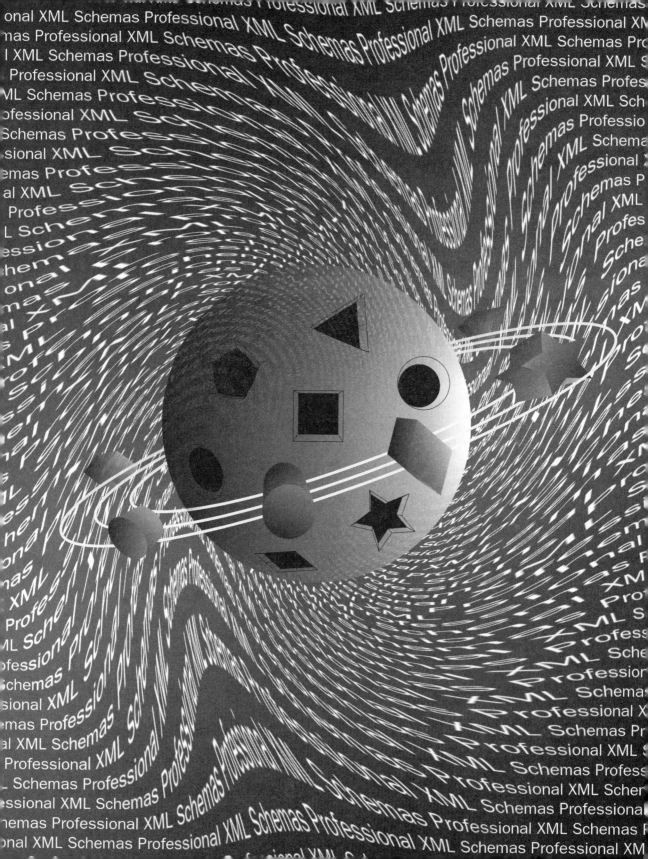

XML System Modeling

Incorporating XML into a business system will require modeling in order to best integrate the new technology into the existing process. This chapter will discuss the two main areas of modeling relevant to such an undertaking:

- ❑ **Information Modeling** – how to identify and represent the objects, properties, and relationships between those objects within the system.

- ❑ **Process Modeling** – what is the business process to be implemented and how the objects are processed throughout their lifetime within the system.

This chapter will take you through the following areas:

- ❑ Establishing system requirements and business process analysis

- ❑ Where in the project to apply XML and XML Schema

- ❑ Graphical UML modeling techniques and system abstraction

- ❑ Information modeling, datatypes, and business rules

- ❑ Creating XML instance documents and a data model for them in XML Schema

In this chapter, we will survey the field of system modeling and cover a basic methodology for taking high-level business goals and creating a cohesive system, effectively incorporating XML. The discussion will focus on the XML and XML Schema side of the system, looking in detail at building the framework that XML will fit into, but often only touching on issues of project management, which require significant attention in their own right but are beyond the scope of this book.

Principles for Data Modeling

A healthy dose of pragmatism and goal-oriented attitudes are required when embarking on this system modeling excursion, in case we find ourselves in:

> *"...the discouraging experience of watching the work funnel into a black hole of diagrams and documents, seldom allowing the escape of an illuminating ray of understanding." – Applied Information Science (www.aisintl.com).*

There are five broad principles that will guide our modeling efforts:

❑ **Complete** – the information model must capture the full set of necessary data, and the processing model must cover a well defined set of use cases

❑ **Meaningful** – the information model aims to represent the "real world" data in a way that is intuitive

❑ **Efficient** – the data organization and syntax is simple and clear

❑ **Unambiguous** – boundaries between acceptable and unacceptable data must exist, and processing behavior under all possible paths must be defined

❑ **Maintainable** – the overall model and its components must be clearly organized and sufficiently simple to be easily maintained in order to be useful during the projects development phase and into its active use

A Simplified Modeling Approach

The modeling world has a vocabulary of its own, with each tool vendor creating their own variations. Historically there are three modeling camps:

❑ **Systems Architects** – concerned with high level system design, business requirements, and process interaction. Generally process centric.

❑ **Database Designers** – concerned almost exclusively with data definitions, usually represented in relational database tables, therefore in the data normalization process. Generally data centric.

❑ **Software Developers** – designing object-oriented (OO) software with class hierarchies and functionality encapsulated with the associated data. Generally object-behavior and application centric.

Modeling for XML is a cross between database design and object-oriented software design. Database design is very data-centric, as is XML, and OO software focuses very much on hierarchical constructs. XML combines both of these; however, the Entity/Attribute terms from database modeling conflict with key terms used in XML but have completely different meanings, and Class/Property from OO software design do not have the right semantics for XML. As a result, we have chosen to use terms which do not clash with common XML vocabulary, are less associated with DB or programming constructs, and are relatively free of vendor specific variations. Furthermore, we have endeavored to simplify the range of terms into something manageable for someone new to this field.

Please note that my usage of modeling terms does not adhere strictly to those defined by UML. Please see the section on *UML and XML Modeling* at the end of this chapter for a further discussion on this.

Summarized below is a glossary of useful terms, which will crop up throughout this chapter:

❑ **Actor** – a person who interacts with the system in some well defined way.
❑ **Agent** – an external system that interacts with the system in question.

Synonyms:	Actor (in UML)

❑ **Information Model** – a description of all objects, properties, hierarchies, and relationships.

Synonyms:	Static Model
Related terms:	Data Model, Entity Relationship Diagram, Conceptual Data Model (CDM) Diagram, Class Diagram, Object Diagram, Physical Data Model (PDM), Object Oriented Model (OOM), Object Model

❑ **Instance** – The actual instantiation of an object within the live system (as opposed to the object representation within the model).

Synonyms:	Object (in software design terms)

❑ **Object** – a logical information block generally encapsulating real world items. This is different from OO software where an object is an instance of a class. One example is an "Address" *object*, which has a specific definition (street, city, postcode, etc.) – compare this to an "Address" *instance* (34 Elm Street, Chester, CH7652).

Synonyms:	Entity, Class
Related terms:	Package, Component

❑ **Processing Model** – a description of how the objects move through the system when it is in operation. This includes the generation, manipulation, and transmission of objects. Sequence and use case diagrams graphically illustrate aspects of the processing model.

Synonyms:	Process Model, Object Interaction Diagram, Implementation Diagram, Dynamic Model
Related terms:	Deployment Diagram, Component Diagram

❑ **Property** – a descriptive aspect of an object.

Synonyms:	Attribute

❑ **Relationship** – a link between related objects also containing the terms of that relationship. This could apply either to specific instances or to general types.

Synonyms:	Association
Related terms:	Composition, Aggregation, Inheritance

❑ **Sequence Model** – the time ordered sequence of events, which occur for a given operation. Usually details the steps of a particular use case.

Related terms:	Activity Graph, Collaboration Diagram, State Chart, State Machine, Work Flow Model, Data Flow Model, Object Life Histories

❑ **State** – the "value" of an object instance at a particular point in time, *or* the place in the processing system that a particular transaction lies.

❑ **Use Case** – describes a common operation within the system and the parties involved in that operation.

The figure below illustrates the associations between these terms and acts as a checklist for the modeling process, which we will repeatedly refer back to. The arrows point from more specific components to more general components, with the dotted line indicating a non-hierarchical association between two components:

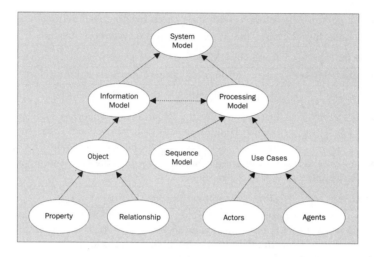

Actors are people who interact with the system and have particular expectations for the behavior of the system and goals in mind, which are motivating their use of the system. **Agents** are external systems whose behavior is fixed and which interact with the system. The actors and agents interact in various **use cases**, which describe a particular use for the system. The **sequence model** captures all possible paths through the system. Together the use cases and sequence model represent the **processing model**, which captures on one level the application processing model, and on another realizes the business goals, process, or problem that the system is meant to improve or implement. The application-processing model is quite distinct from the business process model. However, at a "pre-implementation" level, the overview of the application-processing model must be such that it achieves the goals of the business process.

The processing model is tied to the **information model**, which represents the information objects within the system and the relationships between those objects. **Objects** represent the pieces of information within the system. A set of **properties** belongs to an object and contains the actual information about the object. Objects are associated with each other through **relationships**, which may describe a hierarchy of objects, or may represent inter-object dependencies. Together the information model and the processing model make up the **system model**.

Objects versus Instances

Finally there are **instances,** which have a particular **state**. These are best described by contrasting them to **objects** and **properties**. Take a postal address for example. An Address object would have properties such as `Street`, `City`, and `Postal Code`, and certain general restrictions on these properties (`City` must be from a restricted list, or `Postal Code` must match a particular pattern). The `Address` object would have a certain place within the system and have general relationships to other objects (such as `Person`, `Business`, and `Shipping Details`), as well as the places in the processing model where it is used (say `Order Delivery`, or `Mail Shot`). The object and its properties are a template for a particular instance. An Address instance could be "34 Elm Street, Chester, CH7652", or "5423 High Street, Newcastle, NC1184", or any other combination of `Street`, `City`, and `Postal Code`, however there is only one definition of the `Address` object within this system (note that another system may have multiple types of `Address` object). "34 Elm Street", "Chester", and "CH7652" are the state of a particular instance. Instances only "exist" within the live system, whereas objects are an overview of the "sorts of things" the system can contain. Put another way, objects are a part of the information model of the system, whereas the set of instances and their state comprise the information within the live system at any given point in time.

A further point is that there are two distinct types of "state": the state of the application or system, and the state of instances within the system. Application state would be things such as "Collating Totals" or "Verifying Credentials" or "Entering Phone Number". This sort of state is well represented by finite state machines (FSM) or process flow diagrams. Instance state refers to the specific values of the information within an instance such as "546" or "Golf Balls" or "Charles Gough". This kind of state would often be stored in a database if it were necessary for it to persist.

We will use "application state" or "instance state" as appropriate if the context does not clearly disambiguate it. However, in the process of modeling we will generally be more interested in objects, and will only refer to instances when covering examples in a functioning system.

Magazine Publisher Goes XML

Now that we have familiarized ourselves with some basic modeling terminology and charted a plan for preparing a system model, let's start to build up an example that we can follow through the chapter. The directors of "Bike Zone Magazine" want to improve their business organization and have hired us to modernize their IT system. After the infrastructure issues have been sorted out, we decide to focus on two aspects of their publishing business: distribution, and a paperless editing and production system. Online publication is also a big issue for them, and we are aiming to arrange the editing and production process such that it will easily integrate with a web server and a web design department, although we will not focus here on discussing the online publication process.

Establishing System Requirements

The first stage of any project will be to establish exactly what the goal or problem to be solved is. It is important to establish where in the planning stage we have come in. Occasionally the project will be very well specified, with clear goals and timelines, a full project team, and the support of all the people affected by the process. Other times we are in complete control and perhaps have even initiated the project ourselves. We are both the business domain expert and the technical expert, who will single handedly put together a data management, processing, and archiving system. In this case we have complete freedom to do what we like with the project in the time available. In some instances it will be difficult to establish who is in control or what the objectives are – this is an excellent opportunity for an organized individual to bring order out of chaos and save the project with a whiz-bang buzz-word compliant B2B XML EAI solution leveraging peer to peer web services and producing a secure Internet based digital marketplace.

Most of the time, however, we will be happy to simply improve a real world business process using Internet technology and our knowledge of XML, XML Schemas, and data modeling.

When gathering requirements, remember the following adage:

> **The Customer is King!**

You must identify who the "customer" is for the system and then always keep in mind that the system must be working to provide for their needs, rather than your desire for a feature packed application. The end users must specify their list of prioritized "must see" items for product acceptance, and where the project is speculative you should appoint someone to be the customer by proxy.

Although these techniques apply equally well to projects starting from scratch as to existing system redesigns, we will choose the point of view that the project is adding XML as a new and improved aspect of some business process. Furthermore, for the purposes of this chapter we will assume that we are involved in the project as technical experts rather than as the business domain expert, and therefore will be relying on the business expert to convey their understanding of the process, which we are implementing (whether from new, or through an upgrade).

XML is generally applied to some combination of the following three functions:

❑ **Data archiving** – characterized by long-term storage and information representation.

❑ **Message passing** – characterized by transient information with a short lifespan, usually application to application, where process is the predominant feature.

❑ **Presentation documents** – descriptive documents where formatting markup is likely to be mixed with data markup and readability/presentation quality is the primary goal.

There will be a different emphasis for what and how we model, depending on the particular system. Consider the following questions:

1. Who has initiated this project and why?

2. What are the goals and timelines, and what will be used to measure success of the project?

3. What are our terms of reference? In other words, what is the sphere of influence we have on the project?

4. How is the business process currently handled?

5. Who is affected by the project?

6. Who are the domain experts who understand the business requirements for the data being processed?

7. What are the source and destination of the data in the system?

In order to answer these, we should consider ourselves on an investigation, armed with notepad and pen, and be prepared to make phone calls, hold interviews, and arrange meetings with the people in the know. From this we will have established a contact list consisting of domain experts who define the data, data users who are involved in the actual receipt, distribution, and manipulation of the data, and generators who create the data in the first place.

While we are assuming people are involved at each stage, it may be that some or all of the existing system is already automated; however, the same principles apply. If there are existing automated systems which are to be replaced or integrated with the new system, it is critical to have clear interface definitions of the expected input and output, keeping in mind that there are usually two categories of input/output: the actual data under question, and the control information which tells the automated system how to operate on the data. If interface documentation is unavailable, you must proceed with great caution and consider any access to that system as risky, as its behavior under different circumstances is unknown.

Magazine Publisher Background

We have asked the above questions of the Vice President of Bike Zone Magazine, and discovered that this project is part of an aggressive business expansion initiative aimed at modernizing the infrastructure and expanding the profile and distribution of Bike Zone Magazine. Specifically, the VP has stated that they want to have a much larger online presence, possibly moving to full online publication of the magazine. They also want to streamline their distribution mechanism and go to more of a paperless production and editorial system to facilitate regional contributors and home workers. They do not have much in-house technical experience for their IT systems, so it is fairly open territory, however, they are looking to get something into place in the next three months, and have budgeted for a team of four external consultants. The distribution department consists of seven staff and one manager, while the production and editorial department consists of thirty staff, with a number of editors and two production managers. They currently have a professional publishing software suite that utilizes a data warehouse for archiving stories, photos, and production material. The rest of the business runs off a combination of paper files and an assortment of software packages on the company intranet.

Expect the Unexpected

Even in the presence of strong documentation and technical experts for the existing system, it is possible to have unexpected complications late in the game. A case in point: days before the go-live date on a new XML message processing system, our client realized that the old system, to which we were passing data, did not accept the pipe character (|) as part of the input, since it was used internally as a field delimiter. This sparked a debate over whether to modify and reissue the schemas for the system to the developers, or add in additional processing to transform or remove the pipe character. Neither were desirable because the developers had been told some time earlier that the schema for the XML messages was fixed, and because the system was supposed to retain the submitted data in its original form (no filtering or transformations). The opening section of the new system documentation (which was available months earlier) clearly documented the proposed character set, and so detailed that the pipe character was to be included.

We had clear documentation of the intended implementation and acceptance by the administrators of the legacy system to which we were going to interface, and still at the 11th hour we discovered unacceptable incompatibilities. This particular problem was solved by a schema change to remove the offending character, although an alternative could have been to filter out all pipe characters, and document this as an addendum of the system behavior. While this particular problem could have been revealed by more exhaustive testing, the greater lesson learned is the need for flexibility.

Identify Key Players

The key players must be identified and should be solicited to sign off on the acceptance of the final system. It is important to gain the support and input of those who will be involved in working with the data on a day-to-day basis; however, the responsibility of producing the information model, the processing model, and the system implementation should be reserved for the technical experts such as ourselves – design by committee is doomed to failure.

I recall sitting in meetings with over fifteen people and a whiteboard trying to agree on the arrangement of an XML document and its corresponding schema. Not surprisingly, after several meetings, and no noticeable progress, we decided to hand the task over to XML consultants to prepare on their own, with reports back to the committee at regular intervals. This allowed the business domain experts to focus on the task of ensuring that all the required business data was represented, while the technical domain experts were able to apply their expertise to the organization and modeling of that business data into XML and a corresponding processing application. The meetings that followed then consisted of discussing the business process and the information model, rather than the specifics of an XML Schema and its implied instance documents.

Requirements Definition and Analysis

Based on the gathered feedback it will now be necessary to summarize a list of what we understand to be the requirements of the system. It is very rare that the people who initiated the project will have taken the time or even had sufficient understanding of their own needs to formalize a complete and succinct list of requirements. It is not acceptable to assume that the business domain experts completely understand their own requirements – so we must take it upon ourselves to draft a proposal of the system requirements.

Having gathered the requirements it will be necessary for both business analysts and technical analysts to consider the implications. What aspects have been overlooked? What issues aren't really strict requirements? Is it technically feasible to implement a system that will achieve these requirements? For which requirements will the implementation probably be complex and therefore risky? After answering these questions it will be possible to refine the initial system requirements. You should be comfortable with the requirements continually being refined throughout the development of the project. However, it will also require great discipline to control the degree of revision to the requirements in order to manage and control the project suitably.

On completion of the establishing system requirements stage, we should have the following information:

❑ Management level expectations for the new system (expectations from an external perspective)

❑ Contact group of business domain experts and data users

❑ General understanding of the existing system to be replaced/augmented

❑ General idea of the system design (implementation)

UML and XML Modeling

> *"The Unified Modeling Language (UML) is a language for specifying, visualizing, constructing, and documenting the artifacts of software systems, as well as for business modeling and other non-software systems. The UML represents a collection of the best engineering practices that have proven successful in the modeling of large and complex systems." – OMG Unified Modeling Language Specification (http://www.rational.com/uml).*

In 1995 UML brought together a wide range of software modeling techniques, which had been developed in the preceding decade. Its particular strengths are:

- ❑ Documentation
- ❑ Visualization
- ❑ Collaboration
- ❑ Abstraction

In many ways it is the union of all modeling approaches, as we discover if we venture into the over 800 pages of specification, or any of the plethora of books on the subject (Amazon.com reports over 80). UML centers on diagrams for graphically representing models, and formally describes nine types of diagrams:

- ❑ Object Diagram
- ❑ Class Diagram
- ❑ Use Case Diagram
- ❑ Statechart Diagram
- ❑ Activity Graph
- ❑ Sequence Diagram
- ❑ Collaboration Diagram
- ❑ Component Diagram
- ❑ Deployment Diagram

While each of these imply their own associated model, UML combines them into five broad model categories:

- ❑ Datatypes – defining data structures.
- ❑ State Machine – state transition network for system.
- ❑ Activity Graph – a variation of a state machine that focuses on the transition rather than the state.
- ❑ Collaboration – interaction of objects and model entities.
- ❑ Use Case – behavior of an entity within the system.

The UML specification has fairly strict definitions for all of these things, as well as the associated items used to build up these models and diagrams; the body UML exhaustively covers all options for software system modeling. One of its objectives was not just to unify modeling techniques, but also to merge a vast range of modeling terminology. However, in our discussion we will frequently stretch UML definitions and modeling techniques to simplify an approach suitable for those new to the field of modeling. The entire modeling process is meant to facilitate communication and understanding of the system under development, and the full extent of UML can be an intimidating force possibly stifling discussion and obfuscating the meaning of the models being developed. At times, we take liberties with the modeling terms in order to make this chapter accessible to those who do not have the time or inclination to study the field in depth. For those who are familiar with UML, it may require patience not to continually be identifying terms that are "misused" or diagrams that are incomplete, or possibly not included.

There are numerous software packages available to assist in creating the various UML diagrams. Rational Rose is one of the most exhaustive packages for modeling, and has a cost to match. These are generally designed for object modeling for software development rather than XML data models. Power Designer 8 from Sybase has integrated XML Schema generation as well as reverse engineering of schemas into object models. Both Rational Rose and Power Designer are Enterprise class software, offering exceptional functionality, but with an Enterprise price tag. For most people Visio is considered to provide all the required functionality for creating modeling diagrams and is positioned to allow cost effective deployment throughout an organization. Several other UML design packages are also available covering a range of features at a range of prices. There is even a Java Open Source project developing ArgoUML (http://argouml.tigris.org/).

The important thing to keep in mind is that all software modeling packages or modeling methodologies are simply tools for the purpose of creating coherent and correct data models and processing models, which will be implemented in the actual system. The size of the project must be taken into consideration before investing effort into extensive formal modeling approaches. Large projects will probably benefit immensely from the documentation and visualization that UML software tools provide, as well as the common language it provides to the various parties involved in or affected by the project. UML is becoming more widely used and many technical and non-technical people are familiar with graphical models allowing efficient sharing of ideas and specifications. For smaller projects, designers may find that use cases and object models are beneficial, but only as far as some sketches in a lab book, on a white board, or a flip chart.

Business Process Analysis

Now that we have a better idea about the project and its expectations, the most important thing is to get out there and record a list of all the general information items required by the system. Once we have that in place, we can build an information model of how the information objects relate to each other, and move on from there to actually create some XML documents and Schemas. Finally we will be able to pull it all together into a processing model, through which the XML documents move and are manipulated by the application. In order to do all of this it is necessary to get an overview of the business process that is in place so we have a guide for our investigation into what information items are necessary. This is not part of the process modeling stage, which will come later, but rather a conceptual overview of what is done by the system.

The following figure illustrates the cyclic nature of modeling and the movement from requirements, to analysis, to modeling, and back to re-evaluate the requirements and repeat the cycle. At least two cycles are usually necessary in any healthy system design, while more than three will almost certainly be commercially unviable – remember our earlier warning against the risk of the modeling stage consuming the project. Process analysis is primarily for our benefit to facilitate the information and process modeling, and for this reason should largely be informal.

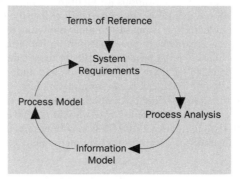

Depending on the system, we will be looking for different types of background information to assist with building an information model. These are as follows:

- ❑ **General Business Domain** – one of the most critical things to focus on, since it will guide you on the appropriate paradigms, vocabulary, and process. This is especially critical for new systems, which lack any applications for comparison or reference.

- ❑ **Database** – schemas describing the tables and columns will contain the sum total of all persistent information required by an existing system. Integrity constraints and stored procedures will further add to our understanding of the *existing* data requirements, but we will have to contend with normalization, which can obfuscate the meaning of the data. We must also accept that the new system may require more data in some areas and less in others. Object definitions will be a strong starting point for an information model if an object or object-relational database is used.

- ❑ **Digital messages** – any existing message passing systems related to our new system can provide useful information about the kind of information required and also about the organization of that information.

- ❑ **Existing application** – this may involve a painful trawl through source code to find interface definitions or class definitions of data objects. Depending on the quality of the application documentation there may be object models to reference.

- ❑ **Paper based system** – get all the forms and any available information describing how to fill them in, or how to process completed forms.

- ❑ **Data dictionary** – containing definitions of information items occurring in the system. May be primarily for business domain users, with business constraints for certain items (for example, a person must be identified as male or female), or more technical in nature for others (for example, the message timestamp must be less than or equal to the receiving system timestamp). If it is prepared well, this will be an important reference, although there must be awareness that the new system may contain more or less data than is found in the data dictionary, and it may be necessary to arrange the data differently in the new system. Generating our own data dictionary can be a valuable part of the modeling process.

Armed with the contact list we will now be faced with the daunting task of sifting through our notes and accumulated resources. Where the existing system is similar to the new system or is well established, we will repeatedly encounter the users *expectation* of identical behavior in the new system, whether this is for data definitions or for the processing model.

> **For this reason you will find that it is *more* important to form an information model for the *existing* system than it is for the new system.**

If our project has no existing reference for behavior, we are likely to lack a detailed specification and will hence have great freedom in the design. In these circumstances we need to establish the anticipated use cases and necessary information items. Hopefully, some formal documentation will already exist, and we will simply be able to tie those sources together into a coherent picture of the existing system, which will then be reviewed by the business domain experts to confirm that it is correct. Our new system can then be based on this model of the old system, and if problems arise, we will be able to refer to the old system's information model to determine where the misunderstanding or error in implementation arose.

However, keep in mind that we are still in the information-gathering mode and to continue the detective work, we want to start two diagrams:

❑ **Object Diagram** – containing anything that we suspect may be a significant piece of information or a grouping of related information items. (Also known as a Class Diagram or Entity Relationship Diagram.)

❑ **Use Case Diagram** – containing all the people and *external* processes that interact with the system, and the ways in which they interact.

The best place for these at this stage is probably in a notebook or on a whiteboard. Both of these diagramming techniques are to facilitate brainstorming and collaborative work with the business domain experts. We suggest that using a software package at this stage will impose a degree of formalism and therefore friction, which will impede the prime objective of information gathering.

Identifying Business Domain Objects

The figure drawn below shows our first attempt at identifying the business domain objects for our magazine publisher. This figure illustrates the various key components of the magazine's business. The magazine roughly consists of stories, photos, advertisements, and the corresponding web versions. The people involved with the magazine consist of writers, photographers, editors, advertisers, and distributors, and of course the readers:

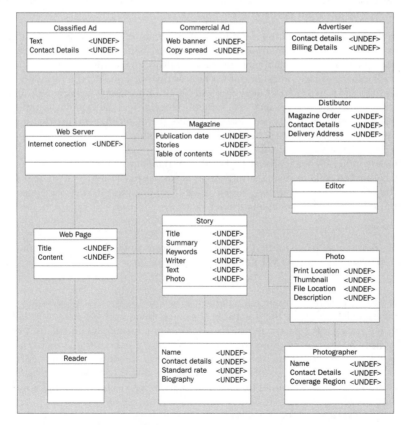

At this stage such a figure would be sketched in a notebook or put up on a whiteboard to facilitate communication regarding the important business objects, without alienating people unfamiliar with more formal modeling notation, which will be generated at a later stage. If we are not working in a group environment, or the developers are never on site with the business domain experts and end users, a simple tabular list may suffice and be more convenient for email distribution.

The figure also illustrates some common aspects: `Stories` are both properties of the `Magazine` object and objects in their own right, and `Photos` exist for the `Story`, and `Writer` objects. We also see certain properties appearing in multiple locations: `Contact Details`, and `Text`, for example. The `Editor` object is included, because the magazine wouldn't be anywhere without an editor, but it is difficult to see what relevant properties the editor has, and in fact that is because the editor is much more involved in the process than in the actual information model of the system. In any case, it is important to identify the editor as part of the system during this phase. The readers are in a similar situation, since they are obviously key to the process, but do not have any particularly relevant properties.

The dashed lines indicate that there are associations between objects, but these are left undefined for the time being, and are not directional. They simply indicate things such as a `Reader` may access either the `Magazine` or a `Web Page`, and that a `Photo` is associated both with a `Story` and a `Photographer`.

Later on we will refine this into a more formal object model and deal with the issues mentioned above, but for now we have simply begun the process of recording and organizing the important aspects of the system. It is important at this stage to accept inconsistencies in the draft object model, such as multiple `Contact Detail` properties. There should be no implication that `Contact Details` is the same in all occurrences (although it may be). Other properties such as `Text` are allowed to have completely different meanings depending on where they are used. Finally, while we should endeavor to include all important business domain objects, we will expect that there will be omissions of some objects and properties, as well as the inclusion of some extraneous ones. While the system develops, it will be necessary to revisit the object model several times, so there is no point struggling to attempt a perfect specification the first time round.

> **Understanding that this is an iterative process will allow for a progression from a high level overview of the information and processing models to the detail and final specification required for actual system implementation and deployment.**

Later in the modeling stage much more subtle discrepancies will arise and learning how to deal with the obvious ones now will facilitate the process of resolving the more difficult issues yet to come.

Use Case Diagram

We also want outlines of the use cases we have gathered. The following figure identifies a number of use cases for the system:

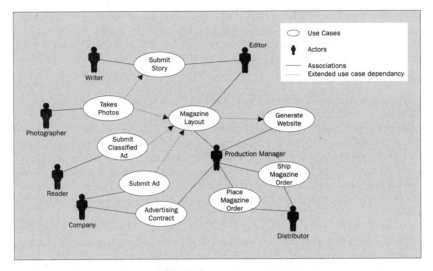

In this diagram we have identified nine use cases and seven actors who participate with the various use cases. Solid lines indicate the actors' involvement in a particular use case. Dashed arrows point from one use case into another use case, which the first feeds into (for example, the Takes Photos use case involving the Photographer actor, feeds into both the Submit Story use case and the Magazine Layout use case). Our use case diagram has revealed the Production Manager actor who actually seems to be much more the center of attention than the Editor (at least in this contrived arrangement). It has also begun to bring out some more of the business process that was not represented in our object diagram. Companies will generally establish advertising contracts with the publisher prior to submitting advertisements, and Distributors both place and receive orders. If, during the process of creating the use case diagram, we think of new objects or properties, we may add them to our draft object model.

We must keep in mind that a use case diagram is, at best, an outline of the use cases within a system. Alistair Cockburn, in *Writing Effective Use Cases* (Addison Wesley, ISBN: 0201702258) describes use cases as follows:

> *"A use case expresses a contract between the stakeholders of a system about its behavior. It describes the system's behavior and interactions under various conditions as it responds to a request on behalf of the stakeholders, the primary actor, showing how the primary actor's goal gets delivered or fails. The use case collects together the scenarios related to the primary actor's goal."*

Note: The stakeholders are anyone who cares about the information that goes into or out of the system, and those involved in the operation of the system itself.

We are using use case diagrams to facilitate our brainstorming – once our understanding of the system has improved, we can produce an object diagram and refine our use case diagram, and then dive into the job of detailing each use case. Furthermore, even detailed use cases provide only an anecdotal specification for the behavior of the system. They are important because people are good at describing what they want to do with a system, or how a business process is executed – they understand the process because they are intimately involved in it, even if they do not necessarily have a complete understanding of the purpose. Specification by example, as with use cases, does not provide any insight into common processing requirements for application design, or sufficient detail to build a complete information model. It does, however, point the designer in the right direction and give scenarios that must be handled, something that is invaluable for acceptance testing.

The testing aspect is one of critical importance in the application life cycle. Use cases allow QA people to insure that new versions of the application have the "same" (to within expected limits) functionality as the current system, and for the generation of automated tests which can be run on the system while it goes through development.

System Decomposition and Abstraction

Now we are at a stage to abstract and decompose components of the system so that we can deal with more manageable blocks. A reasonable breakdown would be Advertising, Distribution, Editorial, and Production/Layout; this is illustrated in the following diagram:

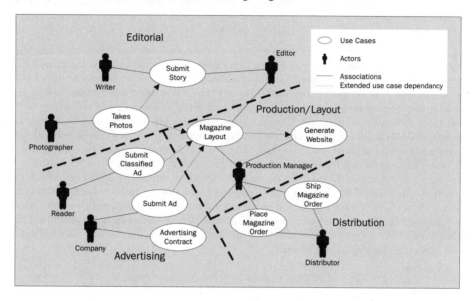

Each of these components will have different characteristics. The Editorial group will mainly be focused on production of text and images for inclusion in the magazine. This group will primarily use the system for archiving stories and photos, and for performing editorial tasks on presentation documents. The Distribution group will contain very *transactional* messages (that is, messages with a short life span whose purpose is mostly to carry information from one point to another) for the submission of magazine orders. Production and Layout will be a combination of data retrieval for accessing stories and photos, and also formatting details.

Once we have decomposed the system into groups, it may reveal that our initial intentions were not appropriate. In our magazine publishing example, for instance, we may decide that Production and Layout are best left as completely human controlled processes. Similarly, it may also reveal more efficient mechanisms for achieving the same goals, since we will be able to focus on a subsection of the overall system. In our divided system, we may see that Advertising could be the most easily to implement, and therefore act as a trial system for the overall concept.

> **Decomposition and abstraction is a critical part of any system modeling or design initiative. It provides encapsulation of related objects and simplification of interfaces between blocks of the system.**

The challenge is to use decomposition to simplify the design without obfuscating the intent of the system – too little (a very flat model) and it will be difficult to see patterns or keep track of relationships, and too much (lots of hierarchy) conceals the meaning of the model. Establishing the right level is a hard learned skill; however, some rules of thumb are:

❑ Never let a graphical representation of part of the system get bigger than what we could clearly represent on a single piece of paper. If it does, either the system is too complex, or we should be able to group and abstract a part of it into a separate block.

❑ Don't put more than two levels of decomposition onto a single diagram.

❑ Keep the number of levels of decomposition to a minimum. Just because we can decompose some part does not necessarily mean we should.

Abstraction is about re-usability, and abstracting the various groups that have come out of our decomposition efforts means finding common blocks and creating definitions for those blocks that are not tied to some specific business problem or application. There is always a trade off when abstracting: on one side, it will provide a more durable component of the system; but on the other, it may lack some required functionality specific to the business problem being addressed, and will often, in the short term, be more difficult to implement. Bespoke systems and applications generally do not, and should not, be distracted by abstraction except in so far as it improves the specific system being designed. However, commercial products or those that will be re-used extensively within a large organization will benefit tremendously from effectively abstracting components – this applies both to object definitions and processing components. Good abstraction provides clear interface definitions, which can be applied in a variety of circumstances, allowing either an object or a process to be reused. An example of abstraction would be to create a common definition for a `Person` object, which could then be used for storing information about the various "people" within a system. An associated abstracted processing component may have a generic mechanism for working with `Person` objects – storing them in a database, updating, querying, and so on.

We are now drawing to the end of the Business Process Analysis stage, at which point we have:

❑ A draft object model suggesting the key objects in the system and their properties

❑ Information regarding the relations between objects

❑ An overview use case diagram illustrating the anticipated uses for the system

❑ General system abstraction dividing the system into blocks

Information Modeling

In this section we will discuss the five components of the Information Model:

❑ **Primary Objects** – the key information groups in the system

❑ **Secondary Objects** – information groups which support or detail an aspect of a primary object

❑ **Properties** – the actual descriptive values for an object

❑ **Constraints** – acceptable values for properties or dependency rules between objects

❑ **Relationships** – descriptions of the relationships between objects

Now we are going to refine our draft object model into a complete information model. This will necessitate stronger definitions of objects and properties. In our draft object model we identified what we will call *primary* objects – the main information items in the system. The fact that these things came to mind first is probably a strong indication that they really are the core pieces of information in the system, although you should feel free to add or remove things from the primary objects list if circumstance demands. Our more rigorous definition of a property is anything that does not contain sub fields itself. Some examples are Email Address, Age, First Name, Quantity, and Cost. If a property can be divided into sub-fields, then it is an object in its own right, although to allow us to distinguish Address, a fairly generic object, from Writer, a specific and key object in our system, we will term these new objects, such as Address, as *secondary* objects. Any properties that are converted to objects themselves are represented as sub-objects of their parent object. It is also quite reasonable to have primary objects as sub-objects of other primary objects (for example, Story is a sub object of Magazine), and for secondary objects to be sub-objects of other secondary objects (for example, Address as a sub-object of Contact Details).

Cardinality

It is also a good time now to consider the **cardinality** of properties and sub-objects. Cardinality refers to the number of times a sub-object is allowed to occur in its parent, and is part of the description of the relationship between an object and its sub-objects. For the time being, do not confuse properties with XML attributes, and objects with XML elements. It is quite reasonable for some properties to occur multiple times for the same object, for instance Email Address may be a property of a Contact Details object, and the system could reasonably allow multiple Email Addresses for a single Contact Details object. At the very least we should begin to get an idea if the sub-object or property is, with respect to its parent object, one of:

- ❑ **Optional** or **Mandatory** – is permitted to be absent, or must be present (is its minimum occurrence 0 or 1?)

- ❑ **Singular** or **Plural** – can occur at most once, or can occur multiple times (is its maximum occurrence 1 or more than 1?)

Kinds of Relationship

We also need to consider the nature of the relationships between objects. There are four basic relationships:

- ❑ **Inheritance**– one object inherits its definition (either in terms of structure or data field definitions) from another object and modifies it in some way. A common example is an International Address object inheriting the definition of Address and adding the international component to the inherited definition. This is represented graphically by arrow **A** in the figure below.

- ❑ **Association** – generally represents processing dependencies or business rules. A Monthly Billing Summary object may be associated with all the Purchase Order objects for that month (perhaps it contains a sum of all purchase orders and also the volume purchased), but there is no direct hierarchical relationship between the two. This is represented graphically by arrow **B** in the figure below.

❑ **Composition** – one object contains another as its child as in a tree relationship, such that the child is intrinsically bound to the parent. Without the parent the child object has no meaning. An example is a `Table of Contents` object as a child of the `Magazine` object – without the `Magazine` there is no meaning to the details of the `Table of Contents` object. This is represented graphically by arrow **C** in the figure below.

❑ **Aggregation** – one object refers to another object as one of its children, but the referenced child object can exist without the parent. An example is a Story object as a child of a Magazine object. Even if the Magazine is removed from the system, the Story should persist. This is represented graphically by arrow **D** in the figure below.

The following figure illustrates the standard notation for representing each of these relationships in a diagram, with the arrow pointing *towards* the containing or superior object (although in the case of associations (dashed lines) these could be mutual associations with bi-directional arrows):

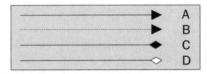

In XML instance documents containing data or messages, composition is the most common and most straightforward type of relationship. What we might call simple XML documents consist primarily of composition relationships. Aggregation is also easily achieved if fragments (or sub-trees) of an XML document can be extracted and stand in their own right. Association relationships are bound to occur wherever one part of an XML document depends on another part. This is usually achieved via `ID` and `IDREF` (from DTDs) or `key` and `keyref` (from XML Schema) within an XML instance document. Inheritance is something new to XML, which the XML Schema language provides. Associations are almost exclusively handled by application specific logic, but the `key` / `keyref` mechanism of XML Schema greatly enhances the ability of schema and document designers to assert consistency and scope of association relationships, while RDF, XLink, and XPointer/XPath can also be harnessed to bind information across the XML tree structure, or even between separate XML documents.

Make sure that you are clear that structure re-use is completely different from aggregation. For our magazine publisher, the `Contact Details` property is listed in several locations on the draft Object Model. From earlier, we realize this will need to become a secondary object in its own right, likely containing `Name`, `Email`, and `Address` properties (again, some of those will likely be split off into further secondary objects). Repetition of the same structure *syntax* is different from reference to the same structure *instance*. In this application each `Contact Details` object is meaningless without its parent (`Photographer`, `Advertiser`, `Distributor`) object, so the relationship is a composition. If the parent object is removed, then the `Contact Details` object is also removed.

Primary Object List

With these things in mind we can start another object diagram, or an object list. In my experience, tabularized object lists are very straightforward and easily understood by non-XML people. In some respects this makes the collaboration or confirmation of the work much easier, since tabular data can easily be transmitted via email and has no special software requirements, although it does lose some of the "big picture" that can be gained from diagrams.

The first task it to come up with definitions for our primary objects, describing them in general terms. This will be the start of a Data Dictionary for our model; however, we can expect that by the end of the project, rather than having a single row in a table for each primary object, there could be as much as a section of several pages describing the key objects within the system.

Object	Description
Magazine	A single edition of the magazine, containing all the information necessary for both print and online publication.
Story	Consisting of the text, formatting, photos, and authorship information for a given story.
Photo	A single photo with associated format, description, and photographer information.
Writer	Contains information regarding the writer's specialization and geographic location. Also contains a bibliography of their work.
Photographer	Contains information on a photographer. Must identify if they are staff or freelance. Must contain geographic location, and a record of their work within the company.

Now start with the primary objects and list their properties and sub-objects, as well as the type of relationship, description, and cardinality rules for each. We will use the short form for specifying cardinality of $x..y$, where x is the minimum occurrence and y is the maximum occurrence; $*$ will mean unbounded (obviously only appropriate for the maximum occurrence). The following table shows the primary objects and their properties and sub-objects for the Editorial model group:

Object	Property or Sub-Object	Cardinality	Type of Relationship	Description
Magazine	Publication Month	1..1	Composition	Must be one of the full month names. Describes the month of publication for a particular Magazine instance.
Magazine	Story	0..*	Aggregation	The magazine may have some stories
Story	Title	1..1	Composition	The story must have a title
Story	Summary	1..1	Composition	The story must have a summary
Story	Keyword	0..*	Composition	The story may have some key words
Story	Photo	0..*	Aggregation	The story may include some photos
Story	Text	1..1	Composition	The story must have its body

Table continued on following page

Object	Property or Sub-Object	Cardinality	Type of Relationship	Description
Story	Writer	1..*	Aggregation	The story must have one or more writers
Photo	File Location	1..1	Composition	The photo must indicate its file location
Photo	Photographer	1..1	Aggregation	The photo must have a photographer
Writer	Name	1..1	Composition	The writer must have a name
Writer	Biography	0..1	Composition	The writer may have a biography
Writer	Photo	0..*	Composition	The writer may have some photos (of him or herself)
Writer	Standard Rate	0..1	Composition	The writer may have a standard rate
Writer	Contact Details	1..1	Composition	The writer must have contact details
Photographer	Name	1..1	Composition	The photographer must have a name
Photographer	Contact Details	1..1	Composition	The photographer must have contact details
Photographer	Coverage Region	1..*	Composition	The photographer must be listed with at least one coverage region

The organization of this table started from the high level object Magazine, and worked its way downwards to the Story, Photo, Writer, and Photographer objects. Grouping our primary objects and defining them within their abstract model groups provides organization and clarity to the presentation of the model. If the primary objects in a group do not have a logical hierarchy or contain multiple hierarchies (multiple possible root objects), then an alphabetical arrangement may be best. It is quite likely that secondary objects will be shared across multiple abstract groups, therefore defining them in a separate table or set of diagrams may be best.

Note that where each primary object contains a primary sub-object, the relationship is an aggregation. This is because primary objects will usually have meaning in their own right, regardless of their association with other objects. We should be careful about the use of the word "meaning". When used, it should always be interpreted within the context of the overall system. Our Magazine Publisher would only ever include an Address object as a compositional relationship of some other object (the Address object has no meaning without knowing what it is an address of). However, a City Planning system, or Postal system would quite happily have addresses as primary objects, with meaning independent of any other context.

> **Two primary objects in a composition relationship should send out warning signals. You should confirm if the sub-object is really dependent upon the context of the parent object in order for it to have meaning. If the sub-object has meaning in its own right, then it should probably be in an aggregation relationship.**

The class diagram below shows the basic structure of our objects:

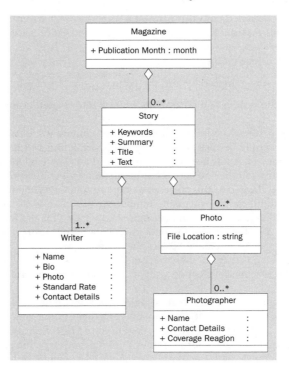

All the primary objects have aggregation relationships with their containers. To simplify the diagram we have shown `Photo` of the `Writer` object as a property, when in fact it is a primary sub-object.

Although this is an implementation detail, the reality is that we will always have in the back of our heads an image of how this model is going to come together once we start designing the data structures. Aggregation relationships at first seem to suggest that they will only provide some indirection from the container object to the "real" contained object. For instance, we may be tempted to imagine that a `Writer` object contained by aggregation within a `Story` object would consist of something like a `WriterID` field in the implementation. For database design, this is likely to be the case, and for software implementations we would imagine a pointer or reference to the "actual" `Writer` object. The temptation of thinking this way will mean that if we want all the information for a contained object to exist within the container, then we will conclude that it must be a composition relationship – this is incorrect.

In our `Story` example, as we visualize the XML, we may feel that it is necessary to have more than just an attribute `WriterID="hsmith7632"`, where `hsmith7632` refers to some `Writer` object elsewhere within the system. Rather, we want to actually have the writer's `Name`, `Photo`, and `Biography` included. This is perfectly reasonable, and still allows the `Story/Writer` relationship to be one of aggregation; it is just necessary to document that the information contained in a `Story` object about a `Writer` is *copied* from a definitive source, the `Writer` object `hsmith7632`. The point of this is not to assume that just because you want a *copy* of the information rather than an *indirection* to the information that you are dealing with a composition relationship. Copies of objects can still be aggregation relationships.

Future Proofing and Scope of the Model

Real life data should be modeled, and this may be a superset of what is required by the processing application. Efficient and meaningful organization of the information should be achieved by:

❑   Identifying the primary objects

❑   Deciding on an object hierarchy and the nature of the object relationships

❑   Decomposing the system and abstracting objects into related groups

A successful strategy is to allow the information model to contain a superset of what is required by the system, since this stage simply consists of *gathering* the information, and in order to establish that a particular item is extraneous, it still needs to be found and analyzed against the requirements of the system and its relationship to other objects. That item can now be incorporated into a broad information model and perhaps even flagged at this stage as being extraneous. When it actually comes to producing the data model and the application processing model, the best plan is certainly to start with a small subset of the full information model, even less than is acceptable for the final system implementation. This allows the gradual development of the data model and application. The priority is simplicity. Applying the 80:20 rule, we will achieve 80% of the systems goals with 20% of the information model. A corollary that can be added is that for software systems, there is a point where increasing complexity as a result of over ambitious scope results in negative returns and an unusable system.

We must make sure we understand new technologies that are coming on line at the same time as our new system, and also take into account any upcoming changes in the way the organization does business – will there be a new enterprise wide inventory system in the next 6 months we will have to interface with? Are we going to be using the Internet rather than a proprietary Intranet system for inter-departmental networks? Have digital marketplaces matured enough that we will be using these in the near future? We must be aware of new standards, technology and larger corporate decisions that should be considered when designing our new system. All these are appropriate areas for limited "future-proofing" of our system, but it is necessary to not let this get out of hand.

Secondary Object List

We will now also detail all the secondary objects referenced from this set of primary objects – see the following table. As the model develops, these descriptions will have to be flushed out to contain more information regarding what constitutes a particular object or property.

Object	Property or Sub-Object	Cardinality	Type of Relationship	Description
Name	First	`1..1`	Composition	A name must have a first name property
Name	Initial	`0..1`	Composition	A name may have a single initial
Name	Last	`1..1`	Composition	A name must have a last name property
Contact Details	Phone Number	`0..*`	Composition	Zero or more phone numbers are permitted

Object	Property or Sub-Object	Cardinality	Type of Relationship	Description
Contact Details	Fax Number	0..*	Composition	Zero or more fax numbers are permitted
Contact Details	Email	0..*	Composition	Zero or more email address are permitted
Contact Details	Address	1..*	Composition	One or more addresses are required
Phone Number	Country Code	1..1	Composition	A phone number must have a country code
Phone Number	Area Code	1..1	Composition	A phone number must have an area code
Phone Number	Local Number	1..1	Composition	A phone number must have a local number
Phone Number	Extension	0..1	Composition	A phone number may an extension
Fax Number	Country Code	1..1	Composition	A fax number must have a country code
Fax Number	Area Code	1..1	Composition	A fax number must have an area code
Fax Number	Local Number	1..1	Composition	A fax number must have a local number
Fax Number	Extension	0..1	Composition	A fax number may have an extension
Address	Line	1..4	Composition	An address must have 1 to 4 general line entries
Address	Town	1..1	Composition	An address must have a town
Address	County	1..1	Composition	An address must have a county
Address	Postal Code	1..1	Composition	An address must have a postal code
Address	Country	1..1	Composition	An address must have a country

At this stage all primary and secondary objects should have been described, leaving only properties. The cardinality of the properties will already have been described so now we are left to provide some description of the permitted values.

Now we have characterized the primary information items for the Editorial model group, the supporting secondary objects, and all properties. So far this has been driven very much by tangible objects: Magazine, Story, Writer, Photographer, Photo. To contrast this, let us turn our attention to the Distribution model group. Here we will see an example of how process-based information items will be modeled.

Sequence Diagrams

Referring back to our use case diagram, we see that the two high-level use cases for the Distribution model group are **Place Magazine Order** and **Ship Magazine Order**. We will propose a simple transaction system, whereby a **Distributor** submits an order message to the publishers automated system, to which the publisher will return a receipt. When the publisher ships the order, the **Distributor** is notified with a delivery message.

In order to specify the objects for this message-based system, we must consider the processing model framework. The process will dictate the nature and composition of these objects. It is for that reason we need to have a general understanding of the business process to be implemented by the system and some idea of the application-processing model.

To illustrate the process we will use a sequence diagram. The sequence diagram includes the actors who are involved in the process and the message objects that are generated:

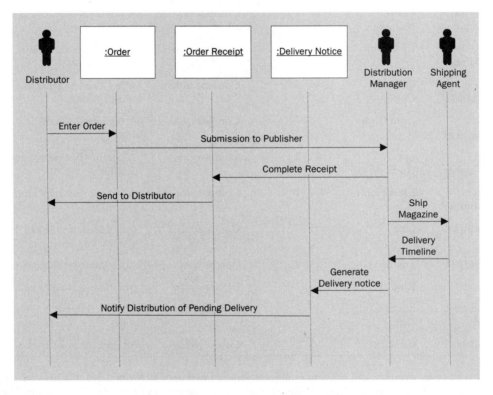

Besides the objects and actors, the vertical axis represents time, and the arrows represent actions or events occurring between actors and objects. This sequence diagram introduces two new Actors to the system: a **Distribution Manager** and a **Shipping Agent**. It will not be uncommon for a system to have objects that represent actors in a system. Our magazine publisher must store information within their distribution system describing their various shipping agents, but the actual business process does not involve these object representations of the shipping agents – instead, it involves real people communicating by phone, fax, email, or post (purchase orders, contracts, and so on).

The following object diagram illustrates the three messages and their associated properties and sub-objects:

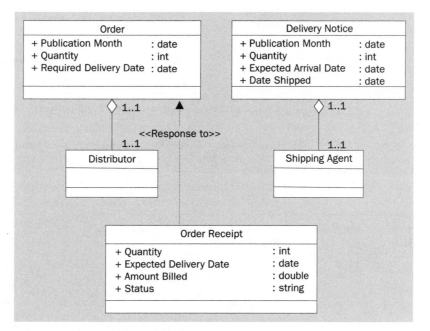

We have indicated an association between **Order** and **Order Receipt** (the dashed line), because **Order Receipt** depends on an **Order** object. This can be counter-intuitive, because the direction of process flow is from **Order** to **Order Receipt**. However, object diagrams do not illustrate the process, only the information items which participate in the process and the relationships or dependencies between those objects.

To complete the description of this process we need our object definitions. Below are the object definitions for the order process:

Object	Description
Order	Sent by a **Distributor** to the **Distribution Manager** specifying a quantity of magazines to be delivered for a particular month. Also includes the required delivery date.
Order Receipt	Sent by the **Distribution Manager** in response to an **Order** from a **Distributor**. Specifies the quantity that has been ordered (which may be different from the actual order placed), the amount billed for the order, and the expected shipping date, as well as an order **Status**, which will be used by the application to flag any issues with the original order.
Delivery Notice	Sent by the **Distribution Manager** to the **Distributor** after the publication has been delivered to the **Shipping Agent**. Specifies the date shipped, the expected delivery date, the quantity, and the publication month.

Here are the properties of the `Order` object in more detail:

Property or Sub-Object	Cardinality	Type of Relationship	Description
Quantity	1..1	Composition	An order must have a quantity specified, indicating the number of magazines required
Distributor	1..1	Aggregation	An order must have a distributor specified
Required Delivery Date	0..1	Composition	An order may have a delivery date specified
Publication Month	1..1	Composition	An order must specify a publication month

And those for the `Order Receipt` object:

Property or Sub-Object	Cardinality	Type of Relationship	Description
Quantity	1..1	Composition	An order receipt must confirm the order quantity
Status	1..1	Composition	An order receipt must specify the status of the order. Status will specify whether or not the order can be filled
Expected Delivery Date	0..1	Composition	An order receipt may specify an expected delivery date
Amount Billed	1..1	Composition	An order receipt must specify the amount billed for the order

And for the `Delivery Notice` object:

Property or Sub-Object	Cardinality	Type of Relationship	Description
Quantity	1..1	Composition	A delivery notice must specify the quantity delivered
Date Shipped	1..1	Composition	A delivery notice must specify the shipping date
Shipping Agent	1..1	Aggregation	A delivery notice must specify the shipping agent
Expected Arrival Date	1..1	Composition	A delivery notice must specify the expected arrival date
Publication Month	1..1	Composition	A delivery notice must specify the publication month

Notice how both Distributor and Shipping Agent sub-objects have been specified as aggregation relationships, because a Shipping Agent exists not only within a Delivery Notice, nor a Distributor in an Order, but rather each have meaning in their own right. For this reason, they are included as their own objects, although we do not go into the detail of specifying their properties here.

Defining Properties

Finally, we need to move on to detailing the properties in the system. The cardinality rules have already been specified in the primary and secondary object diagrams or tables, so we are primarily considering the definitions of permitted values for the properties, and descriptions for the meaning of the properties.

> **The object hierarchy and inter-relationships represent the structure of the information model. However, the information detail is contained in the properties.**

As we have already seen, there are a number of XML Schema datatypes that most properties will fall into (see Chapter 2 for more details). These act as a good starting place for specifying the legal property values:

Datatype	Description
string	A general text string, such as a sentence or paragraph. A Summary property would probably be assigned a string datatype.
NMTOKEN	A whitespace-free character sequence. e.g. distID72, 35-233-8812.
integer	Used for quantities, codes, indices, and measures of whole numbers. Also includes negative values, for example 732301, 0, -7.
decimal	Includes a decimal point and represents numeric values that have a fractional component, for example, 0.8920, 789.0, -42.112.
date	Gregorian calendar dates in the format YYYY-MM-DD.
time	Indicates a time of day in the format HH:MM:SS.MMM with optional time zone notation –HH:MM, for example, 13:20:00.000, 13:20:00.000-05:00.

It is worth noting here that the XML Schema language only supports the period "." as the decimal separator, even though many countries use a comma instead. While patterns can be used to constrain an arbitrary text string to represent fractional numbers using a comma for the decimal separator, this would prevent the use of numeric facets such as maxInclusive, fractionDigits, and totalDigits (the last two could be simulated with appropriate $\{x,y\}$ cardinality constraints on the pattern regular expression). The specific expression consisting for comma separated monetary values of the form "digits, comma, two digits" can be expressed as: $[0-9]+,[0-9]\{2,2\}$.

Applying one of the following constraints (which map to facets in XML Schema) can provide further restrictions:

Constraint	Restriction
Enumeration	The field must exactly match one of a list of items ("London", "Tokyo", "New York", for example)
Length	The field must match certain length restrictions (exactly 10 characters, more than 3 characters, for example)
Value	The field must fall within certain value restrictions (less than 100, greater than or equal to 0, for example)
Pattern	The field must correspond to some fixed syntax (must start with the letter M, must contain the number 7, for example)

Distinguishing Business Rules from Application Rules

Whatever definitions we record now will not necessarily map directly to the final schema; be cautious when using XML Schema terminology such as facets. One of the greatest problems we encounter at this stage is separating business rules from application rules. Business rules are everything that the business domain experts, end users, and management assert on the system. These rules are often described using natural language and may defy quantifying or strict limits. An example would be "A phone number must include the area code". Application rules are not dictated by the business but are either necessary to provide strict boundaries for a "soft" business rule or due to the architecture of the system itself. An example of the first would be "Phone numbers may consist of no more than 15 digits", while an example of the second may be "The pipe character is not permitted" (a purely application dependent restriction). The information model should endeavor to be free of any application-based restrictions, but we usually find that the specification of the information items combines business restrictions with application restrictions. Maintaining a distinction allows us to re-evaluate if application rules continue to exist as the application evolves or is replaced.

Consider the Last Name property: our project may have a design precedent of setting a finite limit on all property sizes (perhaps to limit the maximum size of a message or document), though there may be no precedent for the "real" maximum length that is permitted by the business. Allowing unspecified values in your information model is acceptable, and should actually be explicitly recorded as such. This way, future developers will not have to speculate if something is unspecified or undocumented, a subtle but significant difference. For another example, we may consider it "common sense" to disallow the symbols "^, %, $, *" from a Last Name property. However, on what basis do we make this decision? In some legal jurisdictions, unexpected characters are perfectly acceptable in a name (or perhaps even *as* a name – imagine the result of filtering or rejecting a name in these circumstances!). It is important to keep in mind that XML is international and supports Unicode encoding, therefore thinking that the English alphabet and punctuation is the limit of acceptable characters for any given string is not acceptable. While it may be that due to interfaces with existing systems it is necessary to assert *application* rules to disallow accented characters (take Spanish for instance), it may be that the business rules actually explicitly allow these.

A common problem is when supposed "business" restrictions actually originate from a paper form with the notorious string of single character boxes. These usually originated to aid in legibility and force character spacing. If a person completing the paper form happened to exceed the limit they either squeezed letters in, or wrapped onto the next line, and the operator performing the data entry simply took this into account. Along comes an electronic form completion system and an eager application developer, lacking any other reference for a particular data field, and has suddenly limited City or Family names to, say, twelve characters. Years later this decision has become entrenched as a "Business Rule", and by then it may very well be; since the legacy data processing systems may continue to exist and enforce this rule, we could be forced to as well.

As we have already discussed in Chapter 4, it is now possible to define our own custom datatypes by taking a set of restrictions applied to an existing datatype and giving it a name. This will come quite naturally to anyone with a programming background, or for those now familiar with XML Schema.

Being aware that we can create our own datatypes is important; however, we will not speculate on a set of custom datatypes, which we *may* need for our model. Instead, we will take the pragmatic approach and simply continue to define our property fields and if we feel that one of the existing datatypes is insufficient, we will create the name for a new datatype *first* and then define its specifics *later*. This is very much in line with the approach we used when defining sub-objects and secondary objects in our initial object model:

Property	Datatype	Restrictions	Definition
Amount Billed	`monetary`	Non negative	Contains the amount billed to a distributor by the publisher
Area Code	`integer`	Non negative	
Biography	`string`	Not longer than 150 words	Writer biography
Country	`CountryEnum`		A list of acceptable country names
Country Code	`integer`		Telephone country code
County	`string`		
Coverage Region	`string`		Description of the region covered by a photographer
Date Shipped	`dateTime`		Shipping date of magazine by publisher
Distributor	`NMTOKEN`	Must reference a known distributor code	A code given to each distributor to uniquely identify them
Email	`EmailType`	Must be a legal email pattern	
Expected Arrival Date	`dateTime`		Expected arrival date from publisher to distributor
Expected Delivery Date	`dateTime`		Expected delivery date from publisher to distributor
Extension	`integer`		Phone extension
File Location	`string`		References to a photo file in the database or photo filing system
First	`NMTOKEN`	Can only contain a single name	First name

Property	Datatype	Restrictions	Definition
Initial	string	Maximum length 1, upper case characters A-Z permitted.	Person's name initial
Keyword	string	Phrases are OK	Key words for story
Last	string	May contain multiple names	Person's last name
Line	string	Not longer than 70 characters	General address line
Local Number	integer		Local part of phone number
Postal Code	string	Not longer than 70 characters	
Publication Month	month		
Quantity	integer	Non negative	
Required Delivery Date	dateTime		Distributor specified delivery date
Shipping Agent	word	Must reference a known shipping agent code	A code given to each shipper to uniquely identify them
Standard Rate	monetary	Non negative	Standard story rate for a writer
Status	ReceiptStatusType		Status in response to a distributor order
Summary	string	Not longer than 150 words	Summary of the story
Text	DocBook		A DocBook copy of the text
Title	string	Not longer than 20 words	The title of the story
Town	string	Not longer than 70 characters	

The table above describes all of the properties within the Editorial and Distribution model groups. It has also revealed a common problem when tabularizing properties: name collision and ambiguity. Properties should seem meaningful when viewed within the context of their containing object, but left on their own, properties such as Text, Summary, and Status could mean a variety of things. On large projects, a good solution is to provide an additional column indicating the context of the property. Expanding property names to embed additional meaning is generally not recommended, as the property will only ever exist within the context of the containing object. Therefore, it would be redundant to rename Summary to StorySummary, resulting in the StorySummary property of the Story object. When context is required to uniquely identify a property or disambiguate it, provide it as additional information.

Custom Datatypes

In defining the property fields we are likely to have created a number of custom datatypes. In our example above, we created four: DocBook, ReceiptStatusType, EmailType, and CountryEnum. In fact, DocBook is actually an externally defined type which describes the DocBook DTD (see http://www.oasis-open.org/docbook/), meaning this property should be converted to a secondary object whose structure is defined by an external system. Notice also that several of the string type properties have a common "less than 70 characters" restriction. If these are all due to some common view, such as "certain types of strings ought to not be longer than 70 characters in length", then this constitutes a custom datatype. We saw this kind of thing back in Chapter 5. Any sort of common restriction should be captured as a datatype, rather than repeating restrictions on a case-by-case basis, but only when those restrictions are common because of an association between the objects, and not just coincidental. Following this reasoning, integer and monetary will both have non-negative versions, and the "not longer than 150 words" string will also become its own type. This will provide us with the following custom types and corresponding definitions:

Type Name	Definition
CountryEnum	An enumerated list of the legal countries based on ISO 3661-1
EmailType	String corresponds to pattern: `[A-Za-z0-9\.\-_]{1,64}@[A-Za-z0-9\.\-_]{1,64}`. Consider this for illustrative purposes only. As this is correct for 99% of all email addresses; however, this is *not* the pattern for RFC 822, which specifies legal email address syntax – please refer to the RFC directly or to http://www.ex-parrot.com/~pdw/Mail-RFC822-Address.html for a detailed regular expression for Internet Email validation.
Monetary	A monetary field with at least one integer digit and exactly two fractional digits. Assumes a single currency.
NonNegativeMonetary	Monetary fields $>=$ 0.00.
NonNegativeInteger	Integers with values $>=$ 0
ReceiptStatusType	An enumerated list of {confirmed, denied, error}
String150word	A string consisting of at most 150 words
String70char	A string consisting of at most 70 characters

Business Rules

Business rules apply to the objects and properties we have identified as part of the information model. They specify some issue, policy, or requirement of the business that must be met. Some Business Rules have already been guiding the process of building the information model we currently have. While objects can often be seen as implicit requirements of the system, the cardinality rules, property restrictions, and custom datatypes are largely drawn from business rules. The following statements are all business rules:

1. "We must have a biography for all our writers"

2. "We will not send out a single shipment of less than 200 copies"

3. "If a phone extension is specified then so too must the rest of the phone number"

4. "The distribution total must equal the sum of all shipments to all distributors"

5. "If we cannot fill a full order from a Distributor, we will send them a partial order"

6. "We will only accept one email address per person"

7. "We don't care what the mailing address is"

As we would expect with these kinds of statements, the full set of them is not written down anywhere, and it is often difficult to find even more than a handful, yet they are the fundamental statements that specify the business problem or business process we are involved in. Hopefully, our careful detective work will have drawn out the important business rules from the business domain experts. However, we should expect to find new business rules on an almost continuous basis throughout the life of the project.

Also keep in mind that application decisions will imply rules, even if they haven't been stated. Take statement 3 for instance, where it is conceivable that a staff Writer in our publishing example only has an extension provided, because his office is within the company. An information model will have to decide if an extension can exist without a full phone number, and without statement 3 this may be become a decision made entirely by the implementers, implicitly setting the rule. If the business really doesn't care whether or not the the there is a full phone number with every extension, then even that can be seen as a business rule "We don't care if there is an accompanying phone number with an extension", meaning the decision one way or another makes this an application rule that future applications or revisions may choose to change. You may be tempted to think that "not caring" about a particular issue is the same as making something optional. This is not the case. Making something optional is a particular decision that would be stated as "An extension can optionally have a phone number" (admittedly, the logic of that statement sounds badly backwards), and this as well as future applications would be obliged to implement it. A "don't care" position allows us to implement what is best now, record and justify it as an application rule, and then allow future developers to re-evaluate if they will maintain the same operation, or change it to suit other priorities.

During the early modeling, design, and development of the system, such ongoing "discoveries" can probably be incorporated, provided we allow for an iterative design process. There will come a point when it will be necessary to weigh the importance of newly discovered business rules against the impact on the established system and possibly elect not to incorporate late rules, although they certainly should be recorded.

In reality, collecting business rules will rarely be as simple as documenting statements such as those listed above. Many of these will have come up from conversations, off hand comments, meetings, or emails. To aid in classifying the business rules, we should place them into these four categories:

❑ **Definition** – declares the need for an object or property. (Statements 1 and 6, above, for example)

❑ **Constraint** – limits the allowable values for a given property. (Statements 2 and 7, above, for example)

- ❑ **Fact** – states a relationship between any two objects or properties. (Statements 3 and 5, above, for example)

- ❑ **Derivation** – defines how one property's value is derived via some formula from other properties. (Statement 4, above, for example)

In order to complete our object model, all Definition and Constraint business rules must be correctly represented. It is best to go through the list of these business rules and check them off one at a time. The set of Fact and Derivation business rules must be grouped and listed. If we have an object diagram, then every Fact and Derivation business rule implies an association between the affected objects. With the business rules sorted, clarified, and recorded we will have the first version of our information model.

Due to the importance of business rules in driving the information model design, it could be argued that formalization of the business rules should be done at the beginning of the process rather than at the end. The argument against this is that the business rules aren't sufficiently clear at the start of the project. During the business analysis stage we will have facilitated discussion and improved our own perspective on the general business process, such that business rules will have surfaced as a by-product. With an understanding of the business process, we will also be in a better position to probe the business domain experts for greater detail as they respond to our developing model. Once we near completion of the information model, at least for this iteration, we can formalize the accumulated business rules and use them to sanity check the object model.

In this section, we have built the information model by establishing a list of primary and secondary objects with associated properties. Using different types of relationships, a hierarchy of objects has been established along with cardinality rules. Hierarchy and cardinality have been used to represent the structure of the information model, while the actual content has been defined by assigning datatypes to the properties and, where necessary, creating custom datatypes to represent common field definitions. Finally the set of business rules has been solidified and categorized. Some of these business rules are directly implemented in the object model, while others will be necessary for the processing model.

By now, we should have:

- ❑ An object model
- ❑ A set of business rules

Process Model

This stage of modeling is much more dependent upon the exact system requirements and will rely heavily on the details of the use cases and sequence diagrams. It is a good time to return to the use case diagram and expand it. For each use case, we will want to create a report detailing:

- ❑ Actors
- ❑ General goals
- ❑ Preconditions for the use case
- ❑ Guarantees of how the use case will behave
- ❑ Success conditions
- ❑ Failure conditions
- ❑ Any sub use cases, or associated use cases

Sequence diagrams will also outline the operational flow of the system, and what messages or results are returned when in response to what inputs.

Guaranteeing that our system is processing the right data is also critical, and this starts with receipt of an XML document from an authorized sender, possibly having signed the contents to guarantee their integrity. While XML Schema provides for strong document-centric schema validation (where the documents declare their namespace and schema), applications are better off anticipating the message or document category and then forcing schema validation against a system controlled namespace and Schema document.

Systems that can receive documents from multiple sources will require a mechanism to authenticate the document's source. This sort of system can be done efficiently outside of the XML by the lower level network services, although XML Digital Signatures could be used (see http://www.w3.org/Signature/). What is important is that any sender identification stored in a received document is confirmed to be consistent with the authenticated sender. This is simply an extension of the general principle of consistent data: if any information is duplicated, it should be confirmed to be consistent.

Iterative Development

One of the surest ways to establish a robust system model is to build into the project timeline room for at least two full iterations through the Business Analysis, Information Modeling, Data Modeling, and Process Modeling cycle. If there is no major redesign, successive iterations should take half the time of their forerunner. Your experience and improved relationships with the project team and related stakeholders will facilitate a greater understanding of the needs, objectives, and implementation of the system.

Data Model

It is now necessary to convert the Information Model developed in the last section into a data model. While it would be possible to use some abstract representation for this data model, we will maintain that XML Schema, and example instance documents are as effective a data modeling medium as any, and cut out a level of representation. This is akin to example tables in Entity-Relationship models for database design. As we are now finally moving into XML and XML Schema territory, it is necessary to make a comment on three components of XML data models with XML Schema: namespaces, schemas, and schema instance documents.

Namespaces, Schemas, and Instance Documents

It is important to understand the relationship between these three components of the XML Schema language. It is perfectly legal for one schema to define two completely unrelated documents.

> **A schema does not necessarily define a single instance document, or even a set of instance documents with the same document element.**

Likewise, a namespace is not a schema. A namespace defines a certain XML vocabulary and makes an element called `Title` in one namespace completely separate from an element called `Title` in another namespace. Instance documents contain elements and attributes that are found in the null namespace, one namespace, or possibly multiple namespaces. A single namespace may be used in multiple schemas, and a single schema may refer to multiple namespaces, so neither can be said to be a superset of the other, and therefore cannot provide a complete definition of the other. For more on Namespaces, see Chapter 6.

An XML Schema document, which defines a subset (and possibly the complete set) of a particular schema, may define elements and attributes to belong to a given namespace. In this way it is *possible*, although not at all mandatory, that the complete definition of all elements and attributes in a given namespace are defined in a set of XML Schema documents. Given this namespace defined in our set of XML Schema documents, it is possible for an instance document to then create its own elements in this namespace, which are not defined in the set of Schema documents. Unless the Schema documents for that namespace make appropriate use of any elements, this instance document will not be schema valid against the schemas that define the namespace.

An XML Schema document can define elements and attributes into one given namespace, the null namespace, or a combination of a given namespace and the null namespace. Due to these restrictions on schema documents, in order to build an XML Schema that spans multiple namespaces, it is necessary to make use of multiple schema documents (see Chapter 8). Furthermore, in a system with multiple kinds of instance documents it is a matter of personal choice whether you wish to declare a separate schema for each document type, or to simply group them under the umbrella of one schema that permits multiple document types. My preference would be to declare a different XML Schema for each document type, as this provides the ability to couple schema documents for validation with a set of instance documents that validate against them. However, for certain document designs it may be more practical to have a single schema document, which defines multiple related document types. This would be the case if the various document types are all very similar or if they are all related and quite small. Splitting schemas also benefits the validation process, as schema validators only need to store information relevant to the documents they are validating.

Creating Schema and Instance Documents

The Information Model is the obvious starting point for some sample instance documents. In order to begin this process, we need to decide on three things:

- ❑   What are the instance documents going to contain?
- ❑   How will we map objects and properties to elements and attributes?
- ❑   What are we going to name the elements and attributes?

The first question depends greatly on the system architecture and how the objects interact with each other and the application. There are two broad alternatives here: either the instance document structure could be set by some collaborative body, or instance documents are custom designed to support a particular business application. It is possible to combine these by wrapping one with the other – either contain the generic instance document inside an application specific wrapper, or use a generic envelope with some application specific payload. We will not dwell on the case of pre-determined instance documents, since in such a circumstance there would be no need to model an instance document or schema. Instead, we will focus on the task of creating instance documents, which work with a particular application and business process.

When deciding on instance documents that will exist within the application, one possibility would be to allow any primary object to be an instance document in its own right. These can be used for storing and transporting information regarding a primary object. Preparing an instance document structure for each primary object is useful even if these are never used on their own, simply because they can easily become fragments inserted into other instance documents as required.

The next place to look for possible instance document requirements is interfaces between systems or between the application and users. Any external system interfacing with the application will be a prime target for an XML instance document to act as the format for passing information. Interactions within the application may not be best served by XML – if the application will already have some computer internal representation of the object then it is probably unnecessary to either use binary DOM trees or serialized XML documents to move information between tightly coupled systems – simply leave it in the application specific data structure. With respect to the interfaces with external systems, it is necessary to establish what transmission information is necessary. Will we need timestamps and authentication? Do we need to be able to identify the specific external system, if multiple systems can connect to our application via some port? What control information do we need in order to know what to do with the information we receive? Is there an expected response, either on receipt of the information, or on completion of the processing? Answers to these questions will guide our development of the instance documents we produce.

Once we know what instance documents the system will require, we need to establish exactly what will go into them and how that will be arranged. This comes down to the question of how to arrange elements and attributes to make a meaningful instance document. The question of what to make an attribute is fairly straightforward. Consider the objects included in the instance document, and if we can answer *yes* to each of the following five questions, then the item should definitely be assigned to an attribute.

1. Is it a property?

2. Would the property never occur more than once in a given object?

3. Does the property have no ordering dependence?

4. Does the property have only a single data field?

5. Would the resulting attribute:
   a. describe its parent element;
   b. describe the group of child elements; or
   c. be a modifier on the element value?

We have already looked at naming conventions in Chapter 7, but let's have a quick reiteration – in a large project such as this one, naming conventions are very important. We encourage efficient, meaningful, and unambiguous names. Element and attribute names should be short and to the point, but avoid abbreviations and contractions wherever possible. The names should describe the expected content: either of the children of an element, or the element or attribute values directly, and the names should not be confused with other names within the system *when context is taken into consideration.*

It was an unfortunate shortcoming of DTDs that all element and attribute names had to be globally unique, and many policies to maintain globally unique names arose from this. Names within the context of their immediate parent element should be unambiguous and descriptive (of course, in the case of some common repeated structures it may be necessary to gain the context by referring to a grandparent or great grandparent, as may be the case with a PostCode element in a Contact Details structure). What is critical is that we are consistent with our naming convention, especially with regards to capitalization.

The first object we will look at is the `Writer` object. Below is the current class definition:

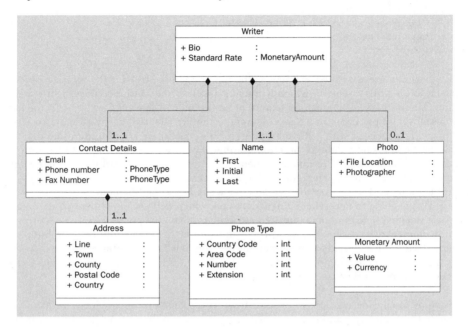

This object diagram shows some of the datatype assignments and cardinality constraints, as well as including the definitions for two custom datatypes: `PhoneType` and `MonetaryAmount`. It does not show any information regarding ordering, or explicitly imply which properties are elements or attributes. The following example XML fragment will provide us with further insight into the structure. In this case, the XML structure matches the object diagram. However, it is quite likely that when creating the sample XML fragment for a structure, we will discover properties that we needed or different arrangements of the internal objects, thus leading to a revision of our object model. Similarly, when we create the XML Schema definition for the structure we may decide on further enhancements or modifications to our object model. The point is to be open to this and not be of the mindset of exactly producing the content of the object model. If XML is the ultimate medium for the representation of the information model, then we should let it influence our ideas about the organization and content of the objects in the information model.

```xml
<?xml version="1.0" encoding="utf-8"?>
<!-- writer.xml -->
<Writer xmlns="http://www.thebikezone.org/xmlSchema/common-20010612">
    <Name First="Gavin" Initial="P" Last="McGynn"/>
    <Biography>A brief write up about Gavin McGwynn</Biography>
    <Photo FileLocation="GavinMcGynn.jpg" Photographer="phillips"/>
    <StandardRate Currency="GBP" >1200.00</StandardRate>
    <ContactDetails>
        <PhoneNumber CountryCode="44" AreaCode="1265" LocalNumber="803234"
                 Extension="126" />
        <Email>gavin@freemail.org</Email>
        <Address>
            <Line>Harbour Cottage</Line>
            <Town>Wallingford</Town>
            <County>Oxfordshire</County>
```

```
                <PostalCode>OX33 5PQ</PostalCode>
                <Country>UK</Country>
            </Address>
        </ContactDetails>
    </Writer>
```

We have chosen to use a `Writer` element as the top node in the tree for the `Writer` object, and have presented it as an XML fragment, which will make a well-formed instance document ready for validation. The primary distinguishing feature of an instance of the `Writer` object is the name of the writer, therefore, we put name in a `Name` element as the first element of the `Writer` structure. While a `Photo` object is associated with a Photographer, in this context we are not interested in actually reproducing the information about the Photographer, rather we choose simply to have an identifier `phillips`, which can be used to uniquely identify a Photographer record within the system. With respect to the `StandardRate` element, we have now reached the stage of actually representing a monetary amount, and we realize that we do have `Writers` whom the company needs to pay in foreign currency. This is going to necessitate a new datatype, which defines an element containing an appropriate decimal field, and an associated attribute on that element to specify the currency (see the `Currency` element above). Finally, we also see an example of abstraction; because both Phone Number and Fax Number had identical definitions from our Object definitions, we therefore elected to create a `PhoneType` consisting of `Country Code`, `Area Code`, `Local Number`, and `Extension` – PhoneNumber is of this type (see below for more on this).

We now come to considering how we would structure a schema for this object. We have already identified both `PhoneType` and `MonetaryAmount` as types in their own right, but are there any other pieces of the `Writer` object that can be abstracted to allow for re-use? `ContactDetails` certainly comes to mind, and within that there is `Address`. When deciding if `Address` should be removed into its own type we must ask ourselves if `Address` will ever be used separately from `ContactDetails`, and if the conclusion we come to is "yes". The same question can be asked of all aspects of this sample, from which we will conclude that `Photo` and `Name` may appear in other locations within our system and therefore can be removed to their own types, while `Biography` we decide only has meaning as a child element of `Writer`. This gives us the following list of types to define in our XML Schema:

❑ Writer

❑ Name

❑ Photo

❑ ContactDetails

❑ Address

❑ PhoneType

❑ MonetaryAmount

We have observed that the last two items on the list, `PhoneType` and `MonetaryAmount`, do not themselves exist in the instance document, rather they are used to assign their content to a named element. This is in contrast to the first five, where the actual element names match the type names. Whenever a new type is created we must decide if in the XML we always want it to have the same element or attribute name, or if it is preferable to assign the content of the type to some arbitrarily named element or attribute. In this case, we decide that `Writer`, `Name`, `Photo`, `ContactDetails`, and `Address` should always have those element names. Therefore in the XML Schema we define them as global elements, which can then be referenced into a particular location.

The following is an XML Schema document that will validate instance documents with `Writer` as the document element:

```xml
<?xml version="1.0" encoding="utf-8"?>
<!-- writer.xsd -->
<!--
Global Element declarations:
    Writer
    Photo
    Name
    Address
    ContactDetails
Global Type declarations:
    MonetaryAmount
    PhoneType
-->
<xs:schema targetNamespace="http://www.thebikezone.org/xmlSchema/common-20010612"
xmlns="http://www.thebikezone.org/xmlSchema/common-20010612"
xmlns:xs="http://www.w3.org/2001/XMLSchema"
elementFormDefault="qualified" id="WriterDraft" version="0.1">

<!-- Writer Global Element definition -->
<xs:element name="Writer">
<xs:complexType>
<xs:sequence>
   <xs:element ref="Name"/>
   <xs:element name="Biography" type="xs:string" maxOccurs="unbounded" />
   <xs:element ref="Photo" maxOccurs="unbounded"/>
   <xs:element name="StandardRate" type="MonetaryAmount" maxOccurs="unbounded"/>
   <xs:element ref="ContactDetails"/>
</xs:sequence>
</xs:complexType>
</xs:element>

<!-- Photo Global Element definition -->
<xs:element name="Photo">
<xs:complexType>
   <xs:attribute name="FileLocation" type="xs:string" use="required" />
   <xs:attribute name="Photographer" type="xs:string" use="required" />
   <xs:attribute name="Description" type="xs:string"  use="optional" />
</xs:complexType>
</xs:element>

<!-- Name Global Element definition -->
<xs:element name="Name">
<xs:complexType>
   <xs:attribute name="First"   type="xs:string" use="required" />
   <xs:attribute name="Initial" type="xs:string" use="optional" />
   <xs:attribute name="Last"    type="xs:string" use="required" />
</xs:complexType>
</xs:element>

<!-- Address Global Element definition -->
<xs:element name="Address">
<xs:complexType>
```

```
<xs:sequence>
    <xs:element name="Line"       type="xs:string" maxOccurs="4" />
    <xs:element name="Town"       type="xs:string" />
    <xs:element name="County"     type="xs:string" />
    <xs:element name="PostalCode" type="xs:string" />
    <xs:element name="Country"    type="xs:string" />
</xs:sequence>
</xs:complexType>
</xs:element>

<!-- ContactDetails Global Element definition -->
<xs:element name="ContactDetails">
<xs:complexType>
<xs:sequence>
    <xs:element name="PhoneNumber" type="PhoneType" minOccurs="1"
maxOccurs="unbounded"/>
    <xs:element name="FaxNumber"   type="PhoneType" minOccurs="0"
maxOccurs="unbounded"/>
    <xs:element name="Email"       type="xs:string" minOccurs="0"
maxOccurs="unbounded" />
    <xs:element ref="Address" maxOccurs="unbounded"/>
</xs:sequence>
</xs:complexType>
</xs:element>

<!-- MonetaryAmount Type definition -->
<xs:complexType name="MonetaryAmount">
<xs:simpleContent>
    <xs:extension base="xs:string">
        <xs:attribute name="Currency" type="xs:string" use="required" />
    </xs:extension>
</xs:simpleContent>
</xs:complexType>

<!-- PhoneType Type definition -->
<xs:complexType name="PhoneType">
    <xs:attribute name="CountryCode" type="xs:string" use="required" />
    <xs:attribute name="AreaCode"    type="xs:string" use="required" />
    <xs:attribute name="LocalNumber" type="xs:string" use="required" />
    <xs:attribute name="Extension"   type="xs:string" use="optional" />
</xs:complexType>

</xs:schema>
```

This schema has now detailed the specific ordering conditions for elements and asserted cardinality rules, but we notice that there is nothing special about the Writer global element, which marks it as a legal document element. This is because XML Schema does not distinguish between global elements meant for element ref="" statements, and those meant to be legal document elements. If we were to try validating the following instance document against the above schema, we would find that it does, in fact validate successfully:

```
<?xml version="1.0" encoding="utf-8"?>
<!-- name.xml -->
<Name xmlns="http://www.thebikezone.org/xmlSchema/common-20010612"
    First="Gavin" Initial="P" Last="McGynn"/>
```

To cope with this, a simple solution is to wrap all the global elements other than `Writer` (or more generally other than those that you want to be legal document elements) each in a `<group name="">` tag. For example, rather than using `<element ref="" />`, simply use `<group ref="" />`. We could reformat our definition of the `Name` type as follows:

```
<!-- Name Global Group definition -->
<xs:group name="Name">
   <xs:element name="Name">
   <xs:complexType>
      <xs:attribute name="First"   type="xs:string" use="required" />
      <xs:attribute name="Initial" type="xs:string" use="optional" />
      <xs:attribute name="Last"    type="xs:string" use="required" />
   </xs:complexType>
   </xs:element>
</xs:group>
```

Now, inside the `Writer` type definition we can replace the following line:

```
<xs:element ref="Name"/>
```

with this one:

```
<xs:group ref="Name"/>
```

and the effect is to include all the elments in the global group `Name`, which by design happens to consist of only one element, also called `Name`. Since global `groups` are not legal document elements (because they can store multiple elements, and a well-formed document can only contain a single document element) we therefore have achieved our goal of effectively allowing element references without creating unwanted legal instance documents.

Representing Relationships in XML Schema

We identified four types of relationships for the objects in our information model: composition, aggregation, inheritance, and association. Each can be represented in XML Schema. When converting our information model to a data model (that is, to XML Schema), we will look at each of the relationships we have defined and build our instance documents, first according to which objects a specific instance document requires, and second, based on the objects definition, which includes its properties, sub-objects, and cardinality rules, business rules, and relationships.

Composition

We have already said that composition is the most straightforward relationship, as it is a simple nesting of one object within a container. In XML this translates to defining one element or attribute as the child of another element. An example is the `Biography` element within `Writer`. Compositions will be represented by creating an anonymous sub-type and placing the contained object inside it.

Aggregation

Aggregation is somewhat more complicated. In circumstances where the instance of an aggregated object only occurs once in a document it is possible to include it using the same technique as composition: simply define the aggregated object to exist inside its containing element. This is exactly what has been done with the `Photo` object in our `Writer` schema above. Although the `Photo` object exists on its own, we have elected to copy the information about an instance of a `Photo` object into the `Writer` object. The key issue here is that it is *copied* from a definitive source.

433

To contrast this, imagine an instance document consisting of all the instances of all the objects in the system. In such a situation we would not want to have multiple occurrences of popular photos, or of a `Writer` object with every one of their stories. Instead we would make use of an indirection mechanism that would provide an index to the actual definition of the writer or photo. This approach can also be applied when a particular instance document includes an object that has mandatory sub-objects joined by aggregation.

The `Photographer` attribute on the `Writer` object's `Photo` object is just such an example. With each photo we don't really need to see the details of the particular photographer, but we do need some mechanism by which we can fetch that information when it is necessary. We do that using an index:

```
<Photo FileLocation="GavinMcGynn.jpg" Photographer="phillips"/>
```

So the `Photographer` attribute is not an instance of a `Photographer` object, but an index, which our application can use to fetch the appropriate `Photographer` object if required.

When aggregations within a document are such that the aggregated instance object is contained within the document in one location and referred to in another, we can use XML Schema to assert the consistency of these indexes. Imagine in our example a document that contains instance objects for all the information items within the system. We would have a massive document, one section of which that would contain all the `Photo` elements, and another which would contain all the `Photographer` elements. Using `key` and `keyref` we can assert that all `Photographer` indexes must refer to an actual photographer. To achieve this, the `Photographer` attribute on `Photo` is marked as a `keyref` to the `key` attribute of a `Photographer` element within the schema:

```
<Photos>
    <Photo FileLocation="GavinMcGynn.jpg" Photographer="phillips"/>
    <Photo FileLocation="RedRocks.jpg"   Photographer="westwood"/>
    <Photo FileLocation="GXK7000.jpg"    Photographer="cooper"/>
    <Photo FileLocation="FinishLine.jpg" Photographer="cooper"/>
</Photos>
<Photographers>
    <Photographer key="cooper">   <!-- content here --> </Photographer>
    <Photographer key="phillips"> <!-- content here --> </Photographer>
    <Photographer key="westwood"> <!-- content here --> </Photographer>
</Photographers>
```

The corresponding schema fragment would look like:

```
<element name="Photos">
    <!-- annonymous content definition for Photo goes here -->
    <keyref refer="photographerIndex" name="dummy">
        <selector xpath="Photo"/>
        <field xpath="@Photographer"/>
    </keyref>
</element>
<element name="Photographers">
    <!-- annonymous content definition for Photographer goes here -->
    <key name="photographerIndex">
        <selector xpath="Photographer"/>
        <field xpath="@key"/>
    </key>
</element>
```

This is very similar to the functionality provided by ID and IDREF under DTDs. However, XML Schema keys and keyrefs are contextual, don't only work on attribute values, and can use any field as a key, rather than just ID attributes. (Identity constraints were covered in detail in Chapter 9.)

Inheritance

Inheritance relationships only apply to types. The inheritance structure in XML Schema is very straightforward, and was covered in detail in Chapter 4. There are two basic complexities for XML Schema types: simple types and complex types. However, there is also a hybrid complex type that inherits from a simple type, thus allowing an element to contain sub-elements and attributes while at the same time having a defined text content field. Simple types can be applied to elements and attributes, while complex types and hybrid simple/complex types can only be applied to elements. The following table illustrates the general effects of applying restriction or extension when inheriting from a simple or complex type in order to create a new type:

Inherited type	Restriction	Extension
Simple Type	New type is a simple type, which defines a subset of the inherited type.	New type is a complex type, which adds attributes to the element, and allows the element value to be of a simple type.
Complex Type	New type is a complex type, which defines a subset of the inherited type.	New type is a complex type, which adds elements or attributes to the inherited type.

Association

Where two objects or properties are related to each other it is possible create a link within the XML instance document tying the two items together. This is done by creating a key / keyref pair for the associated items using the same mechanism shown for aggregation relationships.

Global Declarations

It is important to understand that our schema "connects" to instance documents and other schemas at two points: through global declarations and via the any element, the first being at the "top" of a schema document and the second only legal at "leaf" nodes.

We are going to look at the various ways to access information in a schema document, how to share it with other schemas, and how to tie these into an instance document. A schema document allows us to define five kinds of global items, which can be reused elsewhere, either within the same schema document or inside other schemas. Global declarations are immediate children of the schema element, and do not have cardinality constraints since they would have no meaning. The five types of global declarations are as follows:

- ❑ **Global Element** – these can make legal document elements in instance documents and also can be used by reference.

- ❑ **Global Attribute** – defines attributes that can be used by reference within a schema or instance document. These are particularly important for allowing special "generic" attributes, which can occur anywhere to be placed on any element in an instance document.

❑ **Element Group** – groups can only be declared globally. All group declarations must be named, so the group can be referenced in at any location that an element can be created. Global element groups provide a mechanism for defining a block of structure.

❑ **Attribute Group** – similar to element groups, but define blocks of attributes. These can only be referenced at a location where an attribute can be created.

❑ **Type Definitions** – named simple (data field only) and complex (data field and structural) types that can be re-used.

Because of these, each schema document should list the global items it defines in a comment. It is also useful to know where the "exit" points are from the Schema, and, if they are reasonably limited, declare which externally defined items are used in the schema and where. Of course, XML Schema base types should not be included in this list. Our `Writer` schema above illustrates this.

As we saw in Chapter 8, the `include` statement is equivalent to copying the contents of the included file into the current schema document, so `include` can be used to break up a schema document or a set of definitions for the same namespace into multiple documents. An interesting effect is the use of null namespace schema documents that are included, since the behavior is for them to assume the namespace of the including schema, thus allowing what is termed "Chameleon" schemas. Again, we saw this in Chapter 8. The `import` instruction declares an alternate namespace to be made available within the current schema. The validating application can fetch as many schema documents as it wishes from that namespace, although `import` will probably specify a specific schema document containing the relevant schema definitions. Any global declarations made within these imported schemas are now available for use within the current schema.

Global declarations, therefore, can come from one of three sources: the current schema document, `include` statements, and `import` statements. They can be used in one of three ways: by assigning an element or attribute to be of a particular type, deriving a new type from an existing type, or referencing a global element, attribute or group.

The alternative mechanism of using `any` elements allows us to specify any element, either from the local namespace (`namespace="##local"`), any *other* namespace (`##other`), some specific namespace (`http://some.other.namespace/`), or any namespace at all (`##any`). In these cases, any globally defined element from the appropriate namespace may exist where the `any` element is in the schema. `anyAttribute` has a similar function, but for attributes, and these apply to the element containing the `anyAttribute` statement.

Guidelines for Schema Design

Now it is necessary to begin the process of refining type definitions and applying facets such that all the business rules are satisfied. Many business rules are not achievable with XML Schema alone, such as our example business rule #4 from the earlier section ("The distribution total must equal the sum of all shipments to all distributors"), or strict validation – which an email address string corresponds to the RFC 822 grammar. In these cases, additional processing will be required. Some general guidelines can facilitate this process and lead to a better XML Schema:

❑ Do not allow empty elements or attributes. Instead, ensure that they either have some value or are not present. If an element or attribute is mandatory (such as `minOccurs="1"` or `use="required"`), allowing an empty string as the value is questionable. If they are "allowed" to be empty, then it is better to set `minOccurs="0"` or `use="optional"`, and take their absence to mean "no value"; if they do exist, force them to have some content.

- ❏ Since whitespace can increase the size of an instance document significantly, it may be necessary for an application receiving an XML instance document to confirm the file size is under a certain limit. Also, individual fields should generally be of restricted length since a processing application will often have some limit as to the size of the data structure it can create for a given fragment of a parsed instance document. Furthermore, many databases will have size restrictions on certain types of fields, especially if they are keys, or are being used as part of triggers.

- ❏ Create limited versions of the base types `string`, `decimal`, and `integer` in order to restrict character set and field size – for example, define `myDecimal` to disallow more than one leading zero. Otherwise, be prepared to accept all XML Schema base type definitions with their Unicode variant.

- ❏ Make use of the `unique` element to assert uniqueness of element or attribute values.

- ❏ Use `key` / `keyref` elements to associate two locations in a document. Any path in the document can be specified as a named `key`, such that all paths that are a `keyref` to that named `key` must contain a value specified as a `key`.

- ❏ If the schema is in danger of becoming large, consider moving sections into other files using the group reference method. The principle of abstraction applies equally here. These secondary schema files do not need to have even one global element. We may have one file containing all the named simple type definitions, one for named complex type definitions, and one for groups; we may choose to divide them into related blocks. A very powerful representation of our data model would then be via a *header* XML Schema file consisting essentially of prototypes for all the important elements, attributes, groups, and type declarations, and then including a number of `include` statements, which have the effect of adding the specified file to the current XML Schema document.

- ❏ Wherever we change namespaces in an instance document, use an `any` element and explicitly specify the namespace and number of child elements permitted at that location, or include an `element ref="..."` element to explicitly name the element in the new namespace. Either of these techniques can be used to build a schema, which spans several namespaces and therefore schema documents.

- ❏ If an element or attribute does not exist, does the application take this to mean there is a default value? If so, this can explicitly be stated by using the `default` attribute on the element or attribute declaration.

- ❏ Include the `blockDefault="#all"` attribute on the `schema` element. This will prevent derived types being allowed to substitute in an instance document. This is a security issue, and depends on the application's mechanism for schema validation. It is safer to take the position that derived types cannot be substituted when validating, and if the explicit decision is made, allow derivations substituting in when validating, so this restriction can be lifted, or only applied selectively with the `block` attribute.

- ❏ Include the `finalDefault="#all"` attribute on the `schema` element. This will prevent any new types deriving from those declared in this schema. This is a much stricter constraint than `blockDefault`, but again should probably be the default schema rule. If an explicit decision is made to allow derivations then this can be lifted or applied selectively with the `final` attribute on type definitions.

Testing the Data Model

Now that we have created a number of sample instance documents and refined their corresponding schemas, it is critical to test the validity and functionality of the schema and sample documents. Firstly, we should make sure that both the schemas and their instance documents are valid (that is, according to XML rules), and that the instance documents are successfully validated against the schemas (that is, that they contain the right information). Secondly, we should make sure that the schemas and XML documents actually meet the criteria we laid out, and do what we had planned. For every business rule and data field, we should consider several pass cases and several failure cases. Particular attention should be given to the boundary cases. A minimal rule of thumb would be to incorporate at least three tests per business rule, but for Facts and Derivations, we probably want to have around ten tests per business rule. The business domain experts will also be familiar with the problem scenarios and exceptional cases. These should be included in a regression test system to allow us to test our model after any changes.

Maintaining a set of tests can be tedious but pays great dividends when changes to the system or schema are required. Whenever we come across a bug we create tests that expose that bug and then add them to the test suite to insure that any future changes will not break the fix again.

Summary

By following the simplified system modeling techniques described in this chapter, you will build up a picture of the required system and produce a model that will aid your implementation efforts and the quality of the project documentation. The emphasis must be on reaching the actual implementation stage with a firm understanding of the requirements, and a model to facilitate the development. Any modeling that is done must be Complete, Meaningful, Efficient, and Unambiguous. Diagramming techniques are not in and of themselves the complete system model, but only tools for aiding in the collaborative and organizational process, which will build up appropriate levels of abstraction to allow designers to focus on related objects and functionality without being overwhelmed by the overall system.

To recap, the key steps in the system modeling process are:

1. Establish system requirements, to get a background on the project and what our role is.

2. Identify the key players, such as end users, business domain experts, and managers who are involved with the system.

3. Business process analysis, to allow us to understand the business problem, and the general business domain.

4. Create an information model for any existing system, both to confirm understanding of existing systems and also to act as reference for new system.

5. Information gathering to identify the primary objects in the system, relationships between those objects, and any associated business rules.

6. Object model to arrange objects, record initial properties, and mark known associations.

7. Use case diagram to overview actors and major use cases for system.

8. System decomposition and abstraction to group related objects and actions.

9. Information modeling: establish cardinality, relationships, and business rules between objects. Create tabular object lists with object definitions.

10. Sequence diagrams to illustrate processing model, and related event object definitions.

11. Define properties of objects, and datatypes.

12. Instance document definitions, determining what instance documents are required and what namespaces and schemas they will be defined in.

13. Schema document definitions.

The field of system, information, data, and process modeling is vast, and there are specialists who spend their lives mastering the techniques, so it is difficult to consider these few pages as having done it full justice, but you should now have a framework to operate in and sufficient knowledge to be able to systematically analyze and model XML documents or messages within systems of reasonable complexity.

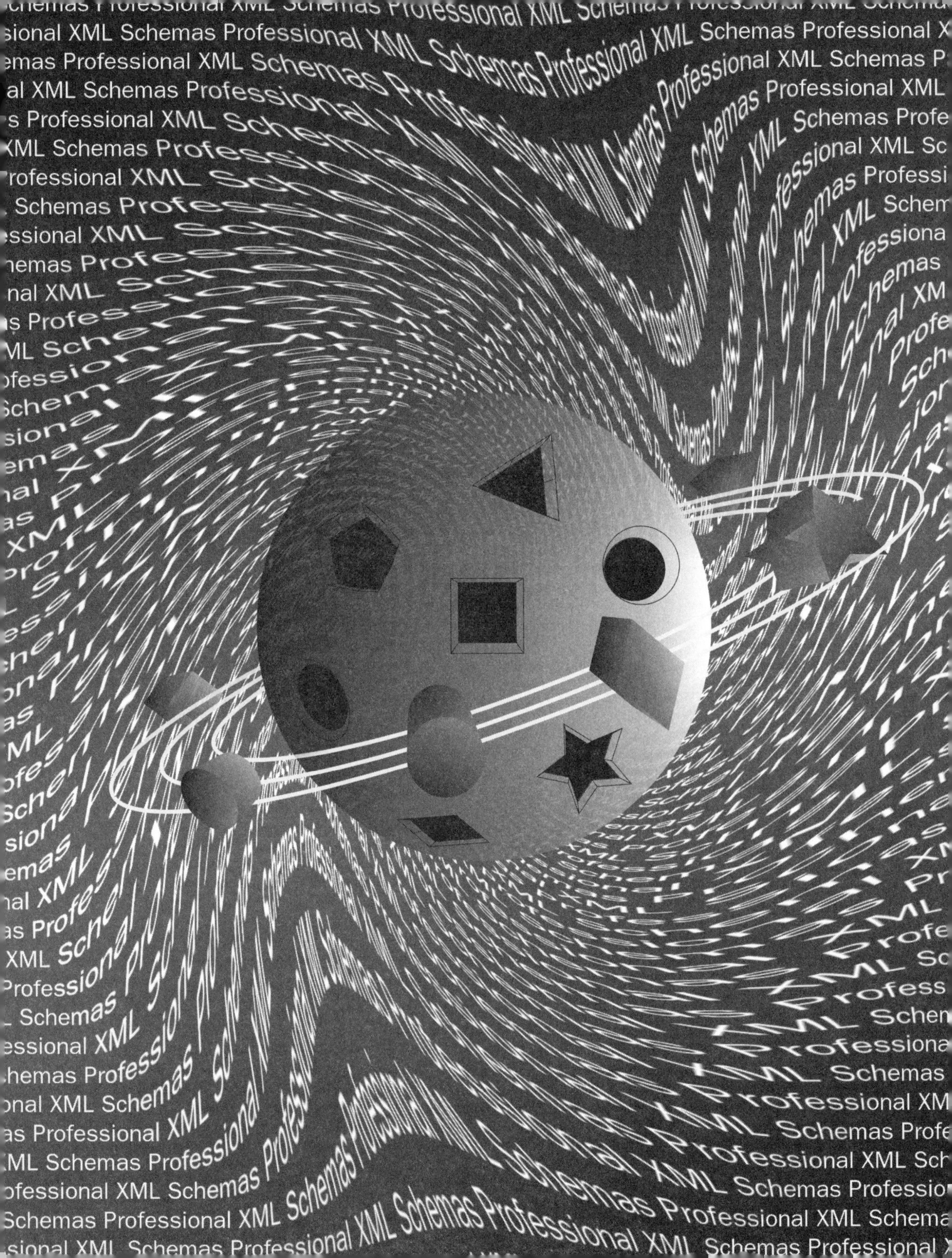
Professional XML Schemas

Creating XML Schema for an Existing Database

In this chapter, we will look at some examples of taking a relational database structure and designing XML Schemas to model that structure. The techniques used to create the schemas in this case study build on the rules for designing XML structures from existing databases that were enumerated in the Wrox book, *Professional XML Databases*, by Kevin Williams et al. (ISBN: 1-861003-58-7). We have extended those rules here to show how type information may be transformed into W3C XML Schema specifications. We will also look at the construction of user-defined types and how they may be used to make your XML Schema easier to comprehend and adopt.

The Business Problem

The fictional company in our case study is a company that resells manufactured items to its customers. The company's invoice system uses a relational database to store the information about the invoices – the type and quantity of parts ordered on each invoice and the related customer information. The company would like to design two document types from the information in the database. The first will be used to provide online information to the customers about the status of all the orders they currently have outstanding, and the second will be used to transmit part and order date information to the manufacturer for invoices in a particular time period so that the orders may be filled in bulk. We will walk through the design of these two documents using XML Schema.

Technologies to Be Used

This chapter is deliberately platform-agnostic – the techniques demonstrated in this chapter may be applied with equal success to any relational database. Similarly, some of the other development tasks associated with the overall business goals – such as the creation of XSLT stylesheets for the presentation of status information for multiple platforms – are outside the scope of this chapter. For more information on how to tackle these kinds of tasks, please refer to *Professional XSL*, by Kurt Cagle et al. (ISBN: 1-861003-57-9), also by Wrox Press.

Unfortunately, the worlds of relational database design and XML Schema have a significant number of terminology clashes. Terms like schema, attribute, and entity can be difficult to resolve. In this chapter, we use the prefix logical or logical schema to indicate that we are discussing the relational database side of the design, while the prefix XML or XML Schema is used to indicate information about the resultant XML documents or the W3C Recommendation itself.

In this chapter, we are only dealing with the analysis and design of the XML Schemas for the two documents we have outlined above. Other programming functions, such as the actual generation and consumption of these documents, are outside the scope of this case study.

The Relational Database Schema

The system we are working with in this example already has a relational schema defined for it. We will be working with a strongly typed logical schema model, as that is the best starting point for creating XML Schemas. XML Schemas can also be created from physical models, but it is easier to see archetypes in the logical model (as we'll see later in the chapter).

The logical schema for our system looks like this:

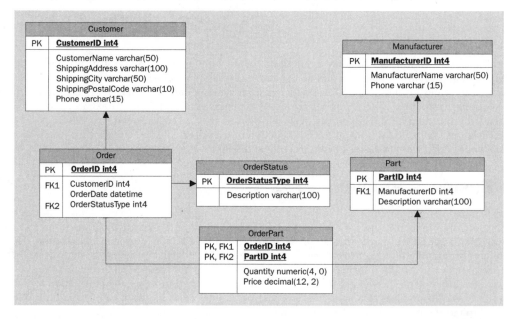

As you can see, we have an OrderPart table, which is central to the schema. It has a relationship with the Part table, which stores information on the parts that can be ordered and who makes them, and the Order table, which stores the details of orders made, and by whom. These two tables are in turn related to the Manufacturer table and the Customer table respectively. In addition, there is a lookup table, OrderStatus, which is connected to the Order table, and provides it with OrderStatusType definitions. This design allows full order information to be brought together easily and quickly, but keeps the information separate and therefore flexible.

Migrating our Database to XML

When wishing to represent a relational database using XML Schema, there are some major considerations that you need to make before you even start:

❑   Determining document scope – deciding on the purpose of the document, and hence its content.

❑   Representing type information – determining the information types of our content, and then going on to decide what XML Schema data types to use to represent these.

❑   Creating a Traversal Path – working out how to structure our document, by looking at how the data we wish to present is structured and accessed in the database, and modeling it accordingly in XML so that the path used to access it is as easy and logical to use as possible.

Determining the Document's Scope

The first step in creating an XML Schema from a relational database is to determine the **scope** of the document being defined by the XML Schema. This includes the document's purpose, and it's content and structure. These follow on from one another – the purpose we give to our XML documents may not require all the tables in the relational database to be modeled in XML, as we may only be looking at a particular subset of the information. After we have decided on the content to include, we then need to think about how to structure that content.

As we talk about these techniques, we'll work through the first example scenario – that of presenting our customers with information about their orders.

Representational or Transactional

The first decision that has to be made is whether the XML document is intended to represent the data for a prolonged period of time (such as an archival copy of an application) or if it instead should be created on the fly and discarded after it is used (such as a transaction request sent to a service). Typically, representational models can be derived entirely from the source relational database model, while transactional models may need to be augmented with other information (such as credentials, in the case of a transaction request). In the first example, we are creating a transactional document that will be styled to present status information to a customer for a particular order.

Determining the Content

We now need to decide on the content we want to use in our XML document, that is, what portion of the relational data structure is important in the XML document type we are defining? Often, our relational databases will contain internal tracking or reference information (such as automatically-generated primary keys) that is not relevant to the representation of that information in an XML Schema. By removing information that is not important in the document being produced, document size and generation time will be reduced, and the document will (in all likelihood) be easier to manipulate.

For our example, we want to use all the information necessary to supply the customer with the status and date of their orders. Note that for the purposes of this example we assume that the user has authenticated in some other part of the system, and can be sent this information without any privacy concerns.

Based on the business requirements for our first example, we determine that the interesting data points to represent in our XML Schema are the following (marked by asterisks in our diagram):

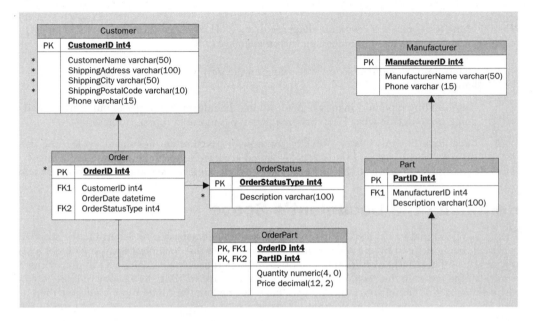

Representing Type Information

When designing XML Schemas for data, it is perfectly acceptable to use only the primitive data types defined in the W3C XML Schema Recommendation. However, our schemas may be made more understandable if user-defined data types are used. This makes the schema easier to read and implement, as well as ensuring consistency across similar data elements (for example, all descriptions will allow a maximum of 100 characters). We'll see how these user-defined data types come into play later in the chapter.

Creating a Traversal Path

Next, we need to work out how we are going to structure our XML document. A good place to start is by getting an understanding of how we will obtain the information we want from our relational database. This is where the **traversal path** comes in: the traversal path is the path used by the program to access the data, that is, which tables it must step through to reach the relevant entry. In an XML document, we mimic the traversal path in the nesting structures to facilitate programmatic access to the data.

Why Is a Traversal Path Important?

Imagine that you are a consumer of an XML document built from our sample schema. If you need to obtain information about customers, but instead you are presented with order information as well, this makes your job (both from a programming and a processing time perspective) more troublesome. If we design the document with the consumer in mind, as all good XML documents should be designed, then we should find that it lends itself better to our purpose, and we won't waste time presenting information that our consumer doesn't need to see.

The other important thing about the design of XML documents is that they are naturally hierarchical in form – most XML libraries are designed to most easily retrieve related information when it is found in a parent-child relationship. Therefore, it makes sense to (where possible) create parent-child relationships that follow the natural way we will access the information in the tables in our relational schema, that is, to follow the relationships between the tables.

For example, let's say we want to reconstruct a particular order. First we would go to the Order table – after all, we probably have an OrderID we're starting with – and get the information there. Next, we would go to the OrderPart table and retrieve all of the quantities and prices of each part ordered. Finally, we would go to the Part table and get the description of all the parts we are showing on the invoice. As you can see, there's a natural join order we need to follow to access the information. This is our traversal path.

XML documents are naturally hierarchical in form – most XML libraries are designed to allow easy retrieval of related information when it is found in a parent-child relationship. Therefore, it makes sense to (where possible) create parent-child relationships that follow the natural way we will access the information in the tables in our relational schema.

Traversing Our First Example

The main point of our example is to store the information and status of all outstanding orders, and report this information to the customer. If we refer to the previous diagram, we see that we have only elected to show information from the Customer and Order tables – it wouldn't make much sense to report back individual line items to the customer, for example!

Let's say we want to reconstruct a particular order from our sample database. To do this, first we would go to the Customer table – after all, we are probably starting with a customerID – and get relevant information from there. Next, we would go to the order table to pick up the relevant orderID, orderStatus (the description of which needs to be looked up in the OrderStatus table), and orderDate. Of course, we could probably return some or all of this information in "one shot" using a join – but there's still a natural join order we need to follow to access the information.

So, the traversal path of our first example is Customer, Order, OrderStatus. We can use this to get an idea of how to model our chosen data in our XML Schema – we will see this below.

Note that we do not need to represent the information in the OrderStatus table – it is a lookup table, and when writing our Schema, we will model it as a user-defined type with a list of possible values, as opposed to creating a separate element structure for it.

Creating the Schema

Now that we have identified the pieces of information and the traversal path that will be relevant to the XML Schema we are defining, we can start building the components of the schema itself. This breaks down into four steps:

❑   Creating the user-defined data types

❑   Modeling the relational entities

❑   Modeling the relational attributes

❑   Modeling the relationships between the tables in the logical model

Creating User-Defined Data types

Before we start defining the structures to hold the data we have selected for inclusion in our model, we first need to create some user-defined data types. These will make our schema more human-readable and the documents created more usable. These user-defined data types come in two flavors – lookup table handlers and common primitive definitions.

Lookup Tables

In almost all relational database designs, there is the concept of a lookup table – a table that provides text descriptions of an enumeration, together with a (usually) numeric value that represents that meaning. The numeric value is then used in the table that references the lookup table, saving space in the relational database structure.

In our example, we are accessing the OrderStatus lookup table, which contains the following entries:

OrderStatusType	Description
1	Received
2	Sent to manufacturer
3	Received from manufacturer
4	In transit
5	Delivered

There are a few ways we could implement this in our design. One way might be to simply use the integer built-in type, with some restrictions on the allowable values:

```
<xs:simpleType name="allowableOrderStatusTypes">
    <xs:restriction base="xs:integer">
        <xs:minInclusive value="1"/>
        <xs:maxInclusive value="5"/>
    </xs:restriction>
</xs:simpleType>
```

However, this doesn't help someone who's trying to understand the document outside of the context of your database. A much better definition would be one that provides human-readable versions of the application status types, such as the one below, in which we model these lookup tables with XML Schema enumerated data types:

```
<xs:simpleType name="allowableOrderStatusTypes">
    <xs:restriction base="xs:string">
        <xs:enumeration value="Received" />
        <xs:enumeration value="SentToManufacturer" />
        <xs:enumeration value="ReceivedFromManufacturer" />
        <xs:enumeration value="InTransit" />
        <xs:enumeration value="Delivered" />
    </xs:restriction>
</xs:simpleType>
```

Remember, when there is a choice to be made when designing an XML document it is almost always better to make the decision that simplifies the consumer's programming job, rather than the producer's. You never know who might need to consume your documents!

Common User-Defined Type Definitions

It also makes sense at this point to decide on some common user-defined data types that we can add to our schema definitions. By defining new data types (rather than just using the primitive types where appropriate), we can ensure that similar concepts are constrained in the same way and that global changes (like changing a date from two year digits to four) do not require a great deal of effort.

Based on the relational schema we are using as our starting point, we can isolate the following candidates for common user-defined types:

- ❑ dollarAmount – decimal(12, 2)
- ❑ quantity – decimal(4, 0)
- ❑ entityName – varchar(50)
- ❑ stateCode – varchar(2)
- ❑ postalCode – varchar(10)
- ❑ description – varchar(100)

Note that it makes sense to define these once for all the information in the relational structure, even though some or all of them may not be used in the specific document structure we are defining. Keeping these definitions consistent across all XML documents derived from this relational data source will make it easier for producers and consumers who are familiar with one type of document derived from this source to pick up and use another document type derived from it.

The definitions for these types are as follows:

```xml
<xs:simpleType name="dollarAmount">
   <xs:restriction base="xs:decimal">
      <xs:totalDigits value="12"/>
      <xs:fractionDigits value="2"/>
   </xs:restriction>
</xs:simpleType>

<xs:simpleType name="quantity">
   <xs:restriction base="xs:integer">
      <xs:totalDigits value="4"/>
   </xs:restriction>
</xs:simpleType>

<xs:simpleType name="entityName">
   <xs:restriction base="xs:string">
      <xs:maxLength value="50"/>
   </xs:restriction>
</xs:simpleType>

<xs:simpleType name="stateCode">
   <xs:restriction base="xs:string">
      <xs:maxLength value="2"/>
```

```
        </xs:restriction>
    </xs:simpleType>

    <xs:simpleType name="postalCode">
        <xs:restriction base="xs:string">
            <xs:maxLength value="10"/>
        </xs:restriction>
    </xs:simpleType>

    <xs:simpleType name="description">
        <xs:restriction base="xs:string">
            <xs:maxLength value="100"/>
        </xs:restriction>
    </xs:simpleType>
```

Modeling the Logical Schema Entities

Next, we model the logical schema entities (or "tables") in our XML Schema. Each logical schema entity should be modeled as an element in our XML structure. Later when we discuss relationships, we'll add the parent-child and pointing relationships as necessary to connect the various elements together. In our example, we only need to model two elements: Customer and Order (remember that we don't need to model OrderStatus since it's a lookup table). Here are the initial content models for these elements (we'll be filling in the complex types for these later in the example):

```
<xs:element name="customer" type="customerType" />

<xs:complexType name="customerType">
</xs:complexType>

<xs:complexType name="orderType" >
</xs:complexType>
```

Modeling the Logical Schema Attributes

Next, we need to model the logical schema attributes we have selected to be part of our XML Schema – in other words, the columns from the source relational database tables. Before we can do so, however, we need to tackle one of everyone's favorite XML modeling issues – do we use elements or attributes for our columns?

Elements or Attributes

Ask any two people who do XML for a living whether elements or attributes are more appropriate for data points in an XML structure, and chances are, you'll get two different answers, which might be diametrically opposed to one another. Here, we'll summarize some general guidelines to follow. When using XML to represent data items from a relational database, it makes much more sense to use attributes, for the following reasons:

❑   Accessing the information programmatically (via the DOM, for example) is easier

❑   Documents are smaller, and therefore take up less space

❑   The disambiguation of structure and data closely mirrors the way that structure and data are disambiguated in a relational database

However, if you choose to instead use elements for this purpose, it's simple enough to change the complex type declaration to declare the data points as a sequence of elements rather than as individual attributes. For our purposes, we'll declare these data points as attributes.

Adding the attribute definitions that represent our data elements to our complex type definitions (and taking into account the user-defined types we created earlier in the chapter), our complex type definitions for our two elements now look like this:

```
<xs:complexType name="customerType">
    <xs:attribute name="customerName" type="entityName" />
    <xs:attribute name="shippingAddress" type="description" />
    <xs:attribute name="shippingCity" type="entityName" />
    <xs:attribute name="shippingState" type="stateCode" />
    <xs:attribute name="shippingPostalCode" type="postalCode" />
</xs:complexType>

<xs:complexType name="orderType" >
    <xs:attribute name="orderID" type="xs:integer" />
    <xs:attribute name="orderDate" type="xs:date" />
    <xs:attribute name="orderStatusType" type="allowableOrderStatusTypes" />
</xs:complexType>
```

Modeling the Logical Schema Relationships

Finally, we need to model the relationships in our logical schema. In an XML Schema, naturally, every element must appear as the child of another element (with the exception of the root element). We may also need to add additional relating mechanisms, such as key structures, that do not fall easily into a parent-child hierarchical model. We build the parent-child relationships based on the traversal path we defined for the XML Schema earlier in the design process.

Using Parent-Child Relationships

As we traverse the path we defined for the schema, each relationship hop down the path should be implemented as a parent-child relationship if possible. This can be done if the following conditions are met:

❑   The relationship is one-to-zero, one-to-one, one-to-zero-or-more, or one-to-one-or-more *in the direction of the traversal*. Note that this may differ from the direction of the relationship as it is defined in the logical schema!

❑   The logical entity at the end of the traversal has not previously been reached by another path in the traversal (if it has, you may still be able to use a parent-child relationship, but it has to be weighed against the actual usage of the data).

If the traversal is zero-or-more-to one or one-or-more-to-one in the direction of the traversal, then a pointing relationship (see below) must be used to show the relationship between the two entities – after all, an element in an XML document can't have more than one parent.

Using Key-Keyref(s) Relationships

If we need to use a pointing relationship in our XML document, we can do so by using a key / keyref pair. XML Schemas introduce this idea, as we saw back in Chapter 9 – they are like ID / IDREF pairs, but much more flexible and useful. To implement one of these relationships, we need to add the following to our structures:

❑ If it's not already present, add an attribute that will be unique across all elements of the given type to the element representing the end point of the traversal path we are dealing with.

❑ Declare the added attribute to be a key for the element at the end point of the traversal.

❑ Add an attribute to the element representing the start point of the traversal with the same name as the unique attribute added to the end point element.

❑ Declare the added attribute as a key reference that refers to the key created at the beginning of the process.

You then need to add a `keyref` element to the definition of the start point of the relationship – again, in the direction of the traversal – that points to an appropriate `key` on the child elements.

Orphaned Elements

Finally, any orphaned elements (elements that are only pointed to, and are not defined as being children of any other element in the structure) must appear as children of the root element of the document. This ensures that orphaned elements, which may only be reached by pointing relationships, have somewhere to live in the resulting XML documents.

For the purposes of our example, there's only one relationship – that between `Customer` and `Order`, in that direction. Since the relationship is one-to-one-or-more in the traversal direction, we can add an `Order` element to the `CustomerType` complex type, and implement the relationship with nested elements. Note that we add a `sequence` compositor, even though it's a sequence of one item – this is to future-proof our design, as we might have to pull data from more than one table at a later date. Also note that we use `minOccurs` and `maxOccurs` to define how often the `Order` children may appear:

```
<xs:complexType name="customerType">
    <xs:sequence>
        <xs:element name="order" type="orderType" minOccurs="1"
                    maxOccurs="unbounded" />
    </xs:sequence>
    <xs:attribute name="customerName" type="entityName" />
    <xs:attribute name="shippingAddress" type="description" />
    <xs:attribute name="shippingCity" type="entityName" />
    <xs:attribute name="shippingState" type="stateCode" />
    <xs:attribute name="shippingPostalCode" type="postalCode" />
</xs:complexType>

<xs:complexType name="orderType" >
    <xs:attribute name="orderID" type="xs:integer" />
    <xs:attribute name="orderDate" type="xs:date" />
    <xs:attribute name="orderStatusType" type="allowableOrderStatusTypes" />
</xs:complexType>
```

After adding in the proper namespace declarations and the user-defined types we created that go with this document, the final schema for our first example looks like this:

```
<?xml version="1.0" encoding="utf-8"?>
<!--databaseSchema1.xsd -->

<xs:schema xmlns:xs="http://www.w3.org/2001/XMLSchema">
```

```
        <xs:element name="customer" type="customerType" />

        <xs:complexType name="customerType">
           <xs:sequence>
              <xs:element name="order" type="orderType" minOccurs="1"
                       maxOccurs="unbounded" />
           </xs:sequence>
           <xs:attribute name="customerName" type="entityName" />
           <xs:attribute name="shippingAddress" type="description" />
           <xs:attribute name="shippingCity" type="entityName" />
           <xs:attribute name="shippingState" type="stateCode" />
           <xs:attribute name="shippingPostalCode" type="postalCode" />
        </xs:complexType>

        <xs:complexType name="orderType" >
           <xs:attribute name="orderID" type="xs:integer" />
           <xs:attribute name="orderDate" type="xs:date" />
           <xs:attribute name="orderStatusType"
              type="allowableOrderStatusTypes" />
        </xs:complexType>

        <xs:simpleType name="entityName">
           <xs:restriction base="xs:string">
              <xs:maxLength value="50"/>
           </xs:restriction>
        </xs:simpleType>

        <xs:simpleType name="stateCode">
           <xs:restriction base="xs:string">
              <xs:maxLength value="2"/>
           </xs:restriction>
        </xs:simpleType>

        <xs:simpleType name="postalCode">
           <xs:restriction base="xs:string">
              <xs:maxLength value="10"/>
           </xs:restriction>
        </xs:simpleType>

        <xs:simpleType name="description">
           <xs:restriction base="xs:string">
              <xs:maxLength value="100"/>
           </xs:restriction>
        </xs:simpleType>

        <xs:simpleType name="allowableOrderStatusTypes">
           <xs:restriction base="xs:string">
              <xs:enumeration value="Received" />
              <xs:enumeration value="SentToManufacturer" />
              <xs:enumeration value="ReceivedFromManufacturer" />
              <xs:enumeration value="InTransit" />
              <xs:enumeration value="Delivered" />
           </xs:restriction>
        </xs:simpleType>

   </xs:schema>
```

An example of a document that conforms to this schema might be:

```xml
<?xml version="1.0" encoding="utf-8"?>
<!-- databaseSchema1.xml -->

<customer customerName="Fred's Steel Works"
          shippingAddress="100 Steel Works Place"
          shippingCity="Steel City"
          shippingState="PA"
          shippingPostalCode="12345">
  <order orderID="20187"
         orderDate="5/12/2001"
         orderStatus="InTransit" />
  <order orderID="21098"
         orderDate="5/15/2001"
         orderStatus="Received" />
</customer>
```

A More Complex Example

Next, we'll take a look at a more complex example – that of an XML Schema for defining a document to list all the parts that are required to be provided by a particular manufacturer for a given time period. Each part will be listed along with information about the order for that part, so that the manufacturer can fulfill the orders in a timely fashion.

Document Scope

First, we need to decide what information in the document is germane to the business problem at hand. In this example, we need to pass back all the parts that correspond to a particular manufacturer that have orders in a given time period, along with the information about those orders. We can conclude that the following starred fields are relevant to the document, therefore should be modeled in the schema:

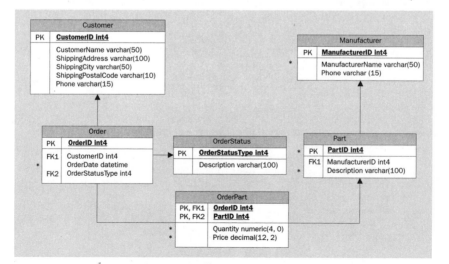

The core concept being conveyed is the manufacturer, so that's where the traversal path needs to start.

The Traversal Path

On analysis of the required fields for our document, we see that there is a direct traversal path from the concept table (the manufacturer) through all the remaining data points. As we will see, the traversal path will include a hop that is one-or-more-to-one in the direction of the traversal, necessitating a pointing relationship to describe the data.

The traversal path for this schema is shown in the following diagram (represented by the dotted arrows):

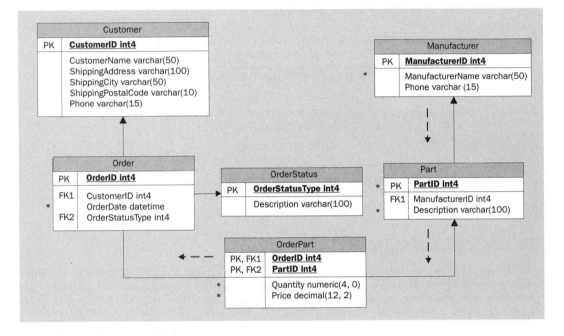

The Logical Schema Entities

In this example, our starting point is the Manufacturer logical schema entity. We also need to define elements to represent the Part, Order, and OrderPart elements. This gives us the following partial structure, which we'll flesh out later:

```
<xs:element name="manufacturer" type="manufacturerType" />

<xs:complexType name="manufacturerType">
</xs:complexType>

<xs:complexType name="partType" >
</xs:complexType>

<xs:complexType name="orderType" >
</xs:complexType>

<xs:complexType name="orderPartType" >
</xs:complexType>
```

The Logical Schema Attributes

Next, we need to create XML attributes on the appropriate elements that represent each of the logical schema attributes we have chosen to model in our XML Schema. Note that we are taking advantage of the same set of user-defined data types from the first example – these declarations should be included in our final schema:

```
<xs:element name="manufacturer" type="manufacturerType" />

<xs:complexType name="manufacturerType">
   <xs:attribute name="manufacturerName" type="entityName" />
</xs:complexType>

<xs:complexType name="partType" >
   <xs:attribute name="partID" type="xs:integer" />
   <xs:attribute name="description" type="description" />
</xs:complexType>

<xs:complexType name="orderType" >
   <xs:attribute name="orderDate" type="xs:date" />
</xs:complexType>

<xs:complexType name="orderPartType" >
   <xs:attribute name="quantity" type="quantity" />
   <xs:attribute name="price" type="dollarAmount" />
</xs:complexType>
```

The Logical Schema Relationships

Finally, we have to map each of the traversals in our traversal path. Since all of these relationships (except one) meet the criteria we defined above, they can be mapped as parent-to-child relationships. However, the relationship from orderPart to order fails under these rules – it is one-or-more-to-one in the direction of the traversal. For this relationship, we need to use a pointing mechanism of some kind – let's use a key / keyref pair, as is discussed earlier. In order to show the relationship between orderPart and order, we'll add the appropriate attributes to each.

After adding the parent-child relationships to our structures, and the key and keyref attributes where needed, we have the following complex type definitions:

```
<xs:element name="manufacturer" type="manufacturerType" />

<xs:complexType name="manufacturerType">
   <xs:sequence>
      <xs:element name="part" type="partType" maxOccurs="unbounded" />
   </xs:sequence>
   <xs:attribute name="manufacturerName" type="entityName" />
</xs:complexType>

<xs:complexType name="partType" >
   <xs:sequence>
      <xs:element name="orderPart" type="orderPartType"
         maxOccurs="unbounded">
```

```
        <xs:keyref name="orderFK" refer="orderKey">
            <xs:selector xpath=".//orderPart" />
            <xs:field xpath="@orderID" />
        </xs:keyref>
    </xs:element>
  </xs:sequence>
  <xs:attribute name="partID" type="xs:integer" />
  <xs:attribute name="description" type="description" />
</xs:complexType>

<xs:complexType name="orderType" >
  <xs:attribute name="orderDate" type="xs:date" />
  <xs:attribute name="orderID" type="xs:integer" />
</xs:complexType>

<xs:complexType name="orderPartType" >
  <xs:attribute name="quantity" type="quantity" />
  <xs:attribute name="price" type="dollarAmount" />
  <xs:attribute name="orderID" type="xs:integer" />
</xs:complexType>
```

Orphans

At this point, upon reviewing for orphans, we discover that the `orderType` complex type is not represented as an element anywhere in our structure. To remedy this, we need to add references to them in the root element type definition:

```
<xs:complexType name="manufacturerType">
  <xs:sequence>
    <xs:element name="part" type="partType" maxOccurs="unbounded" />
    <xs:element name="order" type="orderType" maxOccurs="unbounded">
      <xs:key name="orderKey">
        <xs:selector xpath=".//order" />
        <xs:field xpath="@orderID" />
      </xs:key>
    </xs:element>
  </xs:sequence>
  <xs:attribute name="manufacturerName" type="entityName" />
</xs:complexType>
```

At this point, adding the simple type definitions for the user-defined data types and the appropriate XML Schema Namespace declaration, we have the following final XML Schema structure for this example:

```
<?xml version="1.0" encoding="utf-8"?>
<!-- databaseSchema2.xsd -->

<xs:schema xmlns:xs="http://www.w3.org/2001/XMLSchema">

  <xs:element name="manufacturer" type="manufacturerType" />

  <xs:complexType name="manufacturerType">
    <xs:sequence>
```

```
            <xs:element name="part" type="partType" maxOccurs="unbounded" />
            <xs:element name="order" type="orderType" maxOccurs="unbounded">
               <xs:key name="orderKey">
                   <xs:selector xpath=".//order" />
                   <xs:field xpath="@orderID" />
               </xs:key>
            </xs:element>
         </xs:sequence>
         <xs:attribute name="manufacturerName" type="entityName" />
      </xs:complexType>

   <xs:complexType name="partType" >
      <xs:sequence>
         <xs:element name="orderPart" type="orderPartType"
            maxOccurs="unbounded">
            <xs:keyref name="orderFK" refer="orderKey">
               <xs:selector xpath=".//orderPart" />
               <xs:field xpath="@orderID" />
            </xs:keyref>
         </xs:element>
      </xs:sequence>
      <xs:attribute name="partID" type="xs:integer" />
      <xs:attribute name="description" type="description" />
   </xs:complexType>

   <xs:complexType name="orderType" >
      <xs:attribute name="orderDate" type="xs:date" />
      <xs:attribute name="orderID" type="xs:integer" />
   </xs:complexType>

   <xs:complexType name="orderPartType" >
      <xs:attribute name="quantity" type="quantity" />
      <xs:attribute name="price" type="dollarAmount" />
      <xs:attribute name="orderID" type="xs:integer" />
   </xs:complexType>

   <xs:simpleType name="dollarAmount">
      <xs:restriction base="xs:decimal">
         <xs:totalDigits value="12"/>
         <xs:fractionDigits value="2"/>
      </xs:restriction>
   </xs:simpleType>

   <xs:simpleType name="quantity">
      <xs:restriction base="xs:integer">
         <xs:totalDigits value="3"/>
      </xs:restriction>
   </xs:simpleType>

   <xs:simpleType name="entityName">
      <xs:restriction base="xs:string">
         <xs:maxLength value="50"/>
      </xs:restriction>
   </xs:simpleType>

   <xs:simpleType name="description">
```

```
      <xs:restriction base="xs:string">
         <xs:maxLength value="100"/>
      </xs:restriction>
   </xs:simpleType>

</xs:schema>
```

A sample document using this structure might look like the following:

```
<?xml version="1.0" encoding="utf-8"?>
<!-- databaseSchema2.xml -->

<manufacturer manufacturerName="Bob's Widgets">
   <part partID="20178" description="3 in. widgets">
      <orderPart orderID="1762" quantity="7" price="0.20" />
      <orderPart orderID="1899" quantity="12" price="0.20" />
   </part>
   <part partID="18273" description="2 in. grommets">
      <orderPart orderID="1762" quantity="11" price="0.50" />
   </part>
   <part partID="26334" description="1 in. flanges">
      <orderPart orderID="1899" quantity="20" price="0.15" />
   </part>
   <order orderID="1762" orderDate="5/17/2001" />
   <order orderID="1899" orderDate="5/22/2001" />
</manufacturer>
```

Summary

In this chapter, we've taken a look at a couple of examples of designing XML Schema structures to accommodate information from an existing relational database. Apart from the strong typing and user-defined datatype design aspects of what we've done, these techniques are effectively the same as those defined for DTD design, and described in *Professional XML Databases*. If you want to know more about designing XML structures for databases, you are encouraged to read that book and use the techniques touched on in this chapter to augment the techniques learned there. If you use the structured approach we describe here, you will be able to easily leverage your existing relational data into structures that are defined using XML Schemas.

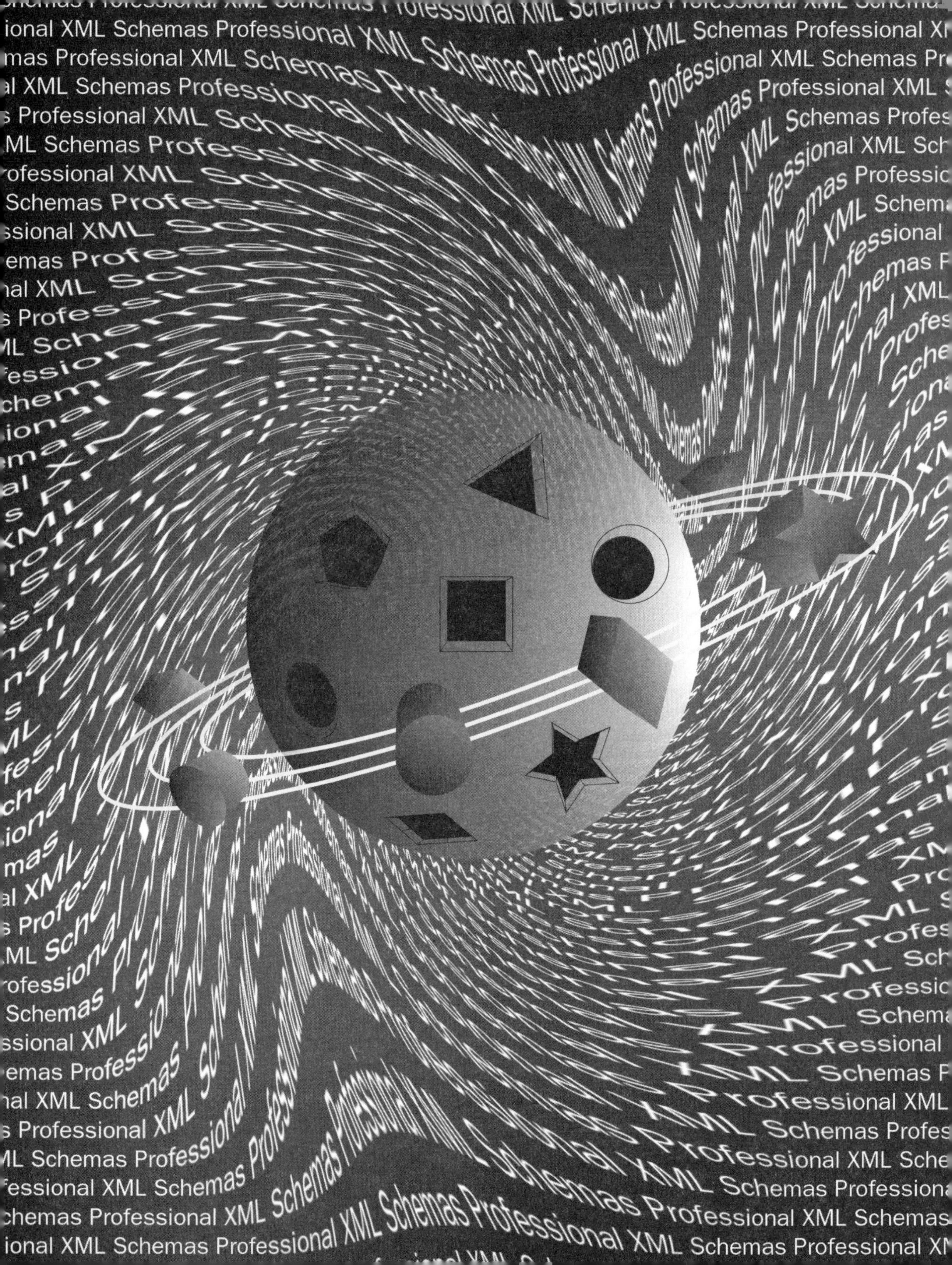
Professional XML Schemas

13

W3C XML Schemas for Document Management

In this chapter we are going to consider developing XML Schemas for documents rather than data. We might ask what the difference is, particularly as the W3C XML Recommendation uses the term XML documents to represent any file that contains XML data, even if it contains, say, data taken from a database of car parts. Equally, we also talk about XML data meaning any XML file or collection of files, even if they are, for example, chapters of a book. Therefore, it's important to understand the difference between XML documents that are data-centric, and XML documents that are document-centric.

Here's some brief history to put this in context. **SGML** (Standard Generalized Markup Language), which is the predecessor of XML and a superset of the XML Recommendation, came out of a project in IBM in the 1960s, concerned with inventing a *Generalized Markup Language* (**GML**) for law office information systems. The idea was that instead of coding documents to indicate *how* they should appear on paper (for example, 14 point Times New Roman bold), the codes should say *what* the different parts of the document were – so there should be codes to indicate headings, paragraphs, emphasis, and so on. The processing of these codes into real typographical specifications was separated from the content creation.

Most of the main concepts of SGML, and hence XML, came out of this project, including formally defined document types and nested element structures. In 1986, after much complexity had been added to these simple ideas, SGML became an international standard (ISO 8879). Partly because it was so complex, SGML took hold slowly, but it began to be used across the world by manufacturers, publishers, governments, and other organizations that created large and complex documents. Its best-known implementation, however, was as HTML, a markup language for web pages, which is an application of SGML (and now, as XHTML, an application of XML).

XML has become important to the data community because it offers an open format for coding data for exchange between and within systems, and because, largely thanks to schemas, it does a lot of the work in validating data that programmers used to do. However, it's worth remembering that there is a growing community of XML users for whom XML is primarily a means of publishing documents. Many of these people were using SGML long before the Web was invented. They are in the publishing industry (mostly in academic, scientific, technical, and medical publishing), technical documentation publishing (mainly defense and transport manufacturing), and business publishing and document management. Many in this community are now moving over to XML to take advantage of its lower costs, larger user base, and the fact that it is simpler to use than SGML.

Document Schemas versus Data Schemas

So what is the difference between XML data and XML documents? Actually there is no technical difference, no point at which data becomes document or vice versa. It's a matter of degree. Look at these examples, one of XML data, one of an XML document:

Typical XML Data

```
<parts>
   <part>
      <partNumber>ECBE5485</partNumber>
      <description>big end</description>
      <partof>crankshaft</partof>
      <fromCar>GAL99</fromCar>
   </part>
</parts>
```

Typical XML Document (fragment)

```
<chapter id="d574dfj">
   <title>XML schemas for document management</title>
   <para>In this chapter we are going to consider developing XML schemas for
         documents rather than data. We might ask what&apos;s the
         difference, particularly as we often talk about XML documents to
         mean any file which contains XML data, even if it contains, say,
         data taken from a database of car parts. Equally we also talk about
         XML data meaning any XML file or collection of files, even if they
         are, say, chapters of a book.
   </para>
</chapter>
```

The first difference we might notice between these two examples is that the first contains discrete *grains* of data, described by the elements that surround them. The second is a flow of text in which some structures (the title for example) have been identified by tags. The XML mechanisms are exactly the same (though the tag names are different), but the way they are used in relation to the content is very different. While XML data instances contain mainly element content or datatypes (at the leaf nodes), XML document instances typically contain a lot of mixed content, literally a mixture of elements and text, as in the above example.

Another way of looking at the difference is the ratio of tags to content. The first contains five words in six elements: a ratio of approximately 1:1. The second contains 77 words in three elements: a ratio of approximately 25:1, which is a dramatic and quantifiable difference.

It's not just in the XML instances that documents look different from data. As we might expect, their schemas look very different too. An XML car part database might define only a handful of elements, because although there may be many parts in a car, they fall into a few categories. Therefore, we might have container elements such as parts and part, and descriptive elements such as partNumber and fromCar.

Many document schemas define upwards of 200 elements (some more than 600), which might include containers such as book, foreword, chapter, list, paragraph, and leaf elements, such as author, publishedDate, and so on. These elements are likely to produce more complex structures than data schemas, simply because documents are usually more complex than fragments of data.

At this point it is worth noting that, to date, there have been very few document schemas developed. SGML introduced Document Type Definitions (DTDs) as a way of defining the potential structures of documents, and until very recently everyone used DTDs for XML. The difference between DTDs and XML Schemas has been covered elsewhere in this book so we won't go into it again, but suffice to say that XML Schemas will eventually replace DTDs because of the extra validation facilities they offer. However, because the major part of designing both DTDs and XML Schemas is understanding and modeling data or documents, there's a lot we can learn from the experience of DTD design.

What XML Documents Model and What They Leave Out

There's another major difference between document and data schemas. With data schemas it's relatively easy to discover what data should be modeled. If the data is coming from a database, or is modeled on a paper form, the different parts of information to be captured will be self-evident – they may be in different fields in the database or appear in a different box on the form.

With documents it's not so easy. As an example, think about the structure of the pages you are reading now. The production people at Wrox have taken the Microsoft Word file this chapter was provided in, and converted it into clear, well-printed type – a process called typesetting. Typesetting (and pagination) involves deciding where column and page breaks go, how different types of title and heading should appear; in short, formatting the text and placing it on the page to make it easy to read.

But all this formatting information – the data that's specific to the printed page – may be irrelevant if this text were delivered over the Internet – to a web client or even a mobile phone. We wouldn't want to know where column breaks occurred because if there are columns of text in the web browser, they are going to be in different places. When we design a schema to model such a document, we have to make a lot of decisions about what is genuine structure (and therefore relevant to all forms the document might take) and what is there as part of its presentation on the printed page.

We're getting to the reason why publishers and other people use XML for publishing. For most it is so that they don't have to create one set of content for paper books, one set for web browsers, and another for, say, voice browsers. Removing the formatting from the text itself gives them the flexibility to process the text in any way they like, so long as they know the structure of what they are processing.

Case Study: Physics Press Goes Online

Let's look at an example of the publishing process. Physics Press is a small, independent (and fictitious) publisher of physics textbooks. Until now they have been a traditional print publisher, and all their content appears as print-on-paper books. This year they have decided to meet the demand there has been for their content to be available both on the web, and by people such as university lecturers who want to re-purpose parts of their books (for example in their own course notes).

The production director of Physics Press has decided that an XML-based production system is required to enable their department to publish on paper and electronically simultaneously. Why use XML though?

XML, whether for documents or data, is about *intelligent content*, that is content which describes itself. This applies to the car parts data, where tags identify the partNumber, and it's true of the XML chapter, where tags also identify the title. This allows the production department of Physics Press to process the same content in any number of different ways. The title might be typeset as 14 point Garamond bold type, or as an H1 (first level heading) element in HTML. It might even be spoken as the title on a voice browser, or used to identify the title of the book by an online bookseller.

At the same time, storing their content in XML will allow Physics Press to *re-purpose* (re-use the same content in different formats or publications) sections of it, and create new publications, or offer it in a modular form to the university lecturers who want a bit from this book, a bit from that, in order to create custom course notes.

The production director of the Press has also learned that if they want to get their content into XML, they will need a schema to define the structure of that content. A schema is the foundation of an XML publishing system, and just like the foundations of a building, it has to be right before we can build the rest of the system on top of it.

In the rest of this chapter we will be considering how to put together a schema for document management, and looking specifically at a schema for publishing.

Managing Document Schema Development

Document schemas are not usually developed in isolation by a single developer, and they break the rule that "too many cooks spoil the broth". Schemas represent much more than the structure of publications or documents – they represent business practice, production methods, and many other aspects of the real world in which they will be used.

Developing a document schema within an organization requires input from many different people because it represents many parts of that organization. It represents the:

❑   Production or document management department who are going to use it to create documents

❑   Development team who will create the systems around it

❑   Marketing department who will have ideas on what products the XML content will be used for

❑   Management team, who need to know what everyone else is up to

To go back to our example of Physics Press, imagine that the marketing department wanted to create a reference web site based on the content of some of the Press's books. The content on this new web site will be taken from specific sections of those books – so whoever is designing the schema needs to know that these sections will be taken out and used on their own, and should therefore be designed in such a way as to allow them to exist in isolation (with their own digital identifiers, IDs, meta data, etc.).

Perhaps the best way to ensure all these people have their say in the design of the schema is to bring them together as a **schema development group**. We would arrange an initial meeting at which the design process is outlined, the group members get to understand why they are involved, and then are pointed towards any material which will help them understand schemas better.

We may want to produce a steering document which forms the basis of discussions about the overall direction the schema design will take – which willinclude considerations of the big issues, such as the scope of the schema, and what it will be used for, and the details such as element naming conventions.

The Schema Design Process: An Overview

Most of the work in developing a document schema is in making decisions about the design of the schema. Perhaps only twenty percent of our time will be coding the actual schema. The rest of our time will be spent:

- ❑ Gathering requirements from different parts of the organization
- ❑ Analyzing the documents we want to model
- ❑ Looking at legacy data that will be converted to the new schema
- ❑ Proposing content models and getting agreement on them from the development group

Only when we have a *map* of the schema fixed will we put it all together in the actual schema. Incidentally, it's because the implementation is such a small part of the process that we can learn a great deal from DTD development (both for SGML and XML documents). The bulk of the work in designing an XML Schema or a DTD for documents is exactly the same.

Document Analysis

Document analysis is the formal process of mapping the structures of the **document set** (the set of documents that the schema is designed to model). It's a way of finding out and describing the material that our XML documents will contain, a parallel to analyzing the data that we would contain within a database, or an XML data schema.

Once we have identified the scope of our schema – the set of documents it will model – we should find representative examples of those documents. To take a simple example, if we wanted to create a schema to model memoranda used by an organization, we would find lots of real samples of memos created by real people in the business. If we missed an example, which contained a new structure that didn't appear in any of the other examples (say a "blind cc" field), our schema wouldn't model that structure, and anyone who wanted to use it would have to come back to us and ask to add it to the schema, and release a new version. This process is essentially the same as creating "use cases" in application design, where the designer tries to capture as many ways of using an application as possible with a view to specifying the functionality that is required of it.

Analyzing Structures

Therefore, with the pile of sample documents in front of us, we can start mapping the major structures within them. We can draw this on a large sheet of paper, use a drawing application, or type it into a word processor, but what we want to end up with is a generic tree view of the structures (something like this, using our memo example):

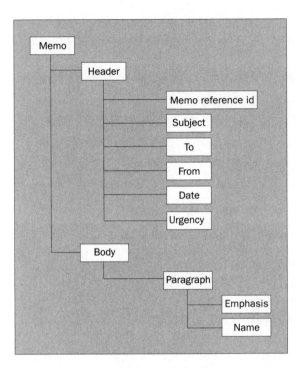

This is the document analysis of the memo document set: every memo analyzed fits *within* this model, but as it's a superset, every memo does not have to fit this model precisely. Some may not contain the Urgency field, but some do, therefore we need to represent it in the document analysis.

We could have gone further – some of the memos contained places, web addresses, and other structures within paragraphs. We might have gone further still and said that paragraphs contain sentences, which contain prepositions, adverbs, verbs, and so on, but clearly we have to draw a line somewhere, and before we start the document analysis we will have decided that it isn't useful to know what part of speech a particular word is. Incidentally, there are some SGML DTDs that go down to this level, because the people who use them will derive value from knowing the grammatical structure of the sentences within their documents. We will look at how to make the decision of what and what not to include in schemas later on, but we should have some idea of what level of granularity our document analysis will go to even at this early stage.

When we are considering larger sets of documents, such as a set of text books, it is sometimes helpful to carry out individual document analysis on a representative sample of them, rather than creating one generic map straight away. This allows the schema development group to see where particular structures (such as an appendix or a bibliography) are used – if they only appear in one book out of a set of a hundred, they might decide that in future, no books will contain these. This shows to what extent schema development can help standardize document production.

To continue with our case study, the document analysis of a physics textbook would run to several pages of A4, but as an example here is part of it, for the book meta data (which is data centric):

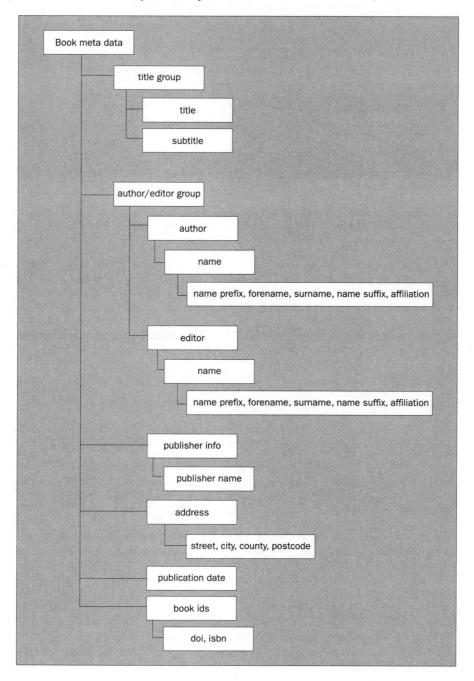

Here is the analysis for chapters (which is document centric):

Identifying Datatypes

As well as identifying the structures that the document set will contain, we need to look at the content of those structures at the leaf node level.

With DTDs, the content of leaf node elements is usually simply PCDATA, as DTDs offer very little in the way of content validation. With schemas, we can be more specific about what that content should look like, by defining datatypes and assigning them to elements.

During the document analysis stage we should be identifying content which falls in particular patterns, such as dates, standard identification schemes (for example: Digital Object Identifier or DOI, an internationally-agreed numbering scheme for identifying a piece of intellectual property on a digital network, for example "10.12345") and any other content which can be described using XML Schema datatype mechanisms. Remember that at this stage we are only describing what is there – we don't need to decide exactly what datatypes we will choose for the schema, but knowing what date formats appear in the document set will help us make those decisions later.

For example, if our memo includes a company memo reference which uses the pattern:

```
[Sender's initials]/[recipient's initials]/[six digit date YYMMDD]/[number]
```

then we should identify the above pattern as the content of the memo reference ID structure. We can turn it into a string data-type using regular expressions later in the development phase.

At this stage we can go back to the schema development group and discuss the document analysis and what it says about the final design of the schema. We may decide that one type of document that we originally intended to be modeled by the schema is too different from the others in the set, and will mean that the schema would have to be too loose to accommodate it.

In terms of Physics Press's schema, pubDate could make use of the built-in date datatypes – but we will need to identify whether the publication date is an exact date (day, month, year), or just the month and year. For the book IDs, new datatypes would be required for the different numbering schemes, which can usually be expressed as regular expressions. ISBNs for example are always 10 digits, grouped together to denote:

- ❑ A group identifier – the language or region in which the book was published (1 to 5 digits)
- ❑ A publisher prefix – identifying the publisher (2 to 7 digits)
- ❑ A title number – identifying the particular edition and binding of a particular book (the length of which is 9 minus the total number of digits used in the first two groups)
- ❑ A check digit to pick up errors in transcription (0-X where X is 10).

We'll see how we might use this analysis to create a new datatype later in the chapter.

Schema Design: Strategic Issues

With the document analysis done, you should have a map, or a set of maps, of the documents that your schema will model. It's now time to think about designing content models, which will contain documents that conform to that map.

Let's look at the decisions you and the schema development group will have to make at this stage.

Choosing an Appropriate Level of Granularity

We have already introduced the concept of granularity in terms of deciding how detailed our document analysis should be. This is a bigger issue in designing the schema itself – do we really need an element to represent this or that structure?

The answer to this sort of question is actually fairly simple: will the element effectively pay for itself? Or, to put it another way, will we derive any value from marking up that particular structure? Going back to the example of the memo, what value would there be in marking up a person's name when it appears in the body text of the memo? We know from the document analysis that names appear in the body text, but is it worthwhile marking them up? The difference in the final document would be something like this. First, without a name element for body text:

```
<body>
    <para>Will anyone who wants to go on the company ski trip please make
        sure that they give their holiday booking form to Nicola Black by
        next Friday.
    </para>
</body>
```

Now with a name element, which can be used in body text:

```
<body>
    <para>Will anyone who wants to go on the company ski trip please make
        sure that they give their holiday booking form to <name>Nicola
        Black</name> by next Friday.
    </para>
</body>
```

Realistically, will anyone need to search for the name? (Names, being "unique" identifiers, are pretty good at identifying themselves!) Does the text within the name tag need to be rendered differently? Probably not, so on balance, we would decide that a name element is not required within body text.

Remember that any tag will also need to be keyed or generated somehow in the authoring of the document. Adding markup costs time and effort (and therefore money) – we have to be sure that every tag will (literally) pay for itself in the end.

Let's consider the question of granularity with reference to the Physics Press schema. Typesetting is typically priced by the effort it takes to key text, format it or tag it up, so the issue of whether an element pays for itself is particularly pertinent in book production.

We mentioned earlier that the marketing department had some ideas on using the material in physics textbooks to create new products or generate revenues. One idea is to link all references to laboratory equipment, to a web site offering the kit at special prices. For example, if the text contains a reference to an aneroid barometer, we would want to mark it up so that a link could be generated. The XML might look like this:

```
<para>Three common ways of measuring air pressure are with the barometer, the
manometer and the Bourdon Gauge. In the next experiment we are going to use an
<labEquipment>aneroid barometer</labEquipment> to measure atmospheric
pressure.</para>
```

If marketing tells us that they can generate revenue from having access to all references of laboratory equipment, then that is what the schema must contain.

Rendering

Another reason we might want to mark up a particular structure is because it is rendered differently from the text around it. Scientific names for plants and animals are usually rendered in italic, for example *Ateles fusciceps robustus*. You may think we should create an italic element to mark up this text, but remember that the XML should capture structure not format. While italic rendering would normally be acceptable for the zoological name, it might be that in another publication the same text should appear in bold – and for that matter, how do we represent *italic* in a voice browser?

So the general rule is that if text is rendered differently, the difference in appearance represents a distinct structure, which should therefore be captured. In this case we might create a zooName element and use it as so:

```
<para>The Columbian Spider Monkey <zooName>Ateles fusciceps robustus</zooName> is
extremely well adapted to life in the forest canopy.</para>
```

Domain-Specific Markup

Different knowledge domains will require a different set of structures to be tagged. The above example of the zooName element might appear in a book on biology, but is unlikely to be required by the Physics Press. Physics textbooks, on the other hand, contain mathematical equations, and this content will have to be captured and represented somehow.

Math is a particular problem for publishers and typesetters. There is a typesetting language called **TeX**, which many mathematicians and physicists are happy to use to write their equations, and it may be best for the Physics Press to use the TeX setting created by their authors instead of attempting to capture it in XML. If they did the latter, there is a standard mathematical XML markup language called MathML (see http://www.w3.org/TR/REC-MathML/). This is currently expressed as a DTD, which can be imported wholesale into a larger DTD, but it is expected that a schema version will be developed in the near future, which Physics Press could incorporate into their textbook schema. Incidentally, a number of authoring tools for generating MathML equations are being developed.

As the root element of MathML is math, we need to consider where in the Physics Press schema mathematical equations are likely to appear. A look at the document analysis would tell us that equations appear both inline (within paragraphs) and as separate block structures. So the content model for paragraphs will need to include math:

```
<xs:element name = "p">
  <xs:complexType mixed = "true">
    <xs:choice>
      <xs:element name = "emphasis" type = "xs:string"/>
      <xs:element name = "xref" type = "xs:string"/>
      <xs:element name = "mathFormula" type = "xs:string"/>
      <xs:element name = "url" type = "xs:anyURI"/>
      <xs:element ref = "email"/>
      <xs:element ref = "math"/>
    </xs:choice>
  </xs:complexType>
</xs:element>
```

As it is likely that users will need to create cross-references to block displayed math, we will need to create a separate `mathBlock` element, containing maths, with an `id` attribute to allow linking:

```
<xs:element name = "blockMath">
  <xs:complexType>
    <xs:sequence>
      <xs:element ref = "math" />
    </xs:sequence>
    <xs:attribute name = "id" type = "xs:ID" />
  </xs:complexType>
</xs:element>
```

Coping with Legacy Data

Most of us work in organizations that don't reinvent themselves every year, and as a result we all have to cope with the legacy of our forebears (and sometimes ourselves) in terms of systems, data, and methods. In the world of documents it's the same. Publishers and document managers are beginning to move to XML Schema-based publishing systems from those based on SGML DTDs.

The question this raises is how much of the legacy data will be converted to conform to the new XML Schema we are developing.

If none, then we still will want to look at the old DTD and document sets to see how the data was modeled before – DTDs and schemas that have proved themselves in the real world are very valuable to XML Schema designers as they show what models work within a specific context. We might even want to base our schema on an element-by-element conversion of DTD to XML Schema syntax (or use a tool to do this automatically). If legacy data does form part of the document sets to be modeled, then we treat it as we would the document analysis: it represents data that the schema will have to model.

Our organizations might also have legacy DTDs that we now want to convert to XML Schemas, to add content validation to structures defined in the DTDs. If this is the case then we will still have to analyze the content of leaf structures, choose or develop datatypes, then add these to the new schema (we will consider data typing issues later in the chapter).

How Prescriptive Should Our Schema Be?

When developing schemas, we can very tightly control the structure of the documents, or we can allow a wide variety of models within the same schema. As an example, consider the high level elements of a textbook. The document analysis might look like this:

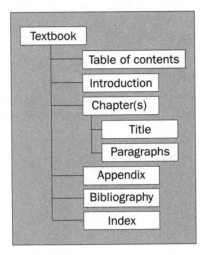

If we wanted all textbooks that were modeled by the schema to have all these elements, in this order, the content model for the textbook element could look like this:

```
<xs:element name="textbook">
  <xs:complexType>
    <xs:sequence>
      <xs:element ref="toc" minOccurs="1" maxOccurs="1" />
      <xs:element ref="introduction" minOccurs="1" maxOccurs="1" />
      <xs:element ref="chapter" minOccurs="1" maxOccurs="unbounded" />
      <xs:element ref="appendix" minOccurs="1" maxOccurs="1" />
      <xs:element ref="bibliography" minOccurs="1" maxOccurs="1" />
      <xs:element ref="index" minOccurs="1" maxOccurs="1" />
    </xs:sequence>
  </xs:complexType>
</xs:element>
```

Alternatively, we could specify that some parts of the book, such as the introduction, appendix, and bibliography are optional because they occur in some books but not in others. The following content model for the textbook element is less prescriptive, because it allows for a degree of choice in documents valid to the schema:

```
<xs:element name="textbook">
   <xs:complexType>
      <xs:sequence>
         <xs:element ref="toc" minOccurs="1" maxOccurs="1"/>
         <xs:element ref="introduction" minOccurs="0" maxOccurs="1"/>
         <xs:element ref="chapter" minOccurs="1" maxOccurs="unbounded"/>
         <xs:element ref="appendix" minOccurs="0" maxOccurs="1"/>
         <xs:element ref="bibliography" minOccurs="0" maxOccurs="1"/>
         <xs:element ref="index" minOccurs="1" maxOccurs="1"/>
      </xs:sequence>
   </xs:complexType>
</xs:element>
```

Note that you can declare an element by reference or directly within its parent's declaration. In this chapter, we've chosen to declare by reference for the simple reason that it helps when reading and editing the schema.

Some parts of the schema will require more prescription than others, because we want to be sure that certain information is included in every document instance. A good example of this is found in meta data. Earlier, in the document analysis, we identified the meta data that was found in a textbook. We found that all books had an author, some had an editor, and some had more than one of each. We agree with the schema development group that every book we publish must have at least an author, but not all books have editors, so the content model for `authorEditorGroup` will look like this:

```
<xs:element name = "authorEditorGroup">
   <xs:complexType>
      <xs:sequence>
         <xs:element ref="author" maxOccurs="unbounded"/>
         <xs:element ref="editor" minOccurs="0" maxOccurs="unbounded"/>
      </xs:sequence>
   </xs:complexType>
</xs:element>
```

On the other hand, with the `name` element (which contains the names of authors and editors) we can be much less prescriptive, because names come in many forms.

In the document analysis, we decided that the best way to describe names was with a `forename` and `surname` element, but that some names have a prefix (Doctor, Professor, Sir, etc.) and some a suffix (Jnr, II, etc.), and some both. Therefore, the `name` element is modeled like this:

```
<xs:element name = "name">
   <xs:complexType>
      <xs:sequence>
         <xs:element ref = "namePre" minOccurs = "0"/>
         <xs:element ref = "forenames"/>
         <xs:element ref = "surname"/>
         <xs:element ref = "namePost" minOccurs = "0"/>
      </xs:sequence>
   </xs:complexType>
</xs:element>
```

There is no right or wrong answer to the question of how prescriptive a schema should be. If we insist on absolute prescription (no optional elements), then we would almost need a different schema for every document we wanted to write, which would be unworkable in reality. On the other hand, if we allow too much choice, then structural validation becomes meaningless. We should aim to have as much control as possible on the structure of the documents, while ensuring that the schema models all documents in the document set.

Smallest Licensable Unit

One reason we go to the trouble of coding documents in XML is to allow parts of the document to be taken out of their original context and re-used elsewhere. This is known as **re-purposing** documents.

Physics Press has the opportunity to make more money from its content by re-purposing parts of its textbooks as course notes for university lecturers. The people designing the schema will have to decide how small these sections of information will have to be – or what constitutes the **smallest licensable unit** of this schema. They need to know this because:

❑ Sections need to be identified in the world outside their documents

❑ Publishers need to know who owns the rights to each section

❑ Someone may need to know what a section is called, where it came from, and who wrote it

In recent years, a group of publishers have designed a standard numbering scheme for identifying content on the Web, called DOI or Digital Object Identifiers. On the whole, if the content is published electronically, it should have a unique number to identify it. We won't go into details here, but it's clear that if a section of our textbook is to be cut out and published on its own, it needs a DOI to identify where it came from.

Similarly, if we make up a set of course notes that took chapters from several books, then we need to know who wrote each chapter. We should also be able to tell who owns the rights to the content, who published it, and so on. This type of information is usually termed meta data – literally data about data, or in this case, data about the chapter.

If we decide that the smallest licensable unit the chapter, then every chapter has to have a DOI (or enough information to create one automatically), author, rights information, and other meta data. So our schema should include a `chapterMeta` (data) element to hold all this:

```
<xs:element name = "chapter">
    <xs:complexType>
        <xs:sequence>
            <xs:element ref = "chapterMeta"/>
            <xs:element ref = "sectLevel1" maxOccurs = "unbounded"/>
            <xs:element ref = "notes" minOccurs = "0"/>
            <xs:element ref = "bibliography" minOccurs = "0"/>
            <xs:element ref = "glossary" minOccurs = "0"/>
        </xs:sequence>
    </xs:complexType>
</xs:element>
<xs:element name = "chapterMeta">
    <xs:complexType>
        <xs:sequence>
            <xs:element ref = "title"/>
            <xs:element ref = "authorEditorGroup"/>
```

```
            <xs:element ref = "rights"/>
            <xs:element ref = "chapterIds"/>
        </xs:sequence>
    </xs:complexType>
</xs:element>
```

Many Specific or Few General Elements

Another major issue on the design of the schema is whether to aim for many specific elements, or reduce the element count by creating general elements that have several roles.

In general we should aim to have as few elements in our schema as possible. Apart from creating work when actually writing the schema, more elements mean:

❏ It takes users longer to become familiar with the schema

❏ More elements for stylesheet and application developers to cope with

❏ More confusion when choosing the correct element

❏ More complex templates for authors and editors

❏ It's harder for authoring tools to be developed and used

So in principle, we should aim to reduce the number of elements to a minimum by sharing elements where possible between structures.

As an example, let's say that Physics Press wants to identify books, articles, conference proceedings, lectures, and other works when they are cited in their content. One way of doing this would be to create many elements for each type of object, as follows:

```
<xs:element name="article" type="string" />
<xs:element name="book" type="string" />
<xs:element name="conference" type="string" />
<xs:element name="lecture" type="string" />
<xs:element name="seminar" type="string" />
```

Alternatively, we could save four (possibly many more) of these elements by creating a single citedObject element and giving it a name attribute to represent the type of object:

```
<xs:element name="citedObject">
    <xs:complexType>
        <xs:simpleContent>
            <xs:extension base="xs:string">
                <xs:attribute name="objectType" type="xs:string"
                              use="required"/>
            </xs:extension>
        </xs:simpleContent>
    </xs:complexType>
</xs:element>
```

If we wanted to restrict the types of object, we could enumerate the values of the `objectType` attribute:

```
<xs:element name = "citedObject">
    <xs:complexType>
        <xs:simpleContent>
            <xs:extension base = "xs:string">
                <xs:attribute name = "objectType" use = "required">
                    <xs:simpleType>
                        <xs:restriction base = "xs:string">
                            <xs:enumeration value = "article" />
                            <xs:enumeration value = "book" />
                            <xs:enumeration value = "conference" />
                            <xs:enumeration value = "lecture" />
                            <xs:enumeration value = "seminar" />
                        </xs:restriction>
                    </xs:simpleType>
                </xs:attribute>
            </xs:extension>
        </xs:simpleContent>
    </xs:complexType>
</xs:element>
```

The advantage of enumerating the different types of cited object is that it gives the schema more control over the content that is created. If we didn't enumerate the types then someone might use paper to indicate an article. Of course they are the same thing, but the schema doesn't know that. If we then wanted to create a list of citedObjects of type paper that appeared in a particular book then we would miss the one that was labeled as article.

Extensibility and Future Proofing

There are times, however, when it is better not to enumerate attributes; specifically to give the schema flexibility to cope with content that has not appeared in the document analysis or that we haven't anticipated – in other words, to make it more future proof.

In the above example we could combine enumerated types with another attribute on the citedObject element named otherType, which would be a simple string attribute:

```
<xs:attribute name="otherType" type="xs:string" use="required"/>
```

This way we acknowledge that there may be other types of cited object that we don't know about yet, but we retain control over the types that we do know about.

Future proofing is a major issue in schema design. In some cases, our document analysis is a complete representation of the document set, past, present, and future. It may be that Physics Press has always created textbooks in the same way and always will, but it sounds unlikely. In reality, authors and the editorial department are always thinking of new ways to present content, the production department is always coming up with new requirements for the XML markup, and marketing just won't stop thinking of new products which require changes to the structure of the content.

Of course, when these changes occur we could sit down and change the schema, to reflect the fact that, say, marketing wanted to link all references to journal articles to the actual article on its publisher's web site (requiring additional data in journal citations) although even the smallest change to a schema in effect creates a completely new one, and documents valid to the old schema will not necessarily be valid to the new one. Changing a large legacy XML document set can be an expensive and time-consuming job, so it's in our interest to anticipate any future requirements within the current schema.

Generic Elements

A danger inherent in the use of XML is the use of inappropriate elements – users often reach for what they consider to be the closest equivalent element if they can't find an element that fits their needs exactly. As an example, supposing someone writing a physics textbook needed to mark up the name of a plant or animal according to the Linnaean *genus-species* taxonomy (let's say *Homo sapiens*). They find that the schema designer hasn't anticipated that this structure might appear in the document set, so they look for the nearest equivalent. The schema does contain an element called `foreignPhrase` and the author can see that content in this element appears in italics, just as he wants *Homo sapiens* to appear, so this is what he uses.

```
<para>When intelligent man, <foreignPhrase>Homo sapiens</foreignPhrase>, first
walked the earth...</para>
```

The result of this inappropriate choice of tags is bad data, and it can have serious consequences. Supposing someone wanted to build an index of foreign phrases as part of the textbook, and pulls out every instance of this element to create the list. The script that does this won't know that *Homo sapiens* is a genus-species name, but as it is marked as a `foreignPhrase`, that's what it assumes it is.

One way of coping with future structures that we can't anticipate is to create one or more generic elements. A generic element for use within paragraphs could be declared as follows:

```
<xs:element name="genericInline">
   <xs:complexType>
      <xs:simpleContent>
         <xs:extension base="xs:string">
            <xs:attribute name="role" type="xs:string" use="required"/>
         </xs:extension>
      </xs:simpleContent>
   </xs:complexType>
</xs:element>
```

This element would appear in inline content models (in paragraphs, list items, etc.). So when an author comes across something they can't find an element for, they can reach for this generic element to describe it:

```
<para>When intelligent man, <genericInline role="genusSpecies">Homo
sapiens</genericInline>, first walked the earth...</para>
```

In addition, when the schema development group meets again to consider what changes are required to the schema, they will have a ready-made list of structures that the old schema couldn't cope with. A simple script could search the document set for uses of the generic elements, and enumerate the content of their `role` attributes. Then when the next version of the schema is released, the structure will be given the correct tagging:

```
<para>When intelligent man, <genusSpecies>Homo sapiens<genusSpecies>, first walked
the earth...</para>
```

To increase the extensibility of our schema, we might consider applying the `role` attribute to other elements as well as generic elements. This can allow users to be more specific about the element they are using as, for example, on a `list` element:

```
<list role="abbreviations">
```

Documentation and Usage Guidelines

Of course, in the above example, the author or editor marking up the text needs to know that they should use the genericInline element when there is no other choice. This information is best communicated via documentation or usage guidelines (sometimes this is the same document), which highlights the importance of documenting the schema and providing anyone using the schema with comprehensive usage guidelines in a clear and accessible format.

We will cover the use of the xs:document element later in this chapter, but from a strategic point of view we should be aware that a document schema is of little use without full descriptions of each element and explanations and examples of its use. We wouldn't expect a pilot to know their way around the cockpit of a passenger jet without some sort of instruction manual, not to mention training.

For example, when a typesetter is coding up the name of the author, they need to know how the naming model is to be used. They have four name elements at their disposal – namePre, forenames, surname, and namePost, but the purpose of the elements may not be self-evident. Given a name such as "Professor Harry Bigsworth", which parts go in what elements?

The typesetter can check the usage guidelines and discover that namePre is designed to hold titles, all forenames go into one forenames element, and surnames go in surname; producing the following markup:

```
<author>
   <name>
      <namePre>Professor</namePre>
      <forenames>Harry</forenames>
      <surname>Bigsworth</surname>
   </name>
</author>
```

The typesetter will also discover from the usage guidelines that the name component tags (namePre, forenames, surname, namePost) should not include whitespace – the stylesheets or templates will control the spaces between the words.

While it is tempting to put-off documentation and usage guideline writing until the end of the project (and preferably get someone else to do it!) these documents should be written concurrently and hand-in-hand with the development of the schema, and by the people who are making the decisions about the schema design (you and the rest of the schema development group).

Schema Design: Tactical Issues

Let's look at some tactical considerations of XML Schema design for documents, before moving on to look at how we might manage and implement the schema design.

Using Standard Modules

Document-centric schemas haven't been around long enough for standard modules to be developed, but here, we anticipate that there will be many, and where possible we should use them. In the SGML world, some organizations developed standard DTDs, including the US military under the Continuous Acquisition and Life-cycle Support (CALS) project. Standardization of entire DTDs never took off in the SGML world, and when we consider the differences between organizations in the way they create and use documents, it would be surprising if many standard *document* XML Schemas are developed, let alone adopted. Document schemas are emphasized because many standard data schemas have already been developed, and rightly so, because a key use of XML is to share data between organizations. Ideally this should be done through the use of standard schemas (though, having said that, XSLT makes it fairly straightforward to transform from one type of document to another).

However, in the SGML world, some modules have become *de facto* standards, the most notable being the CALS exchange table model, which a few years ago was taken over by the (civilian) OASIS group and is so therefore now known as the OASIS model (see http://www.oasis-open.org).

Developing a table markup language is a major project in its own right, and we wouldn't recommend anyone develop their own, particularly as the OASIS model copes with every type and style of table that we might ever come across. It's also highly user-configurable, and if we really need to, it allows us to alter the content models without going too far from the standard.

Another advantage of using a standard module is that someone, somewhere (probably on the Web) will have gone to the trouble of writing a processing or rendering script, which we can then pick up and use in our own scripts (with the author's permission of course). The OASIS table model provides another good example of this – Norman Walsh has written both DSSSL and XSLT modules for rendering OASIS tables into HTML. Writing a fully compliant table rendering XSLT stylesheet is also a major undertaking and we recommend that you save yourself the trouble.

For publishers there is a further advantage to using standard modules – typesetters soon get used to using particular DTDs and schemas and the more familiar they are with a set of elements, the more accurately they will use them, hopefully passing on the ensuing cost benefits to their customers.

When developing the meta data part of a publication schema, we should consider the work done to standardize this, known as the Dublin Core Metadata Initiative. The Dublin Core (the work was done in Dublin, Ohio, not Dublin, Ireland) includes a set of 15 standard meta data elements for published works, specifically: `title`, `creator`, `subject`, `description`, `publisher`, `contributor`, `date`, `type`, `format`, `identifier`, `source`, `language`, `relation`, `coverage`, and `rights`. Our Physics Press schema, were we to develop it fully, would contain all these elements, and sub-elements to describe the data in more detail.

Instead of attempting to design a standard meta data module, which is unlikely to be used since publishers often have widely differing requirements, the idea is that publishers who sign up to the standard will have a minimum set of meta data, which makes it easier to exchange information and content in the future. See http://dublincore.org for details.

Datatypes

XML Schemas offer one major advantage over DTDs – the ability to define or control the content of leaf elements, not only the elements that another element may contain. With both schemas and DTDs there is no absolute control over what goes into a particular leaf element – there is nothing to stop us populating a `title` tag with an author's name, for example. It is only convention (backed up by rigorous checking!) that ensures that the title goes within the `title` element, and the author's name appears in the `author` tag. Once again this stresses the need for clear and easily available documentation and usage guidelines.

Built-in

But with schemas we can go much further than simply declaring content as `#PCDATA`, which is (practically speaking) the limit of DTDs. To begin with there are the built-in data-types. For those developing document schemas, the most interesting are likely to be:

- ❑ `string` – the content of most leaf nodes
- ❑ `date` types – for meta data including date of publication, etc.
- ❑ `language` – for structures such as `foreignPhrase` and meta data such as language of publication

477

- ❑ integer – for identifying section levels, etc

- ❑ IDs and IDREFs – for linking inside and outside articles (these are available in DTDs)

The ability to define the content as, say, a standard date type, and know that it will be validated, is very comforting for those people responsible for the integrity of the data. It can be embarrassing to discover, as we could with DTD-validated XML, that someone has swapped round the publicationDate with the publicationPlace, and that the book was published in the year "New York".

Creating Our Own Datatypes

Of course, we can go beyond these built-in datatypes and define our own. We have already looked at describing leaf element data as part of the document analysis, and we will now look at using this knowledge of the content of our document set to develop our own datatypes.

Let's go back to the memo schema example we mentioned earlier, where we analyzed the memo ID number and found the pattern was:

```
[Sender's initials]/[recipient's initials]/[six digit date YYMMDD]/[number]
```

We can make an assumption that initials are two or three characters long, in which case the element declaration for memoRef is as follows:

```
<xs:element name="memoRef" type="memoRefType"/>

<xs:simpleType name="memoRefType">
    <xs:restriction base="xs:string">
        <xs:pattern value="...?/...?/\d\d\d\d\d\d/\d" />
    </xs:restriction>
</xs:simpleType>
```

Similarly, we can define a datatype for ISBNs (International Standard Book Numbers), which follow a fixed pattern that we can describe with a regular expression: ([0-9]([-]?)){9}[0-9X] (you can find more detailed discussion of regular expressions in Chapter 4 – Derived Datatypes). This isn't perfect because the ISBN syntax can't be described using XML Schema regular expressions (see the analysis of ISBNs earlier in this chapter).

This translates into a datatype with the following declaration:

```
<xs:element name = "isbn">
    <xs:simpleType>
        <xs:restriction base="xs:string">
            <xs:length value = "10" />
            <xs:pattern value = "([0-9]+){1,5}-([0-9]+){2,7}-([0-9]+){1,6}-
                                ([0-9X])" />
        </xs:restriction>
    </xs:simpleType>
</xs:element>
```

Element Naming

Element names are largely a matter of taste, fashion, and practicality. Some people use UpperCamelCase for elements and lowerCamelCase for attributes, while some use lowerCamelCase for both. These both get round the need for further punctuation such as underscores or hyphens (remember spaces are not allowed in element names). For those of you used to SGML DTDs, remember XML element names are case sensitive, so TITLE is a different element from title or Title.

Inevitably we will want to abbreviate element names, but there is a caveat. In the early days of SGML many DTD designers chose short, unintuitive names such as `st` for section title, or `br` for bibliographic reference. Doing this saved on a few keystrokes, but left users a little bewildered, especially in DTDs containing many hundreds of elements.

The answer to this question, as always, lies somewhere between the choice of full, verbose names such as `paragraph`, and using unfathomable abbreviations. Accordingly, `para` is an acceptable abbreviation, and is unlikely to cause confusion, while `sectTitle` might also be considered for section titles. It's a matter of common sense and consideration of the environment in which the schema is going to be used. Publishing is an international business these days, so we must consider the needs of offshore typists and typesetters as well as our own production department.

Section Schemes

The body text of a chapter, article, in fact of most documents, is usually divided into sections, and these bring with them special problems for the schema designer. Consider the sections of this chapter. We can tell intuitively where one section ends and another begins by the appearance of a title or heading. The importance of that section break is indicated by the size and style of the heading – the larger or bolder the typeface, the more important the section.

In XML document schemas, these section levels can be created in several ways. One is to create a section model that allows sections within each section, *ad infinitum*. The content model for this is straightforward and saves many elements:

```xml
<xs:element name="section">
   <xs:complexType mixed="true">
      <xs:sequence>
         <xs:element name="title" type="xs:string" minOccurs="1"
            maxOccurs="1" />
         <xs:element ref="section" minOccurs="0" maxOccurs="unbounded" />
      </xs:sequence>
   </xs:complexType>
</xs:element>
```

Technically there's nothing wrong with allowing a `section` to be nested within a `section`. However, some people (particularly typesetters) who create XML documents containing sections like to see what level of section they are using – in other words they need specific section numbering. If we take this approach we will have to check the number of section levels our document set contains, but most documents don't go further than six levels of nesting. Nonetheless, it is good practice to allow an infinitely nest-able section after the last numbered section. Schematically the model looks like this:

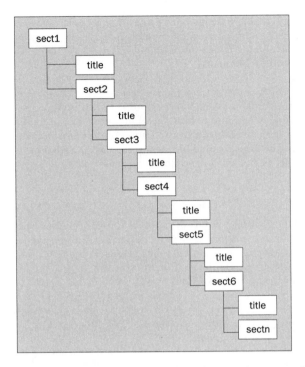

In reality though, sections are not always strictly nested. Looking at the section headings we might see, for example, a jump from section 2 to section 4 without a section 3 heading in between. We might then change the model to allow section 2, 3, 4, 5, or 6 within a section 1, and within section 2 allow section 3, 4, 5, and 6, and so on for each section. Apart from making content models which are unnecessarily complex, this also makes processing or rendering of sections difficult as we have to allow for a large number of possible combinations.

One way round this problem is to enforce strict section nesting, but make the title or heading optional. If your information requires a more seamless flow across section boundaries, but needs to retain the option to be re-used elsewhere, it can be useful to state specifically that the section has no title, by creating an empty noTitle element and making the content model either title or noTitle as in this declaration of sect1:

```
<xs:element name="section">
   <xs:complexType mixed="true">
      <xs:sequence>
         <xs:choice>
            <xs:element name="title" type="xs:string" minOccurs="1"
                     maxOccurs="1" />
            <xs:element name="noTitle" type="xs:string" minOccurs="1"
                     maxOccurs="1" />
         </xs:choice>
         <xs:element ref="section" minOccurs="0" maxOccurs="unbounded" />
      </xs:sequence>
   </xs:complexType>
</xs:element>
```

Managing the Schema Design Phase

As we begin to consider the detailed design of the schema, we will need to provide proposals and manage the discussion and decision-making on elements and their content models among the schema development group. Any complex task is usually better dealt with in small, discrete sections (familiar to developers as the "divide and conquer" approach to problem solving), and in this case dividing the types of elements into categories and working on one at a time, will help us to get through the task.

As we work on the Physics Press schema, we might want to divide the task as follows:

- ❑ Inline elements, block elements and chapter structure
- ❑ Science and graphics
- ❑ Tables
- ❑ Bibliographic material
- ❑ Notes, links, and references
- ❑ High-level structure and meta data

We can work on each section in turn, allowing a proportion of time for each, and make sure everyone knows what is being proposed in terms of elements and their content models. One way of doing this is to create simple XML documents to describe each element, which might look like this:

```xml
<?xml version="1.0"?>
<elements>
   <category>High level structures</category>
   <element>
      <name>sectLevel1</name>
      <description>Top level section element</description>
      <content>
         Mixed, with required title or noTitle, and zero or more
         sectLevel2s
      </content>
      <attributes>id (type ID), role (type string)</attributes>
      <use>
         sectLevel1 is the first section element and is used as the
         container for chapter body content.
      </use>
   </element>
   <!-- Other elements in this category would be described below -->
</elements>
```

As well as presenting the proposed elements in a clear, logical manner, a document such as this might also be used to build the documentation (in XML of course!) with some simple XSLT stylesheets to pull out the relevant sections. In any case we may want to render it as a web page, and post it on our organization's intranet so the schema development group can review it.

We will probably need to go back to earlier sections as we work through all the categories, as new requirements will emerge that will impact on the overall design. This should not be a problem – the design of the schema will not be fixed until after the final review stage.

Turning the Design Into a Schema

You should already be familiar with the syntax of XML Schemas from reading the rest of this book. Coding a document schema is no different from coding any schema, once we have a clear design for the elements and their content models to work from.

An important aspect of writing schemas is identifying element types by their content models. XML Schemas offer simple and complex types, with further subdivision of types according to whether they have attributes, contain text as well as other elements, and so on. These are covered elsewhere in this book (see Chapter 2) but in general document schemas will contain a mixture of:

❑ Text only content (which can be any text (character data), but no elements)

❑ Element only content (which is child elements, but no text outside of those children)

❑ Mixed content (which is text plus a sequence of sub-structures)

Exactly how we write the schema is up to us. Once the design has been agreed, the actual coding of the schema should not take too long. We may want to use a schema design tool such as XML Authority, or simply code it ourselves in a text editor.

We should be wary of attempting to create the schema by first writing a sample document instance and then feeding it into a tool (there are several on the market) that automatically create a schema to model it. An XML document is just one instance of many that the schema could model – so if our instance doesn't model bibliographies, for example, then a `bibliography` element won't appear in the schema. The cardinalities are usually incorrect too.

Let's have a look at the Physics Press schema as it might be developed. Bear in mind that this is not intended to be complete – a full schema for textbooks would probably contain 150-200 elements, and this doesn't contain much documentation. However, it shows how the various sections fit together:

```
<?xml version = "1.0" encoding = "UTF-8"?>
<xs:schema xmlns:xs = "http://www.w3.org/2001/XMLSchema">

    <!-- textbook.xsd -->
    <!-- Partial schema to model physics textbooks -->
    <!-- author: Oliver Griffin -->

    <xs:element name = "textbook">
        <xs:complexType>
            <xs:sequence>
                <xs:element ref = "bookMetadata" />
                <xs:element ref = "chapter" maxOccurs = "unbounded" />
            </xs:sequence>
        </xs:complexType>
    </xs:element>
```

As mentioned previously, we've chosen to declare elements by reference to help with reading and editing the schema.

```
<xs:element name = "bookMetadata">
   <xs:complexType>
      <xs:sequence>
         <xs:element ref = "titleGroup" />
         <xs:element ref = "authorEditorGroup" />
         <xs:element ref = "pubInfo" />
         <xs:element ref = "bookIds" />
      </xs:sequence>
   </xs:complexType>
</xs:element>

<xs:element name = "titleGroup">
   <xs:complexType>
      <xs:sequence>
         <xs:element ref = "title" />
         <xs:element ref = "subtitle" />
      </xs:sequence>
   </xs:complexType>
</xs:element>

<xs:element name = "title" type = "xs:string" />

<xs:element name = "subtitle" type = "xs:string" />
```

The `authorEditorGroup` element is a container for sequences of authors and editors. Using container elements to group elements together helps with processing and rendering, but "costs" an extra element and means more tags need to be written.

```
<xs:element name = "authorEditorGroup">
   <xs:complexType>
      <xs:sequence>
         <xs:element ref = "author" minOccurs = "1"
                     maxOccurs = "unbounded" />
         <xs:element ref = "editor" minOccurs = "0"
                     maxOccurs = "unbounded" />
      </xs:sequence>
   </xs:complexType>
</xs:element>

<xs:element name = "author">
   <xs:complexType>
      <xs:sequence>
         <xs:element ref = "name" />
         <xs:element ref = "affiliation" minOccurs = "0" />
      </xs:sequence>
   </xs:complexType>
</xs:element>

<xs:element name = "editor">
   <xs:complexType>
      <xs:sequence>
```

```
                <xs:element ref = "name" />
                <xs:element ref = "affiliation" minOccurs = "0" />
            </xs:sequence>
        </xs:complexType>
    </xs:element>

    <xs:element name = "name">
        <xs:complexType>
            <xs:sequence>
                <xs:element ref = "namePre" minOccurs = "0" />
                <xs:element ref = "forenames" />
                <xs:element ref = "surname" />
                <xs:element ref = "namePost" minOccurs = "0" />
            </xs:sequence>
        </xs:complexType>
    </xs:element>

    <xs:element name = "namePre" type = "xs:string" />

    <xs:element name = "forenames" type = "xs:string" />

    <xs:element name = "surname" type = "xs:string" />

    <xs:element name = "namePost" type = "xs:string" />

    <xs:element name = "affiliation" type = "xs:string" />

    <xs:element name = "address">
        <xs:complexType>
            <xs:sequence>
                <xs:element ref = "street" minOccurs = "0"
                               maxOccurs = "unbounded" />
                <xs:element ref = "city" minOccurs = "0" />
                <xs:element ref = "country" minOccurs = "0" />
                <xs:element ref = "postCode" minOccurs = "0" />
            </xs:sequence>
        </xs:complexType>
    </xs:element>

    <xs:element name = "street" type = "xs:string" />

    <xs:element name = "city" type = "xs:string" />

    <xs:element name = "country" type = "xs:string" />

    <xs:element name = "postCode" type = "xs:string" />

    <xs:element name = "pubInfo">
        <xs:complexType>
            <xs:sequence>
                <xs:element ref = "pubName" />
                <xs:element ref = "address" minOccurs = "0" />
            </xs:sequence>
        </xs:complexType>
    </xs:element>
```

```
<xs:element name = "pubName" type = "xs:string" />

<xs:element name = "chapter">
   <xs:complexType>
      <xs:sequence>
         <xs:element ref = "chapterMeta" />
         <xs:element ref = "sectLevel1" maxOccurs = "unbounded" />
         <xs:element ref = "notes" minOccurs = "0" />
         <xs:element ref = "bibliography" minOccurs = "0" />
         <xs:element ref = "glossary" minOccurs = "0" />
      </xs:sequence>
   </xs:complexType>
</xs:element>

<xs:element name = "sectLevel1">
   <xs:complexType>
      <xs:sequence>
         <xs:choice>
            <xs:element ref = "title" />
            <xs:element ref = "noTitle" />
         </xs:choice>
         <xs:element ref = "p" minOccurs = "0" maxOccurs = "unbounded" />
         <xs:element ref = "sectLevel2" minOccurs = "0"
                     maxOccurs = "unbounded" />
      </xs:sequence>
   </xs:complexType>
</xs:element>
```

The element `sectLevel1` is the container for chapter content – there must be at least one per chapter.

```
<xs:element name = "notes">
   <xs:complexType>
      <xs:sequence>
         <xs:element ref = "note" maxOccurs = "unbounded" />
      </xs:sequence>
   </xs:complexType>
</xs:element>

<xs:element name = "bibliography">
   <xs:complexType />
   <!-- The bibliography element is declared as empty to save space -->
</xs:element>
```

As this schema isn't complete, we have left out the content models for bibliography and other large structures. Bibliographies contain lists of works (books, articles, etc.) referenced in the text. Bibliographic entries can be quite complicated, with author names, publishers, titles, and other pieces of information that will all help the reader identify the work that's being cited.

```
<xs:element name = "glossary">
   <xs:complexType />
   <!-- The glossary element is declared as empty to save space -->
</xs:element>
```

```
<xs:element name = "chapterMeta">
   <xs:complexType>
      <xs:sequence>
         <xs:element ref = "title" />
         <xs:element ref = "authorEditorGroup" />
         <xs:element ref = "rights" />
         <xs:element ref = "chapterIds" />
      </xs:sequence>
   </xs:complexType>
</xs:element>
```

The chapterMeta element is only shown in part, but notice the difference between the meta data we would hold about a chapter and meta data about the textbook (bookMetadata).

```
<xs:element name = "sectLevel2">
   <xs:complexType>
      <xs:sequence>
         <xs:choice>
            <xs:element ref = "title" />
            <xs:element ref = "noTitle" />
         </xs:choice>
         <xs:element ref = "p" minOccurs = "0" maxOccurs = "unbounded" />
         <xs:element ref = "sectLevel3" minOccurs = "0"
            maxOccurs = "unbounded" />
      </xs:sequence>
   </xs:complexType>
</xs:element>

<xs:element name = "noTitle">
   <xs:complexType />
   <!-- The noTitle element is declared as empty because it has no content -->
</xs:element>
```

The element noTitle is an empty element, but indicates specifically that the section has no title. This is a useful alternative to optional elements as it forces whoever is tagging the material to specify that content does not exist. If the element is optional, they may just leave it out by accident.

```
<xs:element name = "p">
   <xs:complexType mixed = "true">
      <xs:choice>
         <xs:element ref = "emphasis" minOccurs = "0"
                     maxOccurs = "unbounded" />
         <xs:element ref = "xref" minOccurs = "0"
                     maxOccurs = "unbounded" />
         <xs:element ref = "mathFormula" />
         <xs:element ref = "url" minOccurs = "0"
                     maxOccurs = "unbounded" />
         <xs:element ref = "email" minOccurs = "0"
                     maxOccurs = "unbounded" />
         <xs:element ref = "math" minOccurs = "0"
                     maxOccurs = "unbounded" />
```

```
                  <xs:element ref = "citedObject" minOccurs = "0"
                            maxOccurs = "unbounded" />
          </xs:choice>
      </xs:complexType>
</xs:element>

<xs:element name = "sectLevel3">
    <xs:complexType>
        <xs:sequence>
          <xs:choice>
             <xs:element ref = "title" />
             <xs:element ref = "noTitle" />
          </xs:choice>
          <xs:element ref = "p" minOccurs = "0" maxOccurs = "unbounded" />
          <xs:element ref = "sectLevel4" minOccurs = "0"
             maxOccurs = "unbounded" />
        </xs:sequence>
    </xs:complexType>
</xs:element>

<xs:element name = "sectLevel4">
    <xs:complexType>
        <xs:sequence>
          <xs:choice>
             <xs:element ref = "title" />
                <xs:element ref = "noTitle" />
          </xs:choice>
          <xs:element ref = "p" minOccurs = "0" maxOccurs = "unbounded" />
          <xs:element ref = "sectLevel5" minOccurs = "0"
             maxOccurs = "unbounded" />
        </xs:sequence>
    </xs:complexType>
</xs:element>

<xs:element name = "sectLevel5">
    <xs:complexType>
        <xs:sequence>
          <xs:choice>
             <xs:element ref = "title" />
             <xs:element ref = "noTitle" />
          </xs:choice>
          <xs:element ref = "p" minOccurs = "0" maxOccurs = "unbounded" />
          <xs:element ref = "sectLeveln" minOccurs = "0"
             maxOccurs = "unbounded" />
        </xs:sequence>
    </xs:complexType>
</xs:element>

<xs:element name = "sectLeveln">
    <xs:complexType>
        <xs:sequence>
          <xs:choice>
             <xs:element ref = "title" />
             <xs:element ref = "noTitle" />
          </xs:choice>
          <xs:element ref = "p" minOccurs = "0" maxOccurs = "unbounded" />
```

```
                    <xs:element ref = "sectLeveln" minOccurs = "0"
                        maxOccurs = "unbounded" />
            </xs:sequence>
        </xs:complexType>
    </xs:element>

    <xs:element name = "bookIds">
        <xs:complexType>
            <xs:sequence>
                <xs:element ref = "doi" />
                <xs:element ref = "isbn" />
            </xs:sequence>
        </xs:complexType>
    </xs:element>

    <xs:element name = "doi" type = "xs:string" />

<xs:element name = "isbn">
    <xs:simpleType>
        <xs:restriction base="xs:string">
            <xs:length value = "10"/>
            <xs:pattern value = "([0-9]+){1,5}-([0-9]+){2,7}-([0-9]+){1,6}-
                        ([0-9X])"/>
        </xs:restriction>
    </xs:simpleType>
</xs:element>
```

The following inline elements could (and probably would) contain each other – for example, you might want an xref within an emphasis, but to keep things simple, we have declared them simply as strings.

```
    <xs:element name = "emphasis" type = "xs:string" />

    <xs:element name = "xref" type = "xs:string" />

    <xs:element name = "mathFormula" type = "xs:string" />

    <xs:element name = "url" type = "xs:string" />

    <xs:element name = "email" type = "xs:string" />

    <xs:element name = "math">
        <xs:complexType />
        <!-- The math element is declared as empty to save space -->
    </xs:element>

    <xs:element name = "blockMath">
        <xs:complexType>
            <xs:sequence>
                <xs:element ref = "math" />
            </xs:sequence>
            <xs:attribute name = "id" type = "xs:string" />
        </xs:complexType>
    </xs:element>
```

```
<xs:element name = "rights" type = "xs:string"/>
<xs:element name = "chapterIds">
    <xs:complexType>
        <xs:sequence>
            <xs:element ref = "doi" />
            <xs:element ref = "physicsPressId" />
        </xs:sequence>
        <xs:attribute name = "id" type = "xs:string" />
    </xs:complexType>
</xs:element>

<xs:element name = "physicsPressId" type = "xs:string" />

<xs:element name = "note" type = "xs:string" />

<xs:element name = "citedObject">
    <xs:complexType>
        <xs:simpleContent>
            <xs:extension base = "xs:string">
                <xs:attribute name = "objectType" use = "required">
                    <xs:simpleType>
                        <xs:restriction base = "xs:string">
                            <xs:enumeration value = "article" />
                            <xs:enumeration value = "book" />
                            <xs:enumeration value = "conference" />
                            <xs:enumeration value = "lecture" />
                            <xs:enumeration value = "seminar" />
                        </xs:restriction>
                    </xs:simpleType>
                </xs:attribute>
            </xs:extension>
        </xs:simpleContent>
    </xs:complexType>
</xs:element>

</xs:schema>
```

Testing the Schema

It is important that as we write the schema, we create test instances to check the models against. We may be able to create content models based on a mental image of how it will be used in practice, but turning that image into an XML document, or more likely fragment, will confirm that the model will work in reality.

Ideally we should draw from examples that we created in the schema design phase, another reason to develop content models, documentation, and samples as we go rather than waiting until the end of the project. However, we must remember to work from our design documents, not from the schema itself, as we create the test instances – we are testing whether our idea of what the schema should model matches the schema itself.

The more test instances we can create, the better, though it may not be possible to test every possible permutation of a content model, particularly if it contains many optional elements. We may also want to ask third parties to create test instances, for us to check that their idea of what the schema models matches our own. In the publishing world, this might include typesetters, authors, and production staff.

Just as with any software testing regime, the idea is to try to "break" the code, or in this case the content model, before the schema is released so that any potential problems can be trapped and fixed.

Documentation

We have emphasized the need to develop documentation, samples, and usage guidelines from the beginning of the project, and now we will consider the support built into XML Schemas for documenting the schema itself.

With SGML or XML DTDs, the only way to include descriptions or comments within the file was to use comment tags:

```
<!-- comments here -->
```

XML Schemas introduce the annotation element, which contains documentation and/or appinfo. annotation can appear as the first child of the element or attribute declaration.

The documentation element is for human-readable commentary on the schema, while the content of appinfo should be designed for applications to interpret. The content of both documentation and appinfo is any well-formed XML, which allows us to embed our own markup within the descriptions, as in the following example:

```
<xs:element name="citedObject">
    <xs:annotation>
        <xs:documentation>
            An object cited in inline text. Role attribute describes the type
            of object (film, play, etc). File pointed to by the sysId attribute
            is to be processed by media player application.
        </xs:documentation>
        <xs:appinfo><processingApp>media player</processingApp></xs:appinfo>
    </xs:annotation>
    <xs:complexType>
        <xs:simpleContent>
            <xs:extension base="xs:string">
                <xs:attribute name="role" type="xs:string" use="required" />
                <xs:attribute name="sysId" type="xs:string" use="required" />
            </xs:extension>
        </xs:simpleContent>
    </xs:complexType>
</xs:element>
```

One shortcut to creating HTML-based, hyper-linked documentation for our schema is to write XSLT stylesheets (see Chapter 10 – Schema and XSLT) to process the schema file (which is why the normal comment tags: <!-- --> should not be used, as they will not be parsed), pulling out element declarations and their documentation. Even a simple XSLT script could produce something like the following fragment of HTML from the above declaration:

```
<h2><a name="citedObject"/>CitedObject</h2>
<p><b>Attributes:</b> role (required), sysId (required)
<p><b>Content model: </b> simple <b>Base:</b> string</p>
<p><b>Description:</b> An object cited in inline text. Role attribute describes
the type of object (film, play, etc). File pointed to by the sysId attribute is to
be processed by media player application.</p>
```

To take our documentation one step further, look at DocBook (see http://www.docbook.org), a modular, extensible, general-purpose markup language for technical documentation. It is currently expressed as both an SGML and an XML DTD (not an XML Schema at the time of writing). DocBook comes with stylesheets for transforming the SGML or XML to HTML (to be viewed on a standard web browser), or Rich Text Format (to be printed). The results are worth the trouble of authoring in XML, and add a degree of professionalism to our documents. Additionally, we could adopt the same strategy as above of writing XSLT scripts to create DocBook XML directly from the schema files.

Managing Ongoing Development

In an ideal world, a schema would require no changes after its release, but in reality the document set that it models will change over time, new requirements will emerge and we may discover that we left an important element type out of the design. All these will require a new version of the schema.

To regulate the process of handling new requirements, fixing errors or omissions, and releasing new versions, we should designate a group of people responsible for future development – a good place to start would be the current schema development group. We could set up a site on the intranet if the schema is only to be used within our organization, or a web site if we have third parties, vendors, and suppliers who will be using the schema. The site should give access to the documentation and usage guidelines, and as much of the development documents as are available in HTML format. It should also offer links to other sites that explain the technology, and the W3C XML Schema site (http://www.w3.org/XML/Schema) would be a good start.

Summary

We hope you can see from this chapter that XML Schemas for documents are really rather different beasts from data schemas, and designing them therefore requires a very different approach. A document schema designed by one person will only represent that person's view of a process (in our example, publishing). Document schemas represent far more than the documents they model, so the scope of the development process is far ranging, and requires input from many different perspectives:

- authors
- editors
- production
- IT
- marketing
- management

Once finalized and adopted by an organization, a schema will form the heart of a publishing system. As the power of schemas lies in the precision with which we can define the documents that we create, so this power can work against us if the design isn't right. Moreover, correcting those mistakes at a later date can be very costly.

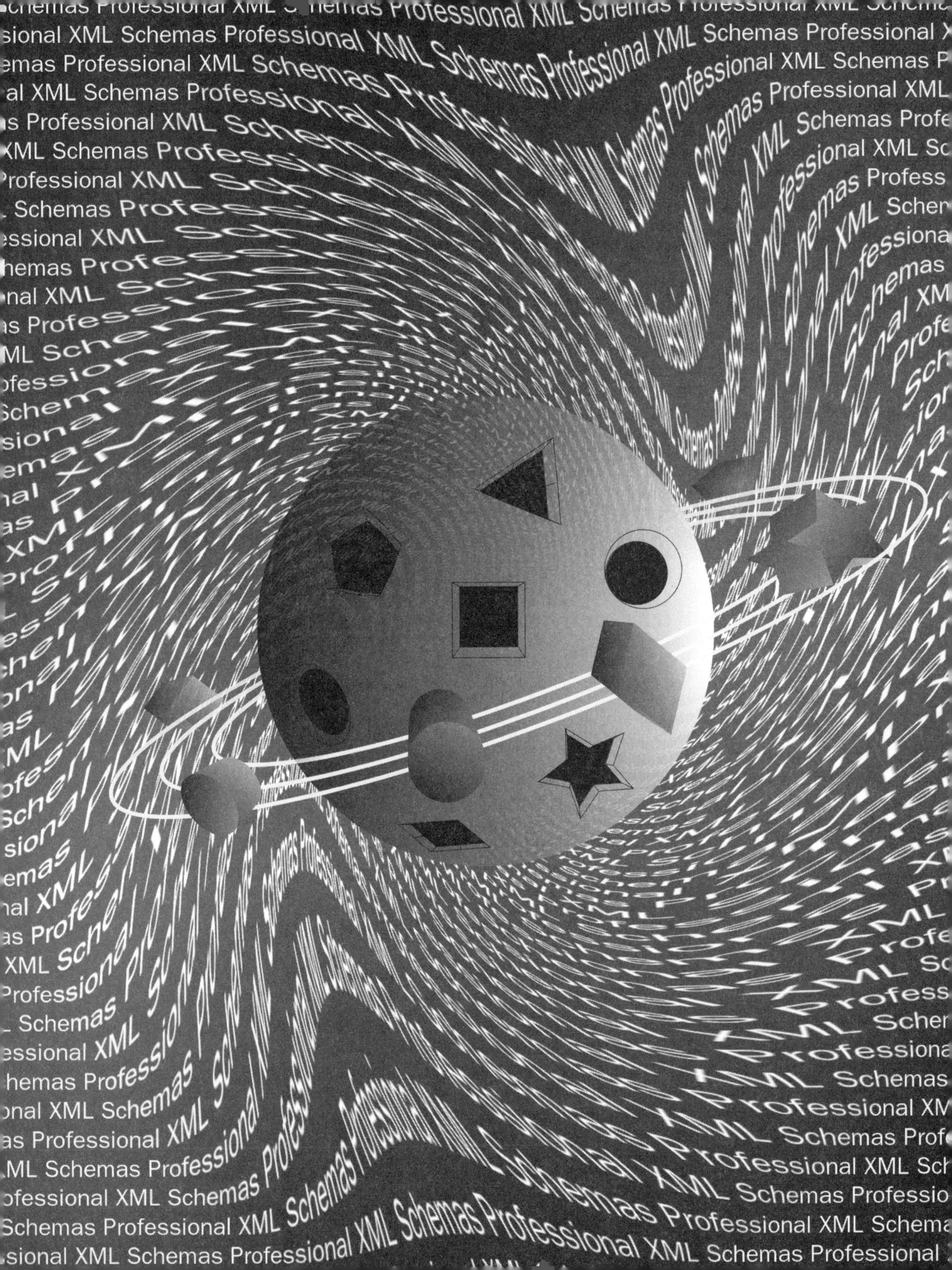
Professional XML Schemas

Schematron and Other Schema Technologies

XML Schemas will solve many of the previous problems with DTDs, but unfortunately there are still needs that are not met by the Recommendation. In this chapter we will look at some other schema technologies. Some of these technologies could be seen as competitors to XML Schema, while others are more complementary in the sense that they address areas untouched by XML Schema.

First, we will take an in-depth look at Schematron, which is relatively mature and seems particularly well suited to being used in partnership with XML Schema. Then we will take an overview of three other more competitive schema projects that offer a healthy diversity of relative strengths and weaknesses.

It's worth noting that XML Schema only became an official W3C Recommendation on May 2nd 2001, and that some of these alternatives are still very much under development.

Schematron

Rick Jelliffe, a member of the W3C XML SCHEMA WORKING GROUP, and developer of XML's naming rules and encoding-detection algorithm designed Schematron. It is a language that allows you to write schemas (which we will normally refer to as Schematron schemas to avoid confusion with W3C XML Schemas) consisting of patterns containing rules, which enforce logical constraints.

Schematron is intended to provide an alternative to the regular expression type of content model in DTDs, and to allow "usage" schemas to be layered on top of the basic "definitional" schemas. Usage schemas address constraints appropriate to various user contexts, such as being halfway through editing a document or ensuring that HTML documents conform to W3C Web Accessibility Initiative Guidelines.

All this means that Schematron has radically different strengths to XML Schema and is in fact highly complementary.

It is very lightweight – no compiled code is needed to run it, just an XSLT processor (such as Saxon for Java, or MSXML3 for Windows) and some open source transforms. It shares not only this lightness, but also its XPath and XSLT implementation with Examplotron, which is discussed later in this chapter. Both are used to generate a stylesheet, which is then run against the instance document that you want to validate. However, the focuses of both technologies are rather different, since Examplotron's primary aim is to express a structure that is visible in an example, whereas Schematron is aimed at expressing additional higher-level constraints.

Schematron is a **rule-based** schema language in contrast to XML Schema, which is **grammar-based**. It says, "*If you have an element matching this context, then the following assertions must be true, and here's what to report when they're not,*" with "context" and "assertions" both being standard XSLT and XPath expressions.

This means that Schematron can express vastly more flexible rules than XML Schema. Since XPath allows access to the document from the root as well as from the context node, Schematron rules effectively have random access to the rest of the document. An XML Schema or DTD effectively validates content depending on the structure (the element names) of parent or ancestor elements. Schematron, on the other hand, allows you to use structural features in ancestors, siblings, descendents or indeed anywhere. This means we can say, for example, "*If delivery contains a US-Address element, the item element must contain a US-Price element,*" or, "*If an item element has a quantity attribute, then it must also have a units attribute.*"

XPath also gives access to the values of the document and allows you to say, for example, "*If delivery country is UK, then Value Added Tax should be 17.5%.*"

In fact, since XSLT adds the `document()` function to the XPath function set, the rules can refer to any conceivable URL that returns an XML result.

Schematron is simple to learn and simple to implement for anyone who already has some understanding of XPath or XSLT. If you're dealing with XML, then learning XPath is a useful investment anyway, given that it is also part of the XSLT, XML Schema and XQuery standards.

Schematron has more focus on making its results more useful to users than XML Schema has. For example, every error message is specified in the schema as part of the assertion, which triggers it, and it is possible to choose at runtime whether the output is delivered as text, XML, or HTML. By contrast, XML Schema does not specify an error message API, structure, or any way of customizing error messages to enhance their semantics.

> *You can find more information from the Schematron site at http://www.ascc.net/xml/resource/schematron/schematron.html, which also has all the utilities you'll need.*

> *The command line examples below use the **Instant Saxon XSLT** engine from http://users.iclway.co.uk/mhkay/saxon/.*

> *There is a good interview with Rick Jelliffe at http://www.xmlhack.com/read.php?item=121.*

Before going into the details, let's walk through a quick example.

A Sample Schematron Schema

By way of illustration, let's take the Purchase Order example from the XML Schema Primer, save it as po.xml and write a Schematron schema for it:

```
<purchaseOrder orderDate="1999-10-20">
    <shipTo country="US">
        <name>Alice Smith</name>
        <street>123 Maple Street</street>
        <city>Mill Valley</city>
        <state>CA</state>
        <zip>90952</zip>
    </shipTo>
    <billTo country="US">
        <name>Robert Smith</name>
        <street>8 Oak Avenue</street>
        <city>Old Town</city>
        <state>PA</state>
        <zip>95819</zip>
    </billTo>
    <comment>Hurry, my lawn is going wild!</comment>
    <items>
        <item partNum="872-AA">
            <productName>Lawnmower</productName>
            <quantity>1</quantity>
            <USPrice>148.95</USPrice>
            <comment>Confirm this is electric</comment>
        </item>
        <item partNum="926-AA">
            <productName>Baby Monitor</productName>
            <quantity>1</quantity>
            <USPrice>39.98</USPrice>
            <shipDate>1999-05-21</shipDate>
        </item>
    </items>
</purchaseOrder>
```

Now let's write a very simple Schematron schema to validate the most obvious possible feature of this document – that it has a purchaseOrder root element. We'll save this as po-0.sch:

```
<sch:schema xmlns:sch="http://www.ascc.net/xml/schematron">
    <sch:title>Schematron Validator for Purchase Orders</sch:title>
    <sch:pattern name="Top Level Purchase Order elements">
        <sch:rule context="/*">
            <sch:assert test="self::purchaseOrder"
            >The root element must be a "purchaseOrder"</sch:assert>
        </sch:rule>
    </sch:pattern>
</sch:schema>
```

What does this schema say? Let's run through these elements from the Schematron namespace:

❑ `schema` – this is the root element, and the obvious place to declare the http://www.ascc.net/xml/schematron namespace

❑ `title` – this may be used by the validator's output

❑ `pattern` – this groups rules together. It should have a descriptive `name` attribute and may have a unique `id` attribute. Unless you're using phases (see below), there needn't be any technical link between the rules. Grouping is done for the convenience of the person writing or reading the schema

❑ `rule` – here's where we do the work of associating target elements with constraints and error messages

❑ `assert` – an assertion will fire its error message when its test expression evaluates to false

❑ `context="/*"` – this rule will be applied to the document's root element

❑ `test="self::purchaseOrder"` – this tests that the current node (as selected by the context attribute above) is itself a `purchaseOrder`

Compiling a Basic Validator

In order to test our simple Schematron schema, we'll need some test data such as a broken purchase order, which has used the wrong case for the root element – `PurchaseOrder` instead of `purchaseOrder`. We will save this as `bad-po-0.xml`.

```
<PurchaseOrder orderDate="1999-10-20">
    ...<!-- rest of xml here -->
</PurchaseOrder>
```

Validating it using the Schematron involves two steps – these are:

❑ Compile the schema into a run-time validator

❑ Run the validator against the schema

This process is illustrated below using a "T-Diagram", where the square blocks are data and the "T" blocks are programs. The program language is displayed on the stem of the "T" (in this case they're all XSL, and just need an XSL processor to run them) and the program's input and output are described on the left and right arms respectively. The key point in the diagram below is that the program represented by the "T" on the right is itself output by the "T" on the left:

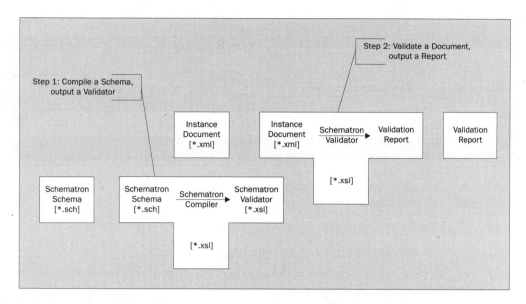

We'll use Saxon to compile a validator – the first parameter is the XML file to be transformed, the second parameter is the name of the transform file, and we'll use the ">" to redirect the output to another file – and then validate a document:

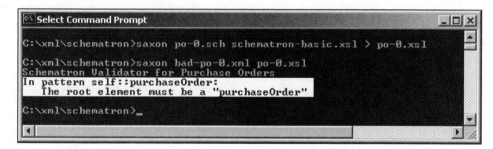

This shows Saxon, an XSLT implementation, compiling the po-0.sch Schematron schema file we listed above with a transform called Schematron-basic.xsl which in turn imports skeleton1-5.xsl (both from the Schematron home page – see the resources box at the start of this section), and redirecting the result into a file called po-0.xsl. This will be our run-time validator.

On the next line we use Saxon again to process bad-po-0.xml with the validator, po-0.xsl, with the result coming out to the DOS console. As we expect, it uses our own error message to report that the root element is in error.

Compiling and Running an XML Validator

Now let's demonstrate Schematron's user focus. The compiler we used last time was designed to generate validators that output their reports as plain text. However, we can use different compilers to generate different kinds of output. For example, Schematron-xml.xsl, which also imports skeleton1-5.xsl (again from the Schematron home page) gives us validators that report in XML, which would be useful if we wanted to run this from a program and automatically parse the results:

```
Select Command Prompt                                                    _ □ ×

C:\xml\schematron>saxon po-0.sch schematron-xml.xsl > po-0.xsl

C:\xml\schematron>saxon bad-po-0.xml po-0.xsl
<?xml version="1.0" encoding="utf-8" standalone="yes"?>
<schematron-output xmlns:sch="http://www.ascc.net/xml/schematron" title="Schematron Validato
r for Purchase Orders" schemaVersion="" phase="#ALL">
   <active-pattern name="Top Level Purchase Order elements"/>
   <fired-rule id="" context="/*" role=""/>
   <failed-assert id="" test="self::purchaseOrder" role="" location="/PurchaseOrder[1]">
      <text>The root element must be a "purchaseOrder"</text>
   </failed-assert>
</schematron-output>
C:\xml\schematron>
```

The key element in the output of a Schematron-XML validator is the `failed-assert` element which is highlighted in the screenshot above.

- ❑ Its presence tells us that there was a validation error
- ❑ Its `text` child element gives us the error message
- ❑ Its `location` attribute contains an XPath expression pointing to the context element in the source document

If this validator is being used by a program, then the program can detect that there has been a validation failure, which rule failed on which node, and what the error message is. This gives the calling program about as much feedback as it can reasonably use (though there is another feature called diagnostics which is described briefly in this chapter and more fully in the Schematron specification).

Compiling and Running an HTML Validator

What else can we do with a validation technology that lets us write our own output modules? In this section, we'll see an example of generating validators, which are targeted at human users. The `schematron-report.xsl` compiler (also from the Schematron home page), which again uses the common compiler library `skeleton1-5.xsl`, generates a report as HTML, complete with "href" links into an HTML image of the document being validated. It comes with `verbid.xsl`, which generates an HTML image of the XML, and `schematron-frame.html` to pull in the error report and the XML image as frames:

```
Command Prompt                                                          _ □ ×

C:\xml\schematron>saxon po-0.sch schematron-report.xsl > po-0.xsl

C:\xml\schematron>saxon bad-po-0.xml po-0.xsl > schematron-errors.html

C:\xml\schematron>saxon bad-po-0.xml verbid.xsl > schematron-out.html

C:\xml\schematron>_
```

When we view schematron-frame.html, we see the error reports and the document image – with IE 5 it looks like this:

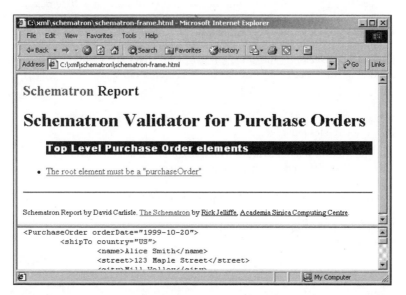

You can click on a validation message to position the XML frame to the context node for that rule. One final point to note after this illustration is that the feature we've chosen to validate – that the root element must be purchaseOrder – is not a rule that can be expressed by an XML Schema.

More Schematron

The above section covers enough to get started with Schematron. In this section we'll look at the remaining Schematron elements and their uses.

Name

The name element can be included in the content of an assert or report message, and allows you to embed the name of the context element. For example:

```
<rule context="USPrice">
    <assert test="/purchaseOrder/shipTo/@country='US'">
    <name/>may only be charged for US delivery</assert>
</rule>
```

This schema rule will produce, when triggered, this message:

```
USPrice may only be charged for US delivery
```

The name element can also take a path attribute containing an XPath expression whose value is used instead of the context node's name.

Diagnostics

Schematron has a strong focus on providing meaningful error messages. The `diagnostics` and `diagnostic` elements, and the `diagnostics` attribute of the `report` and `assert` elements give a way of adding instance data to the error report.

❑ `@diagnostics` – can be in `assert` or `report` elements. Contains a space-separated list of references to the `id` attributes of `diagnostic` elements.

❑ `diagnostics` – must be a child of `schema`. Contains `diagnostic` elements.

❑ `diagnostic` – must be a child of `diagnostics`, has an `id` attribute and contains mixed text and `value-of` elements.

❑ `value-of` – has a select attribute which takes an XPath expression which is evaluated at run-time and substituted for the `value-of` element.

For example, take a look at the constraints in the schema extract below:

```
<pattern name="Shipping and Price">
    <rule context="USPrice">
        <assert test="/purchaseOrder/shipTo/@country='US'"
                diagnostics="actualCountry">
            <name />may only be charged for US delivery
        </assert>
    </rule>
    <!-- ... -->
</pattern>
<diagnostics>
    <diagnostic id="actualCountry">Actual shipTo country was
        <value-of select="/purchaseOrder/shipTo/@country"/>
    </diagnostic>
</diagnostics>
```

These might generate this error report from Schematron-XML validator:

```
<failed-assert id="" test="/purchaseOrder/shipTo/@country='US'" role=""
        location="/purchaseOrder[1]/items[1]/item[1]/USPrice[1]">
    <diagnostic id="actualCountry">Actual shipTo country was UK</diagnostic>
    <text>USPrice may only be charged for US delivery</text>
</failed-assert>
```

This structure also means that diagnostics can be re-used in multiple `assert` and `report` elements.

Phases

Messages and documents frequently have lifecycles, such as when a document gets passed through the workflow of some business process. The most economical and coherent way of describing the validation at each state in the workflow may well be to select the relevant subset of constraints from a single superset.

Schematron allows you to compile a single Schematron schema into different validators for different phases by specifying a phase name at compile time. This requires the use of `pattern` elements' `id` attributes, and of these two new elements:

❑ phase – any phase elements must be children of `schema`, coming immediately before the `pattern` elements. They must have an `id` attribute containing a unique name, and should contain one or more `active` elements.

❑ active – this must have a `pattern` attribute that references the unique `id` attribute of a `pattern` element, and may contain documentary text.

Let see how this works in practice with a phase structured Schematron schema, called `po-1.sch`. This supports two explicit phases, `received` for a newly received order, which may need some further work to ensure that the part numbers and prices are filled in and correct, and `processed`, which should be ready for order, assembly, and delivery:

```xml
<?xml version="1.0" encoding="UTF-8"?>
<schema xmlns="http://www.ascc.net/xml/schematron">
    <title>Schematron Validator for Purchase Orders</title>
    <phase id="received">
        <active pattern="root">Check for correct root element</active>
    </phase>
    <phase id="processed">
        <active pattern="shipAndPrice">
        Ordered items must have match prices to shipment country.</active>
        <active pattern="stock">Ordered items have stock numbers.</active>
    </phase>
    <pattern name="Top Level Purchase Order elements" id="root">
        <rule context="/*">
            <assert test="self::purchaseOrder">
            The root element must be a "purchaseOrder"</assert>
        </rule>
    </pattern>
    <pattern name="Shipping and Price" id="shipAndPrice">
        <rule context="USPrice">
            <assert test="/purchaseOrder/shipTo/@country='US'"
                diagnostics="actualCountry">
            <name />may only be charged for US delivery</assert>
        </rule>
        <rule context="ExportPrice">
            <assert test="/purchaseOrder/shipTo/@country != 'US'">
            <name />may not be charged for US delivery</assert>
        </rule>
    </pattern>
    <pattern name="Processed by Stock Control" id="stock">
        <rule context="item">
            <assert test="@partNum != ''">
            <name/>must have a non-null partNum</assert>
        </rule>
    </pattern>
    <diagnostics>
        <diagnostic id="actualCountry">
        Actual shipTo country was
            <value-of select="/purchaseOrder/shipTo/@country"/>
        </diagnostic>
    </diagnostics>
</schema>
```

(Notice how the `phase/active/@pattern` attributes refer to the `pattern/@id` values.)

We'll apply this schema to the following message (bad-po-1.xml):

```
<?xml version="1.0"?>
<purchaseOrder orderDate="1999-10-20">
    <shipTo country="UK">
        <name>Alice Smith</name>
        <street>123 Maple Street</street>
        <city>Mill Valley</city>
        <state>CA</state>
        <zip>90952</zip>
    </shipTo>
    <billTo country="US">
        <name>Robert Smith</name>
        <street>8 Oak Avenue</street>
        <city>Old Town</city>
        <state>PA</state>
        <zip>95819</zip>
    </billTo>
    <comment>Hurry, my lawn is going wild!</comment>
    <items>
        <item partNum="872-AA">
            <productName>Lawnmower</productName>
            <quantity>1</quantity>
            <ExportPrice>148.95</ExportPrice>
            <comment>Confirm this is electric</comment>
        </item>
        <item partNum="">
            <productName>Baby Monitor</productName>
            <quantity>1</quantity>
            <USPrice>39.98</USPrice>
            <shipDate>1999-05-21</shipDate>
        </item>
    </items>
</purchaseOrder>
```

(Note the blank partNum in the highlighted item, and the clash between the USPrice and the
shipTo/@country.)

Now we'll compile three different validators from the schema, and apply them to the document. First
we'll do one that ignores the phase sub-setting entirely, then one for the received phase and finally
one for the processed phase:

We've used the basic compiler because it gives a nice compact output – if you choose the XML or
report compilers you will get validators that output rather more information, including the diagnostics.

You can see that the document has no errors for the received phase, or when validated against the whole schema, but a couple of errors are thrown up for the processed phase.

> *Note that* phase="processed" *illustrates how Saxon accepts command line parameters to transforms. Though XSLT specifies a single method for referring to external parameters from inside a transform, it doesn't specify an API for XSLT in general, or any specific method for passing in parameters. A program using MSXML 3 as a COM object can pass parameters into a transform with the* addParameter() *method, and Java parsers supporting JAXP or TRAX can use the* setParameter() *method.*

This phase support can be used as a layer over XML Schema to require or deny generally optional elements or attributes. In principle it could even be used to enforce partner-specific variations on allowed and disallowed content, though this would be stretching the purpose of the feature and might not fit in with future Schematron development.

Formatting/Documentation

Schematron provides various elements and attributes for documenting schemas and formatting error messages:

- ❑   p – this is basically a paragraph element, the equivalent of the HTML p element. It is used to document the schema itself, and can be a child of schema, pattern or phase. It can contain the standard formatting elements dir, emph, and span, and can take id, icon, and class attributes, of which id and class can be expected to pass through into HTML unchanged.

- ❑   dir – this can be used inside documentation and output elements to specify the direction in which a language is displayed (left-to-right or right-to-left, with default being left-to-right).

- ❑   emph – this can be used inside documentation and output elements in the same way as its HTML equivalent. (Its HTML equivalent is actually em, rather than emph and is used to render specified text in an emphasized font format).

- ❑   span – this can also be used inside documentation and output elements in the same way as the HTML span element, as a way of applying a class to an inline text sequence.

These elements extend Schematron's ability to add value to the interactive and workflow uses of schema.

Abstract/Extends

Schematron allows rules to implement a form of inheritance using a macro mechanism. The source rule must not have a context attribute, it must have a unique id attribute, and it must have an abstract attribute set to true. Let's consider the extends rule:

- ❑   extends – each rule can contain one or more of these. Each one must have a rule attribute that references the id of an abstract rule. The contents of each referenced abstract rule get copied into the target rule and applied in its context.

Take a look at the po-2.sch schema shown below:

```
<?xml version="1.0" encoding="UTF-8"?>
<schema xmlns="http://www.ascc.net/xml/schematron">
```

```
<title>Schematron Validator for Purchase Orders</title>
<pattern name="abstracts">
    <rule abstract="true" id="childLess">
        <assert test="count(*) = 0">
        <name/>must not have any child elements
        </assert>
    </rule>
</pattern>
<pattern name="Top Level Purchase Order elements" id="root">
    <rule context="/*">
        <assert test="self::purchaseOrder">
        The root element must be a "purchaseOrder"
        </assert>
    </rule>
</pattern>
<pattern name="Shipping and Price" id="shipAndPrice">
    <rule context="USPrice">
        <extends rule="childLess"/>
        <assert test="/purchaseOrder/shipTo/@country = 'US'">
        <name />may only be charged for US delivery
        </assert>
    </rule>
    <rule context="ExportPrice">
        <extends rule="childLess"/>
        <assert test="/purchaseOrder/shipTo/@country != 'US'">
        <name />may not be charged for US delivery
        </assert>
    </rule>
</pattern>
<pattern name="Processed by Stock Control" id="stock">
    <rule context="item">
        <assert test="@partNum != ''">
        <name/>must have a non-null partNum
        </assert>
    </rule>
</pattern>
</schema>
```

If this schema is applied to a document, bad-po-2.xml, which contains the line:

```
<ExportPrice>39.98<comment>this needs to be checked</comment></ExportPrice>
```

then it would generate output including this data:

```
<fired-rule id="" context="ExportPrice" role=""/>
<failed-assert id="" test="count(*) = 0" role=""
        location="/purchaseOrder[1]/items[1]/item[2]/ExportPrice[1]">
    <text>ExportPrice must not have any child elements</text>
```

This also makes a good demonstration of using the name element in output templates.

Key

The key element allows Schematron schemas to access XSLT keys in order to speed up validation needing referential access to large data sets.

❏   key – takes name and path attributes, and applies the XPath expression in the path attribute to each node matching the context expression in the parent rule, to produce an index which can be used (in the similarly named key() function) by the name specified in the name attribute.

For example, take a schema such as assignments.sch:

```
<?xml version="1.0" encoding="UTF-8"?>
<sch:schema xmlns:sch="http://www.ascc.net/xml/schematron">
    <sch:title>Schematron Validator for Staff Assignments</sch:title>
    <sch:pattern name="abstracts">
        <sch:rule abstract="true" id="check-code">
            <sch:assert test="@code">
                <sch:name/>must have a code attribute.
            </sch:assert>
        </sch:rule>
    </sch:pattern>
    <sch:pattern name="groups">
        <sch:rule context="group">
            <sch:key name="group-key" path="@code"/>
            <sch:extends rule="check-code"/>
        </sch:rule>
    </sch:pattern>
    <sch:pattern name="projects">
        <sch:rule context="project">
            <sch:key name="project-key" path="@code"/>
            <sch:extends rule="check-code"/>
        </sch:rule>
    </sch:pattern>
    <sch:pattern name="assignments">
        <sch:rule context="staff">
            <sch:extends rule="check-code"/>
            <sch:assert test="key('group-key', @group)">
                <sch:name/>does not have a valid group code.
            </sch:assert>
            <sch:assert test="key('project-key', @project)">
                <sch:name/>does not have a valid project code.
            </sch:assert>
        </sch:rule>
    </sch:pattern>
</sch:schema>
```

The key points here are how the two highlighted key() calls perform lookups on the named keys using the value of the group or project attributes. The keys are defined to operate on nodes matching the enclosing rule/@context, indexed by the key/@path, and named by key/@name.

Let's try this on assignments.xml below and see what happens with Mr. Oddjob's assignment:

```
<?xml version="1.0" encoding="UTF-8"?>
<assignments>
    <group code="sales">sales</group>
    <group code="r-and-d">research and development</group>
    <group code="consultancy">consultancy</group>
    <project code="abc">ABC Web Banking</project>
    <project code="xyz">XYZ Internet Credit Cards</project>
    <staff code="Joe" group="r-and-d" project="abc"/>
    <staff code="Angela" group="r-and-d" project="abc"/>
    <staff code="Paul" group="sales" project="abc"/>
    <staff code="David" group="sales" project="xyz"/>
    <staff code="Kuldip" group="consultancy" project="abc"/>
    <staff code="Ross" group="consultancy" project="xyz"/>
    <staff code="Oddjob" group="management" project="666"/>
    <!-- ... -->
</assignments>
```

Lightly reformatted, we can expect a result, which includes the following data:

```
<failed-assert id="" test="key('group-key', @group)" role=""
      location="/assignments[1]/staff[7]">
      <text>staff does not have a valid group code.</text>
</failed-assert>
<failed-assert id="" test="key('project-key', @project)" role=""
      location="/assignments[1]/staff[7]">
      <text>staff does not have a valid project code.</text>
</failed-assert>
```

The important thing to remember about keys is that they don't allow you to do anything that you couldn't logically do without them; they just allow you to do it faster. Given that XSLT processors are now mature enough to be competing on speed rather than completeness, this means that you can expect to cope with fairly large messages, but as always the pre-requisite advice on performance is to test hard and test early.

Complementary Features

Now let's see how some of the features of Schematron and XML Schema allow them to work well together.

XML Schema is Grammar-based – Schematron is Rule-based

This makes XML Schema great at describing content models for element types. It also makes it quite easy to process an XML Schema with XSLT and produce a document showing the dependencies between different definitions – the relationships are visible in the structure of the XML Schema itself. By contrast, it is easy to write and run Schematron validators, but less easy to write programs that understand the semantics of a Schematron schema. For instance, the task of writing a program to generate HTML that shows which elements or attributes are used to validate which would be considerably trickier for Schematron schemas.

Schematron Allows Arbitrary Logical Constraints

On the whole, XML Schema does not permit structure to be determined by values, or by structural features from other parts of the document, whereas Schematron does. For example, we can specify that we will only allow a USPrice in the item if we have a US shipping address:

```
<pattern name="Shipping and Price">
  <rule context="USPrice">
    <assert test="/purchaseOrder/shipTo/@country = 'US'">
      USPrice may only be used for US delivery
    </assert>
  </rule>
  <rule context="ExportPrice">
    <assert test="/purchaseOrder/shipTo/@country != 'US'">
      ExportPrice may not be used for US delivery
    </assert>
  </rule>
</pattern>
```

Expressing this kind of business rule in the schema may well be of critical importance when doing e-commerce, where the cost of each ambiguity in the schema will be multiplied by the number of partners you hope to do business with.

Business rules are the crux of both business processes and good business-oriented data models. Their importance is becoming more recognized all the time. Schematron allows a significant subset of business rules to be specified and implemented declaratively. This means there may be substantial economic forces supporting its take-up.

Specify Root Elements

Schematron allows the schema to specify which elements may be root elements. We mentioned this in the illustration above. It may be that some XML Schema implementations will permit the validating party to specify this as a requirement, but it is not a constraint that can be expressed in the schema itself.

"Expansion Slots" Add User Specified Documentation and Processing Elements

XML Schema has "Expansion Slots" for adding user specified documentation and processing elements. The XML Schema `annotation` element provides a framework for adding structured non-XSDL information to a Schema. It can contain both `documentation` and `appinfo` elements, and though neither will be processed by the Schema processor, the contents must be well-formed XML and are not in danger of being discarded in the same way as extensions concealed inside comments. Schematron was designed to be layered over other schemas. We'll look at embedding Schematron constraints in application elements in the *Co-location* section later.

Schematron Runs in Any Environment that Supports XSLT

This almost certainly includes any environment that supports XML Schema. Sadly, this does not yet include the browser, since (at the time of writing) Netscape 6 and IE 6 do not have native XSLT support, though IE 5 supported an earlier experimental syntax. However, it does mean that it is realistic to include Schematron rules as part of your XML Schema for doing business with other businesses.

Schematron Supports XSLT/XPath Constraints of Any Complexity

This is where Schematron shines. XPath has some limitations, such as no regular expressions and a limited set of types, but it is still powerful:

- ❑ It gives random access to any element or elements in the document, working either from the current context node or from the root.

- ❑ The basic types may be limited to number, string, and Boolean (until XPath 2 brings in XML Schema datatypes), but support for node-sets as a first-class type means XPath can do a lot of things in expressions that would require multi-line constructs in other languages.

- ❑ XPath expressions can be nested as deeply as we like.

- ❑ The XSLT document() function gives access to XML in the stylesheet itself, and can be used with runtime expressions to call any URL which returns XML.

- ❑ Most XSLT implementations have extension functions. These are automatically available to your Schematron constraints. Most XSLT engines also offer some way of defining your own functions, which could be useful for requirements like validating credit card checksums. There is currently no mechanism for including these definitions in a Schematron schema, but because Schematron is so open, it would be a fairly simple extension.

- ❑ XPath and XSLT are now mature enough that implementations are being optimized for performance, which could be important when validating larger documents or large numbers of small documents. Schematron's key element supports the use of XSLT keys, which could make a substantial difference when validating large documents.

Co-location

Co-locating Schematron with an XML Schema refers to the practice of embedding Schematron constraints within an XML Schema so that we have a single source for Schematron and XML Schema validation.

Clearly this leads to an extra step in the Schematron validation process – the Schematron schema must first be extracted from the schema, as shown in the diagram below:

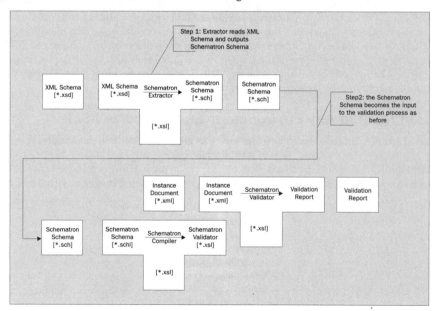

Why Co-locate?

Assuming we're starting a project using XML Schema for data definition, and then realize that we would like to add Schematron features as well, let's consider the reasons for using co-location rather than maintaining a separate Schematron schema:

- ❏ Convenience – for the schema author, it can be part of an integrated validation framework. As constraints can be embedded within the components to which they apply, any changes to an XML Schema definition will bring the relevant constraints into the author's focus.

- ❏ Clarity – for the developer using schemas at build time, it is easy to see which Schematron constraints apply to which Schema definitions.

- ❏ Integrity – because there is a single point of update, co-location will reduce the risk that either development work or runtime validation is carried out with mismatched XML Schema and Schematron.

In short, if we're going to use Schematron with XML Schema, then we should co-locate.

Illustration

Let's take the purchase order example we've been looking at from the XML Schema Primer, and embed some Schematron constraints in it. It's still a valid XML Schema, so I have saved it as `po-sch.xsd`. We need to define the Schematron namespace here so we can use it in the rest of the document:

```xml
<?xml version="1.0" encoding="UTF-8"?>
<xs:schema xmlns:xs=http://www.w3.org/2001/XMLSchema
           xmlns:sch="http://www.ascc.net/xml/schematron">
    <xs:annotation>
        <xs:documentation xml:lang="en">
            Purchase order schema for Example.com.
            Copyright 2000 Example.com. All rights reserved.
        </xs:documentation>
```

The `sch:title` element can be used as part of the validator's output:

```xml
        <xs:appinfo>
            <sch:title>
                Schematron validation schema for the Purchase Orders
            </sch:title>
        </xs:appinfo>
    </xs:annotation>
```

Next, we define some constraints for the top-level element:

```xml
    <xs:element name="purchaseOrder" type="PurchaseOrderType">
        <xs:annotation>
            <xs:appinfo>
                <sch:pattern name="Top Level Purchase Order elements">
                    <sch:rule context="/*">
                        <sch:assert test="self::purchaseOrder">
```

```
                        The root element must be a "purchaseOrder"
                    </sch:assert>
                </sch:rule>
            </sch:pattern>
        </xs:appinfo>
    </xs:annotation>
</xs:element>
<xs:element name="comment" type="xs:string"/>
<xs:complexType name="PurchaseOrderType">
    <xs:sequence>
        <xs:element name="shipTo" type="USAddress"/>
        <xs:element name="billTo" type="USAddress"/>
        <xs:element ref="comment" minOccurs="0"/>
        <xs:element name="items" type="Items"/>
    </xs:sequence>
    <xs:attribute name="orderDate" type="xs:date"/>
</xs:complexType>
<xs:complexType name="USAddress">
    <xs:sequence>
        <xs:element name="name" type="xs:string"/>
        <xs:element name="street" type="xs:string"/>
        <xs:element name="city" type="xs:string"/>
        <xs:element name="state" type="xs:string"/>
        <xs:element name="zip" type="xs:decimal"/>
    </xs:sequence>
    <xs:attribute name="country" type="xs:NMTOKEN" default="US"/>
</xs:complexType>
<xs:complexType name="Items">
    <xs:sequence>
        <xs:element name="item" minOccurs="0" maxOccurs="unbounded">
            <xs:complexType>
```

Now we also define some constraints for the item element:

```
                <xs:annotation>
                    <xs:appinfo>
                        <sch:pattern name="Shipping and Price">
                            <sch:rule context="item/USPrice">
                                <sch:assert test="/purchaseOrder/shipTo/
                                        @country = 'US'">
                                    USPrice may only be used for US delivery
                                </sch:assert>
                            </sch:rule>
                            <sch:rule context="item/ExportPrice">
                                <sch:assert test="/purchaseOrder/shipTo/
                                        @country != 'US'">
                                    ExportPrice may not be used for US delivery
                                </sch:assert>
                            </sch:rule>
                        </sch:pattern>
                    </xs:appinfo>
                </xs:annotation>
                <xs:sequence>
                    <xs:element name="productName" type="xs:string"/>
                    <xs:element name="quantity">
```

```
                    <xs:simpleType>
                        <xs:restriction base="xs:positiveInteger">
                            <xs:maxExclusive value="100"/>
                        </xs:restriction>
                    </xs:simpleType>
                </xs:element>
                <xs:choice>
                    <xs:element name="USPrice" type="xs:decimal"/>
                    <xs:element name="ExportPrice" type="xs:decimal"/>
                </xs:choice>
                <xs:element ref="comment" minOccurs="0"/>
                <xs:element name="shipDate" type="xs:date"
                            minOccurs="0"/>
            </xs:sequence>
            <xs:attribute name="partNum" type="SKU" use="required"/>
        </xs:complexType>
    </xs:element>
  </xs:sequence>
</xs:complexType>
<!-- Stock Keeping Unit, a code for identifying products -->
<xs:simpleType name="SKU">
    <xs:restriction base="xs:string">
        <xs:pattern value="\d{3}-[A-Z]{2}"/>
    </xs:restriction>
</xs:simpleType>
</xs:schema>
```

Two of the highlighted blocks should look familiar – they are the examples we used earlier, but now embedded in XML Schema annotation and application elements. We have also added a sch:title element to clarify the output.

Let's demonstrate this in action. The first step is to generate the Schematron schema, using the xsd2sctrn.xsl utility (available along with the rest of the code that accompanies this book from the Wrox web site). Next we'll compile a basic validator, and then validate good and bad purchase order instances against it. Here's the command line procedure for running this – obviously this would be automated in a real development environment:

```
Command Prompt                                                    _ □ ×

C:\xml\schematron>saxon po-sch.xsd xsd2schtrn.xsl > po-sch.sch

C:\xml\schematron>saxon po-sch.sch schematron-basic.xsl > po-sch.xsl

C:\xml\schematron>saxon po.xml po-sch.xsl
Schematron validation schema for the Purchase Orders

C:\xml\schematron>saxon bad-po-0.xml po-sch.xsl
Schematron validation schema for the Purchase Orders
In pattern self::purchaseOrder:
    The root element must be a "purchaseOrder"
In pattern /purchaseOrder/shipTo/@country = 'US':
    USPrice may only be used for US delivery
In pattern /purchaseOrder/shipTo/@country = 'US':
    USPrice may only be used for US delivery

C:\xml\schematron>_
```

Just for now we'll ignore the XML Schema itself, but the point of embedding Schematron is to give the best of both worlds. In practice you can either create a batch file to validate your instance against XSD and Schematron constraints in one go, or create a validation API that supports both XSD and XSLT, giving a concatenated single result file.

Code Notes

If you're interested in processing XML Schemas with XSLT, you might like to take a look at the `xsd2schtrn.xsl` utility, which was used to extract the Schematron schema:

```xml
<?xml version="1.0" encoding="UTF-8"?>
<!--
    inspired by an original transform by Eddie Robertsson
-->
<xsl:transform version="1.0"
                xmlns:xsl="http://www.w3.org/1999/XSL/Transform"
                xmlns:sch="http://www.ascc.net/xml/schematron"
                xmlns:xsd="http://www.w3.org/2001/XMLSchema">
<!--
    Set the output to be XML with an XML declaration and use indentation
-->
    <xsl:output indent="yes" standalone="yes"/>
```

There are only three templates. This first one matches `xsd:schema`, and is called when the XSLT processor encounters the root schema element in the XML Schema document.

We now call a named template, `gatherSchema`. This is responsible for pulling in any Schematron constraints from `included`, `imported`, or `redefined` XML Schemas, though it treats them all the same. This is worth considering if you are going to embed Schematron rules inside redefined XML Schema files:

```xml
<!--
    match schema and call recursive template to extract included schemas
-->
    <xsl:template match="xsd:schema">

<!-- call the schema definition template ... -->

        <xsl:call-template name="gatherSchema">

<!-- ... with current root as the $schemas parameter ... -->

            <xsl:with-param name="schemas" select="/"/>

<!-- ... and any includes in the $include parameter -->

            <xsl:with-param name="includes" select="document(/xsd:schema/xsd:*
                        [self::xsd:include or self::xsd:import or
                        self::xsd:redefine]/@schemaLocation)"/>
        </xsl:call-template>
    </xsl:template>
```

This loops recursively, building up a node-set of all the documents, which are directly or indirectly referenced from the root document:

```xml
<!-- gather all included schemas into a single parameter variable -->

<xsl:template name="gatherSchema">
    <xsl:param name="schemas"/>
    <xsl:param name="includes"/>
    <xsl:choose>
        <xsl:when test="count($schemas) &lt; count($schemas | $includes)">
            <!-- when $includes includes something new, recurse ... -->
            <xsl:call-template name="gatherSchema">

<!-- ... with current $includes added to the $schemas parameter ... -->

                <xsl:with-param name="schemas" select="$schemas |
                                $includes"/>
```

The line using the document() function to build up the include parameter was probably the single scariest line of XSLT I've ever written – the fact that it works correctly removed the necessity for possibly days worth of design, coding, and testing. It relies on two of the more powerful features of XSLT. The first is that we can have an XPath expression that starts, not with the root node or the current node, but with a variable containing an entire node-set, and that the remainder of the expression will be applied to every node in the set. The second is that document() will accept a node-set of valid URLs as its parameter and return the root node of each document found.

```xml
<!-- ... and any *new* includes in the $include parameter -->

                <xsl:with-param name="includes" select="document
                                ($includes/xsd:schema/xsd:*[self::xsd:include
                                or self::xsd:import or self::xsd:redefine]
                                /@schemaLocation)"/>
            </xsl:call-template>
        </xsl:when>
        <xsl:otherwise>

<!--
    we have the complete set of included schemas, so now let's output the
    embedded schematron
-->

            <xsl:call-template name="output">
                <xsl:with-param name="schemas" select="$schemas"/>
            </xsl:call-template>
        </xsl:otherwise>
    </xsl:choose>
</xsl:template>
```

This is where we construct the output. Schematron requires the `title` and `ns` elements in that order, so we do that first, then loop through the patterns.

```
<!-- output the schematron information -->

   <xsl:template name="output">
      <xsl:param name="schemas"/>


      <sch:schema>

<!-- get header-type elements - eg title and especially ns -->
<!-- title (just one) -->

         <xsl:copy-of select="$schemas//xsd:appinfo/sch:title[1]"/>

<!-- get remaining schematron schema children -->
<!-- get non-blank namespace elements, dropping duplicates -->

         <xsl:for-each select="$schemas//xsd:appinfo/sch:ns">
            <xsl:if test="generate-id(.) = generate-id($schemas//
                  xsd:appinfo/sch:ns[@prefix = current()/@prefix][1])">
               <xsl:copy-of select="."/>
            </xsl:if>
         </xsl:for-each>
         <xsl:copy-of select="$schemas//xsd:appinfo/sch:phase"/>
         <xsl:copy-of select="$schemas//xsd:appinfo/sch:pattern"/>
         <sch:diagnostics>
            <xsl:copy-of select="$schemas//xsd:appinfo/sch:diagnostics/*"/>
         </sch:diagnostics>
      </sch:schema>
   </xsl:template>

</xsl:transform>
```

This transform will generate a valid Schematron schema, though it does not take any notice of whether Schematron constraints are gathered from `include`, `import` or `redefine` elements. We will now look at a few other possible boundaries on this technique.

Limitations of Using Schematron with XML Schema

There are some limitations to how closely we can make Schematron and XML Schema work together, which become particularly apparent when we start using co-location.

Names Versus Types

The first two points spring from the same source – the fact that Schematron depends on element names while XML Schema knows elements' Schema types.

Same Name, Different Type

XSLT 1.0 and XPath 1.0 predate XML Schema and have no specified mechanism for accessing the data type information from the XML Schema validator. Schematron patterns interact with an XML 1.0 and Namespaces view of a document. XML Schema overlays an instance document with grammatical structure and it largely interacts with patterns in the grammatical structure.

What does this mean in practice? Look at the `title` elements and their definitions in the simple `publication.xsd` XML Schema below:

```xml
<?xml version="1.0" encoding="UTF-8" ?>
<xs:schema xmlns:xs="http://www.w3.org/2001/XMLSchema">
    <xs:element name="publication" type="publicationType"/>
    <xs:complexType name="publicationType">
        <xs:sequence>
            <xs:element name="title" type="bookTitleType"/>
            <xs:element name="author" type="authorType" maxOccurs="unbounded"/>
        </xs:sequence>
        <xs:attribute name="ISBN" type="xs:string"/>
    </xs:complexType>
    <xs:complexType name="authorType">
        <xs:sequence>
            <xs:element name="title" type="nameTitleType"/>
            <xs:element name="firstName" type="xs:string"/>
            <xs:element name="lastName" type="xs:string"/>
        </xs:sequence>
    </xs:complexType>
    <xs:simpleType name="bookTitleType">
        <xs:restriction base="xs:string">
            <xs:maxLength value="100"/>
        </xs:restriction>
    </xs:simpleType>
    <xs:simpleType name="nameTitleType">
        <xs:restriction base="xs:string">
            <xs:enumeration value="Mr"/>
            <xs:enumeration value="Miss"/>
            <xs:enumeration value="Mrs"/>
            <xs:enumeration value="Dr"/>
            <!-- etc -->
        </xs:restriction>
    </xs:simpleType>
</xs:schema>
```

This schema defines two elements called `title`, with different meanings and validation. (Elements with the same name and namespace, and in the same content model – in other words, which are used somewhere as siblings – must have the same definition. Elements with the same name and namespace, but in different content models, are not obliged to have the same definition. This is described by the "Schema Component Constraint: Element Declarations Consistent" paragraph in: http://www.w3.org/TR/2001/REC-xmlschema-1-20010502/#cAttribute_Group_Definitions.)

If we really wish to have elements with the same name and namespace but different declarations, then we have to disambiguate them in our Schematron patterns. In the case above, we could match on "author/title" and "publication/title" to validate them separately. But there is a fairly strong case for simply defining it as bad practice and outlawing it under house rules.

Different Names, Same Type

XML Schema allows type definitions to be re-used, through the `type` and `ref` attributes. Elements that are declared to have the same `type` can have different names, which makes it harder to have a single Schematron pattern to validate all elements of a type.

Namespace Re-mapping

XML Schemas may have their target namespaces re-mapped, but Schematron schemas can't detect remapped namespaces. For instance, if a schema without a `targetNamespace` attribute is imported into a schema with a `targetNamespace`, the imported schema's definitions are then used to validate elements and attributes in the `targetNamespace`. XPath expressions cannot easily be parameterized to switch between using some namespace or the Null namespace, so this usage raises problems for using Schematron with XML Schemas.

Schematron and XSLT 2.0

XSLT 2.0 and XPath 2.0 are currently under development, and both specify requirements for XML Schema support. This may improve the capabilities that Schematron can offer.

For XPath these requirements include:

❑ Must support XML Schema regular expressions

❑ Must add support for XML Schema primitive datatypes

❑ Should add support for XML Schema: Structures – this includes various match-by-type features

For XSLT these requirements include:

❑ Must support XML Schema, which expands to:

    ❑ must simplify constructing and copying typed-content

    ❑ must support sorting nodes by XML Schema datatypes

From the point of view of validating, the XPath requirements are most relevant since they allow us to get round one of the key limitations on the use of Schematron to extend XML Schema validation. This limitation is the inability of Schematron rules to refer to XML Schema datatypes (as discussed above).

> *You can find the XSLT 2.0 Requirements Working Draft and the XPath 2.0 Requirements Working Draft at the W3C site at http://www.w3.org/TR.*

> *The Microsoft WSH is available from http://msdn.microsoft.com/scripting/default.htm?/scripting/windowshost/doc/wsVersion.htm. MSXML4 tech preview is available from http://msdn.microsoft.com/code/sample.asp?url=/msdn-files/027/001/594/msdncompositedoc.xml*

Sample Using MSXML 4 Extensions

The W3C has only issued XSLT 2.0 and XPath 2.0 requirements at the time of writing, and there is no proposed syntax for this, let alone compliant implementations. However, Microsoft MSXML 4 Beta 1 implements support with Microsoft extensions, which they have responsibly put in a separate namespace.

While some developers will find working with tools that implement publicly defined specifications more comfortable, the use of pre-specification extensions can be helpful to demonstrate concepts, which is why we have used this here.

If we go back to the example of a schema, which permitted two `title` elements (in different content models) to have the same name but different types, then we can disambiguate our Schematron tests by using the element type to qualify the match expression, as in `publication.sch` below:

```
<sch:schema xmlns:sch="http://www.ascc.net/xml/schematron">
    <sch:ns prefix="ms" uri="urn:schemas-microsoft-com:xslt"/>
    <sch:title>Schematron Validator for Publications</sch:title>
    <sch:pattern name="Book Title">
        <sch:rule context="title[ms:type-is('','bookTitleType')]">
            <sch:assert test="normalize-space(text()) != ''
                    or normalize-space(../@ISBN) = ''">
            Title must not be blank if there is an ISBN.
            </sch:assert>
        </sch:rule>
    </sch:pattern>
</sch:schema>
```

The parameters for the `ms:type-is()` function specify a target namespace (blank in our example) and a type in that target namespace. The function returns a Boolean `true` if the context node is an instance of that type, or one derived from it.

We then have to run the final XSLT transform in a parser that has schema-validated the target document. In MSXML 4 beta 1 this can only be done explicitly, using the `SchemaCache` object. The following JavaScript file will do combined XML schema and Schematron validation using the Windows Script Host from Microsoft (available from http://msdn.microsoft.com/scripting/default.htm?/scripting/windowshost/doc/wsVersion.htm):

```
// This file is:  msxsd-sch.js
// first parameter is an XML file to be read in;
// second parameter is the schema file
// third parameter is an optional schematron validator
```

We'll do some parameter checking in this section:

```
// validate parameters
if((WScript.Arguments.length < 2) || (WScript.Arguments.length > 3))
{
    WScript.Echo("msxsd-sch takes two or three arguments - datafile, schema,
(optional) xsltValidator - eg:");
    WScript.Echo('msxsd books.xml books.xsd books.xslt');
    WScript.Echo('msxsd books.xml books.xsd');
}
else if(WScript.Arguments.length == 3)
{
    validate(WScript.Arguments(0), WScript.Arguments(1), WScript.Arguments(2));
}
else
```

And the validation starts here:

```
{
    validate(WScript.Arguments(0), WScript.Arguments(1), "");
}
```

The third parameter (validator) is not required, so this script could be used simply as a general-purpose utility to validate XML using the XML Schema support in the MSXML4 technology preview. Since this preview doesn't yet support schemaLocation attributes, we will load and cache the schema explicitly:

```
function validate(datafile, schema, validator)
{
    // load the schema
    var xsdDoc = loadXML(schema);

    // find the targetNamespace
    xsdDoc.setProperty("SelectionLanguage", "XPath");
    xsdDoc.setProperty("SelectionNamespaces",
            "xmlns:xsd='http://www.w3.org/2001/XMLSchema'");
    var ns = xsdDoc.selectSingleNode("/xsd:schema/@targetNamespace");
```

We need to associate the schema with the relevant namespace, which we will get from the XML Schema file. (Note that imports that have their own namespaces will require a more sophisticated treatment.)

```
    // add the schema to the cache with the target namespace
    var cache = new ActiveXObject("Msxml2.XMLSchemaCache.4.0");
    if (ns == null)
    {
        cache.add('', xsdDoc);
    }
    else
    {
        cache.add(ns.text, xsdDoc);
    }

    // load the data file and validate against the schema
    var xmlDoc = loadXML(datafile, cache);
```

If everything is OK so far then it's time to load and execute the compiled Schematron validator:

```
    // load validator if specified
    if(validator != "")
    {
        var xslDoc = loadXML(validator);
        WScript.Echo(xmlDoc.transformNode(xslDoc));
    }
}
```

We'll re-use a couple of functions to load XML with or without Schema validation, with error handling:

```
function loadXML(source, schemaCache)
{
   var xmlDoc  = new ActiveXObject("Msxml2.DOMDocument.4.0");
   xmlDoc.async = false;
   if (schemaCache != undefined)
   {
      xmlDoc.schemas = schemaCache;
   }
   xmlDoc.load(source);
   if(xmlDoc.parseError.errorCode != 0)
   {
      loadError(source, xmlDoc);
      WScript.Quit(1);
   }
   return xmlDoc;
}

function loadError(source, xmlDoc)
{
   WScript.Echo("Error loading " + source);
   WScript.Echo("Code: " + xmlDoc.parseError.errorCode);
   WScript.Echo("Source: " + xmlDoc.parseError.srcText);
   WScript.Echo("Line: " + xmlDoc.parseError.line);
   WScript.Echo("Error: " + xmlDoc.parseError.reason);
}
```

We can test this with the following files. Firstly, `publication-0.xml`, which has a type error – title and author in the wrong sequence:

```
<?xml version="1.0" encoding="UTF-8"?>
<publication ISBN="1234-56576-098">
   <author>
      <title>Mr</title>
      <firstName>Herman</firstName>
      <lastName>Melville</lastName>
   </author>
   <title/>          <!-- wrong position -->
</publication>
```

Next we have an instance file, `publication-1.xml`, which should be valid according to the XML Schema, but should fail validation via the Schematron schema:

```
<?xml version="1.0" encoding="UTF-8"?>
<publication ISBN="1234-56576-098">
   <title/>          <!-- should not be empty if ISBN is non-blank -->
   <author>
      <title>Mr</title>
      <firstName>Herman</firstName>
      <lastName>Melville</lastName>
   </author>
</publication>
```

And finally `publication-2.xml` which should be valid against both:

```
<?xml version="1.0" encoding="UTF-8"?>
<publication ISBN="1234-56576-098">
    <title>Moby Dick</title>
    <author>
        <title>Mr</title>
        <firstName>Herman</firstName>
        <lastName>Melville</lastName>
    </author>
</publication>
```

When we try validating the three instance documents, we should get the following output:

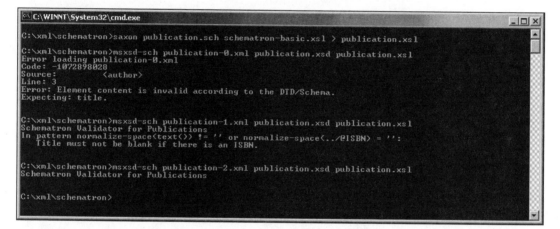

The next steps for a real system would be to embed the Schematron constraints in the main XML Schema, auto-extract the Schematron schema, and deliver the results to the application via a unified exception reporting API.

Topologi – An Interactive Schematron Development Tool

Rick Jelliffe, the designer of Schematron, has started a company called Topologi, where they have developed a graphical validation tool (http://www.topologi.com). The Topologi Transformation Engine is an interactive tool for developing and using XML Schemas and Schematron schemas, with Examplotron and possibly Relax NG also targeted, in line with the general Schematron philosophy of layering validation technologies.

At run time the user can select one or more documents to be validated against one or more schemas. The tool can be configured to present the output as a single screen of combined text, as consecutive screens of text, as an HTML report, or as a two-pane HTML report with links from the output to the relevant XML components. Here's what the output configuration screen for Schematron looks like:

Having chosen the two-pane browser output for Schematron validation, we can now select some documents to validate against a Schematron schema:

Here's how the two-pane output looks:

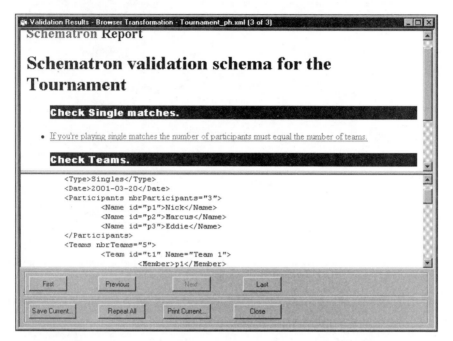

And, just for completeness, here is the output configuration screen for XML Schema, with optional embedded Schematron:

The tool is a "reconfigurable transformation engine", and it appears to have the flexibility to provide a generally useful validation framework while adding weight and plausibility to Schematron's layering approach to validation.

Competitive Schema Technologies

In this section, we'll take a brief look at a few of the other Schematron technologies that compete on the same ground as XML Schema, rather than acting as complementary technologies, in particular:

❑   RELAX NG

❑   Examplotron

❑   ASN.1

RELAX NG

One reason that XML Schema has been controversial is that it is seen by some as too big, and lacking an effective formal model. In a word, it is accused of being inelegant. Two alternatives were put forward that both claimed to remedy this. James Clark, the lead author of the W3C XSLT and XPath specifications developed **TREX** (**Tree REgular eXpressions**). Mr. Makoto Murata, a member of the W3C XML Schema working group, developed the **RELAX** (**REgular LAnguage for XML**) validator. These had similar strengths, and have now been merged to create **Relax NG** (for "Next Generation"; Relax NG is pronounced "relaxing").

Relax NG simplifies and extends the features of DTDs. It simplifies by ignoring non-validation features like defaults and entities. It extends by offering substantially more powerful content modeling and an XML Syntax.

Here's an example of a Relax NG schema, illustrating its support for an ambiguous content model (suggested by Arthur Rother on xml-dev) – a sequence of chess turns.

```
<rng:grammar xmlns:rng="http://relaxng.org/ns/structure/0.9">
   <rng:start>
      <rng:element name="game">
         <rng:element name="white">
            <rng:ref name="move"/>
         </rng:element>
         <rng:zeroOrMore>
            <rng:element name="black">
               <rng:ref name="move"/>
            </rng:element>
            <rng:element name="white">
               <rng:ref name="move"/>
            </rng:element>
         </rng:zeroOrMore>
         <rng:optional>
            <rng:element name="black">
               <rng:ref name="move"/>
            </rng:element>
         </rng:optional>
      </rng:element>
```

```
        </rng:start>
        <rng:define name="move">
            <rng:text/>
        </rng:define>
    </grammar>
```

Note the Relax namespace that needs to be used, `http://relaxng.org/ns/structure/0.9`. Note also that we have added the namespace prefix to the document to demonstrate its use in Relax NG schemas (it wasn't present in the original).

Within the `grammar` wrapper, a single `start` element allows us to define one or more allowable root elements. The grammar can also contain any number of re-usable definitions, declared via use of `define` elements, which can be referenced using a `ref` element with a matching `name` attribute. The `element` (which implies default grouping of exactly one), `optional`, and `zeroOrMore` elements express the same grouping functionality as is provided by DTD content models or basic regular expressions.

For more on the Relax NG syntax, refer to the tutorial listed at the end of this section.

Relax NG Versus XML Schemas and DTDs

Unlike the original Core subset of Relax, Relax NG is no longer positioned as an interim subset of XML Schema, but as a technical competitor and a design influence. Since an in-depth discussion of Relax NG features / syntax is outside the scope of this chapter, we will simply do a comparison of features between Relax NG, XML Schema and DTDs.

The various schema features have been divided into four logical categories in order to make the comparison easier to follow.

Structural Validation

Let's start with mark up based validation – what XML Schema calls Structural Validation.

Feature	Relax NG	XML Schema	DTD	Comment
Specify Root Element	Yes – you can specify a range of possible root elements in the schema	Any global element can be a root element, but there are other reasons why elements may need to be global	Not in the DTD, but possible in the DOCTYPE, which associates a DTD with an instance document	
Ambiguous content	Yes	No	No	Almost any ambiguous content model can be rephrased as an equivalent deterministic content model

Feature	Relax NG	XML Schema	DTD	Comment
Unordered elements	Yes – allows patterns to be interleaved as part of other patterns	Yes: `all` allows you to require a collection of elements at the top level of a content model	No	Relax NG's `interleave` feature is very powerful and could well be useful for this purpose
minOccurs, maxOccurs	Optional one, mandatory one, optional many and mandatory many	`MinOccurs` can be any number from zero, `maxOccurs` can be any number from one to unbounded	Same as Relax NG	Being able to specify arbitrary minimum and maximum numbers of repetitions could be important when specifying messages intended for legacy systems, including several the author has dealt with
Attributes participate in patterns	Yes – for instance, you can allow a choice between including a data item as an attribute or an element	No	No	Useful for RDF 1.0, or for permitting backward-compatible schema evolution.

Namespace Support

Now let's look at namespace support. This is a pre-requisite for e-commerce, since this requires a loosely-coupled, layered architecture to permit rapid evolution and implementation, and the namespace recommendation is the main method for allowing elements and attributes from different layers to co-exist peacefully the same documents and messages.

Feature	Relax NG	XML Schema	DTD	Comment
Support for namespaces	Yes	Yes– and for new "unqualified" usage	Can't support all namespace syntax options	Namespaces and datatypes are the two showstoppers that prevent e-commerce with DTDs.
Multiple namespace in same Schema	Yes – declarations and definitions	Declarations – definitions must be in separate modules	(n/a)	

Modularity

Modularity allows us to re-use sub-schemas in larger schemas.

Feature	Relax NG	XML Schema	DTD	Comment
Re-use definitions for other elements	Yes, using named definitions	Yes, using named types, also see inheritance	Yes, using parameter entities	DTDs are more compact than Relax NG or XML Schema, but the non-XML syntax has proved a hindrance to developer interest
Multi-file definitions	Yes, using the `include` and `externalRef` elements. `include` allows definitions to be overridden, or merged using `choice` or `interleave`	Yes, using `include` for definitions for the target namespace, `import` for definitions for other namespaces and `redefine` to override definitions.	Yes, via external entities – see Norm Walsh's **Docbook DTD*** for a notable example.	
Inheritance and Substitution groups	No, though similar effects can be achieved by composing definitions from other definitions	Yes, though the inheritance model may seem strange to programmers familiar with OO languages	No, though similar effects can be achieved using parameter entities	

*For more on the Docbook DTD, go to http://www.oasis-open.org/docbook/

Validation

This refers to validation of or by the character content of attributes and elements.

Feature	Relax NG	XML Schema	DTD	Comment
Infoset Contribution	None – Relax NG is a pure validator	Default values and type information	Default values and unparsed entity "notations"	The size and complexity of XML Schema's PSVI (Post Schema Validation Infoset) has caused some debate

Feature	Relax NG	XML Schema	DTD	Comment
Co-occurrence constraints	Yes, within a content model, using `value`	No	No	For instance, the ability to specify that any address with a "UK" country attribute has a postcode element, but with "US" requires a zipcode
Cross-references	Yes, with uniqueness scoped to named keys within document	Yes, multi-field keys with uniqueness scoped to named keys within document	Yes, using `ID` and `IDREF` attributes, but uniqueness is only scoped to document	Scoping uniqueness by named keys is a useful feature from a business perspective
Datatypes	Minimal built-in datatypes, but can plug-in XML Schema datatypes using the `xmlschema-datatypes` namespace	Comprehensive and flexible set of datatypes	Minimal tokens and enumerated values	The original XML DTD set of datatypes is not adequate for business or e-commerce uses, and XML Schema part 2 datatypes is a good fit for an urgent requirement.

Why Relax NG?

In some ways, Relax NG can be seen as a reaction to XML Schema, and is perhaps intended as forcefully made comment rather than as a direct replacement. Having said that, it is conceivable that such a simpler alternative to XML Schema could be viable if XML Schema implementations were to prove too large or complex for resource-limited e-commerce platforms like mobile phones, and the alternative could be implemented effectively there. However, the most likely positive outcome is that some of the features get adopted into XML Schema. Perhaps the single strongest aspect of Relax NG is its more powerful content pattern support, as reflected in its support for ambiguous content models, interleaving, and attributes in content models. Since this is based on a sound theoretical model, namely Hedge grammars, the XML Schema restrictions may come to be seen as over restrictive, and the Relax NG model could end up being adopted in a future version of XML Schema, along with co-occurrence constraints, which have already been mentioned by Henry Thompson as a likely feature of XML Schema 1.1. However, it is hard to see how XML Schema could ever be retrofitted with Relax NG's most attractive feature, its overall simplicity.

Relax NG is at still under development, so all these resources are preliminary. The main site is at http://www.oasis-open.org/committees/relax-ng. There is an excellent tutorial at http://www.oasis-open.org/committees/relax-ng/tutorial.html and a Java implementation, **jing**, at http://www.thaiopensource.com/relaxng.

Examplotron

Eric van der Vlist of Dyomedea created Examplotron, which as you may guess from its name, works by examples, and borrows some ideas from Schematron. It is designed to be "the most natural and easy to learn XML schema language defined up to now." The current implementation generates standalone validators, but items 4 and 5 on the to do list at www.examplotron.org suggest generating Schematron, XML Schema or other schema language schemas from Examplotron. Rick Jelliffe has also suggested combining it with a wizard interface to resolve some of the ambiguities inherent in examples.

> *Examplotron, unlike Schematron, currently requires Saxon because it uses Saxon extension functions. Details on where to find Saxon can be found in the Schematron section. See http://www.examplotron.org for* compile.xsl, *which you'll need to run the examples in this chapter, and for further documentation and information about Examplotron.*

Examplotron works by compiling XSL validators directly from sample XML documents. The process is illustrated in the T-diagram below:

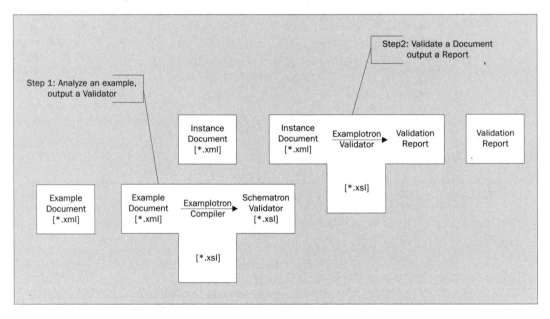

As you can see for the diagram above, there is an interesting comparison to be made with Schematron – both use XSL to compile validators, and both use XSL to run the validators. The big difference is that in principle, there is no separate Examplotron schema. Examplotron compiles XSL validators directly from examples, though as we shall see, these may have additional markup to add schema-like information.

For example, say we create a loan response message:

```
<loanResponse>
    <partnerID>ABC</partnerID>
    <transactionID>12345</transactionID>
```

```
        <loanAmount>575.75</loanAmount>
        <partnerOutlet>Middleham High Street</partnerOutlet>
        <loanType>standard</loanType>
        <decision>accept</decision>
        <decisionID>ACC01234</decisionID>
    </loanResponse>
```

We can now compile a validator for this type of message as shown with the first "T" of the diagram above. We will use the Examplotron utility: compile.xsl. When we validate the original message using the stylesheet generated by the Examplotron utility we get this no-error response:

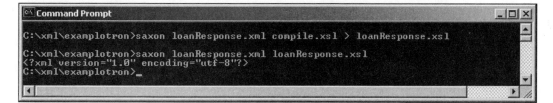

We will now introduce a deliberate error into the message – note the plutonium element:

```
    <?xml version="1.0" encoding="UTF-8"?>
    <loanResponse>
        <plutonium><!-- this element shouldn't be here! --></plutonium>
        <partnerID>ABC</partnerID>
        <transactionID>12345</transactionID>
        <loanAmount>575.75</loanAmount>
        <partnerOutlet>Middleham High Street</partnerOutlet>
        <loanType>standard</loanType>
        <decision>accept</decision>
        <decisionID>ACC01234</decisionID>
    </loanResponse>
```

Next we check it with the validator we created earlier:

This time we get an error element in response. There are several namespace attributes which we can ignore, but the type and path attributes are highlighted in the screenshot above which tell us that the message has an "Unexpected element" and that the unexpected element can be found at "/loanResponse[1]/plutonium[1]".

From the example it has generated a validator, assumes that each of the elements present in the loanResponse content model must be there precisely once, and that no other element or attribute is permitted.

Some things cannot easily be demonstrated by example, such as repetition and logical constraints. This can be demonstrated by using any tool that does automatic Schema or DTD generation, such as XML Spy (http://www.xmlspy.com/download.html). Additional input is typically required from the user to resolve questions such as:

❑   Can this element be repeated?

❑   Is this element optional?

❑   Are the values for this attribute that appear in this document the only ones allowed?

Examplotron has attributes – for example: `occurs` and `assert` – which can be added to the elements in the example to specify optionality, repetition and, in Schematron style, any XPath rules. These elements will be recognized by `compile.xsl` and appropriate constraints generated in the validator.

More Examplotron

Apart from working with unadorned examples, Examplotron does deviate from the path of strict minimalism far enough to provide a grammar containing three attributes and an element in the Examplotron namespace.

❑   `@eg:occurs` – this attribute can be added to any element to specify a repetition constraint. Permissible values are `"*"` (zero, one or many), `"+"` (one or many), `"?"` (zero or one) and `"."` (exactly one). The default is `"."`

❑   `@eg:assert` – this attribute can be added to an element to specify Schematron-style XPath assertions which must be true for that element.

❑   `eg:import` – this element can be placed anywhere in an example document to import another Examplotron example. The validator that is then generated includes rules for both sets of elements.

❑   `@eg:placeHolder` – this attribute can be added to any element in an example that has an `eg:include` element, in order that the imported validation rules don't get over-written outside the `placeHolder`'s parent element.

Here is an example of an Examplotron schema (`loanResponse-occurs.xml`) illustrating the two elements with `eg:occurs` and `eg:asserts` attributes:

```
<?xml version="1.0" encoding="UTF-8"?>
<loanResponse xmlns:eg="http://examplotron.org/0/">
    <partnerID>ABC</partnerID>
    <transactionID>12345</transactionID>
    <loanAmount eg:assert=". = sum(../goods/item/@value)">1.44</loanAmount>
    <partnerOutlet>Middleham High Street</partnerOutlet>
    <goods>
        <item partNo="23561" price="0.12" quantity="12" value="1.44"
            eg:occurs="+"  eg:assert="@value = @price * @quantity">
        Staplers
        </item>
    </goods>
    <loanType>standard</loanType>
    <decision>accept</decision>
    <decisionID>ACC01234</decisionID>
</loanResponse>
```

This generates a validator that permits multiple item elements, and verifies that each item value is the product of its price multiplied by its quantity, and that the overall loanAmount is the sum of the item values.

Why use Examplotron?

Examplotron is an incredibly intuitive way to create schemas and might be useful for relatively simple applications where there is resistance to the initial learning curve of XML Schema. Its great strength is how it fits human psychology – both developers and analysts may find XML Schema fairly opaque, and there is a strong demand for "specification by example". We can imagine circumstances where Examplotron might perform a useful communications role, though we would probably be more inclined to use it to document examples for human readability than to use it as a central validation technology.

ASN.1

ASN.1 (for Abstract Syntax Notation One) is an existing telecoms standard for message definition and serialization (see http://asn1.elibel.tm.fr/xml/) from the International Telecommunications Union. They are working on a standard (which will be called ITU-T Rec. X.694 | ISO/IEC 8825-5) to convert XML Schemas into ASN.1 schemas.

Potentially this offers greater runtime speed to XML Schema users. To see how, we need to look at how messages get sent and received with XML and XML Schema.

We have used a UML action diagram to illustrate this, which simply shows a flow of actions from a start state to one or more end states. The arrows represent sequence, so it is similar to a flow chart. Action diagrams allow you to specify the actors as well as the actions by placing the actions in "swim lanes" belonging to the various components of the system:

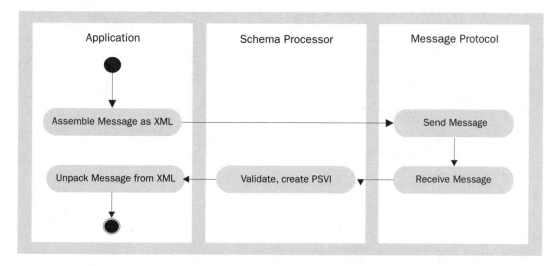

In the action diagram above, the XML Schema of course validates the message as correctly formatted, but the only direct contribution it makes to run-time speed and efficiency is to add any missing attributes with declared default values, or to fill in any empty elements with declared defaults.

ASN.1 has followed a different evolutionary path to XML. It started as a specification technology, and developed various binary "transfer" encoding rules, which specify how ASN.1 datatypes can be represented. BER (Basic Encoding Rule) is optimized for simplicity. PER is optimized for compression and security and the extra information needed to decode and decompress a message means that the ASN.1 schema or its equivalent is needed at runtime. One strand of the reaction to XML is to provide an XML encoding so that ASN.1 messages may more easily be debugged at build-time, but we are more interested here in what ASN.1 can provide for XML rather than what XML can provide for ASN.1.

An ASN.1 toolkit will accept an ASN.1 schema and an encoding, and at build-time will generate run-time components to encode and decode conformant messages, as illustrated by the sequence of actions in the action diagram below:

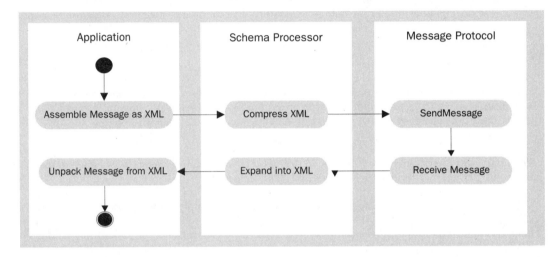

There are two related projects underway – one is to create an XML encoding so that ASN.1 messages can be viewed and debugged. The other, as mentioned above, is to convert XML Schemas to ASN.1 schemas so that high-performance BER or PER messaging can be used. It is also true that a number of standards are specified in ASN.1, where we could actually use XML in real messages. An XML encoding of ASN.1 messages would allow you to use XML and still be fully conformant to the ASN.1 of the standard. This is the situation for a draft standard for Advanced Traveller Information Systems (ATIS) being developed by the Society of Automotive Engineers. In this case, ASN.1 would in fact be the schema for the XML documents.

This (from http://asn1.elibel.tm.fr/xml/example.htm) is what an ASN.1 Schema looks like (note the double dash is the ASN.1 comment delimiter):

```
-- Example of an ASN.1 type definition :
PersonnelRecord ::= [APPLICATION 0] SET
{       name            Name,
        title           VisibleString,
        number          EmployeeNumber,
        dateOfHire      Date,
        nameOfSpouse    Name,
        children        SEQUENCE OF ChildInformation DEFAULT {} }
ChildInformation ::= SET
{       name                    Name,
```

```
           dateOfBirth              Date }
Name ::= [APPLICATION 1] SEQUENCE
{          givenName               VisibleString,
           initial                 VisibleString,
           familyName              VisibleString }
EmployeeNumber ::= [APPLICATION 2] INTEGER
Date ::= [APPLICATION 3] VisibleString  --  YYYY MMDD
```

The same page shows how an instance of this looks encoded in XML:

```
-- XML notation for a value that conforms to the type previously defined:
person ::=
<PersonnelRecord>
   <name>
      <givenName>John</givenName>
      <initial>P</initial>
      <familyName>Smith</familyName>
   </name>
   <title>Director</title>
   <number>51</number>
   <dateOfHire>19710917</dateOfHire>
   <nameOfSpouse>
      <givenName>Mary</givenName>
      <initial>T</initial>
      <familyName>Smith</familyName>
   </nameOfSpouse>
   <children>
      <ChildInformation>
         <name>
            <givenName>Ralph</givenName>
            <initial>T</initial>
            <familyName>Smith</familyName>
         </name>
         <dateOfBirth>19571111</dateOfBirth>
      </ChildInformation>
      <ChildInformation>
         <name>
            <givenName>Susan</givenName>
            <initial>B</initial>
            <familyName>Jones</familyName>
         </name>
         <dateOfBirth>19590717</dateOfBirth>
      </ChildInformation>
   </children>
</PersonnelRecord>
```

Who Will Use It?

The ASN.1 XML projects are targeted at communications infrastructure and telemetry sectors. This makes sense, since these have a high volume of messages that conform to stable engineering standards. A sample message is shown on http://asn-1.com/x968.htm that serializes to 93 bytes using BER. When the XML version of the message was stripped of all format whitespace it was 1065 bytes long, which compressed to 506 bytes using Zip. This admittedly unscientific comparison suggests that ASN.1 could well make a significant difference for restricted bandwidth devices such as mobile phones, but the issue is still subject to hot debate.

On the other hand, the advantages will be less obvious for high-bandwidth commercial applications. The main disadvantage may be the recompilation, linking, and testing of encoders and decoders every time a schema changes. This frequently occurs all the way through the development process of this kind of business application as opposed to more stable communication functions.

Summary

We have taken a close look at Schematron and seen:

- How it can easily be implemented
- The kind of rules Schematron can express that XML Schema can't and its focus on usability of error messages and the support for phases
- How to embed Schematron constraints in XML Schemas and extract them, so that you can maintain a single declarative specification for your messages

Finally, we had a higher-level look at three competitive schema technologies and saw how they hope to help us in the future.

It is hard to avoid concluding that this is an area where much value may be added to the XML processing infrastructure. It is not surprising that XML Schema is seen by some as too complex, but by others as inadequate. A pessimistic view of the technology area would suggest that it is likely to be mired in confusion and discord for some time as technologies reflecting genuinely different values compete for survival. A more optimistic view would be to note that some of these technologies are quite layerable, and that there have been proposals to allow Schematron to be embedded in RELAX, giving us a potential ability to mix and match them according to our current requirements.

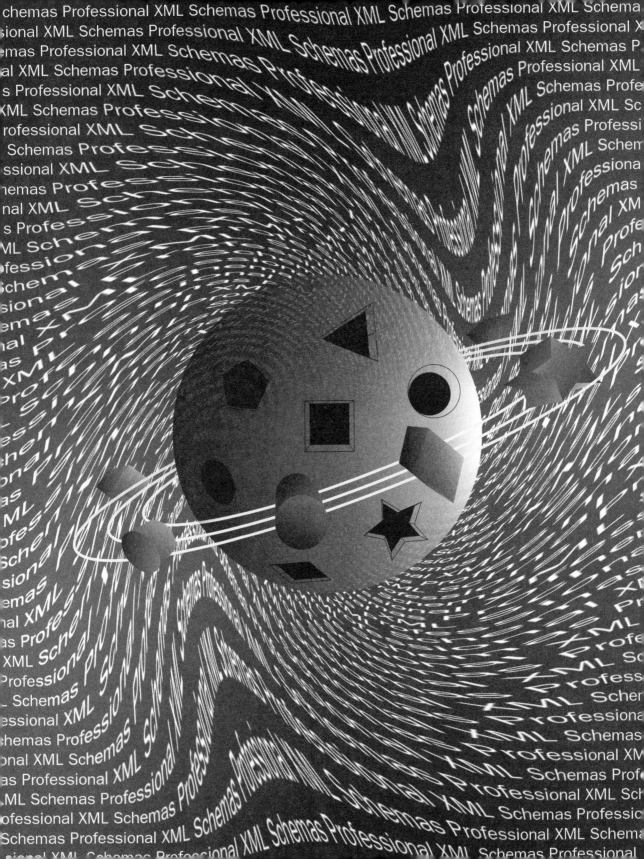

E-Commerce Case Study

Introduction

This chapter aims to show how SOAP can provide a transport layer that exploits the benefits of XML Schema, and is based on a project that was successfully implemented using W3C XML Schema for data specification and a project-specific SOAP implementation for interoperable transport.

We will look at the business requirements of an e-commerce project, and see how they shape the technology, conversation flow, and data structures of a solution. We need to know:

❑ Who is communicating with whom, and how

❑ Where will we use SOAP and why

❑ How we derive our schemas from existing back-end databases

❑ How XML Schemas and Schematron work with SOAP

We shall go from the use case to a three partner conversation analysis, and highlight the SOAP/XML messages within the overall conversation.

The back-end database tables will be used to build XML Schemas to describe SOAP messages that map to the messages. We will also look at extra information that has to be included in the messages to allow the conversation to be continued asynchronously and across different message media. Higher-level business logic constraints will be added to the schema by embedding Schematron constraints.

Finally we'll consider how the continuing development of the web services infrastructure might affect this project.

Automating E-Commerce

Malcom McLean started a world-changing demonstration of the power of standardization when "[I]n 1956 he used a converted World War II oil tanker to sail 58 cargo-filled containers from Port Newark in New Jersey to Houston. [...] Ninety percent of all cargo is now transported by container." (*International Herald Tribune*, May 28, 2001)

The simple fact that so many types of cargo – from fluids, grain, and coal to furniture and refrigerated foodstuffs – could all be loaded, transported by road, rail, and sea, and unloaded by standard machinery revolutionized the economics of the industry and allowed it to offer a better, cheaper, faster service to its customers.

Now think about e-commerce. We will need to pass messages between systems implemented on different platforms and operating systems, using any combination of, for instance, ASCII, EBCDIC, Perl, C++, Java, COBOL, and maybe SQL. Those of us who did pre-XML PC-to-mainframe, client-server projects know how appallingly frustrating and time-wasting these problems can be.

XML, like containerization, reaps compelling cost-savings by allowing a common infrastructure, which works regardless of content, source, transport, or destination. XML containerizes the markup of messages. Any well-formed XML, written with any XML parser, or by hand, can be read with any XML parser, regardless of platform and OS. But e-commerce involves passing messages between strangers, and that raises more areas of communication and security that must also be containerized if we are to avoid expensive ad hoc infrastructure solutions for each new project. Building a common infrastructure for all of these areas is the goal of web services.

The first of these areas is the structure and meaning of the message – what we can expect to write or read in the data, and what you can expect to do with it. The ad hoc solution is writing prose specifications, possibly backed up with DTDs and/or namespaces, and fleshed out by trial and error (also known as integration testing). This is ambiguous, unproductive, and expensive. XML Schema solves a big part of the problem. By giving us a language to specify data structures and a powerful set of common datatypes, it helps us to automate the writing, reading, validation, and usage of messages that conform to a spec. And again, we get these benefits regardless of differences between the technical environments of the message writer and message reader, or what kind of message is being specified.

The next area is how these messages are to be transported. For internal projects it may be acceptable to use a prose description of how the message will be transported to the correct transaction in an application, and how responses or exceptions will be reported back, but once again this does not provide a common infrastructure. Simple Object Access Protocol (SOAP), which we'll learn more about below, is designed to provide a toolkit for sending and receiving XML over HTTP and other transport layers such as SMTP and MQ Series and, in the W3C successor currently under development, BEEP, UDP, and TCP. We need to be aware of certain design options, which are needed to implement web-services architecture as opposed to a component-to-component approach that tries to emulate COM or CORBA.

There are more layers of automation to the web-services architecture which are not directly applicable to this case study, but which will be touched on later.

Project Scenario

This case study is based on a project for a bank moving into a new business area – establishing partnerships with web retailers so that the bank can issue loans to the retailers' customers to pay for the goods. The bank already has an AS/400 back-office system for issuing loans to its customers via call centers, so we will be reading and writing data to its database tables from our Windows NT application servers. We'll call our system Web Retail Loans, or WRL for short. We will refer to the project as WRL from now on.

SOAP – An Overview

SOAP is based on some earlier work on XML-RPC from Don Box of DevelopMentor, Dave Winer of UserLand, and Microsoft. This was, and is, a simple and widely supported protocol that uses XML to implement Remote Procedure Calls. To a PC developer, XML-RPC feels like remote APIs implemented in XML. Calls have synchronous responses. Parameters have atomic typing – individual data items can be named and explicitly typed, and there is support for simple collections, such as arrays. It runs over HTTP, which by default makes it acceptable to firewalls.

The SOAP specification itself was written by DevelopMentor, IBM, Microsoft, Lotus, and UserLand, and was published as a W3C note on the 8th May 2000. It can be seen as a superset of XML-RPC. It continues to support RPC functionality, but has a number of extensions. Calls can now be asynchronous as well as synchronous. It is no longer bound exclusively to HTTP, but can support other protocols such as SMTP. And, as well as having its own API-style encoding for parameter names and types, it also permits other encoding styles, such as having a single XML document for the message or response. The W3C is rewriting and renaming the SOAP specification as XML Protocol (XMLP), which is currently at Working Draft status.

Although it is more complex than XML-RPC, SOAP is still relatively easy to implement and deploy. The HTTP binding defaults to port 80, so it should communicate through most firewalls. It also specifies a mandatory HTTP header, so that firewall administrators can filter it out if they choose, and to overcome the accusation that it is a "stealth" protocol.

As of the time of writing, there was no standard API for communicating with a SOAP component, so I'm going to discuss the SOAP message structure, expanding on those parts that have most relevance for our case study and for XML Schema design.

SOAP Message Structure

The message structure is fairly simple, consisting of an envelope containing an optional SOAP header, and a body that holds the information to be transmitted. However, some of the strategies it supports are quite complicated. Here is a message based on one of the SOAP messages from the system case study:

```
<SOAP-ENV:Envelope
   xmlns:SOAP-ENV="http://schemas.xmlsoap.org/soap/envelope/">
   <SOAP-ENV:Header>
      <tk:transactionToken
         xmlns:tk="http://www.example.com/distributedCommit"
         SOAP-ENV:mustUnderstand="1" value="125" />
   </SOAP-ENV:Header>
   <SOAP-ENV:Body>
```

```
        <loanRequestResponse
            xmlns="http://www.example.com/xml/application.xsd"
            xmlns:xsi="http://www.w3.org/2001/XMLSchema-instance"
            xsi:schemaLocation="http://www.example.com/xml/application.xsd
                wrl-sch.xsd">
            <partnerTransId>ABC000123</partnerTransId>
            <wrlTransId>0000-tnSff-43243</wrlTransId>
        </loanRequestResponse>
    </SOAP-ENV:Body>
</SOAP-ENV:Envelope>
```

We will look at the different SOAP constituents below.

SOAP Envelope

The envelope is the outer wrapper element. It will normally use the SOAP envelope namespace. The specification says a processor "... MAY process SOAP messages without SOAP namespaces as though they had the correct SOAP namespaces", but this clearly invites trouble.

```
<SOAP-ENV:Envelope
        xmlns:SOAP-ENV="http://schemas.xmlsoap.org/soap/envelope/">
    <!-- rest of SOAP message -->
</SOAP-ENV:Envelope>
```

The `Envelope` may contain a `Header` and an `encodingStyle` attribute (see *SOAP Body* below) and must contain a `Body`. There is in fact a schema located at the location used for the namespace, but at the time of writing, this was written to the 1999 XML Schema draft.

SOAP Header

The optional header allows sophisticated communication strategies to be implemented. The specification refers to the "message path" and the possibility of intermediaries partially processing the message.

The specification terminology is a little confusing – **header elements** is the term used to refer to the content elements of the SOAP `Header` element, even though they may have any element name whatsoever, as long as they are not in the `SOAP-ENV` namespace. So, take note of capitalization in the `Header` element name. This element is *not* "a header element", in the first (content) sense; it is the SOAP Header element in the container sense.

```
<SOAP-ENV:Envelope
    xmlns:SOAP-ENV="http://schemas.xmlsoap.org/soap/envelope/">

    <SOAP-ENV:Header>

        <tk:transactionToken
            xmlns:tk="http://www.example.com/distributedCommit"
            SOAP-ENV:mustUnderstand="1" value="125" />

    </SOAP-ENV:Header>

    <!-- rest of SOAP message -->
</SOAP-ENV:Envelope>
```

The header elements can also be used for any other processing data that is required to process the content of the message using this protocol, but would not otherwise be part of the message. For example, they can contain the name of the target transaction within the server, or as mentioned in section 7.2 of the SOAP specification, they could be used for transaction IDs. This would be useful for managing state on an otherwise (largely) stateless protocol, and further down the line for implementing infrastructure features like distributed commit/rollback.

Although headers must be in non-SOAP namespaces, they may use two SOAP-ENV attributes to ensure that they are processed correctly:

- ❑ actor – A SOAP message may travel from the original sender to the ultimate destination via a set of SOAP intermediaries, which are applications that can process the message and then route it further. The actor attribute takes a URI value, and identifies which processor in such a message chain should process this element. When this attribute is omitted, the SOAP message's ultimate recipient is the first recipient. Using the attribute with the special value of http://schemas.xmlsoap.org/soap/actor/next means that it is targeted at the next processor, whichever it may be.

- ❑ mustUnderstand – Takes a "1" or "0", where a "1" specifies that the target processor must return a fault if it cannot process this header. When this attribute is not included, the value is defaulted to "0".

For comparison, the spec states that Body elements are processed as if they had mustUnderstand="1" and actor="", though the exact semantics of this are still under discussion in the XMLP Working Group.

All these uses are quite a long way from XML Schema design concerns, and we will not use the SOAP-ENV:Header element in this case study.

SOAP Body

This mandatory element is where the XML data we want to be processed goes. It's that simple.

```
<SOAP-ENV:Envelope
    xmlns:SOAP-ENV="http://schemas.xmlsoap.org/soap/envelope/">

    <SOAP-ENV:Body SOAP-ENV:encodingStyle="">

        <loanRequestResponse
            xmlns="http://www.example.com/xml/application.xsd"
            xmlns:xsi="http://www.w3.org/2001/XMLSchema-instance"
            xsi:schemaLocation="http://www.example.com/xml/application.xsd
                wrl-sch.xsd">
            <partnerTransId>ABC000123</partnerTransId>
            <wrlTransId>0000-tnSff-43243</wrlTransId>
        </loanRequestResponse>

    </SOAP-ENV:Body>

</SOAP-ENV:Envelope>
```

The Body element may have one or more child elements. We are interested in passing our parameters or responses as a single schema-valid XML document, so we will be using a single child element.

The `Body` element, like any other in the SOAP namespace, can take an `encodingStyle` attribute. The only defined value for `encodingStyle` is: `http://schemas.xmlsoap.org/soap/encoding/`, which means that the names, types, and values of parameters or responses are represented as described in Section 5 of the spec, *SOAP Encoding* – here's an example of an integer array encoded using it:

```
<myFavoriteNumbers  SOAP-ENC:arrayType="xs:int[2]">
    <number>3</number>
    <number>4</number>
</myFavoriteNumbers>
```

As we won't be honoring any use of SOAP Encoding except as far as it supports literal XML, we will signal that we are passing our parameters as literal XML by setting the `encodingStyle` attribute to the empty string.

The reason we don't need to use a general-purpose SOAP encoding is that our messages will already be encoded in XML, using XML Schemas that we'll specify later in this chapter.

SOAP Fault

A SOAP response message may contain one `Fault` element in its body to report exceptions. The SOAP fault carries error or status information that can be expressed using specified, but unqualified, `Fault` elements and a structured fault code.

```
<SOAP-ENV:Envelope
    xmlns:SOAP-ENV="http://schemas.xmlsoap.org/soap/envelope/">
    <SOAP-ENV:Header>
        <tk:transactionToken xmlns:tk="http://www.example.com/distributedCommit"
            SOAP-ENV:mustUnderstand="1" value="125" />
    </SOAP-ENV:Header>
    <SOAP-ENV:Body>
        <SOAP-ENV:Fault>
            <faultcode>SOAP-ENV:Server</faultcode>
            <faultstring>Server Error</faultstring>
            <detail>
            <!-- application error data, not in SOAP namespace -->
            </detail>
        </SOAP-ENV:Fault>
    </SOAP-ENV:Body>
</SOAP-ENV:Envelope>
```

If a SOAP response contains a `Fault` element it cannot contain any other elements – a SOAP response must succeed or fail, and returning a Fault means that the transaction has failed.

Some SOAP Links

We may find specifications and software at several locations:

❑ A W3C note (http://www.w3.org/TR/SOAP) by Microsoft, IBM, DevelopMentor, and UserLand

❑ The IBM implementation is now being run as open source software by Apache at http://xml.apache.org/soap/

❑   Microsoft's support can be found at http://msdn.microsoft.com/soap/default.asp

❑   There is also a note on using SOAP with MIME at http://www.w3.org/TR/SOAP-attachments; this is to allow attachments, including binaries

❑   SOAP developers use the SOAP mailing list at http://discuss.develop.com/soap.html

❑   The SOAP FAQ is at http://www.develop.com/soap/soapfaq.htm

❑   The W3C has an XML Protocol Working Group at http://www.w3.org/2000/xp/ to "develop technologies which allow two or more peers to communicate in a distributed environment, using XML as its encapsulation language"; they have issued a requirements document and may well have a profound affect on the future of SOAP

Project Requirements

It is really important to get a good high level requirements analysis in this kind of system – projects involving inter-platform communications are complicated and risky enough anyway without the ill-feeling and cost explosions that can be caused by misunderstandings over business requirements. The authors are not wedded to any particular methodology, but we have found UML Activity diagrams an effective way of agreeing and signing off high-level project scope.

Main Use Case

Our client, a bank, wants to move into an emerging e-market: that of providing loans online to people buying goods from web retailers. The web retailers will be the bank's **partners**, the purchasers its **customers**.

Say a customer has been shopping for some new kitchen components – a fridge and a freezer. Having selected the goods from our partner they get the option of paying by credit card or of taking out a loan. They decide to take a loan. They receive a loan application form, pre-filled with their purchase details, fill in some financial details, and submit the application form. A response tells them that the application is acceptable and offers them a loan based on it. They decide to accept the loan and complete the purchase – once they have printed out the loan agreement, signed it and sent it to the bank, their goods will be delivered.

There are also three variations on this use case:

❑   Our customer cancels the process at any point short of returning the signed loan agreement

❑   The bank declines to offer them an agreement

❑   The bank "refers" the loan application for a later decision – in which case it will have to inform the partner and customer of the decision, and if it accepts the loan, help the customer to return to the appropriate point in the purchase process, for example by pointing them to a web page containing their shopping basket.

The following UML activity diagram shows this flow for the main use case and variations:

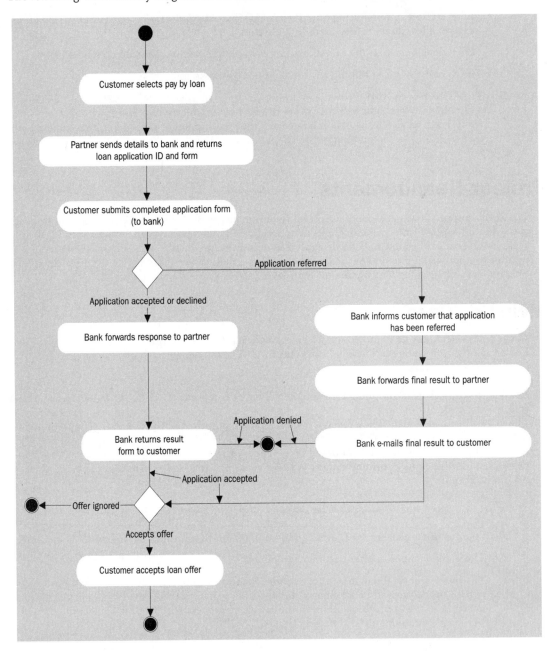

The system may be extended later to give the customer various self-service options, for instance viewing the amount outstanding or changing monthly repayments.

Design Goals

Apart from supporting the use case above, our client has specified various other desirable features for the system we're building:

1. The system must be secure

2. The system must have scalable performance

3. A partner's cost of joining and required development effort should be as low as possible

4. Partners should not be discouraged from joining by operating system or programming language constraints

5. The cost to the bank of acquiring each new partner should be as low as possible

6. The cost of each transaction should be minimized as much as possible

7. It should prove to be a good fit with the bank's existing back-end system

And, of course, the system should be as cheap as possible, stable, and completed yesterday.

Architecture

Based on the Project Requirements, we decide to use the following architecture

Communication with the Customer

This will be done over the web using ordinary HTML forms with standard web security (HTTP over SSL), through e-mail for read-only data, and traditional postal services for sending and returning the loan agreement form. This should provide adequate security (Requirement 1) and doesn't introduce any scalability problems (Requirement 2).

Communication Between the Bank and Partner

This will be via SOAP over secure sockets, and by mail. The bank has accepted that SSL can provide an appropriate level of encryption. The SOAP messages will be Schema-validated, and we will build Schemas for them from the back-end application's database tables.

Why Pass Documents, not Ordinary Parameters?

We chose this approach because we felt it likely that the messages would evolve as the market matured and new partners were signed up. Taking this approach minimizes the potential impact because:

❑ Changing the schema will be the most efficient way to communicate alterations to business partners

❑ We still get run-time transport and validation, without re-coding or even re-compiling

❑ Unaffected parts of the application – or unaffected partners – should be able to ignore missing or added elements and attributes

It will also fit well with the bank's audit requirements since it is easy to log XML messages. This supports Requirements 1, 5, and 7.

Why SOAP?

SOAP was not in fact the first choice for the project on which this case study is loosely based. Originally advice was asked for on whether it would be possible to write a client component in Perl, on the grounds that this would run on most web servers.

Once the requirements were understood we recommended SOAP over Perl on the grounds that:

❑   Although Perl supports web applications and has good XML support, specifying SOAP directly would increase partner productivity even on Perl platforms, and reduce the handicap for non-Perl Partners. This makes SOAP a more portable solution than Perl and supports Requirements 3 and 4.

❑   Given a Perl solution, taking on any non-Perl Partners would have involved either creating a new client in the partner's preferred technology, or thorough and defensive testing for problems caused by the Partner's re-implementation of the client component in their different technology – SOAP reduced costs for the bank, and supported Requirement 5.

The idea of having a data API rather than a program API was compelling, and if we hadn't gone for SOAP, we would probably have gone for CGI POSTs with the XML content in a single large URL-encoded variable. The advantages of SOAP over this approach are that by the time we had defined a protocol for handling errors and content, we would probably have re-invented a substantial part of what is a reasonably simple specification, but would not be able to take advantage of future developments such as third-party components and related protocols.

We also found the firewall aspect very important. The bank was understandably protective about its production web and application servers, so the fact that SOAP would pass through the default SSL port and didn't require any loosening of the firewall helped to speed up both the initial decision to go ahead with the project, and the development and deployment.

The fact that SOAP passes all its parameters at once, and uses HTTP, supports the speed and transaction cost requirements.

Design

Now we'll use an effective technique – we'll take the activity diagram that we used to describe and agree the requirements, and derive transactions from it. We've already decided which actors in the system we are interested in – Customers, Partners, and ourselves (WRL). We will go through the activity diagram and pick out any activities that are communications between these actors. Then we'll use a Sequence diagram to describe these transactions: which protocol they use, what message they pass, and who sends and receives each.

Conversation Sequence Diagram

The transactions are shown in context with the UML Sequence Diagram below, which highlights the start- and end-points of each transaction, and the overall order:

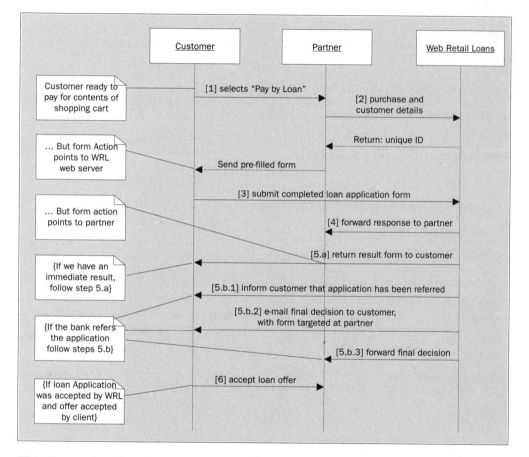

This diagram describes the same use case as the action diagram, but we are now moving from a business perspective to an implementation perspective as we start to categorize the various system actors and transactions. To keep it simple, and because these don't effect the message structures, we haven't shown:

❑ whether the application is accepted or declined by the bank

❑ time limits if the customer takes no action

❑ the customer completing an accepted application by receiving the loan form in the mail, signing it, and sending it to the partner in order to have their goods delivered

❑ the partner passing the signed loan application back to the bank

In this project the implementation has followed the business logic, with both Partner and WRL initiating SOAP calls. In other words, each may act as a SOAP client, and each may act as a SOAP server. In some environments this could cause difficulties. Any firewall is likely to be more restrictive about server applications receiving calls from outside than it is about client applications making calls, and with good reason.

However, since both the partner and the bank are running web sites, and running an SSL SOAP server requires no greater firewall loosening than running a secure web server, this is probably a reasonable choice.

If this was seen as a difficulty then the Partner could be implemented as a pure SOAP client, and fake its server transactions by polling WRL, but it's best to avoid this kind of solution – infrequent polling leads to lagged transactions, and frequent polling slows the server.

Transactions and Messages

As we can see from the sequence diagram, three operations connect the partner and WRL. These are:

❑ [2] Purchase and Customer Details – initiated by the Partner

❑ [5.a.1] forward response to partner – initiated by WRL

❑ [5.b.3] forward final decision – initiated by WRL

The SOAP messages sent and received in each of these operations are shown in the following table:

Operation	Client	Server	Message Sent	Message Received
[2] send purchase and customer details	Partner	WRL	LoanRequest	LoanRequestRespon se
[4] forward response to partner	WRL	Partner	LoanResult	LoanResultRespons e
[5.b.3] forward final decision	WRL	Partner	LoanResult	LoanResultRespons e

So two of the transactions use the same messages – leaving us with just four message bodies:

❑ LoanRequest – The partner passes its own details, known customer details, and purchase details to the bank.

❑ LoanRequestResponse – The bank passes back to the partner the bank's transaction ID for the remainder of this business transaction.

❑ LoanResult – The bank passes an *accept, decline,* or *refer back* message to the partner, including both the partner's and the bank's transaction ID. If the customer has been validated against the electoral roll, their address details are also passed back. If the bank has accepted the application the acceptance details are listed.

❑ LoanResultResponse – the partner passes back to the bank the two transaction IDs and a URL that, when clicked on by the customer, will take them to the next stage in the purchase process.

These are the four messages that need to be specified and validated at build time and run-time with XML Schemas. Neither the action nor the sequence diagram will tell us much about the content details of these messages – for that we need to look at the back-end system with which we are communicating.

Data Structures

The bank already has a back-end system for processing loan requests. The requirements of this system will dictate what data we need to create loan applications and loan agreements.

We will start by looking at the back-end system's database. Since the database is designed to hold all the data that the application will need at any time in a loan's life-cycle, and since the structure is designed to eliminate redundancy rather than to reflect transactions, we have to filter out which tables and fields within those tables are relevant to our four message bodies, by looking at the loan system's API. We shall assume that the bank staff familiar with the back-end system have done this analysis for us.

Since the back-end application is only interested in complete and valid loan applications we'll keep the intermediate data on a local database and then use a normal PC client API to update the AS/400 once the loan application has been completed.

Some Tables from the Database

Here is how we modeled the local database:

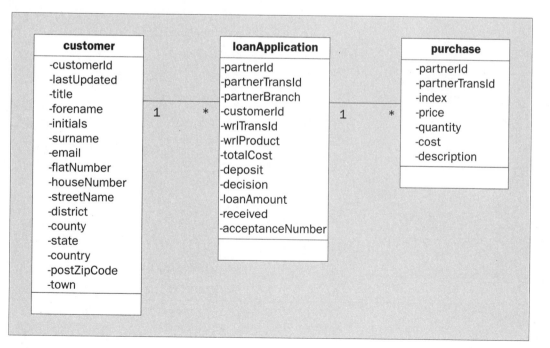

This is the normalized view of the data, as a static structure. There are two main differences between the data as it held on this database, and as it will be sent and received. The first is that the tables here implement a relational model of a hierarchical association. Each purchase references one `loanApplication`, each `loanApplication` references one customer, and this is how data will in fact be grouped in our messages. This allows us to view the message data as a hierarchy. XML models hierarchies more effectively and simply, by nesting data rather than using foreign keys, so this is what we shall do in the message structures. The second difference is that the database model is designed to hold all the information that might be associated with each entity at any time in its life cycle. Our messages will be designed to hold whatever subset of Customer, `loanApplication`, or purchase data is potentially required for the operations that use the messages.

The Message Schema

Starting with the four messages that we need to send and receive, and populating those message with the database fields that the back-end system staff tell us are needed, we can start to build an XML Schema to describe the messages. We haven't used table qualifiers here because any time the same field appears in different tables it holds the same data.

Message	Fields needed
loanRequest	partnerId
	partnerTransId
	partnerBranch
	totalCost
	deposit
	amountRequired
	deposit
	wrlProduct
	title
	forename
	initials
	surname
	email
loanRequestResponse	partnerTransId,
	wrlTransId

Message	Fields needed
loanResult	partnerTransId
	wrlTransId
	acceptanceNumber
	wrlProduct
	decision
	flatNo
	houseNumber
	houseName
	streetName
	district
	town
	county
	state
	postZipCode
loanResultResponse	partnerTransId
	wrlTransId
	redirectURL

Logically we could do this with a schema for each message, but we preferred to use a single schema in order to maximize reuse of definitions, and to provide a single point to validate the schema itself. Note that the full SOAP schema code can be found in the code download for this book, available from http://www.wrox.com/.

```
<?xml version="1.0" encoding="utf-8"?>
<xs:schema xmlns:sch="http://www.ascc.net/xml/schematron"
           xmlns:xs="http://www.w3.org/2001/XMLSchema"
           xmlns="http://www.example.com/xml/application.xsd"
           targetNamespace="http://www.example.com/xml/application.xsd"
           elementFormDefault="qualified">
  <xs:annotation>
    <xs:documentation>
       Loan Request Types, copyright WRL 2000.
    </xs:documentation>
  </xs:annotation>
</xs:schema>
```

First we'll declare the document elements of our four SOAP message types:

```
<!--
    root elements
-->
<xs:element name="loanRequest" type="loanRequestType" />
<xs:element name="loanRequestResponse" type="loanRequestResponseType" />
<xs:element name="loanResult" type="loanResultType" />
<xs:element name="loanResultResponse" type="loanResultResponseType" />
```

Now we'll define the four types, starting with the `loanRequestType`. The apparently arbitrary `maxOccurs="10"` applied to the `product` element is to protect the back-end system, which also has this restriction. The possibly mysterious `wrlProduct` element refers to the financial product that the partner is requesting, in other words the type of loan. All loans in this application will be of the same type in the first place, but we're leaving room for expansion.

```
<!-- top level complex types -->
<!-- loanRequestType: incoming loan request message -->
<xs:complexType name="loanRequestType">
    <xs:sequence>
        <xs:element name="partnerId">
            <xs:simpleType>
                <xs:restriction base="xs:string">
                    <xs:maxLength value="5" />
                </xs:restriction>
            </xs:simpleType>
        </xs:element>
        <xs:element name="partnerTransId" type="transIdType" />
        <xs:element name="partnerBranch" type="threeChar" minOccurs="0" />
        <xs:element name="totalCost" type="totalType" />
        <xs:element name="deposit" type="totalType" />
        <xs:element name="amountRequired" type="totalType" />
        <xs:element name="product" type="productType" maxOccurs="10" />
        <xs:element name="wrlProduct" type="threeChar" minOccurs="0" />
        <xs:element name="title" type="titleType" minOccurs="0" />
        <xs:element name="forename" type="nameString" minOccurs="0" />
        <xs:element name="initials" type="fourChar" minOccurs="0" />
        <xs:element name="surname" type="nameString" minOccurs="0" />
        <xs:element name="email" minOccurs="0">
            <xs:simpleType>
                <xs:restriction base="xs:string">
                    <xs:maxLength value="80" />
                </xs:restriction>
            </xs:simpleType>
        </xs:element>
    </xs:sequence>
</xs:complexType>
```

You'll notice that we've used several common simple types in order to make the schema more compact and legible, and to make it easier to maintain. These will be defined below.

Look at the `loanRequestResponseType` – there's nothing too mysterious here. We return the partner's business transaction ID and our own. By using the `wrlTransId` in future transactions the partner can refer straight back to this application.

```
<!-- loanRequestResponseType: immediate response to a loanRequest -->
<xs:complexType name="loanRequestResponseType">
    <xs:sequence>
        <xs:element name="partnerTransId" type="transIdType" />
        <xs:element name="wrlTransId" type="transIdType" />
    </xs:sequence>
</xs:complexType>
```

The `loanResultType` has the usual transaction IDs, and conversation flow is controlled by the sixth element, `decision` – this is where we send our *accept*, *decline*, or *refer* code.

```xml
<!-- loanResultType: result of a loan request -->
<xs:complexType name="loanResultType">
   <xs:sequence>
      <xs:element name="partnerTransId" type="transIdType" />
      <xs:element name="wrlTransId" type="transIdType" />
      <xs:element name="acceptanceNumber" type="documentNumber" />
      <xs:element name="loanAmount" type="totalType" />
      <xs:element name="wrlProduct" type="threeChar" />
      <xs:element name="decision" type="threeChar" />
      <xs:choice>
         <xs:element name="flatNo" type="fourChar" />
         <xs:element name="houseNumber" type="fourChar" />
         <xs:element name="houseName" type="addressString" />
      </xs:choice>
      <xs:element name="streetName" type="addressString" />
      <xs:element name="district" type="addressString" />
      <xs:element name="town" type="addressString" />
      <xs:element name="county" type="addressString" />
      <xs:element name="state" type="addressString" />
      <xs:element name="postZipCode" type="postZipCodeType" />
   </xs:sequence>
</xs:complexType>
```

The final root element is the `loanResultResponseType`. This is the response back from the partner to the bank, and includes a `redirectURL`, which, in the case of an acceptance, can be used to redirect the customer to his or her shopping basket on the partner's web site.

```xml
<!-- loanResultResponse: immediate response to a loanResult -->
<xs:complexType name="loanResultResponseType">
   <xs:sequence>
      <xs:element name="partnerTransId" type="transIdType" />
      <xs:element name="wrlTransId" type="transIdType" />
      <xs:element name="redirectURL" type="xs:anyURI" />
   </xs:sequence>
</xs:complexType>
```

There's only one other complex type – the `productType`:

```xml
<!-- other complex types -->
<xs:complexType name="productType">
   <xs:sequence>
      <xs:element name="productPrice">
         <xs:simpleType>
            <xs:restriction base="xs:decimal">
               <xs:totalDigits value="6" />
               <xs:fractionDigits value="2" />
            </xs:restriction>
         </xs:simpleType>
      </xs:element>
      <xs:element name="quantity" type="xs:positiveInteger" />
      <xs:element name="cost" type="totalType" />
```

```
        <xs:element name="productDescription">
            <xs:simpleType>
                <xs:restriction base="xs:string">
                    <xs:maxLength value="50" />
                </xs:restriction>
            </xs:simpleType>
        </xs:element>
    </xs:sequence>
</xs:complexType>
```

These elements map directly onto the back-end database, which is why we have, for example,
`productDescription` with a maximum length of fifty characters. This kind of arbitrary restriction
may not be elegant, but the ability to specify XML datatypes which are guaranteed to conform to
database datatypes appears to have been a major goal of the XML Schema working group, and will be
invaluable to anyone involved in enabling existing systems for e-commerce.

The rest of the schema is enumerations and the common simple types referred to in the schema so far:

```
<!-- simple types: enumerated types -->
<xs:simpleType name="titleType">
    <xs:restriction base="xs:string">
        <xs:enumeration value="Miss"/>
        <xs:enumeration value="Mr"/>
        <xs:enumeration value="Mrs"/>
        <xs:enumeration value="Ms"/>
        <xs:enumeration value="Dr"/>
        <!-- etc -->
    </xs:restriction>
</xs:simpleType>

<!-- simple types - strings and numbers -->
<xs:simpleType name="transIdType">
    <xs:restriction base="xs:string">
        <xs:maxLength value="26"/>
    </xs:restriction>
</xs:simpleType>
<xs:simpleType name="addressString">
    <xs:restriction base="xs:string">
        <xs:maxLength value="24"/>
    </xs:restriction>
</xs:simpleType>
<xs:simpleType name="nameString">
    <xs:restriction base="xs:string">
        <xs:minLength value="2"/>
        <xs:maxLength value="20"/>
    </xs:restriction>
</xs:simpleType>
<xs:simpleType name="documentNumber">
<xs:restriction base="xs:string">
        <xs:maxLength value="10"/>
    </xs:restriction>
</xs:simpleType>
<xs:simpleType name="totalType">
    <xs:restriction base="xs:decimal">
        <xs:totalDigits value="8"/>
```

```
                <xs:fractionDigits value="2"/>
            </xs:restriction>
        </xs:simpleType>
        <xs:simpleType name="fourChar">
            <xs:restriction base="xs:string">
                <xs:maxLength value="4"/>
            </xs:restriction>
        </xs:simpleType>
        <xs:simpleType name="threeChar">
            <xs:restriction base="xs:string">
                <xs:maxLength value="3"/>
            </xs:restriction>
        </xs:simpleType>
        <xs:simpleType name="postZipCodeType">
            <xs:restriction base="xs:string">
                <xs:pattern
                    value="\s*[A-Za-z]{1,2}\d{1,2}[A-Za-z]?\s?\d{1}[A-Za-z]{2}\s*"
                />
                <!-- Matches any amount of whitespace, followed by first part of
                     postcode, followed by 0 or 1 spaces, followed by second
                     half of postcode, followed by any amount of whitespace -->
                <!-- Country-specific regular expression -->
            </xs:restriction>
        </xs:simpleType>
    </xs:schema>
```

Sample Messages

In this section, we'll look at some examples of the four message types, the first two as used in the Partner-to-WRL operation "send Purchase and Customer Details":

❑   LoanRequest

❑   LoanRequestResponse

The other two, as needed for the "forward response to partner" and "forward final decision" WRL-to-Partner operations:

❑   LoanResult

❑   LoanResultResponse

LoanRequest

```
<SOAP-ENV:Envelope
    xmlns:SOAP-ENV="http://schemas.xmlsoap.org/soap/envelope/">
    <SOAP-ENV:Body>
        <loanRequest xmlns="http://www.example.com/xml/application.xsd"
            xmlns:xsi="http://www.w3.org/2001/XMLSchema-instance"
            xsi:schemaLocation="http://www.example.com/xml/application.xsd
                wrl-sch.xsd">
            <partnerId>ABC</partnerId>
            <partnerTransId>ABC000123</partnerTransId>
            <partnerBranch>LCS</partnerBranch>
            <totalCost>100</totalCost>
```

```
            <deposit>0</deposit>
            <amountRequired>100</amountRequired>
            <product>
                <productPrice>100</productPrice>
                <quantity>1</quantity>
                <cost>100</cost>
                <productDescription>gramophone</productDescription>
            </product>
            <wrlProduct>wrl</wrlProduct>
            <title>Mr</title>
            <forename>Philip</forename>
            <initials/>
            <surname>Larkin</surname>
            <email>p.larkin@largecoolstore.com</email>
        </loanRequest>
    </SOAP-ENV:Body>
</SOAP-ENV:Envelope>
```

LoanRequestResponse

```
<SOAP-ENV:Envelope
    xmlns:SOAP-ENV="http:// schemas.xmlsoap.org/soap/envelope/">
    <SOAP-ENV:Body>
        <loanRequestResponse
            xmlns="http://www.example.com/xml/application.xsd"
            xmlns:xsi="http://www.w3.org/2001/XMLSchema-instance"
            xsi:schemaLocation="http://www.example.com/xml/application.xsd
                wrl-sch.xsd">
            <partnerTransId>ABC000123</partnerTransId>
            <wrlTransId>0000-tnSff-43243</wrlTransId>
        </loanRequestResponse>
    </SOAP-ENV:Body>
</SOAP-ENV:Envelope>
```

LoanResult

```
<SOAP-ENV:Envelope
    xmlns:SOAP-ENV="http:// schemas.xmlsoap.org/soap/envelope/">
    <SOAP-ENV:Body>
        <loanResult
            xmlns="http://www.example.com/xml/application.xsd"
            xmlns:xsi="http://www.w3.org/2001/XMLSchema-instance"
            xsi:schemaLocation="http://www.example.com/xml/application.xsd
                wrl-sch.xsd">
            <partnerTransId>ABC000123</partnerTransId>
            <wrlTransId>0000-tnSff-43243</wrlTransId>
            <acceptanceNumber>wrl-FG-19</acceptanceNumber>
            <loanAmount>100</loanAmount>
            <wrlProduct>wrl</wrlProduct>
            <decision>YES</decision>
            <houseNumber>31</houseNumber>
            <streetName>Dockery Street</streetName>
            <district></district>
            <town>Hull</town>
            <county>Humberside</county>
            <state></state>
            <postZipCode>HD1-1AB</postZipCode>
        </loanResult>
    </SOAP-ENV:Body>
</SOAP-ENV:Envelope>
```

LoanResultResponse

```
<SOAP-ENV:Envelope
    xmlns:SOAP-ENV="http://schemas.xmlsoap.org/soap/envelope/">
    <SOAP-ENV:Body>
        <loanResultResponse
            xmlns="http://www.example.com/xml/application.xsd"
            xmlns:xsi="http://www.w3.org/2001/XMLSchema-instance"
            xsi:schemaLocation="http://www.example.com/xml/application.xsd
                wrl-sch.xsd">
            <partnerTransId>ABC000123</partnerTransId>
            <wrlTransId>0000-tnSff-43243</wrlTransId>
            <redirectURL>
                http://www.wrl.example.com/myloan?id=ABC000123
            </redirectURL>
        </loanResultResponse>
    </SOAP-ENV:Body>
</SOAP-ENV:Envelope>
```

Having the XML Schema `schemaLocation` attribute embedded in each message body is probably unnecessary in practice but it does reduce the scope for misunderstandings with new partners.

Let's take a look at what we've gained so far by using Schema-valid XML for our messages:

❑ We've eliminated an entire category of encoding and parsing problems

❑ We've simplified testing and diagnosis by decoupling transport and validation problems

❑ We've made the data specification process faster and clearer by providing a declarative, platform-neutral way of defining application-specific restrictions like 50 character length limits

❑ We've given ourselves more time to concentrate on specifying higher value business rules

Using Schematron with XML Schema

If we wanted, we could add some more validation to our system by using a Schematron schema. We can use Schematron to implement some higher-level business rules that reference the values of elements or attributes, and can even call external documents or web transactions.

Non-XML Schema Constraints

We can specify further constraints that will be automatically validated from the Schema, using a co-located Schematron, a technique that we saw in the last chapter. We will have to write code to execute the generated Schematron validator, but we can still get the same benefits of automatic message validation from a single specification document.

We'll specify some simple Schematron constraints – just check that the numbers are OK, which is the kind of non-syntax-based rule where Schematron adds functionality beyond XML Schema. We will:

❑ Validate purchase cost against price and quantity
❑ Validate total cost against sum of purchase costs

As the XML Schema is getting rather large we'll simply show the bits where the Schematron constraints are embedded.

```
<xs:schema xmlns:sch="http://www.ascc.net/xml/schematron"
           xmlns:xs="http://www.w3.org/2001/XMLSchema"
           xmlns="http://www.example.com/xml/application.xsd"
           targetNamespace="http://www.example.com/xml/application.xsd"
           elementFormDefault="qualified">
```

We need to declare the Schematron namespace above (the obvious sch: prefix has been used) so that the Schematron elements can be identified and processed.

```
<xs:annotation>
   <xs:appinfo>
      <sch:title>Schematron validation schema for WRS</sch:title>
      <sch:ns prefix="w"
              uri="http://www.example.com/xml/application.xsd" />
   </xs:appinfo>
</xs:annotation>
```

The `appinfo` element above contains a `sch:title`, which will be used in output reports, and a `sch:ns` namespace instruction, which will ensure that there is an appropriate namespace declared for the `w:` prefix by the time the Schematron XPath expressions below come to be evaluated.

```
<!-- top level complex types -->
<!-- loanRequestType: incoming loan request message -->
<xs:complexType name="loanRequestType">
   <xs:annotation>
      <xs:appinfo>
         <sch:pattern>
            <sch:rule context="w:loanRequest">
               <sch:assert test="w:totalCost = sum(w:product/w:cost)">
                  The totalCost must add up to the sum of the product
                  costs
               </sch:assert>
            </sch:rule>
         </sch:pattern>
      </xs:appinfo>
   </xs:annotation>
```

Here we write a Schematron pattern containing a rule, which applies to the `w:loanRequest` element, and asserts that `totalCost` must equal the sum of the costs of its product children.

```
<xs:sequence>
   <!-- ... -->
</xs:sequence>
```

```
      </xs:complexType>
   <!-- other complex types -->
   <xs:complexType name="productType">
      <xs:annotation>
      <xs:appinfo>
            <sch:pattern>
               <sch:rule context="w:product">
                  <sch:assert test="w:cost = w:price * w:quantity">
                     The product cost must equal the price times the
                     quantity
                  </sch:assert>
               </sch:rule>
            </sch:pattern>
      </xs:appinfo>
      </xs:annotation>
```

Here we have a similar constraint – a rule that applies to every w:product, and asserts that the cost of each must equal its price times its quantity. Again this is the kind of value-based constraint that cannot be expressed in XML Schema.

```
      <xs:sequence>
         <!-- ... -->
      </xs:sequence>
   </xs:complexType>
   <!-- ... -->
</xs:schema>
```

For a more complete discussion of the Schematron elements above, see the previous chapter.

There's one other Schematron feature I'd like to mention, the ability to call external documents or web transactions. If we were receiving Addresses rather than sending them, and assuming we had access to a CGI transaction to validate names against street numbers and postal or zip codes, we could write a validation test that used the XSLT document() function to call this transaction, since document() takes as its parameter a string expression that resolves to a URL. So we could create a different URL for each message, containing the street number, name, and post a zip code as CGI parameters, and even apply XPath to the results if the transaction returns well-formed XML. An example, which calls a completely hypothetical local transaction addr.pl, might look like this:

```
<sch:rule context="w:loanRequest">
  <sch:assert
      test="document(\cgi\addr.pl?name={w:surname};code={w:postZipCode})">
      Address validator could not find evidence of name at
      postcode.
   </sch:assert>
</sch:rule>
```

This is possibly controversial – it has performance implications, and means that the Schema could produce different results from one site to another, or from one run to another, but it is something to consider.

Looking Ahead – A Web Services View

Transport and validation are only two of the functions that have to be performed in order to perform e-commerce. The project described in the case study involves doing business with a small number of high-value partners. This makes it worthwhile even if other communication functions have to be specified and coded using traditional methods. Now we'll look over the horizon at new or future technologies that build on XML and XML Schema to automate some other necessary functions.

There are several technology proposals aimed at automating e-commerce, several derived from EDI. We are going to discuss one cluster, the SOAP/WSDL/UDDI technology stack, which aims to allow plug-and-play business-to-business integration, and possibly even to spread out to provide the same service automation internally.

WSDL

WSDL stands for Web Services Description Language and allows a host site to offer human and machine-readable documentation of the web services offered there. It isn't dependent on the services being implemented as SOAP transactions (it also has an HTTP GET/POST binding), but SOAP is the primary target.

Our project, for example, has a SOAP interface. We could now document the messages, XML parameters, that get sent, the operations (calls) that send and return these messages, and a protocol binding to the SOAP server(s) that will accept these operations, all in machine-readable form. This will automate the whole process of a partner connecting up with WRL. If the messages follow industry standard XML Schemas (as they emerge), and if the potential client can already interface to these structures, then signing up really will be plug and play. If not, but they use XML, they may choose to use some XSLT to convert their own structures to the specified message structures.

UDDI

Walk out of the front door, board the waiting helicopter and climb a few thousand feet. Can you still recognize your office on that murky map below you? Possibly. Can you see who else is hosting web services, what business they're doing, with which transactions? Clearly not – we need a more practical way of answering these questions.

This is where UDDI (Universal Discovery, Description, and Integration) comes in. It's both a set of directory services and an infrastructure, and is currently in version 2 of the proposed standard.

The directory services can be grouped into:

❑ "White pages" that describe a registered company through human-readable prose, existing codes such as DUNS numbers and tax IDs, and structured information like contact lists (described in the UDDI XML Schema)

❑ "Yellow pages" that describe the business of the company by reference to geographical, service and product indexes, and standard industry codes

❑ "Green pages" that list technical information about the available transactions

As an infrastructure, any UDDI node should support both the enquiry API and the publishing API. Both APIs are implemented via SOAP transporting schema-valid messages. Although the excitement tends to be associated with the vision of the "cloud" of public UDDI servers (or "node"), UDDI will serve in other nodes too – there will be public UDDI nodes that interoperate, there will be portal UDDI nodes providing services for a specific business area to a closed group – maybe one marketplace, maybe the customers of one web service provider, maybe the suppliers of a large vehicle manufacturer or a major government department. There will also be private UDDI nodes for automating what we used to call client-server, and there will be test and development UDDI nodes.

It is important to keep track of UDDI's scope – it is intended to enable technical discovery of services, not to form a full-featured discovery service. Basically it is aimed at allowing you to find potential business partners and to connect to them, but more advanced queries involving time or region are expected to be layered over UDDI in separate protocols.

Some Web Services Links

We'll find explanations, specifications, downloads and demonstrations at the following addresses, among others:

❏   A good general-purpose site is http://www.webservices.org. There are articles and downloads on IBM Developer Works at http://www-106.ibm.com/developerworks/webservices (many good articles, especially those by Uche Ogbuji and Steve Graham), and at Microsoft on http://msdn.microsoft.com/webservices, also with much useful information.

❏   The WSDL note at the W3C is at http://www.w3.org/TR/wsdl.

❏   WSDL support is now being built into SOAP tools from Microsoft, Apache, and others.

❏   UDDI white papers and specifications are at http://www.uddi.org, also see Robin Cover's UDDI Cover Pages at http://xml.coverpages.org/uddi.html

❏   MS, IBM, and others have UDDI test servers that demonstrate interoperability, as described in http://msdn.microsoft.com/xml/articles/xml12182000.asp.

❏   Many EDI standards are being developed in XML – too many to list here – though most of these have not yet taken advantage of XML Schema.

Summary

We have looked at why we want to use XML Schema with SOAP, and how SOAP works. We then derived messages and message structures from an agreed business analysis and an existing database. We extended the idea of declarative message specification and validation by using Schematron to add XPath based rules, and finally looked ahead to the place WSDL, UDDI, and future web services standards might play in our case study.

We have shown:

❏   How a SOAP message is structured and where our transaction specific XML goes
❏   How to design XML Schemas for these transactions, and associate the messages with them
❏   How to model the business practices on specific messages, and how to design the datatypes based on the back-end database
❏   How to use Schematron to add more functionality to our schemas, allowing further numerical relationships to be defined between datatypes
❏   The different web service discovery languages, UDDI and WSDL, what they do, and where we can find more information about them.

This case study shows a real-life implementation of a SOAP B2B system. The design could vary from system to system, but this shows you how to get started when creating these systems and the kinds of things to look out for when designing the schemas.

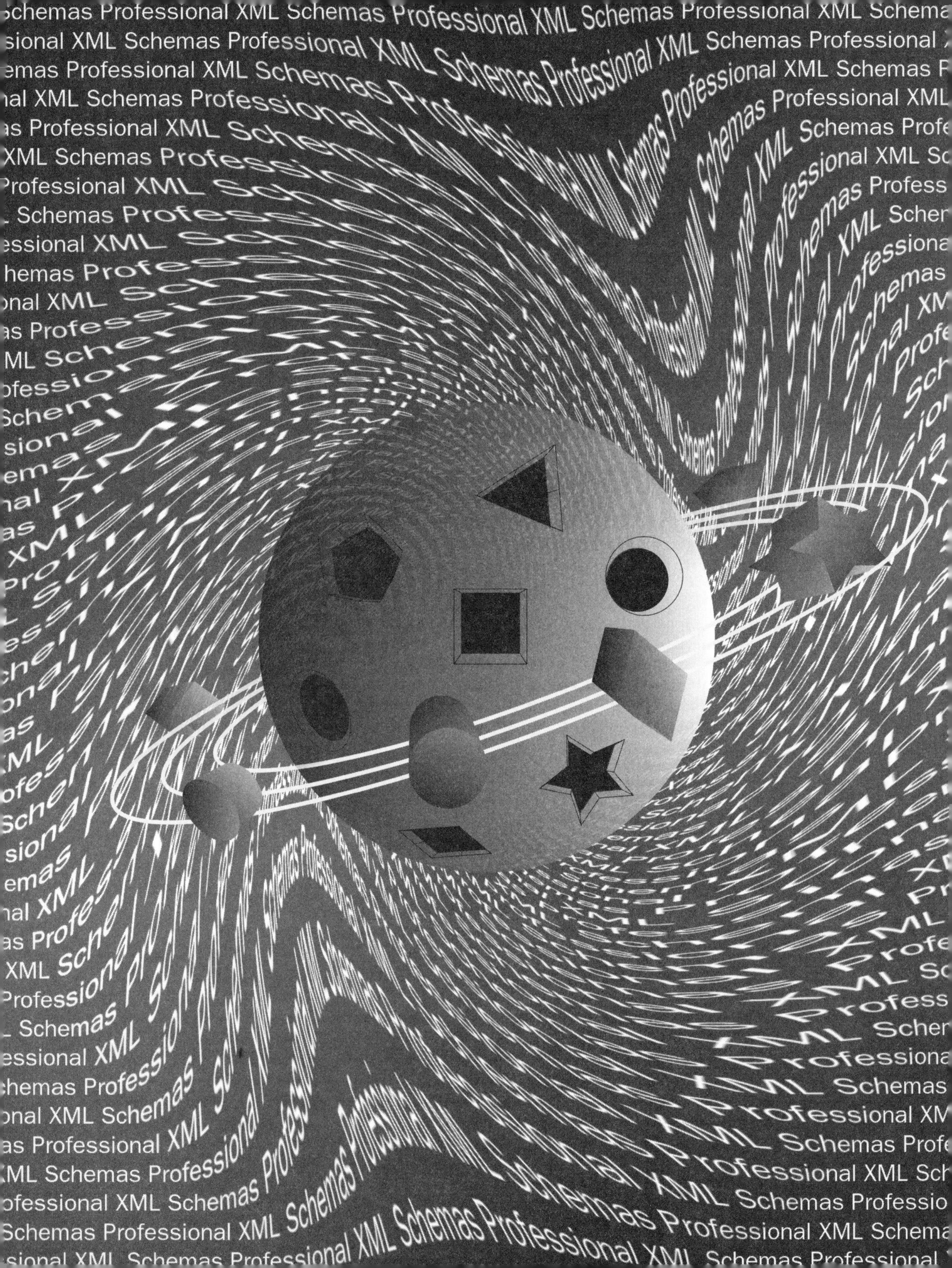
Professional XML Schemas

Schema-Based Programming

It is easy to focus on schemas solely in terms of how they specify the form and shape, if you will, of XML documents. All too often, we as programmers, treat schemas as second-class citizens. It is useful during development to be free of the constraints of validation, able to modify the syntax of our vocabulary without modifying a formal schema document. In production, with the software (hopefully) well tested, validation imposes a performance penalty. If you have ever programmed an application to take data from various sources, particularly a web-based application, you'll realize the value in having a schema to enforce integrity when data enters your application. Even in this situation, though, a schema has peripheral impact. Data is validated, and then admitted to the heart of the application. Within the application, however, schemas have little use.

To get you thinking about the importance of data, we'd like to present the current results of a small, ongoing research project. This project is called Schema-Based Programming (SBP). Pioneered by Michael Corning, SBP is an ongoing effort to implement everything in an application – user interface, internal state, and behavior – using XML and declarative tools. SBP takes its name and inspiration from the phrase "the schema is the API". In this chapter, we'll introduce the basics of SBP and implement a simple application. In particular, we aim to teach:

❑   How decisions made in designing a Schema affect the processing capabilities of an SBP application.

❑   How to implement a Model-View-Controller application using XML, XSLT, and a limited amount of script code.

❑   How to implement internal state and behavior using Petri Nets and XSLT

❑   How formal design methods and declarative techniques like XSLT can be used to improve software development.

We stress that SBP is a work in progress and a research effort. You will exercise your XML schema development skills and your abilities as an XSLT programmer. SBP is not yet ready for the development of production applications, and it may not be the simplest way to build applications. Still, we believe that the exercise of embracing a declarative model – making the "schema your API" – is an interesting one for experienced programmers. If nothing else, it will challenge you and show the way toward using formal methods in programming.

Declarative Programming

Most programs written in mainstream languages are **procedural**. The code tells the computer what to do, when to do it, and how to go about it. The programmer has full control over the outcome, and it is very easy for a programmer to stray from the incoming data. The ability to create structures and internal data regardless of the incoming data stream, is a powerful tool, but one that is all too susceptible to incorrect assumptions and improperly coded business rules.

SBP is an example of **declarative programming**. The programmer declares his intentions with respect to the input data. You might think of this in terms of rules that say "When you see this type of data, do the following." To some extent, this is the same as procedural programming. The programmer is telling the computer what to do.

Declarative programs respond to incoming data. Scheduling problems in when and how to respond arise, but the programmer is shielded from them. The processor implementing the declarative application handles these decisions. The programmer is freed of the details of "when" and "how", but is constrained in what he can do by the structure of the data. He cannot easily create massive new internal data structures, and it is very hard for him to create data on the output stream out of nothing. There is always a tie between what comes in, what happens, and what comes out.

Perhaps the most common example of declarative programming, is SQL. When we compose a SQL query, we tell the SQL command processor where to look and what we want back. Internally, the processor goes through very sophisticated algorithms to turn our text query into a set of instructions that most efficiently executes our intentions. We do not care what happens internally so long as the proper data comes out in the proper order. The processor, moreover, cannot show us anything that does not exist in the specified database. To generate a wholly spurious result set, the programmer must resort to calculated fields and lengthy stored procedures (which may be more procedural than the query language).

This is not to say that all procedural programs are bad, and that all declarative programs are good and correct. Bad code can be written in any language, and we have all pulled off prodigious feats of programming in spite of a bad development environment. It is our belief (the testing of which is one goal of the present effort), that declarative programming is more likely to help the programmer produce correct code when used for tasks suited to this approach.

Formal Tools for Program Development

The field of computer science has a number of techniques intended to make programming more a matter of engineering and less a matter of art. These formal methods are mathematical techniques that model the behavior of systems. They are formal, therefore mathematical techniques, a given design can be proven correct. Contrast that with the current practice of programming in most organizations. We design an application in general terms. Perhaps we use a formal design methodology like the Unified Modeling Language (UML). Such methodologies, though, are used for carefully documenting a design. They cannot make verifiable predictions about the performance of applications built to those specifications. The methodology may be sound, but the outcome is only as good as the fallible humans who implemented it. There is no rigorous, repeatable way to look at the outcome and verify it. It is not until testing begins that the programmer knows whether the design is correct or not. Fixing all the known bugs does not guarantee that the program is now correct; there may be an as-yet undetected bug.

Why, then, don't we routinely use formal methods in the day-to-day practice of software development? One reason, is that there is a very steep learning curve. It is far easier to learn a new programming language to the level where we can be productive than it is to learn a formal method. Education alone though, cannot explain the lack of formal methods in ordinary development. Some of these methods have been around for decades, more than enough time for a sizable body of programmers to pass through school and enter the field armed with one or more formal methods. A bigger problem is the inherent disconnect between formal methods and programming languages. Formal methods are declarative, and most mainstream languages are procedural. Tools to help programmers use formal methods in software design stop at the design stage. It is then necessary to write code that adheres to the design produced using the formal method. When we do that, we have lost many of the advantages of using a formal method in the first place. We no longer have to prove that our design is correct, but now you have to prove that the implementation adheres to the design. How is that done? We have to test the software... clearly, formal methods would have a better reputation if they were combined with a declarative language in an integrated design and development environment.

That is among the long-term goals for SBP. We would, at the very least, like to have an environment that uses formal methods to prove a design and implement a simulation of the finished software. Ideally, the final application implementation would be generated from the tool as well. We are far from that goal, but we will see an early example of merging a formal method with the declarative approach of SBP to produce a small application in this chapter.

Implementing Applications with SBP

An ideal SBP application, would be written wholly as a series of XSLT transformations applied to an XML document. The current state of Internet programming in general, and XSLT in particular does not allow that, so a certain amount of script code will be necessary. With the right development model, though, we can keep the procedural code to a small amount of standardized code that does not vary between SBP applications, a tiny amount of procedural code custom to each SBP application, and a large amount of XML and XSLT. Another goal is the use of formal methods for the creation of provably correct applications, therefore we also want to develop a structure that permits experimentation with different formal methods. There is, conveniently enough, an existing architecture that meets these requirements called the **Model-View-Controller** (**MVC**) paradigm. MVC will be one of the two pillars of SBP development.

Model – View – Controller

MVC separates the core state and behavior of an application from the visual interface. The data is termed the **Model** as it typically represents something in the real world. At any rate, it represents what we wish to study, or model. The visual interface is called the **View**. More than one view is permitted in an application to allow users to have different views of the model data or to provide different ways of working with the data. If the application is to have any integrity, however, there can only be one Model. A small amount of code executing independently of the model serves to connect the two. This is called the **Controller** as it funnels events between the Model and the Views:

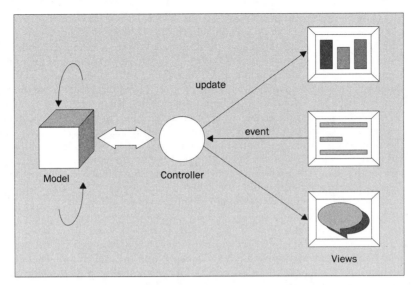

You may already be using MVC without knowing it. The Microsoft Foundation Classes, a staple of application programming on the Windows platform, are designed around MVC. The core Java user interface classes also reflect MVC to some extent, and many other commercial programming libraries from third parties use MVC. As we shall see shortly, MVC provides a certain discipline to the programming process. Let's look briefly at each component of this architecture before we see how SBP will use MVC.

Model

The Model consists of all the core data in the application, as well as all the code needed to provide the essential functionality of the application. We use these qualifiers, because small amounts of data and code may be needed to operate the different interfaces. The Model assumes that an application is about, or represents, one thing. All the information to describe the current state of that thing is isolated and placed in the Model. The core behavior of that thing, the functionality provided by the application, is placed with the data in the Model. This has the advantage of making it easy for programmers to locate the right section of code to modify when an enhancement is desired. If it is core functionality, it must be found in the Model.

More important to our present concerns, this segregation of behavior and the data on which it acts away from the rest of the application promotes the overall integrity of application data and the correctness of how the application, runs. The behavior of the interface, the presentation of the data, is segregated *from* the data. State information is recorded exactly once, in the Model. No matter how many times that data is shown to the user, and no matter in what form – what visual behavior – that data is displayed, it exists in only one place. So long as that one representation is correct, the application state must be correct. If an interface displays erroneous data, the fault must be found in the interface.

Consider a spreadsheet application. We might show the same data in several places. We will certainly enter the data on one sheet. Depending on our application, we might create links to that data, causing it to appear on one or more additional worksheets. If we wish to see the data as a graph, the data is again linked to another page. All these worksheets can have different ways of formatting and displaying the data, but they must all reflect the same thing. Somewhere in the application code is a data structure containing the true value of the data. When the user changes the data in one of the worksheets, the representation of the data in that model structure is changed.

View

A View, by contrast, has no core data within it, nor does it contain code implementing the core features of the application. All code is dedicated to visual representation and interaction, and any data found in a View is limited to housekeeping data needed to implement the visual interface, for example; information about the size and placement of the view window.

We may have as many views as we wish; indeed, it is desirable to have multiple views. Each view is dedicated to one way of looking at or interacting with the data. A tabular spreadsheet (to continue our example) is different from a bar graph, and both differ in behavior from a dialog box. We might, for example, have three windows open: a tabular worksheet, a bar graph, and a dialog box for editing the data displayed in the views – not that each view shouldn't render all the data. The tabular display could represent everything, with the bar graph rendering a selected subset of the data, and the dialog showing the properties of a single cell. Each display is linked to the Model; a change in one effects a change in the Model, which ripples out to the other views as the application ensures a consistent view of the Model data.

Controller

As we have already noted, the function of the Controller is to implement the linkage between the Model and the View. The Controller is a small body of event dispatching code. Notification of changes in the Model must be passed on to the Views. Since a View may be linked to a subset of the Model, not all Views need to be notified of every internal event. In fact, efficiency dictates that the Controller should use the association of events and Views to regulate how events are propagated to Views. Similarly, events in the Views – our user interface – must be passed on to the Model. This is the only way the Model is made aware of the outside world.

SBP Schema

Let's turn from the arena of theory toward a practical implementation. We'll begin by presenting a schema to describe SBP applications. Documents conforming to this schema will be a static and persistent representation of the MVC architecture. At runtime, such documents will become the basis of SBP applications.

Each SBP application must contain within it the full body of code and data for the Model, as well as the code and data for the Views, and enough code to form a runtime Controller. Since the Controller must manage the association of events and Views, SBP documents must also contain a record of such associations. The following fragment is the start of the SBP schema we will use in this chapter. The full text of the schema is found in the file SBP.xsd:

```
<?xml version = "1.0" encoding = "UTF-8"?>
<xs:schema xmlns:xsl = "http://www.w3.org/1999/XSL/Transform"
          xmlns:xs = "http://www.w3.org/2001/XMLSchema">
   <xs:import namespace = "http://www.w3.org/1999/XSL/Transform"
              schemaLocation = "http:/www.w3.org/1999/XSL/Transform"/>
   <xs:element name = "Application">
      <xs:complexType>
         <xs:sequence>
            <xs:element ref = "Model"/>
            <xs:element ref = "Intentions"/>
```

```
            <xs:element ref = "event" maxOccurs = "unbounded"/>
            <xs:element ref = "view" maxOccurs = "unbounded"/>
        </xs:sequence>
      </xs:complexType>
    </xs:element>
    . . . <!-- additional declarations follow -->
  </xs:schema>
```

We've already stated that we're going to use XSLT as our declarative implementation language, therefore it should be no surprise to see references to the XSLT namespace. Our study really begins with the top-level `Application` element. Everything in our SBP document will be a child of `Application`. Such applications' consist of a Model element within which is found all information needed to recreate the Model of this application in the MVC architecture. Following this element is an `Intentions` element. Intentions are not a part of MVC; instead, they contain the script functions that will need to be loaded into the client browser so as to form the Controller. When we turn to implementing SBP applications in the next section, we shall see that a bit of work is needed to put the code into place and start the Controller. The `event` elements help the runtime Controller by recording the association of events and Views. The remaining `view` elements will require a bit more explanation, but for now, let it suffice to say that they contain the XSLT transforms to properly respond to events. As such, they are the persistent form of the View or Views in the application.

Here is the shell of a compliant SBP document:

```
<?xml version="1.0" ?>
   . . .
<Application>
  <Model>
     . . .
  </Model>
  <Intentions>
     . . .
  </Intentions>
  <event id="pulse" notify="net"/>
  <view id="net" boundTo="netView">
     . . .
  </view>
</Application>
```

Let's consider the `Model` element for a moment, as it is one of the most important parts of an SBP application.

Model

Here's the declaration for the `Model` element:

```
<xs:element name = "Model"/>
```

This may be shocking at first glance. We just finished telling you that this is one of the most important parts of an SBP application, and now we present a content model with no restrictions. To a certain extent, there is no avoiding this in a Schema meant to fit many applications. Part of the Model element will be given over to structures that represent the internal state of the application; this necessarily will change from application to application, but what about the code needed to power the Model?

We want to use formal methods to power SBP applications. In theory, we should be able to generalize a good deal of the code needed to operate a model based on a particular method. With that in mind, we could qualify the content model to reflect a known method. Each part of the MVC triad is designed to operate without knowledge of the internal workings of the others. We should be able, therefore, to replace one Model implementation with another. It is for this reason – making the inner operation of the Model plug-replaceable – that we leave the content model unrestricted. In practice, as we shall see in the next section, we will be very particular about what we put into the Model element as child content.

View

The view element implements the View portion of the MVC model. There is a runtime part as well, but that is not part of the SBP application document. Here is the formal declaration for the view element:

```
<xs:element name = "view">
   <xs:complexType>
      <xs:sequence>
         <xs:element ref = "xsl:transform"/>
      </xs:sequence>
      <xs:attribute name = "boundTo" use = "required" type = "xs:string"/>
      <xs:attribute name = "id" use = "required" type = "xs:ID"/>
   </xs:complexType>
</xs:element>
```

The value of the id attribute, uniquely identifies the view element within the Application document and is used by the Controller, as we shall shortly see, to retrieve Views for notification when an event comes into it.

The visual interface – the physical manifestation of the MVC View – is implemented in this application as HTML displayed within the client browser. Specifically, at application start-up (initial load of the document), we create named div elements to serve as containers for each View's HTML. Recall that a div is a block element that contains other HTML content. These are the physical manifestation of the View, and receive the HTML generated by the logical view in response to an event. That logical view is what is contained in the view element. It is, if you will, the "code" needed to operate the View. In our case, it is a transform element (complete XSLT stylesheet) drawn from the XSLT namespace. This is very important. If the "schema is the API", then our View code must be declarative, driven by the current state of the Model. That is exactly what XSLT does. Here is a sample view element:

```
<view id="net" boundTo="netView">
   <xsl:transform version="1.0"
                  xmlns:xsl="http://www.w3.org/1999/XSL/Transform">
      <xsl:template match="/">
         <!-- XSLT here -->
      </xsl:template>
   </xsl:transform>
</view>
```

The transformation within this `view` acts on the contents of the Model to produce output HTML that is to be placed within a `div` named **netView**. That HTML, when rendered in the `div` by the browser, becomes the physical manifestation of the MVC View. The value of the `boundTo` attribute on `view`, then, is the name of the `div` into which the HTML output of the transform must be placed. This controller uses this information to complete processing of an event.

Controller

The Controller is unique in the SBP schema, in that it is the only object that possesses procedural code. This is contained within the `Intentions` element:

```
<xs:element name = "Intentions">
  <xs:complexType>
    <xs:sequence>
      <xs:element ref = "codeBlock" maxOccurs = "unbounded"/>
    </xs:sequence>
  </xs:complexType>
</xs:element>
```

`Intentions` is merely a collection of `codeBlock` elements. These are further defined as follows:

```
<xs:element name = "codeBlock">
  <xs:complexType mixed = "true">
    <xs:sequence minOccurs = "0" maxOccurs = "unbounded">
      <xs:element ref = "code"/>
    </xs:sequence>
    <xs:attribute name = "mode" use = "required">
      <xs:simpleType>
        <xs:restriction base = "xs:NMTOKEN">
          <xs:enumeration value = "XML"/>
          <xs:enumeration value = "ASP"/>
        </xs:restriction>
      </xs:simpleType>
    </xs:attribute>
    <xs:attribute name = "id" use = "required" type = "xs:ID"/>
  </xs:complexType>
</xs:element>
```

Each `codeBlock` element contains zero or more `code` elements. It may also contain text, as indicated by the value of **true** for the `mixed` attribute. As we shall see below, the code elements contain the procedural code needed to operate the Controller at runtime. In addition to the element content, `codeBlock` possesses `mode` and `id` attributes. The `mode` attribute is used to distinguish between client-side and server-side SBP implementations. A client-side implementation executes solely on the client. After the initial download, events are passed through the Controller and execute within the client. In the server-side case, events are passed back to the server. Server side implementations should be used when we cannot be sure of having a robust client (robust in terms of XML and XSLT support.) The server-side portion of the Controller passes the event to the correct View, which executes its XSLT transformation and returns fully formed HTML to the client.

As you might expect, the Controller code differs depending on the implementation. Client-side Controller code is found in `codeBlock` elements whose `mode` attribute bears the value `XML`, while server-side procedural code is in `codeBlock` elements whose mode attribute takes the value `ASP`. The enumeration values are somewhat arbitrary – we've selected the ones shown here, because the client-side implementation consists of viewing the XML document directly, while server-side implementations have traditionally been executed as ASP. The `id` attribute uniquely identifies the `codeBlock`.

*The example in this chapter will only show the client-side implementation. For an example of a dual implementation, see **Professional XML second edition**, by Nik Ozu et al (ISBN: 1-861005-05-9), published by Wrox Press.*

Now, if the `codeBlock` can contain text, that is, it is a mixed content element, why do we need the `code` element? We could, and sometimes will, just place the procedural script code into the textual content of the `codeBlock` element. We need the `code` element for specific event handlers, or more explicitly, the event-specific portion of the Controller. Here is the formal declaration of this element:

```
<xs:element name = "code">
   <xs:complexType>
      <xs:simpleContent>
         <xs:extension base = "xs:string">
            <xs:attribute name = "event" type = "xs:string"/>
            <xs:attribute name = "boundTo" type = "xs:string"/>
            <xs:attribute name = "id" use = "required" type = "xs:ID"/>
         </xs:extension>
      </xs:simpleContent>
   </xs:complexType>
</xs:element>
```

The value of `event` is the name of the event to which this procedural code applies. The value of `boundTo` is the View – the name of the `div` where the results of the event processing will be rendered. The `id` attribute, finally, is needed to uniquely identify this element. Note that `event` and `boundTo` are optional attributes. This gives us some flexibility. Sometimes we will place procedural code into `code` elements, rather than into the textual portion of a `codeBlock` for modularity and source code control. In that case, we would not need `event` and `boundTo`. Here is a sample `codeBlock` with a child `code` element written in JavaScript:

```
<codeBlock id="eventHandlers" mode="XML">
   <code id="OnViewClick" boundTo="netView" event="pulse">
   function OnViewClick()
      {
         ... // procedural code here
      }
   </code>
</codeBlock>
```

Now that we have completely specified the contents of `codeBlock`, we return to the other half of the Controller, the `event` element. Remember, this is the association between an event in the application and one or more Views. Here is the portion of our schema that declares this element:

```
<xs:element name = "event">
   <xs:complexType>
      <xs:attribute name = "notify" use = "required" type = "xs:IDREFS"/>
      <xs:attribute name = "id" use = "required" type = "xs:ID"/>
   </xs:complexType>
</xs:element>
```

An event element is empty of child elements. It exists solely to support its two attributes, which tell the Controller which runtime Views need to be notified when a particular event fires. The value of the id attribute is the name of the event. This value will be passed into the Controller from the visual interface to trigger the event. The value of notify is a whitespace-delimited string of ID references. The references point to view elements. The Controller will parse the notify attribute and retrieve each view element in turn, instructing each view element to update itself in response to the event. Here is a sample event element:

```
<event id="pulse" notify="net"/>
```

The view element whose id is net needs to be notified of the pulse event. When a pulse event comes into the Controller, it will use this element to retrieve the view element whose ID is net, perform the transformation contained in that element, and place the output HTML into the div whose ID is referenced in the boundTo attribute on the view.

This takes us deeper into the actual implementation of an SBP application. So far, we've avoided direct discussion of our scheme for implementing SBP applications, in favor of discussing the structure of SBP Application documents. Now that you know where everything is found, it is time to discuss how that data is used to implement a functioning SBP program.

Implementing an SBP Application

We've told you where the various pieces of the Model, View, and Controller are found in an Application document, and we've even hinted at what happens when the application is loaded into a browser. Key pieces of the puzzle remain, though. We'll start by explaining the main sequence of events in the life of an SBP application. From there, we'll examine the details of the steps, with particular attention paid to the procedural code behind the Controller. This constitutes the vast majority of the procedural code in an SBP application, and it is almost entirely generalized and reusable across SBP applications.

Next, we'll look at one specific formal method, Petri Nets, as a tool for implementing the Model. This will bring in a third party schema, the Petri Net Markup Language (PNML), as well as a general purpose XSLT stylesheet. Taken together, PNML documents and the stylesheet will power our Model.

Scheme of Processing

Here is the lifecycle of a client-side SBP application:

❑ Browser requests XML document conforming to Application schema

❑ Browser requests XSLT stylesheet referenced in the XML document

❑ XML document is rendered as shell user interface

❑ Controller is started

❑ Model responds to user interface events by executing XSLT transformations

Note that after the second step, everything in the application occurs entirely within the client. Everything apart from the Controller is declarative XSLT. At that time, the application is up and running on a thin layer of procedural code in the Controller and great big chunks of XSLT in the Model and the Views. Let's examine each step in turn.

The scheme that follows relies on robust XML, XPath, and XSLT support on the client. In particular, it relies on the browser to process a link to a stylesheet automatically. The processing instruction shown in the next section is a Microsoft extension. For this reason, you will require Microsoft Internet Explorer 5.0 or later, as well as Microsoft's XML parser, MSXML, version 3.0 or later installed in replace mode. Instructions for installing MSXML 3 in this mode are found on http@//msdn.microsoft.com/xml

The Controller code we'll examine later is also dependent on Internet Explorer and MSXML 3.0, but could readily be modified to accommodate another XML parser and XSLT processor.

Initial Download Actions

A user starts an SBP application by providing a browser with the URL of a document conforming to the Application schema we discussed above. When the document is delivered to the client, it encounters a link like this within the document:

```
<?xml-stylesheet type="text/xsl" href="ChemNet.xsl"?>
```

This is a processing instruction instructing the XML parser to retrieve an XSLT stylesheet named `ChemNet.xsl`. Note the `type` attribute; this is what tells the parser the MIME type of the linked document. The default behavior in Internet Explorer is to request the XSLT stylesheet that is referenced, apply the transformation contained therein, and push the resultant document into the browser window.

Two critical things happen when the stylesheet is applied: a shell user interface is created, and the contents of the relevant `codeBlock` elements are loaded into that shell and started.

User Interface Creation

The static, non-interactive elements of the user interface are generated directly by the XSLT stylesheet. These may be hard-coded into the stylesheet or created based on templates that respond to the contents of the `Application` document's `Model` element. The point is to get the unchanging parts of the application interface onto the screen immediately and with a minimum of effort. Here is the form of such a stylesheet:

```
<xsl:transform version="1.0"
               xmlns:xsl="http://www.w3.org/1999/XSL/Transform" >
    <xsl:output method="html" indent="yes" omit-xml-declaration="yes" />
    <xsl:param name="mode">XML</xsl:param>
<xsl:template match="/">
    <html>
        <head>
            <title>Your title here</title>
            <script language="Javascript">

        <!-- Controller-related XSLT here -->

        </script>
        </head>
```

```
            <body>

            <!-- Static HTML here -->
            <!-- One or more named, empty divs follow -->

                <div id="netView">
                </div>
                ...
            </body>
        </html>
    </xsl:template>
```

The standard XSLT stylesheet element (in this case `transform` is used, but its equivalent `stylesheet` will also work) contains the XSLT version and namespace declaration. That is followed with an `output` element to instruct the client XSLT processor to generate HTML output and omit the usual XML declaration (the `method` and `omit-xml-declaration` attributes, respectively). Next, we have an XSLT parameter declaration (the `param` element) so that the stylesheet receives the appropriate `mode` parameter.

> *A server-side implementation will override this by setting the value ASP in code before executing the transformation.*

The root template is shown above. This creates the shell of an HTML document, by directly outputting the markup for an HTML page, that is, the `html`, `head`, `title`, and `body` elements. Skipping over the `script` element for a moment – we shall return to it in the very next section – we come to more HTML. Much of this will vary from application to application, but all SBP applications have one thing in common: they all contain one or more `div` or `span` elements that are initially empty. These are the physical manifestations of the Views that we mentioned earlier. The IDs of these `div`s – `netView` in the example above – are referenced in the `Application` document in the `view` elements. These containers are the ones that will receive dynamic HTML in response to an event.

At this point, we have an HTML document in the display with placeholders for interactive content, but it is a dead document. Without the Controller, we do not have an application. Let's fill in the part of the stylesheet that gives us a Controller.

Controller Activation

We've stated that the Controller is based on procedural script code, and from the template shown above, you can see where it might be expected to go – the script element – and you know from prior discussion where it comes from: the `codeBlock` elements in the `Application` document. Getting it there is the task of the following additions to the stylesheet `ChemNet.xsl`:

```
<xsl:transform version="1.0"
               xmlns:xsl="http://www.w3.org/1999/XSL/Transform">
    <xsl:output method="html" indent="yes" omit-xml-declaration="yes" />
    <xsl:param name="mode">XML</xsl:param>

<xsl:template match="/">
    <html>
        <head>
            <title>Your title here</title>
            <script language="Javascript">
```

```
                    <xsl:for-each select="Application/Intentions">
                        <xsl:apply-templates />
                    </xsl:for-each>
                </script>
            </head>
            <body>
                <!-- Static HTML here -->
                <!-- One or more named, empty divs follow -->
            </body>
        </html>
    </xsl:template>
```

```
<xsl:template match="codeBlock">
    <xsl:if test="@mode=$mode">
        <xsl:apply-templates />
    </xsl:if>
</xsl:template>
```

```
</xsl:transform>
```

Within the HTML `script` element, we select the `Intentions` elements within the Application document and tell the XSLT processor to continue processing templates from that point (with the `for-each` element). The processor will find the template that matches the `codeBlock` element. If the mode parameter value – which in our case is "XML" – matches the value of the mode attribute on the `codeBlock` element, processing continues. Since there are no more templates in the stylesheet, the default behavior of copying the child contents occurs. This has the effect of copying the textual content of `codeBlock` and `code` elements into the body of the output HTML page. The vast majority of the Controller code never changes from one SBP application to another, and may be copied into the `Application` document without change. Unfortunately, there is as yet, no good way to write this in one place and reuse it. XLink would be ideal, but it is not yet a Recommendation and not widely supported. We could use an XSLT `import` element and keep the code in a separate stylesheet, but that would be a bit obscure. Rather than appearing with the application, the Controller code would be buried under two layers of indirection – a stylesheet copied into a stylesheet. Until we have XLink, then, we shall continue to copy the unchanging parts of the Controller from application to application. Here is that markup. It is found in `ChemNet.xml` within the `Intentions` element:

```
<Intentions>
<codeBlock id="declarations" mode="XML">
    var model=document.XMLDocument;

    var nlstEvent=model.getElementsByTagName("event");

    <code id="initialize">
        window.onload=initialize;
        function initialize()
        {
            // application-specific code here!
        }
    </code>
</codeBlock>

<codeBlock id="permanentBlock" mode="XML">
    <code id="notify" >
        function notify(event)
```

```
          {
             var aNotify=getEvent(event).getAttribute("notify").split(" ");
             for (each in aNotify)
             {
                view=model.selectSingleNode(
                            "/Application/view[@id='"+aNotify[each]+"']");
                document.all(view.getAttribute
                            ("boundTo")).transform(view.firstChild);
             }
          }
       </code>

       <code id="transform">
          function transform(xslView)
          {
             try
             {
                this.innerHTML= model.transformNode(xslView)
             }
             catch(e)
             {
                alert("Error during transform:\n\n"+e.description)
             }
          }
       </code>

       <code id="getEvent">
          function getEvent(strID)
          {
             return getNodeFromID(strID, nlstEvent)
          }
       </code>

       <code id="getNodeFromID">
          function getNodeFromID(strID, nlst)
          {
             var node=null;
             nlst.reset()
             while(node=nlst.nextNode())
             if(strID==node.getAttribute("id")) break
             return node
          }
       </code>
    </codeBlock>
 </intentions>
```

Note that the first codeBlock element begins with textual content, allowing us to get some global code and variable declarations into the final script element. By far the most important thing to do, is get a reference to the original XML document into the variable model so that we can refer to the XML throughout the application's life. We will need to refer to the MVC Model, in particular. Next, we declare a useful variable, a list of the event elements. This will enable the Controller to conveniently find the association between the events it receives, and the logical view elements that need to be notified.

This still hasn't started the Controller. That is the function of the assignment of an event handler for the window object's onload event:

```
window.onload=initialize;
function initialize()
{
    // application-specific code here!
}
```

When the stylesheet is finished, the browser will then parse the outputted HTML document. The embedded script code will automatically begin to execute, so the initialize function will be assigned as the event handler. When the browser has finished rendering the document, initialize is called in response to the firing of the onload event. The body of initialize will vary from application to application, but one very important task must be accomplished. Event handlers for user interface events must be assigned to the physical Views (remember, these are div or span elements in the HTML document) in response to these user interface events by firing events in the controller and calling XSLT transformations taken from the Application document. The initialize function also fires an event to start the application. Here is a sample initialize function, which we shall see again when we take up the sample application:

```
function initialize()
{
    netView.onclick=OnViewClick;
    netView.transform=transform;
    notify("pulse");
}
```

This implementation works with an application that has a single View. The physical view for it, is a div named netView. We wish to respond to user-initiated click events on the view, so we assign an event handler for the onclick event. This is an application-specific function named OnViewClick. That is a short piece of procedural code. The heavy lifting involved in rendering the view is accomplished through declarative XSLT, so we extend netView to include a method named transform. That function implements finding the logical view associated with the physical view and executing the XSLT transformation found within the logical view:

```
function transform(xslView)
{
    try
    {
        this.innerHTML= model.transformNode(xslView)
    }
    catch(e)
    {
        alert("Error during transform:\n\n"+e.description)
    }
}
```

We've implemented transform as a DHTML expansion property of the physical view therefore, we can take advantage of this object; no code is needed to find the correct physical view. We call the XML transformNode method on the Application document (which we captured in the model variable) and stuff the results into the innerHTML property of the physical view. How, though, does the XSLT get from the logical view in the Application document to transform, and how is transform called? That takes us back to the very last line of the sample initialize function above, and a function called notify.

Event Processing

We assigned event handlers to the physical views in the main code section. They will be application-specific, but they all have two things in common: they update the MVC Model based on the event, and they fire the event into the MVC Views by calling `notify`. In our initialize function, above, we didn't need to update the Model as the initial state of the model is captured in the `Model` element of the Application document. Consequently, we called `notify` directly to render the interactive portion of the user interface based on the contents of the Model. We will discuss the event handlers later, but let's begin by taking a look at `notify`:

```
function notify(event)
{
   var aNotify=getEvent(event).getAttribute("notify").split(" ")
   for (each in aNotify)
   {
      view=model.selectSingleNode(
              "/Application/view[@id='"+aNotify[each]+"']");
      document.all(view.getAttribute("boundTo")).transform(view.firstChild);
   }
}
```

This code does not change from application to application. It accepts a string parameter, `event`, consisting of the name of the event fired. It uses a utility function called `getEvent` to retrieve the `event` element corresponding to the event named in the parameter. For the `pulse` event, that element looks like this:

```
<event id="pulse" notify="net"/>
```

You may recall that the `notify` attribute is an `IDREFS` type that names all the logical views requiring notification. In this case, there is only one such view, and it is named `net`. We retrieve the logical view using MSXML's proprietary XPath method, `selectSingleNode`, giving it the XPath expression that denotes the location of the `view` elements. These are direct children of the `Application` document element. The correct `view` element to retrieve is the one whose `id` attribute value equals the individual `IDREF` value taken from the value of the `notify` attribute on the `event` element. For the `event` element shown above, the XPath expression is:

```
/Application/view[@id='net']
```

The first (and only) child of the `view` element retrieved by that expression is the XSLT, `transform` element we wish to apply to render the physical view. The ID of that physical view (the `div` or `span`) is the value of the `view` element's `boundTo` attribute. Here is the outer shell of the `view` element retrieved by our example:

```
<view id="net" boundTo="netView">
   <xsl:transform version="1.0"
               xmlns:xsl="http://www.w3.org/1999/XSL/Transform"
               xmlns:p="urn:pnml-working">
   <!-- XSLT templates here -->
   </xsl:transform>
</view>
```

Note that it is bound to the div whose ID is netView. The last line of notify, then, calls the transform method of the div named netView, passing it the XSLT stylesheet it extracted from the view element named net:

```
document.all(view.getAttribute("boundTo")).transform(view.firstChild);
```

We've seen that the transform function applies the XSLT and stuffs the resultant markup into the physical View. The browser takes things from there, rendering the HTML into human-viewable content. All that remains of the invariant Controller code are the utility functions getEvent and getNodeFromID:

```
function getEvent(strID)
{
    return getNodeFromID(strID, nlstEvent)
}

function getNodeFromID(strID, nlst)
{
    var node=null;
    nlst.reset()
    while(node=nlst.nextNode())
    if(strID==node.getAttribute("id"))
    break;
    return node;
}
```

The getEvent function serves to encapsulate our XML conventions. It accepts the name of an event and calls getNodeFromID, passing it the name of the event and the nlstEvent variable. That variable, you will recall, was set up in the main code body as a list of event elements. The getNodeFromID function walks that list until it finds an element whose id attribute matches the event name passed in by getEvent. This processing relies on a simple, but important, convention: the id of the event element must match the name of the event fired.

When the application reaches this point, it has accomplished all but the last task in our processing scheme. That task is responding to events as they are fired in the user interface. We've seen the Controller code for this, but we haven't seen any application-specific event handler code – event handler code first modifies the Model.

To talk about event handlers, then, we must finally come to grips with the Model element. For the purposes of this chapter, we will use Petri Nets as the formal method that powers our application.

Implementing the Model with Petri Nets

Petri Nets are the work of Carl Adam Petri, which was begun in the 1960s. They are a form of mathematical **graphs**. Graphs are a collection of **nodes** and **edges** between nodes. Nodes represent a place or thing, while edges serve to connect nodes to form a path or relationship between them. In some forms of graphs, named **digraphs** (from "directed graph"), the edges have a direction and hence, control the navigation through the graph by specifying a set of possible paths.

There are many types of Petri Nets, and a rich body of literature about them. They have found wide use throughout a number of fields. For example, they are used in computer science to study concurrency. The particular form of Petri Net we shall use is a **place/transition net**, or **P/T net**.

There is a rich introduction to Petri Nets is maintained by the University of Aarhus, Denmark, at the Petri Net World site, http://www.daimi.au.dk/PetriNets/. A classification of Petri Net types is found there at http://www.daimi.au.dk/PetriNets/classification/. Be warned, however, this site takes a formal mathematical approach to the topic.

Petri Nets make use of digraphs as follows. Each node is called a **place**. A place represents a state in the overall system. If the system is in a particular state, it is said to be: "marked with a **token**". When the system transitions to another state, it must pass through a **transition**. When the conditions of the transition are satisfied, the token is removed from the losing state (or place) and copied to the gaining state. Directed edges, termed **arcs**, connect places to transitions. A place may be connected to multiple transitions, and a transition may similarly be connected to multiple places. When either of the two situations occurs, a transition may result in the creation of multiple tokens and multiple marked places.

It is useful to have a graphical representation of P/T nets. Conventionally, circles indicate places. If a place is marked, it has a dark fill. Transitions are usually indicated by rectangles. The diagram below shows a sample P/T net with four places (the set {S1, S2, S3, S4}) and three transitions: {T1, T2, T3}):

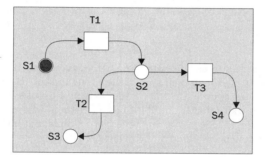

For a transition to fire, all places leading into it must be marked. Given the initial marking, called generation 0, shown above, the first generation of the P/T net shown will result in a token at place S2. In the following generation, the marking at S2 causes both T2 and T3 to fire, leading to tokens at S3 and S4. Those places have no transitions leading out of them, therefore the net will end with a terminal state in which S3 and S4 are marked.

Why bother with this? P/T nets are particularly well suited to the implementation of state transition machines, a well-known computing mechanism. Internet protocols are often specified as a series of state transitions. Chances are that the HTTP protocol in your browser is implemented as a state transition machine. Using P/T nets as our formal method takes us onto familiar and respected territory in computing.

Petri Nets, as a formal mathematical discipline, have many algorithms and theorems proven for them. Once we have a system specified as a Petri Net, we may use one of these algorithms to predict the behavior of that system. For example, if we search the Microsoft Developer Network for Petri Nets, we find three articles written in 1994 by Ruediger Asche. In that series, Asche develops an application that uses Petri Nets to detect deadlocks and predict the behavior of concurrent systems.

To find these articles, go to http://search.microsoft.com/us/dev/default.asp, select MSDN Library as the search target, and enter petri net as the search words. As of this writing (May 2001) the articles we refer to are the first three entries on the main search results list.

Petri Net Markup Language

The great fans of XML that we are, we intend to implement a P/T net for our Model using an XML document as the declaration of the net and an XSLT stylesheet as the declarative code that moves the token from place to place. To this end, we add two child elements to the content model of the Model element: PNEngine, which contains an XSLT transform element that powers the net, and pnml, an XML representation of the net. The pnml element is the more important of the two as PNEngine, like all declarative engines, can only respond to what it finds in the pnml element. Here is what the Model element will look like:

```
<Model>
    <PNEngine>
        <xsl:transform>
        ... <!-- XSLT stylesheet to power P/T net from net -->
        </xsl:transform>
    </PNEngine>
    <pnml>
    ... <!-- persistent net representation here -->
    </pnml>
</Model>
```

Fortunately for us, there is an existing XML vocabulary we can adapt to our needs. This is the Petri Net Markup Language (PNML). PNML is the work of Matthias Jüngel, Ekkart Kindler, and Michael Weber, at Humboldt University in Berlin. PNML was intended as a language for the exchange of Petri Nets between programs. As such, it is all about the structure of the net and does not contain any mechanism for simulating nets. It is a work in progress, so it is at present suited to the representation of simple Petri Nets. It also contains optional structures meant to convey a graphical representation of the net described in the document, structures which are of no use in our situation. We will be able to accomplish our immediate aims through one small addition to PNML and the deletion of the graphical information.

PNML is fully discussed at http://www.informatik.hu-berlin.de/top/pnml/. There is even a schema for PNML, but it conforms to an early draft of the W3C Schema effort and is not readily translated into the current syntax. Nevertheless, you will find several papers and a worked example to help you explore PNML. PNML is the most up to date and readily supported proposal; pointers to alternative markup vocabularies may be found at http://xml.coverpages.org/xmlAndPetriNets.html.

General Structure of a PNML Document

Here is the outer shell of a PNML document, as we shall use it:

```
<p:pnml xmlns:p="urn:pnml-working">
    <p:net id="SBP-sample" type="stNet">
        <p:place id="S1">
            ...
        </p:place>
```

```
        <p:transition id="T1">
            ...
        </p:transition>
        <p:arc id="a1" source="S1" target="T1"/>
    </p:net>
</p:pnml>
```

The document element for a PNML document, and the root of PNML sub tree in our `Application` vocabulary, is the `pnml` element. We are making ad hoc changes to the PNML schema, so we have chosen to use a URN of our own devising in lieu of the formal PNML namespace, as given by Jungel et al. Further, since this entire document will be contained within our own document and must be referenced in mixed XSLT, we have found it convenient to explicitly scope each PNML name with a namespace prefix.

Note that a PNML document consists of a single child `net` element, which contains a mix of `place`, `transition`, and `arc` elements in any order. The fragment shown has one instance of each type, and the `arc` element has the place as its `source` and the transition as its `target`.

Places

A `place` element does little more than declare a place in a Petri Net. It has an `id` attribute to uniquely identify it. It may also, optionally, have a child `name` element. Throughout PNML documents, that element is used to contain a human-readable description or label for the parent of the `name` element. The authors of PNML have chosen to declare `name`, which is used on `transition` elements as well, to contain a `value` element. The latter element is text-only and contains a descriptive string meant for human use. In the context of the place element, it is intended as a label for the visual depiction of the net. While this is, strictly speaking, a visual data item, we retain it in our use to make the Model more readable.

In PNML, as defined by its authors, the `place` element can have a `marking` element when the place has a token. PNML's authors envisioned the token as a simple marking, but we wish to open the vocabulary up to more robust use. In general, the `marking` element will have open content. We can use this content to contain arbitrary data, which has meaning to the application, powered by the net. We can envisage conditional transitions based on the content of the token as well as XSLT transformations of the token based on its passage through a given transition. The structure and use of tokens in PNML as used in SBP is very much an open issue for SBP researchers. For the purposes of this chapter, we'll use a text element to describe the real-world item represented by the contents of the token.

Here is an expansion of the `place` element we looked at above:

```
<p:place id="S1">
    <p:name>
        <p:value>This place is the initial state of the system</p:value>
    </p:name>
    <p:marking>
        <p:token>
            <!-- rich content here -->
        </p:token>
    </p:marking>
</p:place>
```

Transitions

A transition, in our current usage, is little more than a declaration of a simple item. Like place, it has an `id` attribute and an optional `name` element. In the future, we envision developing some sort of mechanism for performing conditional tests on tokens attempting to pass through the transition, as well as a container for an XSLT `transform` element meant to act on tokens making the transition. For now, however, transition remains a very simple structure as shown in this expansion of the transition given earlier:

```
<p:transition id="T1">
   <p:name>
      <p:value>First state transition in the application</p:value>
   </p:name>
</p:transition>
```

Arcs

Arcs are the edges that describe the permissible paths through the graph. In the context of a P/T net, they describe what happens in the system. They connect places representing states of the system with transitions; as such, they indicate what can happen to the system in any particular state. In and of themselves, they are not important – they have no labels and no internal state. This makes them particularly easy to model in XML, as all we need are two references, one to a place and one to a transition. Arcs have an explicit direction, one reference will be the `source` of the arc and the other will be the `target`. With this information, we can always tell what places feed a transition, and what places gain tokens when a transition occurs. Here is a sample `arc` element:

```
<p:arc id="a1" source="S1" target="T1"/>
```

XSLT Stylesheet for PNML

PNML helps us fill in one half of the `Model` element. The other half is the dynamic behavior of the Model. In a P/T net, this means a way of moving tokens through the net according to the rules of a P/T net. In this section, we will study an XSLT stylesheet, which will be embedded in the Model. Whenever an event occurs that effects the Model, the event handler procedural code will apply this stylesheet to the current PNML document, replacing the current document (the current state) with the PNML document resulting from the transformation (the succeeding state). Put another way, the input to the transformation is a PNML document representing the Model before the event, and the output is a PNML document representing the Model after the event.

The stylesheet that we'll discuss in this section is substantially the work of Michael Corning of Microsoft. The current author made limited modifications to accommodate the task of moving a rich token such as we have described.

Identifying States that Gain and Lose Tokens

Much of the stylesheet will be given over to simply copying existing elements and attributes into the output PNML document without change. After all, the structure of the P/T net remains unchanged in spite of the occurrence of the event. XSLT handles this very well with little help from the programmer. The key to the PNML-manipulating stylesheet is to identify which places are losing tokens and which are gaining them, based on the current marking of the net. To do this, we'll need to declare eight key variables. We'll need some supporting variables to construct these declarations, but these eight represent important concepts in the P/T net and are not merely supporting structures:

- ❑ Holding states – places that are currently marked with tokens

- ❑ Waiting states – places that are not marked with tokens

- ❑ Hot arcs – arcs leading from holding state places

- ❑ Cold arcs – arcs leading from waiting state places

- ❑ Enabled transitions – transitions all of whose source places are marked

- ❑ Disabled transitions – transitions with one or more unmarked source places

- ❑ Places losing tokens – places which are sources of enabled transitions

- ❑ Places gaining tokens – places which are the target of enabled transitions

It might seem, upon casual inspection, that places losing tokens are the same as holding states, and places gaining tokens are the same as waiting states. This is not the case; each is distinct. A holding state need not lose a token; in fact, it will not lose a token when one of the other sources of the transition to which it is connected as a source is not marked with a token. All sources must lose their tokens or none do. Similarly, waiting states will not gain tokens unless the transition, which is their source, is enabled. Let's take a look at how these variables are declared in our stylesheet. We'll assume that the context of the transformation is the pnml element. The first step is to declare some utility variables that locate the net itself, its places, transitions, and arcs:

```
<xsl:variable name="net" select="/p:pnml/p:net"/>

<xsl:variable name="places" select="$net/p:place"/>

<xsl:variable name="transitions" select="$net/p:transition"/>

<xsl:variable name="arcs" select="$net/p:arc"/>
```

Now we'll build up our eight essential variables in terms of these basics and their markings. Recall the definition of a holding state: a place that is marked. In PNML, that means we need an XPath expression that finds places that have a token element:

```
<xsl:variable name="holdingStates"
    select="$places[p:marking/p:token]"/>
```

Conversely, a waiting state is a place element that does *not* have a token:

```
<xsl:variable name="waitingStates"
    select="$places[not(p:marking/p:token)]"/>
```

Hot arcs are those whose source, identified by the source attribute, is a holding state. That means finding arc elements whose source value matches the value of an id attribute on a holding state. As we did with holding and waiting states, we can negate the condition to find cold arcs:

```
<xsl:variable name="hotArcs"
    select="$arcs[@source = $holdingStates/@id]"/>

<xsl:variable name="coldArcs"
    select="$arcs[not(@source = $holdingStates/@id)]"/>
```

Finding enabled transitions is a bit convoluted. We are looking for transitions which are targets of hot arcs (that is, arcs leading from a holding state) and which are not targets of cold arcs (that is, arcs leading from waiting states). Identifying the former means finding those transitions whose id attribute has a value that matches the value of the target attribute of a hot arc; satisfying the latter means negating the condition where the id of the transition matches the target attribute value of a cold arc. This is how the variable declaration looks in XSLT:

```
<xsl:variable name="enabledTransitions"
              select="$transitions[@id = $hotArcs/@target and
              not(@id = $coldArcs/@target)]"/>
```

Finding a disabled transition is easier. A transition is disabled whenever it is the target of a cold arc. We do not need to check whether or not it is also the target of a hot arc. One cold arc leading into the transition is sufficient to place the transition into the set of disabled transitions:

```
<xsl:variable name="disabledTransitions"
              select="$transitions[@id = $coldArcs/@target]"/>
```

Losing tokens are identified by the source attribute of hot arcs whose target is an enabled transition:

```
<xsl:variable name="loseTokens"
              select="$hotArcs[@target = $enabledTransitions/@id]/@source"/>
```

Gaining tokens requires a bit more explanation. They are identified by the target attribute of cold arcs whose source is an enabled transition. Hot arcs are those which are connected to a holding state - they are about to provide a path for the transition of a token. Cold arcs then, are those that are not connected to a holding state; this makes sense, as the source of an arc leading to a gaining state must be a transition. We need to narrow down the set of cold arcs, though. The source must be an enabled transition. If the source is not enabled, no token will pass through the arc to the place, so the place cannot be expected to gain a token. If the arc is cold, but the transition at its source is enabled, a token is about to pass through the transition, over the arc, and into the place. Such a place, then, is about to gain a token:

```
<xsl:variable name="gainTokens"
              select="$coldArcs[@source = $enabledTransitions/@id]/@target"/>
```

Controlling the Transformation

The stylesheet begins processing with the pnml element. Since this node will remain unchanged, we want to copy it intact with all its attributes, as they exist in the input:

```
<xsl:template match="/p:pnml">
   <xsl:copy>
      <xsl:copy-of select="@*"/>
```

Still within the copy element, we want to execute the remainder of the stylesheet's processing for each net element found, just in case we store more than one net within a PNML document. We copy the original net element's attributes to the newly copied net element, and then apply the template that matches nodes and attributes – essentially everything in the remainder of the document. When this is done, our processing is complete. This template, therefore, controls the overall flow of the transformation and is mainly a controlled copy of the input document:

```
<xsl:template match="/p:pnml">
    <xsl:copy>
        <xsl:copy-of select="@*"/>
        <xsl:for-each select="p:net">
            <xsl:copy>
                <xsl:copy-of select="@*"/>
                <xsl:apply-templates select="node()|@*"/>
            </xsl:copy>
        </xsl:for-each>
    </xsl:copy>
</xsl:template>
```

Below the level of the net element, we have to exercise some caution. The controlling template just shown passes control to a template that begins like this:

```
<xsl:template match="node()|@*">
    <xsl:if test="name() != 'p:token'">
        <xsl:copy>
            ... <!-- special conditions apply here -->
        </xsl:copy>
    </xsl:if>
</xsl:template>
```

This template is called recursively, as we shall see in a moment, so we cannot make any assumptions about what node is the current context when this template is called. We need special processing for tokens, therefore the very first thing we are going to do is test to see if the current node is a token element. If it is, we exit the template. We will move the token while we are processing waiting states that will gain tokens, but the recursive nature of this template is such that the token element of a losing state place node will be encountered anyway and we do not wish to copy it to the output document. Tokens encountered must, therefore, disappear, that is, be removed from the losing state.

Within the copy element, we are concerned with three conditions:

- ❑ The current context is a place losing a token

- ❑ The current context is a place gaining a token

- ❑ The current context is any other node

Here is what happens to places losing tokens:

```
<xsl:choose>
    <xsl:when test=".=$holdingStates[@id=$loseTokens]">
        <xsl:apply-templates select="node()|@*" mode="moveTokens"/>
    </xsl:when>
```

Note the addition of the mode attribute. This invokes a template that simply copies the node and, through recursion, all its children:

```
<xsl:template match="node()|@*" mode="moveTokens">
    <xsl:copy>
        <xsl:apply-templates select="node()|@*" mode="moveTokens"/>
    </xsl:copy>
</xsl:template>
```

Now return to the original node and attribute template. Let's skip over the gaining place case for a moment and look at the default processing case:

```
<xsl:otherwise>
    <xsl:apply-templates select="node()|@*"/>
</xsl:otherwise>
```

Since there is no mode attribute, the apply-templates element calls the template in which it appears (the one matching the expression node()|@*) recursively. This, incidentally, is how this template can encounter a token and why we had to insert the if element at the start of the template. A waiting state place, which is not losing a token, will satisfy this condition (name() != 'p:token') and recourse through its children using this template, that is, the one matching all nodes and attributes. This occurs when the transition, which is a target of the place, is disabled, that is, it has other sources, which are not marked.

The really interesting case is the one in which the current context is a place which is gaining a token. The condition met in this case is .=$waitingStates[@id=$gainTokens], as you can see below. We are showing the entire template to give context to the conditions we have just discussed in isolation:

```
<xsl:template match="node()|@*">
    <xsl:if test="name() != 'p:token'">
        <xsl:copy>
            <xsl:choose>
                <xsl:when test=".=$holdingStates[@id=$loseTokens]">
                    <xsl:apply-templates select="node()|@*" mode="moveTokens"/>
                </xsl:when>
                <xsl:when test=".=$waitingStates[@id=$gainTokens]">
                    <xsl:apply-templates select="node()|@*" mode="moveTokens"/>
                    <xsl:call-template name="state-transition">
                        <xsl:with-param name="target-id" select="@id"/>
                    </xsl:call-template>
                </xsl:when>
                <xsl:otherwise>
                    <xsl:apply-templates select="node()|@*"/>
                </xsl:otherwise>
            </xsl:choose>
        </xsl:copy>
    </xsl:if>
</xsl:template>
```

In the highlighted when element, we first apply the template that copies the place from the input document to the output. Next, we have to copy the token from the losing state place to this place in the output. We have moved those instructions to a named template called state-transition. That template takes one parameter, the id of the gaining state place, that is, the current node.

Rich Tokens

Recall that we are invoking the state-transition template from within the body of a gaining state place element and passing it the id of the place. Since we are creating a new token within the gaining place, we begin like this:

```
<xsl:template name="state-transition">
    <xsl:param name="target-id"/>
    <xsl:element name="p:marking">
        <xsl:element name="p:token">
```

This gives us a `marking` element with a child `token` element. Next, we want to copy the contents of the `token` node from the place that is losing the token. This is where the template becomes complex. To find that source, we have to look back at the transition, which is the source of the arc leading to the gaining place, and then back through that to all its sources. We may have more than one losing place.

> *There are a variety of ways to handle tokens in Petri Nets. Some permit only a single token per place, while others permit multiple tokens. This implementation will copy tokens from each losing place to each gaining place.*

The stylesheet was not originally set up for this sort of traversal, though the PNML vocabulary obviously is. The "schema is the API" and the schema supports the traversal, therefore we can get there, but we are certainly stretching the "API" to its limit. We declare a variable named `source`, which is a collection of places that are losing tokens, to the current gaining place:

```
<xsl:variable name="source"
              select="$holdingStates[@id=$loseTokens and @id=
              $hotArcs[@target=$enabledTransitions[@id=
              $coldArcs[@target=$target-id]/@source]/@id]/@source]"/>
```

You will notice that the `select` attribute has as its value what is perhaps the most ugly XPath expression we have ever written. We begin with the collection of holding states; tokens are obviously going to come from that collection. The filter pattern has two clauses conjoined. The first checks to see if a particular holding state is also in the list of losing states:

```
@id=$loseTokens
```

The next looks to see if the holding state is the source of a hot arc:

```
@id=$hotArcs[. . .]/@source
```

If only we could leave the filter pattern on `hotArcs` elided! Obviously though, we can't; the list of hot arcs includes every hot arc in the net. We need the subset of hot arcs, which happen to lead from a losing state to the transition in which we are interested. That transition, of course, is the one leading to the gaining state. The value of the `target` attribute on a candidate hot arc must be found in the list of enabled transitions in order to be considered:

```
[@target=$enabledTransitions[. . .]/@id
```

We refine the list of enabled transitions by looking for those enabled transitions whose `id` is the source of a cold arc. Remember, the arc from the transition to the gaining place will be cold:

```
@id=$coldArcs[. . .]/@source
```

Now we are very, very close. We need the particular cold arc whose target matches the target `id` passed into the template – the `id` of the gaining `place`:

```
@target=$target-id]/@source
```

Now that we have a list of source (or losing state) `place` nodes, we iterate through the list, copying their tokens to the gaining `place` element of the output document:

```
            <xsl:for-each select="$source">
                <xsl:copy-of select="$source/p:marking/p:token/*"/>
            </xsl:for-each>
        </xsl:element>
    </xsl:element>
</xsl:template>
```

That extended XPath expression that we saw above, is not nearly as elegant as the rest of the stylesheet – indeed, it's pretty gruesome as such things go, but it suffices to traverse the arcs from gaining places to their source losing places. When this stylesheet is used to transform the PNML document that records the state of our application, the result is a PNML document recording the state of the application's Model after the event. We can replace the old Model document in our `Application` XML document with the new Model document (a PNML document reflecting the transition) to update the state of the application. To see how that happens, let's apply our approach to a sample problem.

Sample Application

Our application will be a simulation of a very simple (and completely imaginary) chemical manufacturing process. In its initial state, the process takes in raw materials and loads them into a chemical reactor. The reactor produces refined unobtainium*. The bulk of the manufactured batch goes to a laboratory for quality control testing, although a small amount of unobtainium is recycled to the input step as seed material. At the completion of testing, the unobtanium goes to the loading dock for delivery to a client.

> *Unobtanium is, of course, that mythical substance engineers like to invoke when a desirable machine can't be made to work with materials found in the real world.*

A schematic of the process is depicted below:

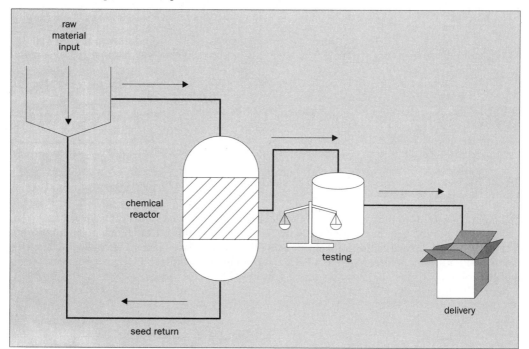

Our application must track the flow of unobtainium through the system. Initially, unobtainium will be present at the input step and nowhere else. The user of our application should be able to click on the user-interface to advance the system to the next time step. At each step, the user-interface should show where unobtainium is present in the system.

We are taking advantage of the DHTML model in Internet Explorer, as well as the XSLT implementation in Microsoft's MSXML 3.0 XML processor. You must have the latter installed as your default parser (that is, in replace mode), and you must use Internet Explorer as your browser. The application shown is intended to demonstrate the SBP technique, not provide a general technology for everyday use. We note, however, that there is nothing in SBP that cannot be implemented in other XML parsers and browsers. The technique itself relies on open technology. For simplicity and clarity in the code, we are providing an implementation tied to a very specific platform.

Model

The first step toward implementation is to devise a P/T (place/transition) net for the system. This is readily done from the schematic above. The graphical representation of the net is depicted below for the initial state of the system:

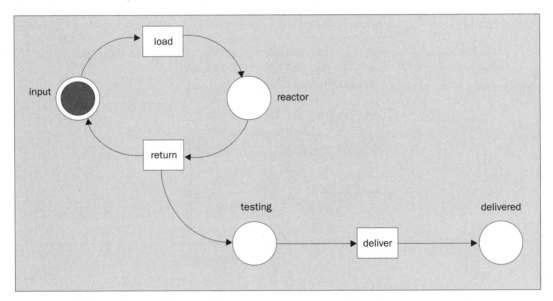

The input place leads to the reactor place through the load transition. The reactor place leads to both testing and input through the return transition. Note that when this transition occurs, both the input and testing places will be marked with tokens. Finally, the testing place leads to the delivered state through the deliver transition. Before we get to a PNML representation of this P/T net, lets consider the states of the application:

Time step	Input	Reactor	Testing	Delivered
0	X			
1		X		
2	X		X	
3		X		X

After the third time step, the net enters an endless cycle in which the markings of steps 2 and 3 alternate. So long as raw material is available for the input state, the net will cycle. Now, let's proceed to a PNML representation of the net. It will be embedded within the Model element of ChemNet.xml, immediately following the PNEngine element:

```
<p:pnml xmlns:p="urn:pnml-working">
    <p:net id="SBP-sample" type="stNet">
        <p:place id="input">
            <p:name>
<p:value>raw material input</p:value>
            </p:name>
            <p:marking>
                <p:token>
                    <p:RawMaterial>unobtainium</p:RawMaterial>
                </p:token>
            </p:marking>
        </p:place>
        <p:transition id="load">
            <p:name>
                <p:value>load chemical reactor</p:value>
            </p:name>
        </p:transition>
        <p:place id="reactor">
            <p:name>
                <p:value>chemical reactor</p:value>
            </p:name>
        </p:place>
        <p:transition id="return">
            <p:name>
                <p:value>return seed material</p:value>
            </p:name>
        </p:transition>
```

Note the marking element on the place element whose id has the value input. It has a child element token, which in turn has a textual element RawMaterial. We'll use the content of RawMaterial when we create our user interface. Having created the two places and two transitions that form the loop on the left side of the graph, we need to connect them with arcs:

```
<p:arc id="a1" source="input" target="load"/>
<p:arc id="a2" source="load" target="reactor"/>
<p:arc id="a3" source="reactor" target="return"/>
<p:arc id="a4" source="return" target="input"/>
```

Now, we'll finish the net. Note that we can mix places, transitions, and arcs in any order within the sequence without violating the content model of the net element:

```
<p:place id="testing">
    <p:name>
        <p:value>quality tests</p:value>
```

```
        </p:name>
      </p:place>
      <p:transition id="deliver">
        <p:name>
          <p:value>package and delivery</p:value>
        </p:name>
      </p:transition>
      <p:place id="dock">
        <p:name>
          <p:value>loading dock</p:value>
        </p:name>
      </p:place>
      <p:arc id="a5" source="return" target="testing"/>
      <p:arc id="a6" source="testing" target="delivery"/>
      <p:arc id="a7" source="delivery" target="dock"/>
    </p:net>
  </p:pnml>
```

This is fairly simple, albeit tedious. The important thing to remember when writing a PNML document by hand is to make sure the values in the `source` and `target` attributes of `arc` elements correctly refer to `place` and `transition` elements elsewhere in the document. Also, note that the `dock` place represents the delivered state in the above table and diagram.

View

We don't really want to watch tokens fly around a P/T net's graphical depiction. We want something to show to an end user. Here is the prototype of the user interface:

The interactive portion of the interface, our sole View, is the HTML table found between the horizontal rules. The first row consists of labels drawn from the places in the Model. The second row should take the value of the tokens and display them under the label of the marked place. The screen shot above shows the application at time step 3. When the application starts, the View should reflect step 0. Clicking anywhere on the table will advance the Model to the next time step.

You'll recall that the XML document (ChemNet.xml in the software download) is linked via a processing instruction to an initial XSLT stylesheet (ChemNet.xsl). That stylesheet generates the static parts of the interface and inserts an empty physical view. Here is how ChemNet.xsl begins:

```
<xsl:transform version="1.0"
               xmlns:xsl="http://www.w3.org/1999/XSL/Transform"
               xmlns:p="urn:pnml-working">
    <xsl:output method="html" indent="yes" omit-xml-declaration="yes" />
    <xsl:param name="mode">XML</xsl:param>
    <xsl:template match="/">
        <html>
            <head>
                <title>ChemNet SBP Demonstration</title>
```

The PNML namespace declaration has been added to the transform element. We've also started the shell of an HTML document and created a title. While we are still in the head element, we need to copy the Intentions into a script element. This inserts the Controller into the application:

```
<script language="Javascript">
    <xsl:for-each select="Application/Intentions">
        <xsl:apply-templates />
    </xsl:for-each>
</script>
```

Now we'll generate some of the static parts of the interface:

```
</head>
<body>
    <font face="Verdana" font-size="12pt">
        <strong>Chemical Manufacturing Simulation</strong>
    </font>
    <p/>
    <font face="Verdana" font-size="10pt">
        Powered by SBP and Petri Nets
    </font>
    <p/>
    <hr/>
```

Next, we insert the physical container for the View in the form of a div bearing the ID of netView. Note that this physical View is initially empty:

```
<div id="netView">
</div>
<hr/>
<font face="Verdana" font-size="8pt">
    Click table to advance one generation
</font>
</body>
</html>
</xsl:template>
```

That's the root-matching template. We need one more template – one that matches `codeBlock` elements and recursively copies their contents into the HTML page:

```
<xsl:template match="codeBlock">
    <xsl:if test="@mode=$mode">
        <xsl:apply-templates />
    </xsl:if>
</xsl:template>
</xsl:transform>
```

Note that we are testing the `codeBlock` element's `mode` attribute against the `mode` parameter set at the beginning of the stylesheet. This is not important in the client-only version, but if we were to mix in Controller information for a server-side version, it would be important to distinguish between the two versions.

The stylesheet is only a small part of the overall MVC View, a one shot affair that only executes once on startup of the application. When the program is running, it takes its transforms from the `view` elements in the `Application` document. There is a one-to-one relationship between physical views and logical views, so we expect to find a `view` element associated with the physical view `netView`. This transform, found in `ChemNet.xml`, has to generate the HTML table we saw in the screen shot above, taking labels and token information from the `pnml` document embedded in the Model. Here is how it starts:

```
<view id="net" boundTo="netView">
    <xsl:transform version="1.0"
                   xmlns:xsl="http://www.w3.org/1999/XSL/Transform"
                   xmlns:p="urn:pnml-working">
```

The `id` of this `view` element is `net`. The value of the `boundTo` element refers to the physical view (`div`) in the HTML page. Note that we've had to declare the PNML namespace again. When this stylesheet is encountered, it is the only stylesheet running; the separate stylesheet is long gone.

The root-matching template of this stylesheet will set out the HTML table structure, and populate the first row with the labels found in the `name` elements of the PNML document:

```
<xsl:template match="/">
    <table border="1">
        <tr>
            <xsl:for-each select="Application/Model/p:pnml/p:net/p:place">
                <td align="middle">
                    <font face="Verdana" font-size="10pt">
                        <xsl:value-of select="p:name/p:value"/>
                    </font>
                </td>
            </xsl:for-each>
```

The `for-each` element iterates through every `place` in the net, causing the `value-of` element within it to copy the labels from the source document. Next, we close the first row of the table and look for tokens:

```
        </tr>
        <tr>
            <xsl:for-each select="Application/Model/p:pnml/p:net/p:place">
```

The `for-each` element makes each `place` element in the source document the context node in turn. For each one of these, we want to check for a token and copy some information from the token, if found. We'll delegate that to a named template. We're setting a `font` element with a `color` attribute of red: if any text is copied from the `token` element, it will appear in the table as red text:

```
            <td align="middle">
                <font face="Verdana" color="red" font-size="8pt">
                    <xsl:call-template name="token-out">
                        <xsl:with-param name="token"
                                        select="p:marking/p:token"/>
                    </xsl:call-template>
                </font>
            </td>
        </xsl:for-each>
    </tr>
</table>
</xsl:template>
```

We called the `token-out` template with the `token` element, if any, as a parameter. This is what `token-out` looks like:

```
<xsl:template name="token-out">
    <xsl:param name="token"/>
    <xsl:if test="$token">
        <xsl:value-of select="$token/p:RawMaterial"/>
    </xsl:if>
</xsl:template>
</xsl:transform>
</view>
```

We call `token-out` for every `place`, therefore we first want to check and see if that `place` was marked. If it isn't, the `token` parameter will be `null` and the `test` expression of the `if` element will fail. If a token exists, the place was marked and we copy the text of the token's `RawMaterial` child element into the table.

`ChemNet.xsl` worked with the model to give us the shell of our interface. The contents of the `view` element gave us a transform that regenerates the HTML table every time the event fires. So long as it is invoked after the Model is updated, our interface will faithfully reflect the state of the system following the event. Making that happen is the job of the Controller.

Controller

We need to do three things to implement a Controller for our application: define an event for a user click on the view, write the `initialize` function that starts the Controller when the page loads, and write an event handler that invokes the `view` transform when the event occurs.

Define an Event

This task is simple. We create an `event` element in the `Application` document following the `Intensions` element. The `event` element does two things: provide a name for the event, and refer to the logical view that must receive the event.

The event name is an arbitrary string. Our user click serves as a pulse that moves the system ahead one generation, therefore we will call that event **pulse**. The sole logical view in our application is `net`. This is also the logical view behind the physical view where the event occurred, so it makes sense to notify that view (`net`) of the event occurrence. Here is the event element, found in `ChemNet.xml` immediately after the `Intensions` element's closing tag and right before the `view` elements:

```
<event id="pulse" notify="net"/>
```

Write the Initialize Function

When we covered the `codeBlock` element in the Application schema we showed a series of functions that are common to all SBP applications. At that time, we mentioned a mandatory function, `initialize`, which is called by the main code section after the page loads. It serves to add event handler functions to the views as well as adding the `transform` function to the `view` object. Usually, `initialize` also fires the first event of the application's lifecycle.

Views vary from application to application, and applications will have different events, therefore we cannot write a common `initialize` function. Consequently, it is our responsibility to write one from scratch for this application. We have but one event and one view, so our implementation will be short. Remember, this function is found within a `code` element in `ChemNet.xml`:

```
function initialize()
{
   netView.onclick=OnViewClick;
   netView.transform=transform;
   notify("pulse");
}
```

Remember that `netView` is the name of the `div` acting as our physical view. We want to connect the DHTML `onclick` event to our application so that Internet Explorer will notify us when an event has occurred. The first line informs Internet Explorer that it needs to call our script function `OnViewClick` when a user click occurs on the `netView` div. The second line makes our `transform` function, which is common code in any SBP application, an expansion function of the view. The `notify` function, also common code, calls the `transform` method on the current page object without knowing exactly which object that is. If we want our `transform` function to be called correctly, we need to connect it to `netView` in this way.

The `initialize` function is called after `ChemNet.xsl` has created an HTML page and that page is loaded into the browser window. That stylesheet created the shell of the interface. In particular, `netView` was empty. If we want the user to see anything when the application appears on screen, we have to fire the pulse event. We do not want to call the event handler, however. The event handler function will update the Model before it calls `notify`. When the application starts, however, the Model PNML document already reflects the initial state of the system. All we want to do is update the View. Consequently, we call `notify` ourselves. When `initialize` completes following the call to `notify`, the user interface is complete and a table reflecting time step 0 is visible to the user.

Writing the Event Handler

The event handler resides in its own `code` element within `ChemNet.xml`. Once the initial stylesheet has loaded this code into the running document, `ChemNet.xml` becomes a wholly self-contained application. The Controller is going to use attributes of this element to locate the physical view that receives the results of the XSLT as well as associating this handler with the pulse event. The content of the element is a JavaScript function. In `initialize`, we told Internet Explorer to call a function named `OnViewClick` when a DHTML `onclick` event occurred, so the function we write here had better be named `OnViewClick`:

```
<code id="OnViewClick" boundTo="netView" event="pulse">
   function OnViewClick()
   {
       ...  // implementation here
   }
</code>
```

The event handler has tasks: update the Model and call `notify`, passing it the string `pulse` as a parameter. In order to update the Model, we must locate the PNML document and the XSLT transform inside the `PNEngine` element, apply the latter to the former, and insert the result back into the `Model` element, replacing the old `pnml` element:

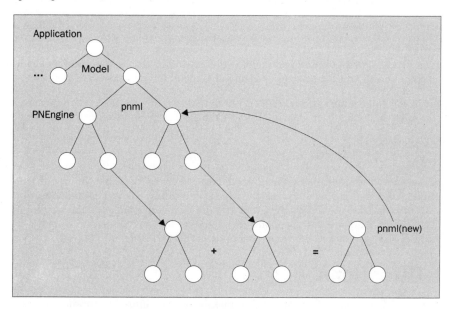

We begin by locating the two documents (`PNEngine` and `pnml`) with which we wish to work using MSXML's `selectSingleNode` method, and XPath expressions:

```
function OnViewClick()
{
    var parent;
    var stateTransform=
        model.selectSingleNode("/Application/Model/PNEngine").firstChild;
    var stateModel = model.selectSingleNode("/Application/Model/p:pnml");
```

The stylesheet we need is actually the immediate child of the `PNEngine` element. Now, we need the result of the XSLT transformation to be an object we can insert into the `Application` document. MSXML's `transformNodeToObject` method will do this for us, but, unhappily, it only accepts streams and XML documents as output targets. It will not take a node. Further, the transform we wrote to power the P/T net only works on whole documents. Given these conditions, it makes sense to load the pnml subtree we located in the last step into a new instance of the MSXML parser and ready an empty instance to receive the results of the transformation:

```
    var newState = new ActiveXObject("MSXML2.DOMDocument.3.0");
    var oldState = new ActiveXObject("MSXML2.DOMDocument.3.0");
```

```
    newState.async=false;
    oldState.async=false;
    oldState.loadXML(stateModel.xml);
```

Now we perform the transformation, starting with the document element of the pnml document:

```
    oldState.transformNodeToObject(stateTransform, newState);
```

We can use the replaceChild method to swap the new pnml document (now resident in newState), but that requires finding the Model element, which is the parent of the old pnml document subtree:

```
    parent = stateModel.parentNode;
    parent.replaceChild(newState.documentElement, stateModel);
```

The replaceChild method's first parameter is the new node, that is, the node replacing an existing node in the document, while the second parameter is the old node we wish to replace.

At this point, the application's Model reflects the time step following the event, so we can go ahead and instruct the View to update itself. We do this by calling notify and passing in the name of the event:

```
    notify("pulse");
}
```

That's all there is to the Controller. Whenever the user clicks on the table, Internet Explorer will call the event handler. OnViewClick will update the Model and call notify. That function will rely on common Controller code to identify the event and the view requiring notification from information in the event element. At that point, the Controller retrieves the view transform from the logical view, performs the XSLT, and inserts the results, an updated HTML table, into the physical view.

Future Directions

As you can see, SBP is just getting started. Happily, the tools required to conduct research into SBP are modest. There is no good reason why you cannot get busy with the tools you have at hand and begin constructing SBP applications.

There is much room for improvement in the area of development tools. An effective XSLT debugger has long been desired in the XML community, and yet the tools currently available are rudimentary when compared to their procedural counterparts. We need a debugger that allows developers to dynamically attach to an XSLT from within a procedural script debugger, or permit a programmer to set a breakpoint on a transform element so that the XSLT debugger will trigger when the transform comes into use.

If we are going to continue to use Petri Nets, we need modeling tools for their graphical construction that can export PNML documents. Drawing tools like Visio could be adapted. Once a net has been created, a simulation tool would be highly desirable. For example, instead of the interface we provided in our sample application, it would be useful at design time to see a graphical depiction of the underlying net that could be animated. With a PNML representation of the system, we could apply an XSLT that would result in a Scalable Vector Graphics (SVG) document. Viewers for SVG are slowly becoming available, most notably Adobe's plug-in for Netscape and Internet Explorer (see http://www.adobe.com/svg for the free download). This capability should be folded into an SBP debugger, allowing programmers to replace the runtime user interface of an SBP application with a dynamically generated view of the Model. In fact, this would be something wholly new to programmers.

Currently, when working in procedural languages, developers cannot directly view the Model. They must infer defects in operation, based on viewing the user interface and taking measurements through debuggers. Formal design tools are used at design time ,but rarely allow simulation of the system. Certainly, they cannot be invoked from a debugger to examine the behavior of an application in a rigorous way. Since our Model is based on a formal method and we are using a known representation of the data (PNML), it becomes possible for a third party debugger to attach to a running SBP application, examine its Model, and provide the developer with a direct view into the internal behavior of the system.

While we are congratulating ourselves on the use of formal methods, we should note that we haven't taken advantage of the predictive algorithms proven for Petri Nets. We envision a future design tool that would let a developer draw a net for his application, then check for potential deadlocks and race conditions. By applying spanning algorithms (see a good computing algorithms book such as **Algorithms in C++** by Robert Sedgwick (*ISBN 0-201-51059-6*) published by Addison-Wesley, 1992) to the net, the development tool could display a list of the possible code paths, that is, different ways the program can execute, together with an estimate of their performance. This would be something new in the practice of software development – prediction through design, rather than development from a static design. Prediction avoids bugs; development from a static design requires testing to uncover bugs and can never guarantee that the design will always be completely defect free. Prediction relies on a formal model proceeding from a theory, such as Petri Nets. The reason is that only a formal theory, with proven mathematical results, lets us make rigorous predictions and assertions. The practice of software as an art, with only a loose connection to rigorous theory, does not allow us to make provable assertions.

Of more immediate concern is the task of improving the expressive potential of Petri Nets as used in SBP. Two areas under investigation are conditional transitions and transformation of rich tokens in the course of a transition.

Right now, with P/T nets as we have implemented them in this chapter, the only condition controlling the movement from one state to another through a transition is the one that says all source places of a transition must be marked before the transition can occur. This is satisfactory if tokens are simple integer markings. Rich tokens, though, are desirable because they give us the ability to use data structures as tokens. Instead of the string we used, we could have XML fragments capturing some state that changed over the course of moving through the net. In such cases, we might like to associate some programmer-supplied conditions on transitions. You might wish to allow a transition if and only if all source places are marked with tokens and the state of the token meets some condition. XPath permits conditional expressions, but unfortunately XSLT does not allow variables to be evaluated as part of an if element. For example, if the PNML document contained a condition element as a child of transition such as <condition> token/MyData/item/@cost > 50 </condition>, the PNEngine transform cannot do the following to check the condition:

```
<xsl:variable name="condition" select="condition"/>
<xsl:if test="$condition">
```

The if element will evaluate true whenever there is a condition element because the variable is not null. The condition we desire – a check of the token's cost attribute – will not be evaluated. The condition would have to be explicitly written into the PNEngine transform in order to work as we expect, thereby negating the advantage of having a general-purpose Petri Net engine. We could resort to XSLT extensions – Java classes or script code depending on the processor vendor – but these would be procedural, losing the advantage of transparency.

At the moment, transformation of rich tokens appears amenable to a declarative solution. This will involve yet another layer of transforms, however. Now, the token will have to be extracted in the way we extracted the pnml document in our Model. Following a transformation using a `transform` element embedded in the pnml document – preferably linked in so that programmers do not have to rewrite the basic transform! – the resultant token would be inserted into the new pnml within the gaining place. As the number of transformation steps in our scheme grows, serious thought will have to be given to performance, particularly how document structure – the Schema – impacts performance.

Summary

This chapter was intended to give you motivation for writing schemas beyond their use in document validation. With SBP, the structure of your XML vocabulary directly controls what that vocabulary can accomplish. The declarative code – view transforms and PNML-manipulating stylesheets – react to input documents. Side effects occur only when the pattern of data presented satisfy the XPath expressions governing the selection of templates in the XSLT stylesheets. Even validation takes on new meaning. When rich tokens become broadly supported, we can validate tokens following a transition to ensure the integrity and correct functioning of our application. As such, they become an internal check in the engine to detect errors in processing. SBP applications that validate to a schema would warn of impending problems before bugs occur rather than crashing as a result of their execution.

Central to our implementation of SBP are two techniques that predate SBP: the Model-View-Controller paradigm and Petri Nets. MVC gave us a framework on which to build our `Application` schema. The separation of visual interface from internal processing allowed us to create XSLT transforms for the views in isolation from the transform needed to power the Model. We were able to introduce Petri Nets, with all the promise of formal methods, without concerning ourselves unduly with the code needed to implement the visual interface.

The basic operation of an SBP application is generalized. We have common procedural code and XML structures to implement the Controller. An XSLT stylesheet distinct from the XML document containing the main application jumpstarts the process, rendering the shell of the interface and copying the controller code into the running application. Although the amount of code written for an SBP application appears formidable on first inspection, the amount of custom code is really quite small and limited to application features unique to the application. An SBP programmer writes the following:

- ❑ User interface (view) transforms and `view` elements
- ❑ `event` elements and event handler functions
- ❑ The body of the `initialize` function
- ❑ The static portion (pnml in our example) of the Model

SBP is an interesting research problem well suited to amateur investigation. It holds promise for advancing the state of programming practice through the use of declarative languages for implementation and formal methods for design and prediction. Even if this promise is not realized, the practice of SBP gives you new insight into the implications inherent in an XML Schema, and a thorough test of your XSLT skills.

> *Presently, there is very little on the Web regarding SBP. Michael Corning's work is described at* http://www.aspalliance.com/mcorning *and* http://www.terracogito.redmond.wa.us/blueprints.htm.

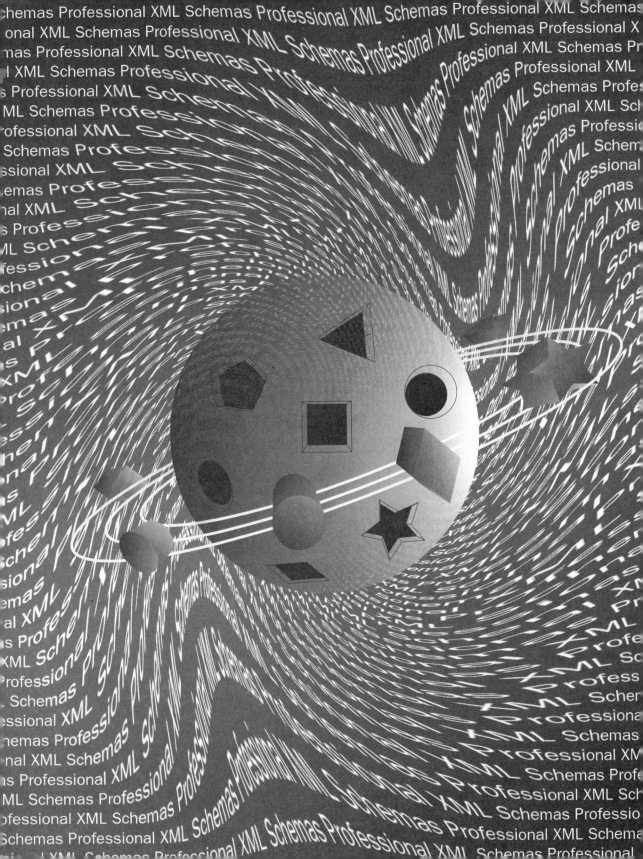

Schema Element and Attribute Reference

In this appendix, we provide a full listing of all the elements that form part of the XML Schema Structures Recommendation (found at http://www.w3.org/TR/xmlschema-1/). The elements are given in alphabetical order, and each element is described, an example or two is given, followed by a table detailing all of those attributes that element can carry. Required attributes are denoted by bold text.

Note that the constraining facets are not included here, but in the next appendix, together with a listing of all the built-in datatypes to which they apply.

At the end of this appendix, we present a table of the XML Schema attributes that can be used in instance documents, and are in the XMLSchema-Instance namespace.

all

The elements contained within this element, are allowed to appear in any order within the instance documents. The `all` element may be declared within a `complexType` or a `group`. It can contain `element` or `annotation` elements. Note that when using `minOccurs` and `maxOccurs` on element declarations within an `all` element, you cannot set a multiplicity higher than 1 with `maxOccurs`, although you can make an element optional with `minOccurs`. These limitations do not apply to these attributes when they are applied to the `all` element itself.

Example

```
<xs:element name = "Rucksack">
  <xs:complexType>
    <xs:all>
      <xs:element name = "Sunglasses" type = "xs:string"
```

```
                          minOccurs = "0" maxOccurs = "1" />
        <xs:element name = "Sweater" type = "xs:string" />
                              minOccurs = "0" maxOccurs = "1" />
        <xs:element name = "Book" type = "xs:string" />
        <xs:element name = "Lunchbox" type = "xs:string" />
        <xs:element name = "Flask" type = "xs:string" />
      </xs:all>
    </xs:complexType>
  </xs:element>
```

Attributes

Attribute	Value Space	Description
id	ID	Gives a unique identifier to the element.
maxOccurs	nonNegativeInteger or unbounded	The maximum number of times the model group can occur.
minOccurs	nonNegativeInteger	The minimum number of times the model group can occur.

For more information: see Chapter 3, and §3.8.2 of the Recommendation.

annotation

The annotation element is used to provide informative / explanatory data to be read by machines or humans. It may contain appinfo, or documentation elements, which are used to contain instructions for the processing application and schema documentation comments respectively. It is contained by most elements (excluding itself); specific cases are detailed below.

Example

An example of using annotation with documentation:

```
<xs:element name = "Person">
   <xs:annotation>
      <xs:documentation>
         Used to contain personal information. Note that the last name
         is mandatory, while the first name is optional.
      </xs:documentation>
   </xs:annotation>
   <!-- definition of Person element goes here -->
</xs:element>
```

An example of using annotation with appinfo:

```
<xs:element name="purchaseOrder" type="PurchaseOrderType">
   <xs:annotation>
      <xs:appinfo>
         <sch:pattern name="Top Level Purchase Order elements">
            <sch:rule context="/*">
               <sch:assert test="self::purchaseOrder">
                  The root element must be a "purchaseOrder"
```

```
                </sch:assert>
              </sch:rule>
            </sch:pattern>
          </xs:appinfo>
        </xs:annotation>
      </xs:element>
```

In this second example, the `annotation` element is used to contain a schematron schema inside the `appinfo` element.

For more information: see Chapters 1, 9 and 14, and §3.13.2 of the Recommendation.

any

This is wildcard element that acts as a placeholder for any element in a model group; the `any` element is never the direct child of an `element` element. The content may be validated against another namespace if desired. This is useful, for instance, if unspecified XHTML, or MathML content may be included within the instance document. It may contain an `annotation` element, and can be contained by `choice` or `sequence`.

Example

```
<xs:element name = "XHTMLSection">
   <xs:complexType>
      <xs:sequence>
         <xs:any namespace = "http://www.w3.org/1999/xhtml"
              minOccurs = "0" maxOccurs = "unbounded"
              processContents = "lax" />
      </xs:sequence>
   </xs:complexType>
</xs:element>
```

Here, an `XHTMLSection` element in an instance document can contain any well-formed markup that is valid in the XHTML namespace.

Attributes

Attribute	Value Space	Description
id	ID	Gives a unique identifier to the element.
maxOccurs	nonNegativeInteger or unbounded	The maximum number of times the model group can occur.
minOccurs	nonNegativeInteger	The minimum number of times the model group can occur.

Table continued on following page

Attribute	Value Space	Description
namespace	##any | ##other | List of (anyURI | ##targetNamespace | ##local)	##any means that the content can be of any namespace. ##other refers to any namespace other than the target namespace of the schema. Otherwise, a whitespace separated list of the namespaces of allowed elements, which can include ##targetNamespace to allow elements in the target namespace of the schema and ##local to allow elements in no namespace. The default is ##any.
processContents	lax | skip | strict	If lax, validation is performed if possible. If skip, then no validation occurs. If strict, validation is enforced, and 'the validator needs to be able to find declarations for the elements used. The default is skip.

For more information: see Chapter 3, and §3.10.2 of the Recommendation.

anyAttribute

Like any, this element is a wildcard element, only this allows unspecified attributes to be present. Again, these can be validated against a specific namespace. For example, XML Schema allows elements to have any attributes as long as they're not in the XML Schema namespace or no namespace. You might find this useful to allow the use of any XLink attribute on an element. Can be contained by attributeGroup, complexType, extension, or restriction, and like most elements and can contain an annotation.

Example

```
<xs:element name = "SomeElement">
   <xs:complexType>
      <!-- content definition goes here-->
      <xs:anyAttribute namespace = "http://www.w3.org/1999/xlink" />
   </xs:complexType>
</xs:element>
```

Attributes

Attribute	Value Space	Description
id	ID	Gives a unique identifier to the element.
namespace	##any | ##other | List of (anyURI | ##targetNamespace | ##local)"	The same rules and defaults apply as for the any element, described above.
processContents	skip | lax | strict	The same rules and defaults apply as for the any element, described above.

For more information: see Chapter 3, and §3.4.2 of the Recommendation.

appinfo

This allows information to be supplied to an application reading the schema, perhaps containing unique identifiers, or additional tags to help an application perform further processing on the schema. It is always used inside the `annotation` element, as described above.

Example

```
<xs:element name="purchaseOrder" type="PurchaseOrderType">
   <xs:annotation>
      <xs:appinfo>
         <sch:pattern name="Top Level Purchase Order elements">
            <sch:rule context="/*">
               <sch:assert test="self::purchaseOrder">
                  The root element must be a "purchaseOrder"
               </sch:assert>
            </sch:rule>
         </sch:pattern>
      </xs:appinfo>
   </xs:annotation>
</xs:element>
```

Attributes

Attribute	Value Space	Description
source	anyURI	Specifies a URI where the parser can acquire the required appinfo content.

For more information: see Chapters 1, 10, and 14, and §3.13.2 of the Recommendation.

attribute

This is used to declare attributes and/or indicate the presence of an attribute. It is usually found within an `attributeGroup` or a `complexType` and so defines the attributes for that particular content model. It can also be used in an `extension` or `restriction` element, however, when deriving a new type, or inside the root `schema` element to create global attribute definitions that can be referenced from other declarations. The `attribute` element may contain an `annotation`. It may also contain an anonymous `simpleType` declaration, if there's no `type` attribute.

Example

```
<xs:attribute name = "Amount">
   <xs:simpleType name="positiveDecimalN.2" >
      <xs:restriction base="xs:decimal" >
         <xs:minInclusive value="0" />
         <xs:fractionDigits value="2" />
      </xs:restriction>
   </xs:simpleType>
</xs:attribute>

<xs:element name = "Payment">
   <xs:complexType >
```

```
        <xs:attribute ref = "Amount" />
        <xs:attribute name = "currency" type = "xs:string" default = "US$"
                                                    use = "optional" />

    </xs:complexType>
  </xs:element>
```

Attributes

Attribute	Value Space	Description
default	string	A string containing the value of the attribute, if the attribute has not been specified in an instance document.
fixed	string	If present, the value of the attribute in an instance document must always match the value specified by fixed.
form	qualified| unqualified	If qualified, then the attribute must be namespace qualified in the instance document. Note that if the form attribute is present on the attribute element then it overrides attributeFormDefault on the schema element.
id	ID	Gives a unique identifier to the element.
name	NCName	The name of the attribute, conforming to the XML NCNAME datatype.
ref	QName	Specify a previously defined attribute name, allows us to inherit its properties.
type	QName	The datatype of the attribute.
use	optional | prohibited | required	If optional, then the attribute may be omitted in the instance document. If required, it must be included, and if prohibited, it cannot be included. The default is optional.

For more information: see Chapters 1, 6 (for more on namespace qualification), and §3.3.2 of the Recommendation.

attributeGroup

This allows us to specify and refer to a group of attribute definitions for multiple use – that is, when we want more than one element to carry the same group of elements. It may contain annotation, attribute, attributeGroup, and anyAttribute. There are two ways that attributeGroup (and group) elements are used. Initially, we can define the group at the top level of the schema (as a child of the schema element), and secondly, we can reference that definition from within a complexType definition. Attribute group definitions can be nested, so attributeGroup can contain or be contained by another attributeGroup. It can also be referenced from within a redefine, extension, or restriction when creating a new type.

Example

```
<xs:attributeGroup name = "myAttrGroup">
   <xs:attribute name = "weight" type = "xs:decimal" use = "optional" />
   <xs:attribute name = "height" type = "xs:decimal" use = "optional" />
</xs:attributeGroup>

<xs:element name = "Person">
   <xs:complexType>
      <xs:sequence>
         <!-- element content here -->
      </xs:sequence>
      <xs:attributeGroup ref = "myAttrGroup" />
   </xs:complexType>
</xs:element>
```

Attributes

Attribute	Value Space	Description
id	ID	Gives a unique identifier to the element.
name	NCName	The name of this attribute group.
ref	QName	Reference to another attribute group; used when referring back to a previously defined group.

For more information: see Chapter 3 and §3.6.2 of the Recommendation.

choice

When the choice element is used, we can specify that the contents specified within this tag are *mutually exclusive*. That is, one and only one of its immediate children can appear in the instance document. It may contain annotation, element, group, choice, sequence, or any elements, so we can nest content models. Similarly, it can be contained by choice, complexType, group, or sequence.

Example

```
<xs:element name = "IceCream">
   <xs:complexType>
      <xs:sequence>
         <xs:choice>
            <xs:element name = "Strawberry" type = "xs:string" />
            <xs:element name = "Chocolate" type = "xs:string" />
         </xs:choice>
         <xs:choice>
            <xs:element name = "Cone" type = "xs:string" />
            <xs:element name = "Tub" type = "xs:string" />
         </xs:choice>
      </xs:sequence>
   </xs:complexType>
</xs:element>
```

Attributes

Attribute	Value Space	Description
id	ID	Gives a unique identifier to the element.
maxOccurs	nonNegativeInteger or unbounded	The maximum number of times the model group can occur.
minOccurs	nonNegativeInteger	The minimum number of times the model group can occur.

For more information: see Chapter 3, and §3.8.2 of the Recommendation.

complexContent

This element is used to extend or restrict complex types. It indicates that the resulting content model can carry attributes, and will contain element content or mixed content, or even be empty. This element is used inside a complexType, and can contain annotation, restriction, or extension.

Example

```
<xs:complexType name="CAN_Address">
    <xs:complexContent>
        <xs:extension base="Address">
            <xs:sequence>
                <xs:element name="Province" type="xs:string" />
                <xs:element name="PostalCode" type="CAN_PostalCode"/>
            </xs:sequence>
        </xs:extension>
    </xs:complexContent>
</xs:complexType>
```

Attributes

Attribute	Value Space	Description
id	ID	Gives a unique identifier to the element.
mixed	boolean	If true, then the content is specified as being mixed. The default is false.

For more information: see Chapter 4 and §3.4.2 of the Recommendation.

complexType

This specifies that the type is complex type – that is, it can have element content and/or carry attributes. Complex type definitions are the key to the creation of complex structures and content models in XML Schema. Anything that is more complex than simple character data is essentially a complex type. They are usually declared within an element element, or globally within the schema element, but they can also be used from within redefine. A complexType has an optional annotation element. It may be derived from another type, in which case it contains simpleContent or complexContent element. Alternatively, it can specify a model group directly using group, all, choice, or sequence, followed by an attribute declaration using attribute, attributeGroup, or anyAttribute elements.

610

Example

```
<xs:element name = "ResearchPaper">
  <xs:complexType mixed = "true">
    <xs:sequence>
      <xs:element name = "Hypothesis" type = "xs:string" />
      <xs:element name = "Conclusion" type = "ConclusionType" />
    </xs:sequence>
    <xs:attribute name = "paperID" type = "xs:integer" />
  </xs:complexType>
</xs:element>
<xs:complexType name = "ConclusionType" block = "#all">
  <xs:simpleContent>
    <xs:extension base="xs:string">
      <xs:attribute name = "accepted" type = "xs:boolean" />
    </xs:extension>
  </xs:simpleContent>
</xs:complexType>
```

Attributes

Attribute	Value Space	Description
abstract	boolean	This specifies whether the complex type can be used to validate an element. If abstract is true, then it can't – you have to derive other types from it for it to be useful. Note that this behavior is distinct from using the abstract attribute on the element element (see below). The default is false.
block	#all | List of (extension | restriction)	Allows the schema author to prevent derived types being used in the instance document in place of this type (which can be done with the xsi:type attribute). extension and restriction, prevent the use of types derived by extension and restriction respectively, and #all prevents the use of any derived type.
final	all | List of (extension | restriction)	This attribute restricts the derivation of a new datatype by extension or restriction within the schema. The values it takes act in the same way as those for block.
id	ID	Gives a unique identifier to the type.
mixed	boolean	Specifies whether or not the content of this datatype is mixed.
name	NCName	The name of the datatype specified.

For more information: see Chapter 1, Chapter 3 and §3.4.2 of the Recommendation.

documentation

Content is used in this to help document the schema, for example, on an element-by-element basis, to indicate how certain structures should be used and so forth. This facilitates automatic generation of documentation for a schema. Complex content is permitted within the documentation tag, so you could include, for example, well-formed XHTML. The `documentation` tag is always contained within `annotation`.

Example

```
<xs:element name = "Person">
   <xs:annotation>
      <xs:documentation>
         Used to contain personal information. Note that the last name
         is mandatory, while the first name is optional.
      </xs:documentation>
   </xs:annotation>
   <!-- definition of Person element goes here -->
</xs:element>
```

Attributes

Attribute	Value Space	Description
source	anyURI	Specifies the URI where the content of this element may be found. You don't need this attribute, if the content is specified within the documentation tag as in the example above.
xml:lang	language	Specifies the language, using a code defined by RFC 3066. Most languages can be identifies by a simple two letter code.

For more information: see Chapters 1 and 9, and §3.13.2 of the Recommendation.

element

Possibly the most important schema namespace element, this declares the elements that can occur in the instance document. It can contain a `simpleType` or a `complexType` depending on the content definition, and `unique`, `key`, or `keyref` elements to define identity constraints. As with most elements, it can also contain an `annotation`. Elements are declared within model groups using `all`, `choice`, or `sequence`, or can be declared globally as children of the `schema` element.

Example

```
<xs:element name = "Customer">
   <xs:complexType>
      <xs:sequence>
         <xs:element name = "FirstName" type = "xs:string" />
         <xs:element name = "MiddleInitial" type = "xs:string" />
         <xs:element name = "LastName" type = "xs:string" />
      </xs:sequence>
      <xs:attribute name = "customerID" type = "xs:string" />
   </xs:complexType>
</xs:element>
```

Attributes

Attribute	Value Space	Description
abstract	boolean	Specifies that the element is abstract, and so it cannot appear in the instance document, but must be substituted with another element. The default is `false`.
block	`#all` | List of (substitution | extension | restriction)	Prevents derived types being used in place of this element, in the instance document (which can be done with the `xsi:type` attribute) and/or substituting another element in its place. `extension` and `restriction` prevent the use of types derived by extension and restriction respectively, and `#all` prevents the use of any derived type.
default	string	Allows us to specify a default value for the element, if a value is not included in the instance document.
final	`#all` | List of (extension | restriction)	This prevents the element being nominated as the head element in a substitution group, which has members derived by `extension` and/or `restriction` as appropriate.
fixed	string	If present in the instance document, the value of the element must always match the specified string value.
form	qualified | unqualified	If `qualified`, then the element must be namespace qualified in the instance document. The value of this attribute overrides whatever is specified by the `elementFormDefault` on the `schema` element.
id	ID	Gives a unique identifier to the type.
maxOccurs	nonNegativeInteger | unbounded	The maximum number of times the element can occur.
minOccurs	nonNegativeInteger	The minimum number of times the element can occur.
name	NCName	The name of the element.
nillable	boolean	If true, the element may have a nil value specified with `xsi:nil` in the instance document. The default is `false`.

Table continued on following page

Attribute	Value Space	Description
ref	QName	This attribute allows us to reference a globally defined element, using the value of that element's name attribute.
substitutionGroup	QName	The element becomes a member of the substitution group, specified by this attribute. Wherever the head element of the substitution group is used in a model group, we can substitute this element in its place.
type	QName	The type of the content of this element, which could be simple or complex.

For more information: see Chapters 1, 3 and 6, and §3.3.2 of the Recommendation.

extension

This element is used to extend a base type with further element or attribute declarations. When adding element content to a type, the extension element may contain one or more of element, group, choice or sequence. When adding attributes, it will contain the attribute, attributeGroup or anyAttribute elements. Note that when extension is contained inside complexContent, then it can introduce new element and / or attribute content, whereas when it is inside a simpleContent element, then it can only be used to add attributes to a type.

Example

Extending a complex type:

```
<xs:complexType name="CAN_Address">
   <xs:complexContent>
      <xs:extension base="Address">
         <xs:sequence>
            <xs:element name="Province" type="xs:string" />
            <xs:element name="PostalCode" type="CAN_PostalCode"/>
         </xs:sequence>
      </xs:extension>
   </xs:complexContent>
</xs:complexType>
```

Extending a simple type to produce a complex type with simple content:

```
<xs:complexType name = "ConclusionType" block = "#all">
   <xs:simpleContent>
     <xs:extension base="xs:string">
         <xs:attribute name = "accepted" type = "xs:boolean" />
     </xs:extension>
   </xs:simpleContent>
</xs:complexType>
```

Attributes

Attribute	Value Space	Description
base	QName	Specify the base internal or derived datatype that will be extended.
id	ID	Gives a unique identifier to the element.

For more information: see Chapter 4, and §3.4.2 of the Recommendation.

field

Allows us to specify an XPath node for an element or attribute used to give a key or unique value (see the key, keyref, and unique elements). It can contain an annotation element, and is used within a key, keyref, or unique elements.

Example

```
<xs:element name = "Employees" minOccurs = "1" maxOccurs = "1" >
   <xs:complexType>
      <xs:sequence>
         <xs:element ref = "Employee" minOccurs = "1"
                                      maxOccurs = "unbounded" />
      </xs:sequence>
   </xs:complexType>
   <xs:unique name = "employeeIdentificationNumber">
      <xs:selector xpath = "Employee" />
      <xs:field xpath = "@employeeID" />
   </xs:unique>
</xs:element>
```

Attributes

Attribute	Value Space	Description
id	ID	Gives a unique identifier to the element.
xpath	XPath	This attribute points to a value that's used to index the elements selected by the identity constraint, relative to those elements.

For more information: see Chapter 9, and §3.11.2 of the Recommendation.

group

Allows us to define model groups that can be reused in different structures in our schema. The group element can be used in one of two ways: firstly, to define a named model group, and secondly, to reference a globally defined named model group. The group element may contain an annotation element, and if it is being used to define a group, rather than reference one, then it contains one of all, choice, or sequence. It is used as a child of the schema element when creating a global model group definition, or within choice, sequence, complexType, or redefine when referencing a group.

Example

```
<xs:element name = "Customer">
   <xs:complexType>
      <xs:group ref = "FirstOrLastNameGroup" />
   </xs:complexType>
</xs:element>

<xs:group name = "FirstOrLastNameGroup">
   <xs:choice>
      <xs:element name = "FirstName" type = "xs:string" />
      <xs:element name = "LastName" type = "xs:string" />
   </xs:choice>
</xs:group>
```

Attributes

Attribute	Value Space	Description
id	ID	Gives a unique identifier to the element.
maxOccurs	nonNegativeInteger | unbounded	The maximum number of times the element can occur.
minOccurs	nonNegativeInteger	The minimum number of times the element can occur.
name	NCNAME	Defines the name of the model group. In this case we are creating a named model group, so ref, minOccurs, and maxOccurs attributes are not permitted.
ref	QName	This points towards a previously defined model group. When using this attribute, we can't use name, but we can set occurrence constraints with minOccurs and / or maxOccurs.

For more information: see Chapter 3, and §3.7.2 of the Recommendation.

import

This element imports a schema for another namespace. It's declared as a child of the root schema element, and has an optional annotation. A schema may import multiple other schemas.

Example

```
<xs:schema xmlns:xs = "http://www.w3.org/2001/XMLSchema"
           targetNamespace = "http://www.example.com/ECommerce"
           xmlns = "http://www.example.com/ECommerce"
           elementFormDefault = "qualified"
           xmlns:wrox = "http://www.wrox.com/ECommerce">

   <xs:import  schemaLocation = "http://file_Location/Products.xsd"
      namespace = "http://www.wrox.com/ECommerce" />
   <xs:import  schemaLocation = "http://file_Location/TypeLib.xsd"
      namespace = "http://www.wrox.com/ECommerce" />

   <!-- rest of schema definition here -->

</xs:schema>
```

Attributes

Attribute	Value Space	Description
id	ID	Gives a unique identifier to the element.
namespace	anyURI	The target namespace of the imported data.
schemaLocation	anyURI	The location of the schema to import.

For more information: see Chapter 8, and §4.2.3 of the Recommendation.

include

This element is used to include a schema from the same target namespace, or adopt one from no namespace. Like import, it is declared as a child of the root schema element, and may contain an annotation. A schema may include any number of include elements.

Example

```
<xs:schema xmlns:xs = "http://www.w3.org/2001/XMLSchema"
           targetNamespace = "http://www.example.com/ECommerce"
           xmlns = "http://www.example.com/ECommerce"
           elementFormDefault = "qualified">

    <xs:include  schemaLocation = "http://location_of_schema/Products.xsd" />
    <xs:include  schemaLocation = "http://location_of_schema/TypeLib.xsd" />

    <!-- rest of schema definition here -->

</xs:schema>
```

Attributes

Attribute	Value Space	Description
id	ID	Gives a unique identifier to the element.
schemaLocation	anyURI	The location of the schema to include.

For more information: see Chapter 8, and §4.2.1 of the Recommendation.

key

The key element, along with its partner keyref, allows us to define a relationship between two elements. For example, element A might contain a key that is unique within a specified scope. Element B can then refer back to element A using a keyref element. A key is always defined inside an element. It contains selector and field elements to define the element that is the key, and the scope in which it applies. Like other elements, it can also contain an annotation.

Example

```
<xs:key name = "KeyDepartmentByID">
    <xs:selector xpath = "Departments/Department" />
    <xs:field xpath = "@departmentID" />
</xs:key>
```

Attributes

Attribute	Value Space	Description
id	ID	Gives a unique identifier to the element.
name	NCName	The name of the key used.

For more information: see Chapter 9, and §3.11.2 of the Recommendation.

keyref

The `keyref` element is used to specify a reference to a `key` (see the discussion of `key` above.) Like key, it is declared within an `element` element, and contains an optional annotation element, and `selector` and `field` elements.

Example

```
<xs:keyref name = "RefEmployeeToDepartment" refer = "KeyDepartmentByID">
    <xs:selector xpath = "Employees/Employee" />
    <xs:field xpath = "Department/@refDepartmentID" />
</xs:keyref>
```

Attributes

Attribute	Value Space	Description
id	ID	Gives a unique identifier to the element.
name	NCName	The name of the key reference.
refer	QName	The name of the key to which this key reference refers.

For more information: see Chapter 9, and §3.11.2 of the Recommendation.

list

A `list` is a special sort of simple type – it is a finite-length sequence of whitespace-separated atomic values. The `itemType` attribute defines the item type of which the list consists. The `itemType` cannot be a list type, however. We cannot have a list of lists, or a list of a type that can contains whitespace. A `list` is defined within a `simpleType` definition, and can contain an optional `annotation` and `simpleType` elements.

Example

```
<xs:simpleType name="AgesList">
    <xs:list itemType="xs:integer" />
</xs:simpleType>
```

Attributes

Attribute	Value Space	Description
id	ID	Gives a unique identifier to the element.
itemType	QName	A base datatype of which the elements of a list in an instance document consist.

For more information: see Chapter 9, and §3.14.2 of the Recommendation.

notation

A notation is used to associate a particular file type with the location of a processing application. The name of the notation should correspond to a value that is declared as a NOTATION datatype (or rather, derived from this type, since it cannot be used directly in the schema). A notation is declared inside the root schema element, and can contain an optional annotation.

Example

```
<xs:notation name="jpeg" public="image/jpeg" system="JPEG_Viewer.exe" />
<xs:notation name="png" public="image/png" system="PNG_Viewer.exe" />

<xs:simpleType name="notation.Image" >
   <xs:restriction base="xs:NOTATION">
      <xs:enumeration value="jpeg"/>
      <xs:enumeration value="png"/>
   </xs:restriction>
</xs:simpleType>
```

Attributes

Attribute	Value Space	Description
id	ID	Gives a unique identifier to the element.
name	NCName	The name of the specified NOTATION datatype.
public	anyURI	Any URI; usually some relevant identifier, like a MIME type.
system	anyURI	Any URI; usually some local processing application.

For more information: see Chapter 9, and §3.12.2 of the Recommendation.

redefine

This allows us to redefine complex types, simple types, model groups, or attribute groups from another external schema. The external schema needs to have the same target namespace as the one where redefine is used, however, or no namespace. Within the element, we refer to an existing type and amend it as necessary using extension or restriction. redefine is used within the root schema element, and may contain annotation, simpleType, complexType, group, or attributeGroup elements.

Example

From one schema we have:

```
<xs:complexType name = "NameType">
  <xs:sequence>
    <xs:element name = "FirstName" type = "xs:string" />
    <xs:element name = "MiddleInitial" type = "xs:string" />
    <xs:element name = "LastName" type = "xs:string" />
  </xs:sequence>
</xs:complexType>
```

We can redefine this in another schema like so:

```
<xs:redefine schemaLocation = "http://file_location/firstSchema.xsd">
  <xs:complexType name = "NameType">
    <xs:complexContent>
      <xs:restriction base = "NameType">
        <xs:sequence>
          <xs:element name = "FirstName" type = "xs:string" />
          <xs:element name = "LastName" type = "xs:string" />
        </xs:sequence>
      </xs:restriction>
    </xs:complexContent>
  </xs:complexType>
</xs:redefine>
```

Attributes

Attribute	Value Space	Description
id	ID	Gives a unique identifier to the element.
schemaLocation	anyURI	Specifies the location of the schema.

For more information: see Chapter 8, and §4.2.2 of the Recommendation.

restriction

This element is used to constrain an existing complex or simple type, using various constraining elements. There are three different situations where we might use restriction: to restrict a simple type, to restrict a complex type using simple content, or to restrict a complex type using complex content. Therefore, the restrict element may appear inside simpleType, simpleContent, or complexContent. In the first two situations, the element may contain a simpleType element, and one of the constraining facets – minExclusive, maxExlusive, minInclusive, maxInclusive, totalDigits, fractionDigits, length, minLength, maxLength, enumeration, whitespace, or pattern. When restricting a complex type, restriction may also contain attribute, attributeGroup, anyAttribute, and if the restriction is inside a complexContent element, then it may also include group, all, choice, and sequence. The restriction element also has an optional annotation element.

Example

Deriving a simple type:

```
<xs:simpleType name="Char">
  <xs:restriction base="xs:string">
     <xs:length value="1" />
  </xs:restriction>
</xs:simpleType>
```

Deriving complex type with simple content:

```
<xs:complexType name = "Person">
  <xs:simpleContent>
    <xs:extension base="xs:string">
        <xs:attribute name = "age" type = "xs:integer" />
    </xs:extension>
  </xs:simpleContent>
</xs:complexType>
```

```
<xs:complexType name = "RestrictedPerson">
    <xs:simpleContent>
        <xs:restriction base="Person">
            <xs:attribute name = "age">
                <xs:simpleType>
                    <xs:restriction base = "xs:integer">
                        <xs:minInclusive value="1" />
                        <xs:maxInclusive value="120" />
                    </xs:restriction>
                </xs:simpleType>
            </xs:attribute>
        </xs:restriction>
    </xs:simpleContent>
</xs:complexType>
```

Deriving a complex type with complex content:

```
<xs:complexType name="ShortAddress">
    <xs:complexContent>
        <xs:restriction base="Address" >
            <xs:sequence>
                <xs:element name="Name" type="xs:string" />
                <xs:element name="Street" type="xs:string" minOccurs="1"
                    maxOccurs="2" />
                <xs:element name="City" type="xs:string" />
            </xs:sequence>
        </xs:restriction>
    </xs:complexContent>
</xs:complexType>
```

Attributes

Attribute	Value Space	Description
id	ID	Gives a unique identifier to the element.
base	QName	The base type from which the new type is derived.

For more information: see Chapters 2 and 4, and §3.4.2 and §3.14.2 of the Recommendation.

schema

This is the parent element of all other schema elements. Details such as target namespace are specified here, as well as various other useful properties, detailed below. It may contain include, import, redefine, annotation, simpleType, complexType, group, attributeGroup, element, attribute, or notation.

Example

```
<?xml version = "1.0" encoding = "UTF-8"?>
<xs:schema xmlns:xs = "http://www.w3.org/2001/XMLSchema">
   <!--rest of content goes here-->
</xs:schema>
```

Attributes

Attribute	Value Space	Description
attributeFormDefault	qualified | unqualified	Specifies the default attribute if the attribute is missing.
blockDefault	#all | List of extension | restriction | substitution	Allows us to block some or all of derivations of datatypes using substitution groups, with the extension, restriction, and substitution element, from being used in the schema; except where overridden by the block attribute of an element or complexType element in the schema.
elementFormDefault	qualified | unqualified	Similar to the attributeFormDefault attribute above, only applies to namespace qualification of elements instead.
finalDefault	#all | List of extension | restriction	Similar to blockDefault, only this blocks all derivations.
id	ID	Gives a unique identifier to the element.

Attribute	Value Space	Description
targetNamespace	anyURI	This is used to specify the namespace that this schema refers to.
version	token	Used to specify the version of the schema. This can take a token datatype.
xml:lang	language	Specifies the language, using a code defined by RFC 3066. Most languages can be identifies by a simple two letter code.

For more information: see Chapter 1, and §3.15.2 of the Recommendation.

selector

This is used within the context of key, keyref, or unique to define elements that have unique values. The position of the key, keyref and unique element indicates its scope within the document. It may contain annotation.

Example

```
<xs:key name = "KeyDepartmentByID">
    <xs:selector xpath = "Departments/Department" />
    <xs:field xpath = "@departmentID" />
</xs:key>
```

Attributes

Attribute	Value Space	Description
id	ID	Gives a unique identifier to the element.
xpath	XPath	A *relative* XPath expression (relative to the element on which the identity constraint is defined) that specifies which elements the identity constraint applies to.

For more information: see Chapter 9, and §3.11.2 of the Recommendation.

sequence

Items that are specified inside this element must also appear in the instance document in the same order. We can specify the frequency in which this sequence may appear within the parent node. It is contained within choice, complexType, group, or sequence and may contain annotation, element, group, choice, sequence, or any.

Example

```
<xs:sequence>
    <xs:element name = "FirstName" type = "xs:string" />
    <xs:element name = "MiddleInitial" type = "xs:string" />
    <xs:element name = "LastName" type = "xs:string" />
</xs:sequence>
```

Attributes

Attribute	Value Space	Description
id	ID	Gives a unique identifier to the element.
maxOccurs	nonNegativeInteger or unbounded	The maximum number of times the model group can occur.
minOccurs	nonNegativeInteger	The minimum number of times the model group can occur.

For more information: see Chapter 3, and §3.8.2 of the Recommendation.

simpleContent

This specifies that the content of a datatype is simpleContent (no tagged data). We would normally restrict or extend it using the extension or restriction elements. It is contained within complexType and may contain annotation, restriction, or extension.

Example

```
<xs:complexType name="length1">
   <xs:simpleContent>
      <xs:extension base="xs:nonNegativeInteger">
         <xs:attribute name="unit" type="xs:NMTOKEN"/>
      </xs:extension>
   </xs:simpleContent>
</xs:complexType>
```

Attributes

Attribute	Value Space	Description
id	ID	Gives a unique identifier to the element.

For more information: see Chapter 4, and §3.4.2 of the Recommendation.

simpleType

This declares or references a simple type (no element content). It can be contained within attribute, element, list, redefine, restriction, schema, or union, and may contain annotation, list, restriction, or union.

Example

```
<xs:simpleType name="FixedLengthString">
   <xs:restriction base="xs:string">
      <xs:length value="120" />
   </xs:restriction>
</xs:simpleType>
```

```
<simpleType name="Size" >
    <restriction base="xs:string" >
        <enumeration value="S" />
        <enumeration value="M" />
        <enumeration value="L" />
        <enumeration value="XL" />
    </restriction>
</simpleType>
```

Attributes

Attribute	Value Space	Description
final	#all | List of (union | restriction)	Restricts how new datatypes may be derived from this simple type.
id	ID	Gives a unique identifier to the element.
name	NCName	The name of the datatype that this element is defining.

For more information: see Chapters 1 and 2, and §3.14.2 of the Recommendation.

union

This allows us to join numerous simple data types together. Specify a whitespace-separated list of datatypes and they will be joined together to form the new datatype. It is contained by `simpleType` and may contain `annotation`, or `simpleType`.

Example

```
<xs:simpleType name="union.ShoeSizes">
    <xs:union memberTypes="list.size list.sizenum" />
</xs:simpleType>
```

Attributes

Attribute	Value Space	Description
id	ID	Gives a unique identifier to the element.
memberTypes	List of QName	A whitespace-separated list of simple datatypes that we wish to join together to become a new simpleType.

For more information: see Chapters 2 and 4, and §3.14.2 of the Recommendation.

unique

It allows us to specify that elements must have a unique value within a document, where the value might be their value, or the value of one of their ancestors or attributes, or a combination. Any `unique` datatype cannot have the same value more than once within the instance document, subject to the conditions specified in the `selector` or `field` elements. It is contained by `element` and may contain `annotation`, `selector`, or `field`.

Example

```
<xs:unique name = "employeeIdentificationNumber">
  <xs:selector xpath = "Employees/Employee" />
  <xs:field xpath = "@employeeID" />
</xs:unique>
```

Attributes

Attribute	Value Space	Description
id	ID	Gives a unique identifier to the element.
name	NCName	Is simply a name for the identity constraint, subject to any constraints/exceptions applied by the `selector` and `field` elements.

For more information: see Chapter 9, and §3.11.2 of the Recommendation.

XML Schema Instance Attributes

The XML Schema Instance namespace is declared in an instance document to refer to instance specific XML Schema attributes. (the namespace does not include any elements.) For example, the document can indicate to the parser the location of the schema to which it conforms using the `schemaLocation` attribute. The namespace is: `http://www.w3.org/2001/XMLSchema-instance`, and is declared in the document element like this:

```
<element-name xmlns:xsi="http://www.w3.org/2001/XMLSchema-instance">
```

All the attributes detailed in the table below would be prefixed by `xsi:` in the above case.

Attribute	Type	Description
nil	boolean	Used to indicate that an element is valid despite having an empty value. Necessary for simple types, such as dates and numbers, for which empty values aren't valid. For example: `<OrderDate xsi:nil = "true"></OrderDate>`
noNamespaceSchemaLocation	anyURI	Used to specify the location of a schema without a target namespace. For example: `xsi:noNamespaceSchemaLocation= "name.xsd"`

Attribute	Type	Description
schemaLocation	list of anyURI	Used to specify the location of a schema with a target namespace. The namespace of the schema is specified first, then after a space there is the location of the schema. Multiple schema / namespace pairs can be given as a whitespace separated list. For example: `xsi:schemaLocation="http://www.example.org example.xsd"`
type	QName	Allows us to override the current element type by specifying the qualified name of a type in an existing XML Schema. Note that the datatype has to be derived from the one that the element is declared with, and it can't have been blocked. For example: `<returnAddress xsi:type="ipo:USAddress">`

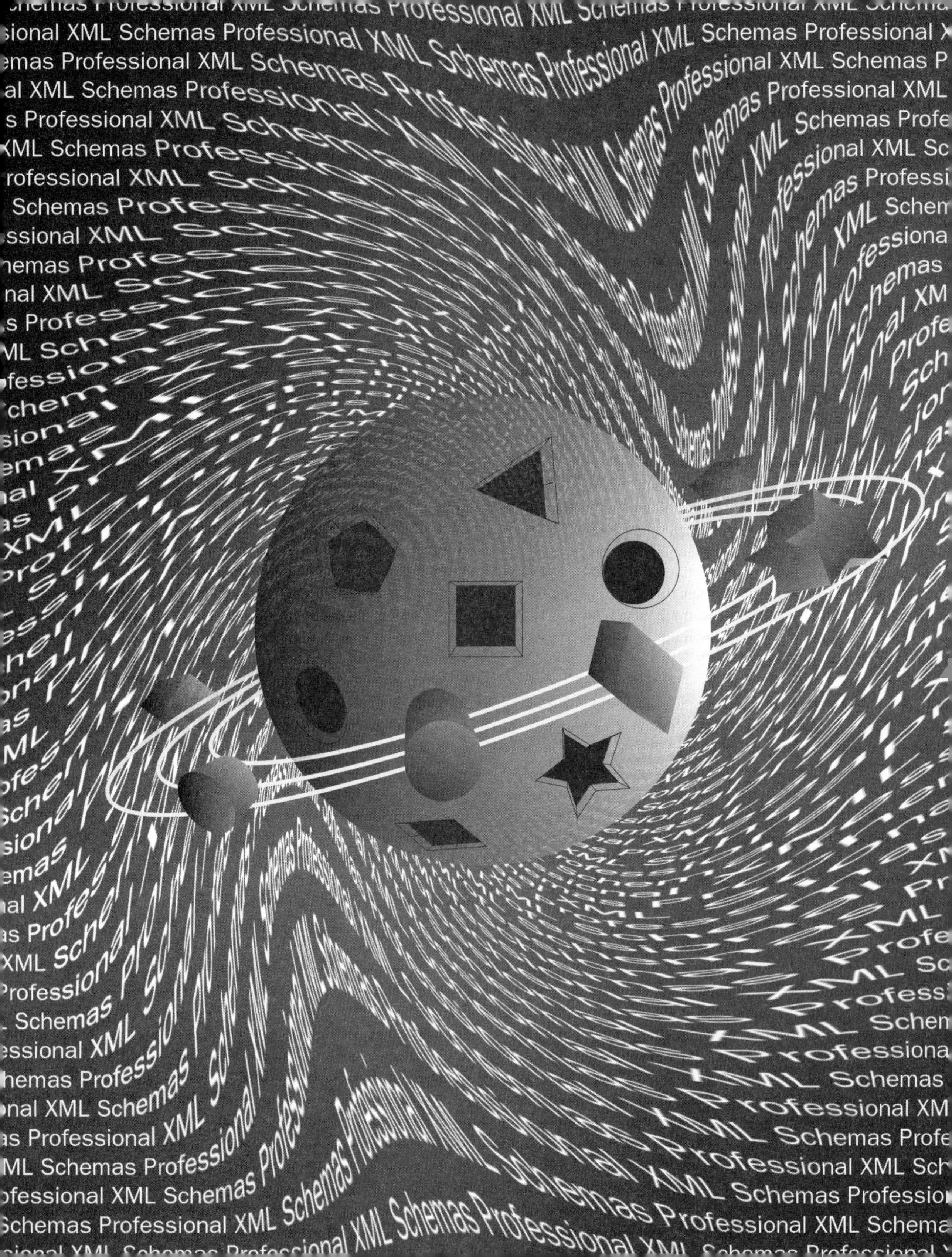
Professional XML Schemas

Schema Datatypes Reference

In this appendix, we will give a quick reference to the W3C Recommendation for XML Schema, Part 2: Datatypes. Datatypes were separated out into a specification in their own right, so that they can be used by other XML-related technologies as well as XML Schema, for example, Relax NG.

XML Schema defines a number of **built-in** types that we can use to indicate the intended type of content, and indeed to validate it. We can further restrict these types using **facets** to create our own datatypes, known as **derived types**. The second part of the XML Schema Recommendation defines two sorts of datatype:

- ❑ **Built-in types**, which are available to all XML Schema authors, and should be implemented by a conforming processor.
- ❑ **User-derived types**, which are defined in individual schema instances, and are particular to that schema (although it is possible to import these definitions into other definitions.)

Remember, there are two sub-groups of built-in type:

- ❑ **Primitive types**, which are types in there own right. They are not defined in terms of other datatypes. Primitive types are also known as base types, because they are the basis from which all other types are built.
- ❑ **Derived types**, which are built from definitions of other datatypes.

In first part of this appendix, we will provide a quick overview of all the XML built-in datatypes, both primitive and derived. In the second part, we will give details of all of the constraining facets of these datatypes that can be used to restrict the allowed value space thereby deriving new types. Finally, for completeness, we will reproduce the tables shown in Chapter 4, which illustrate which of these constraining facets can be applied to which datatype.

XML Schema Built-in Datatypes

Here are the primitive types that XML Schema offers, from which we can derive other datatypes:

Primitive type	Description	Example
string	Represents any legal character strings in XML that matches the Char production in XML 1.0 Second Edition (http://www.w3.org/TR/REC-xml)	Bob Watkins Note, if you need to use these characters in some text (in element content or an attribute value), you will need to escape them according to the XML rules: < or &#60 for < (an opening angled bracket) > or > for > (a closing angled bracket) & or &#30 for & (an ampersand) ' or ' for ' (an apostrophe) " or " for " (a quotation mark)
boolean	Represents binary logic, true or false.	true, false, 1, 0 (These are the only permitted values for this datatype.)
decimal	Represents arbitrary precision decimal numbers.	3.141 The ASCII plus (+) and minus (−) characters are used to represent positive or negative numbers, for example: -1.23, +00042.00.
float	Standard concept of real numbers corresponding to a single precision 32 bit floating point type.	-INF, -1E4, 4.5E-2, 37, INF, NaN NaN denotes not a number INF denotes infinity

Primitive type	Description	Example
double	Standard concept of real numbers corresponding to a double precision 64 bit floating point type.	-INF, 765.4321234E11, 7E7, 1.0, INF, NaN NaN denotes not a number INF denotes infinity
duration	Represents a duration of time in the format PnYnMnDTnHnMnS, where: P is a designator that must always be present nY represents number of years nM represents number of months nD represents number of days T is the date/time separator nH is number of hours nM is number of minutes nS is number of seconds	P1Y0M1DT20H25M30S 1 year and a day, 20 hours, 25 minutes and 30 seconds Limited forms of this lexical production are also allowed. For example, P120D denotes 120 days.
dateTime	A specific instance in time in the format: CCYY-MM-DDThh:mm:ss where: CC represents the century YY represents the year MM represents the month DD represents the day T is the date/time separator hh represents hours mm represents minutes ss represents seconds (Fractional seconds can be added to arbitrary precision) There is also an optional time zone indicator.	2001-04-16T15:23:15 Represents the 16th of April 2001, at 3:23 and 15 seconds in the afternoon. (Note that the year 0000 is prohibited, and each of the fields CC, YY, MM and DD must be exactly 2 digits).

Table continued on following page

Primitive type	Description	Example
time	Represents an instance of time that occurs every day in the format HH:MM:SS. Fractional seconds can be added to arbitrary precision and there is also an optional time zone indicator.	14:12:30 Represents 12 minutes and thirty seconds past two in the afternoon.
date	Represents a calendar date from the Gregorian calendar (the whole day) in the format CCYY-MM-DD. There is also an optional time zone indicator. This complies with the ISO Standard 8601.	2001-04-16 Represents the 16th of April 2001.
gYearMonth	Represents a month in a year in the Gregorian calendar, in the format CCYY-MM.	1999-02 Represents February 1999.
gYear	Represents a year in the Gregorian calendar in the format CCYY. There is also an optional time zone indicator and optional leading minus sign.	1986 Represents 1986.
gMonthDay	Represents a recurring day of a recurring month in the Gregorian calendar in the format --MM-DD. There is also an optional time zone indicator.	--04-16 Represents the 16th of April, ideal for birthdays, holidays, and recurring events.
gDay	Represents a recurring day in the Gregorian calendar in the format --DD.	--16 Represents the sixteenth day of a month. Ideal for monthly occurrences, such as pay day.
gMonth	Represents a recurring month in the Gregorian calendar in the format --MM--. There is also an optional time zone indicator.	--12-- Represents December.

Primitive type	Description	Example
hexBinary	Represents hex-encoded arbitrary binary data.	0FB7
base64Binary	Represents Base64-encoded arbitrary binary data.	GpM7
anyURI	Represents a URI. The value can be absolute or relative, and may have an optional fragment identifier, so it can be a URI Reference.	http://www.example.com mailto://info@example.com mySchemafile.xsd
QName	Represents any XML element together with a prefix bound to a namespace, both separated by a colon. *The XML Namespace Recommendation can be found at:* http://www.w3.org/TR/REC-xml-names/	xs:element
NOTATION	Represents the NOTATION type from XML 1.0 Second Edition. Only datatypes derived from a NOTATION base type (by specifying a value for enumeration) are allowed to be used in a schema. Should only be used for attribute values.	

In order to create new simple datatypes – known as **derived types** – you place further restrictions on an existing built-in type (or another simple type that has been defined). The type that you place the restrictions upon is known as the new type's **base-type**. Here is a list of the **built-in derived types**:

Derived type	Description	Base type	Example
normalizedString	Represents white space normalized strings. Whitespace normalized strings do not contain carriage return (#xD), line feed (#xA) or tab (#x9) characters.	string	Like this

Table continued on following page

Derived type	Description	Base type	Example
`token`	Represents tokenized strings, they do not contain line feed or tab characters and contain no leading or trailing spaces, and no internal sequences of more than two spaces.	`normalizedString`	`One Two Three`
`language`	Natural language identifiers, as defined in RFC 1766, and valid values for `xml:lang` as defined in XML 1.0 Second Edition.	`token`	`en-GB, en-US, fr`
`NMTOKEN`	XML 1.0 Second Edition `NMTOKEN`.	`token`	`small`
`Name`	Represents XML Names.	`token`	`for:example`
`NCName`	Represents XML "non-colonized" Names, without the prefix and colon.	`Name`	`Address`
`ID`	Represents the `ID` attribute type from XML 1.0 Second Edition.	`NCName`	
`IDREF`	Represents the `IDREF` attribute type from XML 1.0 Second Edition.	`NCName`	
`IDREFS`	`IDREFS` attribute type from XML 1.0 Second Edition. (An aggregation with one and only one member type: `ENTITY`.)	`A list with itemType IDREF`	
`ENTITY`	Represents the `ENTITY` attribute type from XML 1.0 Second Edition.	`NCName`	Note that the `ENTITY` has to be declared externally to the schema in a DTD.
`ENTITIES`	Represents the `ENTITIES` attribute type from XML 1.0 Second Edition. `ENTITIES` is a set of `ENTITY` elements separated by an XML whitespace character.	`A list with itemType ENTITY` *All elements of an ENTITIES instance are of type ENTITY, which also forms some kind of base type*	Note that the `ENTITIES` list has to be declared externally to the schema in a DTD.

Derived type	Description	Base type	Example
integer	Standard mathematical concept of integer numbers.	decimal	-4, 0, 2, 7
nonPositiveInteger	Standard mathematical concept of a non-positive integer (includes 0).	integer	-4, -1, 0
negativeInteger	Standard mathematical concept of negative integers (does not include 0).	nonPositiveInteger	-4, -1
long	An integer between -9223372036854775808 and 9223372036854775807.	integer	-23568323, 52883773203895
int	An integer between -2147483648 and 2147483647.	long	-24781982, 24781924
short	An integer between -32768 and 32767.	int	-31353, -43, 345, 31347
byte	An integer between -128 and 127.	short	-127, -42, 0, 54, 125
nonNegativeInteger	A positive integer including zero.	integer	0, 1, 42
unsignedLong	A nonNegativeInteger between 0 and 18446744073709551615.	nonNegativeInteger	0, 356, 38753829383
unsignedInt	An unsignedLong between 0 and 4294967295.	unsignedLong	46, 4255774, 2342823723
unsignedShort	An unsignedInt between 0 and 65535.	unsignedInt	78, 64328

Table continued on following page

Derived type	Description	Base type	Example
unsignedByte	An unsignedShort between 0 and 255.	unsignedShort	0, 46, 247
positiveInteger	An integer of 1 or higher.	nonNegativeInteger	1, 24, 345343

Constraining Facets

The constraining facets defined in the XML Schema Datatypes specification are:

- ❏ length
- ❏ minLength
- ❏ maxLength
- ❏ pattern
- ❏ enumeration
- ❏ whitespace
- ❏ maxInclusive
- ❏ minInclusive
- ❏ maxExclusive
- ❏ minExclusive
- ❏ totalDigits
- ❏ fractionDigits

length

This allows us to specify the exact length of a datatype. If the datatype is a string, then it specifies the number of characters in it. If it's a list, then it specifies the number of items in the list. It is always used inside a restriction element, and can in turn contain an annotation element.

Example

```
<xs:simpleType name="USA_SSN">
   <xs:restriction base="xs:string">
      <xs:length value="11" />
   </xs:restriction>
</xs:simpleType>
```

Attributes

Attribute	Value Space	Description
fixed	boolean	If a simple type has its length facet's fixed attribute set to true, then it cannot be used to derive another simple type with a different length facet. Default is false.
id	ID	Gives a unique identifier to the type.
value	nonNegativeInteger	The actual length of the datatype.

For more information: see Chapter 4 and §4.3.1 of the Datatypes Recommendation.

minLength

This sets the minimum length of a datatype. If the base type is string, then it sets the minimum number of characters. If it is a list, it sets the minimum number of members. It is always used inside a restriction element to do this. It can contain an annotation element.

Example

```
<xs:simpleType name="USA_LicensePlate">
   <xs:restriction base="xs:string">
      <xs:minLength value="1" />
      <xs:maxLength value="9" />
   </xs:restriction>
</xs:simpleType>
```

Attributes

Attribute	Value Space	Description
fixed	boolean	If true, then any datatypes derived from the one in which this is set cannot alter the value of minLength. The default is false.
id	ID	Gives a unique identifier to the type.
value	nonNegativeInteger	Sets the minimum length of the datatype, if applicable; must be a non-negative integer.

For more information: see Chapter 4 and §4.3.2 of the Datatypes Recommendation.

maxLength

This sets the maximum length of a datatype. If the base type is string, then it sets the maximum number of characters. If it is a list, it sets the maximum number of members. It is always used inside a restriction element to do this. It can contain an annotation element.

Example

```
<xs:simpleType name="USA_LicensePlate">
   <xs:restriction base="xs:string">
      <xs:minLength value="1" />
      <xs:maxLength value="9" />
   </xs:restriction>
</xs:simpleType>
```

Attributes

Attribute	Value Space	Description
fixed	boolean	If fixed is true, then any datatypes derived the one in which this is set, cannot alter the value of maxLength. The default is false.
id	ID	Gives a unique identifier to the type.
value	nonNegativeInteger	Sets the maximum length of the datatype, if applicable; must be a non-negative integer.

For more information: see Chapter 4 and §4.3.3 of the Datatypes Recommendation.

pattern

This allows us to restrict any simple datatype by specifying a regular expression. It acts on the lexical representation of the type, rather than the value itself. It is always used inside a restriction element to do this. It can contain an annotation element.

Example

```
<xs:simpleType name="USA_SSN">
   <xs:restriction base="xs:string">
      <xs:pattern value="[0-9]{3}-[0-9]{2}-[0-9]{4}" />
   </xs:restriction>
</xs:simpleType>
```

Attributes

Attribute	Value Space	Description
id	ID	Gives a unique identifier to the type.
value	anySimpleType	The value contained within this attribute is any valid regular expression.

For more information: see Chapter 4 and §4.3.4 of the Datatypes Recommendation.

enumeration

The `enumeration` element is used to restrict the values allowed within a datatype to a set of specified values. It is always used inside a `restriction` element to do this. It can contain an `annotation` element.

Example

```
<xs:simpleType name="Sizes">
    <xs:restriction base="xs:string">
        <xs:enumeration value="S" />
        <xs:enumeration value="M" />
        <xs:enumeration value="L" />
        <xs:enumeration value="XL" />
    </xs:restriction>
</xs:simpleType>
```

Attributes

Attribute	Value Space	Description
id	ID	Gives a unique identifier to the element.
value	anySimpleType	One of the values of an enumerated datatype. Multiple `enumeration` elements are used for the different choices of value.

For more information: see Chapter 2 and §4.3.5 of the Datatypes Recommendation.

whiteSpace

This dictates what (if any) whitespace transformation is performed upon the XML instances data, before validation constraints are tested. It is always used inside a `restriction` element to do this. It can contain an `annotation` element.

Example

```
<xs:simpleType name="token">
    <xs:restriction base="xs:normalizedString">
        <xs:whiteSpace value="collapse" />
    </xs:restriction>
</xs:simpleType>
```

Attributes

Attribute	Value Space	Description
fixed	boolean	If `fixed` is `true`, then any type derived from this one cannot set `whiteSpace` to a value other than the one specified. The default is `false`.
id	ID	Gives a unique identifier to the type.

Table continued on following page

Attribute	Value Space	Description
value	collapse | preserve | replace	preserve means that all whitespace is preserved as it is declared in the element. If replace is used, then all whitespace characters such as carriage return and tab and so on are replaced by single whitespace characters. collapse means that any series of whitespace characters are collapsed into a single whitespace character.
		Note that a type with its whiteSpace attribute set to preserve, cannot be derived from one where with a value of replace or collapse, and similarly, one with a value of replace, cannot be derived from one with a value of collapse.

For more information: see Chapter 2 and §4.3.6 of the Datatypes Recommendation.

maxInclusive

This sets the *inclusive* upper limit of an ordered datatype (number, date type or ordered list). So, the value stated here is therefore, the highest value that can be used in this datatype. maxInclusive must be equal to or greater than, any value of minInclusive and greater than the value of minExclusive. It is always used inside a restriction element to do this. It can contain an annotation element.

Example

```
<xs:simpleType name="TheAnswer">
    <xs:restriction base="xs:integer">
        <xs:minInclusive value="42" />
        <xs:maxInclusive value="42" />
    </xs:restriction>
</xs:simpleType>
```

Attributes

Attribute	Value Space	Description
fixed	boolean	If true, then any datatypes derived from this one cannot alter the value of maxInclusive; the default is false.
id	ID	Gives a unique identifier to the type.
value	anySimpleType	If the base datatype is numerical, this would be a number; if a date, then this would be a date.

For more information: see Chapter 4 and §4.3.7 of the Datatypes Recommendation.

maxExclusive

This sets the *exclusive* upper limit of an ordered datatype (number, date type, or ordered list). The maxExclusive value is therefore one higher than the maximum value that can be used. maxExclusive must be greater than or equal to the value of minExclusive and greater than the value of minInclusive It is always used inside a restriction element to do this. It can contain an annotation element.

Example

```
<xs:simpleType name="TheAnswer">
    <xs:restriction base="xs:integer">
        <xs:minExclusive value="42" />
        <xs:maxExclusive value="42" />
    </xs:restriction>
</xs:simpleType>
```

Attributes

Attribute	Value Space	Description
fixed	boolean	If true, then any datatypes derived from this one cannot alter the value of maxExclusive; the default is false.
id	ID	Gives a unique identifier to the type.
value	anySimpleType	If the base datatype is numerical, this would be a number; if a date, then a date.

For more information: see Chapter 4 and §4.3.8 of the Datatypes Recommendation.

minExclusive

This sets the *exclusive* lower limit of an ordered datatype (number, date type or ordered list). The minExclusive value is therefore one lower than the lowest value the data can take. minExclusive must be less than the value of maxInclusive, and less than or equal to the value of maxExclusive. It is always used inside a restriction element to do this. It can contain an annotation element.

Example

```
<xs:simpleType name="TheAnswer">
    <xs:restriction base="xs:integer">
        <xs:minExclusive value="42" />
        <xs:maxExclusive value="42" />
    </xs:restriction>
</xs:simpleType>
```

Attributes

Attribute	Value Space	Description
fixed	boolean	If true, then any datatypes derived from this one, cannot alter the value of minExclusive; the default is false.
id	ID	Gives a unique identifier to the type.
value	anySimpleType	If the base datatype is numerical, this would be a number; if a date, then a date.

For more information: see Chapter 4 and §4.3.9 of the Datatypes Recommendation.

minInclusive

This sets the *inclusive* lower limit of an ordered datatype (number, date type, or ordered list). The value stated here is therefore the lowest value that can be used in this datatype. minInclusive must be equal to or less than any value of maxInclusive and must be less than the value of maxExclusive. It is always used inside a restriction element to do this. It can contain an annotation element.

Example

```
<xs:simpleType name="TheAnswer">
  <xs:restriction base="xs:integer">
    <xs:minInclusive value="42" />
    <xs:maxInclusive value="42" />
  </xs:restriction>
</xs:simpleType>
```

Attributes

Attribute	Value Space	Description
fixed	boolean	If true, then any datatypes derived from this one cannot alter the value of minInclusive; the default is false.
id	ID	Gives a unique identifier to the type.
value	anySimpleType	If the base datatype is numerical, this would be a number; if a date, then a date.

For more information: see Chapter 4 and §4.3.10 of the Datatypes Recommendation.

totalDigits

This facet applies to all datatypes derived from the decimal type. The value stated is the *maximum* number of decimal digits allowed for the entire number (which must always be a positive integer).

Example

```
<xs:simpleType name="Datapoint">
    <xs:restriction base="xs:decimal">
        <xs:totalDigits value="9" />
        <xs:fractionDigits value="3" />
    </xs:restriction>
</xs:simpleType>
```

Attributes

Attribute	Value Space	Description
fixed	boolean	If true, then any datatypes derived from this one cannot alter the value of totalDigits; the default is false.
id	ID	Gives a unique identifier to the type.
value	positiveInteger	The actual value of the totalDigits attribute.

For more information: see Chapter 4 and §4.3.11 of the Datatypes Recommendation.

fractionDigits

This facet applies to all datatypes derived from the decimal type. The value stated is the *maximum* number of digits in the fractional portion of the number (always a *non-negative* integer that is less than or equal to the value of totalDigits).

Example

```
<xs:simpleType name="Datapoint">
    <xs:restriction base="xs:decimal">
        <xs:totalDigits value="9" />
        <xs:fractionDigits value="3" />
    </xs:restriction>
</xs:simpleType>
```

Attributes

Attribute	Value Space	Description
fixed	boolean	If true, then any datatypes derived from this one cannot alter the value of totalDigits; the default is false.
id	ID	Gives a unique identifier to the type.
value	nonNegativeInteger	The actual value of the value fractionDigits attribute. This cannot be any larger than the totalDigits value.

For more information: see Chapter 4 and §4.3.12 of the Datatypes Recommendation.

The two tables below, indicate which of these constraining facets may be applied to which datatypes, in order to derive new types. First, for the primitive built-in types:

Datatypes	length	minLength	maxLength	whiteSpace	pattern	enumeration	minExclusive	maxExclusive	minInclusive	maxInclusive	totalDigits	fractionDigits
String Types												
string	X	X	X	preserve	X	X						
anyURI	X	X	X	collapse	X	X						
NOTATION	X	X	X	collapse	X	X						
QName	X	X	X	collapse	X	X						
Binary Encoding Types												
boolean				collapse	X							
hexBinary	X	X	X	collapse	X	X						
base64Binary	X	X	X	collapse	X	X						
Numeric Types												
decimal				collapse	X	X	X	X	X	X	X	X
float				collapse	X	X	X	X	X	X		
double				collapse	X	X	X	X	X	X		
Date/Time Types												
duration				collapse	X	X	X	X	X	X		
dateTime				collapse	X	X	X	X	X	X		
date				collapse	X	X	X	X	X	X		
time				collapse	X	X	X	X	X	X		
gYear				collapse	X	X	X	X	X	X		
gYearMonth				collapse	X	X	X	X	X	X		

Datatypes	length	minLength	maxLength	whiteSpace	pattern	enumeration	minExclusive	maxExclusive	minInclusive	maxInclusive	totalDigits	fractionDigits
gMonth				collapse	X	X	X	X	X	X		
gMonthDay				collapse	X	X	X	X	X	X		
gDay				collapse	X	X	X	X	X	X		

Second, and for the derived built-in types:

Datatypes	length	minLength	maxLength	whiteSpace	pattern	enumeration	minExclusive	maxExclusive	minInclusive	maxInclusive	totalDigits	fractionDigits
Types Derived from string												
normalizedString	X	X	X	replace	X	X						
token	X	X	X	collapse	X	X						
language	X	X	X	collapse	X	X						
Name	X	X	X	collapse	X	X						
NCName	X	X	X	collapse	X	X						
ID	X	X	X	collapse	X	X						
IDREF	X	X	X	collapse	X	X						
IDREFS	X	X	X	collapse		X						
NMTOKEN	X	X	X	collapse	X	X						
NMTOKENS	X	X	X	collapse		X						
ENTITY	X	X	X	collapse	X	X						
ENTITIES	X	X	X	collapse		X						
Types Derived from decimal												
integer				collapse	X	X	X	X	X	X	X	0
negativeInteger				collapse	X	X	X	X	X	X	X	0
positiveInteger				collapse	X	X	X	X	X	X	X	0
nonNegativeInteger				collapse	X	X	X	X	X	X	X	0
nonPositiveInteger				collapse	X	X	X	X	X	X	X	0

Table continued on following page

Datatypes	length	minLength	maxLength	whiteSpace	pattern	enumeration	minExclusive	maxExclusive	minInclusive	maxInclusive	totalDigits	fractionDigits
byte				collapse	X	X	X	X	X	X	X	0
short				collapse	X	X	X	X	X	X	X	0
int				collapse	X	X	X	X	X	X	X	0
long				collapse	X	X	X	X	X	X	X	0
unsignedByte				collapse	X	X	X	X	X	X	X	0
unsignedShort				collapse	X	X	X	X	X	X	X	0
unsignedInt				collapse	X	X	X	X	X	X	X	0
unsignedLong				collapse	X	X	X	X	X	X	X	0

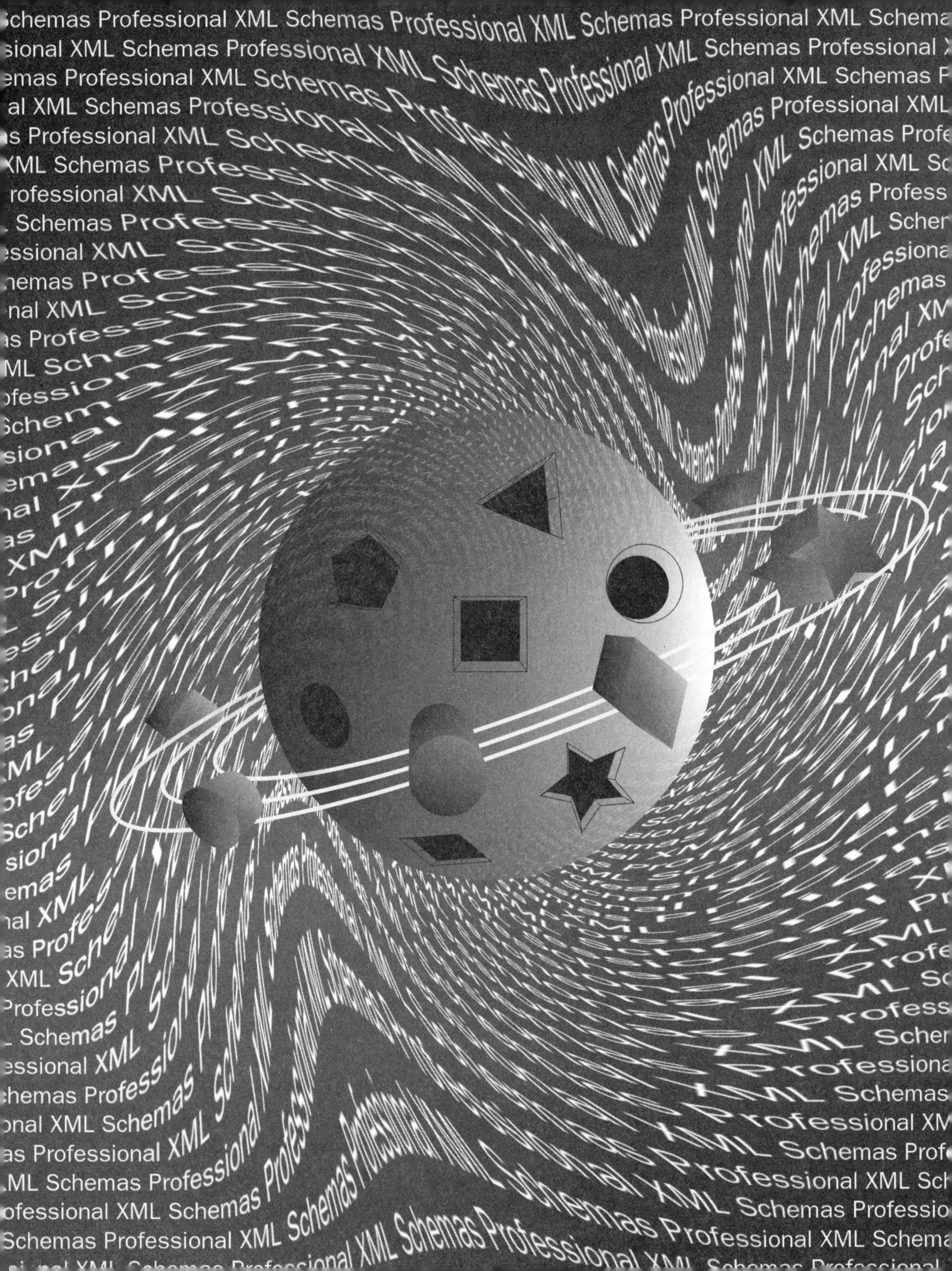
Professional XML Schemas

UML Reference

UML (Universal Modelling Language) is an approach to object-oriented software modeling introduced by Grady Booch, Ivar Jaconbson, and Jim Rumbaugh. UML defines a number of diagrams, which can be used as tools regardless of the design methodology used. There is extensive writing on the principles of UML (see *Instant UML*, ISBN 1861000871, from Wrox Press), but our intention here is simply to give an overview of the notation used in this book where UML is applied.

Classes and Objects

A **class** is represented in the UML like this:

Class
attribute1 attribute2
methodA() methodB()

The rectangle representing the class is divided into three compartments, the top one showing the class name, the second showing the attributes and the third showing the methods.

An **object** looks very similar to a class, except that its name is underlined:

UML defines three visibility levels for attributes and methods:

- ❏ Public – the element is visible to all clients of the class, represented by a + (plus).
- ❏ Protected – the element is visible to subclasses of the class, represented by a # (hash).
- ❏ Private – the element is visible only to the class, represented by a - (minus).

Packages are represented graphically by a folder:

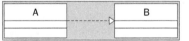

Packages divide and organize models in much the same way that directories organize file systems. Each package corresponds to a subset of a model and can contain classes, objects, relationships, components, or nodes.

Relationships

Relationships between classes are generally represented in class diagrams by a line or an arrow joining the two classes. UML can represent the following, different sorts of object relationships.

Dependency

If **A** depends on **B**, then this is shown by a dashed arrow between **A** and **B**, with the arrowhead pointing at **B**:

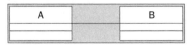

Association

An association between **A** and **B** is shown by a line joining the two classes:

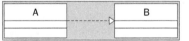

If there is no arrow on the line, the association is taken to be bidirectional. A unidirectional association is indicated like this:

Aggregation

An aggregation relationship is indicated by placing a white diamond at the end of the association next to the aggregate class. If **B** aggregates **A**, then **A** is a part of **B**, but their lifetimes are independent:

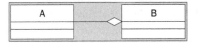

Composition

Composition, on the other hand, is shown by a black diamond on the end of association next to the composite class. If **B** is composed of **A**, then **B** controls the lifetime of **A**.

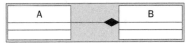

Multiplicity

The multiplicity of a relationship is indicated by a number (or *) placed at the end of an association.

The following diagram indicates a one-to-one relationship between **A** and **B**:

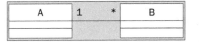

This next diagram indicates a one-to-many relationship:

A multiplicity can also be a range of values. Some examples are shown below:

1 - One and only one

* - Any number from 0 to infinity

0..1 - Either 0 or 1

n..m - Any number in the range *n* to *m* inclusive

1..* - Any positive integer

Naming an Association

To improve the clarity of a class diagram, the association between two objects may be named:

Teacher	teaches	Student		Person	lives in	House

Inheritance

An inheritance (generalization/specialization) relationship is indicated in the UML by an arrow with a triangular arrowhead pointing towards the generalized class.

If **A** is a base class, and **B** and **C** are classes derived from **A**, then this would be represented by the following class diagram:

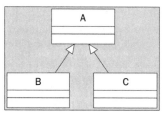

Multiple Inheritance

The next diagram represents the case where class **C** is derived from classes **A** and **B**:

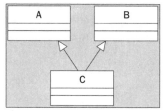

States

States of objects are represented as rectangles with rounded corners. The *transition* between different states is represented as an arrow between states, and a *condition* of that transition occurring may be added between square braces. This condition is called a guard:

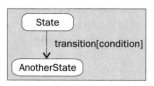

A state chart diagram must not leave any room for ambiguous constructs. This means that it is always necessary to describe the system's initial state. It is possible to have a number of final states that correspond to a different end condition, or not have a final state at all, as in the case of a system that never stops.

The initial state is represented by a big black dot. A final state is represented by a big black dot surrounded by a circle:

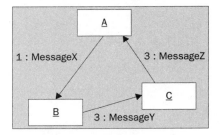

Object Interactions

Interactions between objects are represented by interaction diagrams – both sequence and collaboration diagrams. An example of a collaboration diagram is shown below. Objects are drawn as rectangles, and the lines between them indicate links – a link is an instance of an association. The order of the messages along the links between the objects is indicated by the number at the head of the message:

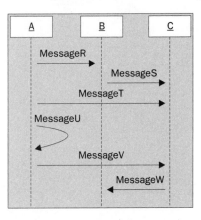

Sequence diagrams show essentially the same information, but concentrate on the time-ordered communication between objects, rather than their relationships. An example of a sequence diagram is shown below. The dashed vertical lines represent the lifeline of the object:

Components

Components represent all kinds of elements that pertain to the piecing together of software applications. Among other things they may be simple files, or libraries, which are downloaded together.

By default each class in the logical model has a specification and a body. The specification contains the class interface; while the body contains the implementation of that same class, represented by the component symbol itself:

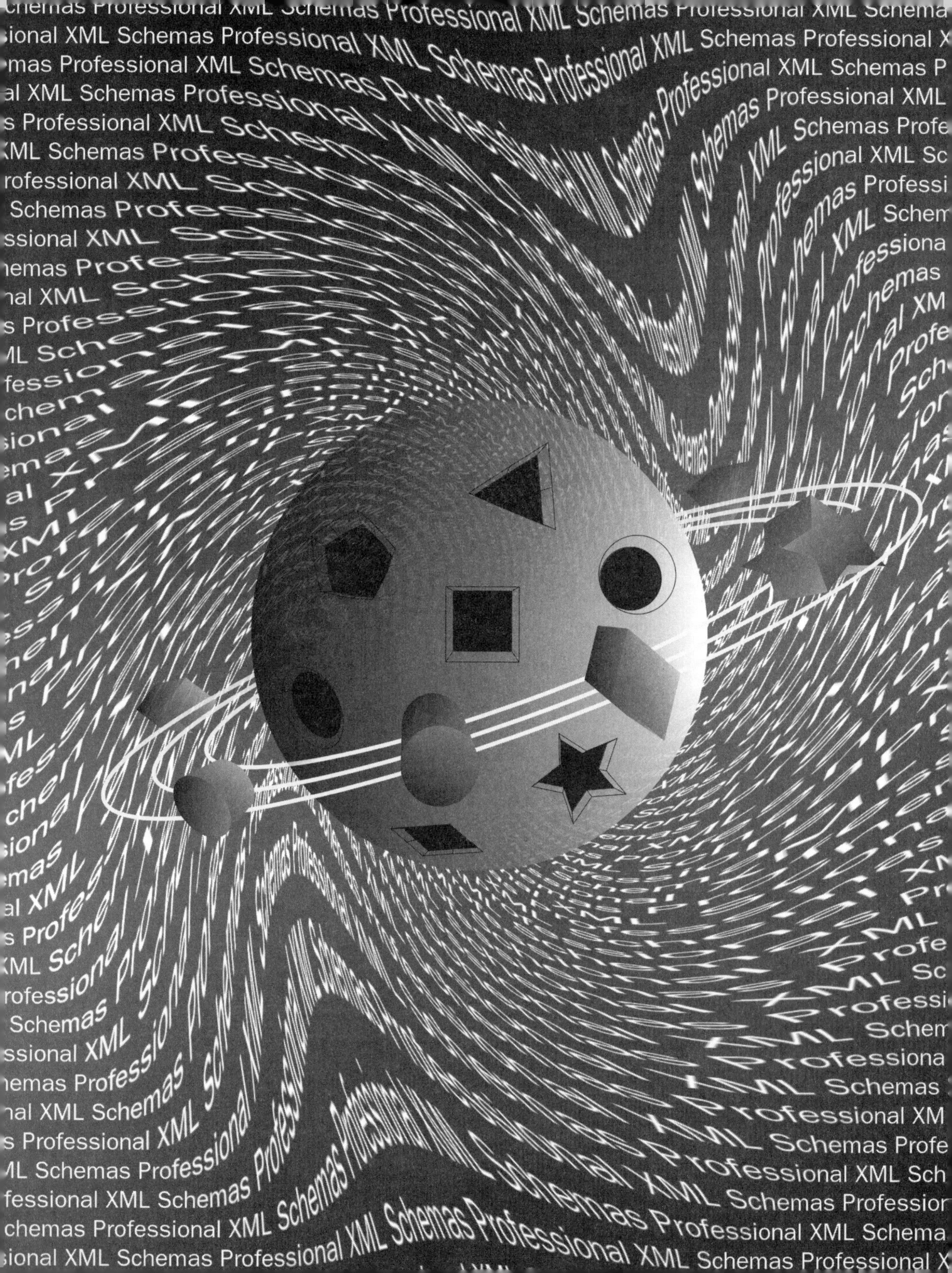
Professional XML Schemas

XML Schema Tools

In this appendix, we will make a survey of XML tools that support the XML Schema Recommendation. These include validating parsers (check some XML data against an XML Schema), *schema* validity checkers (including an online WWW service), conversion tools, and a pair of commercial IDEs (integrated development environments), with built-in validating editors and other tools.

> *Note that the coverage of tools in this appendix is not comprehensive. At the time of writing, the W3C only recently made XML Schema a Recommendation, and so new tools are becoming available all the time. Many are still in beta, but final versions are expected soon. The tools presented here should, however, give you a flavor of what is available and an indication of where to find out more.*

Parsers & XML Development Kits (XDKs)

The first level of software wrapped around XML is a parser. In this book, we are only interested in *validating* parsers, mostly those that handle some version of the XML Schema Recommendation. In several cases, these most basic tools have been supplemented by additional tools, such as schema converters; or an API, usually one that relates to the DOM and/or SAX Recommendations. Often, these are all packaged as an XML Development Kit (XDK). All of these tools require the use of some programming language to invoke the XML parser and schema processors.

The following table shows a quick comparison of some of the parsers and XDKs that support the XML Schema Recommendation (or an earlier draft thereof):

Name	Version#	Updated	Requires?	XML Schema?	Language support?
MSXML4	4.0	2001-04-13 [sic]	Windows 98, Me, NT, or 2000 (Win32)	PR 2001-03-30 (+XDR schemas)	JavaScript, VBScript, VisualBasic, C++
Xerces-c	1.5.0	2001-06-19	Win32, Linux, Unix	1REC 2001-05-02	C++, Perl, COM
Xerces-j	1.4.1	2001-06-22	JRE 1.3	REC 2001-05-02	Java 1.3
XML4C	3.5.0	2001-06-27	Win32, AIX, Linux, Solaris, HP-UX, or AS/400	1REC 2001-05-02	C++
XML4J	3.1.1	2001-01-08	JRE 1.1	2WD 2000-04-07	Java 1.1
XML Schema Processor (and XDK)	v2 (for Oracle 9i)	2001-06-15 (Java beta) 2001-05-01 (Java) 2001-04-13 (C, C++)	Win32, Solaris, Linux, or HP-UX	REC 2001-05-02 3CR 2000-10-24 3CR 2000-10-24	Java, C, C++

[1] *REC 2001-05-02* is a very limited subset of the REC (see details below).
[2] *WD 2000-04-07* is of little use anymore, but XML4J is included in this table as a caution about this important asymmetry in the status of the IBM-Apache parser pairs (which share common code).
[3] *CR 2000-10-24* is more current than any WD, but is less so than a PR, much less the REC
REC= Recommendation, CR= Candidate Rec., PR= Proposed Rec., WD= Working Draft.

Xerces-c, Xerces-j (Apache)

The Apache Software Foundation is well known for its most popular open source web server software. It is not surprising then that Apache has produced some of the leading XML tools as well. In this effort, they have been supported by IBM, who donated the code for their two in-house parsers (see below). The combined effort has produced the **xerces-c** (C++) and **xerces-j** (Java) validating parsers.

> *These two XML parsers are available at http://xml.apache.org/xerces-c/index.html and http://xml.apache.org/xerces-j/index.html.*

XML Schema Conformance

Unfortunately, as of the time of this writing (June 2001), support for XML Schemas has fallen a little behind, with a very limited subset being supported in current stable releases. There are alpha versions with better XML Schema support, and history suggests that Apache will have stable software with full support in the near future (no doubt with additional contributions from IBM).

Xerces-j support for XML Schemas is good, with the following limitations:

❑ `length`, `minLength`, and `maxLength` facets with values larger than 2147483647 (that is, a 32-bit signed integer) will not validate correctly.

❑ year and seconds values in date/time datatypes are similarly limited to a maximum of 2147483647.

❑ only forward references are supported between multiple schemas that are imported or included (using the `import` or `include` elements) in such a way as to cause circular (recursive) references.

Xerces-c has very limited XML Schema support at the moment, with a more complete version in development. There are many unimplemented features, including the following omissions:

❑ most built-in datatypes – the only types implemented are: `string`, `boolean`, `decimal`, `hexBinary`, `base64Binary`, and `integer`!

❑ all simple datatypes derived by list or union.

❑ some complex type support (the `group` and `all` elements).

❑ the `any` and `anyAttribute` elements.

❑ identity constraints.

❑ `redefine` support.

❑ the `xsi:type` attribute.

These four features of XML Schema are implemented as "Experimental Features" and are *not* tested:

❑ complex type derivation support (the `simpleContent` and `complexContent` elements).

❑ element and attribute re-use (the `ref` attribute).

❑ `include` support.

❑ `import` support.

Unfortunately, there is no clear statement about when these missing features will be implemented.

Specifying a Schema

A schema must be associated with an XML data instance, using a `xsi:noNamespaceSchemaLocation` or `xsi:schemaLocation` attribute on the root (more properly, the document) element of the document. This is more restricted than XML Schemas allow, particularly the constraint that the schema be identified on the "root" element. No other means of associating schema and data is currently provided.

Working with Xerces

In order to validate an instance document against a schema using Xerces, you can try running one of the sample programs that is supplied with Xerces, for example `DOMCount` (remember to use the `-v` flag for validation). Alternatively, we have supplied a simple `validate` class, which is available for download from the Wrox web site, along with the rest of the code that accompanies this book. This is a simple command line utility that loads up an XML file and validates it. It is supplied with a simple batch file, which is easiest to run from the folder where you have Xerces installed.

XML4C, XML4J (IBM)

These two validating parsers were among the earliest tools to support XML Schema Working Drafts. While the **XML4J** parser is essentially obsolete, and IBM provides **XML4C** binaries for Win32 (Windows 98, Me, NT, 2000), four different versions of Unix (AIX, Linux, Solaris, and HP/UX), and even the AS/400. Source code distributions support numerous other Unix versions, the Macintosh, and others.

> *These two parsers are available at http://www.alphaworks.ibm.com/tech/xml4c and http://www.alphaworks.ibm.com/tech/xml4c.*

Both of these have gone back and forth with the Apache Foundation's Xerces-c and -j parsers. IBM now uses Xerces-j as its Java-based XML parser, and has stopped further development of IBM4J. However, XML4C remains under active development (in conjunction with Xerces-c).

XML Schema Conformance

As noted, the XML4J parser has not been updated, and so its XML Schema support goes back to the 2000-04-07 Working Draft! The XML4C parser is tied to Xerces-c, so the same limitations apply.

MSXML4 and XDK (Microsoft)

Microsoft was an early proponent of XML (and recent hyperbole from its executives suggests the interest remains white hot). Just a few years ago, beta versions of IE5 and early versions of the **MSXML** parser, were one of the only widely distributed ways to parse and display XML data. Of course, since this is from Microsoft, its use is limited to Windows platforms (Win32 that is, though there *are* older versions without XML Schema support for the MacOS).

> *MSXML4 is available at http://msdn.microsoft.com/xml.*

XML Schema Conformance

Like most early validating parsers, the first version of MSXML only supported schemas in the form of XML 1.0 DTDs. As of the MSXML 2.0 version, however, support was added for an early schema proposal called XML-Data Reduced (XDR). Rather than wait for an official W3C Schema Recommendation, Microsoft chose to call XDR by the generic name "XML Schema", while also promising support for the W3C Recommendation, once it was finalized.

MSXML4 has almost complete support for the XML Schema Recommendation, with the following two exceptions:

❑ identity constraints

❑ regular expression support (the `pattern` facet)

❑ `xsi:schemaLocation` and `xsi:noNamespaceSchemaLocation`

Working with MSXML4

To help you use MSXML 4 to test your schemas, we have created a very basic ASP page using JavaScript, to load the schema and validate an instance document against it. Any errors in the schema or the instance document encountered by the Parser will be written to the browser. Here is the code for `tester.asp`:

```
<% @language = "JScript" %>
<%

    schema = Server.CreateObject("Msxml2.XMLSchemaCache");
    schema.add ("namespaceURI", "locationOfSchema");

    source = Server.CreateObject("Msxml2.DOMDocument");
    source.schemas = schema;

    source.async = false;
    source.validateOnParse = false;
    source.load("locationOfInstanceDocument");

    Response.Write("Parse Error : " + source.parseError.reason + "<br />");

    Response.Write("Validate error: " + source.validate.reason + "<br />");

%>
```

To use this ASP, it must be copied into a web directory, and then accessed through a web browser after you have supplied it with the necessary parameters. We used Microsoft IIS 5.0 to create the necessary web directory, and IE 5.5 to view its output.

Note that you need to use the `add()` method to explicitly specify the schema to which the instance document conforms, since MSXML4 does not support the XMLSchema-Instance attributes `schemaLocation` and `noNamespaceSchemaLocation`.

XML Schema Processor and XDKs (Oracle)

The production versions of Oracle's **XML Schema Processor** use their **XML Parser for Java v2** to validate data against an XML Schema schema, as defined in the one Candidate Recommendation (2000-10-24). However, there *is* a Java beta version that supports the final Recommendation. There are also versions that support JavaBeans, C, C++, and even PL/SQL (though there is not, as yet, an XML Schema processor for this Oracle database language).

Oracle's XDKs, including their XML Parser for Java and XML Schema Processor, are available at http://technet.oracle.com/tech/xml/.

Schema Checkers

Summarized in the table below is a list of tools for checking the validity of a schema document, according to the W3C XML Schema Recommendation.

Name	Version#	Updated	Requires?	XML Schema?	Language support?
XML Schema Quality Checker	1.0.17	2001-05-21	JRE 1.3	REC 2001-05-02	Java 1.3
XML Schema Validator (XSV)	1.196/1.97	2001-06-04	Win32, or browser for online version	REC 2001-05-02	Python 1.6 (with PyLTXML library for validation).

XML Schema Quality Checker (IBM)

In addition to various XML parsers, IBM now provides the XML Schema Quality Checker to validate XML Schema *schemas*. Instead of providing a general validator, this tool verifies that schema components adhere to the W3C XML Schema Recommendation (2001-05-02).

A free version of the XML Schema Quality Checker is available from IBM's alphaWorks at http://www.alphaworks.ibm.com/tech/xmlsqc.

XML Schema Conformance

As a simple schema checker, this tool need not try to offer full conformance as a validating parser. Its purpose is merely to verify schema structures, vocabulary, and even identity constraints (key, keyref, unique) against the W3C XML Schema Recommendation.

XML Schema Validator

There is a service available from the W3C website, at http://www.w3.org/2001/03/webdata/xsv, which offers a form-based validation service using the University of Edinburgh's XML Schema Validator, XSV. Alternatively, you can download this as a Win32 executable, or as Python source files, from http://www.ltg.ed.ac.uk/~ht/xsv-status.html. For more details on using this tool, you can check out the section *Validating with XSV* in Chapter 1, or one of the web references given here.

Note that this tool goes beyond simply checking the validity of an XML Schema, but can also be used for processing XML documents, and checking that they conform to a specified schema.

XML Schema Conformance

This tool generally provides excellent conformance to the specification, and since there are frequent updates to the tool, the level of conformance improves. At the time of writing, however, XSV does not support the following:

❑ Simple type conformance, other than enumerations and max/min for numeric types.

❑ Detailed enforcement of derivation by restriction.

❑ Redefinition of named groups and attribute groups.

❑ Occurrence ranges over 100 for elements or groups in content models (performance limitation).

Authoring Tools

Name	Version#	Requires?	XML Schema?
Turbo XML	2.2	Win32, Unix	REC 2001-05-02
XML Spy	3.5	Win32	CR 2000-10-24
XML Spy	4.0 (beta)	Win32	REC 2001-05-02

Turbo XML (TIBCO Extensibility)

Turbo XML is an easy-to-use XML and schema editor from Tibco Software Inc., available from www.extensibility.com. Evaluation versions are available.

From the main window, you can select to create a new schema or an instance document. Note that by default, a new DTD is created if you select New Schema from the main window. You can change this behavior by editing your preferences – go to the Schema Editor tab and change the Default New Schema To selection to XSD Schema.

If you want to validate an existing XML file, then all you need to do is open it in Turbo XML and it will automatically validate it for you. Note that if there isn't an `xsi:schemaLocation` or similar linking attribute in the instance document, then you'll need to associate a schema with the document, which you can do by hitting the Set Schema... button, and selecting the appropriate schema file. Here's an example of a conforming instance document:

Any errors that are found when validating are shown in the Errors area at the bottom of the window. Clicking on the Source button at the top of the window will bring up the document source for editing, and the Edit Schema... button loads up a different window (XML Authority) enabling us to edit the schema instead:

Again, you can view the source file here, as well as the graphical interface. The Overview/Properties button opens a window that allows you to set the overall attributes of the schema, such as the value for elementFormDefault and the target namespace.

XML Schema Conformance

Turbo XML doesn't appear to support identity constraints. It doesn't return an error if incorrect identity references have been inserted. It can also be a little erratic regarding namespaces and it can also add an xmlns: attribute to your documents, which make your documents not well-formed when other applications read them.

XML Spy 3.5 and 4.0 (Altova)

At the time of writing, XML Spy 4 is in beta, but the full version should be on sale very soon. We'll concentrate on version 4 in this section, as that offers conformance with the W3C XML Schema Recommendation, rather than the Candidate Recommendation.

You can create a new schema or instance document (as well as many other file types) by selecting File|New... from the main window. XML Spy provides both a graphical interface for easy schema creation, and a text view of the source, as an XML Authority (part of Turbo XML). Here's what the simple name.xsd file (that we saw earlier) looks like in the graphical schema design view:

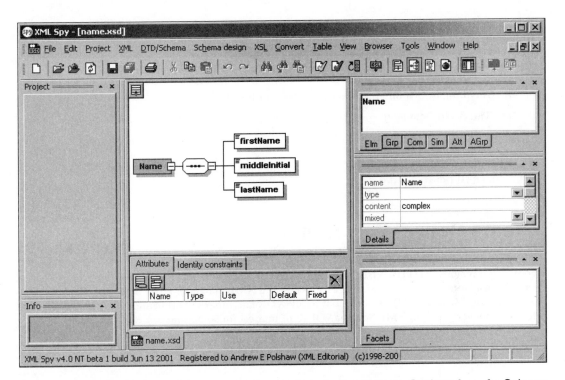

You can specify the attribute of the `schema` element, by selecting **Schema Settings** from the **Schema Design** dialog. This includes things like the values of the `elementFormDefault` attribute. It also allows you to declare a target namespace for your schema.

To validate an instance document against this (or any other) schema, you can simply open the document in XML Spy, and it will automatically perform validation. If there is not already an `xsi:schemaLocation` or `xsi:noNamspaceSchemaLocation` attribute associating the instance document with a schema, then you can select **Assign Schema** from the **DTD/Schema** menu to rectify this. Pressing the yellow or the green check mark buttons will check for well-formedness and validity respectively.

XML Schema Conformance

At the time of writing, XML Spy 4 did not conform to the entire W3C XML Schema Recommendation. Unsupported features are:

- Identity Constraints
- The `redefine` element
- The `final`, `block`, and `nillable` attributes
- The `xsi:nil` attribute

We also found one problem with regular expressions, in that it didn't appear to support character class subtractions properly. That is, if we use as a restriction:

```
<pattern value="[A-Z-[QZ]]" />
```

Rather than allowing any capital ASCII letter, other than Q and Z, it would allow any string at all, without bringing up any kind of error.

There are also some unsupported features in the graphical schema design view; these are:

- Anything from a different namespace cannot be edited.
- The GoTo Definition command only works within the schema design view.
- Find/Replace is not yet included.

Note that the limitations described here apply to the beta version of the product and some may change before the final release version.

Schema Conversion Tools

The commercial XML authoring tools we've just reviewed all have a variety of schema-to-schema converters, including DTDs, XDR, and early drafts of XML Schema. Some parsers, such as MSXML4, can also use different schemas (in this case, XDR and XML Schema). From now on, schema support will probably focus on XML Schema, but many XDR and other experimental schemas exist, so tools that can convert these to XML Schema will be of interest for some time.

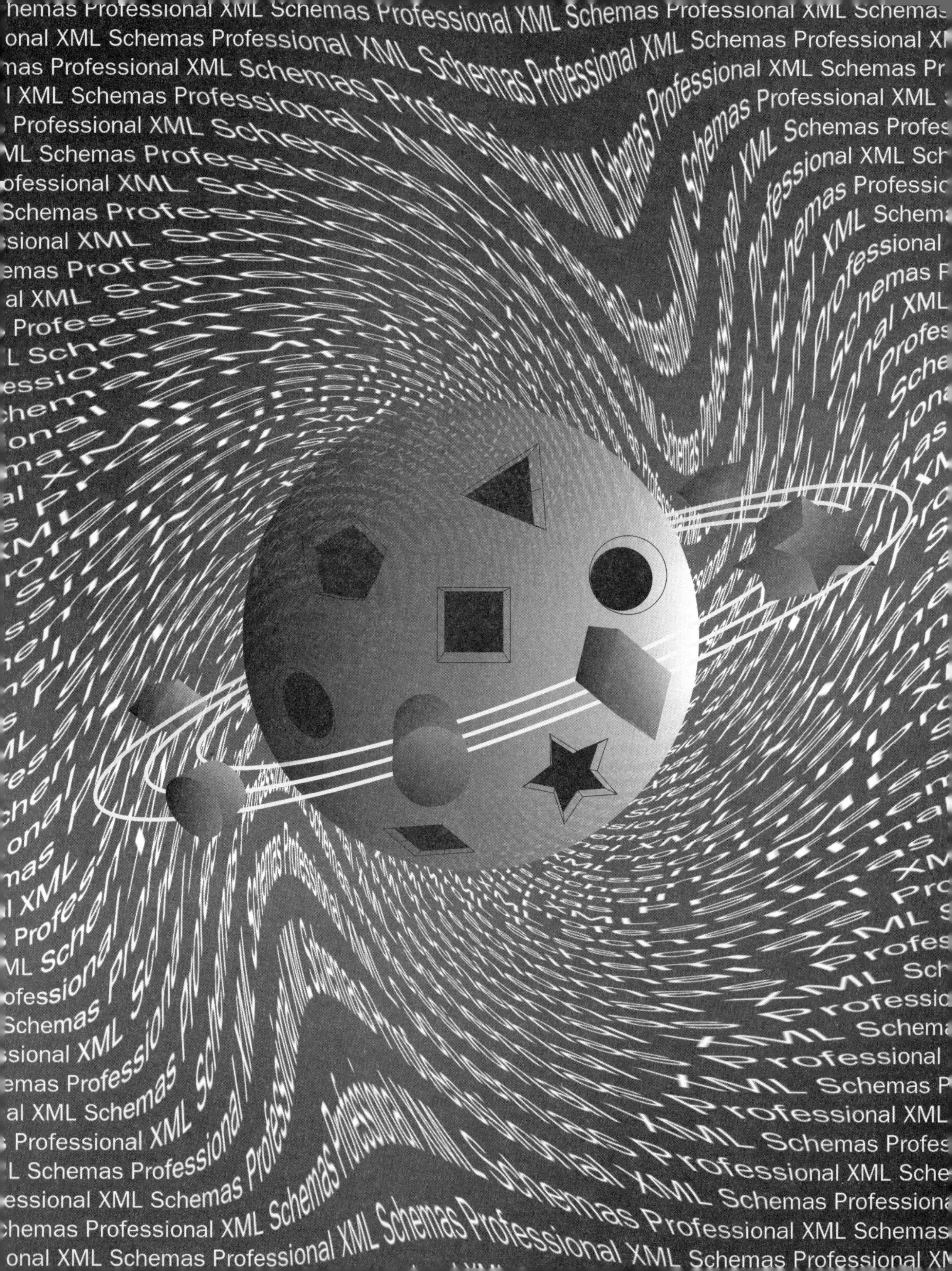
Professional XML Schemas

Bibliography and Further Reading

This listing includes all of the references found throughout the rest of the book, arranged here firstly into 2 sections, URLs and Books, then into subject categories, for ease of use.

URLs

Data Modeling/UML

Rational.com UML resources: http://www.rational.com/uml

ArgoUML Java Open Source UML Project: http://argouml.tigris.org

DocBook DTD: http://www.oasis-open.org/docbook

DocBook site: http://www.docbook.org

Use Cases: http://www.pols.co.uk/usecasezone, http://www.usecases.org

Date/Time Resources

International Earth Rotation Service (IERS): http://maia.usno.navy.mil/

IERS Master Clock and Time Reference: http://tycho.usno.navy.mil/time.html

Miscellany by Dr J R Stockton [2001-05-21]: http://www.merlyn.demon.co.uk/miscdate.htm

A Summary of the International Standard Date and Time Notation by Markus Kuhn [2000-04-17]: http://www.cl.cam.ac.uk/~mgk25/iso-time.html.

Regular Expressions

Definition of XML Schema Regexs: http://www.w3.org/TR/xmlschema-2/#regexs

XML Schema Regex examples: http://www.w3.org/TR/xmlschema-0/#regexAppendix

Unicode Regex definitions: http://www.unicode.org/unicode/reports/tr18/

Implications of Character Case Mappings: http://www.unicode.org/unicode/reports/tr21/

Use of Canonical Character Forms and Character Value Normalization:
http://www.unicode.org/unicode/reports/tr15/

Perl Regex articles and links: http://www.perl.com/reference/query.cgi?regexp

Perl Regex Syntax documentation: http://www.perl.com/CPAN-local/doc/manual/html/pod/perlre.html

SBP Resources

Introduction to Petri Nets: http://www.daimi.au.dk/PetriNets/

Classification of Petri Net types: http://www.daimi.au.dk/PetriNets/classification/

PNML Discussion: http://www.informatik.hu-berlin.de/top/pnml/

XML and Petri Nets resources: http://xml.coverpages.org/xmlAndPetriNets.html

SBP resources: http://www.aspalliance.com/mcorning and
http://www.terracogito.redmond.wa.us/blueprints.htm

Standards

RFCs

RFCs for URIs: http://www.ietf.org/rfc/rfc2396.txt and http://www.ietf.org/rfc/rfc2732.txt

RFCs for URLs: http://www.ietf.org/rfc/rfc1738.txt and http://www.ietf.org/rfc/rfc1808.txt

RFC for URNs: http://www.ietf.org/rfc/rfc2141.txt

RFC 2045: Multipurpose Internet Mail Extensions (MIME) Part One: Format of Internet Message
Bodies: http://www.ietf.org/rfc/rfc2045.txt

RFC 2368: The mailto URI scheme [1998-07]: http://www.ietf.org/rfc/rfc2368.txt (updates RFCs 1738
and 1808).

RFC 3066: Tags for the Identification of Languages [2001-01]: http://www.ietf.org/rfc/rfc3066.txt
Older version at: http://www.ietf.org/rfc/rfc1766.txt

RFC 2373: IP Version 6 Addressing Architecture [1998-07]: http://www.ietf.org/rfc/rfc2373.txt. Their
use in URIs is described in RFC 2732:
Format for Literal IPv6 Addresses in URL's [1999-12]: http://www.ietf.org/rfc/rfc2732.txt

W3C Recommendations

W3C Home: http://www.w3.org/

XML Schema Requirements: http://www.w3.org/TR/NOTE-xml-schema-req

Schema Recommendation Part0: Primer: http://www.w3.org/TR/xmlschema-0/

Schema Recommendation Part1: Structures: http://www.w3.org/TR/xmlschema-1/

Schema Recommendation Part2: Datatypes: http://www.w3.org/TR/xmlschema-2/

Datatypes for DTDs (DT4DTD) 1.0: http://www.w3.org/TR/dt4dtd

SOX Information: http://www.w3.org/TR/NOTE-SOX

XML Data Information: http://www.w3.org/TR/1998/NOTE-XML-data-0105/

Canonical XML Recommendation: http://www.w3.org/TR/xml-c14n

Namespaces in XML Recommendation: http://www.w3.org/TR/REC-xml-names/

XLink 1.0 Recommendation: http://www.w3.org/TR/xlink/

XML Signature Working Group page: http://www.w3.org/Signature/

SOAP

W3C Note on SOAP: http://www.w3.org/TR/SOAP

IBM Implementation of SOAP: http://xml.apache.org/soap

Microsoft Support site for SOAP: http://msdn.microsoft.com/soap/default.asp

SOAP FAQ: http://www.develop.com/soap/soapfaq.htm

SOAP with MIME: http://www.w3.org/TR/SOAP-attachments

SOAP Developers mailing list: http://discuss.develop.com/soap.html

XML Protocol Activity: http://www.w3.org/2000/xp/

ISO Standards

Ordering Information for ISO-11404 (Language Independent Datatypes):
http://www.iso.ch/cate/d19346.html

ISO 3166-1:1997 (E). Codes for the representation of names of countries and their subdivisions – Part 1:
Country codes. Online lists available at:
http://www.din.de/gremien/nas/nabd/iso3166ma/codlstp1/en_listp1.html (two-character "Internet"
codes), or http://www.un.org/Depts/unsd/methods/m49alpha.htm (the three-character codes)

ISO 4217:1995 Codes: http://www.xe.com/iso4217.htm and
http://www.thefinancials.com/vortex/CurrencyFormats.html

ISO 639:1988 (E): Code for the representation of names of languages. Code lists from the US Library of Congress: http://lcweb.loc.gov/standards/iso639-2/termcodes.html
Summary of this standard: http://lcweb.loc.gov/standards/iso639-2/langhome.html. Another source is at http://www.oasis-open.org/cover/iso639a.html

ISO 6709:1983 Standard representation of latitude, longitude, and altitude for geographic point locations (summary of):
http://www.ftp.uni-erlangen.de/pub/doc/ISO/english/ISO-6709-summary

You can find ordering info for any of the other ISO Standards at http://www.iso.ch as well.

Postal Standards

Universal Postal Union (UPU): http://www.upu.org

UPU Postage rates and addressing formats for 189 member nations:
http://www.upu.org/ap/layout.startup?p_language=AN&p_theme=addrsyst&p_content_url=/ap/postco de.choice?p_language=AN.

USPS (United States Postal Service) state and territorial abbreviations:
http://www.usps.gov/ncsc/lookups/usps_abbreviations.html

Other Standards

Another codes resource: http://www.oasis-open.org/cover/country3166.html

IEEE Standard for Binary Floating-Point Arithmetic (IEEE 754-1985):
http://standards.ieee.org/reading/ieee/std_public/description/busarch/754-1985_desc.html

Internet Assigned Numbers Authority (IANA): http://www.iana.org

Oasis group home page: http://www.oasis-open.org

DublinCore meta data initiative: http://dublincore.org

Tools

XSV download: http://www.ltg.ed.ac.uk/~ht/xsv-status.html

Use XSV online: http://www.w3.org/2001/03/webdata/xsv

SAXON XSLT Engine: http://users.iclway.co.uk/mhkay/saxon/

Microsoft WSH download:
http://msdn.microsoft.com/scripting/default.htm?/scripting/windowshost/doc/wsVersion.htm

MSXML 4 technology preview:
http://msdn.microsoft.com/code/sample.asp?url=/msdn-files/027/001/594/msdncompositedoc.xml

Topologi Schematron development tool: http://www.topologi.com

Adobe SVG viewer plugin for IE and Netscape: http://www.adobe.com/svg

Turbo XML 2.2 (download trial copy): http://www.extensibility.com

XML Spy: http://www.xmlspy.com/download.html

Unicode

Unicode 3.0 database (revision 3.1.0 as of 2001-02-28):
http://www.unicode.org/Public/UNIDATA/UnicodeCharacterDatabase.html

General Categories and other properties for all Unicode characters: http://www.unicode.org/Public/3.1-Update/PropList-3.1.0.txt

Blocks-4.txt file (Block escapes): http://www.unicode.org/Public/3.1-Update/

Web Services

IBM Developer Works: http://www.ibm.com/developerworks/webservices

Microsoft (Web Services): http://msdn.microsoft.com/webservices

Web Services general-purpose site: http://www.webservices.org

WSDL note at the W3C: http://www.w3.org/TR/wsdl

UDDI white papers and specifications: http://www.uddi.org

Robin Cover's UDDI Cover Pages: http://xml.coverpages.org/uddi.html

UDDI test servers: http://msdn.microsoft.com/xml/articles/xml12182000.asp

Wrox Resources

Wrox home: http://www.wrox.com/

Professional XML Schemas book page:
http://www.wrox.com/Books/Book_Details.asp?sub_section=1_2&isbn=1861005474&subject=XML&subject_id=30

Wrox P2P XML discussion lists: http://p2p.wrox.com/xml

Wrox support mail address: mailto:support@wrox.com

Wrox feedback mail address: mailto:feedback@wrox.com

XML

Global versus Local Namespace declarations, best practices, by Roger Costello:
http://www.xfront.com/BestPractices.html

XML Schema Alternatives

Schematron Site: http://www.ascc.net/xml/resource/schematron/schematron.html

Schematron related interview with Rick Jellife: http://www.xmlhack.com/read.php?item=121

Relax NG main site: http://www.oasis-open.org/committees/relax-ng

Relax NG tutorial: http://www.oasis-open.org/committees/relax-ng/tutorial.html

Jing (Java open source Relax NG implementation): http://www.thaiopensource.com/relaxng

Examplotron main site: www.examplotron.org

ASN.1 example schema: http://asn1.elibel.tm.fr/xml/example.htm

Books

XML

Professional XML Second Edition, by Nik Ozu et al (ISBN: 1-861005-05-9), published by Wrox Press, 2001

Professional XSL, by Kurt Cagle et al (ISBN: 1-861003-57-9), published by Wrox Press, 2001

XSLT Programmer's Reference, by Michael Kay (ISBN: 1-861005-06-7), published by Wrox Press, 2001

Professional XML Databases, by Kevin Williams et al (ISBN: 1-861003-58-7), published by Wrox Press, 2000

Professional XML Meta Data, by David Dodds et al (ISBN: 1-861004-51-6), published by Wrox Press, 2001

Data Modeling/UML

Writing Effective Use Cases, by Alistair Cockburn (ISBN: 0-201702-25-8), published by Addison-Wesley, 2000

UML Distilled, Second Edition, by Martin Fowler, Kendall Scott (ISBN: 0-201657-83-X), published by Addison-Wesley, 1999

Data Modeling Essentials, by Graeme Simsion (ISBN: 1-850328-77-3), published by Van Nostrand Reinhold, 1994

Instant UML, by Pierre-Alain Muller (ISBN: 1-861000-87-1), published by Wrox Press, 1997

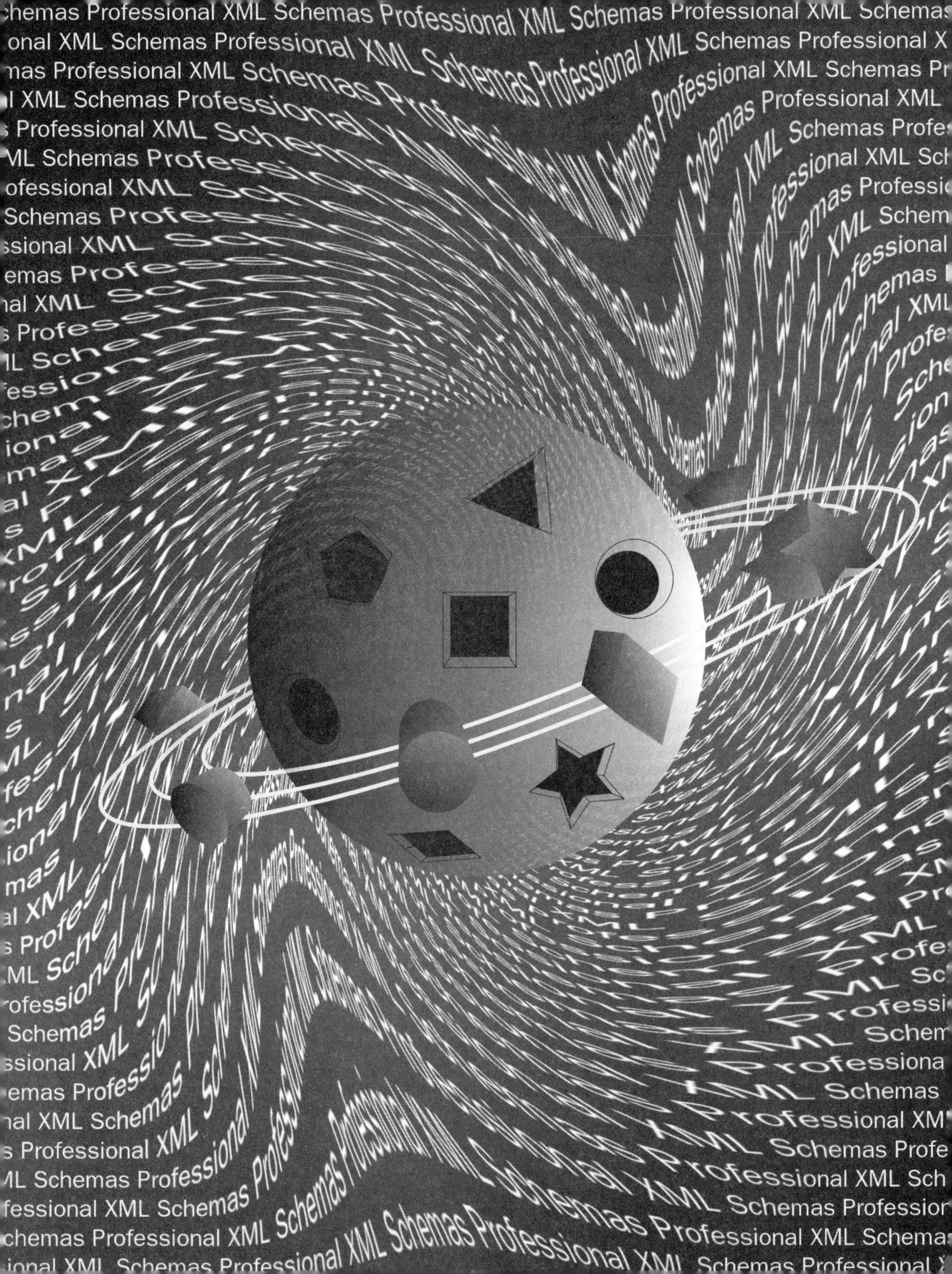
Professional XML Schemas

Index

A Guide to the Index

The index is arranged hierarchically, in alphabetical order, with symbols preceding the letter A. Most second-level entries and many third-level entries also occur as first-level entries. This is to ensure that users will find the information they require however they choose to search for it.

Elements are XML Schema elements unless indicated otherwise.

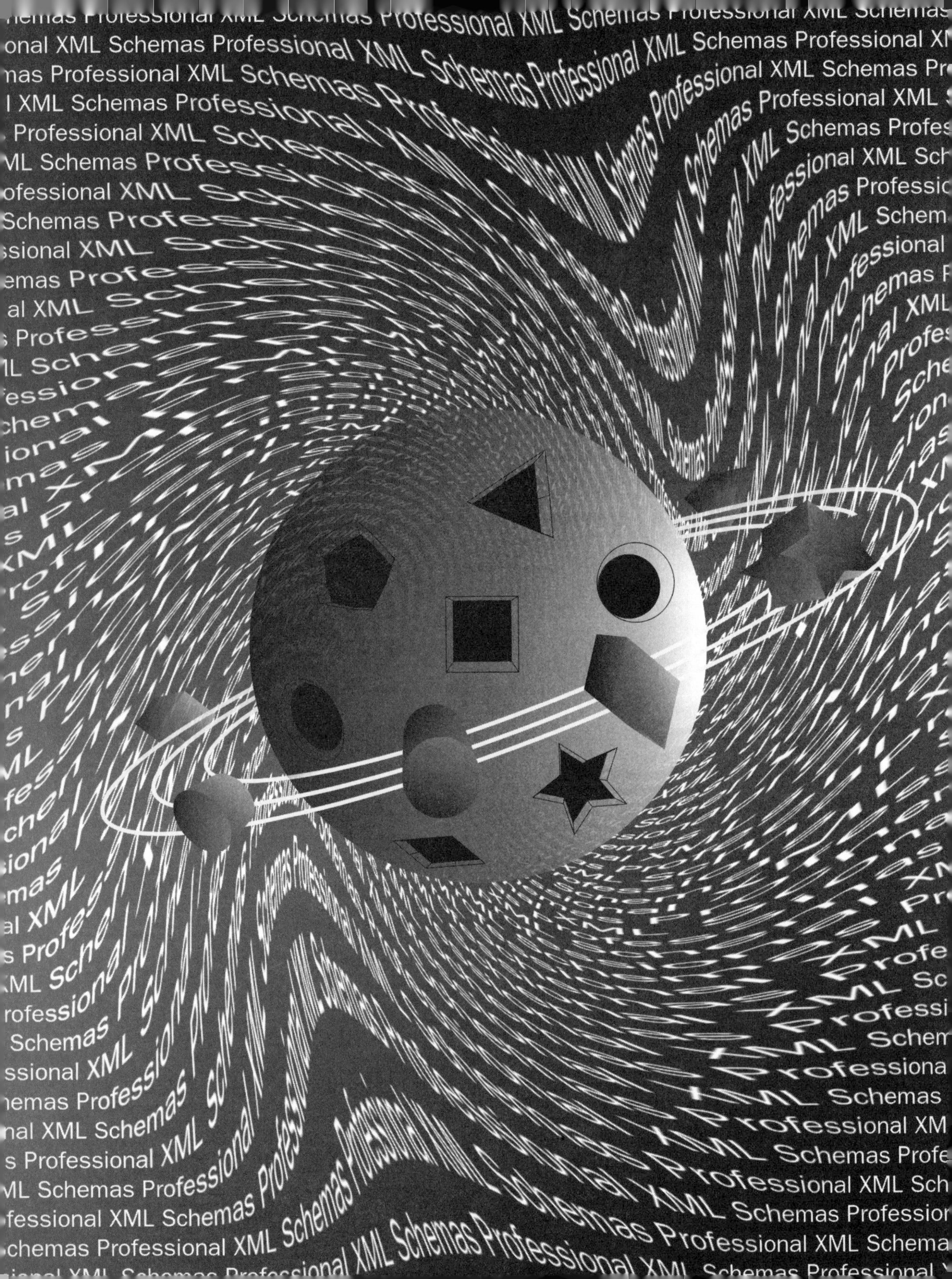
Professional XML Schemas

wrox

Programmer to Programmer™

Wrox writes books for you. Any suggestions, or ideas about how you want
information given in your ideal book will be studied by our team.
Your comments are always valued at Wrox.

Free phone in USA 800-USE-WROX
Fax (312) 893 8001

UK Tel.: (0121) 687 4100   Fax: (0121) 687 4101

Professional XML Schemas – Registration Card

Name _____

Address _____

_____

_____

City _____ State/Region _____

Country _____ Postcode/Zip _____

E-Mail _____

Occupation _____

How did you hear about this book?

☐ Book review (name) _____

☐ Advertisement (name) _____

☐ Recommendation _____

☐ Catalog _____

☐ Other _____

Where did you buy this book?

☐ Bookstore (name) _____ City_____

☐ Computer store (name) _____

☐ Mail order _____

☐ Other _____

What influenced you in the purchase of this book?

☐ Cover Design ☐ Contents ☐ Other (please specify):

_____

How did you rate the overall content of this book?

☐ Excellent ☐ Good ☐ Average ☐ Poor

What did you find most useful about this book? _____

_____

What did you find least useful about this book? _____

_____

Please add any additional comments._____

_____

What other subjects will you buy a computer book on soon?

_____

What is the best computer book you have used this year?

_____

wrox

Programmer to Programmer™

Note: If you post the bounce back card below in the UK, please send it to:

Wrox Press Limited, Arden House, 1102 Warwick Road,
Acocks Green, Birmingham B27 6HB. UK.

Computer Book Publishers